Ex Libris

Katie Boehler

# Encyclopedia Of Pieced Quilt Patterns

Compiled by
**Barbara Brackman**

American Quilter's Society
P. O. Box 3290 • Paducah, KY 42002-3290

Library of Congress
Cataloging-in-Publication Data

Brackman, Barbara.
Encyclopedia of pieced quilt patterns/compiled by Barbara Brackman
p. cm.
Includes bibliographical references and index.
ISBN 0-89145-815-8: $34.95
1. Quilting – Patterns. 2. Patchwork – Patterns. 3. Quilting – Patterns – Periodicals – Indexes. 4. Patchwork – Patterns – Periodicals – Indexes.
I. Title.
TT835.B64 1993
746.46'041'03 – dc20
93-7669
CIP

Additional copies of this book may be ordered from:
**American Quilter's Society**
P.O. Box 3290
Paducah, KY 42002-3290
@ $34.95. Add $1.00 for postage & handling ($1.50 international)

Copyright: Barbara Brackman, 1993

This book or any part thereof may not be reproduced
without the written consent of the Author and Publisher.

# ENCYCLOPEDIA Of Pieced Quilt Patterns

Compiled by
# Barbara Brackman

**American Quilter's Society**
P. O. Box 3290 • Paducah, KY 42002-3290

# PREFACE TO THE REPRINTED EDITION

*"It is not wise to be didactic about the nomenclature of quilt patterns."*

– **Florence Peto**
*American Quilts and Coverlets*, 1949, pg. 21

If Adam's task was naming the animals[1], it may be that Eve's was naming quilt patterns. I know I am not the only quilt lover who has developed a file to keep track of the pattern names of all the quilts I intended to make. *The Encyclopedia of Pieced Quilt Patterns* grew out of my belief that every quilt pattern had a name if only I could find it.

Today, twenty years after I began indexing patterns, I find myself agreeing with Florence Peto's comment: "It is not wise to be didactic about the nomenclature of quilt patterns." In this preface to the reprinted edition I will caution readers that it is unwise to be didactic because the "facts" are very elusive. I now realize that not every pattern has a name, that there is no "correct" name for any design, and that some of the names we take for granted as authentic nineteenth-century folklore actually have relatively short histories. Names so familiar to us, standards like Mariner's Compass, Flower Garden, and Lone Star, seem to have been unknown to nineteenth century quilters.

Following Peto's advice, I will not present this index as the authority on pattern names. Pattern names, like all vocabulary, change over time. The right name for a pattern is what you call it. This encyclopedia is, however, the most complete index to published names for American quilt design. It indexes patterns that appeared in print as early as the 1830's. The first published pattern was the design I numbered #161, which we call Grandmother's Flower Garden today. In January 1835, *Godey's Lady's Book* published a picture with three names: Hexagon, Six-Sided Patchwork and Honey Comb Patchwork. Following that first appearance, published quilt patterns were sparse for decades. Because magazines had limited technology for creative illustrations, many of the mid-century patterns were copied directly from British magazines, a fact first noted by quilt historian Virginia Gunn[2]. This plagiarism of English publications is a prime reason the published patterns had so little to do with the quilts that American women were making at the time.

# Preface

Magazines printed patterns for pieced quilts constructed in mosaic-style rather than in the block-style designs favored by American seamstresses. The writers also often recommended silk fabric rather than the cotton calicoes that quilters here loved.

A reader looking for pattern names in mid-century publications is usually disappointed. For example, pattern #443, which has appeared in print since the turn of the century as Twist Patchwork, Twisted Rope, Plaited Block, and Round the Twist, was first published in *Godey's* in December, 1851, under the generic caption "Patchwork: Combination Designs."

As magazines increased in the United States and technology for illustration improved, references to quilts also increased. In the 1880's, periodicals began to influence American design as they published pictures of new patterns such as the Fan, the Log Cabin, and the Crazy quilt. During the 1890's, the number of patchwork features increased significantly in the needlework and reader's exchange columns of women's magazines and farm papers. These patterns reflected the look of American quilts. Drawings were of block designs; instructions advised quilters to use cotton fabric and the running-stitch technique rather than the English template method described in earlier decades.

Names for designs took on new importance. Typical of the magazines with rural audiences was the *Ohio Farmer*, which printed eleven designs in 1894. Five were unnamed patterns, but six were printed under names like Bird's Nest, Kaleidoscope, and Ocean Wave. These patterns were usually shared by readers who designed the block or copied it from a family quilt. Names occasionally reflected current events. In 1899 the *Orange Judd Farmer* offered Dewey's Dream and Manila, patterns celebrating our victory in the Spanish-American War.

In the twentieth century, variety in pattern names became the standard. Elizabeth Daingerfield, in a February 1912 article in *Ladies' Home Journal*, reflected the interest in poetic names by showing designs called Lady-Finger, Tulip Wreath, and Sunflower. Generic names like "Pretty Patchwork" became rare.

The growing importance of descriptive names is illustrated by *Hearth and Home* magazine's request for blocks named after states, capital cities, and U.S. territories. In 1907, the editor asked readers to design new blocks or rename old favorites for their region. *Hearth and Home*, like other magazines, printed a small drawing or photo of the finished quilt block and offered full-sized paper patterns to readers who mailed a coin. This combination of a pictured design and a mail-order pattern was the standard periodical format for years. Few newspapers or magazines included the actual pattern pieces.

Many of the names in the *Encyclopedia of Pieced Quilt Patterns* are from the numerous turn-of-the-century magazines. My research included reading runs of national periodicals like *Ladies' Home Journal* and *Successful Farming*, as well as those with smaller circulations. Regional, ephemeral publications like the *Rural New Yorker* and *Dakota Farmer* were a good source for obscure patterns and names. Because I did my research while living in the Midwest I have focused on magazines from those regions. Recent work by pattern historian Wilene Smith has made me realize that I missed many of the ephemeral series of women's magazines printed in Augusta, Maine about 1900. These women's magazines and story magazines were important sources for patterns and pattern names[3]. I did, however, include many patterns from two Augusta magazines, *Hearth and Home* and *Comfort*, which were well-indexed in the 1970's.

The mail-order departments at the periodicals competed with companies that were exclusively devoted to selling quilt patterns by mail. While Montgomery Ward and Sears, Roebuck & Company were taking advantage of rural free delivery to sell American women quilt frames, fabric, and batting through catalogs, H. M. Brockstedt and his Ladies Art Company sold them patchwork patterns from his mail-order catalog that began in 1889. The pamphlet, which underwent many revisions, featured small drawings of 300 to 600 patterns, each captioned with a name. Early

# Preface

twentieth-century catalogs included the Joseph Doyle Company's and Clara Stone's *Practical Needlework*. Because catalogs were revised and reprinted, and because quilters saved them for decades, the catalog names often were more durable than those recorded only in periodicals.

In the late 1920's, metropolitan newspapers began offering pattern features. Among the first was the *Seattle Post-Intelligencer* in which Prudence Penny, editor of the women's page, began publishing an annual series quilt in 1926. One of the most prolific columns was one which appeared in the *Kansas City Star* (1928-1960), and was managed most of that time by Edna Marie Dunn. The Star printed a full-sized pattern once a week; collectors count 1,068 patterns.[4] Most were contributed by readers in the five-state region the *Star* farm weekly served. Like those in most of the other columns the designs were a mix of traditional blocks and a few new designs. There were also many patterns considered "traditional" that had originated twenty or thirty years earlier in the first pattern columns.

The Nancy Cabot column, a daily feature in the *Chicago Tribune* from 1933 through the end of the decade, was also a good source for patterns and names. Loretta Leitner Rising wrote the column without reader assistance and many of the patterns were originals of her own design.

In the late 1920s a new format for selling patterns evolved. The syndicated column looked like a newspaper column but the source was an independent pattern studio. Two early syndicators were Ruby Short McKim, who began designing embroidered blocks in 1916, and Florence LaGanke Harris, whose Nancy Page quilt columns started in 1928. They were joined by numerous companies as the quilt craze peaked in the early 1930s. Colonial Pattern of Kansas City, Home Art of Des Moines, and Needlecraft of New York City ran pattern features in newspapers all over the country, using such names as Aunt Martha, Hetty Winthrop, and Laura Wheeler. Advertisement in thin disguise, syndicated columns included a sketch of a pattern with its name, a short history of the design (usually of questionable historical accuracy) and a few shading and fabric suggestions. The reader who desired a full-sized pattern sent a dime to her local paper, which forwarded the request to the syndicate office. Some syndicates sold single pattern sheets; others sold booklets of many.

With pattern historians Joyce Gross and Cuesta Benberry I have been listing pattern columns. At this point (1992) we have a list of 244 newspapers that carried pattern columns during the 1930's. During World War II, the features began to disappear, victims of the newsprint shortage caused by the war. Few new patterns were generated in the years 1940-1970, and today quilters obtain their patterns from specialty magazines rather than the local newspaper (only a few newspapers now have one-of-a-kind pattern columns; the Laura Wheeler/Alice Brooks names still syndicate).

Because the periodicals published few names before 1890, many earlier names have been lost. For example: Tennessee quilters know what a Nine-diamond is (it's a nine patch set on point in a square block, #2385). But few outside the region know the name because it was not published or indexed; therefore that name is not given in this encyclopedia. Some names went unpublished because they were inelegant or distasteful to the magazine editors. Burgoo Trollop, Ham Shank, and Pigpen went unrecorded in the commercial pattern network, while more elegant names like Lady of the Lake, Delectable Mountains, and Wind Power of the Osages have been published over and over. Patterns honoring the losing side were rarely published. Collectors are not too sure about what a Confederate Rose looked like and no one recorded the pattern KuKlux, although its name appeared in print. Didn't anyone name patterns for losing presidential candidates James G. Blaine or Alton Parker?

A source more durable than newsprint clippings appeared in 1915 when Marie Webster wrote the first quilt book. *Quilts: Their Story and How to Make Them* grew out of her pattern features for *Ladies' Home Journal*.

6

## Preface

She listed many pattern names but illustrated only a few. Most of the names can be traced to earlier sources, particularly the Ladies Art Company catalogs.

Ruth Finley and Ruby McKim added much to pattern identification with their books naming and picturing designs. In 1929, Finley published *Old Patchwork Quilts and the Women Who Made Them*, for which she collected names in Ohio, New England, and New York. McKim collected patterns in the area near her Independence, Missouri, home for *101 Patchwork Patterns*, a compilation of her newspaper columns and patterns from her mail-order studio. In 1935 Carrie Hall took pattern identification a step further with the book she co-wrote with Rose Kretsinger. *The Romance of the Patchwork Quilt in America* indexed over 800 blocks with names Hall found in newspapers, books, and mail-order catalogs.

When I became interested in quilt patterns in the late 1960's, I began my files by indexing the books at the public library: Finley, Webster, McKim, and Hall and Kretsinger. I also kept track of patterns appearing in *Quilter's Newsletter Magazine* and in the new trickle of quilt books like Beth Gutcheon's *Perfect Patchwork Primer* and Lenice Bacon's *American Patchwork Quilts*. Soon the trickle became a deluge and I realized that keeping up with the patterns generated in the 1970's would be a full-time job. Therefore, the *Encyclopedia of Pieced Quilt Patterns* indexes few patterns designed after 1970. Most of the references are to periodicals published between 1890 and 1940.

I could not have attempted this index without the assistance of many friends and correspondents. I discussed pattern construction and classification techniques at length with Jean Mitchell, Helen Crockett, and Thelma Helyar while we volunteered to catalog Carrie Hall's blocks at the Helen F. Spencer Museum of Art in the mid-1970s. After working with the book for the Kansas Quilt Project, Mary Margaret Rowen gave me ideas on changing the key to make things easier to find.

Like every other contemporary quilt historian, I owe much to Cuesta Benberry, who answered my questions and shared her library, her ideas, and her lists. Thanks are due to earlier researchers who indexed designs from numerous publications: Carrie Hall, Louise Townsend, Wilene Smith, Edna Van Das, Elizabeth Szabronski, and Wilma Smith. And thanks to friends Cathy Dwigans and Gregg Blasdel who encouraged me to begin this project, and to Carol and Charles Jones, who have stored thousands of volumes in their attic for years.

– Barbara Brackman
January 1993

### FOOTNOTES

[1] Genesis: Chapter 2:20, "And Adam gave names to all cattle, and to the fowl of the air and to every beast of the field...."

[2] Virginia Gunn, "Victorian Silk Template Patchwork in American Periodicals, 1850-1875," *Uncoverings 1983* (San Francisco: American Quilt Study Group, 1984).

[3] Wilene Smith, "Quilt History in Old Periodicals," *Uncoverings* 1990 (San Francisco: American Quilt Study Group, 1991).

[4] Edith Leeper, "Stalking the Kansas City Star Quilt Patterns," *Lady's Circle Patchwork Quilts*, May 1988, pp. 64, 67, 75.

# TABLE OF CONTENTS

**AN INTRODUCTION, TO THE BOOK, 12**
Overview & Instructions, 12
**KEY FOR LOCATING PATTERNS, 16**

**Pattern Category 1:**
**ONE PATCH, 20**

*Category Key, 21*
Triangles, 22
Rectangles, 24
Diamonds, 26
Misc. Four-Sided Figures, 28
Five-Sided Figures, 28
Hexagons, 30
Misc. Six-Sided Figures, 32
Odd Shapes, 32
Curves, 34
Three-Dimensional Pieces, 34

**Pattern Category 2:**
**NON-SQUARE BLOCKS, 36**

*Category Key, 37*
Triangular Blocks, 38
Rectangular Blocks, 38
Diamond-Shaped Blocks, 46
Hexagonal Blocks, 48
Uneven Six-Sided Blocks, 54
Eight-Sided Blocks, 56
Blocks with more than eight sides, 58
Wedding Ring Types, 58

**Pattern Category 3:**
**MULTI-PATCH, 62**

*Category Key, 63*
Four-Sided Shape as a Piece, 64
Five-Sided Shape as a Piece, 68
Six-Sided Shape as a Piece
  Even Sides, 70
  Uneven Sides, 72
Eight-Sided Shape as a Piece, 74
Curved Pieces, 76
Three-Dimensional Pieces, 78

**Pattern Category 4:**
**STRIP QUILTS, 80**

*Category Key, 81*

**Pattern Category 5:**
**REALISTIC, 84**

*Category Key,* 85
Baskets
  Empty Baskets, 86
  Baskets with Appliquéd Contents, 90
  Baskets Full of Triangles (& Squares), 92
  Baskets Full of Diamonds or Other Shapes, 94
Vases and Misc. Containers, 98
Flowers, 100
Trees
  Trees With Triangles for Leaves, 110
  Trees With Squares and Rectangles for Leaves, 114
  Trees With Diamonds and Other Shapes for Leaves, 114
Leaves, 116
Houses and Other Architecture, 118
Airplanes, 122
Boats, 124
Animals
  Butterflies and Other Insects, 126
  Birds, 128
  Cats and Other Felines, 128
  Other Animals, 130
People, 130
Misc. Subject Matter, 132
Letters, 136

**Pattern Category 6:**
**TWO-BLOCK, 138**

*Category Key,* 139
One Block is a Checkerboard Grid, 140
Neither Block is a Checkerboard Grid, 144
Three Blocks, 144

**Pattern Category 7:**
**SASH & BLOCK, 146**

*Category Key,* 147
Plain Block/Pieced Sashing, 148
Pieced Block/Pieced Sashing, 150

**Pattern Category 8:**
**FOUR PATCH, 154**

*Category Key,* 155
Squares and Rectangles Only, 156
Sixteen Squares, 158
Thirty-six Squares, 162
Sixty-four Squares, 162
Blocks with a Square in Each Patch, 164
Blocks with Specific construction, 164
  *See Category Key for details,* 155
Block is a Star, 170
Blocks with Specific Construction, 172
  *See Category Key for details,* 155
Misc. Pinwheel Types, 180
Misc. Sawtooth Types, 180
Blocks with Specific Construction, 182
  *See Category Key for details,* 155
Asymmetrical Four Patch, 182
Unequal Four Patch, 184
Misc. Four Patch, 184
Blocks with Specific Construction, 190
  *See Category Key for Details,* 155
Four Patch with Curves, 194

**Pattern Category 9:**
**EQUAL NINE PATCH, 202**

*Category Key,* 203
  Block is Squares and/or Rectangles, 204
  Stars with Specific Construction, 206
    *See Category Key for Details,* 203
  Blocks with Specific Construction, 208
    *See Category Key for Details,* 203
  Blocks with Specific Patch Unpieced, 216
    *See Category Key for Details,* 203
  Blocks with Specific Construction, 216
    *See Category Key for Details,* 203
  Asymmetrical Blocks, 218
  Misc. Equal Nine Patch Blocks, 220
  Nine Patch Blocks with Curves, 224

## Table of Contents

**Pattern Category 10:**
**UNEQUAL NINE PATCH WITH SMALL CENTER SQUARE, 226**

*Category Key,* 227
Twenty-Five Squares, 228
Patches are Squares & Rectangles, 232
Blocks with Specific Construction, 234
  *See Category Key for Details,* 227
Blocks with Unpieced Bars, 238
Other Types of Blocks, 244
Blocks With Curves, 250

**Pattern Category 11:**
**UNEQUAL NINE PATCH WITH LARGE CENTER SQUARE, 252**

*Category Key,* 253
Blocks with Unpieced Corners, 254
Blocks with Squares and Rectangles in the Corners, 262
Blocks with Specific Construction, 264
  *See Category Key for Details,* 253
Other Types of Blocks, 270
Blocks with Curved Seams, 274
Feathered Stars, 276
  *Note: Not All of the Feathered Stars Are Really Nine Patch*

**Pattern Category 12:**
**ONE PATCH – SQUARE, 282**

*Category Key,* 283

**Pattern Category 13:**
**FOUR X, 290**

*Category Key,* 291
Four X with No Curves, 292
Four X with Curves, 296

**Pattern Category 14:**
**SQUARE IN A SQUARE, 298**

*Category Key,* 299
Blocks with Unpieced Corners, 300
Blocks with Unpieced Center Square, 302
Center Square Pieced of Squares and Rectangles, 302
Blocks with Specific Construction, 304
  *See Category Key for Details,* 299
Misc. Blocks with Specific Construction, 308
Blocks with Curves, 312
Blocks with Specific Construction, 314
  *See Category Key for Details,* 299
Misc. Blocks with Specific Construction, 324
Blocks with Specific Construction, 326

**Pattern Category 15:**
**MALTESE CROSS, 330**

*Category Key,* 331
Blocks with Specific Patches Unpieced
  *See Section Key for Details,* 331
Blocks with Specific Construction
  *See Section Key for Details,* 331

**Pattern Category 16:**
**NINE X, 338**

*Category Key,* 339
Blocks with Specific Construction, 340
  *See Category Key for Details,* 339
Miscellaneous Nine X Blocks, 374

**Pattern Category 17:**
**TWO-PATCH PATTERNS, 378**

*Category Key,* 379
Diagonal Division, 380
Unequal Diagonal Division, 384
Horizontal or Vertical Division, 384

**Pattern Category 18:**
**THREE-PATCH PATTERNS, 386**

*Category Key,* 387
Horizontal or Vertical Division, 388
Diagonal Division, 392
Off-Center Diagonal Construction, 394
Blocks with Specific Construction, 394
  *See Category Key for Details,* 387

*Table of Contents*

**Pattern Category 19:**
**FANS, 396**

*Category Key,* 397
Single Fans
  Smooth Edge, 398
  Scalloped Edge, 400
  Other Edges, 400
  Blocks with Specific Construction
    *See Category Key for Details,* 397
Double Fans, 402
Miscellaneous Fans, 402
Sets for Fans, 402

**Pattern Category 20:**
**WHEELS, 406**

*Category Key,* 407
Circle in Center
  Spokes, 408
  Spirals, 408
  Four Identical Radiating Petals, 410
  Six Identical Radiating Petals, 410
  Eight Identical Radiating Petals, 412
  More Than Eight Petals, 416
  Miscellaneous, 422
Curved Seams Meet in Center, 424
Intersecting Curved Lines, 426
Intersecting Straight Lines, 426
Square in Center, 430
Hexagon or Octagon in Center, 430
Other Specific Shapes in Center
  *See Category Key for Details,* 407
Odd Curved Shapes in Center, 438

**Pattern Category 21:**
**FIVE- & SIX-POINTED STAR BLOCKS, 440**

*Category Key,* 441
Five-Pointed Stars, 442
Six-Pointed Stars, 444

**Pattern Category 22:**
**EIGHT-POINTED/45°DIAMOND STARS, 450**

*Category Key,* 451
Single Stars, 452
Star Off Center, 452
Center Star Made Up of Odd Pieces, 454
Star Made Up of Many Diamonds, 456
Star Surrounded by Parts of Other Stars, 460
Star Inside Another Star, 462
Star Surrounded By Other Shapes, 464
Stars with Points Oriented Up & Down, 468

**Pattern Category 23:**
**OTHER STARS, 470**

*Category Key,* 471
Multiple Stars, 472
Star Has Eight Equal/Wide Points, 472
Wide Points Oriented Up & Down, 474
Wide Points Oriented Left & Right, 474
Odd Eight-Pointed Stars, 476
Long Diamonds, 478
Points are Triangles or Other Shapes, 478

**Pattern Category 24:**
**WHOLE-TOP DESIGNS, 482**

*Category Key,* 483

**Pattern Category 25:**
**MISCELLANEOUS, 496**

*Category Key,* 497
With Diamonds, 498
With Curves, 502
With Six-Sided Pieces, 506
Assymetrical or Off-Center Blocks, 508
With Octagonal Shapes, 510
Interlocking Horizontals & Verticals, 512
Intersecting Lines in the Center, 512
Square in the Center, 514
Truly Miscellaneous, 518

**REFERENCES, 520**

**ALPHABETICAL INDEXES, 528 - 551**

# An Introduction to the Book

**Overview & Instructions**
**by Barbara Brackman**

The *Encyclopedia of Pieced Quilt Patterns* is an index to published quilt patterns. I originally published it as eight volumes, issuing one volume at a time from 1979 to 1984, and later revised the first two volumes. This edition includes everything from all of those eight volumes with revision for volumes 3 and 4, an improved key for pattern location and an updated cross referencing system.

## PATTERNS INCLUDED

Only pieced patterns are indexed. Pieced patterns with some appliqué or embroidery are also included, but appliqué patterns with a little bit of piecing are not. Appliqué designs are indexed in a separate book, the *Encyclopedia of Appliqué,* which will be published by EPM Publications. Designs that can be either pieced or appliquéd have been included in both books.

Patterns are shown with the shading arrangements the publication specified. If a color scheme seemed important to the design, it is also indicated.

## NUMBERING SYSTEM

Pieced quilt patterns – specific methods of arranging pieces – indexed in the *Encyclopedia* have been assigned identification numbers. Some of the pattern numbers have a decimal point added, so I could insert newly found patterns into the numbering system. Some whole numbers have no pattern and are therefore missing.

There were no home computers available when I began this numbering system, but it works well for a computerized data base. If you want to use a computer to identify patterns numerically, be sure to set up a seven-digit field for these numbers, with four digits before the decimal and three after.

You will then need to enter all numbers as seven-digit numbers. Thus, the hexagon design we call Grandmother's Flower Garden (#160 in Section 1) should be entered as #0160.000 rather than just #160. If entered as 160, your computer will read the pattern as #1600 – which would place the pattern numerically in the Nine-Patches in Section 9.

*Introduction, Overview & Instructions*

Sometimes different names were given to various shadings or color arrangements of the same pattern. If two quilt patterns are identical in their arrangement of pieces but different in shading, I have given them the same number, but they will be differentiated by a letter after the number. For example, Variegated Diamonds is #142a and Baby's Blocks #142b:

Variegated Diamonds, #142a

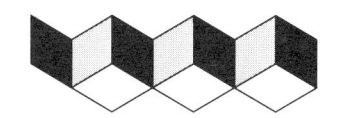

Baby's Blocks, #142b

If, on the other hand, two blocks make use of the same pieces, but the arrangment is different, the number I have assigned them will be different, too. The two patterns shown below are considered two different patterns and therefore have been given two different numbers:

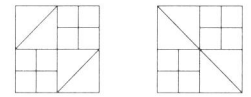

Some writers/designers modify patterns to make them easier or faster to piece. When patterns have been modified this way they are included under both categories, with a cross-reference. For example: Cheyenne #298 and #2113 is shown as an eight-sided block or a square block.

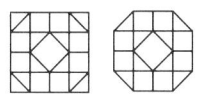

**PATTERN NAMES AND THEIR PUBLISHED SOURCES**

Each pattern in the index appears with not only its ID number, but also its name(s) and the published source(s). Often there were several sources for a particular pattern name, but in the *Encyclopedia* listing I have included only the earliest source.

For example: both the Ladies Art Company's catalog and Carrie Hall and Rose Kretsinger's *Romance of the Patchwork Quilt in America* call pattern #1130b "Devil's Puzzle." The Ladies Art Company's 1889 catalog is an earlier source than the 1935 book, so I listed the Ladies Art Company as the source.

The published sources follow the pattern names, in abbreviated form. The abbreviations used appear listed with their full references in the bibliography, at the back of the book.

In Pattern Categories 1-7, formerly the updated Volumes 1 and 2, I have also indicated patterns that appeared in quilts before periodicals and pattern companies dominated communication about quilt patterns. In these sections, patterns from quilts made prior to 1875 are indicated with the words: "EARLIEST EXAMPLE," indicating these were the oldest examples of that particular design I had been able to find.

**ORGANIZATION OF THE BOOK**

Patterns are classified and grouped into categories on the basis of the basic unit of design and the way it is repeated (its repeat). These visual categories are usually defined by seam lines that organize designs into types. Some of the categories are ones quilters already have names for; Nine Patch and Four Patch describe the way those blocks are assembled. For most, though, I have developed my own descriptions, such as Maltese Cross and Square in a Square.

When using the book, it is important to keep in mind that patterns are classified on the basis of major seam lines. Imaginary seam lines are not used.

For example: Brown Goose is not a Nine Patch, although imaginary lines might make

13

## Introduction, Overview & Instructions

it one. It is a Three Patch with vertical divisions:

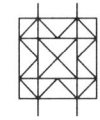

Within each unit of classification, patterns are generally listed from simple to complex. For example:

This pattern...

comes before this pattern...

which comes before this pattern.

Patterns with curved pieces generally are included last within each category.

**LOCATING AN ILLUSTRATION OF A PATTERN WHEN YOU KNOW ITS NAME**

In the *Encyclopedia*, patterns are indexed both visually and alphabetically. One can easily use the alphabetical index of pattern names at the back to find a pattern for which the name is known. The listing will give the pattern's identification number, and you can then find that number in the book.

All pattern drawings are presented in numerical order, beginning with pattern 111 on page 22. In the upper righthand corner of each righthand page you will find the range of identification numbers that will be found on that particular page.

**LOCATING A PATTERN WHEN YOU KNOW WHAT IT LOOKS LIKE BUT DON'T KNOW ITS NAME**

The main index for the book is a classification of patterns by the way they look. With this index you can find the name of an unknown pattern.

The Key For Locating Patterns on page 16 will direct you to a specific category, where a Category Key will help you locate the best pages on which to look for your pattern. To use the key to find a pattern, you will first need to determine what the repeat in your design is.

To do so, think in terms of how the pattern's design unit would have to be drawn for someone who wanted to reproduce the pattern. Consider this pattern:

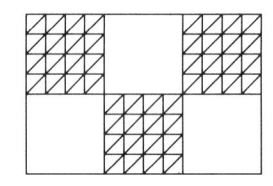

You might decide that the basic unit of design is this:

However, a quiltmaker given only that unit information and asked to draw the full pattern might produce this pattern:

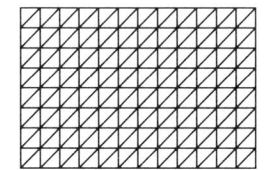

14

*Introduction, Overview & Instructions*

To describe the basic design unit that is repeated, you would have to draw the block below and specify that it is alternated with plain blocks:

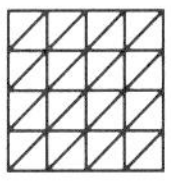

To obtain the repeat, think in terms of isolating the least amount of information necessary to reproduce the pattern.

You may sometimes find that the repeat of the block you decide upon and the repeat I have decided upon are not the same. This is a particular problem with quilts that are set in an all-over pattern.

Consider this pattern:

Its repeat can be seen as this:

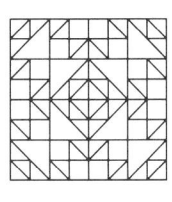

Or this:

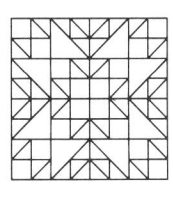

Or this:

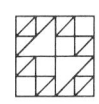

If you cannot find your pattern in the *Encyclopedia*, try looking at the repeat in a different way.

With this information in mind, if you are ready to find a pattern using the visual index, turn to the Key For Locating Patterns on page 16 and begin your search – and your exploration of the wide range of quilt patterns documented in this book.

15

# Key For Locating Pattern Categories

If you are trying to locate a particular pieced pattern in the *Encyclopedia*, please be sure you carefully read the Introduction on pages 12-15. With an understanding of the organization of the book and its patterns, return to this Key for Locating Patterns. You are now ready to look for your pattern.

Beginning with STEP 1 on page 17, read through each of the characteristics until you reach the first one that fits your block. (Be sure to keep in mind that the visual categories in this book are based on major seam lines, not imaginary lines.) When you find a characteristic that fits, follow the instructions in italics, which will either send you to another step, or to a specific category in the book.

When you are directed to a specific pattern category, you will be sent to the category's table of contents and key. You can then use the Category Key on the righthand page to find the pages on which your pattern is most likely to fall. Work with this key the same way you do this Key for Locating Patterns. Continue reading through characteristics until a description fits your block; then follow the instructions. In some cases you may be able to quickly look through the list of contents on the left-hand page and know exactly where to turn without using the Category Key.

If you have trouble locating your design, review the Introduction, particularly the last section. You may need to look at your block in a different way. Often the repeat in a block can be seen in several different ways. That's one of the reasons there are the great numbers of interpretations and variations indexed in this encyclopedia.

Best wishes for all of your searches!

**STEP 1**

**If the pieces are not organized into square blocks,**

•but they *are* organized into blocks, see *Non-Square Blocks, p. 36*

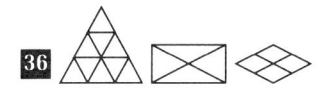

•and there is one shape (that is not a square) repeated over the surface of the quilt, *see One Patch, p. 20*

•and random shapes in no organized pattern make up the design, you will not find the pattern in this book. *Crazy quilts have not been indexed.*

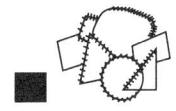

•the top is made of pieces organized into strips, and these strips alternate with unpieced strips to make up the design, *see Strip Quilts, p. 80.*

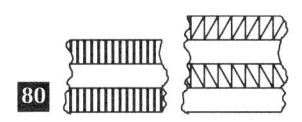

•and the pieces form a repeat, but it is not organized into strips or blocks, *see Multi-Patch Patterns, p. 62*

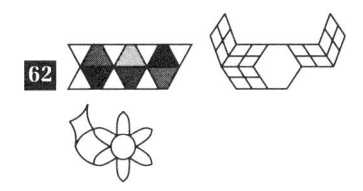

**STEP 2**

**If the pieces are organized into square blocks,**

•and the top is a central medallion, organized so that the whole top must be seen to understand the design repeat, *see Whole Top Designs, p. 482.*

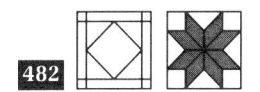

•and the repeat is two separate square blocks, which may each have a name of its own, but which when combined form a distinct pattern with a new name, *see Two-Block, p. 138.*

•and the repeat which makes up the pattern is made of both the blocks and the sashing or set, and both are integral to the design (the blocks may be unpieced), *see Sash Block Patterns, p. 146.*

**STEP 3**

*Go through the rest of the characteristics in order, choose the first one that describes your block, and turn to that page.*

**If your pattern...**

*Key to Locating Pattern Categories*

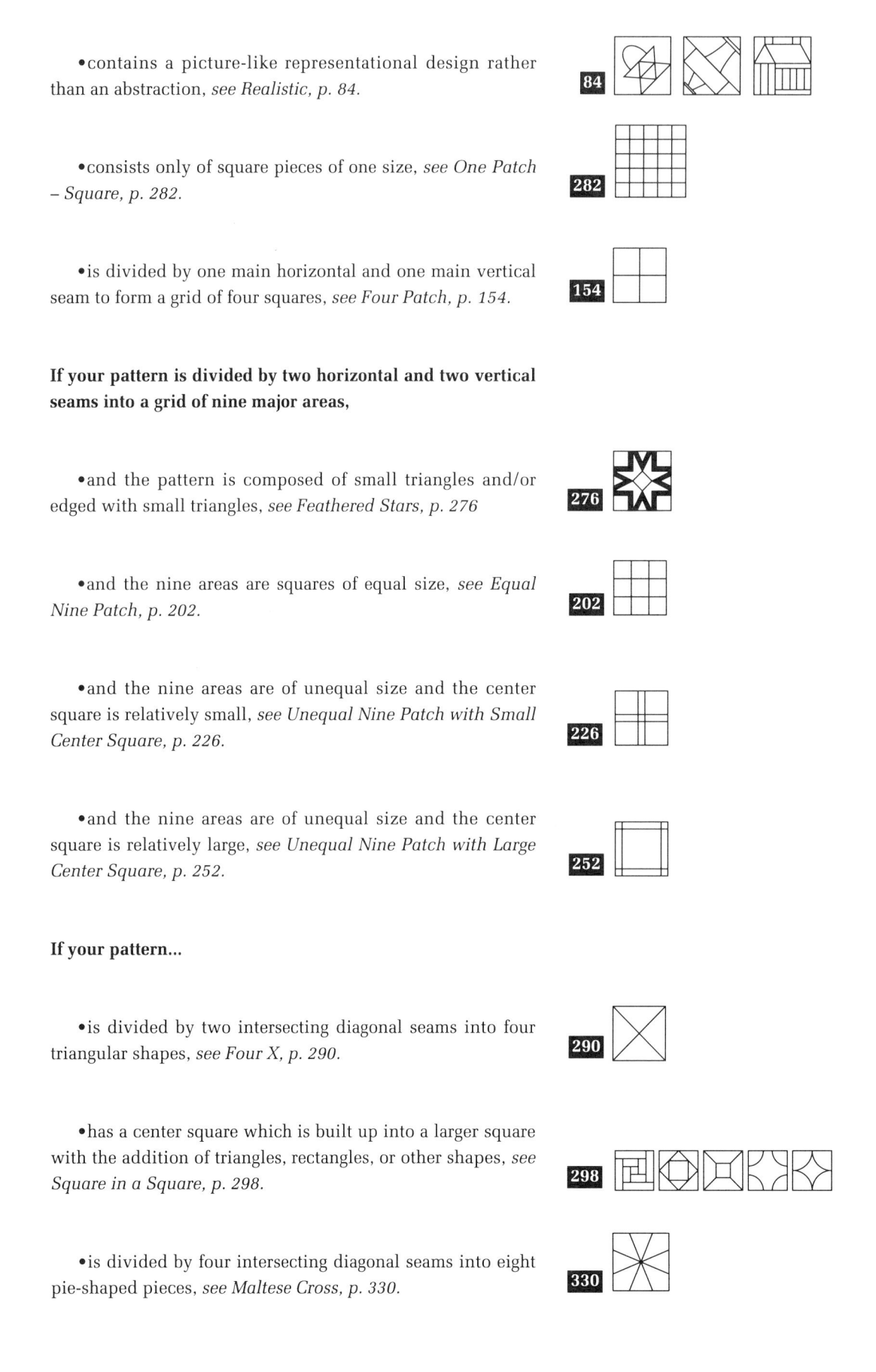

•contains a picture-like representational design rather than an abstraction, see *Realistic, p. 84.*

•consists only of square pieces of one size, see *One Patch – Square, p. 282.*

•is divided by one main horizontal and one main vertical seam to form a grid of four squares, see *Four Patch, p. 154.*

**If your pattern is divided by two horizontal and two vertical seams into a grid of nine major areas,**

•and the pattern is composed of small triangles and/or edged with small triangles, see *Feathered Stars, p. 276*

•and the nine areas are squares of equal size, see *Equal Nine Patch, p. 202.*

•and the nine areas are of unequal size and the center square is relatively small, see *Unequal Nine Patch with Small Center Square, p. 226.*

•and the nine areas are of unequal size and the center square is relatively large, see *Unequal Nine Patch with Large Center Square, p. 252.*

**If your pattern...**

•is divided by two intersecting diagonal seams into four triangular shapes, see *Four X, p. 290.*

•has a center square which is built up into a larger square with the addition of triangles, rectangles, or other shapes, see *Square in a Square, p. 298.*

•is divided by four intersecting diagonal seams into eight pie-shaped pieces, see *Maltese Cross, p. 330.*

18

*Key to Locating Pattern Categories*

•has four diagonal seams that divided it into nine major shapes, *see Nine X Patterns, p. 338.*

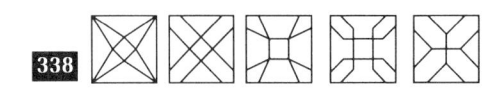

**338**

•has a single seam dividing it into two major shapes; the seam can be horizontal, vertical or diagonal, *see Two-Block Patterns, p. 378.*

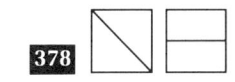

**378**

•is divided into three major shapes by two diagonal, vertical or horizontal seams, *see Three-Block Patterns, p. 286.*

**386**

•contains a shape in the center (circle, hexagon, octagon, square, etc.) from which the other pieces radiate, *see Wheels, p. 406.*

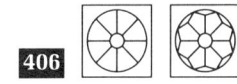

**406**

**If your pattern contains a star as the major design element, hasn't fit into any of the previous categories, and**

•has five points, *see Five- & Six- Pointed Star Blocks, p. 440.*

**440**

•has six radiating points, each a 60° diamond, *see Five & Six Pointed Star Blocks, p. 440.*

**440**

•has eight radiating points with eight 45° diamonds, *see Eight-Pointed/45° Diamond Stars, p. 450.*

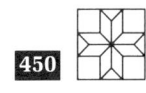

**450**

•and has points made up of shapes other than eight equal 45° diamonds, *see Other Stars, p. 470.*

**470**

**If your pattern...**

•doesn't fit into any previous categories, *see Miscellaneous Patterns, p. 496.*

**496**

19

# Pattern Category 1

## One Patch

**Patterns in Category 1 share these characteristics:**

- The basic design unit is one piece repeated over the whole top
- That piece is not a square
- The pieces are not organized into square blocks

**Category 1 includes:**

- Triangles, 22
- Rectangles, 24
- Diamonds, 26
- Misc. Four-Sided Figures, 28
- Five-Sided Figures, 28
- Hexagons, 30
- Misc. Six-Sided Figures, 32
- Odd Shapes, 32
- Curves, 34
- Three-Dimensional Pieces, 34

# KEY TO PATTERN CATEGORY 1: ONE PATCH

**STEP 1**

If the basic design unit of your pattern is one piece which is repeated over the whole top, and the pieces are not organized into square blocks, your pattern is one-patch
*continue with STEP 2 below*

If the basic design unit of your pattern is a square which is repeated over the whole top,
*category 12, p. 282*

If your pattern is neither of the above,
*return to the Key on p. 17*

**STEP 2**
If pieces are three-dimensional (gathered, folded or cut-work),
*turn to p. 34*

If pieces are flat with no intentional gathers,
*continue with STEP 3 below*

**STEP 3**
If pieces have curves,
*turn to p. 34*

If pieces have straight edges,
*continue with STEP 4 below*

**STEP 4**
If pieces have three sides,
*turn to p. 22*

If pieces have four sides,
*continue with STEP 5 below*

If pieces have five sides,
*turn to p. 28*

If pieces have six sides,
*continue with STEP 6 below*

If pieces have more than six sides,
*turn to p. 32*

**STEP 5**
If pieces are rectangles,
*turn to p. 24*

If pieces are diamonds,
*turn to p. 26*

If pieces have four sides but are odd-shaped,
*turn to p. 28*

**STEP 6**
If pieces have six equal angles and six equal sides,
*turn to p. 30*

If pieces have six unequal angles or six unequal sides,
*turn to p. 32*

Pattern Category 1: *One Patch*

TRIANGLES

**111a**    JOSEPH'S COAT – Doyle
THOUSAND PYRAMIDS – Finley 1929
RED SHIELDS – Nancy Cabot ca. 1935
THE MOWING MACHINE QUILT – KC Star 12/12/43
PYRAMIDS – Bruce Johnson
TRIANGLES – Khin 1980

**111b**    TUMBLERS – Gutcheon PPP. *See 141.*

**111c**    A TRIP TO EGYPT – Home Art ca. 1935
TRIANGLE MOSAIC – QEC 1983
EARLIEST EXAMPLE: ca. 1840, Safford & Bishop pg. 129

**112a**    DOG'S TOOTH – Wooster
LIGHTNING – Nancy Cabot

**112b**    LACE EDGE QUILT – KC Star 1949
LIGHTNING STRIPS – Gutcheon PPP

**112c**    STREAK O' LIGHTNING – Finley 1929
ZIG-ZAG – Finley
RAIL FENCE – Finley
SNAKE FENCE – Finley
DOG'S TOOTH – Colby

**112d**    A THOUSAND PYRAMIDS – Nancy Cabot 1933
CHAINED LIGHTNING – attributed to Nancy Cabot by Wilma Smith
LAND OF THE PHARAOH – Nancy Cabot

**113a**    *OCEAN WAVES – LAC #182, 1898
TENTS OF ARMAGEDDON – University of Kansas
THOUSANDS OF TRIANGLES – McKendry
EARLIEST EXAMPLE: 1854, QEC 1978 pl. 6

**113b**    THE WILD GOOSE CHASE – KC Star 12/28/1938/Comfort

**114**    ZIG ZAG – Doyle
FENCE ROW QUILT – KC Star 10/6/1943
DOG'S TOOTH – Colby
LIGHTNING STREAK – Coats & Clark Bk. 160
SNAKE FENCE – McKendry

**115**    CUPID'S DART – Nancy Cabot

*The triangles in this pattern actually form a square block (see #3150), but they are included in this One Patch section since they are so closely related.*

Triangles (111a – 115)

Pattern Category 1: *One Patch*

RECTANGLES

**131a**    **HIT AND MISS** – Finley 1929

**131b**    **HAIRPIN CATCHER** – Wooster
**BRICKWALL ONE** – Rodgers

**132a**    **BRICKWALL** – Finley 1929
**BRICKWORK** – Hall 1935

132b    **DEPRESSION** – KC Star 5/27/42
**STREAK O' LIGHTNING** – Holstein
**GENERAL SHERMAN'S QUILT** – Capper's/Famous Features, Obenchain
*Bicentennial Quilts* 1976 (red & white bricks with blue starred border)
**ZIG ZAG** – QEC 1981
**OLD GARDEN WALL** – attributed to Union Mill Ends by NNT Summer 1972
EARLIEST EXAMPLE: 1854 QEC 1978 pl. 6

132c    **BRICKWORK QUILT** – LAC #293, 1898

133    **BRICK CRIB QUILT** – McKim

134    **BASKET WEAVE THREE PATCH** – Aunt Kate

135    **FINE WOVEN PATCHWORK** – LAC #240, 1898
**FEATHEREDGE STRIPE** – Orange Judd Farmer 2/4/1899 (feather stitching around pieces)
**FENCE RAIL** – Mountain Artisans, Rhode Island School of Design Catalog
**KULI PAU** (Hawaiian for Bent Knee) – Woodard & Greenstein in *Clarion* Summer 1979
**STREAK OF LIGHTNING** – Bishop/Knopf pg. 62
EARLIEST EXAMPLE: ca. 1860, Bishop/Knopf pg. 62

136    **ORANGE PEKOE** – Nancy Cabot

*Rectangles (131a – 136)*

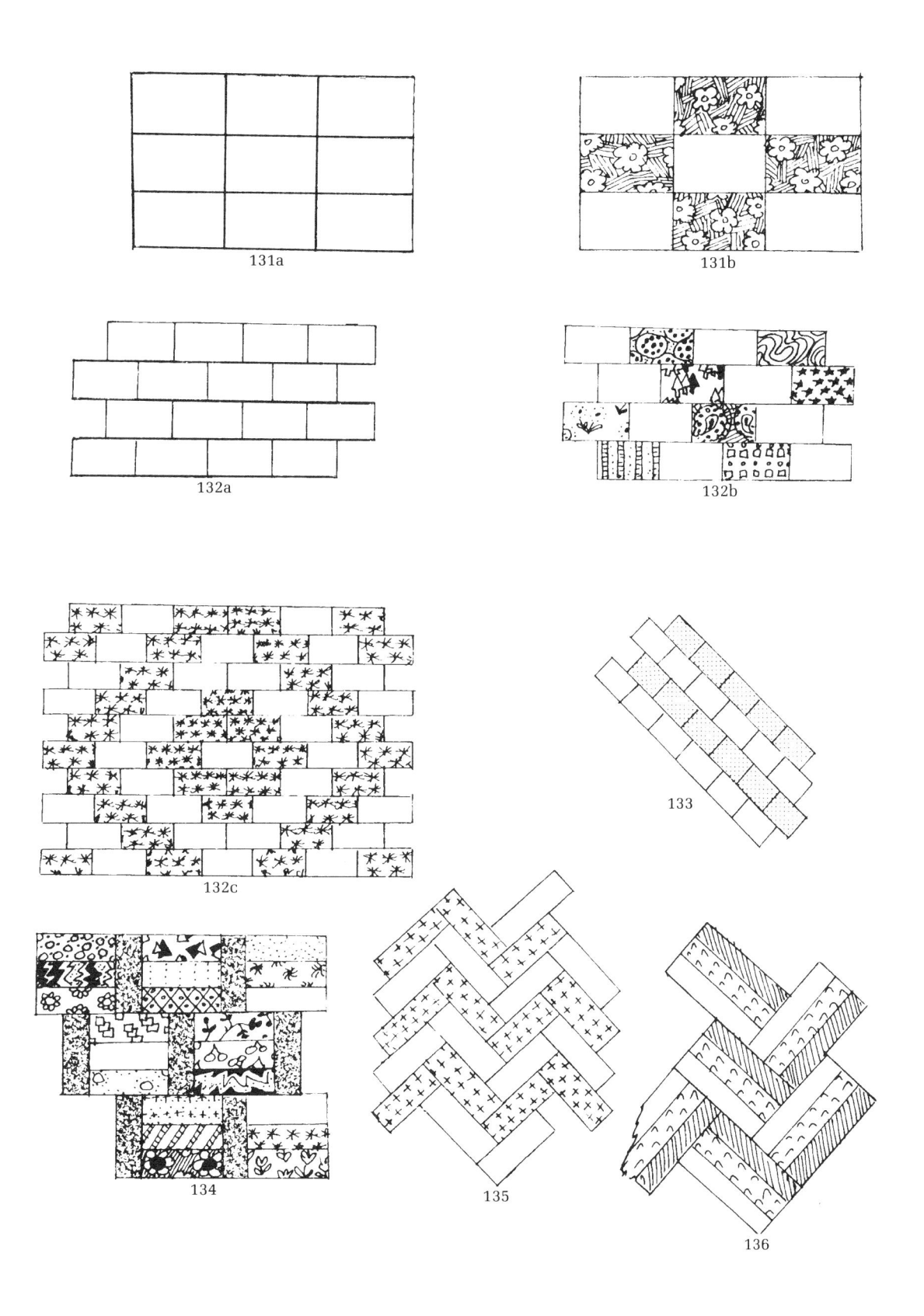

131a

131b

132a

132b

132c

133

134

135

136

# Pattern Category 1: *One Patch*

DIAMONDS

**141a**    **DIAMONDS** – LAC #49 1898
       **HERITAGE QUILT** – QNM/Heirloom Plastics
       **BOSTON CORNERS** – Nancy Cabot
       EARLIEST EXAMPLE: ca. 1850, Safford & Bishop pg 129

**141b**    **DIAMOND DESIGN** – LAC #312, 1898

**141c**    **FORD'S QUILT** – Goodspeed (red, white, & blue)

**141d**    **SPRINGTIME IN THE OZARKS** – KC Star 12/18/1940 (25 prints bordered by row of green or white)

**141e**    **MODERN TULIP** – Aunt Kate Vol. 1 #7. *See 111b.*

**142a**    **VARIEGATED DIAMONDS** – LAC #288, 1898

**142b**    **UNNAMED** – Godey's 1851
       **BLOCK PATTERN** – Caulfeild & Saward 1882
       **BOX PATTERN** – Caulfeild & Saward 1882
       **VARIEGATED DIAMONDS** – Farm & Home ca. 1890
       **SHIFTING CUBES** – Comfort, Hearth & Home
       **BABY'S BLOCKS** – McKim
       **BUILDING BLOCKS** – Rural New Yorker 4/23/32
       **BOX UPON BOX** – Nancy Page
       **CUBEWORK** – Hall 1935
       **GOLDEN CUBES** – Nancy Cabot
       **JACOB'S LADDER** – Woman's Day ca. 1940
       **STAIRSTEP QUILT** – Woman's Day 1940
       **DISAPPEARING BLOCKS** – Mountain Mist
       **STAIRS OF ILLUSION** – NNT Summer 1973
       **TUMBLING BLOCKS** – Bacon
       **STEPS TO THE ALTAR** – Bacon
       **ENGLISH T BOX** – Bacon
       **BOX PATCHWORK** – Shelburne
       EARLIEST EXAMPLE: 1852 Betterton

**142c**    **EISENHOWER QUILT** – This Week 1953
       **JACOB'S LADDER** – This Week 1953
       **STAIR STEP QUILT** – This Week 1953

**142d**    **HEXAGONAL STAR** – Capper's/Famous Features
       **RISING STAR** – Capper's/Famous Features

**142e**    **HEXAGONAL** – Household Journal
       **HEXAGONAL STAR** – Capper's/Famous Features
       **RISING STAR** – Capper's/Famous Features
       *142d & e are the same block in two different sets*

**142f**    **WHIRLING DIAMONDS** – KC Star 11/24/48

**142g**    **TEXAS STAR** – Capper's/Famous Features Bk. Q110 (star embroidered in center)
       **LEMON STAR** – McKendry (no embroidery)

**142h**    **THE STAR & BOX QUILT** – KC Star 9/20/39
       **THE BUILDER'S BLOCKS** – KC Star 10/22/47

**142i**    **TUMBLING BLOCKS** – Mountain Mist
       **BABY BLOCKS & STARS** – McKendry

**142j**    **PLAY BLOCK** – Capper's/Famous Features (one row pink, one row blue). *See 240 & 3700.*

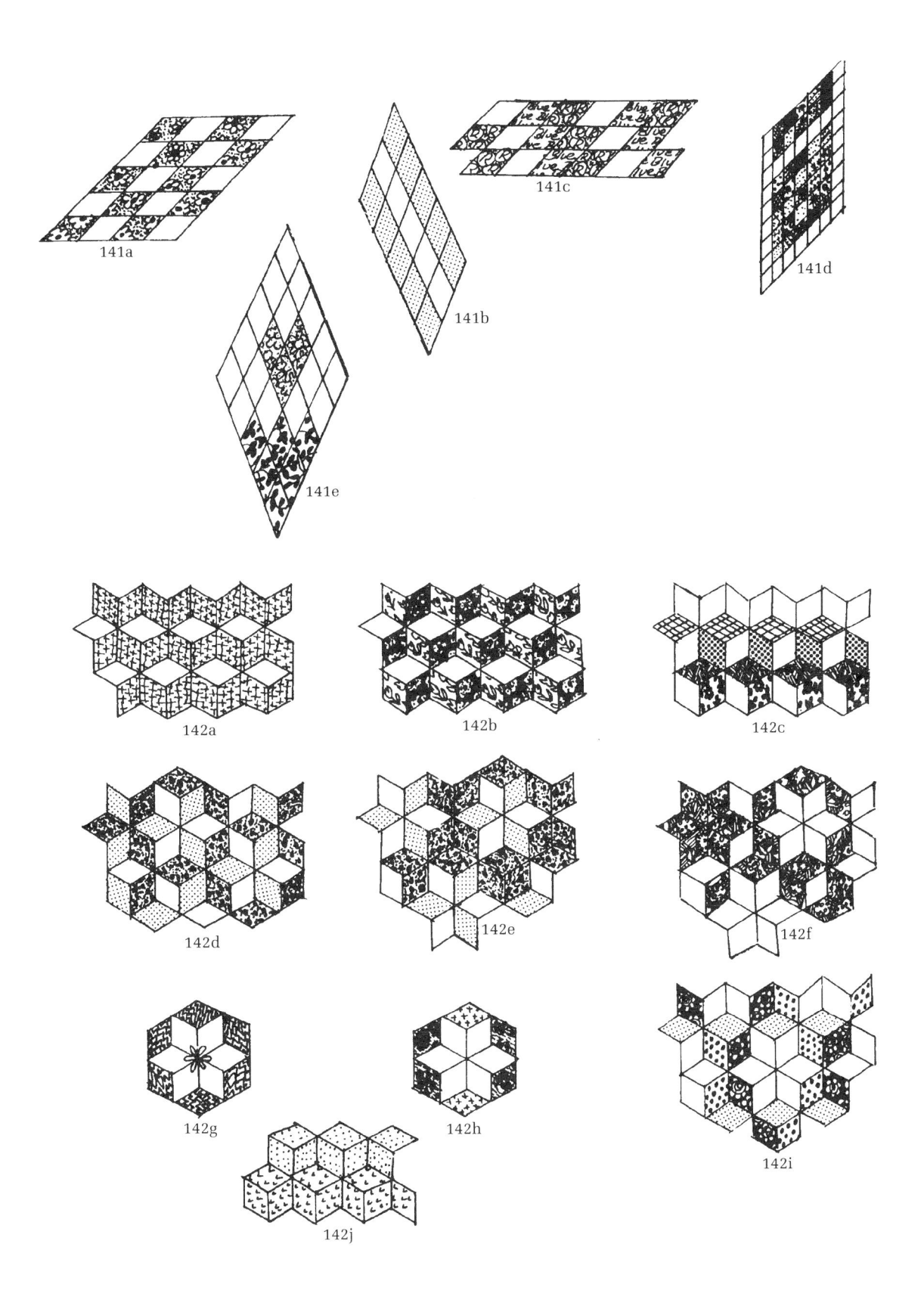

*Diamonds (141a – 142j)*

141a

141b

141c

141d

141e

142a

142b

142c

142d

142e

142f

142g

142h

142i

142j

Pattern Category 1: *One Patch*

| | | |
|---|---|---|
| DIAMONDS | **143a** | **TINY STAR** – Hall 1935<br>**AUNT STELLA'S PATTERN** – Burton/Land of Nod |
| | **143b** | **STAR AND BLOCKS** – Gutcheon PPP #246. *See 427 & 3708.* |
| | **144** | **BUILDING BLOCKS** – Golden Hands |
| | **145a** | **UNNAMED** – Peterson's Magazine ca. 1880<br>**WAVE** – OCS<br>**RAIL FENCE** – OCS<br>EARLIEST EXAMPLE: ca. 1775-1800, Finley pl. 83 |
| | **145b** | **BUTTERFLY QUILT** – Comfort |
| | **146** | **HIT AND MISS VARIATION** – Woodard & Greenstein *Crib Quilts*<br>EARLIEST EXAMPLE: ca. 1850-1875, Woodard & Greenstein, *Crib Quilts* pg 77 |
| | **147** | **ZIG ZAG** – QEC 1981<br>**HERRINGBONE** – Khin<br>*Numbers 145 – 147 vary only in the angle of the diamonds* |
| MISC. FOUR-SIDED FIGURES | **151a** | **TUMBLER** – LAC #368, 1898<br>**OUT OF THIS WORLD** – OCS Bk. 103 |
| | **151b** | **FLOWER POT** – Grandmother Dexter |
| | **152a** | **RIGHT ANGLE PATCHWORK** – Caulfeild & Saward 1882<br>**ECCLESIASTICAL** – LAC #295, 1898<br>**CRAZY TILE** – KC Star 5/24/39 & 1/21/48 |
| | **152b** | **MONK'S PUZZLE** – Nancy Cabot. *See 160.* |
| | **152c** | **INNER CITY** – Jinny Beyer, PP. *See 177.* |
| | **153a** | **COLONIAL GARDEN** – Grandmother Clark Bk. 23, 1932. *See 243 & 4102.* |
| | **153b** | **ROSE STAR ONE PATCH** – OCS/Laura Wheeler ca. 1935<br>**CANADIAN CONVENTIONAL STAR** – McKendry<br>**COLONIAL FLOWER GARDEN** – McKendry<br>**HEXAGONS** – Meeker |
| | **154** | **UNNAMED** – Peterson's Magazine |
| FIVE-SIDED FIGURES | **158** | **BAT WINGS** – Robert Frank, E-Z Patterns |

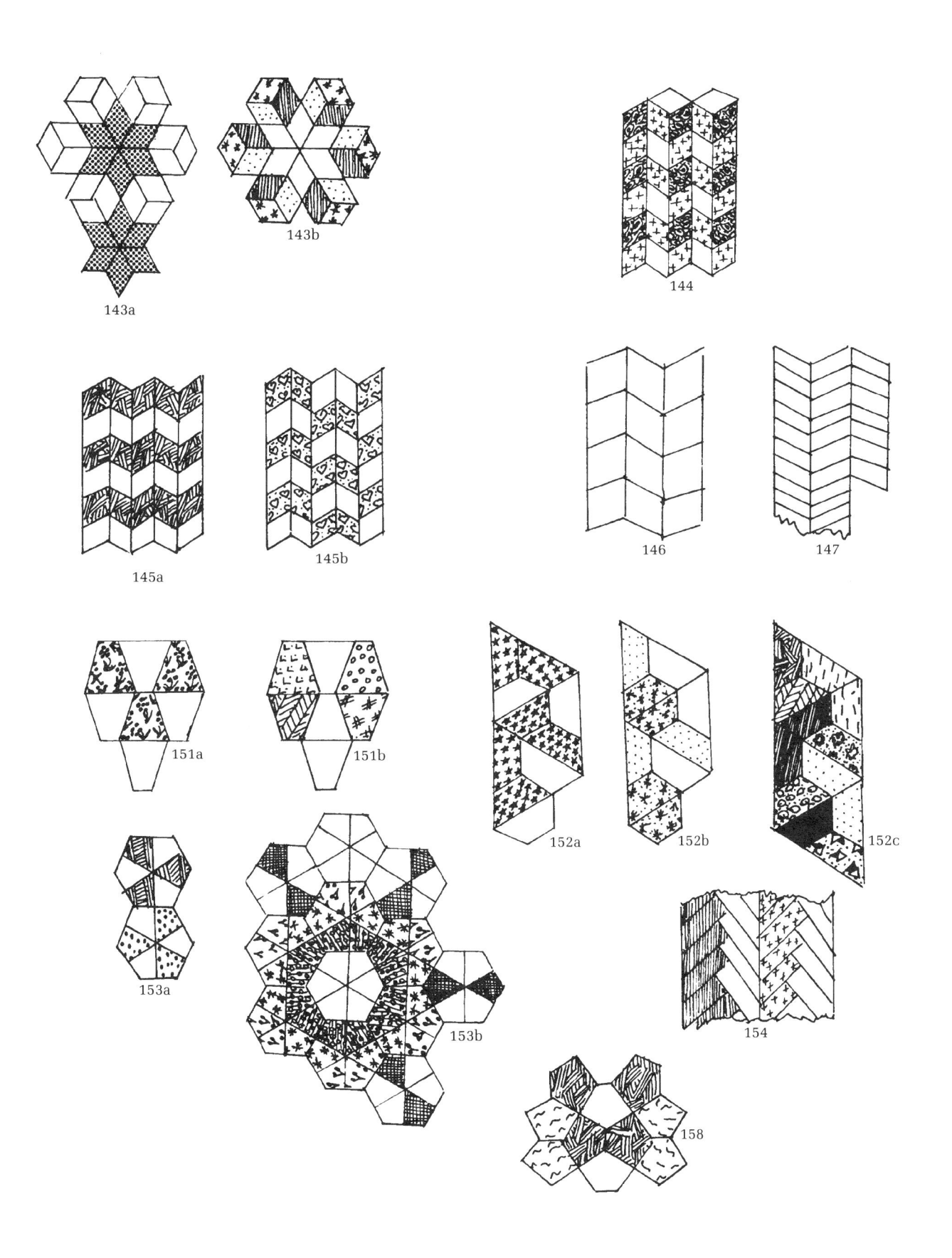

*Diamond, Misc. Four-Sided Figures, Five-Sided Figures (143a – 158)*

## Pattern Category 1: *One Patch*

There is an infinite variety of hexagon patterns. Some of the more common which have names are shown here. According to Finley all hexagon patterns are known as Honeycomb and Mosaic.

HEXAGONS

**160a**
- HEXAGON – Caulfeild & Saward 1882
- HONEYCOMB – Caulfeild & Saward 1882
- MOSAIC – Finley 1929
- CENTURY – Lithgow
- POOR BOY – Marshall
- FRIENDSHIP QUILT – OCS (plain patches have embroidery by friends)
- HIT OR MISS – OCS
- EARLIEST EXAMPLE: 1813, Shelburne #140

**160b**
- UNNAMED – Godey's
- VARIEGATED HEXAGONS – Farm and Home ca. 1890

**160c**
- OCEAN WAVE – Colby

**160d**
- OCEAN WAVE – Colby

**160e**
- OCEAN WAVE – Colby

**160f**
- CHEVRON – OCS Bk. 116

**160g**
- CHARM – Wallace's Farmer 1/18/1929
- A HONEYCOMB PATCH – Hearth & Home
- SIMPLICITY'S DELIGHT – KC Star 1946

**160h**
- ENDLESS CHAIN – Farmer's Wife

**160i**
- GRANDMOTHER'S FLOWER GARDEN – OCS Bk. 116

**160j**
- FRENCH BOUQUET – Hall 1935
- BRIDE'S BOUQUET – Farmer's Wife

**160k**
- THE HEXAGON – Hearth and Home
- OLD FASHIONED FLOWER GARDEN – Oklahoma Farmer Stockman 1931 (yellow center, plain ring, print ring with white paths between flowers)
- AUNT JEMIMA'S FLOWER GARDEN – Oklahoma Farmer Stockman 1931 (yellow, plain, print and white)
- HEXAGONS – Rural New Yorker 1932
- GRANDMOTHER'S ROSE GARDEN – Rural New Yorker 1932
- FRENCH ROSE GARDEN – Rural New Yorker 1932
- MARTHA WASHINGTON'S ROSE GARDEN – Home Art
- RAINBOW TILE – Hall 1935 (shades of solid pastels)
- GRANDMOTHER'S FLOWER GARDEN – Hall 1935
- COUNTRY TILE – OCS (dark paths between flowers)
- EARLIEST EXAMPLE: 1840 QEC 1978

**160l**
- THE WHEEL OF LIFE – Finley in Country Gentleman 1931 (white paths between flowers)
- GARDEN WALK – Capper's/Famous Features
- MARTHA WASHINGTON'S FLOWER GARDEN – Capper's/FF
- OLD FASHIONED FLOWER GARDEN – Capper's/FF
- FLOWER GARDEN – OCS Bk. 116
- JOB'S TROUBLES – University of Kansas

**160m**
- THE DIAMOND FIELD – KC Star 1932
- RAINBOW TILE – Hall 1935
- MARTHA WASHINGTON'S FLOWER GARDEN – Spool Cotton 1940
- EARLIEST EXAMPLE: 1830, Orlofsky pg. 91

**160n**
- HONEYCOMB – Godey's 2/1835
- SIX-SIDED PATCHWORK – Godey's 2/1835
- HEXAGON PATCHWORK – Godey's 2/1835
- COLONIAL BOUQUET – attributed to Union Mill Ends by NNT Summer 1972
- EARLIEST EXAMPLE: 1825-1850, Shelburne #8

*Hexagons (160a – 160n)*

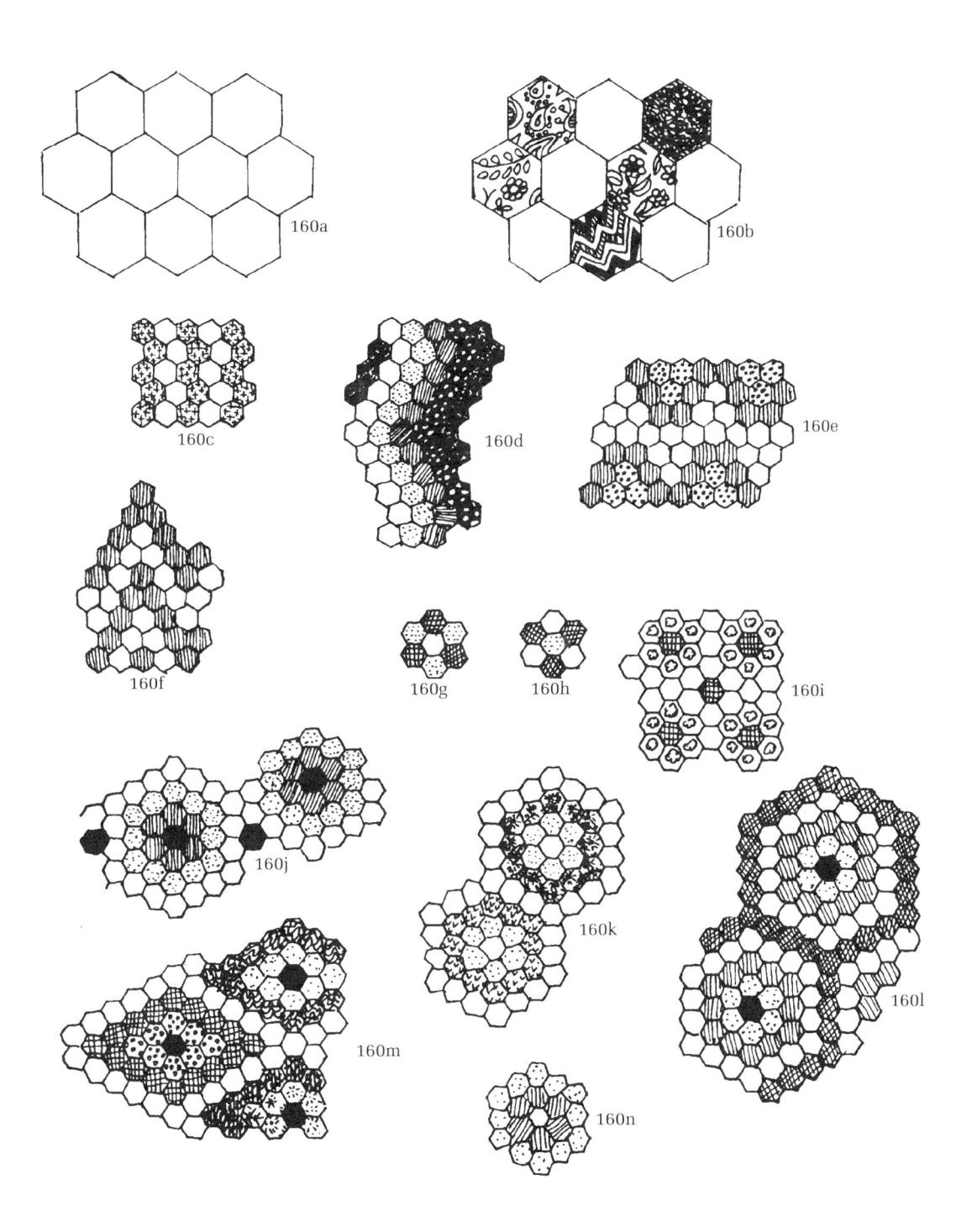

160a
160b
160c
160d
160e
160f
160g
160h
160i
160j
160k
160l
160m
160n

Pattern Category 1: *One Patch*

| | | |
|---|---|---|
| MISC. SIX-SIDED FIGURES | **171a** | **ODDFELLOWS** – Craft Horizons June 1966 |
| | **171b** | **UNNAMED** – Godey's |
| | | **LOZENGE** – Caulfeild & Saward 1882 |
| | | **POINTED OBLONG** – Caulfeild & Saward |
| | | **CHURCH WINDOWS** – Colby |
| | | **BLOSSOM PUFFS** – OCS Bk. 122 |
| | **171c** | **HONEYCOMB PATCHWORK** – LAC #241, 1898 |
| | **172** | **COFFIN** – Colby |
| | **173** | **SQUARE DIAMONDS** – Woman's World ca. 1930 |
| | **174** | **HONEYCOMB** – Gutcheon |
| | **175a** | **PICKET FENCE** – KC Star 1/6/1954 |
| | **175b** | **PICKET FENCE** – KC Star 1/6/1954 |
| | **176a** | **DESIGNER'S CHOICE** – OCS Bk. 116 |
| | **176b** | **THE "L" PATCH** – OCS Bk. 116 |
| | **177** | **RIGHT ANGLES PATCHWORK** – Caulfeild & Saward 1882. *See 152c.* |
| ODD SHAPES | **178** | **UNNAMED** – Godey's 4/1850 pg. 285 |

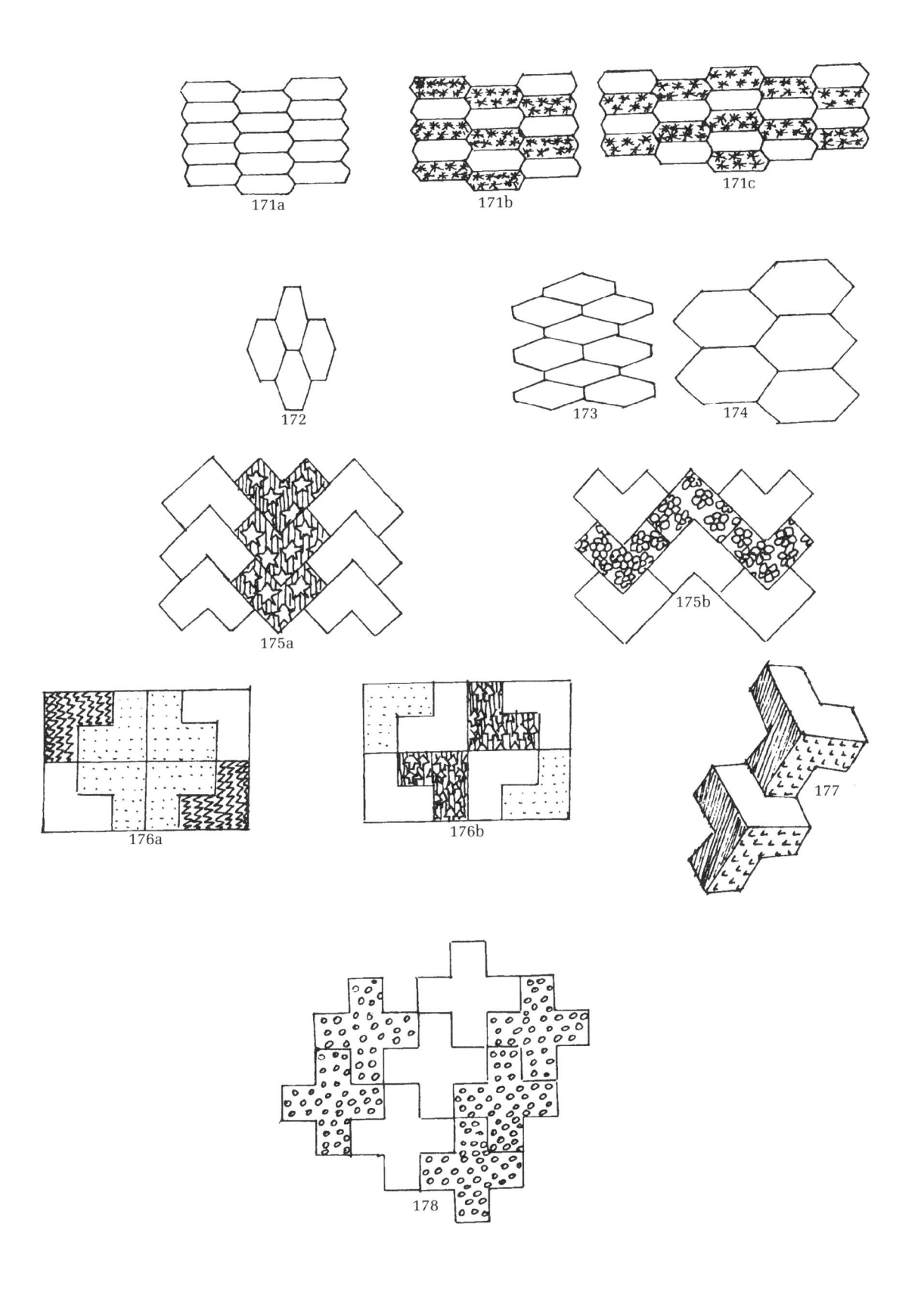

*Misc. Six-Sided Figures, Odd Shapes (171a – 178)*

171a

171b

171c

172

173

174

175a

175b

176a

176b

177

178

33

# Pattern Category 1: *One Patch*

CURVES

181a  CLAMSHELL – Finley 1929
SEASHELL – Grandmother Clark
SHELL – Colby
FISHSCALE – Colby
SUGAR SCOOP – Little 'n Big 2/65

181b  SHELL CHAIN – LAC #62 1898
SEA SHELLS ON THE BEACH – KC Star 6/24/53

181c  MUSHROOM SHELL – OCS

181d  ZIG ZAG SHELL – OCS
EARLIEST EXAMPLE: 1813, Shelburne #140 (appliqué)

182  OVER THE WAVES – OCS

183  UNNAMED – Colby

184  SUGAR SCOOP – Farm & Home ca. 1890

185a  FRIENDSHIP QUILT – KC Star 1930
ALWAYS FRIENDS – QNM, Marshall
SPOOLS – Hinson QC
DOUBLE AX – OCS #7472
FRIENDSHIP CHAIN – Ericson/Danner Bk. 6
DOUBLE BIT AXE – Amarillo Daily News 4/17/74
BADGE OF FRIENDSHIP – Khin
JIGSAW – Khin
THE SPOOL – Quilt World 6/81

185b  CHARM – KC Star 1933
FRIENDSHIP QUILT – KC Star 1933

185c  MOTHER'S ODDITY – Capper's 1928
EARLIEST EXAMPLE: ca. 1875 unpublished

188  OGEE – Evelyn Brown 12/75

189  ECONOMY JUMBLE – attributed to Godey's by Capper's 2/14/31

THREE DIMENSIONAL PIECES

191  RAISED PATCHWORK – Caulfeild & Saward 1882
SWISS PATCHWORK – Caulfeild & Saward 1882
BISCUIT QUILT – Ohio Farmer 10/29/1896
BUN QUILT – QNM/Heirloom Plastics
PUFFED SQUARES – Holstein

192  YO YO – Capper's 10/8/1932 & Grandmother Clark 1932
PUFF – Grandmother Clark 1932
BED OF ROSES – Grandmother Clark 1932
HEIRLOOM PILLOW – Grandmother Dexter
BON-BON – QNM/Heirloom Plastics
YORKSHIRE DAISY – Golden Hands #10
PUFF BALL – Golden Hands #10
SUFFOLK PUFFS – Golden Hands #10
PINWHEEL – Khin
ROSETTE – Khin
POWDER PUFF – Khin
*Illustration shows top and back of spread*

193  RAISED PATCHWORK – Caulfeild & Saward 1882
SWISS PATCHWORK – Caulfeild & Saward 1882

194  RAISED PATCHWORK – Caulfeild & Saward 1882
SWISS PATCHWORK – Caulfeild & Saward 1882

195  WHITE BLOSSOM COVERLET – Woman's Day 7/66
*Similar to 160k but center hexagon is puffed*

*Curves, Three Dimensional Pieces (181a – 195)*

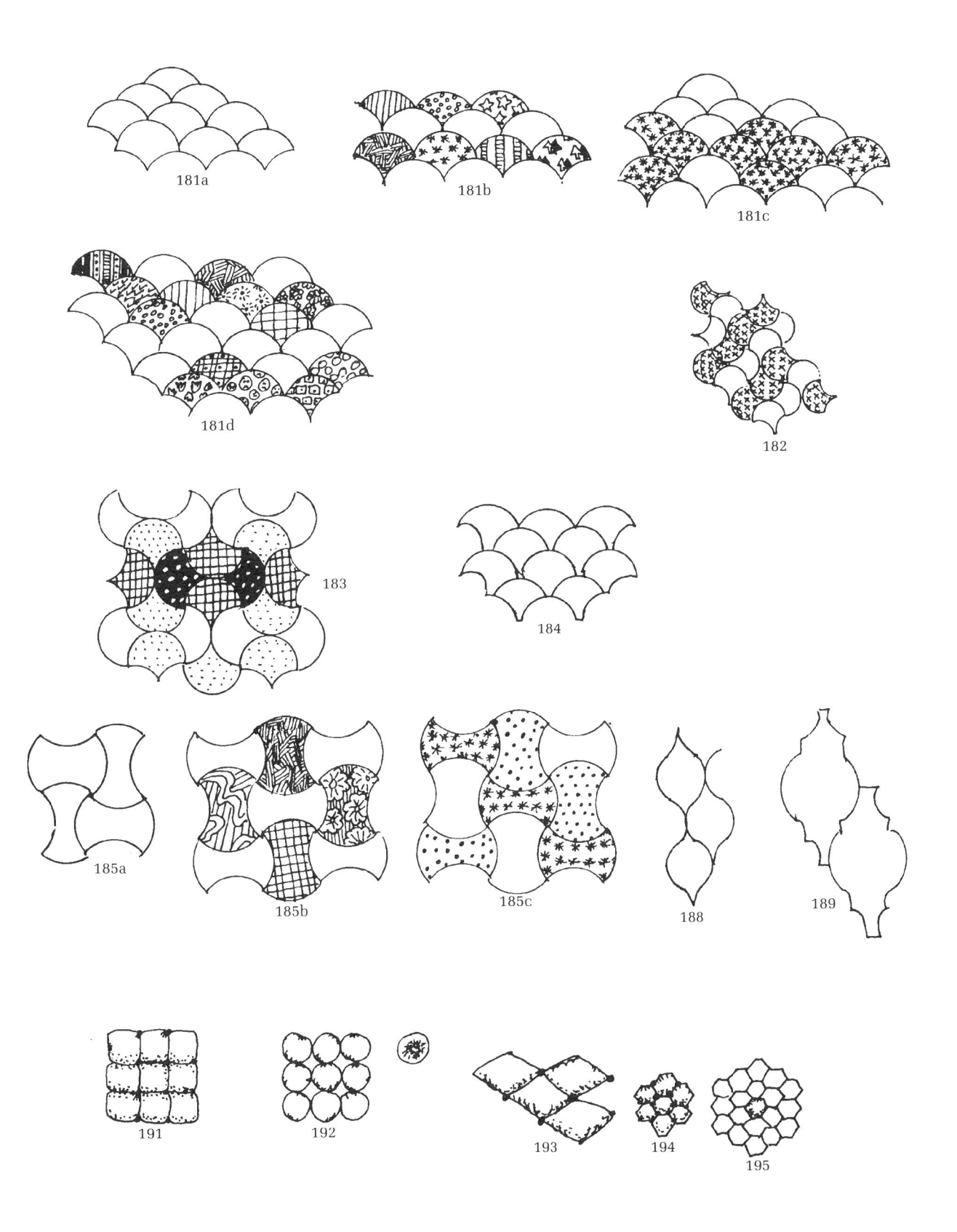

35

# PATTERN CATEGORY 2

## Non-Square Blocks

**Patterns in Category 2 share these characteristics:**

- They are regular, geometrically shaped units, made up of more than one piece of fabric.
- They may be set with other geometric shapes. For example:

**Category 2 includes:**

- Triangular Blocks, 38
- Rectangular Blocks, 38
- Diamond-Shaped Blocks, 46
- Hexagonal Blocks, 48
- Uneven Six-Sided Blocks, 54
- Eight-Sided Blocks, 56
- Blocks with More Than Eight Sides, 58
- Wedding Ring Types, 58

## KEY TO PATTERN CATEGORY 2: NON-SQUARE BLOCKS

Go through the list below in order. Choosing the first applicable description.

| | |
|---|---|
| If the block is a triangle, | ***turn to Triangular Blocks, pg. 38*** |
| If the block is a rectangle, | ***turn to Rectangular Blocks, pg. 38*** |
| If the block is a diamond, | ***turn to Diamond-Shaped Blocks, pg. 46*** |
| If the block is a hexagon, | ***See Hexagonal Blocks, pg. 48*** |
| If the block is an uneven six-sided figure, | ***turn to Uneven Six-Sided Blocks, pg. 54*** |
| If the block is an eight sided figure, | ***turn to Eight-Sided Blocks, pg. 56*** |
| If the block has more than eight sides, | ***turn to pg. 58*** |
| If the block is a circle set with a corresponding squeezed shape such as ⊐ or ⟨⟩ , | ***turn to Wedding Ring Type, pg. 58*** |

Pattern Category 2: *Non-Square Blocks*

| | | |
|---|---|---|
| TRIANGULAR BLOCKS | **201** | **SUGAR LOAF** – NNT, Vol 7 – 2<br>**THE PYRAMID** – Khin |
| | **201.7** | **FLAT IRON PATCHWORK** – The Ohio Farmer 7/23/1896 |
| | **202** | **TRIANGULAR TRIANGLES** – LAC #103 1898<br>**TRIANGLE QUILT** – Quilt World 10/80<br>**TRIANGULAR TREES** – Haders/Warner<br>EARLIEST EXAMPLE: ca. 1865, Haders/Warner pg. 86 |
| | **203** | **PYRAMIDS** – LAC #411 1898<br>**PIECED PYRAMIDS** – Hall 1935 |
| | **204** | **SUGAR LOAF** – KC Star 1931<br>**FLAT IRON** – Nancy Cabot<br>**ARROWHEADS** – Haders/Warner<br>EARLIEST EXAMPLE: ca. 1860, Haders/Warner p. 89. *See 4021.* |
| | **205** | **PYRAMID PATCHWORK** – QNM #90 1977 |
| | **206** | **WONDER OF EGYPT** – Nancy Cabot |
| | **207a** | **ICE CREAM CONE** – Hinson QM |
| | **207b** | **ORANGE PEEL** – OCS/Laura Wheeler |
| | **209** | **ROSE ARBOR** – Home Art Studios ca. 1933 |
| RECTANGULAR BLOCKS | **209.5** | **BASKETWEAVE** – QNM #73 1975 |
| | **209.6** | **RAINBOW WEAVE** – Canada Quilts #39/40 Sum./Aut. 1981 |
| | **210** | **JERICHO WALLS** – KC Star 1943 |
| | **211** | **SALUTE TO LOYALTY** – KC Star 1943 |
| | **212** | **THE WHITE CROSS** – KC Star 1946 |

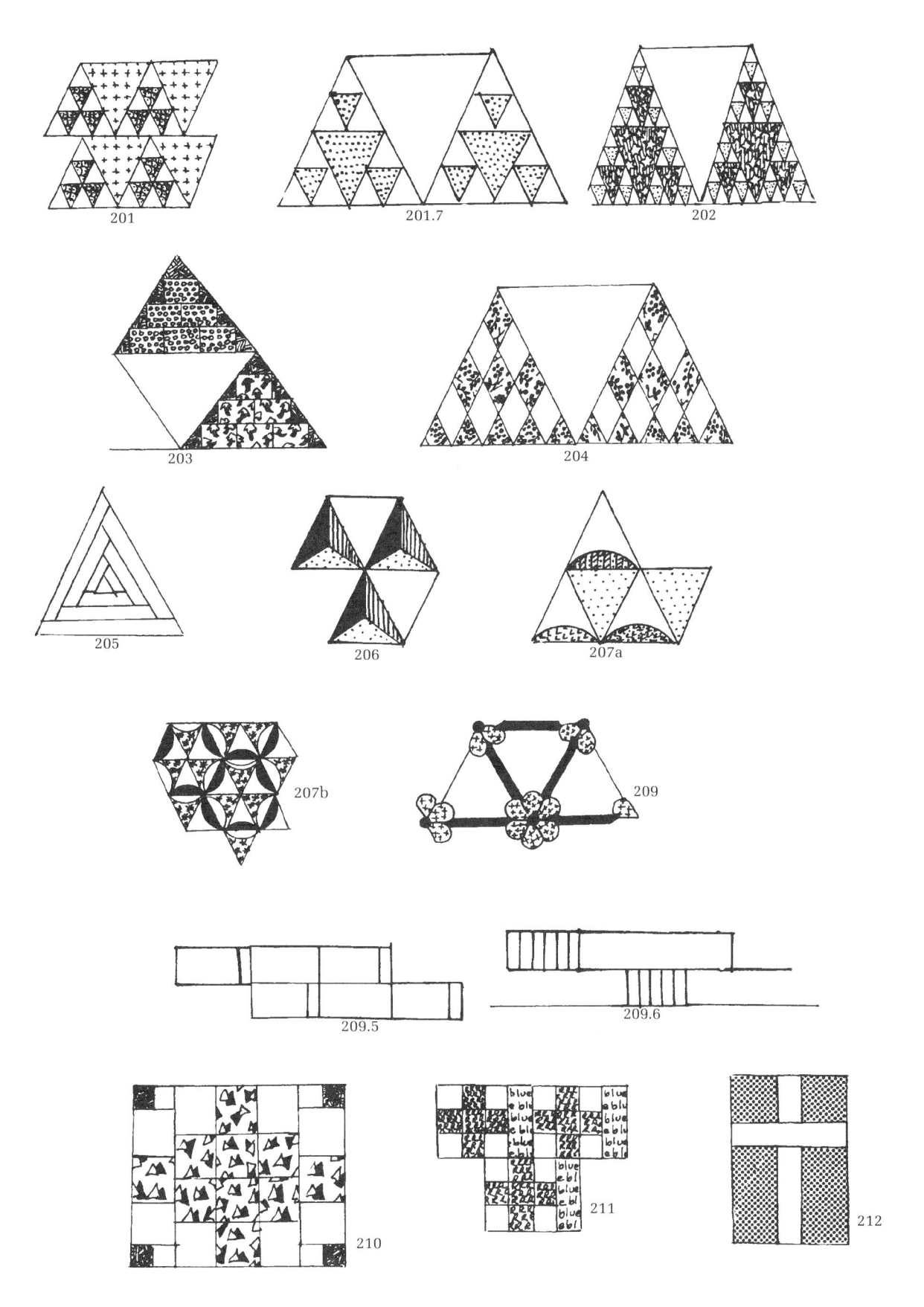

*Triangular Blocks, Rectangular Blocks (201 – 212)*

39

# Pattern Category 2: *Non-Square Blocks*

RECTANGULAR BLOCKS

| | | |
|---|---|---|
| | 212.2 | CHAIN LINKS – Telegraphics/Hagerman 6/12/80 |
| | 212.3 | PLEASANT PATHS – Farm Journal |
| | 212.5 | SHADED DIAMONDS – Nancy Cabot |
| | 213a | TIT FOR TAT – Aunt Kate |
| | 213b | TIT FOR TAT – Aunt Kate |
| | 213c | WILD GOOSE CHASE – Holstein |
| | 213d | WAVY NAVY – Toronto Star ca. 1940-5. *See 480.* |
| | 214 | WILD GOOSE CHASE – Holstein. *See 480.* |
| | 215 | TALL PINE TREE – Hall |
| | 216 | TALL PINE TREES – Household Magazine<br>LONESOME PINE – Home Art Studios |
| | 216.11 | HILL AND VALLEY – Heard |
| | 216.12 | HILL AND VALLEY – Nancy Page |
| | 216.22 | HAWKS IN FLIGHT – Nancy Cabot |
| | 216.27 | SPRING AND FALL – Nancy Cabot |
| | 216.31 | TREE OF PARADISE – Farm Journal<br>PINE TREE – Woman's Day 4/1961. *See 811.* |
| | 216.35 | JOHNNY JUMP UP – Woman's World 1/1933 |
| | 216.38 | PIECED IRIS – McKim 101<br>MODERNISTIC IRIS – Hall |
| | 216.4 | STAR AND DIAMONDS – Nancy Cabot. *See pp. 510-515 for similar stars which can be drawn in a rectangle or a square.* |
| | 217 | DIAMOND FRIENDSHIP – KC Star |
| | 217.5 | BAT'S WINGS – LAC #43, 1898. |

*Rectangular Blocks (212.2 – 217.5)*

212.2

212.3

212.5

213a

213b

213c

213d

214

215

216

216.11

216.12

216.22

216.27

216.31

216.35

216.38

216.4

217

217.5

Pattern Category 2: *Non-Square Blocks*

| | | |
|---|---|---|
| RECTANGULAR BLOCKS | 217.7 | **TEA TIME** – Nancy Cabot<br>**MIXED T'S** – QNM #98 |
| | 218 | **SOLDIER BOY** – KC Star 1944 |
| | 218.2 | **OKLAHOMA BOOMER** – LAC 1898 |
| | 218.3 | **BUG QUILT** – Quilt Fall 1980 |
| | 218.4 | **TEAPOT** – Orange Judd Farmer 8/4/1900 |
| | 219 | **THE WORLD FAIR QUILT** – KC Star 10/27/43 |
| | 220 | **THE ENVELOPE QUILT** – KC Star 9/20/44 |
| | 220.4 | **PICKET FENCE** – Aunt Martha |
| | 220.6 | **THE FLOWING RIBBON** – KC Star 1933 |
| | 220.7 | **WHIRLING NINE-PATCH** – QNM #92 |
| | 220.8 | **BASKET OF DIAMONDS** – KC Star 8/18/37 |
| | 221 | **BOARD MEETING** – Gutcheon QDW |
| | 222 | **REFRACTIONS** – Gutcheon QDW |
| | 222.2 | **THE STAR FISH** – Nancy Cabot. *See 233.* |
| | 222.4 | **YELLOW LILY** – McKim |
| | 222.5 | **ROCK STAR** – QNM #88 |
| | 222.8 | **WHIRLWIND** – Woman's World ca. 1930 |
| | 223 | **42ND STREET** – Evelyn Brown |
| | 224 | **A BUTTERFLY IN ANGLES** – KC Star 2/2/44 |

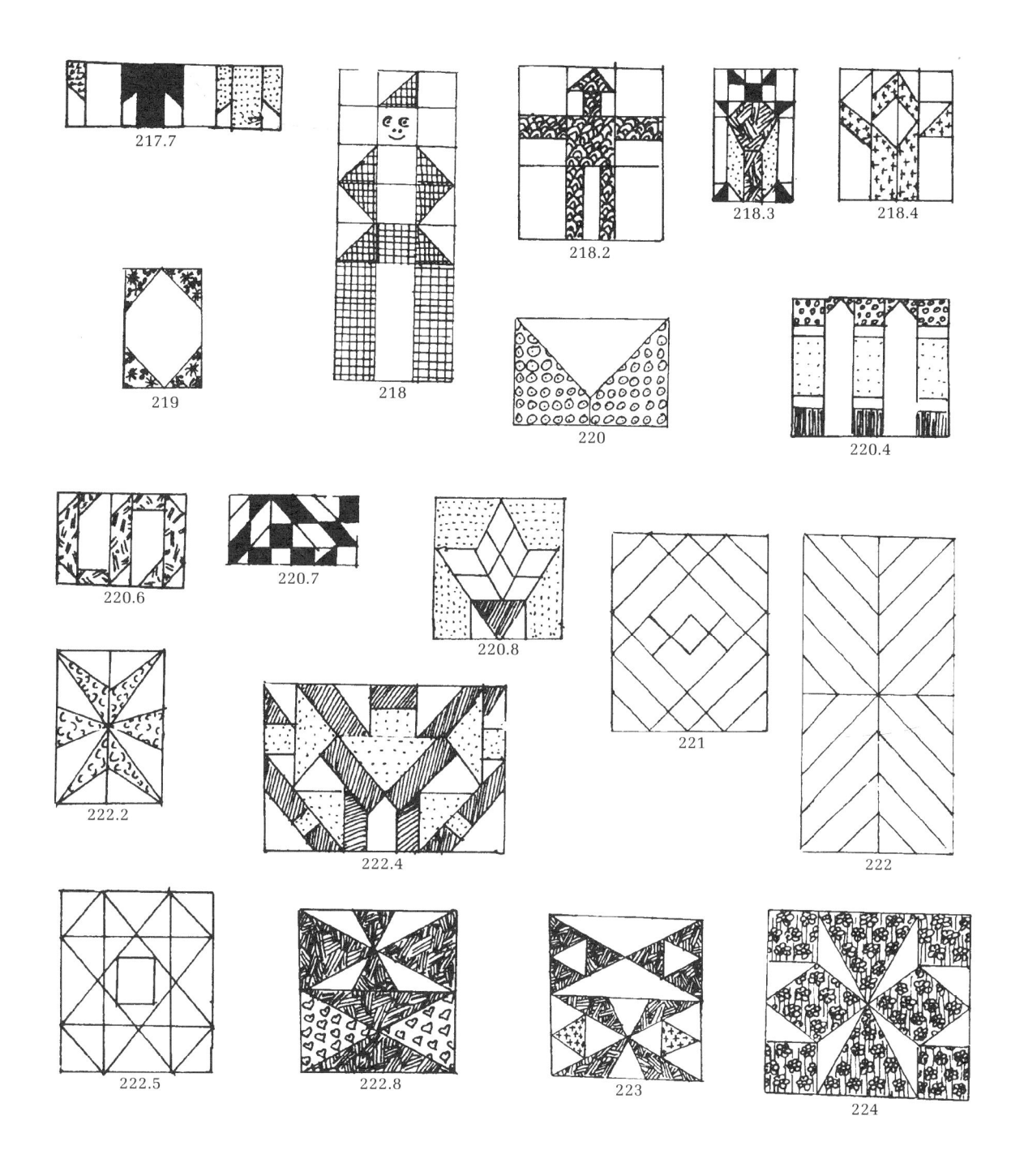

*Rectangular Blocks (217.7 – 224)*

217.7
218
218.2
218.3
218.4
219
220
220.4
220.6
220.7
220.8
221
222
222.2
222.4
222.5
222.8
223
224

## Pattern Category 2: *Non-Square Blocks*

RECTANGULAR BLOCKS

| | | |
|---|---|---|
| **224.2** | **Butterfly Quilt** – Quilt World 5/78 |
| **224.5** | **Rocky Mountain High** – QNM #111, 1979 |
| **224.7** | **Television Quilt** – Quilt World 10/77 |
| **225** | **Sylvia's Bow** – KC Star 12/20/39 |
| **225.3** | **Shooting Star** – Jones, Suzi, *Webfoots & Bunchgrassers: Folk Art of the Oregon Country.* Oregon Arts Commission. Catalog of an Exhibition, 1980. |
| **225.5** | **Concorde Star** – QNM #85, 1976 |
| **226** | **Victory Quilt** – KC Star 4/22/42 |
| **226.5** | **Unnamed** – QNM #70 |
| **226.6** | **Topaz Trail** – Nancy Cabot |
| **226.71** | **Blue Eagle NRA** – Nancy Cabot |
| **226.72** | **The Country Meeting House** – Country Gentleman 7/30 |
| **226.73** | **The Dog Quilt** – KC Star 5/2/36 |
| **226.75** | **Fish** – QNM #66, 1972 |
| **226.76** | **Ararat** – KC Star 6/6/31 |
| **226.77** | **Giddap** – KC Star 7/18/31 |
| **226.8** | **Flags and Ships** – Quilt World 2/79 |
| **227** | **Topiary Garden** – Evelyn Brown |
| **227.3** | **Indian Sunburst** – LCPQ 1981. *See 3344.* |
| **228** | **Aztec** – QNM #54, 1971 |
| **229** | **Japanese Sunburst** – Little 'n Big Aug. 1965. *See 3373.* |

*Rectangular Blocks (224.2 – 229)*

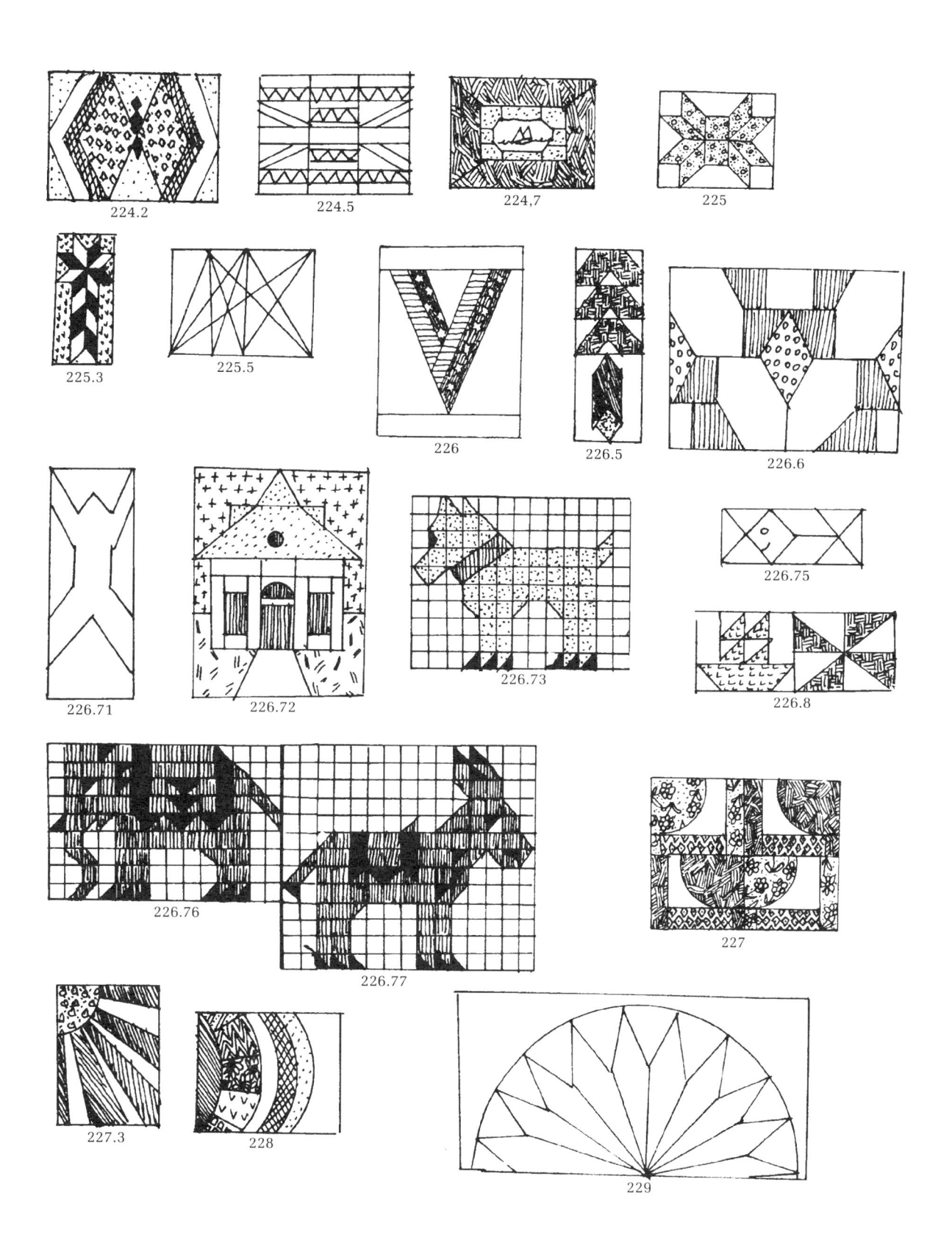

224.2
224.5
224,7
225
225.3
225.5
226
226.5
226.6
226.71
226.72
226.73
226.75
226.8
226.76
226.77
227
227.3
228
229

45

# Pattern Category 2: *Non-Square Blocks*

| | | |
|---|---|---|
| DIAMOND-SHAPED BLOCKS | **231a** | **WALK AROUND** – LAC #527, ca. 1929<br>**GUIDE POST** – Mountain Mist<br>**BOSTON CORNERS** – Nancy Cabot 2/10/34<br>**DOUBLE X'S** – Nancy Cabot<br>**WEB OF DIAMONDS** – Nancy Cabot<br>**COUNTRY CROSSROADS** – Little 'n Big 8/64 |
| | **231b** | **DIAMONDS** – Nancy Page 1933 |
| | **232** | **SHADOW TRAIL** – Mountain Mist |
| | **232a** | **NINE PATCH DIAMOND** – Hinson QM |
| | **232b** | **DIAMOND NINE PATCH** – Mrs. Danner 1970 |
| | **232.4** | **BLOCK AND STAR** – McKendry |
| | **232.8** | **DIAMONDS** – OCS/Alice Brooks |
| | **233** | **STAR FISH** – Home Art. *See 222.2.* |
| | **234** | **SNOWFLAKE** – Woman's World ca. 1930 |
| | **235** | **HANDS** – Haders, Sunshine and Shadow |
| | **236** | **COMET STAR** – Hearth and Home |
| | **237** | **NEIL'S DIAMOND** – QNM #99, 1978 |
| | **237.5** | **JONATHAN LIVINGSTON SEAGULL** – QNM #53, 1971 |
| | **238** | **FOUR WINDMILLS** – Nancy Cabot |

*Diamond-Shaped Blocks (231a – 238)*

# Pattern Category 2: *Non-Square Blocks*

HEXAGONAL BLOCKS

**239**    SIX POINTED STAR – Clara Stone
A LITTLE GIRL'S STAR – KC Star 8/15/50
PENNSYLVANIA HEX – Woman's Day 4/65 (set in concentric rings). *See 142 3700, & 3701.*
EARLIEST EXAMPLE: ca.1820 in Haders/Warner pg. 112.

**240**    DIAMOND CUBE – LAC #91, 1898
TEA BOX – Farm Journal
EARLIEST EXAMPLE: ca. 1820 Haders/Warner pg. 112

**241**    SEVEN STARS – LAC #8, 1898
SEVEN SISTERS – Danner/Ericson
SEVEN STARS IN A CLUSTER – Capper's Weekly 1928
EARLIEST EXAMPLE: ca. 1845 in QEC 1981, Pl.1

**241.1**    TWINKLING STAR – Mountain Mist (set with plain diamonds in strips). *See 3716.*

**241.2**    THE GLISTENING STAR – Country Gentleman 7/30. *See 3707.*

**241.33**    UNNAMED – OCS (when set all over identical to 241.35)

**241.35**    UNNAMED – OCS (when set all over identical to 241.33)

**241.4**    STATE OF KENTUCKY – Hearth & Home. *See 3722.*

**241.6**    HEXAGON SNOWFLAKE – QNM #93, 1977 (set with triangles)

**241.9**    WAGON WHEEL – Aunt Kate 1965 (set with triangles)

**242**    THREE PATCH – OCS/Laura Wheeler

**243**    COLONIAL GARDEN – Grandma Clark
ROSE STAR ONE PATCH – OCS
TUMBLING HEXAGON – QNM #65, 1974. *See 153.* (Can be set in a variety of ways with hexagons, triangles and diamonds to make different mosaic patterns.) *See 415.3.*

**244**    STAR CENTER ON FRENCH BOUQUET – KC Star 1934
SNOW CRYSTALS – KC Star 1932 (set in concentric rings with rings of plain hexagons)

**244.5**    THE DIAMOND HEXAGON – Nancy Page (set with plain hexagons in strips). *See 425.8.*

**245**    WHIRLING HEXAGON – KC Star 7/25/36
THE TEXAS TRELLIS – KC Star 7/28/43
WHIRLING TRIANGLES – QNM #68, 1975

**245.1**    MAPLE LEAF – Canada Quilts Midwinter 1978

**246**    HEXAGON – LAC #353
AN OLD FASHIONED WHEEL QUILT – KC Star 1938
HEXAGON BEAUTY – Farm Journal
SPIDER WEB – LCPQ #16, 1979

**247**    A COBWEB QUILT – Orange Judd Farmer 1/4/1896 (set all over)
SPIDER WEB – KC Star 1930 (set with triangles)

**247.5**    TRIALS AND TROUBLES – Rural New Yorker 8/1/31

**248**    MORNING STAR – OCS/Laura Wheeler

**249**    FLOATING CLOUDS – KC Star 11/23/38

*Hexagonal Blocks (239 – 249)*

# Pattern Category 2: *Non-Square Blocks*

HEXAGONAL BLOCKS

250
MADISON – Hearth & Home
MADISON QUILT BLOCK – LAC #477

251a
HEXAGONAL STAR – Hearth & Home
TEXAS STAR – LAC #466
HEXAGON STARS – Nancy Page
FRIENDSHIP HEXAGON – Nancy Page
DOLLY MADISON'S STAR – Home Art
DOLLY MADISON PATTERN – KC Star
STAR GARDEN – KC Star 1/27/54. *See 424.7.*

251b
PEPPER & SALT SHAKERS – Clarke (set surrounded by plain hexagons)
EARLIEST EXAMPLE: dated 1844 in Bishop/Knopf pg. 134

252
THE DIAMOND – Ohio Farmer 4/16/1896
FLOWER GARDEN BLOCK – KC Star 1937

254
MORNING STAR – KC Star 1936

255a
DUTCH TILE – KC Star 1931
ARABIAN STAR – Capper's/Famous Features
STAR OF BETHLEHEM – Union Mill Ends

255b
DUTCH TILE – KC Star 1931

256
FAVORITE – Ohio Farmer 11/29/1894
DIAMONDS AND ARROW POINTS – KC Star 2/21/45. *See 3715.*

257
OZARK DIAMONDS – KC Star 1931
OZARK STAR – KC Star 1931
MA PERKINS FLOWER GARDEN – KC Star 5/16/36

258
THE OKLAHOMA STAR – KC Star 1/17/45
THE MOUNTAIN STAR – Marshall. *See 3702.*

259
THE OZARK STAR – KC Star 1935

260
HIDDEN STAR – KC Star 7/4/35

261
FIVE PATCH BEAUTY – OCS
STAR STUDDED BEAUTY – OCS

262
BRILLIANT STAR – Nancy Page 1/26/34
POINTING STAR – KC Star 3/2/36

263
THE HEXAGON STAR – KC Star 10/9/40

263.5
EASTERN STAR – OCS. *See 415.7.*

264
THE PINWHEEL – KC Star 5/7/34

*Hexagonal Blocks (250 – 264)*

51

Pattern Category 2: *Non-Square Blocks*

HEXAGONAL BLOCKS

| | | |
|---|---|---|
| | 265 | ARROWHEADS – KC Star ca. 1941-2 |
| | 266A | ORIENTAL SPLENDOR – Home Art & Progressive Farmer 2/35<br>THE SMOOTHING IRON – Progressive Farmer 2/35 |
| | 266B | FLORIDA – Hearth & Home |
| | 266C | NEW HAMPSHIRE – Hearth & Home<br>STAR RAYS – Nancy Page<br>DIAMOND STRING – Nancy Page |
| | 266.5 | SNOWFLAKE QUILT – Workbasket 1945 |
| | 267 | ZODIAC STARS – Home Art |
| | 268 | DUTCH TILE – Home Art |
| | 268.5 | MODERNISTIC STAR – Aunt Martha, Prize Winning Quilts 1931 |
| | 269 | FLORIDA STAR – KC Star 1932 |
| | 269.3 | MORNING STAR – Nancy Cabot |
| | 269.5 | COLLINSVILLE ROSE STAR – QNM #78, 1976 |
| | 269.6 | MONTANA STAR – Hearth & Home<br>STAR OF MONTANA – Hearth & Home |
| | 269.8 | JACOB'S COAT – Aunt Martha, Prize Winning Quilts 1931 |
| | 270 | LOG CABIN – Safford & Bishop |
| | 271 | MILKY WAY – OCS |

*Hexagonal Blocks (265 – 270)*

265

266a

266b

266c

266.5

267

268

268.5

269

269.3

269.5

269.6

269.8

270

271

Pattern Category 2: *Non-Square Blocks*

HEXAGONAL BLOCKS

| | | |
|---|---|---|
| | 271.5 | GRANDMOTHER'S FLOWER BASKET – QNM #124, 1980 |
| | 271.7 | DIAMOND ROWS – Farm Journal 1/37 |
| | 272 | ENDLESS CHAIN – OCS/Alice Brooks, Laura Wheeler, C. Curtis |
| | 272.5 | ROCK WALL – LCPQ #22 |
| | 272.8 | PINWHEEL – OCS |
| | 273 | SIX POINTED STAR – KC Star 10/5/38 |
| | 274 | GAY COSMOS QUILT – Home Art #391<br>COSMOS – Home Art #391 |
| | 274.5 | HEXAGONS AND FLOWERS – OCS |
| | 275 | DAISY CHAIN – Aunt Martha |
| | 275.5 | KANSAS SUNFLOWER – Quilt World July/Aug. 1976 |
| | 275.8A | ROSES OF PICARDY – Progressive Farmer 1971 |
| | 275.8B | THE TOY BALLOON QUILT – Home Art |
| | 276 | TWINKLING STAR – Hall<br>STAR AND CRESCENT – Hall<br>FLOWER STAR – Hall |
| | 277 | SPARKLING DEW – Nancy Cabot |
| | 278 | KALEIDOSCOPE – OCS |

*If you cannot find your pattern here look in Hexagonal Blocks, pg. 48 or Six-Pointed Stars, pg. 511.*

UNEVEN SIX-SIDED BLOCKS

| | | |
|---|---|---|
| | 281a | UNNAMED – Peterson's Magazine last quarter 19th century<br>BOX QUILT – Finley |
| | 281b | PATIENCE CORNERS – LAC #80, 1896 |
| | 281c | THE HEAVENLY STEPS – Finley<br>PANDORA'S BOX – Finley<br>DANCING CUBES – Progressive Farmer |
| | 282 | TUMBLING BLOCKS – Coats and Clark |
| | 282.5 | IRISH CHAIN – Comfort 8/22 |
| | 282.7 | OCEAN WAVE – Nancy Page |
| | 283 | OCEAN WAVE – McKim, Rural New Yorker 2/14/31<br>WAVES OF THE OCEAN – Hearth and Home<br>ODDS AND ENDS – Comfort 1/26<br>OCTAGON – Comfort 1/26<br>ODD FELLOWS QUILT – Rural New Yorker 2/14/31<br>EARLIEST EXAMPLE: ca. 1850-60 in Bishop & Coblentz pg. 112. |

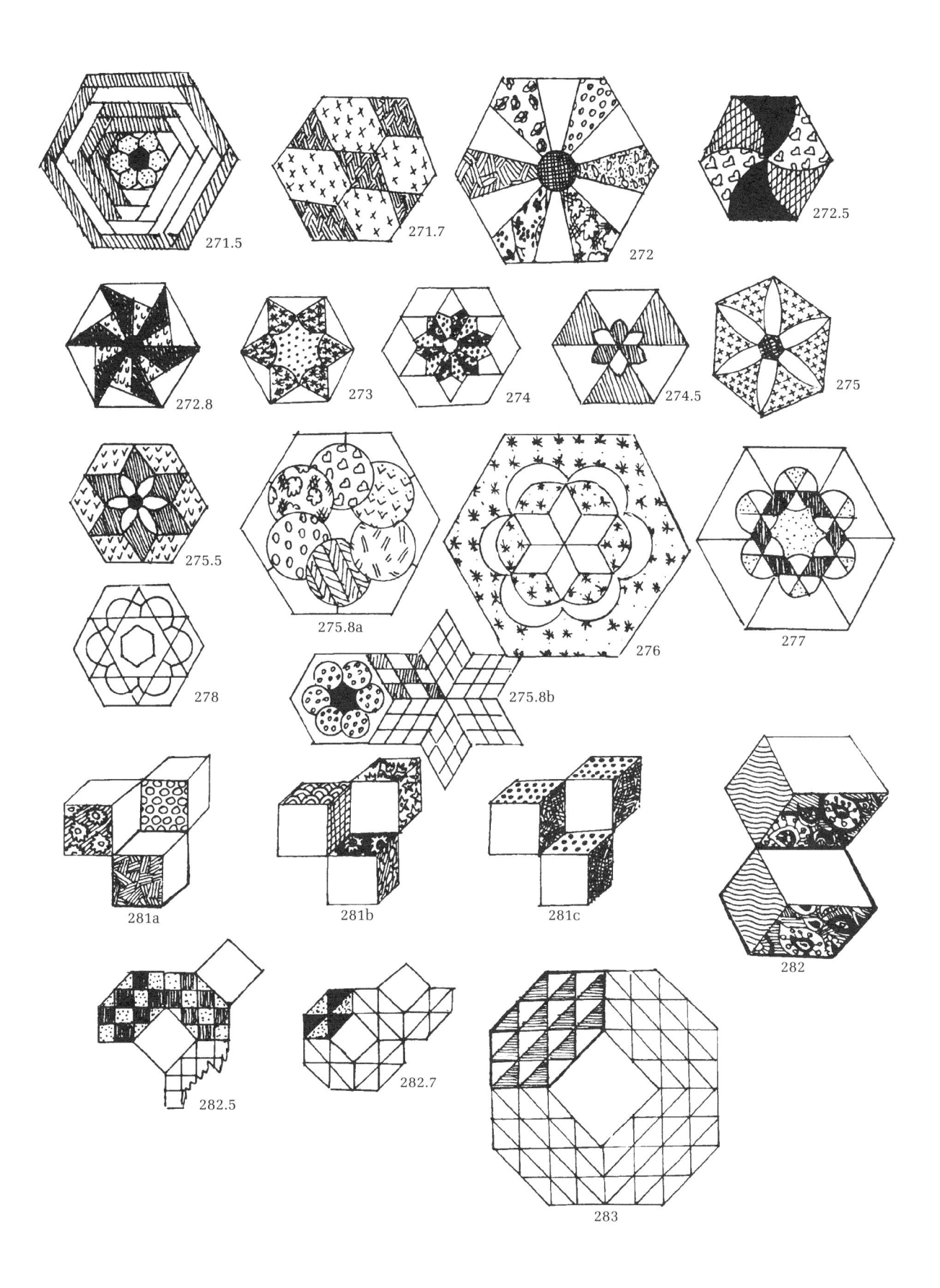

*Hexagonal Blocks, Uneven Six-Sided Blocks (271.5 – 283)*

271.5
271.7
272
272.5
272.8
273
274
274.5
275
275.5
275.8a
276
277
278
275.8b
281a
281b
281c
282
282.5
282.7
283

55

Pattern Category 2: *Non-Square Blocks*

| | | |
|---|---|---|
| UNEVEN SIX-SIDED BLOCKS | **284a** | **UNNAMED** – QEC 1979 |
| | **284b** | **VARIABLE TRIANGLES** – McCall's Bk. of Quilts |
| | **285** | **GLORY DESIGN** – Woman's World ca. 1931<br>**GLORY BLOCK** – KC Star 1933 (red, white, & blue)<br>**OLD GLORY** – Nancy Cabot |
| | **286** | **UNNAMED** – McKim<br>**ORIENTAL TULIP** – Nancy Cabot |
| EIGHT-SIDED BLOCKS | **290** | **PARQUETRY DESIGN FOR PATCHWORK** – Orange Judd Farmer 6/15/1900 |
| | **291** | **THE PEACEFUL VALLEY QUILT** – Marshall. *See 2853.* |
| | **292** | **HEXAGON BEAUTY QUILT** – KC Star 6/14/39. *See 2726.* |
| | **293** | **GOLDEN GATES** – LAC #117, 1898<br>**WINGED SQUARE** – Hall |
| | **294** | **OCTAGON** – Farm Journal |
| | **295** | **DOVE IN THE WINDOW** – Home Art 1933. *See 4214.* |
| | **296** | **WHIRL AROUND** – KC Star 7/31/40. *See 2537.* |
| | **296.5** | **ROLLING STAR** – Capper's Weekly 1927. *See 3805.* |
| | **296.7** | **EVENING STAR** – Mills |
| | **296.8** | *See 3808.* |
| | **296.9** | **EVENING STAR** – KC Star 11/28/31. *See 2736 & 3585.* |
| | **297** | **INDIAN PLUME** – Aunt Martha. *See 2052.* |

*Uneven Six-Sided Blocks, Eight-Sided Blocks (284a – 297)*

57

Pattern Category 2: *Non-Square Blocks*

EIGHT-SIDED BLOCKS

**297.5**    IXL – KC Star 1936
I Excell – KC Star 1936. *See 2798.*

**298a**    Cheyenne – KC Star 1933

**298b**    Rock Garden – Aunt Martha. *See 2113.*

**298.5**    Aerial Beacon – Progressive Farmer 1931. *See 2747.*

**298.7**    Joining Dots – Aunt Kate 6/66

**299**    Montana – Hearth & Home

**299.2**    Ida Red – QNM #66, 1974

**299.4**    Railroad Crossing – QNM #94, 1977

*If you cannot find your block here look under Multi-Patch, pg. 63 or Eight Pointed Stars, pg. 451.*

BLOCKS WITH MORE THAN EIGHT SIDES

**299.9**    Man in the Moon – Aunt Martha. *See 3456.*

WEDDING RING TYPES

**300**    Ohio Beauty – The Country Home 5/28

**301**    Tea Leaf – LAC #69, 1898
Compass – Capper's Weekly 5/20/28
Lover's Knot – Grandmother Clark 1932
Lafayette Orange Peel – Home Art
Circle Upon Circle – Mrs. Danner 1934
Bay Leaf – Grandma Dexter
Pincushion – Shelburne. *See 1519, 2683, 2684, 3620, 3630.*
Earliest Example: ca. 1825-50, Shelburne #164

**301.5**    Cathedral Window – Erica Wilson. (lozenge shapes are open work, squeezed square is bound with bias). *See 460.2.*

**301.7**    Scuppernong Hull – Hearth & Home

**301.8**    A Brand New Presentation of the Wedding Ring – Needle Craft Magazine ca. 1930 (all appliqué)

**301.9**    Wedding Ring Chain – Grandma Dexter

**302**    Double Wedding Ring – Capper's Weekly 10/20/28
The Endless Chain – Capper's Weekly 10/20/28
The Rainbow – Capper's Weekly 10/20/28
Around the World – Carlie Sexton 1930
King Tut – Carlie Sexton
Double Wedding Bands – Mountain Mist. *See 2686.*

**303**    Wedding Ring – McKim 1929
Rainbow Wedding Ring – McKim (colors of the rainbow)
Rainbow – Rural New Yorker 7/4/31

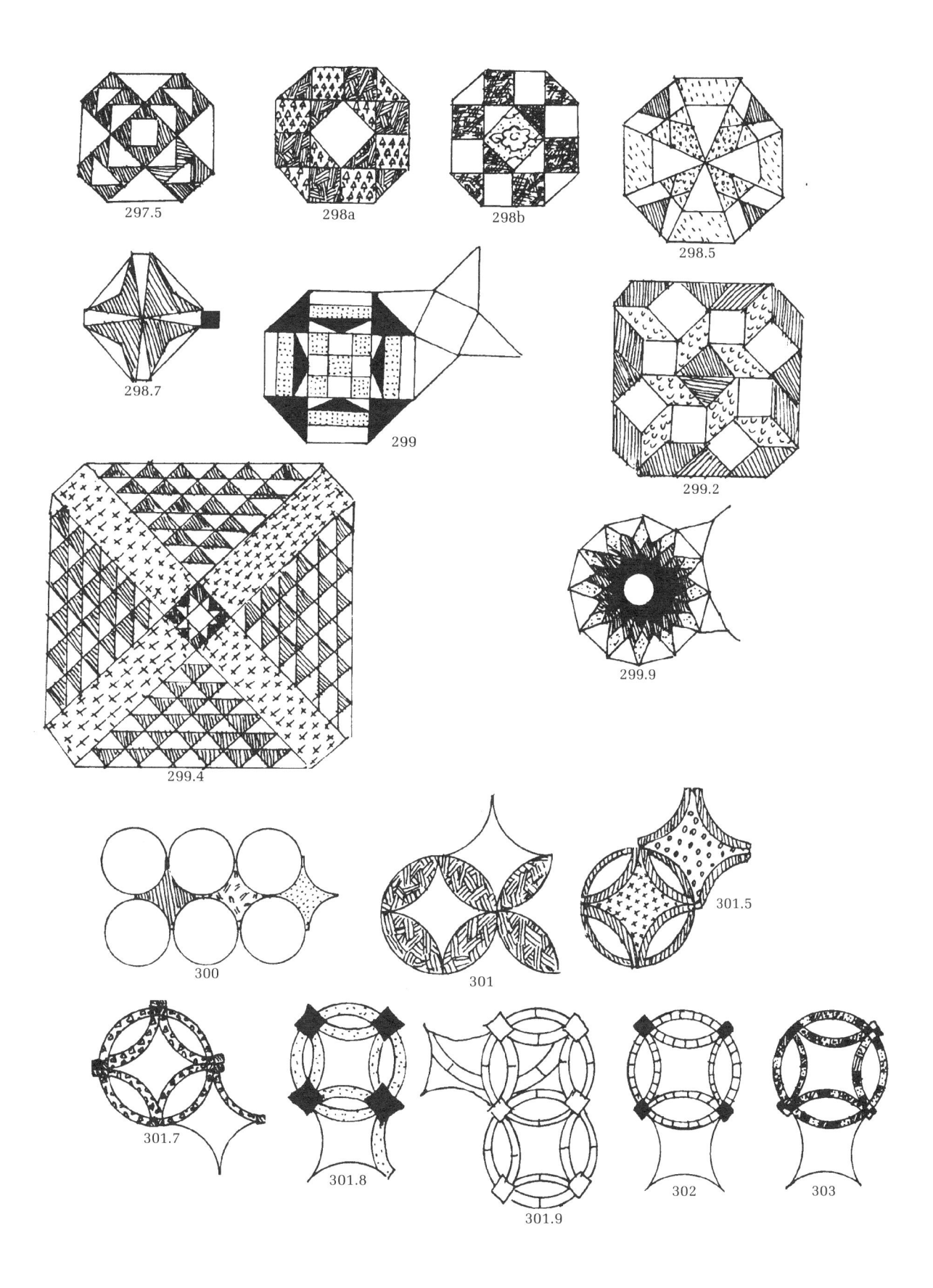

*Eight-Sided Blocks, Blocks with more than eight sides, Wedding Ring Types (297.5 – 303)*

# Pattern Category 2: *Non-Square Blocks*

WEDDING RING TYPES

**304**     **PICKLE DISH** – Lithgow

**305**     **PICKLE DISH** – KC Star 10/24/31
**INDIAN WEDDING RING** – Grandmother Clark 1932
**SWEETWATER QUILT** – Marshall

**305.3**     **WHEN CIRCLES GET TOGETHER** – Capper's Weekly 1/31/31

**305.5**     **WHISPERING LEAVES** – Mountain Mist

**305.6**     **WONDER OF THE WORLD** – Aunt Martha *Prize Winning Quilts*

**305.7**     **BLACK BEAUTY** – Clara Stone
**RED BUDS** – Nancy Cabot

**305.8**     **WASHINGTON SNOWBALL** – Clara Stone. *See 1018, 2656, & 2672.*

**305.9**     **JUPITER'S MOONS** – Meeker (center circle appliqué)

**306**     **IMPROVED NINE PATCH** – Rural New Yorker 2/15/30
**CIRCLE UPON CIRCLE** – KC Star 12/2/33
**FOUR LEAF CLOVER** – KC Star 9/25/35
**NINE PATCH VARIATION** – Hall 1935
**BAILEY NINE PATCH** – Mrs. Danner 1958. *See 2689 & 424.5.*

**307**     **HEARTS AND DIAMONDS** – Home Art

**308**     **BRIDGE QUILT** – KC Star 1933

**308.5**     **LADIES BEAUTIFUL STAR** – Oklahoma Farmer Stockman 4/1/31

**309**     **KENSINGTON CLUB QUILT** – Home Art
**KENSINGTON BLOCK** – Home Art

**310**     **PATRIOT'S PRIDE** – Mountain Mist #84

**311**     **CIRCLE UPON CIRCLE** – Aunt Kate ca. 1963

**311.5**     **WHIG ROSE** – Aunt Martha
**WHITE ROSE** – Aunt Martha

**312**     **THE STAR CHAIN** – KC Star 12/22/48

**313**     **GOLDEN WEDDING RING** – Home Art

Many times these designs are shown inside a square block or actually adapted to the square block. *See pp 350-3 for similar patterns.*

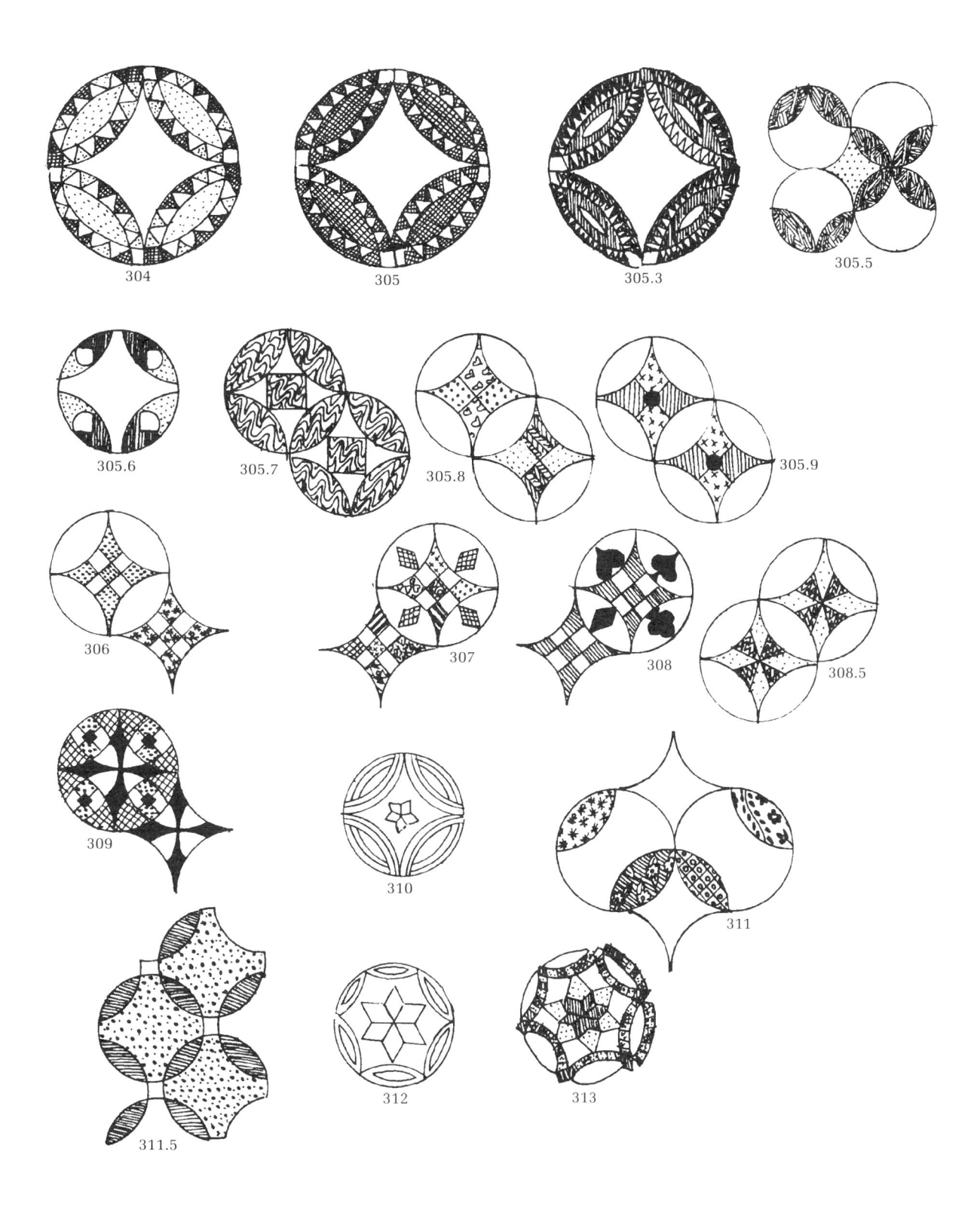

*Wedding Ring Types (304 – 313)*

304

305

305.3

305.5

305.6

305.7

305.8

305.9

306

307

308

308.5

309

310

311

311.5

312

313

# *P*attern
## CATEGORY 3

# Multi-Patch

**Patterns in Category 3 share these characteristics:**

- They are made up of pieces of more than one shape.
- They are made up of pieces which are not organized into repeatable, regular geometric-shaped blocks.

**Category 3 includes:**

- Four-Sided Shape as a Piece, 64
- Five-Sided Shape as a Piece, 68
- Six-Sided Shape as a Piece, 70
- Eight-Sided Shape as a Piece, 74
- Curved Pieces, 76
- Three-Dimensional Pieces, 78

## KEY TO PATTERN CATEGORY 3: MULTI-PATCH

Go through the list below in order, choosing the first applicable description

If the pattern is three dimensional, *turn to pg. 78*

If the pattern includes a piece with curves, *turn to pg. 76*

If the pattern includes an eight-sided piece, *turn to pg. 74*

If the pattern includes a six-sided shape, *turn to pg. 70*

If the pattern includes a five-sided shape, *turn to pg. 68*

If the pattern includes a four-sided shape, *turn to pg. 64*

Pattern Category 3: *Multi-Patch*

FOUR-SIDED SHAPE AS A PIECE

| | | |
|---|---|---|
| | **400.2** | STAR OF DESTINY – Clara Stone |
| | **400.5** | KITES IN THE AIR – Khin |
| | **401** | AUNT SUKEY'S PATCH – LAC #327 |
| | **402** | ZIG ZAG BLOCKS – Grandmother Clark 1931 |
| | **403** | COARSE WOVEN – LAC #242 |
| | | COARSE PATCHWORK – Nancy Cabot |
| | **403.5** | SUMMER TREES – QNM #119, 1981 |
| | **403.7** | UNNAMED – Telegraphics 6/9/83 (red, white, & blue) |
| | **404** | Q QUILT – QNM #101, 1978 |
| | **405** | THIS WAY, THAT WAY – QNM #49, 1973 |
| | **405.5** | LOCKED SQUARES – Nancy Cabot |
| | **406** | TUMBLER – Ruth Finley |
| | **407** | KANSAS STAR – Hall 1935 |
| | **410** | HERITAGE QUILT – Evelyn Brown |
| | **411** | TOMORROW'S HEIRLOOM – OCS |
| | **411.3** | UNNAMED – Godey's ca. 1860 |
| | | MAGIC SQUARES – Meeker |
| | **411.5** | FLYING BATS – Danner/Ericson Bk. 7, 1975 |
| | **411.6** | DIAMOND NINE PATCH – Quilt World June 1982 |
| | **412** | UNNAMED – Godey's 1851 |
| | | BRICK PILE – LAC #410 |
| | **412.3** | BOSTON STREETS – Nancy Cabot. *See 2585.* |
| | **412.5** | CRANBERRY PATCH – Nancy Cabot |
| | **412.7** | LITTLE FOXES – Nancy Cabot |

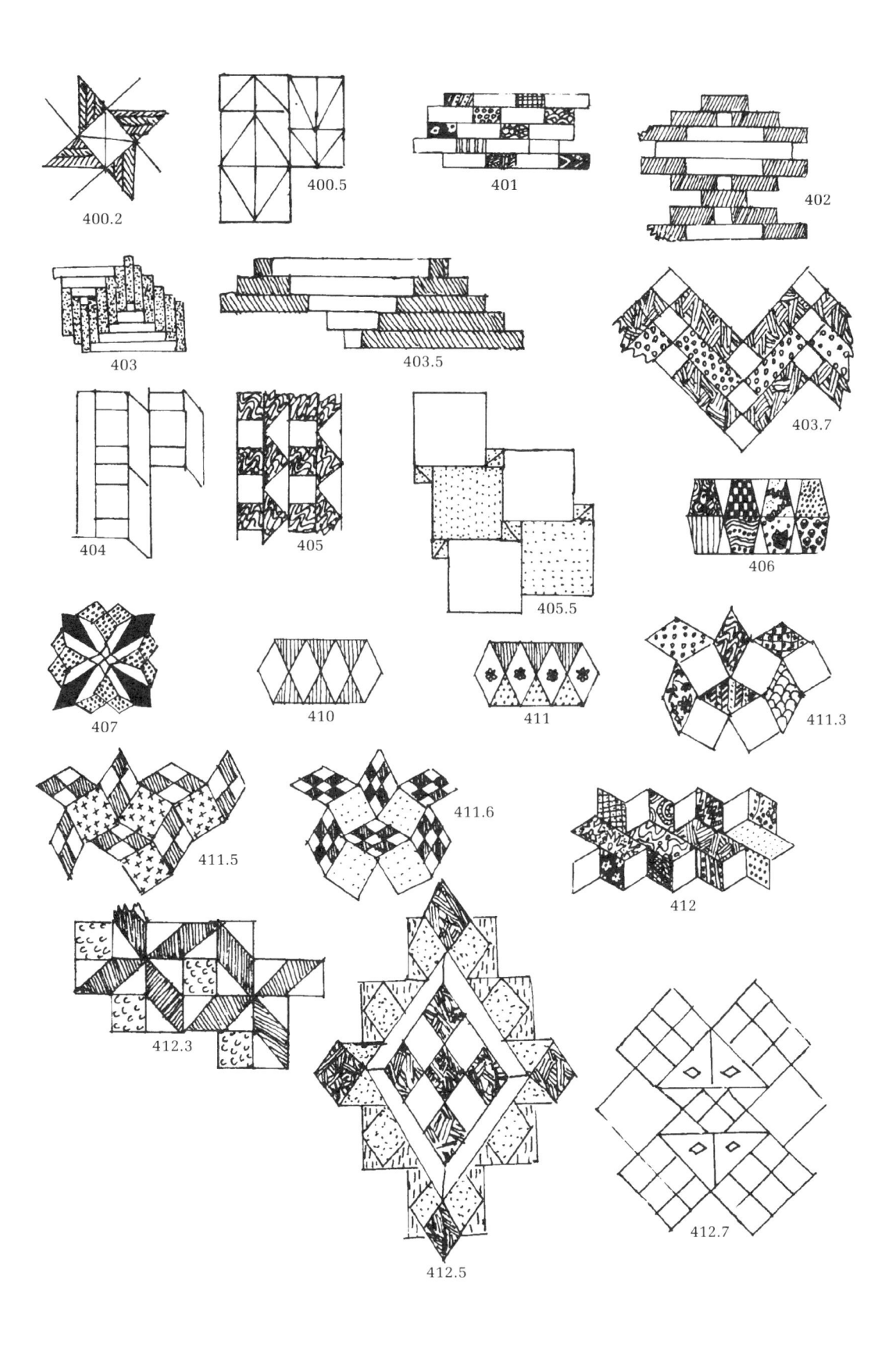

*Four-Sided Shape as a Piece (400.2 – 412.7)*

400.2
400.5
401
402
403
403.5
403.7
404
405
405.5
406
407
410
411
411.3
411.5
411.6
412
412.3
412.5
412.7

65

## Pattern Category 3: *Multi-Patch*

FOUR-SIDED SHAPE AS A PIECE

**412.8**     **DIAMONDS AND SHADOWS** – Nancy Cabot

**413**     **KALEIDOSCOPE PATCHWORK** – Ohio Farmer 1/18/1894
**DIAMOND AND STAR** – LAC #481
**DIAMOND STAR** – Oklahoma Farmer Stockman 1930
*See 1251, 1252, 1259, 2975, 2976, 3873, 3874, & 3945.*

**413.1**     **KALEIDOSCOPE** – Holstein
EARLIEST EXAMPLE: ca. 1860, Holstein

**413.5**     **UNNAMED** – QNM #95, 1977

**414**     **DIAMOND AND STAR** – Hall 1935

**415**     **STAR OF CHAMBLIE** – Clarke

**415.21**     **UNNAMED** – Godey's mid-19th century
**DOVE IN THE WINDOW** – Country Gentleman ca. 1940
**STARRY NIGHT** – Nancy Cabot
EARLIEST EXAMPLE: ca. 1825-50, Woodard & Greenstein, *Crib Quilts*, pg. 27. *See 1258, 3055, 3056, 3872.*

**415.23**     **STAR AND DIAMOND QUILT** – LCPQ.
EARLIEST EXAMPLE: ca. 1875, LCPQ

**415.25**     **ROCKY ROAD TO KANSAS** – Dubois, *Galaxy of Stars*

**415.27**     **LOST CHILDREN** – Clara Stone. *See 1253 and 2984.*

**415.3**     **LONE STAR** – Nancy Page
**LONE STAR OF TEXAS** – Nancy Page
**BLAZING STAR** – Nancy Page
**THE SUNBURST** – Nancy Page. *See 244.*

**415.32**     **DOUBLE STAR** – Meeker. *See 241.33.*

**415.34**     **BABY BLOCKS** – Orlofsky
EARLIEST EXAMPLE: ca. 1863, Orlofsky, Pl. 60

**415.35**     **UNNAMED** – Ohio Farmer 1/25/1894
**A PRETTY PATCHWORK** – Hearth & Home, Comfort
EARLIEST EXAMPLE: ca. 1860, Conroy, pg. 43. *See 263.5.*

**415.6**     **SPARKLING JEWELS** – Home Art

**415.7**     **UNNAMED** – Possibly from Nashville Banner says NNT, Fall 1973

**415.8**     **STAR** – Modern Priscilla
**JOB'S TROUBLES** – Modern Priscilla. *See 441 & 3704.*

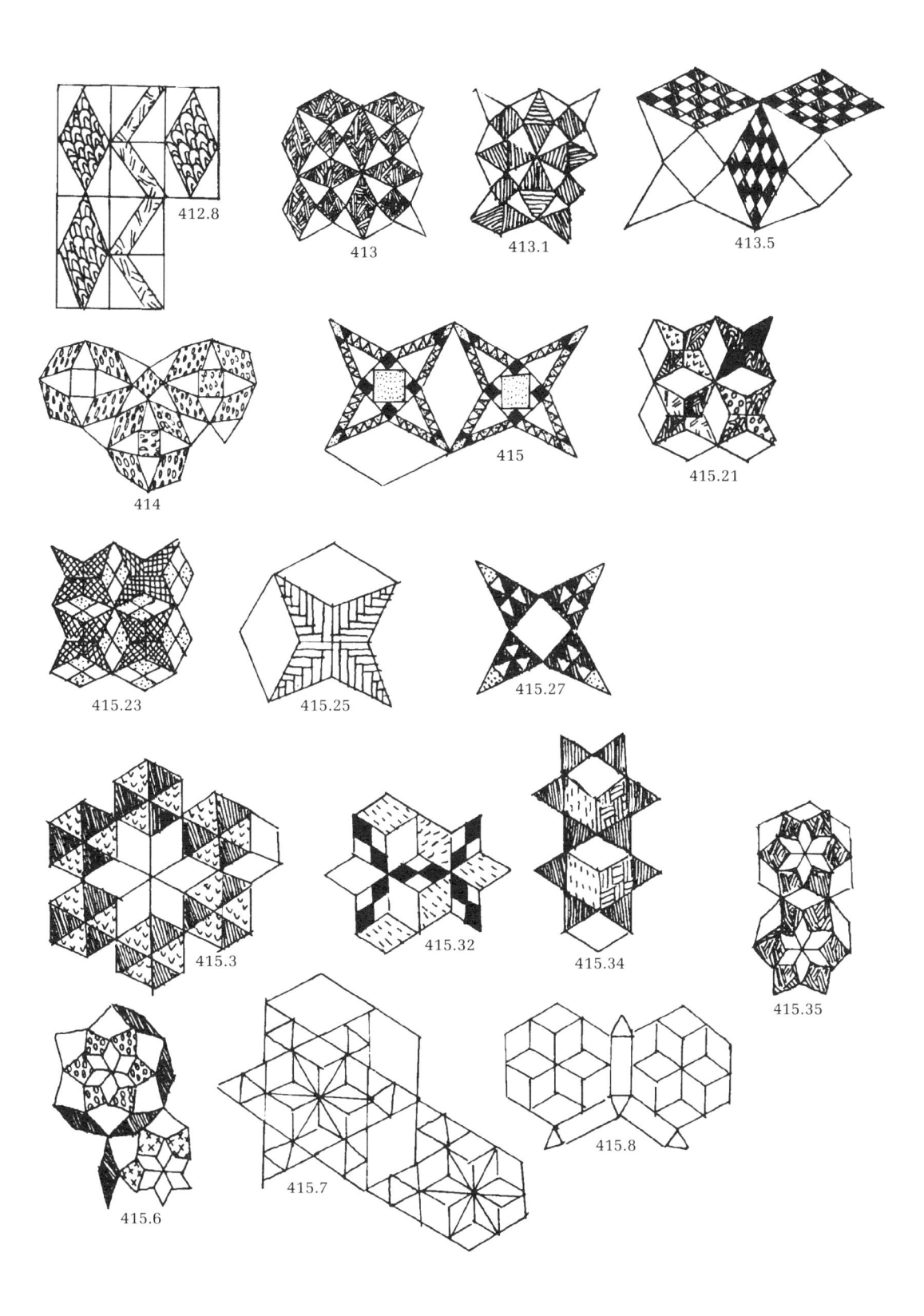

*Four-Sided Shape as a Piece (412.8 – 415.8)*

Pattern Category 3: *Multi-Patch*

| | | |
|---|---|---|
| FOUR-SIDED SHAPE AS A PIECE | 416 | **POINSETTIA QUILT** – Home Art and Rural New Yorker, 12/7/35 **DIAMOND BEAUTY QUILT** – Workbasket Vol 8, #7, 1943 |
| | 416.5 | **VINE BLOCK** – Nancy Cabot |
| | 416.6 | **TANGLED SQUARES** – Nancy Cabot |
| | 416.7 | **SULTAN'S BLOCK** – Nancy Cabot |
| | 416.8 | **EUREKA** – Nancy Cabot. *See 3735 and 3736.* |
| | 416.9 | **CUMBERLAND GAP** – Nancy Cabot |
| | 417.2 | **UNNAMED** – Treasures in Needlework 1870 (cross is outlined with black ribbon). *See 1409.* |
| | 418 | **COUNTRY FARM** – LAC #209. *See 2144 & 2831.* |
| FIVE-SIDED SHAPE AS A PIECE | 420 | **POINTED TILE** – Aunt Martha |
| | 421 | **EMMOND'S FLOOR** – QNM #77, 1975 |
| | 422 | **SQUARE UPON SQUARES** – Nancy Cabot |
| | 422.5 | **PATHWAY TO THE STARS** – QNM #79, 1976 |
| | 423 | **UNNAMED** – Godey's |
| | 423.5 | **STARS OF TWILIGHT** – Home Art |
| | 424 | **CHAIN OF DIAMONDS** – Aunt Martha |

*Four-Sided Shape as a Piece, Five-Sided Shape as a Piece (416 – 424)*

Pattern Category 3: *Multi-Patch*

| | | |
|---|---|---|
| FIVE-SIDED SHAPE AS A PIECE | 424.5 | IMPROVED NINE-PATCH – Nancy Cabot 2/28/33<br>NINE PATCH – Nancy Cabot 2/28/33 |
| | 424.7a | DESERT FLOWER – Mary McElwain<br>DESERT ROSE – attributed to Nancy Cabot by Nancy's |
| | 424.7b | TEXAS STAR – Rural New Yorker 3/13/37, Aunt Martha<br>SOLOMON'S GARDEN – Nancy Cabot (in all of these the flowers are appliquéd on the arms of the star). *See 251.* |
| | 424.8 | BOUTONNIERE – KC Star 9/26/1931<br>STAR BOUQUET – Capper's/Famous Features |
| SIX-SIDED SHAPE AS A PIECE (EVEN SIDES) | 425 | UNNAMED – Godey's 5/1850<br>EARLIEST EXAMPLE: dated 1854 QEC 1976, pl. 6 |
| | 425.2 | GRANDMOTHER'S FLOWER GARDEN<br>EARLIEST EXAMPLE: dated 1866, Clarke, pg. 78 |
| | 425.4 | GRANDMOTHER'S FLOWER GARDEN – Aunt Martha Bk. 3175 (diamonds and triangles specified to be green) |
| | 425.5 | UNNAMED – Burnham.<br>EARLIEST EXAMPLE, ca. 1860, Burnham, pg. 48 |
| | 425.6 | CABLE – Vote. *See 435.2.* |
| | 425.7 | WOVEN PATTERN – Meeker |
| | 425.8 | HEXAGONS – Comfort. *See 244.5.* |
| | 426 | BABY BLOCKS – QEC 1977 |
| | 427 | STAR BOUQUET QUILT – Home Art<br>MORNING STAR – Shelburne<br>EARLIEST EXAMPLE: ca. 1800, Bishop, *New Discoveries* pg. 16. *See 143, 3700, & 3701.* |
| | 427.2 | MORNING STAR – Coats and Clark. *See 3705.* |
| | 427.4 | BOX QUILT – Nancy Page |
| | 427.5 | AUNT ETTA'S DIAMOND QUILT – Workbasket May 1947<br>POINTING STAR – Mrs. Danner Bk. 6. *See 3715.* |
| | 428 | AUNT MARTHA'S ROSE – Aunt Martha |
| | 429 | UNNAMED – Ohio Farmer 1/18/1894<br>BLOCK PATCHWORK – LAC #361<br>THE VENETIAN QUILT – Rural New Yorker 10/14/33<br>WANDERING PATHS – Nancy Cabot<br>MORNING GLORY – KC Star 12/23/33 (morning glory quilted in center) |
| | 430 | ROSALIA FLOWER GARDEN – KC Star 12/13/39<br>JACK'S CHAIN – Puckett & Giberson |
| | 431 | FAITHFUL CIRCLE – Aunt Martha |
| | 431.5 | JOSEPH'S COAT – OCS |
| | 431.8 | WAGON WHEEL – QNM #62, 1974 |

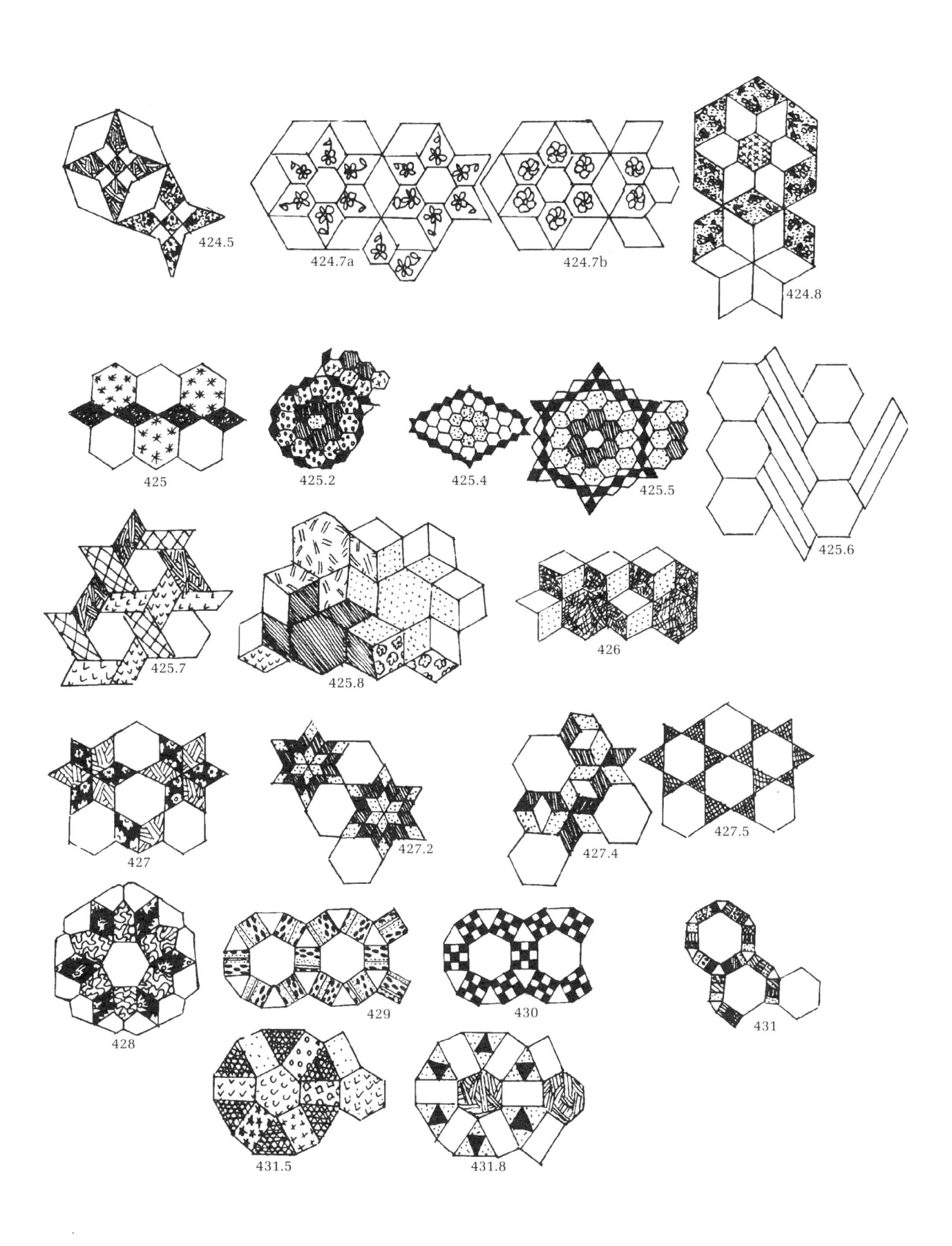

*Five-Sided Shape as a Piece, Six-Sided Shape as a Piece (Even Sides) (424.5 – 431.8)*

# Pattern Category 3: *Multi-Patch*

| | | |
|---|---|---|
| SIX-SIDED SHAPE AS A PIECE (ODD SIDES) | 432a | FANTASTIC PATCHWORK – LAC #290<br>QUINTETTES – Nancy Page<br>STAINED GLASS – Gutcheon |
| | 432b | RAIL FENCE – Nancy Cabot |
| | 433a | FIVE CROSS – Clara Stone<br>LATTICE BLOCK – Nancy Cabot 8/5/34<br>CHURCH WINDOWS – attributed to Nancy Cabot or Nancy Page by various sources<br>OGDEN CORNERS – Workbasket 1935 |
| | 433b | KANSAS DUGOUT – Aunt Martha |
| | 433c | OLD FASHIONED QUILT – KC Star 9/11/37<br>OZARK TILE PATTERN – KC Star. *See 1181, 1187, 3250, 4104, 4106, 4107, & 4108.* |
| | 434 | MOSAIC PATCHWORK #4 – Caulfeild & Saward 1882<br>PUZZLE TILE – LAC #289, 1898<br>ENDLESS CHAIN – attributed to Union Mill Ends by NNT |
| | 435.2 | ROPE – Woman's World. *See 425.6.* |
| | 435.5 | UNNAMED – Godey's 1863 |
| | 435.7 | UNNAMED – Godey's |
| | 436 | MEMORY CHAIN – Aunt Martha |
| | 437 | RED CROSS – KC Star 1932<br>A RED, WHITE & BLUE COLOR SCHEME – KC Star 1/13/43 |
| | 438 | UNNAMED – Peterson's Magazine<br>MOSAIC PATCHWORK #3 – Caulfeild & Saward 1882<br>TILE PATCHWORK – LAC #310<br>CHINESE PUZZLE – KC Star 1936. *See 1430, 4110, & 449.6.* |
| | 438.7 | QUILT OF FOUR BIRDS – Workbasket |
| | 438.8 | STAR AND CROSS – Della Harris |
| | 439 | UNNAMED – OCS 1968 |
| | 440 | POINSETTIA – Aunt Martha |
| | 441 | GOLDEN CIRCLE STAR – KC Star 1937. *See 3704.* |
| | 441.2 | BRUNSWICK STAR – Ohio Farmer 1/25/1894 |
| | 441.7 | BARN BATS – Nancy Cabot |
| | 441.8 | CONTINUOUS STAR – Clara Stone |

*Six-Sided Shape as a Piece (Odd Sides) (432a – 441.8)*

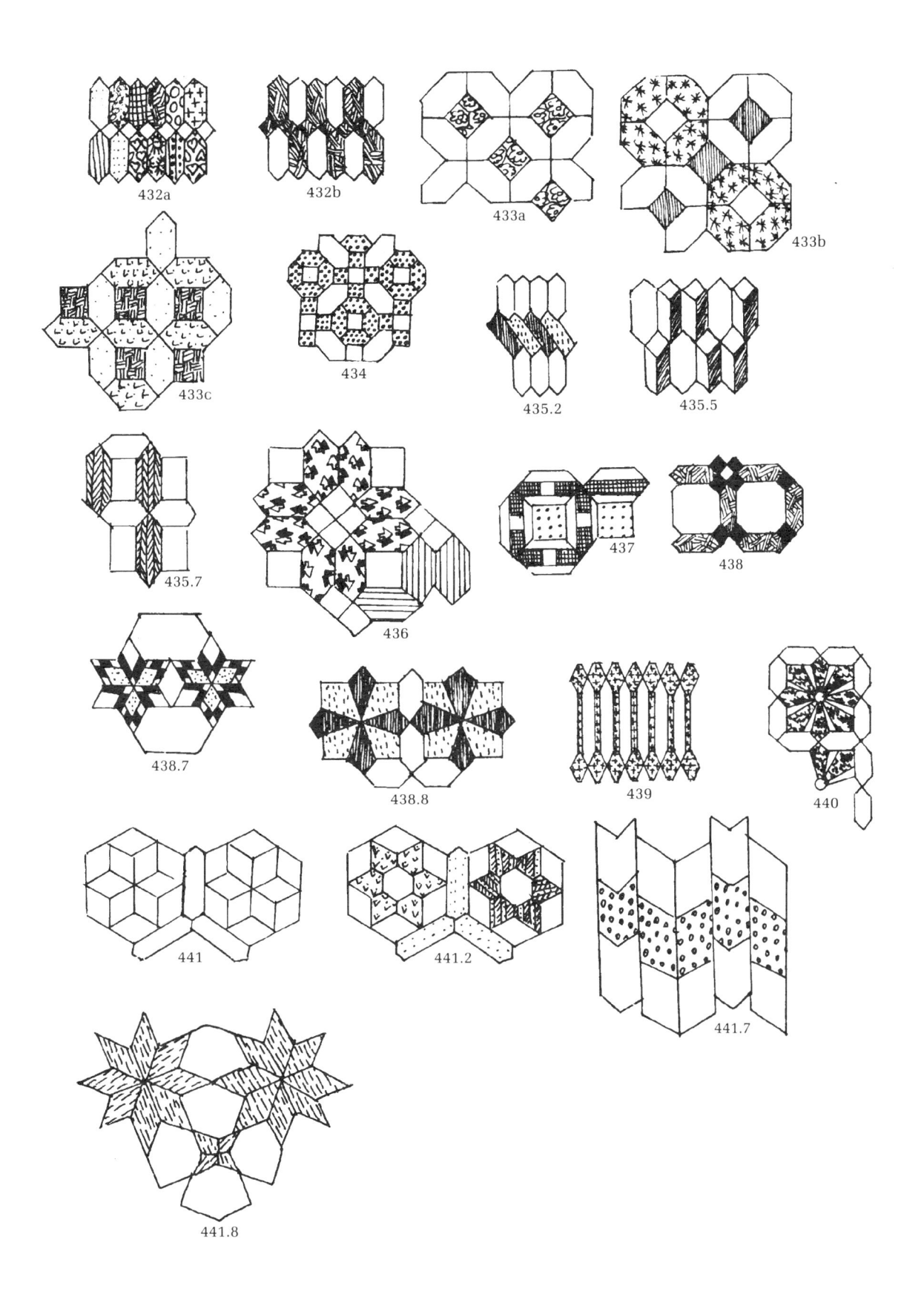

# Pattern Category 3: *Multi-Patch*

| | | |
|---|---|---|
| EIGHT-SIDED SHAPE AS A PIECE | **442** | **Octagon** – LAC #198, 1898 |
| | | **Job's Trouble** – Clara Stone |
| | | **Mechanical Blocks** – Helen Kaufman 1928 |
| | | **Octagonal** – Nancy Cabot 8/6/34 |
| | | **Snowballs** – Nancy Cabot |
| | | **Ozark Cobblestones** – KC Star |
| | | **An All Over Pattern of Octagons** – KC Star 9/23/42 |
| | | **Octagons** – Gutcheon PPP |
| | | Earliest Example: 1850 McKendry, pg. 122. *See 4141 & 4142.* |
| | **442.5** | **Unnamed** – Godey's |
| | **442.8** | **Unnamed** – Treasures in Needlework 1870 |
| | | **White Mountains** – Nancy Cabot |
| | | **Octagon Block** – Nancy Cabot |
| | | **Patriot's Quilt** – Houck & Miller |
| | | Earliest Example: ca. 1860-5, Houck & Miller, pg. 128 |
| | **443** | **Unnamed** – Caulfeild & Saward 1882 |
| | | **Twist Patchwork** – LAC #294 |
| | | **Twisted Rope** – Hearth & Home. *See 4195.* |
| | **444** | **Missouri Wonder** – KC Star 1936 |
| | **444.5** | **Twisted Ribbons** – Nancy Cabot |
| | **445** | **Colonial Garden Quilt** – Aunt Martha |
| | | **The Eight Point Snowflake** – KC Star 4/8/53 |
| | **445.2** | **Paths to Happiness** – Home Art |
| | **445.3** | **Star and Web Quilt** – Orlofsky |
| | | Earliest Example: Mid 19th century, Orlofsky, pg. 106 |
| | **445.7** | **Kaleidoscope Silk Quilt** – The Delineator 5/1891 |
| | **445.8** | **Wedding Ring Tile** – Workbasket 1941 |
| | **445.9** | **Periwinkle** – Wallace's Farmer 2/29 |
| | | **Hummingbird** – Mary McElwain |
| | | **Bluet Quilt** – Nancy Page. *See 1214, 1246, 2324, & 3870.* |
| | **446** | **Periwinkle** – Grandmother Clark 1932 |

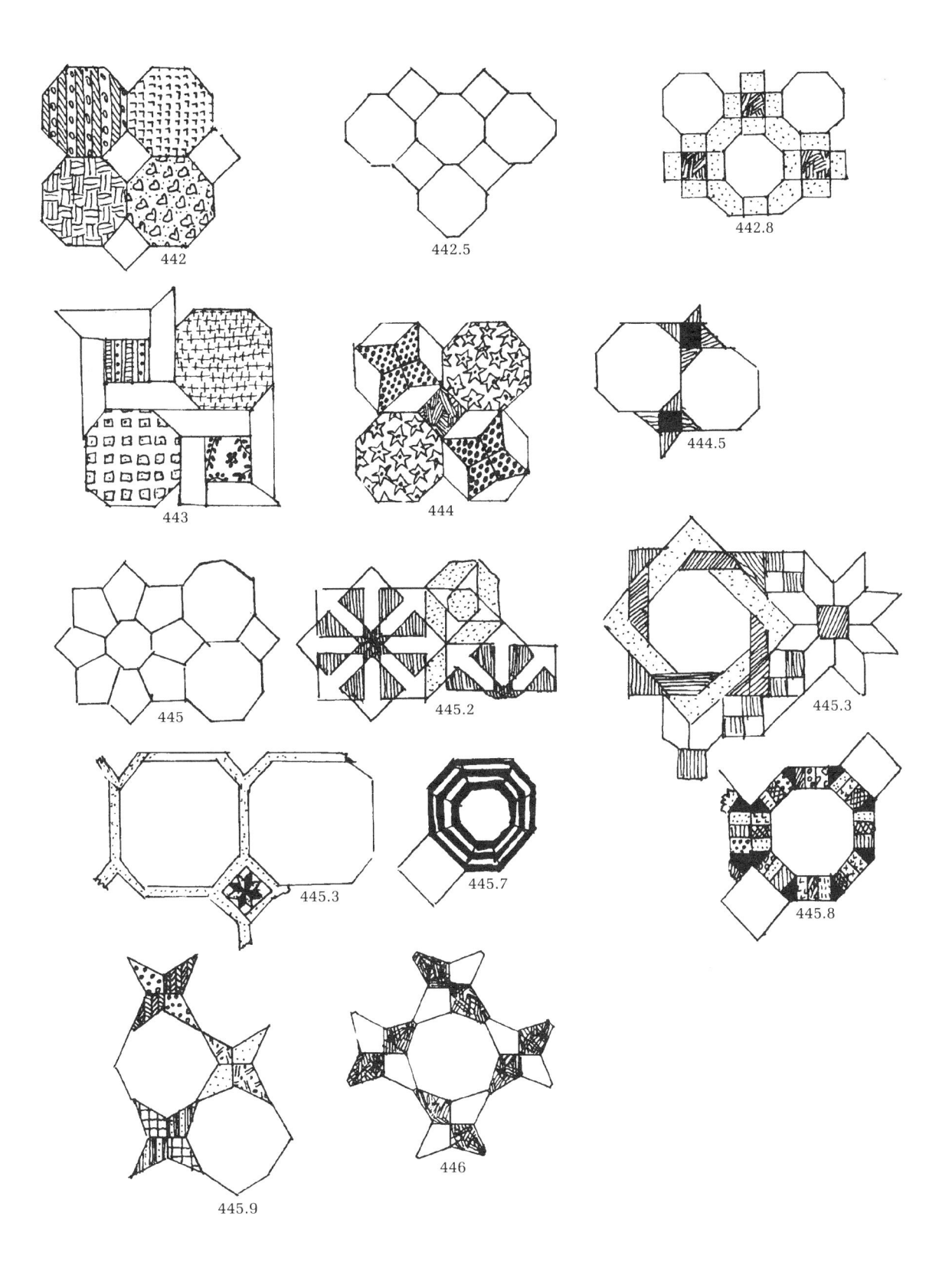

*Eight-Sided Shape as a Piece (442 – 446)*

442
442.5
442.8
443
444
444.5
445
445.2
445.3
445.3
445.7
445.8
445.9
446

75

Pattern Category 3: *Multi-Patch*

| | | |
|---|---|---|
| EIGHT-SIDED SHAPE AS A PIECE | **447** | UNNAMED – Godey's 4/1850 |
| | **447.3** | UNNAMED – QEC 1979.<br>EARLIEST EXAMPLE: ca. 1820, QEC 1979, PL 50 |
| | **447.8** | UNNAMED – Peterson's Magazine |
| | **448** | OCTAGON TILE – LAC #286, 1898 |
| | **449** | TIFFANY BUTTERFLIES – Evelyn Brown |
| | **449.5** | MAY TIME QUILT – Workbasket |
| | **449.6** | UNNAMED – Godey's. *See 438, 1430, & 4110.* |
| | **449.7** | UNNAMED – Treasures in Needlework 1870 |
| | **449.8** | UNNAMED – Godey's |
| | **449.9** | UNNAMED – Treasures in Needlework 1870 |
| | **450** | UNNAMED – Godey's 4/1850 |
| CURVED PIECES | **451** | JOSEPH'S COAT – Home Art 1933<br>PEELED ORANGE – Nancy Cabot 10/1/33<br>EARLIEST EXAMPLE: 1848, Robertson, pg. 127 |
| | **452** | BASKET LATTICE – LAC #417 |
| | **452.3** | UNNAMED – Workbasket 1944 |
| | **452.7** | JACK O'LANTERN – Mountain Mist |
| | **453** | LOVER'S LINKS – LAC #122, 1898<br>THE LOVER'S CHAIN – Hearth & Home |
| | **454** | MOON AND STARS – OCS/Wheeler |

*Eight-Sided Shape as a Piece, Curved Pieces (447 – 454)*

77

Pattern Category 3: *Multi-Patch*

CURVED PIECES

**454.3**    **FANNY'S FAN** – Finley. *See 3305.*

**455**    **UNNAMED** – Godey's 4/1850

**456**    **UNNAMED** – Godey's 4/1850

**457**    **BAMBOO SPREAD** – OCS 1968

**457.3**    **FLUFFY PATCHES** – OCS

**457.8**    **UNNAMED** – Godey's

**457.9**    **EASTER LILLY** (*sic*) **QUILT** – Home Art Master Quilting Album

**458**    **THE SHASTA DAISY QUILT** – Home Art Master Quilting Album

**458.2**    **THE WINDING PATH QUILT** – Home Art Master Quilting Album

**458.5**    **VICTORIA'S CROWN** – Burnham.
EARLIEST EXAMPLE: ca. 1840, Burnham. *See 3640.*

**458.7**    **TRUE LOVER'S LINK** – Aunt Martha, Prize Winning Quilts

**459**    **THE WISHING WELL** – Mountain Mist

**459.13**    **FEATHERED STARS** – QEC 1979. *See 3001-3003.*

**459.15**    **MAYFLOWER QUILT** – Dubois/Stars.
EARLIEST EXAMPLE: ca. 1880, Dubois/Stars. *See 3001-3003.*

**459.2**    **THE FLOWER RING** – KC Star 5/29/40

THREE-DIMENSIONAL PIECES

**460**    **DAISY BLOCK** – Aunt Martha 1933
**ATTIC WINDOWS** – OCS
**CATHEDRAL WINDOW** – Iowa Farm & Home Register 6/56
**PAIN IN THE NECK QUILT** – Quilters Journal 1/80

**460.3**    **MOCK ORANGE QUILT** – Workbasket Vol. 9, #11, 1944 (windows are pieced)

**460.5**    **PRAIRIE STAR** – Grandma Dexter (bias binds cut-work ovals)

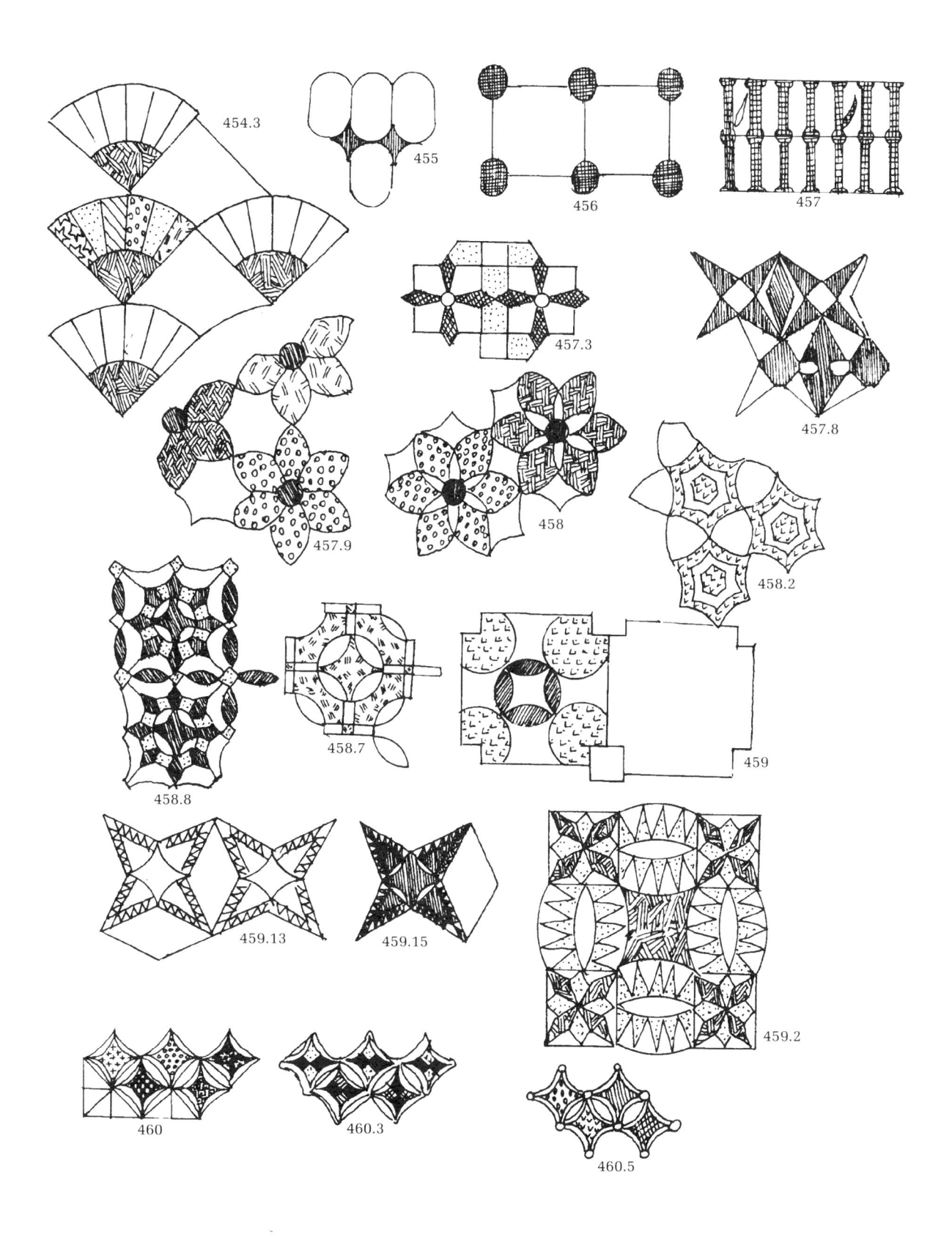

*Curved Pieces, Three-Dimensional Pieces (454.3 – 460.5)*

454.3
455
456
457
457.3
457.8
457.9
458
458.2
458.7
458.8
459
459.13
459.15
459.2
460
460.3
460.5

# PATTERN CATEGORY 4

## Strip Quilts

**Pattens in Category 4 share these characteristics:**

- Some consist only of unpieced strips.
- They are more commonly unpieced strips alternated with pieced strips.

## KEY TO PATTERN CATEGORY 4: STRIP QUILTS

All the Strip Quilts are on page 83.

# Pattern Category 4: *Strip Quilts*

STRIP QUILTS

**475**    **BARS** – Bishop & Safanda
**JOSEPH'S COAT** – Holstein
**RAINBOW** – Holstein (strips pieced in rainbow colors)
Strippy is a British name.

**475.5**    **SPLIT BARS** – Bishop & Safanda

**476**    **CHINESE COINS** – Bruce Johnson

**476.5**    **BARS** – Bishop & Safanda

**476.7**    **UNKNOWN**

**477a**    **ROMAN STRIPE** – Webster
**BARS** – McKendry
EARLIEST EXAMPLE: ca. 1850-75 McKendry, pg. 198

**477b**    **ROMAN SQUARE** – Finley (every 4th patch is dark)

**477c**    **LADDER OF SUCCESS** – QNM #99, 1978

**478**    **FLAGS** – Wooster

**479**    **TREE EVERLASTING** – Finley
**HERRINGBONE** – Finley
**THE PRICKLY PATH** – Finley
**ARROWHEADS** – Finley
EARLIEST EXAMPLE: ca. 1830, Finley, Pl 17

**480**    **WILD GOOSE CHASE** – LAC #94, 1898
**BIRDS IN FLIGHT** – Bacon
**WILD GEESE FLYING** – Bacon
**GEESE IN FLIGHT** – Bruce Johnson
EARLIEST EXAMPLE: ca. 1775-1800, Orlofsky pg. 39. *See 2181, 213, & 214.*

**480.7**    **NOTHING WASTED** – Farm Journal 1937

**481**    **TWIST AND TURN** – LAC #98, 1898

**482**    **UNNAMED** – Ohio Farmer 10/29/1896
**KITE'S TAIL** – Hall 1935 (strips on diagonal)

**483**    **RED CROSS** – QNM #60, 1974
**BARS VARIATION** – Bishop & Safanda

**484**    **GARDEN PATH** – Telegraphics

**485**    **UNNAMED** – Bishop & Safanda

**486**    **ROMAN WALL QUILT** – Bishop & Safanda

*Strip Quilts (475 – 486)*

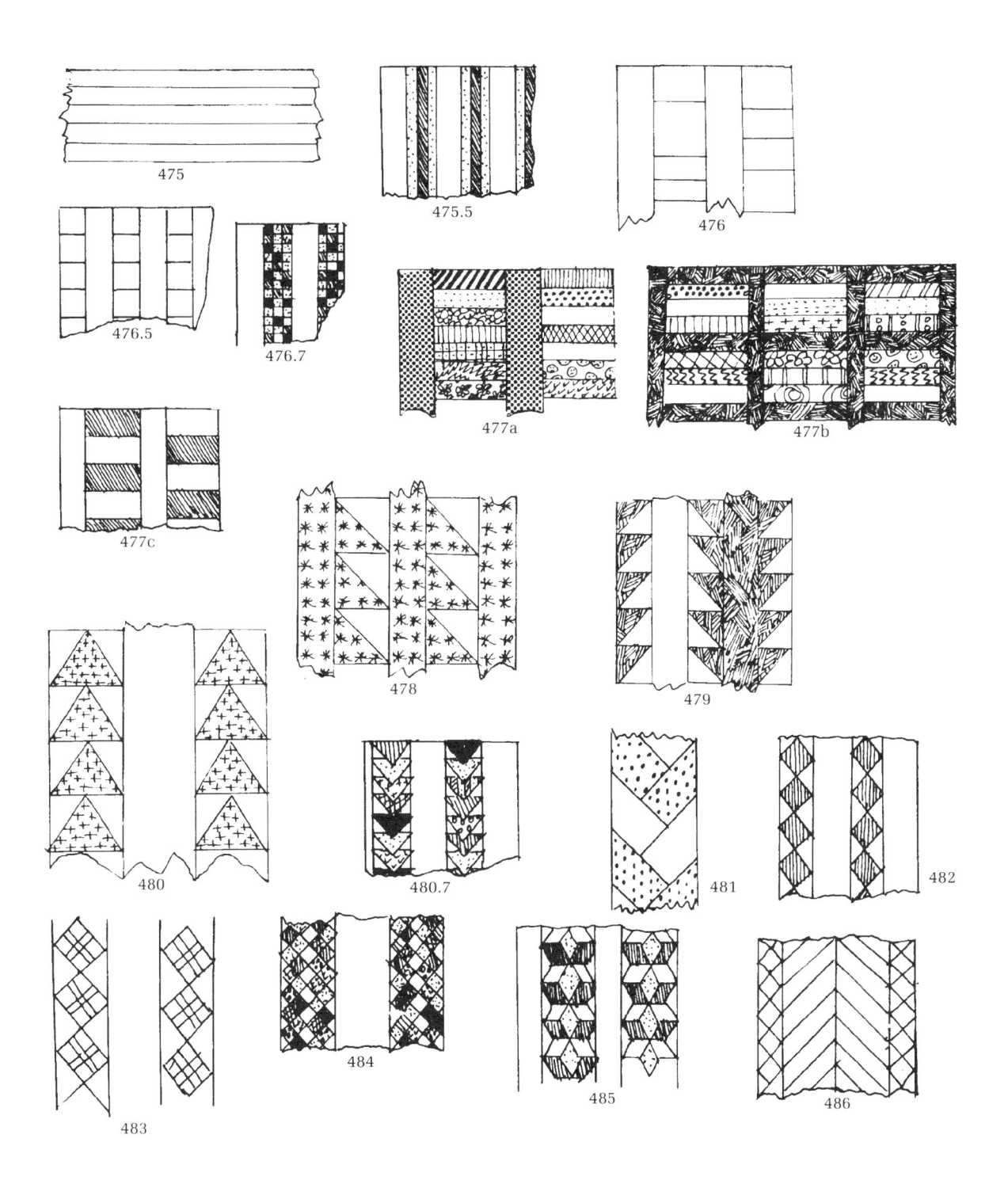

83

# PATTERN CATEGORY 5

## Realistic

**Patterns in Category 5 share these characteristics:**
- They contain a pictorial representation rather than an abstract design.

- While they may be classified another way (such as Nine Patch), they are so recognizable that they are indexed here.

**Category 5 includes:**
- Baskets
  Empty Baskets, 86
  Baskets with Appliquéd Contents, 90
  Baskets Full of Triangles (and Squares), 92
  Baskets Full of Diamonds or Other Shapes, 94
- Vases and Misc. Containers, 98
- Flowers, 100
- Trees
  Trees with Triangles for Leaves, 110
  Trees with Squares and Rectangles for Leaves, 114
  Trees with Diamonds and Other Shapes for Leaves, 114
- Leaves, 116
- Houses and Other Architecture, 118
- Airplanes, 122
- Boats, 124
- Animals
  Butterflies and Other Insects, 126
  Birds, 128
  Cats and Other Felines, 128
  Other Animals, 130
- People, 130
- Misc. Subject Matter, 132
- Letters, 136

# KEY TO PATTERN CATEGORY 5: REALISTIC

**Step 1**

If your block is a basket, go to Step 3 below

If your block is anything other than a basket, go to Step 2 below.

**Step 2**

| | |
|---|---|
| If block is a flower, | *turn to p. 100* |
| If block is a tree, | *turn to p. 110* |
| If block is a leaf, | *turn to p. 116* |
| If block is a house & other architecture, | *turn to p. 118* |
| If block is airplanes, | *turn to p. 122* |
| If block is a boat, | *turn to p. 124* |
| If block is an animal, | *turn to p. 126* |
| If block is a person, | *turn to p. 130* |
| If block is miscellaneous, | *turn to p. 132* |
| If block is a letter, | *turn to p. 136* |

**Step 3**

| | |
|---|---|
| If block is empty basket, | *turn to p. 86* |
| If block is basket with appliquéd contents, | *turn to p. 90* |
| If block is basket full of triangles and squares, | *turn to p. 92* |
| If block is basket full of diamonds & other shapes, | *turn to p. 94* |
| If block is vase & miscellaneous container, | *turn to p. 98* |

Pattern Category 5: *Realistic*

EMPTY BASKETS

| | | |
|---|---|---|
| | 650.2 | BASKET – Dakota Farmer 11/15/27 |
| | 650.3 | LITTLE BASKET – Hearth and Home |
| | | FRUIT BASKET – Hearth and Home |
| | 651 | BABY BASKET – Mary McElwain |
| | | THE MAY BASKET – KC Star 7/2/41 |
| | | BASKET QUILT – on a U.S. commemorative stamp, issued 3/8/78 |
| | 652 | FOUR LITTLE BASKETS – LAC #305 |
| | | FOUR BASKETS – Nancy Cabot |
| | 652.7 | UNNAMED – From a sampler dated 1859 in Bacon |
| | 653 | DRESDEN BASKET – Grandmother Dexter Bk. 36A |
| | | RED BASKET – Danner/Ericson Bk. 6 |
| | 653.5 | BASKET – Comfort |
| | 654 | GRANDMOTHER'S BASKET – KC Star 3/2/1932 |
| | 655 | BASKET WITH HANDLES – From a quilt ca. 1880 in Bruce Johnson |
| | 656 | UNNAMED – Capper's Weekly 1945, possibly Home Art |
| | 656.2 | A BASKET PATCH – Hearth and Home |
| | 656.3 | UNNAMED – From a sampler quilt dated 1862 in Bishop/Knopf |
| | 656.4 | OLD FASHION FRUIT BASKET – NNT 9/70 |
| | 657a | BASKET QUILT – LAC #316 |
| | 657b | BREAD BASKET – Nancy Cabot |
| | 658.2 | FLOWER BASKET – From a quilt ca. 1935, Quilt Engagement Calendar 1983 |
| | 658.5 | BASKET – McKendry. *See 1035.5.* |
| | 659 | THE BASKET – KC Star 5/25/38 |
| | 660 | SUGAR BOWL – Ohio Farmer 1/12/29 |
| | | GRANDMOTHER'S BASKET – Ohio Farmer 1/12/29 |
| | 661 | BASKET – Evelyn Brown in *Tumbling Alleys* |

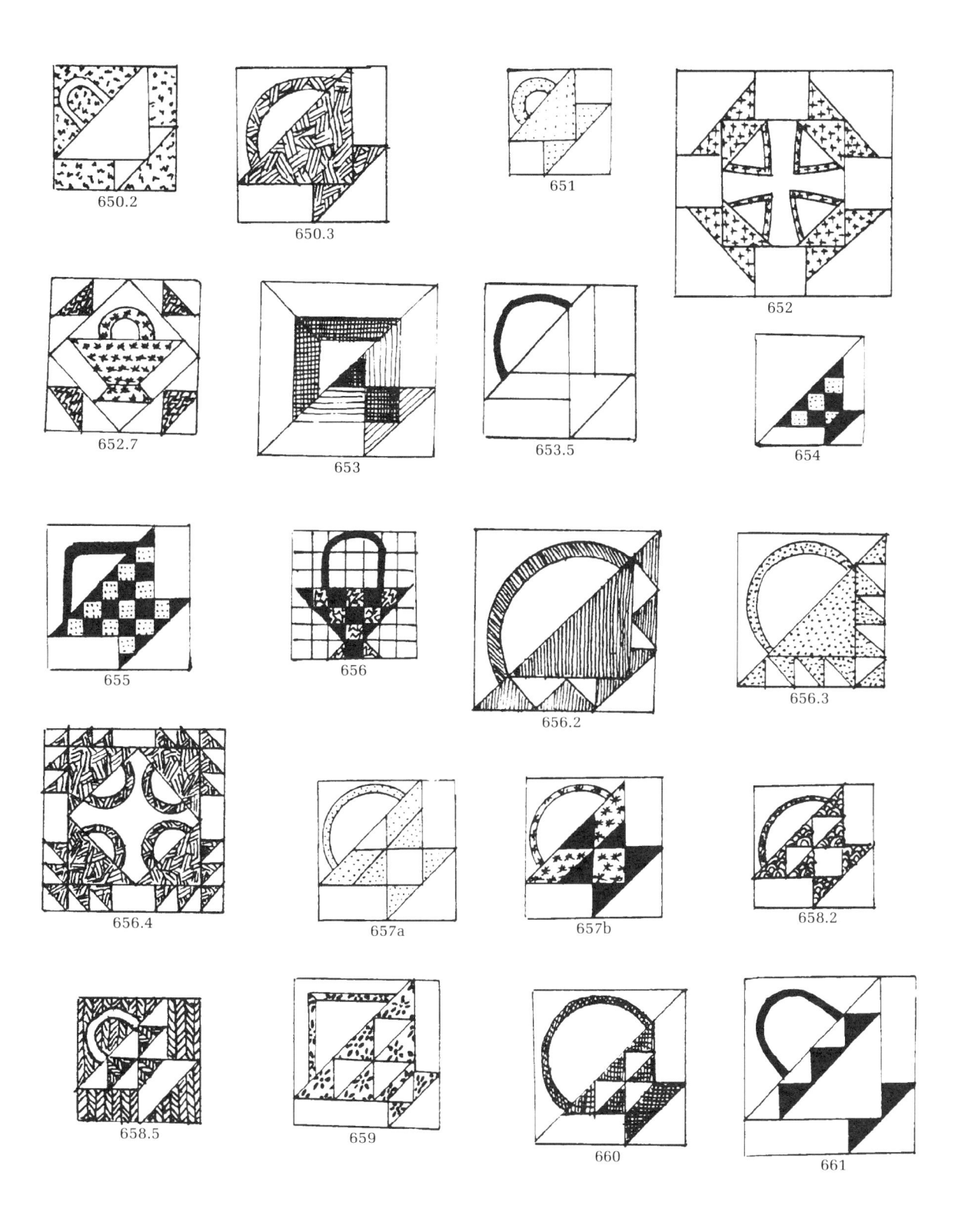

*Empty Baskets (650.2 – 661)*

650.2
650.3
651
652
652.7
653
653.5
654
655
656
656.2
656.3
656.4
657a
657b
658.2
658.5
659
660
661

# Pattern Category 5: *Realistic*

| | | |
|---|---|---|
| EMPTY BASKETS | 662 | **BASKET QUILT** – Orange Judd Farmer 9/2/1899<br>**THE BASKET** – The Family 1913<br>**GRANDMOTHER'S BASKET** – Pennsylvania Farmer ca. 1930<br>**COLONIAL BASKET** – Woman's Day 6/49 from a quilt ca. 1861<br>**CHERRY BASKET** – Woman's Day 6/49<br>**FLOWER BASKET** – Woman's Day 6/49. *See 673.* |
| | 662.5 | **BASKETS** – from a quilt ca. 1850 in McKendry |
| | 663 | **FLOWER BASKET** – from a quilt ca. 1862 in Robertson |
| | 664 | **PIECED BASKETS** – Webster<br>**BASKET BLOCK** – Comfort<br>**CHERRY BASKET** – from a quilt ca. 1860 in Robertson<br>**FLOWER BASKET** – from a quilt ca. 1860 in Robertson<br>EARLIEST EXAMPLE: sampler dated 1852 in Robertson |
| | 665.2 | **BASKET DESIGN** – Needlecraft or Modern Priscilla ca. 1919 |
| | 665.3 | **UNNAMED** – from a quilt ca. 1860-2 in Kolter, Pl 78 |
| | 665.4 | **FLOWER BASKET** – Hearth and Home |
| | 666 | **MAY BASKET** – Hearth and Home |
| | 667 | **BASKETS** – Bruce Johnson |
| | 668 | **CHERRY BASKET** – LAC #58<br>**BERRY BASKET** – Coats and Clark<br>**FRUIT BASKET** – Comfort |
| | 668.5 | **HANGING BASKET** – Rural New Yorker 4/5/30 |
| | 669 | **BASKET** – Grandmother Clark Bk. 20, 1931 |
| | 670a | **BASKET** – Comfort or Hearth and Home ca. 1910 |
| | 670b | **CHERRY BASKET** – McCall's "Antique Quilts" ca. 1973 |
| | 671 | **FLOWER BASKET** – Grandmother Dexter Bk. 36a ca. 1935 |
| | 671.5 | **BASKET DESIGN** – Comfort |
| | 672 | **THE BASKET** – Modern Priscilla<br>**COLONIAL BASKET** – Hall |
| | 673 | **BASKET** – Woman's World, The Patchwork Book. *See 562.* |
| | 674 | **UNNAMED** – OCS (Brooks/Wheeler) #5832 & 7477<br>**BASKET** – McKendry |

*Empty Baskets (662 – 674)*

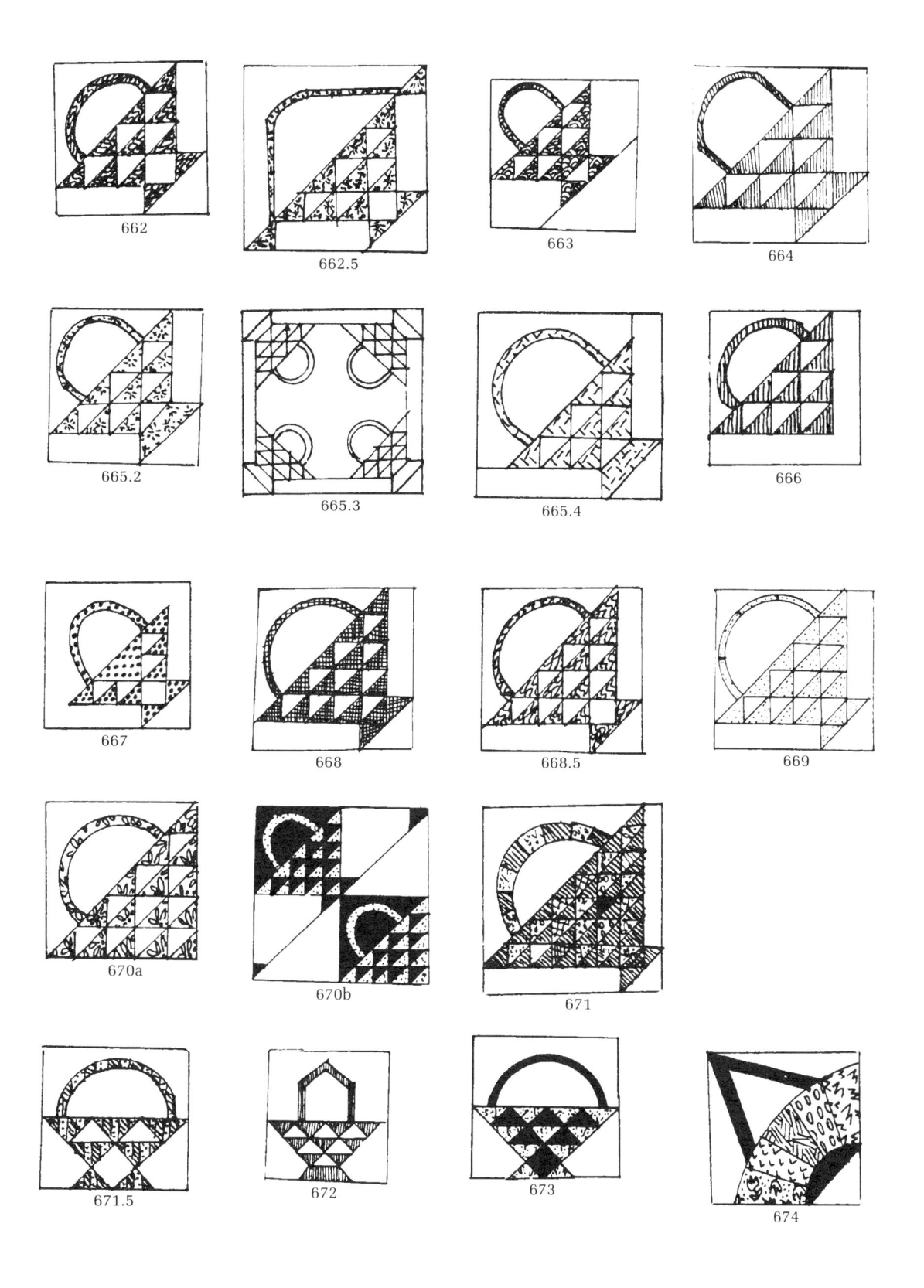

662
662.5
663
664
665.2
665.3
665.4
666
667
668
668.5
669
670a
670b
671
671.5
672
673
674

89

## Pattern Category 5: *Realistic*

BASKETS WITH APPLIQUÉD CONTENTS

| | | |
|---|---|---|
| **674.8** | **FLOWER BASKET** – Carlie Sexton in Successful Farming (striped basket in original) |
| **674.9** | **FRUIT BASKET** – Nancy Page |
| **675** | **FLOWER BASKET** – From a quilt dated 1855 in Bishop's New Discoveries |
| **676** | **BASKET OF ORANGES** – McKim |
| **677** | **BASKET AND IRIS** – Hinson Quilter's Companion |
| **678** | **FLOWER BASKET** – Bishop's New Discoveries |
| **678.5** | **BASKETS QUILT** – Betterton |
| **679** | **BASKET OF FLOWERS** – Mountain Mist |
| **680** | **SPRING FLOWERS** – Home Art |
| **681** | **BASKET AND FLOWERS** – Comfort |
| **682** | **BASKET** – From a 19th century quilt, LCPQ Fall 1982 |
| **685** | **CHERRY BASKET** – Capper's Weekly 2/12/38 |
| **686** | **THE GARDEN BASKET** – Finley (each has different appliqué) |
| **690** | **BASKET FLOWER** – Nancy Cabot |
| **691** | **BASKET AND BLOSSOM** – Nancy Cabot<br>**PIECED FLOWER BASKET** – Nancy Cabot |
| **692** | **TULIP BASKET** – Nancy Cabot 5/25/33 |

*Baskets with Appliquéd Contents (674.8 – 692)*

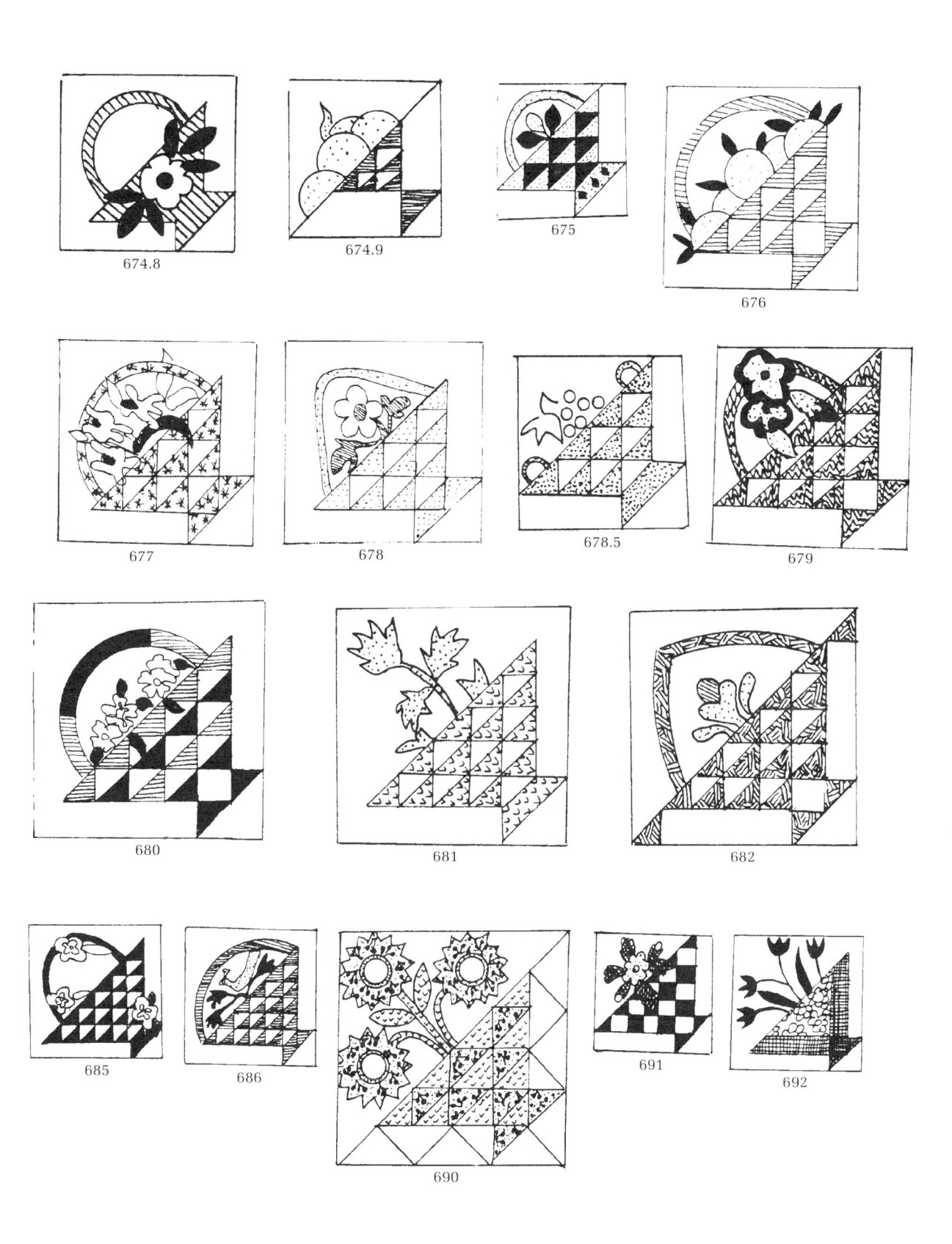

674.8
674.9
675
676
677
678
678.5
679
680
681
682
685
686
690
691
692

# Pattern Category 5: *Realistic*

| | | |
|---|---|---|
| BASKETS FULL OF TRIANGLES (AND SQUARES) | 700 | CACTUS POT – Oklahoma Farmer Stockman 1/1/30 |
| | 701 | SUGAR BOWL – Farm Journal |
| | 702 | SUGAR BOWL – Nancy Cabot |
| | 702.5 | THE SUGAR BOWL – Capper's Weekly 11/26/27 |
| | 703 | BASKET – Nancy Page |
| | 704 | BASKET QUILT – The American Farmer 4/1/1895<br>FLOWER BASKET – LAC #57<br>BETTY'S BASKET – Nancy Page |
| | 705 | SIMPLE FLOWER BASKET – Nancy Cabot |
| | 706 | BABY BUNTING – Orange Judd Farmer 1/26/1900 or 1901 |
| | 707 | CAKE STAND – LAC #59<br>BASKET – Hearth and Home and OCS (Brooks/Wheeler)<br>FRUIT BASKET – Household Magazine 11/29 |
| | 707.5 | BASKET – Ohio Farmer 3/10/1898 |
| | 708 | FRUIT BASKET – Woman's World 2/28 |
| | 709 | FLOWER POT – KC Star 1937 |
| | 710a | FLOWER BASKET – Clara Stone |
| | 710b | MAY BASKET – KC Star 10/17/47 |
| | 711 | CAKE STAND – Nancy Cabot 11/18/33 |
| | 712 | GRAPE BASKET – LAC #387 & Hearth and Home<br>BASKET OF CHIPS – McKim<br>MAY BASKET – Capper's Weekly/Famous Features<br>PICNIC BASKET – Nancy Page |
| | 712.5 | FRUIT BASKET – Gutcheon Perfect Patchwork Primer |
| | 713 | BASKET OF CHIPS – Comfort<br>CHIP BASKET – Farmer's Wife<br>BASKET OF FLOWERS – Coats and Clark<br>FLOWER POT – McCall's Magazine #1651<br>ANNA'S BASKET – Danner/Ericson Bk. 5 1970<br>EARLIEST EXAMPLE: Sampler dated 1862 in Bishop/Knopf |
| | 714 | THE BROKEN SUGAR BOWL – Wallace's Farmer 7/27/28<br>THE BROKEN DISH – Wallace's Farmer 7/27/28<br>THE BASKET QUILT – Wallace's Farmer 7/27/28<br>MAY BASKET DESIGN – Farmer's Wife 1931<br>FRUIT BASKET – McKim<br>BASKET OF TRIANGLES – Mrs. Danner 1934 |
| | 717 | A BASKET QUILT IN TRIANGLES – KC Star 12/16/42 |
| | 718 | BEA'S BASKET – Bets Ramsey, The Chattanooga Times 3/24/81 made ca. 1935 |
| | 719 | MRS. HARDY'S HANGING BASKET – Clara Stone<br>HANGING BASKET – KC Star 8/11/37 |
| | 720 | THE FRUIT BASKET – clipping from unknown newspaper #K1625 |
| | 722 | FRUIT BASKET – The Country Home Magazine 2/33 |
| | 722.5 | BASKET OF FLOWERS – clipping from unknown source |
| | 723 | BASKET OF FLOWERS – possibly Comfort |

*Baskets Full of Triangles (& Squares) (700 – 723)*

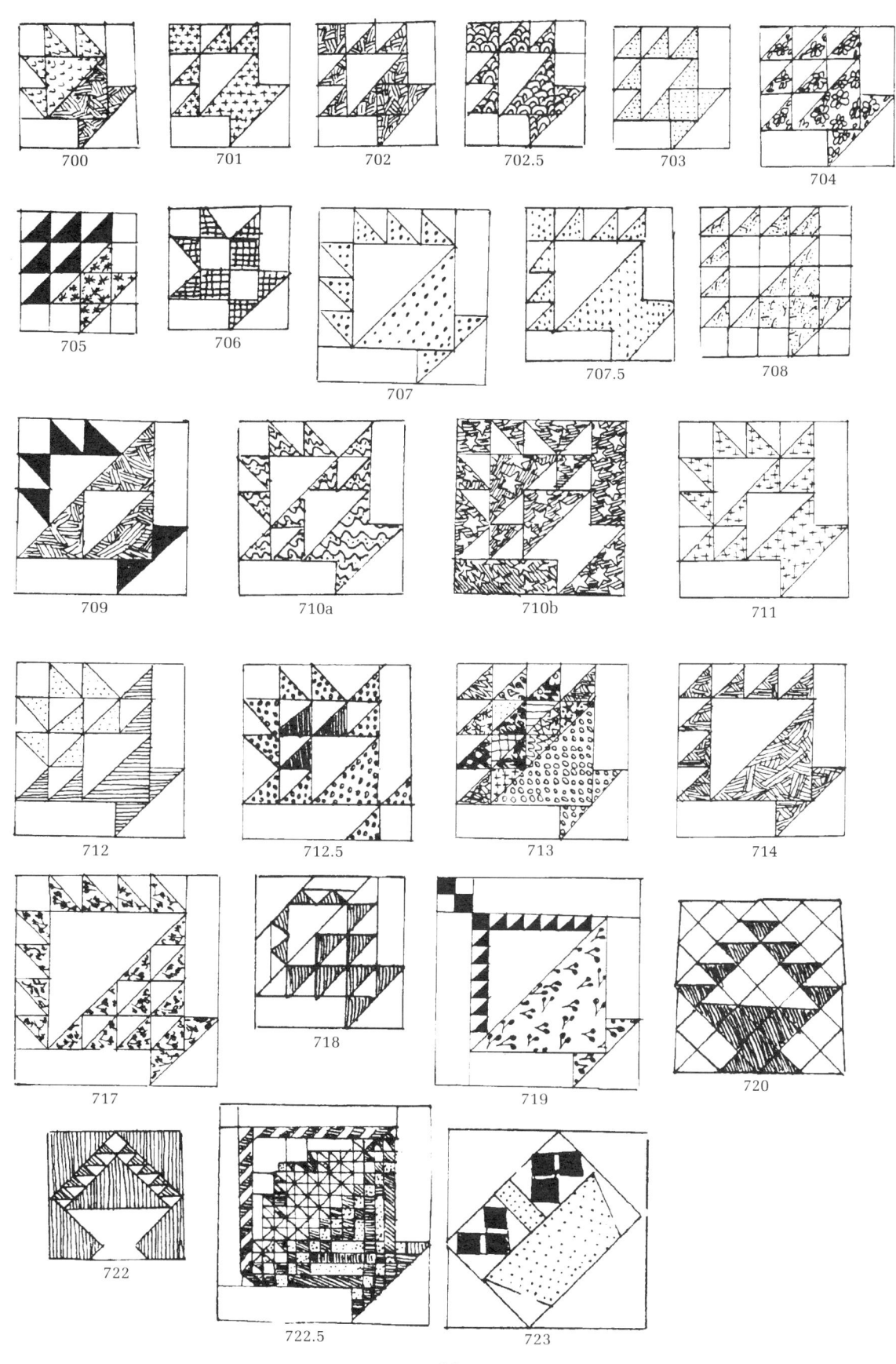

93

Pattern Category 5: *Realistic*

BASKETS FULL OF DIAMONDS OR OTHER SHAPES

| | | |
|---|---|---|
| | 725 | THE DISK – LAC #138<br>FLOWER POT – Hearth & Home and Rural New Yorker 4/11/31<br>FLOWER BASKET – KC Star 7/31/35<br>BASKET OF DIAMONDS – KC Star 11/11/36<br>JERSEY TULIP – Mary McElwain<br>RAINBOW CACTUS – Mary McElwain. *See 4040.* |
| | 725.2 | BASKET OF SCRAPS – McKendry |
| | 725.5 | CACTUS BASKET – Herrschner's "Quilts" |
| | 726 | BASKET OF SCRAPS – Hinson QM |
| | 726.5 | BIRD AT THE WINDOW – Little 'n Big 2/66<br>DOVE AT THE WINDOW – Little 'n Big 2/66 |
| | 727 | UNNAMED – Farm & Home 1/1/1889<br>SOME PRETTY PATCHWORK – LAC #287<br>GARDEN BASKET – Nancy Cabot |
| | 728 | TEXAS CACTUS BASKET – attributed to Nancy Cabot/Wilma Smith<br>SCRAP BASKET – Mrs. Danner Bk. 2, 1934<br>FLOWER BASKET – Holstein |
| | 729 | CACTUS BASKET – Finley<br>DESERT ROSE – Finley<br>TEXAS ROSE – Finley<br>TEXAS TREASURE – Finley |
| | 730 | FLOWER POT – McKim<br>CACTUS BASKET – Nancy Cabot<br>DESERT ROSE – Hall and Della Harris, Cat. #47 |
| | 731 | CACTUS BASKET - Evelyn Brown in Tumbling Alley 1978 |
| | 732 | FLOWER POT – Ladies' Home Journal 2/09<br>BOX – Ladies' Home Journal 2/09 |
| | 733 | FLOWER POT – Clara Stone<br>MAY BASKET – Nancy Cabot<br>HICK'S BASKET – KC Star 3/13/40 |
| | 734 | TULIP BASKET – Aunt Martha #C3230<br>THE GREAT CIRCLE QUILT – NNT |
| | 735 | BASKET OF SCRAPS – Mahler |
| | 736 | CALICO BUSH – Nancy Cabot |
| | 737 | FLOWERS IN A BASKET – KC Star 8/20/41 |

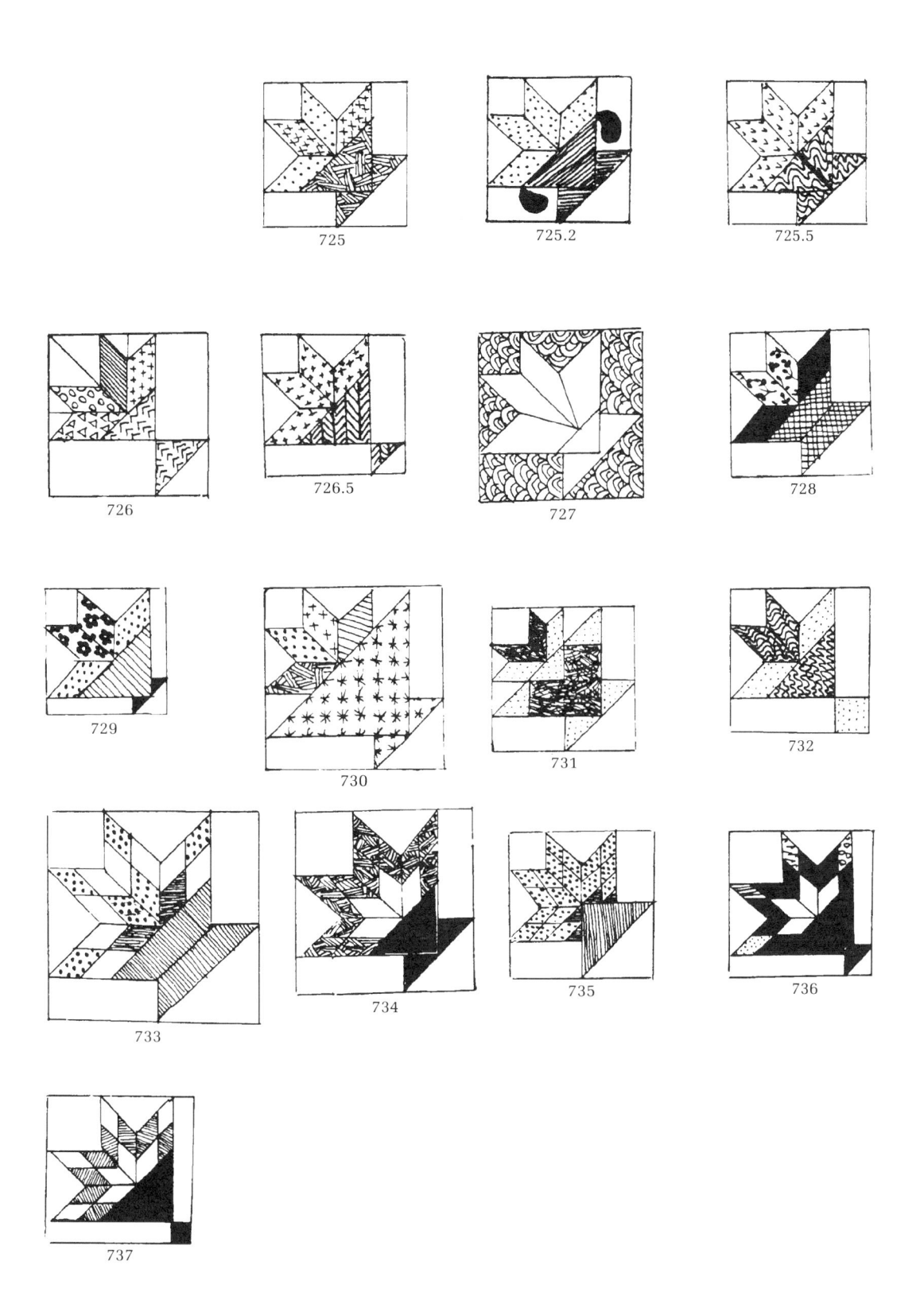

*Baskets Full of Diamonds or Other Shapes (725 – 737)*

95

## Pattern Category 5: *Realistic*

BASKETS FULL OF DIAMONDS OR OTHER SHAPES

| | | |
|---|---|---|
| 740 | Tulip in Vase – Carlie Sexton 1928 |
| 741 | Basket of Lilies – LAC #55 |
| 742 | Basket of Flowers – KC Star 12/7/35 |
| | A Basket of Bright Flowers – KC Star 4/24/46 |
| 743 | Royal Japanese Vase – Farm and Home 2/15/1890 |
| | Royal Dutch Tulip and Vase – Home Art |
| | Carolina Lily – Woodard and Greenstein Crib Quilts |
| 744 | Tulip in Vase – LAC #273 |
| 744.5 | Pot of Flowers – Oklahoma Farmer and Stockman 1/15/29 |
| 744.7 | Martha's Basket – Woman's World 1932 |
| 745 | Flower Vase – Nancy Cabot |
| 745.5 | Lily Corners – Khin |
| 746 | Basket of Lilies – KC Star 4/8/31 |
| 747 | Basket of Tulips – Capper's Weekly |
| 747.5 | The Tulip Basket – Capper's Weekly 1929 |
| 748 | Potted Star Flower – Farm Journal |
| 749 | Friendship Basket – OCS (Brooks/Wheeler) #511 |
| 749.8 | Flower Basket – OCS (Brooks/Wheeler) #7343 |
| 750 | Texas Cactus Basket – Nancy Cabot |
| 751 | Floral Centerpiece – Nancy Cabot |
| 751.5 | Primrose Patch Quilt – Workbasket April 1945 |
| 752 | Leafy Basket – OCS (Brooks/Wheeler) #797 |

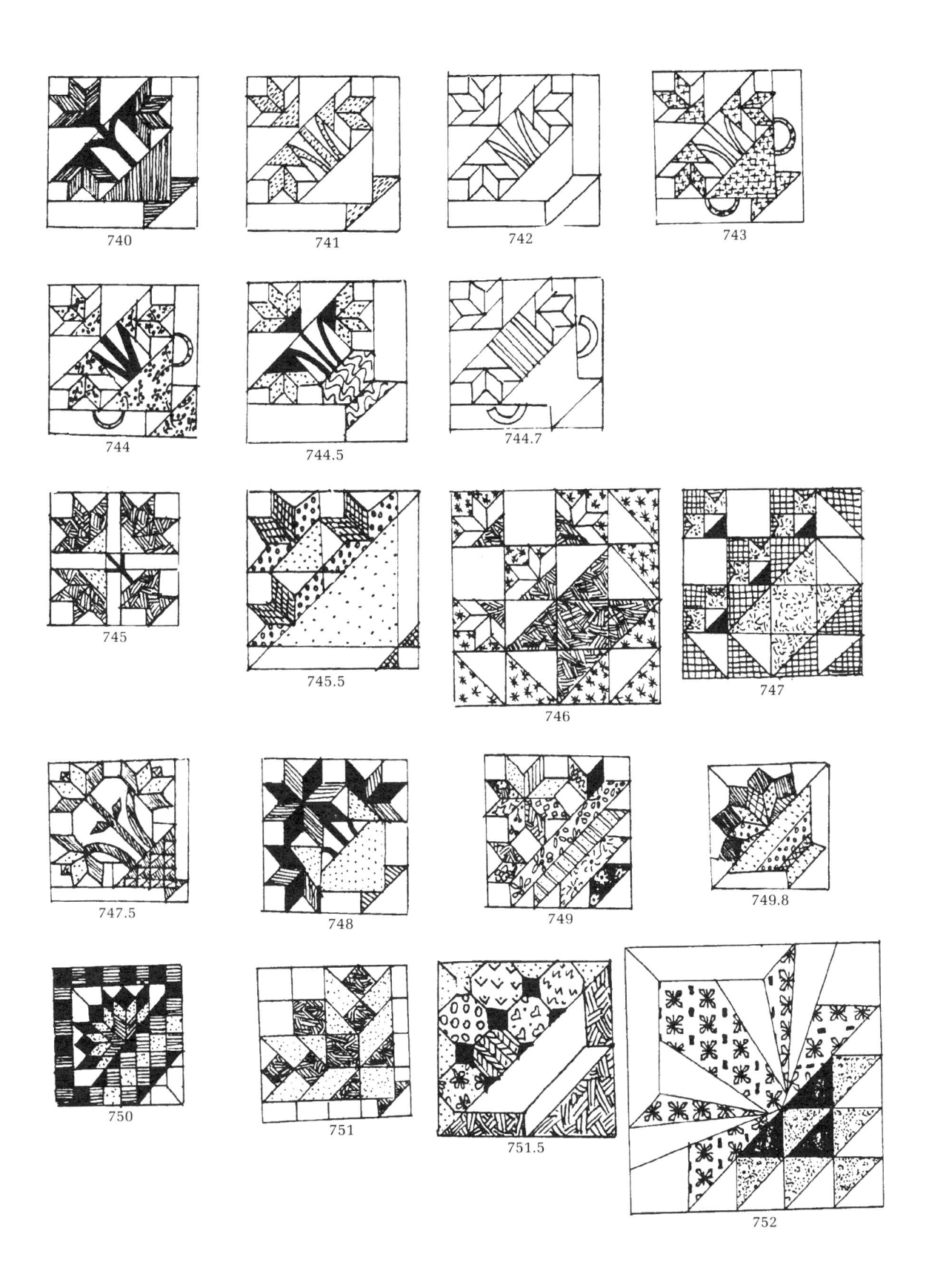

*Baskets Full of Diamonds or Other Shapes (740 – 752)*

97

Pattern Category 5: *Realistic*

| | | |
|---|---|---|
| BASKETS FULL OF DIAMONDS OR OTHER SHAPES | 752.5 | THE FLOWER POT QUILT – Aunt Martha #M 143 (green & white) |
| | 753 | ROSE BASKET – Nancy Cabot |
| | 753.5 | BASKET OF FLOWERS – Prairie Farmer Bk. 1, 1931 |
| | 753.7 | BASKET OF LILIES – OCS (Brooks/Wheeler) #5210 |
| VASES AND MISC. CONTAINERS | 754 | SNOWDROP – (#1 in Bowl of Flowers Serial) OCS (Brooks/Wheeler) #5077a |
| | 755 | ROSE – (#4 in Bowl of Flowers Serial) OCS (Brooks/Wheeler) #5077d |
| | 756 | ASTER – (#2 in Bowl of Flowers Serial) OCS (Brooks/Wheeler) #5077b |
| | 756.3 | TULIP – (#3 in Bowl of Flowers Serial) OCS (Brooks/Wheeler) #5077c |
| | 756.5 | LILY – (#5 in Bowl of Flowers Serial) OCS (Brooks/Wheeler) #5077e |
| | 756.7 | POPPY – (#6 in Bowl of Flowers Serial) OCS (Brooks/Wheeler) #5077f |
| | 758 | GARDEN OF FRIENDSHIP – OCS (Brooks/Wheeler) #5787 |
| | 758.5 | CACTUS FLOWER – Hearth and Home |
| | 759 | STAR BOUQUET – Clara Stone |
| | 760 | VASE OF FLOWERS – "Grandmothers Flower Quilts" source? |
| | 761 | TEA BASKET – Mrs. Danner Bk. 2, 1934 |
| | 762 | COMPOTE QUILT – attributed to Godey's by Little 'n Big |
| | 762.5 | COLONIAL BASKET – OCS (Brooks/Wheeler) #5072 |
| | 763 | VASE OF FLOWERS – OCS (Brooks/Wheeler) #640 |
| | 763.2 | VASE OF FLOWERS – OCS (Brooks/Wheeler) #5204 |
| | 763.7 | CHRYSANTHEMUM – OCS (Brooks/Wheeler) #5194 & 5001 |

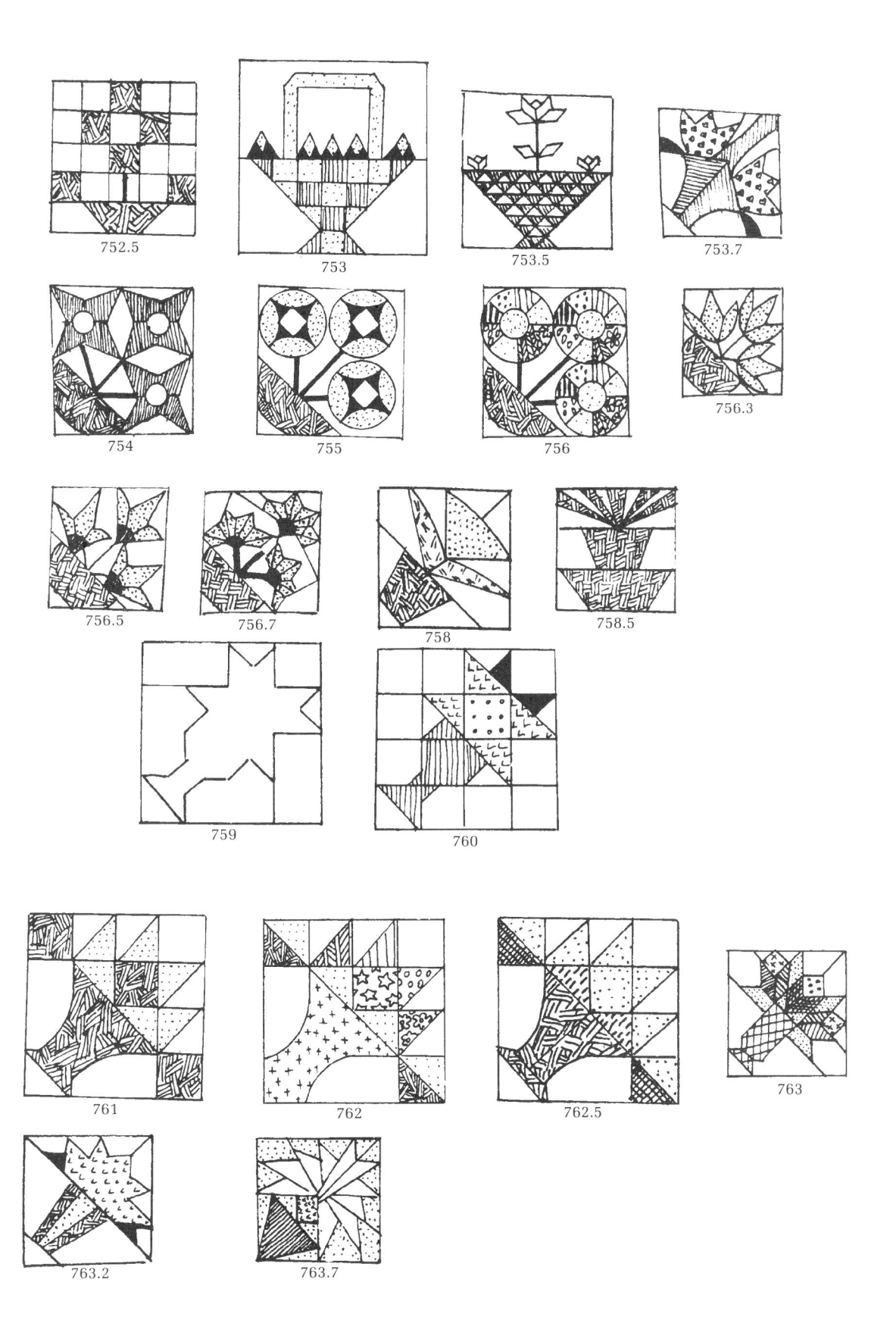

*Baskets Full Of Diamonds or Other Shapes, Vases and Misc. Containers (752.5 – 763.7)*

99

## Pattern Category 5: *Realistic*

FLOWERS

| | | |
|---|---|---|
| | 765.01 | TULIP – attributed to OCS (Brooks/Wheeler) by Khin |
| | 765.02 | TULIP – OCS (Brooks/Wheeler) #508 |
| | 765.10 | MISSISSIPI PINK – Needlecraft 5/29 |
| | 765.11 | ANTIQUE SHOP TULIP – Hinson, Quilter's Companion |
| | 765.12 | NORTH CAROLINA LILY – McKim's, Patchwork Parade of States |
| | 765.13 | KENTUCKY LILY – Edie Pigg & Cora Wright, Kentucky Pride Quilts 1982 |
| | 765.20 | LILY – Goodspeed |
| | 765.21 | DAY LILY BLOCK – Gutcheon PPP |
| | 765.23 | DOUBLE PEONY – Capper's Weekly 1927 |
| | 765.24 | THE DOUBLE TULIP – Mrs. Danner Bk. 2, 1934 |
| | 765.25 | A LILY QUILT – Orange Judd Farmer 1/19/01<br>THE MEADOW LILY – Finley<br>THE WOOD LILY – Finley<br>THE TIGER LILY – Finley<br>THE MOUNTAIN LILY – Finley<br>THE PRAIRIE LILY – Finley<br>THE MARIPOSA LILY – Finley<br>THE FIRE LILY – Finley |
| | 765.30 | CLEVELAND LILIES – LAC #53 |
| | 765.31 | PENNSYLVANIA TULIP – Mountain Mist |
| | 765.4 | NOON DAY LILY – LAC #51<br>POT OF FLOWERS – Grandmother Clark Bk. 20, 1931<br>NORTH CAROLINA LILY – Hall<br>MOUNTAIN LILY – Hall<br>FIRE LILY – Hall<br>PRAIRIE LILY – Hall<br>WOOD LILY – Hall<br>MEADOW LILY – Hall<br>MARIPOSA LILY – Hall |
| | 765.5 | TRIANGLE FLOWER – Grandmother Clark<br>EARLIEST EXAMPLE: of any of the three-lobed flowers #765.1 - 765.5 is dated 1849 in a private collection. There is a variation in Benoni Pearce's sampler dated 1850 in the Smithsonian's collection |
| | 765.6 | MARIPOSA LILY – attributed to Nancy Cabot/Wilma Smith |
| | 766.1 | GRANDMOTHER'S DREAM – Carlie Sexton in The Country Gentleman 7/26 |
| | 766.2 | DOUBLE TULIP – Woman's Home Companion |
| | 766.3 | LILY FLOWER – Good Housekeeping<br>TULIP – Good Housekeeping |

*Flowers (765.01 – 766.3)*

765.01  765.02  765.10  765.11  765.12

765.13  765.20  765.21  765.23  765.24

765.25  765.30  765.31  765.4  765.5

765.6

766.1  766.2  766.3

Pattern Category 5: *Realistic*

FLOWERS
- 767 — CLUSTER OF STARS – Nancy Cabot
- 768.1 — EARLY PEONY – Prudence Penny, Seattle Post Intelligencer
- 768.2 — TREE QUILT PATTERN – Ohio Farmer 1896
  CLEVELAND TULIP – Household Journal
  CAROLINA LILY – Oklahoma Farmer and Stockman 10/1/31
  PINEYS – Needlecraft 1936
- 768.3 — POINSETTIA QUILT – Betterton
- 769 — PRESIDENT'S QUILT – LAC #297
- 770 — DOUBLE PAEONY – LAC #178
  YELLOW LILY – Marshall
  DOUBLE TULIP BOUQUET – Comfort 1923
- 771 — DOUBLE TULIP – The Family 9/13
- 772 — SQUARE AND SWALLOW – Woman's World, "The Patchwork Bk." 1931
  EARLIEST EXAMPLE: of any of these three-lobed flowers is similar to this one in a sampler in the collection of the Baltimore Museum of Art dated 1844 (in Katzenberg).
- 773 — THE PEONY – Finley
- 773.1 — BED OF PEONIES – Mountain Mist #62
- 773.2 — SCARLET CARNATIONS – QNM #124, 1980
- 773.5 — THREE-FLOWERED SUNFLOWER – LAC #74
- 773.6 — TRIPLE SUNFLOWER – Clara Stone and Household Journal
- 773.7 — HATTIE'S SUNFLOWER – Danner/Ericson Bk. 5, 1970
- 773.8 — KANSAS SUNFLOWER – Spool Cotton Co. 1940

*Flowers (767 – 773.8)*

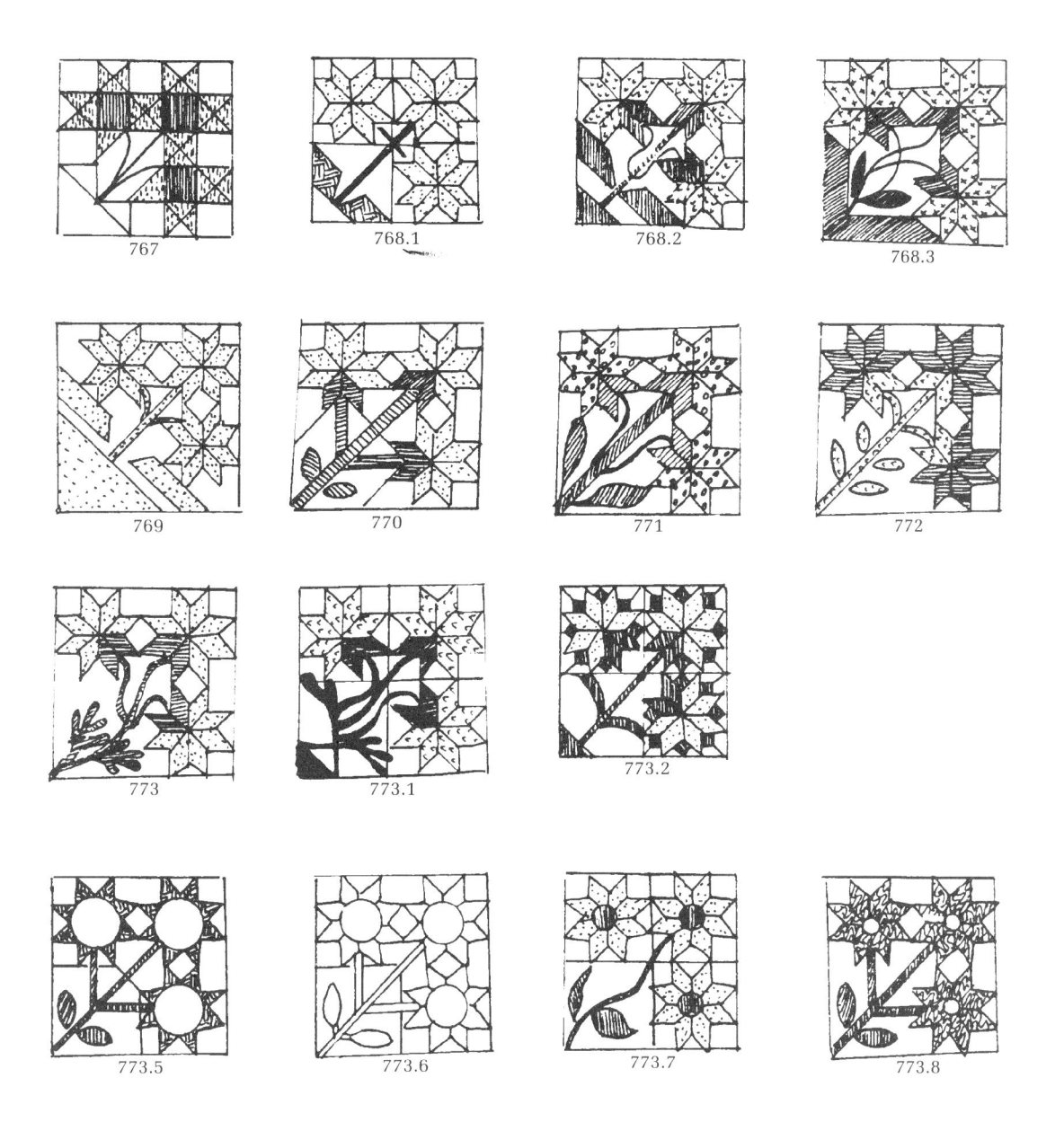

767　768.1　768.2　768.3

769　770　771　772

773　773.1　773.2

773.5　773.6　773.7　773.8

## Pattern Category 5: *Realistic*

FLOWERS
- **774**    Rosebud Patchwork – Needlecraft Magazine 7/29
- **775**    Texas Bluebonnet – by Juanita Watson in Quilter's Newsletter Magazine #128, 1981
- **775.5**    Bluebonnet Beauty – QNM #128, 1981
- **776**    Nosegay – OCS (Brooks/Wheeler) #5419
- **777**    Daffodil – OCS (Brooks/Wheeler) #1030
- **777.2**    Old Fashioned Garden – OCS (Brooks/Wheeler) #5175
- **777.4**    Iris – OCS (Brooks/Wheeler)
- **777.5**    Orange Bud – Aunt Martha "The Quilt Fair Comes To You" 1933
- **777.6**    Floral Bouquet – Nancy Cabot 8/31/34
- **777.7**    Nosegay – OCS (Brooks/Wheeler) #7093
- **778**    Bellflower – OCS (Brooks/Wheeler) #642
- **779**    Flower of Friendship – OCS (Brooks/Wheeler) #694
- **779.1**    Friendship Flowers – OCS (Brooks/Wheeler) #538
- **779.2**    Flower of the Woods – OCS (Brooks/Wheeler) #5367
- **779.5**    Carnation – by Arleta Dennis in Quilt World 4/80
- **780**    Rose – McKim
         Modernistic Rose – Hall
- **780.3**    Oriental Rose – Nancy Cabot 10/13/33
- **780.5**    Iris Rainbow – by Arlene Gutzeit in Quilt World 8/1980
- **781**    Pansy Quilt – Home Art
- **783**    Pansy – McKim
         Modernistic Pansy – Nancy Cabot 9/30/33
- **784**    Trumpet Vine – McKim
         Modernistic Trumpet Vine – Hall
- **784.3**    The Morning Glory Quilt – McKim

*Flowers (774 – 784.3)*

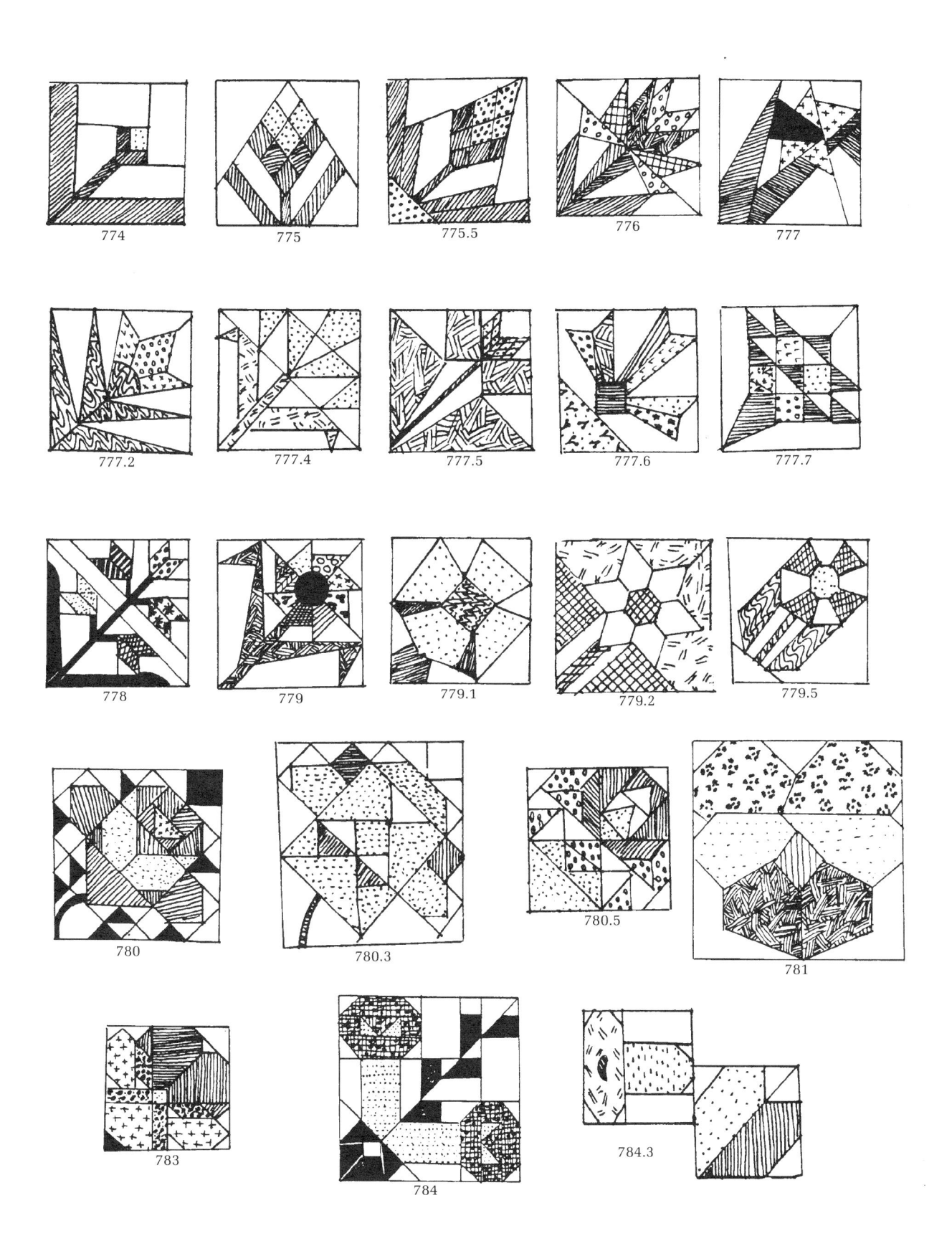

774 775 775.5 776 777
777.2 777.4 777.5 777.6 777.7
778 779 779.1 779.2 779.5
780 780.3 780.5 781
783 784 784.3

## Pattern Category 5: *Realistic*

FLOWERS

| | | |
|---|---|---|
| | **784.5** | OLD FASHIONED GARLAND – OCS (Brooks/Wheeler) #500<br>PINEAPPLE – QNM #79, 1976 |
| | **784.6** | WHITE HOUSE ROSE – Needlecraft Magazine |
| | **785** | WATER BEAUTY –-OCS (Brooks/Wheeler) #792 |
| | **785.2** | UNNAMED – OCS (Brooks/Wheeler) #7023 |
| | **785.5** | TULIP – Hartman |
| | **785.7** | TENNESSEE TULIP – Bets Ramsey in Chattanooga Times 4/28/81 |
| | **786** | CROCUS – OCS (Brooks/Wheeler) #670 |
| | **787** | TULIP GARDEN – OCS (Brooks/Wheeler) #5666 |
| | **788** | ORIENTAL POPPY –-McKim<br>MODERNISTIC CALIFORNIA POPPY – Hall |
| | **788.2** | JOHNNY JUMP-UP – Woman's World 1/33. *See 216.35.* |
| | **788.4** | MORNING GLORY SQUARE – Workbasket ? |
| | **788.5** | EVENING FLOWER – OCS (Brooks/Wheeler) #5189 |
| | **789** | FLEUR DE LIS – OCS (Brooks/Wheeler) #776 |
| | **790** | SPRING FANCY – OCS (Brooks/Wheeler) #969 |
| | **791** | STAR FLOWER – OCS (Brooks/Wheeler) #844 |
| | **791.5** | MARTHA WASHINGTON – Sophie LaCroix<br>MARTHA WASHINGTON ROSE – Sophie LaCroix |
| | **792** | CALLA LILY QUILT – OCS (Brooks/Wheeler) #972 |
| | **793** | DOGWOOD – OCS (Brooks/Wheeler) #5376 |
| | **794** | ARKANSAS MEADOW ROSE – KC Star 10/9/35 |
| | **795** | SUNFLOWER – OCS (Brooks/Wheeler) #1088 |

*Flowers (784.5 – 795)*

107

Pattern Category 5: *Realistic*

FLOWERS

| | | |
|---|---|---|
| | **796** | **FIELD OF DAISIES** – OCS (Brooks/Wheeler) #338 & 953 |
| | **796.2** | **POND LILY** – OCS (Brooks/Wheeler) #1039 |
| | **796.5** | **PEONY** – OCS (Brooks/Wheeler) #722 |
| | **796.7** | **GARDEN TULIP** – Source Unknown |
| | **797** | **GRANDMOTHER'S FAVORITE** – OCS (Brooks/Wheeler) #1044 |
| | **797.5** | **MORNING GLORY** – OCS (Brooks/Wheeler) #5211 |
| | **798** | **WATER LILY** – OCS (Brooks/Wheeler) #696 |
| | **798.5** | **PRAIRIE FLOWER** – OCS (Brooks/Wheeler) #5335 |
| | **798.7** | **CLEOPATRA'S FAN** – OCS (Brooks/Wheeler) #846 |
| | **799** | **FLOWER OF SPRING** – KC Star 1/11/36<br>**FLORAL PATCHWORK** – OCS (Brooks/Wheeler) #7191<br>**A TULIP PATTERN IN HIGH COLORS** – KC Star 1/26/49 |
| | **800** | **JAPANESE MORNING GLORY** – OCS (Brooks/Wheeler) #786 |
| | **800.1** | **GARDEN TREASURE** – OCS (Brooks/Wheeler) #5452 |
| | **800.2** | **TULIP BLOCK** – Hearth and Home |
| | **800.8** | **SWEET SULTAN** – OCS (Brooks/Wheeler) #5138 |
| | **800.9** | **PRISCILLA'S CHOICE** – OCS (Brooks/Wheeler) #959 (when set side-by-side, blocks form flowers and leaves) |

*Flowers (796 – 800.9)*

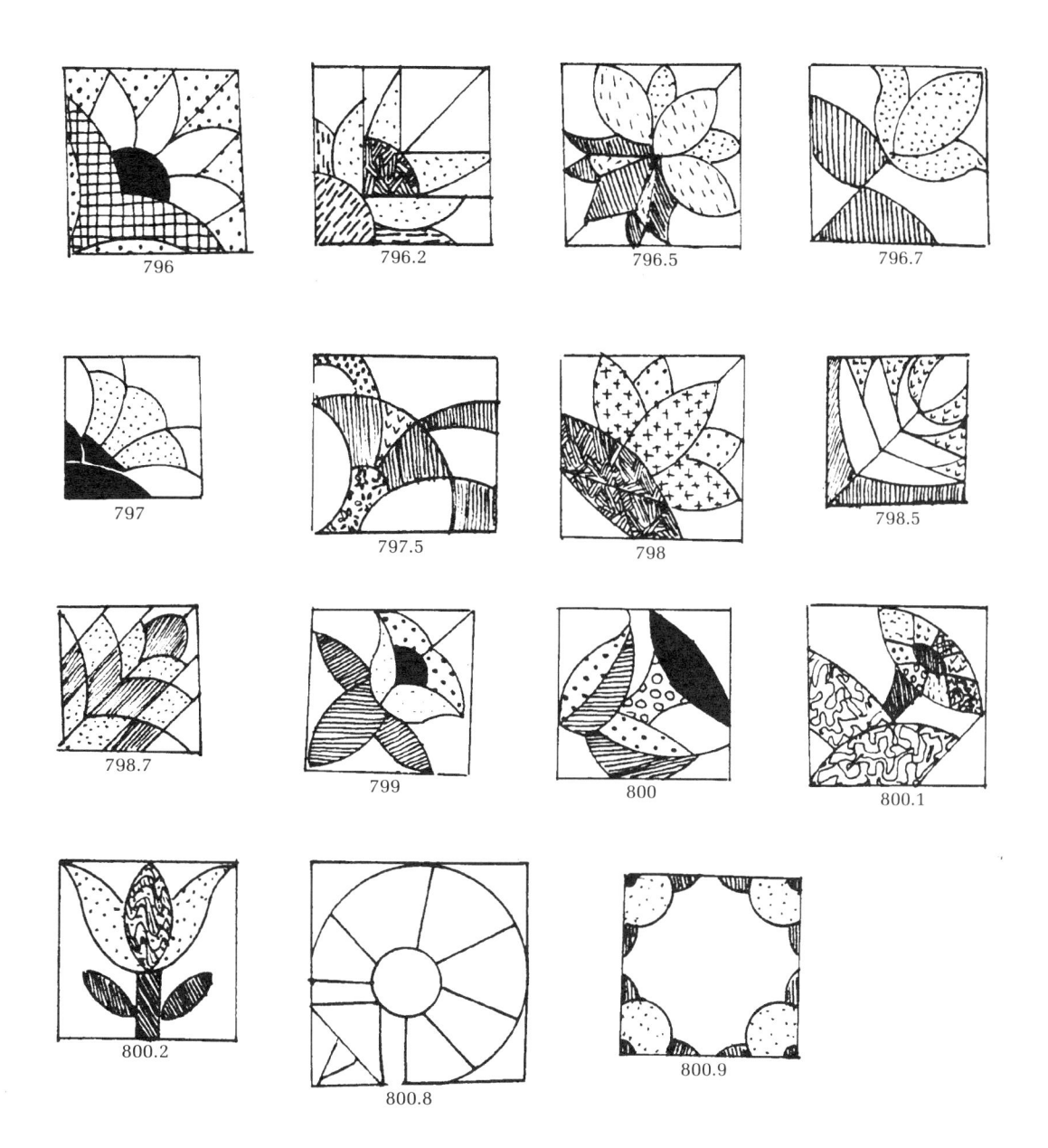

109

# Pattern Category 5: *Realistic*

| | | |
|---|---|---|
| TREES WITH TRIANGLES FOR LEAVES | 801 | PATCH BLOSSOM – Aunt Martha Bk. #3614, 1963 |
| | 802 | CHRISTMAS TREES – QNM #107, 1978 |
| | 805 | NORWAY PINE – Farm Journal<br>PINE TREE – OCS (Brooks/Wheeler) #420 |
| | 806 | PINE TREE – Grandmother Clark |
| | 807 | PINE TREE – McCall's Magazine ca. 1935<br>TEMPERANCE TREE – Hall |
| | 808 | PINE TREE QUILT DESIGN – Wallace's Farmer 5/4/28 |
| | 809 | CHRISTMAS TREE – KC Star 6/2/34<br>PINE TREE – KC Star 6/2/34 |
| | 810 | PINE TREE – Grandmother Clark 1932 |
| | 810.5 | CENTENNIAL TREE – Clara Stone and Hearth and Home |
| | 810.7 | PINE TREE – from a quilt ca. 1900 in McKendry |
| | 811 | TREE OF PARADISE – Woman's World |
| | 811.5 | TEMPERANCE TREE – Ohio Farmer 11/29/1894 |
| | 811.7 | TREE OF PARADISE – Rural New Yorker 4/7/34 |
| | 812 | TREE OF PARADISE – Hall |
| | 813 | TREE OF PARADISE – Carlie Sexton 1928 |
| | 814 | TREE OF LIFE – Safford & Bishop |
| | 815 | PROUD PINE – by Anna Lupkiewicz in M. Johnson's Prize Country Quilts, 1977 |
| | 815.3 | TREE OF PARADISE – Needlecraft Magazine 5/32<br>TEMPERANCE TREE – Needlecraft Magazine 5/32<br>WASHINGTON'S ELM – Needlecraft Magazine 5/32<br>CENTENNIAL TREE – Needlecraft Magazine 5/32<br>WASHINGTON TREE – Woman's Day 9/42 |
| | 815.5 | EVERGREEN TREE – Hearth and Home? |
| | 815.8 | EVERGREEN TREE – Grandma Dexter #2731 (trunk appliqué) |
| | 816 | PINE TREE – Nancy Cabot |
| | 817 | WEEPING WILLOW – Orange Judd Farmer 1896 |

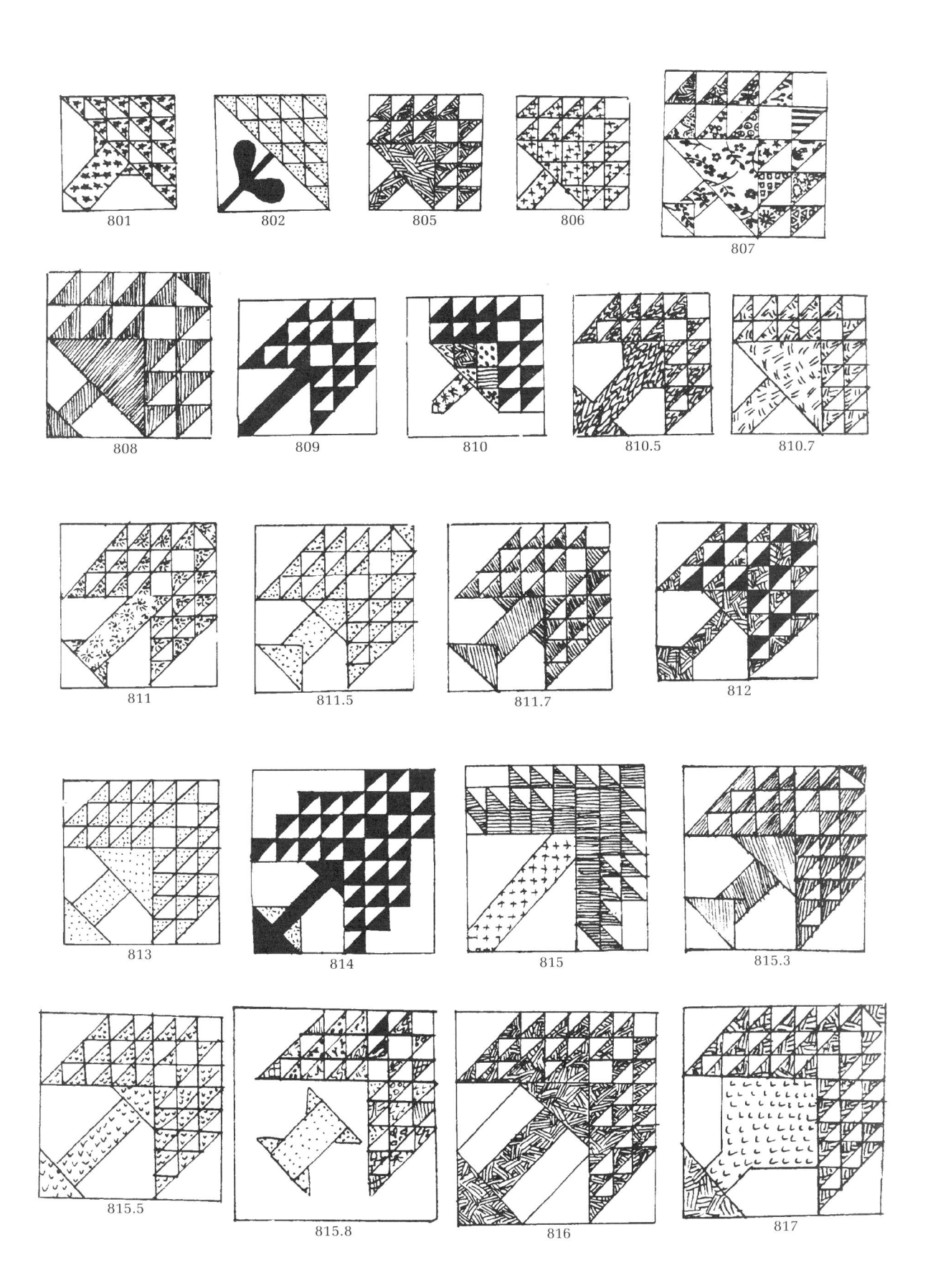

*Trees with Triangles for Leaves (801 – 817)*

111

Pattern Category 5: *Realistic*

| | | |
|---|---|---|
| TREES WITH TRIANGLES FOR LEAVES | 818 | PINE TREE – Nancy Page |
| | 819 | TREE OF PARADISE – LAC #260<br>TREE – Dakota Farmer 11/15/27<br>CHRISTMAS TREE PATCH – Comfort<br>THE PINE TREE – Finley |
| | 820 | TREE OF PARADISE – Webster and Pennsylvania Farmer<br>TREE OF LIFE – Ickes |
| | 820.5 | TREE OF PARADISE – Aunt Martha |
| | 821 | PINE TREE – McKim and The Farmer's Wife 1931<br>TREE OF PARADISE – Hall |
| | 822 | PINE TREE – McKim in KC Star 1928 |
| | 822.5 | TREE OF PARADISE – Helen Kaufman in Bureau Farmer 1/31 |
| | 823 | CHRISTMAS TREE – Hall<br>TREE OF LIFE – Hall |
| | 823.5 | PINE TREE – LCPQ #19, 1980 |
| | 824 | TREE OF LIFE – Mail and Breeze (Capper's) |
| | 824.5 | CHRISTMAS TREE – The Family 9/13 |
| | 825 | PINE TREE – Peto |
| | 826 | TREE OF LIFE – Oklahoma Farmer Stockman 10/25/20 |
| | 827 | TREE OF PARADISE – Mountain Mist |
| | 829 | APPLE TREE – attributed to Nancy Cabot/Wilma Smith |
| | 829.5 | TENNESSEE PINE – Hinson QC |

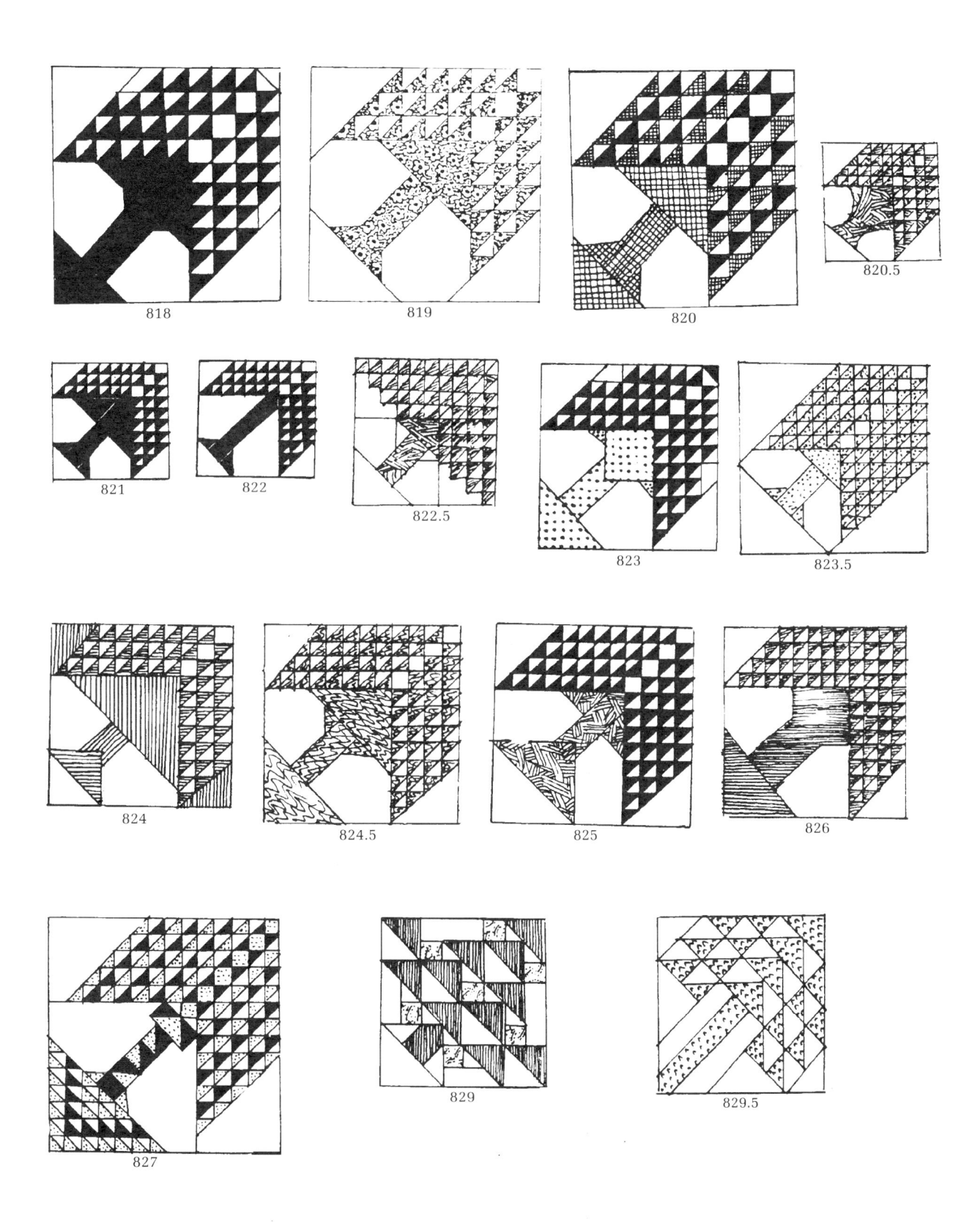

*Trees with Triangles for Leaves (818 – 829.5)*

## Pattern Category 5: *Realistic*

| | | |
|---|---|---|
| TREES WITH TRIANGLES FOR LEAVES | **829.9** | TREE OF PARADISE – Farm Journal 1/25 |
| | **830** | TREE OF PARADISE – Nancy Cabot |
| | **831** | THE TREE OF PARADISE – Modern Priscilla 8/28 |
| | **832** | BALSAM FIR – Nancy Cabot |
| | **833** | TINY PINES – Nancy Page |
| | **834** | PINE TREE – LAC #405<br>THE PINE FOREST (A QUILT FOR MAINE) – McKim Patchwork, Parade of States<br>CHRISTMAS TREE – KC Star 1932 |
| | **835** | THE FOREST FOR THE TREES – Gutcheon Quilt Design Workbook. *See 215 & 216.* |
| TREES WITH SQUARES AND RECTANGLES FOR LEAVES | **836** | TREE OF TEMPTATION – Hall |
| | **837** | TREE OF TEMPTATION – Hinson QM |
| | **838** | CHERRY TREE PATCHWORK DESIGN – Walker 1932 |
| | **839** | LITTLE BEECH TREE – Nancy Cabot |
| | **840** | LITTLE BEECH TREE – LAC #223<br>PINE TREE – McKim and Prudence Penny |
| | **843** | THE WEEPING WILLOW QUILT – Rural New Yorker 4/20/35 and The Indiana Farmers' Guide |
| | **844** | CASCADE PRIDE – by Mary Chartier in Quilt World 12/81 |
| TREES WITH DIAMONDS AND OTHER SHAPES FOR LEAVES | **845** | LOZENGE TREE – Nancy Cabot |
| | **846** | FORBIDDEN FRUIT TREE – LAC #224<br>MAINE'S SPREADING PINE TREE – Workbasket 1935 |
| | **846.5** | WEEPING WILLOW – Prairie Farmer Bk.let #1, 1931 |
| | **847** | MODERN PEONY – Nancy Cabot |
| | **848** | PAEONY BLOCK – LAC #308 |

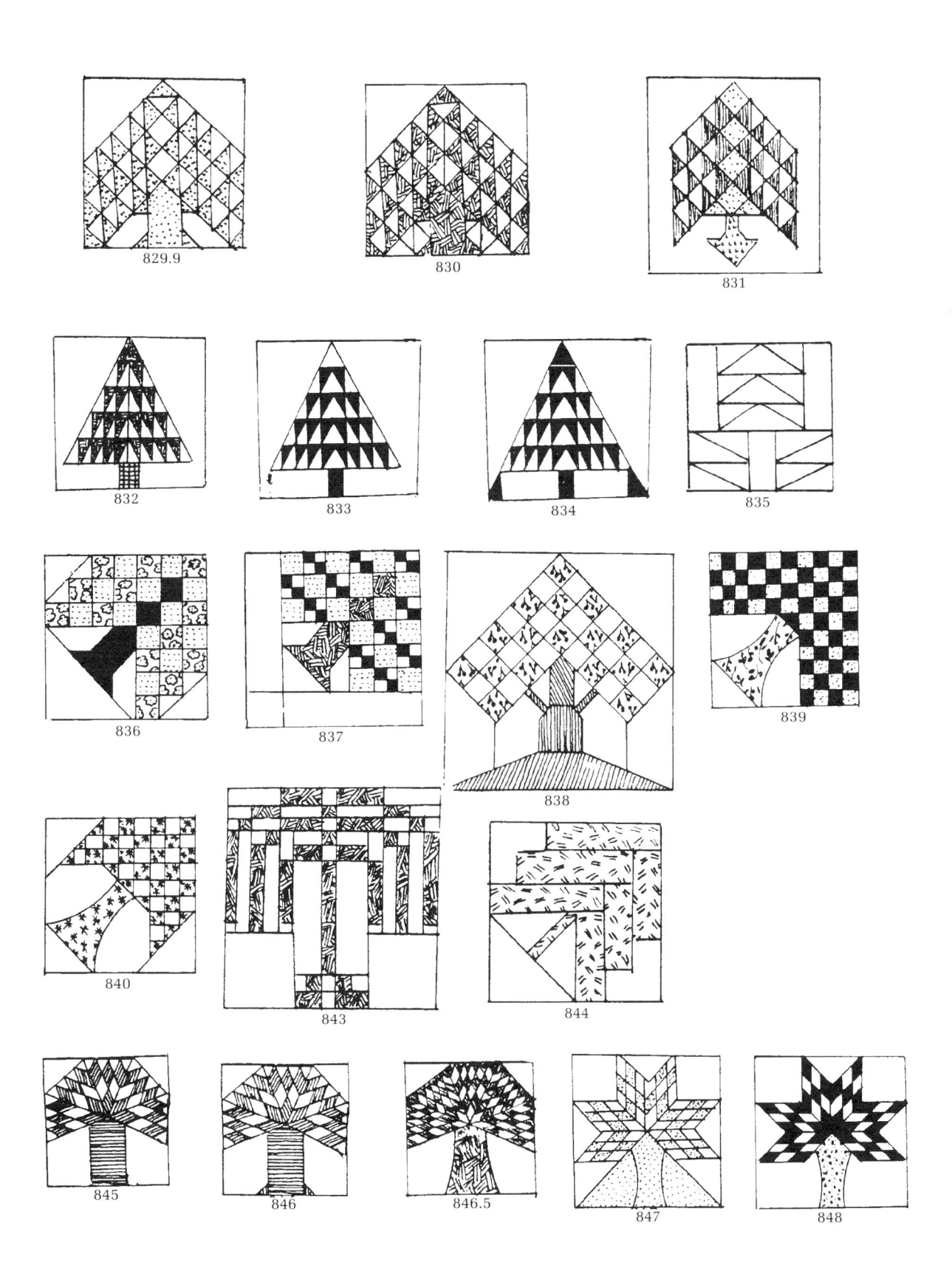

*Trees with Triangles, Squares, Rectangles, Diamonds and Other Shapes for Leaves (829.9 – 848)*

# Pattern Category 5: *Realistic*

| | | |
|---|---|---|
| TREES WITH DIAMONDS AND OTHER SHAPES FOR LEAVES | 849 | LIVE OAK TREE – LAC #222 |
| | 850 | GEORGE WASHINGTON CHERRY TREE – Sophie LaCroix 1916 |
| | 851 | CONE TREE – Nancy Cabot |
| | 852 | TREE OF TEMPTATION – Capper's Weekly 10/5/29 |
| | 854 | PINE TREE QUILT – OCS (Brooks/Wheeler) #535 |
| | 855 | FLORIDA FOREST – by Mabel Wolford in M.E. Johnson's Prize Winning Quilts 1977 |
| | 856 | TRAIL OF THE LONESOME PINE – Capper's Weekly? Nancy Cabot? |
| LEAVES | 857.01 | CENTENNIAL MAPLE – Aunt Kate's Quilting Bee 8/1965 (for Canada's centennial) |
| | 857.02 | MAPLE LEAF – Mountain Mist #81 |
| | 857.031 | SWEET GUM LEAF – KC Star 12/20/30 |
| | 857.032 | SWEET GUM LEAF – Clara Stone |
| | 857.033 | CACTUS ROSE – Betterton |
| | 857.04a | STAR FLOWER – Oklahoma Farmer Stockman ca. 1925 |
| | 857.04b | THE LILY – Carlie Sexton |
| | 857.04c | CACTUS ROSE – Shelburne |
| | 857.04d | WHITE LILY – Lockport Batting Company ca. 1930 |
| | 857.04e | PEONY VARIATION – Woodard and Greenstein *Crib Quilts* EARLIEST EXAMPLE: of any of these 857.04 variations is in a sampler dated 1843-5 in the Smithsonian Collection |
| | 857.06 | TEA LEAF – attributed to Nancy Cabot/Wilma Smith |
| | 857.07 | TEA LEAF – attributed to Nancy Cabot/Wilma Smith |
| | 857.08 | TEA LEAF – Finley |
| | 857.09 | STATE OF OHIO – Hinson<br>BUCKEYE LEAF – Hinson (See 1232) |
| | 857.093 | THE OAK LEAF – Illinois State Register 4/10/32<br>THE HISTORIC OAK LEAF – KC Star 1/4/1961. *See 1328 & 1331.* |

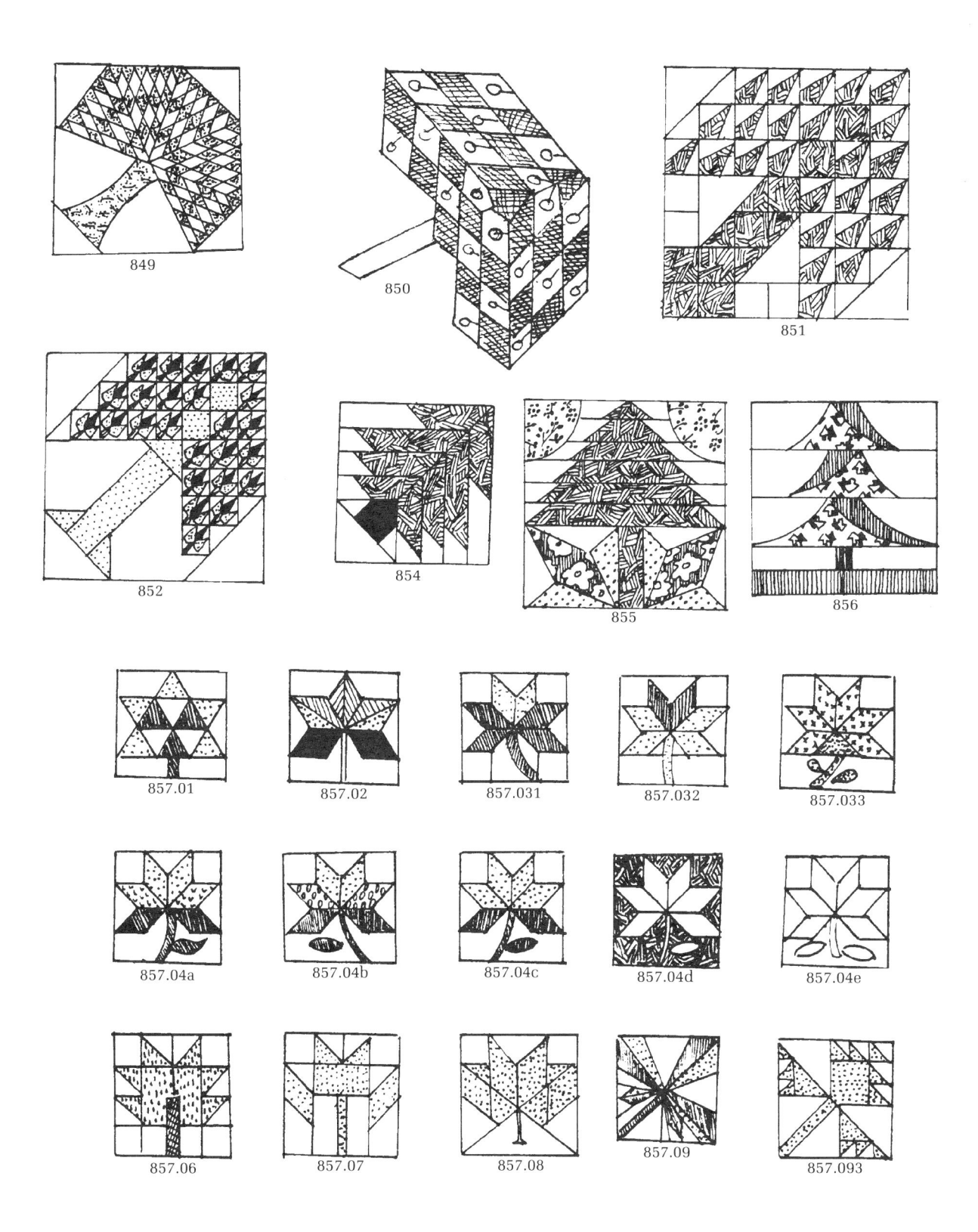

*Trees with Diamonds and Other Shapes for Leaves, Leaves  (849 – 857.093)*

849

850

851

852

854

855

856

857.01

857.02

857.031

857.032

857.033

857.04a

857.04b

857.04c

857.04d

857.04e

857.06

857.07

857.08

857.09

857.093

## Pattern Category 5: *Realistic*

| | | |
|---|---|---|
| HOUSES AND OTHER ARCHITECTURE | 861 | HOUSE – Gutcheon Perfect Patchwork Primer |
| | 862 | HOUSE ON THE HILL – McKim<br>THE STAR'S EXHIBITION HOUSE QUILT BLOCK PATTERN – McKim KC Star 1929<br>LITTLE WHITE HOUSE ON A HILL – Nancy Cabot |
| | 863 | OLD HOME – Comfort and Hearth and Home<br>HOUSE – Hearth and Home<br>LOG CABIN – Hearth and Home<br>LINCOLN'S CABIN HOME – Hearth and Home<br>TIPPECANOE – Hearth and Home<br>OLD KENTUCKY HOME – Needlecraft 1929 |
| | 864 | OLD HOME – Comfort |
| | 865 | LOG CABIN – Oklahoma Farmer Stockman 1920<br>LITTLE RED SCHOOL HOUSE – Finley<br>EARLIEST EXAMPLE: Although there are many house quilts attributed to the last half of the 19th century I was surprised to find that the earliest dated example I can find is 1890 - 92 in Kolter's *Forget Me Not*, Pl 126. |
| | 865.2 | A UNIQUE QUILT – Dakota Farmer 5/15/27 |
| | 865.5 | HOUSES REPEATED – Ickis |
| | 866 | LITTLE RED SCHOOLHOUSE – Hinson |
| | 867 | SCHOOLHOUSE – Nebraska Collections |
| | 868 | THE OLD HOMESTEAD – LAC #108 |
| | 869 | JACK'S HOUSE – LAC #396 |
| | 870 | LITTLE RED HOUSE – LAC #373 |
| | 870.2 | HOUSE JACK BUILT – Capper's Weekly? |
| | 870.3 | THE LOG CABIN – unknown clipping with words "...me Journal" by Patty Shannon ca. 1940 |
| | 870.5 | SCHOOLHOUSE – Life Magazine 9/22/41 |
| | 871 | LOG CABIN – LAC #307<br>WESTERN – Doyle |
| | 872 | THIS OL' HOUSE – June Friend, N.E. Kansas Radio Quilt 1982 |
| | 873 | SCHOOLHOUSE – from a quilt ca. 1926 in Woodard & Greenstein *Crib Quilts* |
| | 873.5 | ABE LINCOLN'S LOG CABIN – Capper's Weekly 2/10/34 Home Art? |
| | 874 | HONEYMOON COTTAGE – McKim |

*Houses and Other Architecture (861 – 874)*

119

# Pattern Category 5: *Realistic*

| | | |
|---|---|---|
| HOUSES AND OTHER ARCHITECTURE | 875 | ALBUM HOUSE QUILT – Orlofsky |
| | 876 | PATCH HOUSES – OCS (Brooks/Wheeler) #805 |
| | 877 | LOG CABIN – by Edith McGlothin in M.E. Johnson's Prize Country Quilts 1977 |
| | 878 | SCHOOL HOUSE – from a quilt ca. 1880, Holstein |
| | 879 | SCHOOL HOUSE – from a quilt ca. 1880, Holstein |
| | 880 | COUNTRY VILLAGE – Women's Household 10/77 |
| | 881 | THE COURTHOUSE SQUARE – by Stella Davis, in M.E. Johnson's Prize Country Quilts 1977 |
| | 882 | LITTLE RED SCHOOLHOUSE – Aunt Kate's Quilting Bee |
| | 883 | RED BARN – by Ann Weeks in M.E. Johnson's Prize Country Quilts 1977 |
| | 884 | OLD COUNTRY CHURCH – by Lois Bruner in M.E. Johnson's Prize Country Quilt 1977 |
| | 884.5 | LITTLE CHURCH ON THE RIDGE – Edie Pigg and Cora Wright, Kentucky Pride Quilts 1982 |
| | 885 | COUNTRY CHURCH – QNM |
| | 886 | VILLAGE SCHOOL HOUSE – (for New Hampshire) in McKim, Patchwork Parade of States |
| | 887 | DUTCH MILL – McKim |
| | 887.5 | WINDMILL – OCS (Brooks/Wheeler) #5903 |
| | 888 | GARFIELD'S MONUMENT – LAC #136 |
| | 889 | THE MONUMENT – Ohio Farmer ca. 1890 |
| | 890 | THE PATCHWORK FENCE – McKim<br>PICKET FENCE BORDER BLOCK – McKim<br>PICKET FENCE – Aunt Martha. *See 220.4.* |
| | 891 | CASTLE – Oppenheimer & Haas in Woman's Home Companion 1928 |

*Houses and Other Architecture (875 – 891)*

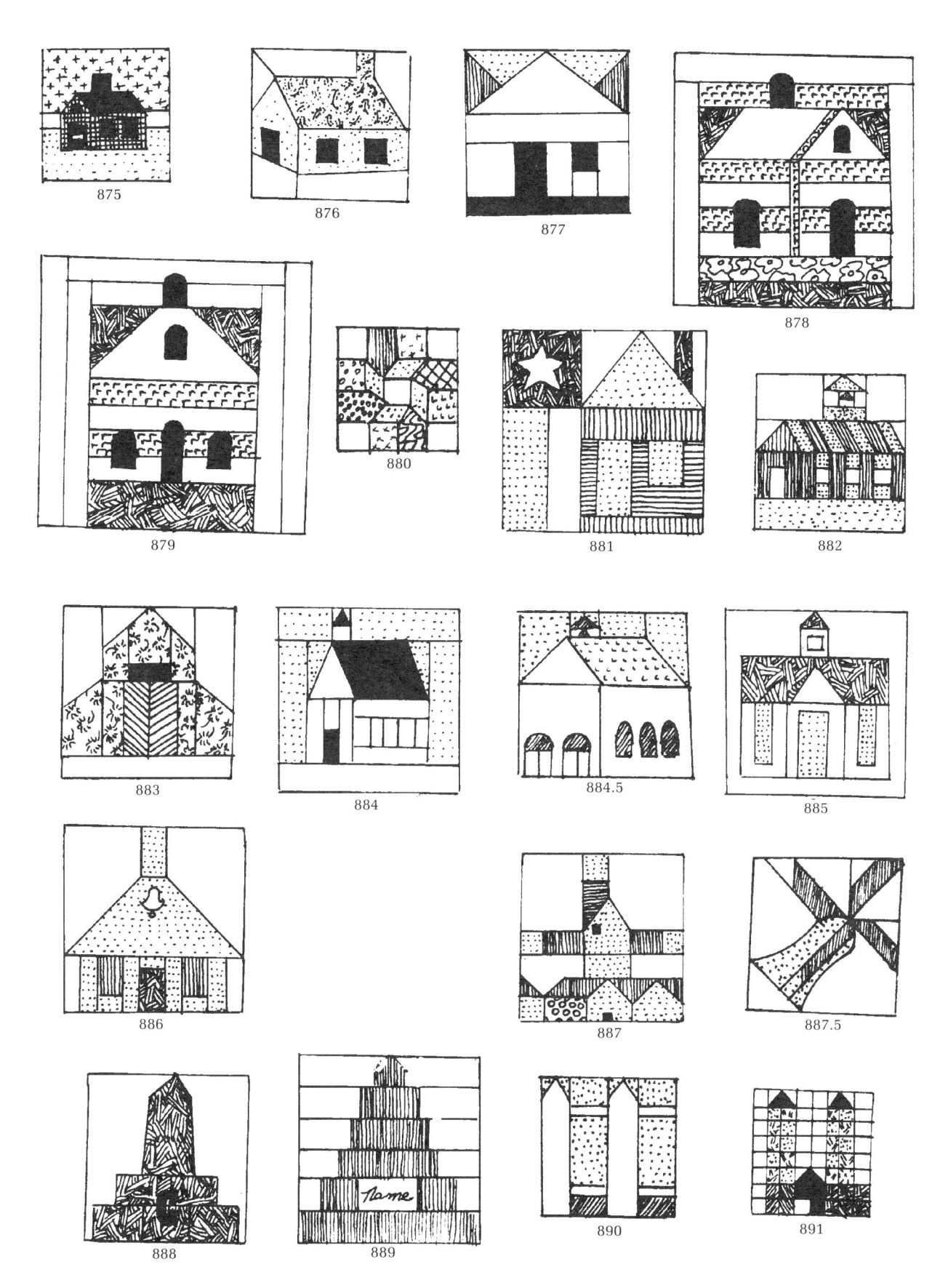

121

Pattern Category 5: *Realistic*

| AIRPLANES | 901 | LONE EAGLE AIRPLANE – Successful Farming 1929 |
| --- | --- | --- |
| | 901.3 | AEROPLANE – Aunt Martha, The Quilt Fair Comes to You 1933 (propeller is appliqué) |
| | 901.5 | AEROPLANES – from a pamphlet that may be Aunt Martha |
| | 902 | THE AIRCRAFT QUILT – KC Star 6/13/29<br>AEROPLANE – Oklahoma Farmer Stockman 1929<br>AIRPLANE – Hall. *See 908.* |
| | 903 | THE AIRPLANE – Capper's Weekly 5/12/30 |
| | 904 | AIR WAYS – (for Washington) McKim, Patchwork Parade of States |
| | 905 | AIRPLANE QUILT – QNM #97, 1977 |
| | 906 | LINDBERGH'S NIGHT FLIGHT – by Ruby Magness in M.E. Johnson's Prize Country Quilts 1977 |
| | 907 | THE ALTA PLANE – QNM #97, 1977 |
| | 907.5 | AIRPLANE – attributed to Nancy Cabot/Wilma Smith |
| | 908 | AIRPLANE AND PROPELLER – Danneman. *See 902.* |

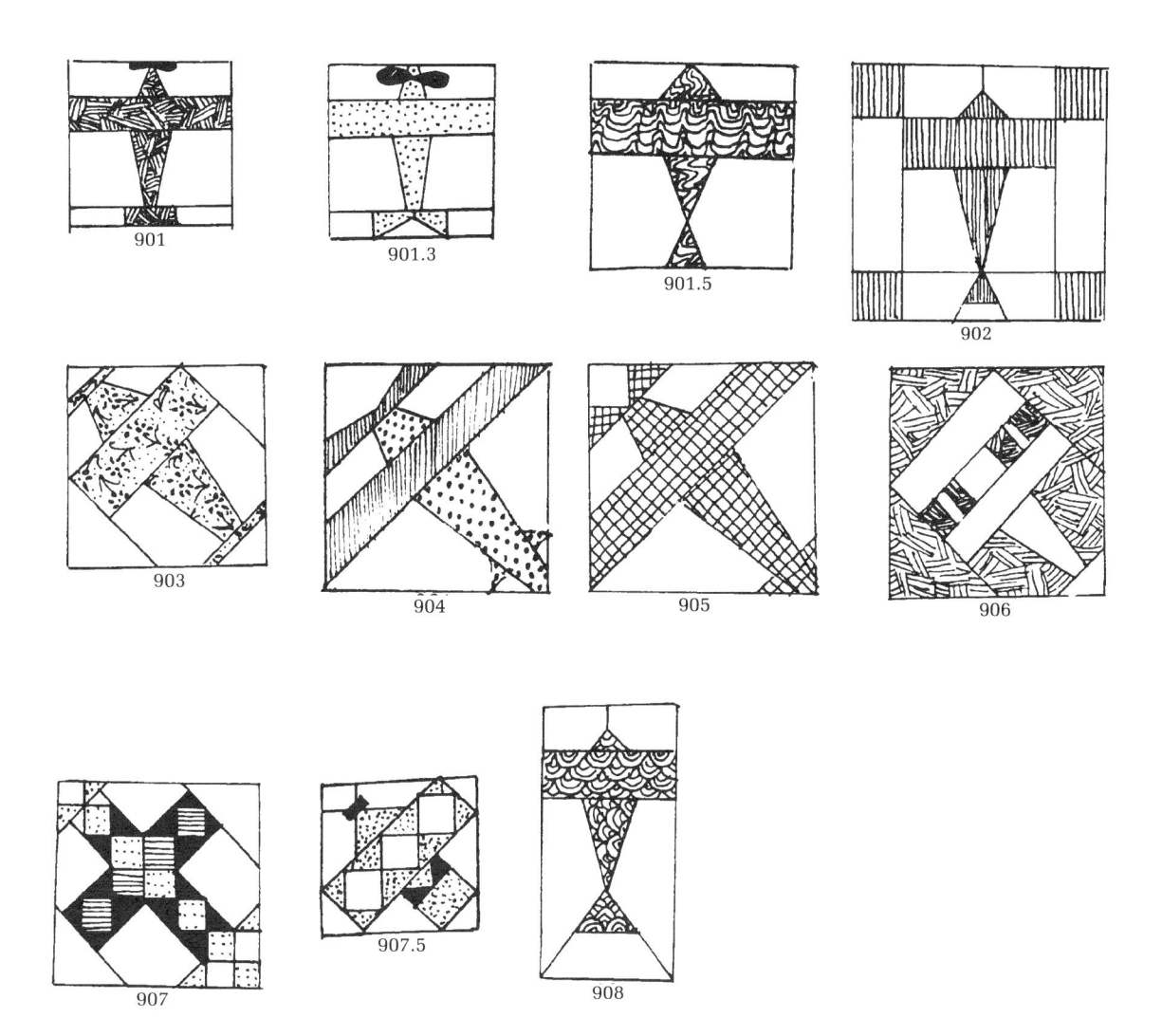

*Airplanes (901 – 908)*

901
901.3
901.5
902
903
904
905
906
907
907.5
908

123

## Pattern Category 5: *Realistic*

BOATS
 **910** SAILING INTO DREAMLAND – Aunt Kate's Quilting Bee 3/65

 **911** THE SHIP – Mrs. Danner

 **912** THE MAYFLOWER – KC Star 8/29/36
   TAD LINCOLN'S SAILBOAT – Famous Features

 **912.3** LITTLE SHIP O' DREAMS – Needlecraft 6/31

 **913** FISHING BOATS – Nancy Cabot

 **914** THE SAILBOAT OKLAHOMA – KC Star 6/28/44

 **915** SAILBOAT QUILT – Nancy Page

 **916** SHIPS IN THE NIGHT – Nancy Cabot
   DREAM SHIP – Mary McElwain

 **917** TALL SHIPS OF '76 – Quilts by Lynn, Minneapolis 1976

 **918** DUTCH BOAT – McKim

 **919** SAILBOAT – OCS (Brooks/Wheeler) #1549

*Boats (910 – 919)*

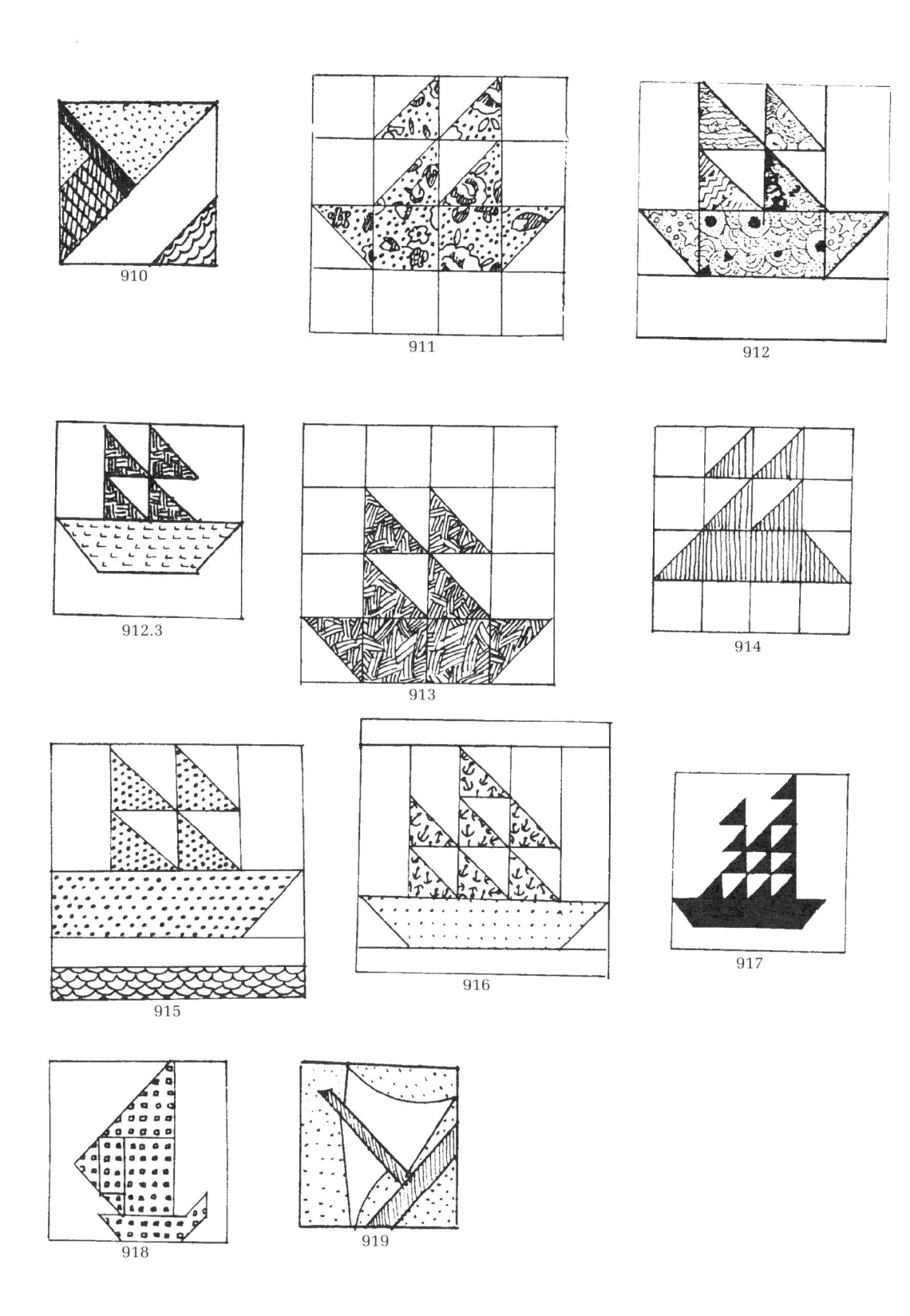

125

## Pattern Category 5: *Realistic*

BUTTERFLIES AND OTHER INSECTS

| | | |
|---|---|---|
| 921 | UNNAMED – Aunt Martha |
| 922 | BUTTERFLY – Verdie Foster in Needlecraft 1928 |
| | EARLIEST EXAMPLE: This is probably the first pattern published for a pieced butterfly quilt. Although appliquéd butterflies appear in earlier quilts, I haven't yet found any pieced butterflies that predate this pattern. |
| 923 | PIECED BUTTERFLY – Home Art and Nancy Cabot |
| 923.5 | A QUILTED BUTTERFLY – Capper's Weekly 5/3/30 |
| 924 | BUTTERFLY – KC Star 1936 |
| 924.5 | FLUTTERING BUTTERFLY – Home Art |
| 924.6 | KATE'S BUTTERFLY – Aunt Kate's Quilting Bee Vol. 2, #5 |
| 924.7 | CONTEMPORARY BUTTERFLY – Aunt Kate's Quilting Bee 3/66 |
| 925 | BUTTERFLY – OCS (Brooks/Wheeler) #663 |
| 925.5 | BUTTERFLY – OCS (Brooks/Wheeler) #5094 |
| 926 | THE BUTTERFLY QUILT – McKim |
| 927 | THE BUTTERFLY QUILT – McKim |
| 927.5 | BUTTERFLY – OCS (Brooks/Wheeler) #5663 |
| 928 | UNNAMED – OCS (Brooks/Wheeler) #7139 |
| 929 | BUTTERFLY QUILT – OCS (Brooks/Wheeler) #2305 |
| 930 | PIECED BUTTERFLY – QNM #70, 1975 |
| 931 | BUTTERFLY QUILT #2 – Aunt Kate's Quilting Bee Vol. 1, #4 |
| 931.5 | PATCHWORK BUTTERFLY – OCS (Brooks/Wheeler) #534. *For a rectangular butterfly see 224.2.* |
| 932 | LADY BUG – Aunt Kate's Quilting Bee 5/66 |

*Butterflies and Other Insects (921 – 932)*

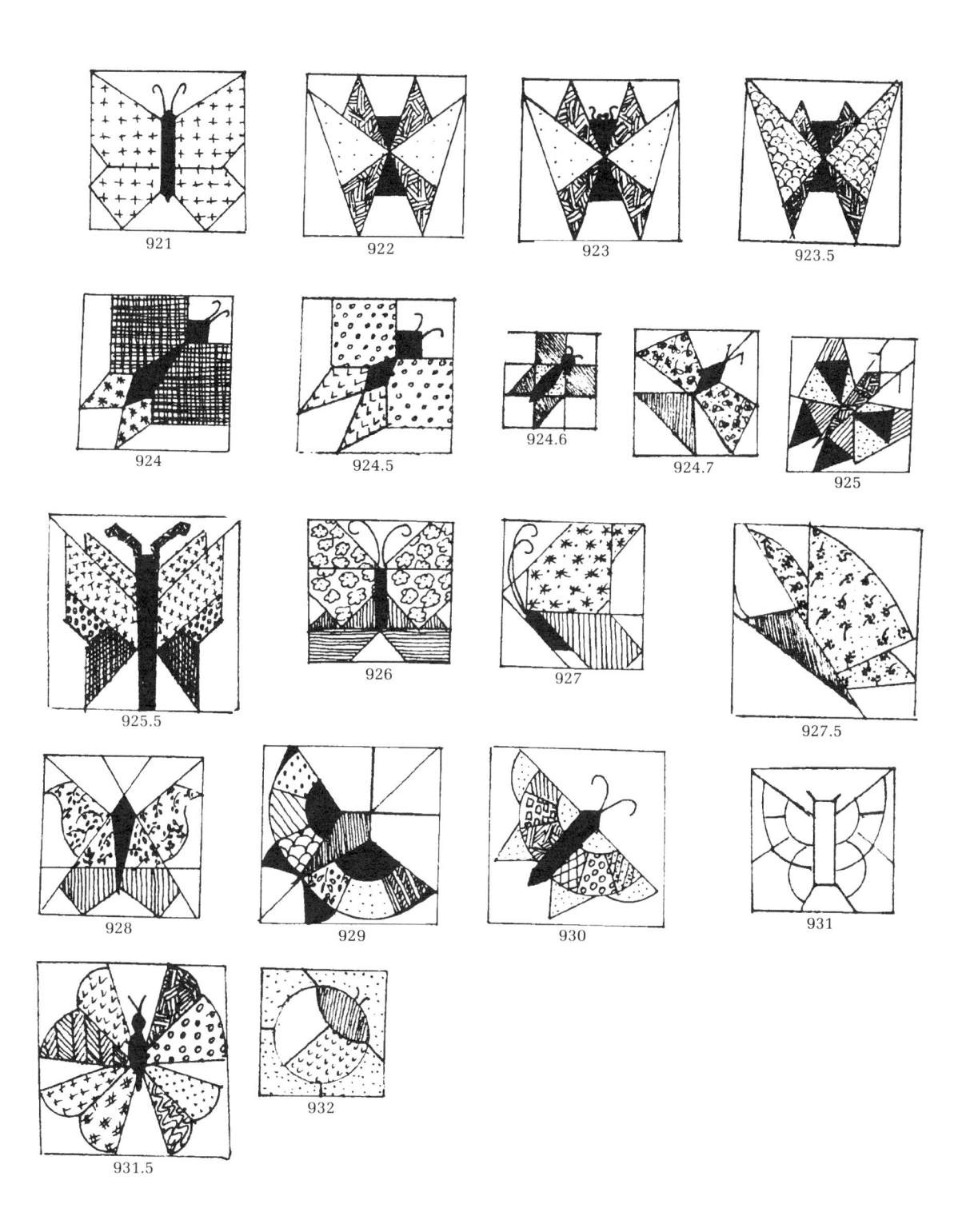

127

## Pattern Category 5: *Realistic*

| | | |
|---|---|---|
| BIRDS | 933 | SWALLOW'S FLIGHT – Aunt Martha, Prize Winning Quilts ca. 1930 |
| | 934 | SWALLOW IN FLIGHT – Aunt Kate's Quilting Bee |
| | 934.4 | FOUR LITTLE BIRDS – LAC #303, 1928 |
| | 934.6 | BLUEBIRDS – Meeker |
| | 935 | PEACOCK PATCHWORK – OCS (Brooks/Wheeler) #1784<br>THE PEAFOWL QUILT – Little 'n Big |
| | 935.5 | STRUTTING PEACOCK – Aunt Kate's Quilting Bee |
| | 935.7 | PEACOCK PATCHWORK – OCS (Brooks/Wheeler) #6110 |
| | 936 | BIRD PATCHWORK – OCS (Brooks/Wheeler) #5580 |
| | 936.4 | RED ROBIN – OCS (Brooks/Wheeler) #7372 |
| | 936.7 | CHICKEN – Needlecraft 3/28 |
| | 936.8 | POLLY AND HER CAGE – Oppenheimer & Haas Needlecraft 3/28 |
| | 936.9 | PENGUINS – Prudence Penny, Seattle Post Intelligencer 1933 |
| | 936.95 | OSTRICH – Prudence Penny, Seattle Post Intelligencer 1933.<br>*For a bird in a diamond shaped block see 237.5.* |
| CATS AND OTHER FELINES | 937.1 | THREE LITTLE KITTENS – Aunt Martha (border) |
| | 937.2 | SCRAP CATS – by Linda Platt, QNM 113, 1979 |
| | 937.3 | UNNAMED – Anne Orr in Good Housekeeping |
| | 937.4 | UNNAMED – Woodard & Greenstein (probably from Oppenheimer and Haas design) |
| | 937.5 | CALICO CAT – OCS (Brooks/Wheeler) #5707<br>PRETTY PUSSY – OCS (Brooks/Wheeler) #5707 |
| | 937.6 | WILD CAT – Prudence Penny, Seattle Post Intelligencer 1933 |
| | 937.7 | LEOPARD – Prudence Penny, Seattle Post Intelligencer 1933 |
| | 937.8 | LION – Prudence Penny, Seattle Post Intelligencer 1933 |

*Birds, Cats and Other Felines (933 – 937.8)*

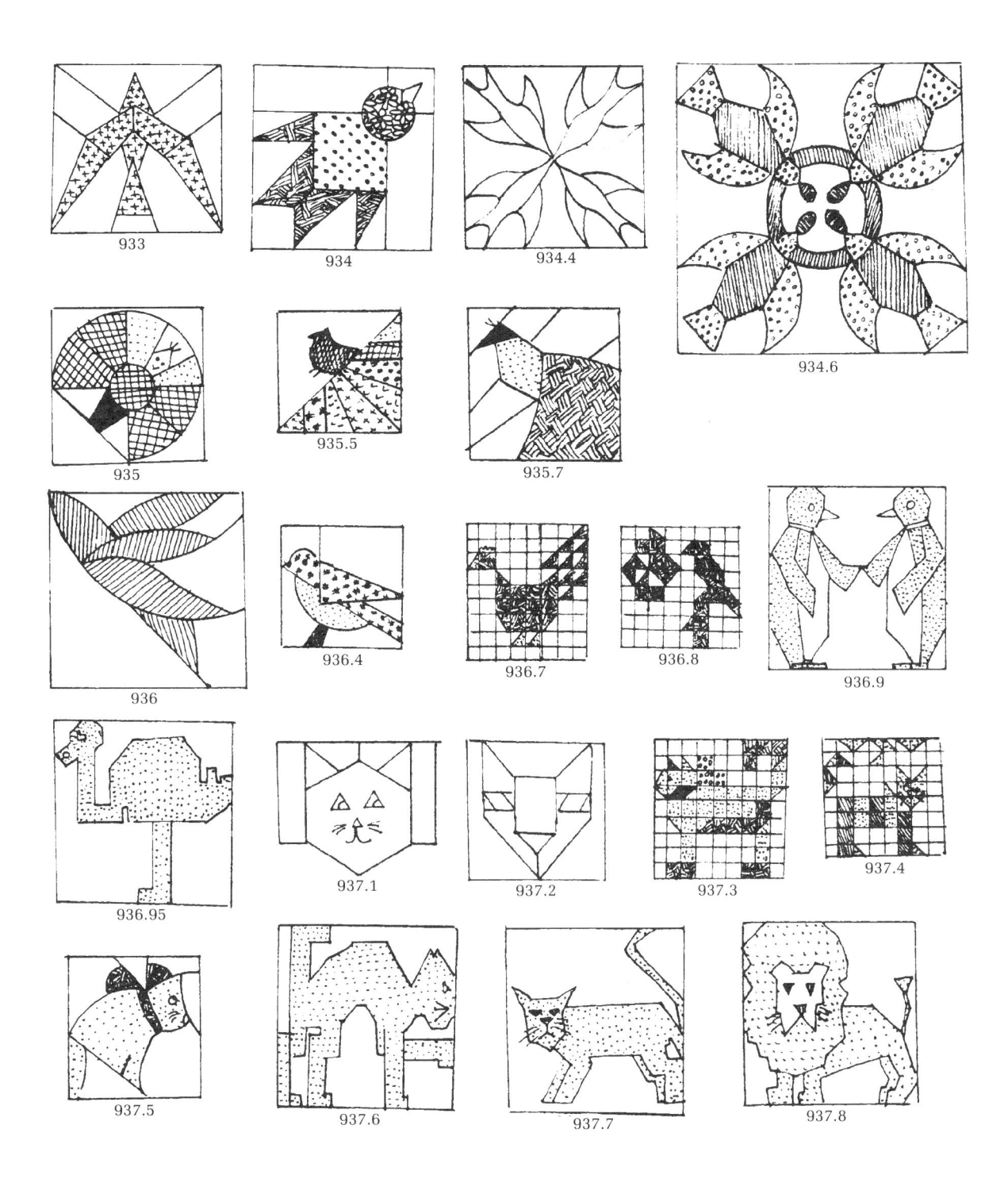

129

Pattern Category 5: *Realistic*

OTHER ANIMALS
- 938.1   UNNAMED – Anne Orr in Good Housekeeping. *See 226.73.*
- 938.2   SCOTTIE PATCHWORK – OCS (Brooks/Wheeler) #5673
  GINGHAM DOG – DuBois in Bye Baby Bunting
  FALA – Telegraphics 1976
- 938.3   SCOTTIE QUILT – OCS (Brooks/Wheeler) #1311
- 938.4   UNNAMED – Oppenheimer & Haas, Woman's Home Companion 1928
- 938.5   UNNAMED – Woodard and Greenstein, Crib Quilts. *For another elephant see 226.76.*
- 938.6   ELEPHANT – Prudence Penny, Seattle Post Intelligencer 1933
- 938.7   UNNAMED – Woodard and Greenstein, Crib Quilts
- 938.8   GIRAFFE – Prudence Penny, Seattle Post Intelligencer 1933
- 938.9   INDIAN ON HORSEBACK – Oppenheimer & Haas Needlecraft 3/28
- 939.1   ZEBRA – Prudence Penny, Seattle Post Intelligencer 1933
- 939.15   PIECED ROCKING HORSE – by Lita Swindle, LCPQ #19 1980. *For a pieced donkey see 226.77.*
- 939.2   POLAR BEAR – Prudence Penny, Seattle Post Intelligencer 1933
- 939.3   DANCING BEAR – Oppenheimer and Haas in Needlecraft 3/28
- 939.4   KANGAROO – Prudence Penny, Seattle Post Intelligencer 1933
- 939.5   CAMEL – Prudence Penny, Seattle Post Intelligencer 1933
- 939.6   HIPPOPOTAMUS – Prudence Penny, Seattle Post Intelligencer 1933
- 939.7   REINDEER – Prudence Penny, Seattle Post Intelligencer 1933
- 939.8   SEAL – Prudence Penny, Seattle Post Intelligencer 1933
- 939.9   SQUIRREL – Prudence Penny, Seattle Post Intelligencer 1933
- 940   BUFFALO – Prudence Penny, Seattle Post Intelligencer 1933
- 940.10   CROCODILE – Prudence Penny, Seattle Post Intelligencer 1933
- 940.15   FOX – Prudence Penny, Seattle Post Intelligencer 1933
- 940.20   MONKEY – Prudence Penny, Seattle Post Intelligencer 1933
- 940.25   BEAVER – Prudence Penny, Seattle Post Intelligencer 1933

PEOPLE
- 940.30   CLOWN – Oppenheimer and Haas Needlecraft 3/28
- 940.33   UNNAMED – Oppenheimer & Haas Woman's Home Companion 1928
- 940.35   UNNAMED – Anne Orr in Good Housekeeping
- 940.36   UNNAMED – Anne Orr in Good Housekeeping
- 940.37   UNNAMED – Anne Orr in Good Housekeeping
- 940.38   UNNAMED – Anne Orr in Good Housekeeping

*Other Animals, People (938.1 – 940.38)*

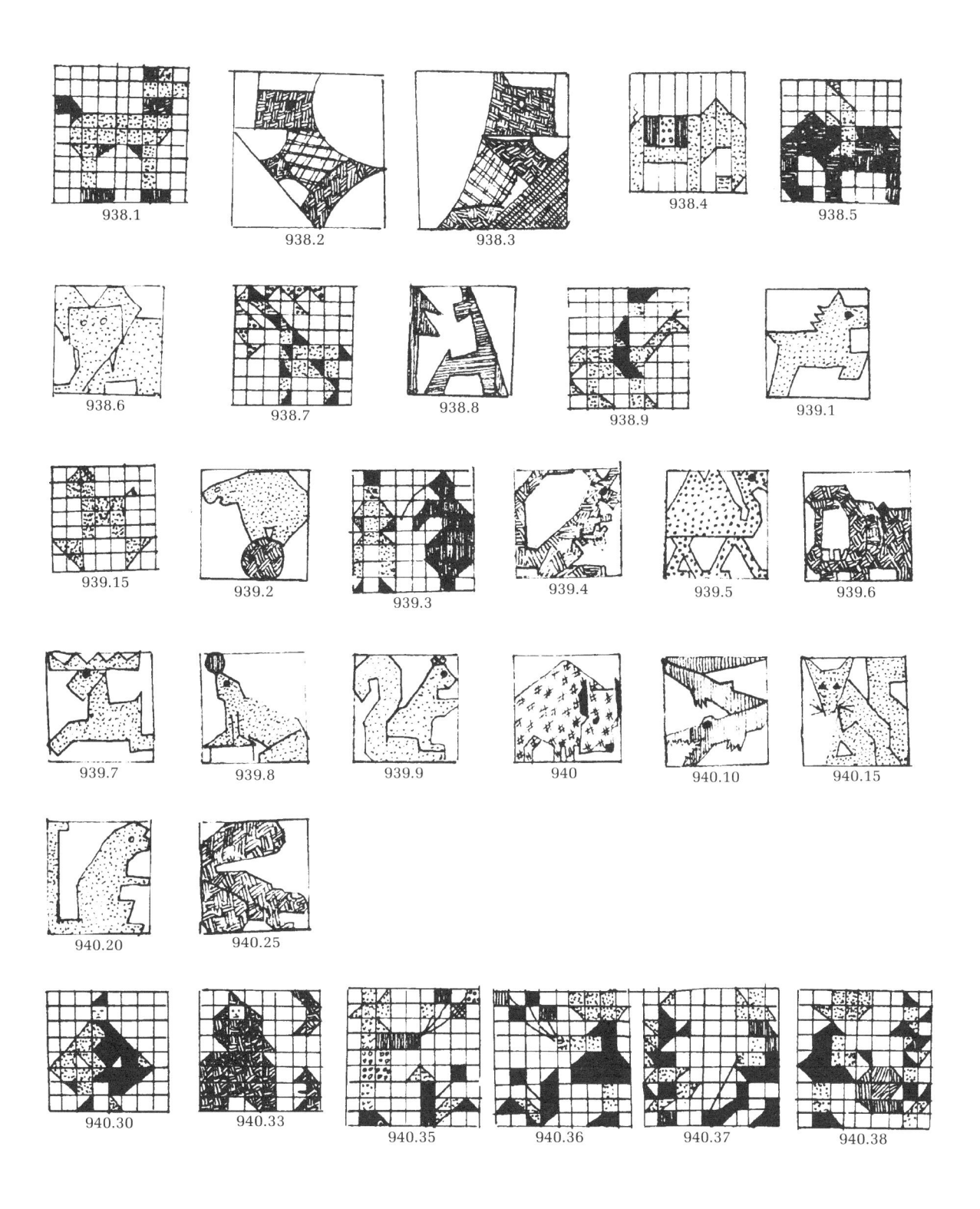

131

# Pattern Category 5: *Realistic*

PEOPLE

**940.40**    **UNNAMED** – Woodard and Greenstein, Crib Quilts. *See 218.*

**940.41**    **NORMANDY GIRLS** – Oppenheimer and Haas Woman's Home Companion 1928

**940.42**    **CHING AND CHOW** – Oppenheimer and Haas Woman's Home Companion 1928

**940.43**    **UNNAMED** – Woodard and Greenstein Crib Quilts

**940.44**    **SOLDIERS** – Oppenheimer and Haas Needlecraft 3/28

**940.45**    **INDIANS** – Oppenheimer and Haas Needlecraft 3/28

**940.5**    **UNNAMED** – from quilt ca. 1900 in Bishop's New Discoveries

**940.6**    **SUNBONNET GIRLS** – Sally Goodspeed ca. 1975

**940.7**    **SUNBONNET GIRLS** – OCS (Brooks/Wheeler) #7322

**940.8**    **SUNBONNET GIRLS** – Little 'n Big

MISC. SUBJECT MATTER

**941**    **COFFEE CUPS** – KC Star 1/12/35
       **THE CUP AND SAUCER** – KC Star 2/27/46

**943**    **GOBLET** – KC Star 9/6/30
       **WATER GLASS** – KC Star 1934

**944**    **THE OLD FASHIONED GOBLET** – KC Star 1937
       **TUMBLER** – attributed to Hearth and Home by Wilma Smith

**945**    **THE WINE GLASS** – Oklahoma Farmer Stockman 1920

**947**    **THE ICE CREAM CONE** – KC Star 10/15/43

**948**    **MOON OVER THE MOUNTAIN** – Ickis

**949**    **THE CROSS** – LAC

**949.3**    **THE CROSS** – Ohio Farmer 5/7/1898

**949.5**    **SISTER NAN'S CROSS** – Hearth and Home

**949.7**    **CROSS AND CROWN** – Clara Stone

**950**    **THE HEART OF THE HOME** – KC Star 6/27/38

**951**    **PATTY'S SUMMER PARASOL** – KC Star 4/1/53

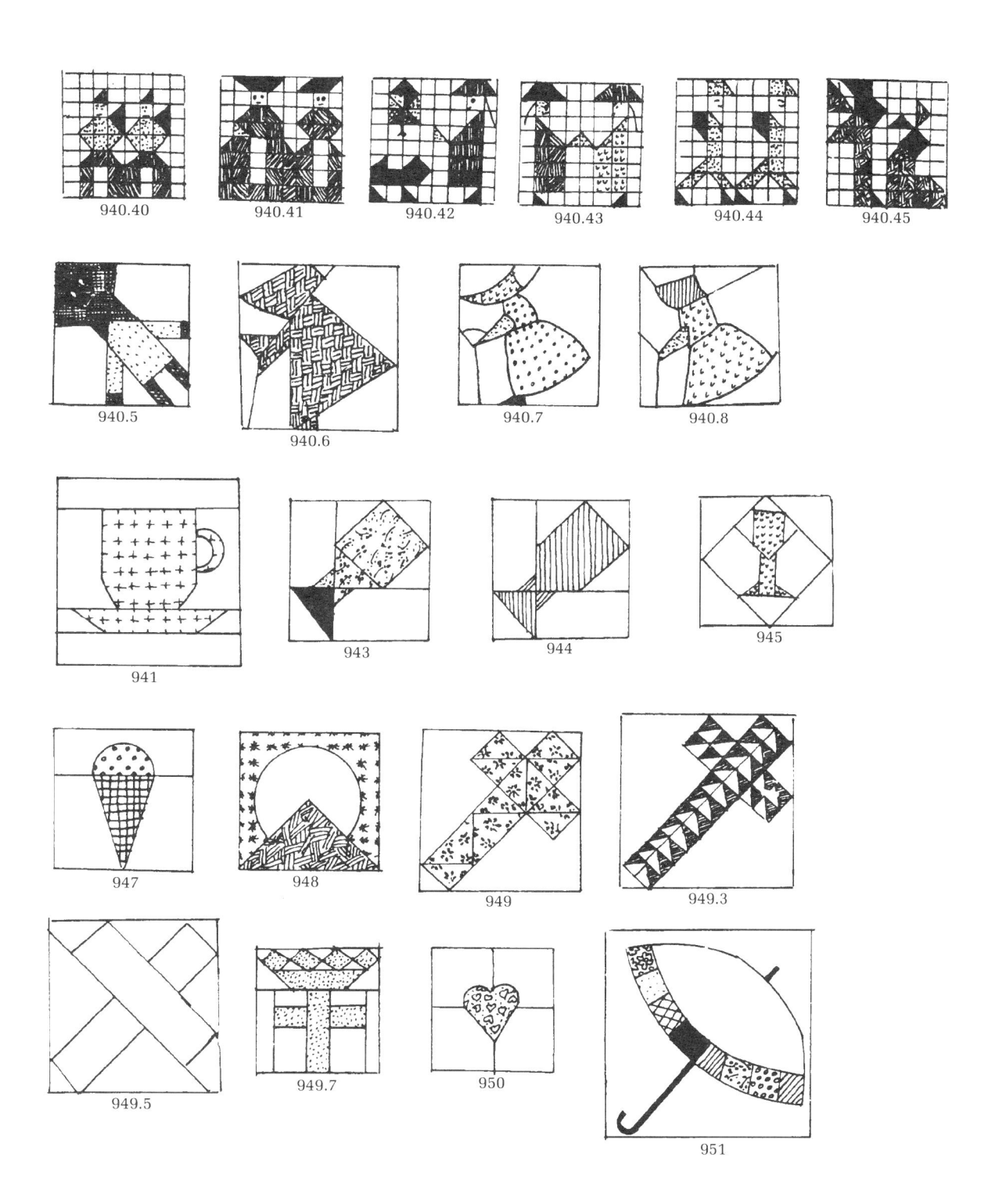

*People, Misc. Subject Matter (940.40 – 951)*

940.40  940.41  940.42  940.43  940.44  940.45

940.5  940.6  940.7  940.8

941  943  944  945

947  948  949  949.3

949.5  949.7  950  951

133

# Pattern Category 5: *Realistic*

| | | |
|---|---|---|
| MISC. SUBJECT MATTER | **953** | **A Japanese Garden** – KC Star 1934 |
| | **954** | **A Quilt Made of Scraps** – OCS (Brooks/Wheeler) #6911<br>**Lantern** – OCS (Brooks/Wheeler) #6911 |
| | **955** | **Lantern** – OCS (Brooks/Wheeler) #2824 |
| | **956** | **Japanese Lantern** – Aunt Martha #C295 |
| | **957** | **Japanese Lantern** – Aunt Martha and Nancy Cabot 6/20/33<br>**Chinese Lantern** – Aunt Martha |
| | **959** | **Acorn** – McKim<br>**Modernistic Acorn** – Hall |
| | **960** | **My Mother's Apron** – KC Star |
| | **962** | **Telephone** – Aunt Kate's Quilting Bee Vol. 2, #11 |
| | **966** | **King Tut Ankh** – Canada Quilts Winter 1979 |
| | **967** | **Unnamed** – Woodard and Greenstein Crib Quilts |
| | **968** | **Space Capsule** – Aunt Kate's Quilting Bee |
| | **969** | **The Bell** – KC Star 3/15/61 |
| | **970** | **Anchors Aweigh** – OCS (Brooks/Wheeler) #7418 |
| | **971** | **Spinster's Spindle** – Union Mill Ends |
| | **973** | **Old Indian Trail** – KC Star 12/24/41 |

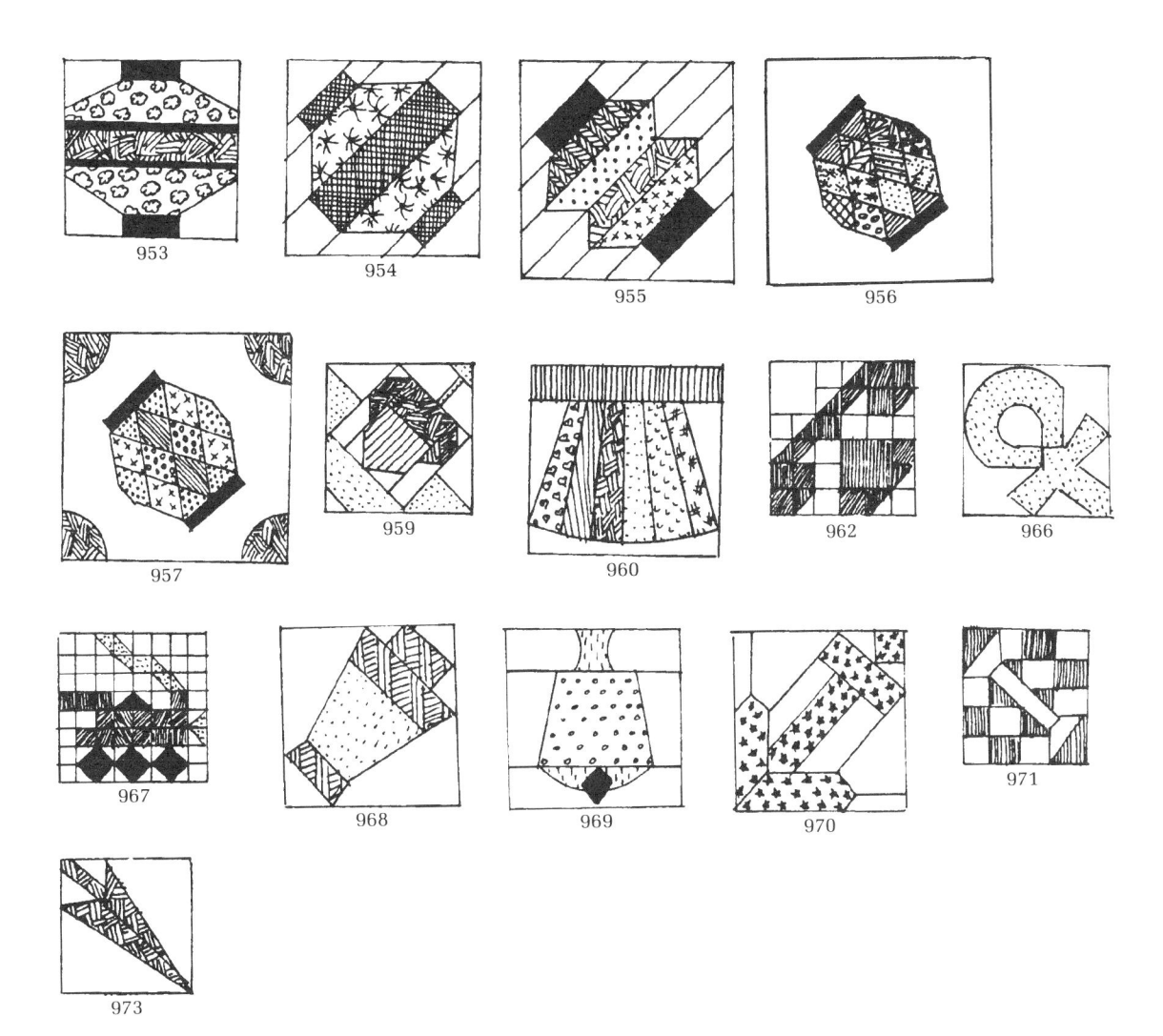

*Misc. Subject Matter (953 – 973)*

953
954
955
956
957
959
960
962
966
967
968
969
970
971
973

# Pattern Category 5: *Realistic*

| | | |
|---|---|---|
| LETTERS | 980 | UNNAMED – LAC #421 |
| | 980.5 | UNNAMED – LAC #422 |
| | 981 | UNNAMED – LAC #423 |
| | 981.5 | UNNAMED – LAC #424 |
| | 981.7 | A "D" THIS TIME – Orange Judd Farmer 2/5/1898 |
| | 982 | UNNAMED – LAC #425 |
| | 982.5 | UNNAMED – LAC #426 |
| | 983 | UNNAMED – LAC #427 |
| | 983.5 | UNNAMED – LAC #428. *See 2384.* |
| | 984 | UNNAMED – LAC #429 |
| | 984.5 | UNNAMED – LAC #430 |
| | 984.6 | ANOTHER J – Orange Judd Farmer 9/9/1899 |
| | 985 | UNNAMED – LAC #431 |
| | 985.5 | UNNAMED – LAC #432 |
| | 986 | UNNAMED – LAC #433 |
| | 986.2 | M QUILT BLOCK – Orange Judd Farmer 5/7/1898 |
| | 986.5 | UNNAMED – LAC #434 |
| | 987 | UNNAMED – LAC #435 |
| | 987.5 | HERE'S YOUR O – Orange Judd Farmer 4/16/1898 |
| | 988 | UNNAMED – LAC #436 |
| | 988.5 | THIS IS FOR THE PEASES – Orange Judd Farmer 3/5/1898 |
| | 988.7 | UNNAMED – LAC #437 |
| | 989 | UNNAMED – LAC #438 |
| | 989.5 | R THERE – Orange Judd Farmer 5/28/1898 (original reversed) |
| | 990 | UNNAMED – LAC #439 |
| | 990.2 | S – Orange Judd Farmer 1/8/1898 (reversed). *See 220.6.* |
| | 990.5 | UNNAMED – LAC #440. *See 217.* |
| | 991 | UNNAMED – LAC #441 |
| | 991.5 | UNNAMED – LAC #442 |
| | 991.7 | VICTORY QUILT – KC Star 4/22/1942. *See 226.* |
| | 991.9 | VICTORY QUILT – Workbasket 3/1942<br>RED, WHITE 'N BLUE "V" QUILT – Capper's Weekly 9/27/41 |
| | 992 | UNNAMED – LAC #443 |
| | 992.5 | A PARALLELOGRAM W – Orange Judd Farmer 9/16/1899 |
| | 993 | UNNAMED – LAC #444 |
| | 993.5 | UNNAMED – LAC #445 |
| | 994 | UNNAMED – LAC #446 |

*Letters (980 – 994)*

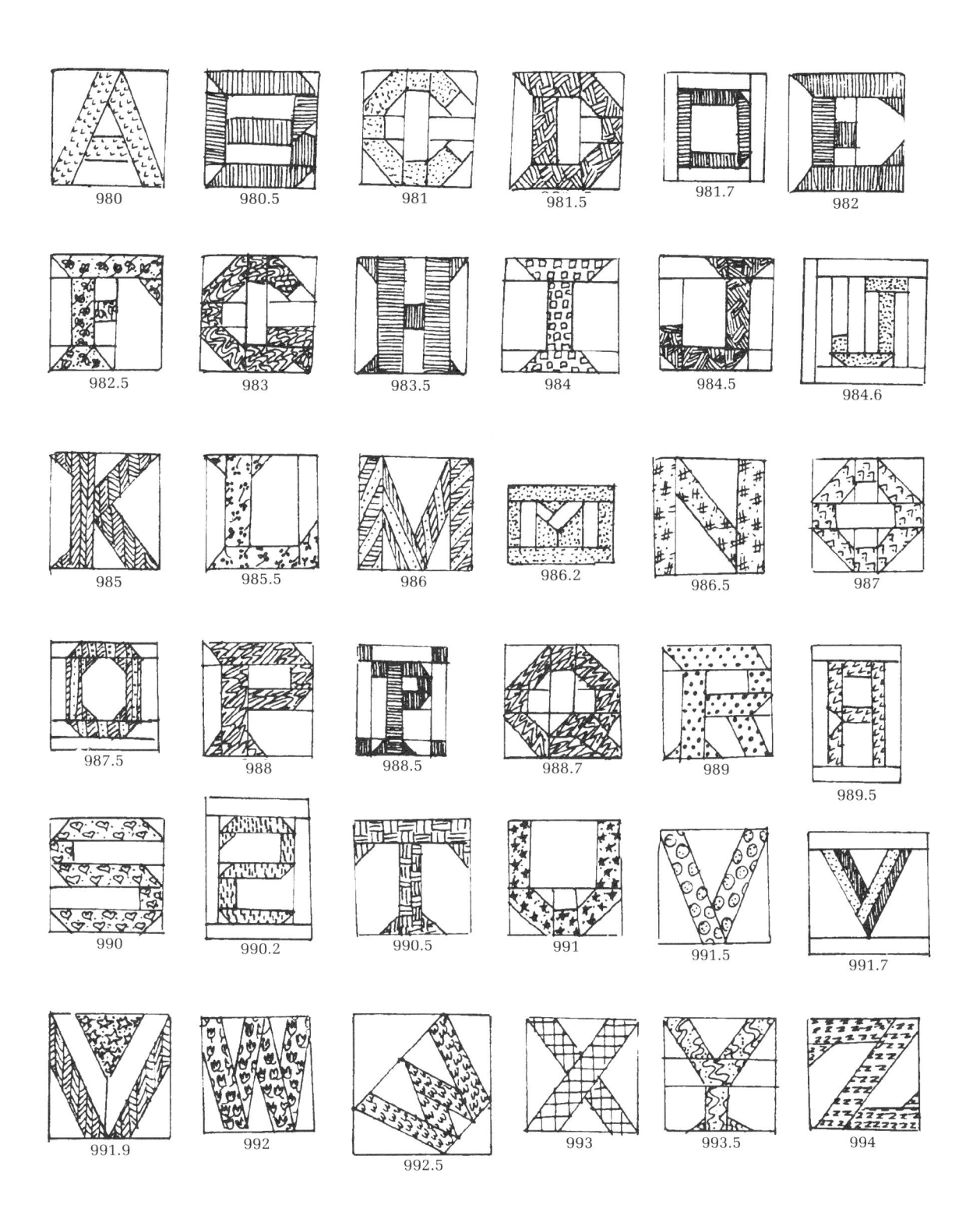

137

# Pattern

## CATEGORY 6

## Two-Block

**Patterns in Category 6 share these characteristics:**

- The repeat is two or more separate blocks. These separate blocks are combined, usually in an alternating pattern, to make a distinct pattern with a specific name.

- The blocks may each have a different name and be indexed under other categories when they appear alone. When combined they have a new name.

**Category 6 includes:**

- One Block Is a Checkerboard Grid, 140
- Neither Block Is a Checkerboard Grid, 144
- Three Blocks, 144

## KEY TO PATTERN CATEGORY 6: TWO-BLOCK

If the repeat is made of three blocks, *turn to p. 144*

If one block is a checkerboard grid, *turn to p. 140*

If neither block is a checkerboard grid, *turn to p. 144*

# Pattern Category 6: *Two-Block*

ONE BLOCK IS A CHECKERBOARD GRID

**1001**  FLAGSTONES – LAC. *See 1601 & 4141.*
NEW SNOWBALL – attributed to Hearth and Home by W. Smith
IMPROVED NINE PATCH – Aunt Martha 1932
SNOWBALL – Doyle
DELAWARE'S FLAGSTONES – Workbasket 1935
FEDERAL CHAIN – Nancy Cabot
AUNT PATTY'S FAVORITE – Farm Journal
AUNT PATSY'S PET – Nancy Cabot
FOUR AND NINE PATCH – Nancy Cabot
NINE AND FOUR PATCH – Progressive Farmer
THE SNOWBALL AND NINE PATCH – Danner/Ericson Bk. 5, 1970
NEW NINE PATCH – Evelyn Brown 1978
GRANDMOTHER SHORT'S QUILT – Goodspeed
DUTCH MILL – LCPQ #22
PULLMAN PUZZLE – LCPQ #22

**1002**  GOOSE CREEK – Nancy Page. *See 1601 & 2375.*

**1003a**  TIC TAC TOE – Nancy Page. *See 1601 & 1645.*

**1003b**  TILE PUZZLE – attributed to Nancy Cabot/Wilma Smith

**1004**  OKLAHOMA TRAILS AND FIELDS – by Mildred Hardin in M.E. Johnson's Prize Country Quilts 1977. *See 1601 & 2702.*

**1005**  UNNAMED – Godey's. *See 1601 & 1631.*

**1006**  GOOD LUCK BLOCK – Nancy Cabot 9/14/33 *See 1601.*
LUCKY BLOCK – attributed to Nancy Cabot/Wilma Smith
LUCKY QUILT – Oklahoma Farmer Stockman 1/1/35
FOUR LEAF CLOVER – Oklahoma Farmer Stockman 1/1/35

**1007**  INDIAN PATCH – Farm Journal. *See 1101 & 1460.*

**1009**  RAILROAD CROSSING – Finley. *See 1102 & 1193.*

**1010**  SUSPENSION BRIDGE – Mrs. Danner Bk. #2, 1934. *See 1037, 1102, 3314, & 2677.*

**1013**  DOUBLE IRISH CHAIN – LAC #60
IRISH CHAIN – Farm Journal
CUBE LATTICE – Farm Journal. *See 2020 & 2279.*

**1014**  MRS. HOOVER'S COLONIAL QUILT – Needlecraft 5/26
CHAINED FIVE PATCH – Finley
DOUBLE IRISH CHAIN – Nancy Cabot
NELLIE'S CHOICE – Mary McElwain. *See 2279.*
EARLIEST EXAMPLE: dated 1822 in Peto

**1014.2**  GRANDMOTHER'S IRISH CHAIN – Clara Stone

**1015**  FEDERAL CHAIN – Nancy Cabot 6/9/33. *See 2279.*

**1016**  DOMINO CHAIN – Woman's World
DOGWOOD BLOSSOMS – Hall. *See 2279.*

**1017**  MARY MOORE'S DOUBLE IRISH CHAIN – Bureau Farmer 1930
DOUBLE IRISH CROSS – McKim
MARY MOORE'S QUILT – Bureau Farmer. *See 2279.*

**1018**  DOUBLE IRISH CHAIN – Capper's Weekly (probably OCS (Brooks/Wheeler). *See 2279.*

**1018.4**  UNNAMED – Quilt World. *See 2279.*

**1018.5**  TIGER LILY – The Farmer's Wife. *See 2279.*

**1019a**  TRIPLE IRISH CHAIN – McKim
SINGLE IRISH CHAIN – Pforr
THREE IRISH CHAINS – Mountain Mist

**1019b**  JEWEL BOX – Mary McElwain 1936

**1020**  THE FORTY-NINERS-- McKim, Patchwork Parade of States

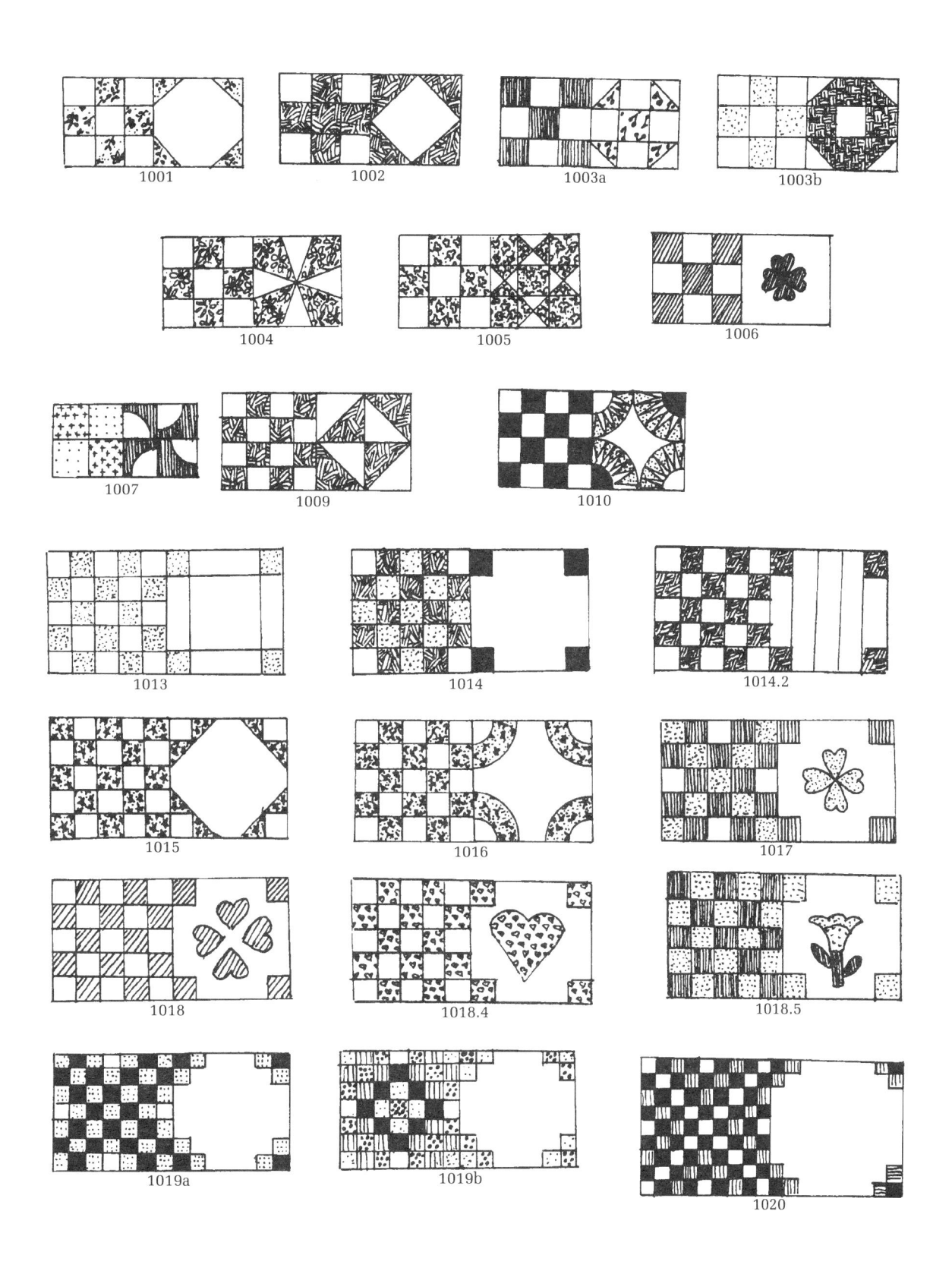

*One Block Is a Checkerboard Grid (1001 – 1020)*

1001  1002  1003a  1003b

1004  1005  1006

1007  1009  1010

1013  1014  1014.2

1015  1016  1017

1018  1018.4  1018.5

1019a  1019b  1020

141

## Pattern Category 6: *Two-Block*

ONE BLOCK IS A CHECKERBOARD GRID

**1020.2**    VIOLA'S SCRAP QUILT – NNT 9/70.
*See 2279 & 2301.*

**1021**    CHECKERED STAR – OCS (Brooks/Wheeler) #624. *See 1283.*

**1021.5**    TRIPLE IRISH CHAIN AND 8 POINT STAR – LCPQ #26, 1982

**1022**    DOUBLE IRISH CHAIN – KC Star 1/17/34

**1023**    ATLANTA – Hearth and Home 8/17
LOVE CHAIN – Prairie Farmer Bk. 1, 1931. *See 1803.*

**1024**    DOUBLE IRISH CHAIN – University of Kansas 1978. *See 1601.*

**1025**    FOUR SQUARES – Nancy Cabot. *See 1103 & 2020.*

**1025.3**    OHIO TRAIL – Nancy Cabot

**1025.5**    STEPS TO GLORY – Nancy Cabot

**1025.7**    MILLER'S DAUGHTER – Hearth and Home. *See 2020 & 4141.*

**1025.9**    MAY FESTIVAL – QNM #132, 1981.
*See 1645 & 4141.*

**1026**    UNNAMED – by Judy Schiedman in QNM #110, 1979. *See 2301.*

**1026.3**    LOUNGE THROW – The Delineator 3/1892. *See 2301 & 2573.*

**1026.5**    CAROLINE'S CHOICE – Nancy Cabot. *See 2301 & 1262.*

**1026.7**    MONASTERY WINDOWS – Nancy Cabot. *See 2375 & 3250.*

**1027**    CONVENTIONAL – Helen Kaufman in Bureau Farmer 2/30

**1027.5**    FLYFOOT – OCS (Brooks/Wheeler) #431. *See 1346.*

**1028**    LIGHTNING – Gutcheon Quilt Design Workbook. *See 4141.*

**1028.5**    ROUND THE TWIST – James. *See 405.5, 2571, & 4141.*

**1028.7**    STAR AND BLOCK – Carlie Sexton. *See 3735 & 2023.*

**1029**    BLOCK STAR – attributed to Nancy Cabot/Wilma Smith

**1030**    SNOWBOUND – Mountain Mist #46. *See 3735.*

*One Block Is a Checkerboard Grid (1020.2 – 1030)*

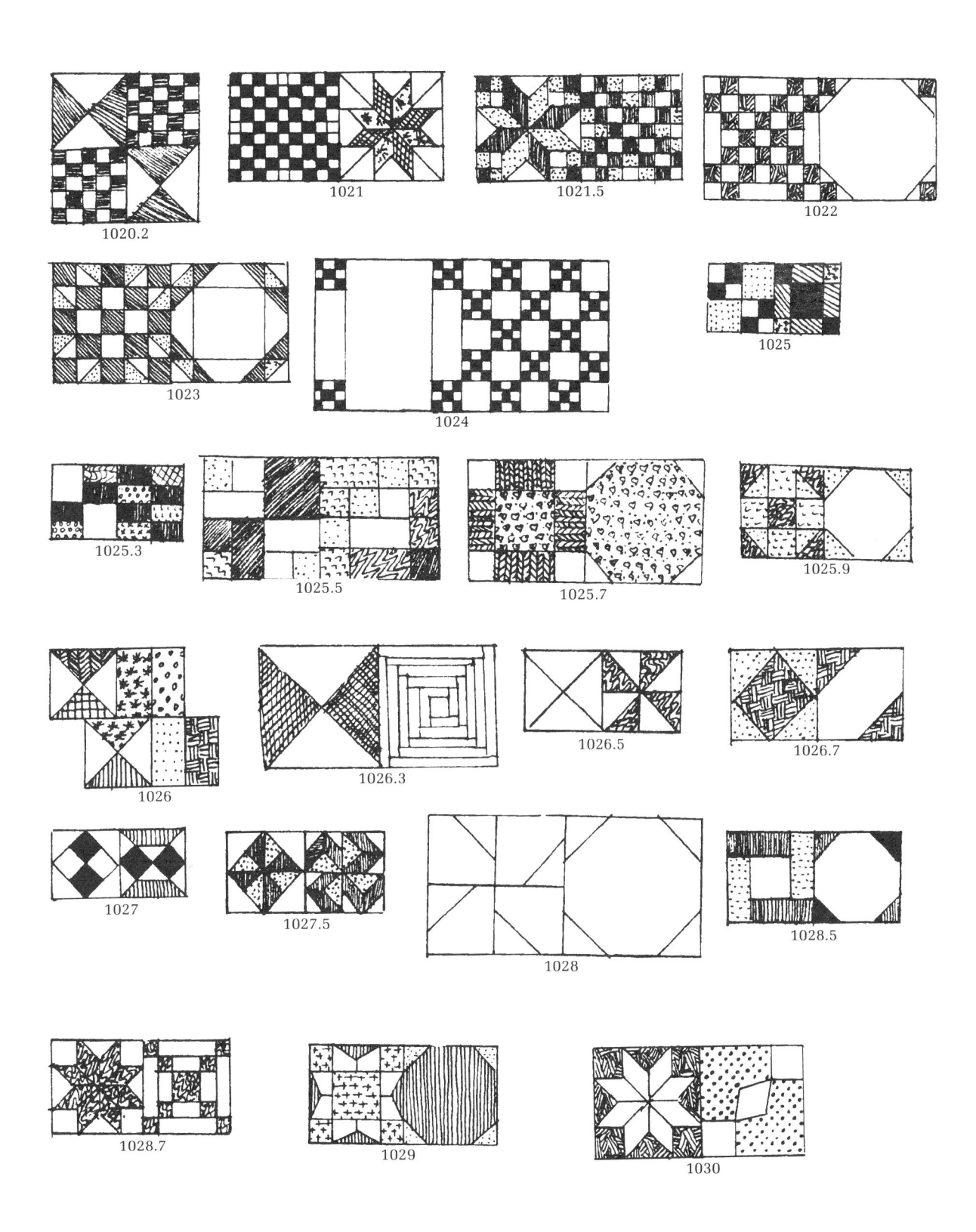

143

# Pattern Category 6: *Two-Block*

**NEITHER BLOCK IS A CHECKERBOARD GRID**

| | | |
|---|---|---|
| | 1031 | COUNTRY GARDENS – Mountain Mist #83. *See 3150.* |
| | 1032 | GREENBERG WEDDING QUILT – Gutcheon Perfect Patchwork Primer<br>WEDDING CHAIN – Gutcheon Quilt Design Workbook. *See 2775.* |
| | 1032.5 | SHADY LANE – Detroit News 1938 |
| | 1033 | LORNA DOONE – Farm Journal |
| | 1034 | UNNAMED – OCS (Brooks/Wheeler) #7287. *See 2758 & 2375.* |
| | 1035 | COUNTRY FAIR – QNM #45, 1973. *See 2376.* |
| | 1035.5 | BASKET AND DAISY – McKendry. *See 658.5.* |
| | 1036 | KALEIDOSCOPE – Nancy Cabot. *See 3092 & 2030.* |
| | 1036.5 | THREE PATCH – OCS (Brooks/Wheeler) #7198. *See 3909.* |
| | 1037 | OKLAHOMA DOGWOOD – Mountain Mist #101. *See 1010 & 2223.* |
| | 1038 | BOWKNOT AND ROSE – OCS (Brooks/Wheeler) #521 |
| | 1038.5 | DOUBLE STAR – The Country Gentleman 7/31 |
| | 1038.6 | CONSTELLATION – Successful Farming 6/33 |
| | 1039a | ALGONQUIN TRAIL – Nancy Cabot |
| | 1039b | WONDER OF THE WORLD – Aunt Jane<br>DRUNKARD'S PATH – LAC<br>DRUNKARD'S TRAIL – Mae Wilford Quilt Patterns (no date)<br>TRAIL OF FRIENDSHIP – Mae Wilford Quilt Patterns (no date)<br>BOSTON TRAIL – Mae Wilford Quilt Patterns (no date)<br>INDIANA PUMPKIN VINE – Mae Wilford Quilt Patterns (no date)<br>OLD MAID'S PUZZLE – Mae Wilford Quilt Patterns (no date)<br>KING TUT'S CROWN – Mae Wilford Quilt Patterns (no date)<br>CLEOPATRA'S PUZZLE – Mae Wilford Quilt Patterns (no date)<br>INDIANA PUZZLE – Mae Wilford Quilt Patterns (no date)<br>GHOST'S WALK – Mae Wilford Quilt Patterns (no date) |
| | 1039c | SOLOMON'S PUZZLE – The Delineator 9/06. *See 1461.* |
| | 1040 | *See 1461* |
| | 1040.5 | NEW STATE – American Woman ca. 1910 |
| | 1040.7 | WONDER OF THE WORLD – Aunt Jane |
| | 1041 | ORANGE SQUEEZER – Evelyn Brown in Quilting: Do It My Way |
| | 1042 | WINGS OF VICTORY QUILT – American Home Magazine 7/42 |
| | 1043 | CORONATION – Finley<br>KING'S CROWN – Finley<br>PRESIDENT'S QUILT – Finley<br>WASHINGTON'S OWN – Finley<br>POTOMAC PRIDE – Finley. *See 2691 & 3914.* |

**THREE BLOCKS**

| | | |
|---|---|---|
| | 1044 | ATTIC STAIRS – Nancy Cabot. *See 2375 & 2301.* |
| | 1046 | CHAIN OF DIAMONDS QUILT – Aunt Martha. *See 1601 & 2702.* |
| | 1048 | CHECKERBOARD SKEW – Gutcheon Quilt Design Workbook |
| | 1048.2 | UNNAMED – Workbasket ca. 1942 |

*Neither Block Is a Checkerboard Grid, Three Blocks (1031 – 1048.2)*

145

# PATTERN CATEGORY 7

## Sash & Block

**Patterns in Category 7 share these characteristics:**

- They are all-over patterns

- The repeat consists of both a block and the set. The set is as important to the identification of the pattern as the block.

- The block may be pieced or plain. In the case of a plain block, the set is the variation that identifies the design.

**Category 7 includes:**

- Plain Block/Pieced Sashing, 148

- Pieced Block/Pieced Sashing, 150

**KEY FOR PATTERN CATEGORY 7: SASH & BLOCK**

If your pattern has plain blocks with pieced sashing *turn to p. 148*

If your pattern has pieced blocks with pieced sashing *turn to p. 150*

If the block is pieced it may be indexed separately under another number and name.

Pattern Category 7: *Sash & Block*

PLAIN BLOCK/
PIECED SASHING

| | | |
|---|---|---|
| | **1051** | CHECKERS – Nancy Cabot<br>EARLIEST EXAMPLE: ca. 1820/Quilt Engagement Calendar 1979 |
| | **1052** | UNNAMED – Godey's 1858 |
| | **1053** | CRISS CROSS PATCHWORK – QNM #90, 1977 |
| | **1053.5** | THE PATIENCE QUILT – Rural New Yorker 6/10/33 |
| | **1053.9** | AUNT LUCINDA'S DOUBLE IRISH CHAIN – Clara Stone<br>AUNT LUCINDA'S BLOCK – Workbasket<br>THE NEW JERSEY STAR – Workbasket 1935 |
| | **1054** | GARDEN MAZE – Finley<br>TANGLED GARTER – Finley<br>TIRZAH'S TREASURE – Finley<br>SUN DIAL – Hall |
| | **1055** | BRIDAL STAIRWAY – Household Magazine 6/30 |
| | **1057a** | VESTIBULE – LAC #383<br>SQUARE CROSS – Nancy Cabot 5/25/34 |
| | **1057b** | MORNING STAR – Aunt Jane in Household Journal 1914 |
| | **1058** | MORNING STAR – Nancy Page<br>SQUARE CROSS – attributed to Nancy Cabot/Wilma Smith.<br>*See 1136, 1710, 2104, & 2138.* |
| | **1059** | DARTING MINNOWS – Bacon |
| | **1059.5** | EIGHT-POINTED STAR – Bishop/Knopf |
| | **1060** | PINEAPPLE QUILT – Aunt Martha Bk. 3540, 1960 |
| | **1061** | UNNAMED – Godey's. *See 3735.* |
| | **1061.5** | STONEWALL JACKSON – Nancy Cabot. *See 3735.*<br>TOUCHING STARS – Quilt Engagement Calendar 1981 |
| | **1062** | CUPID'S ARROWPOINT – KC Star 4/6/29 |
| | **1062.3** | FOUR STAR SQUARE – *Quilt Close Up*, a catalog published by the Hunter Museum of Art, Chattanooga, 1983 |
| | **1062.5** | SPRING – Capper's Weekly 9/20/30 (green and white) |

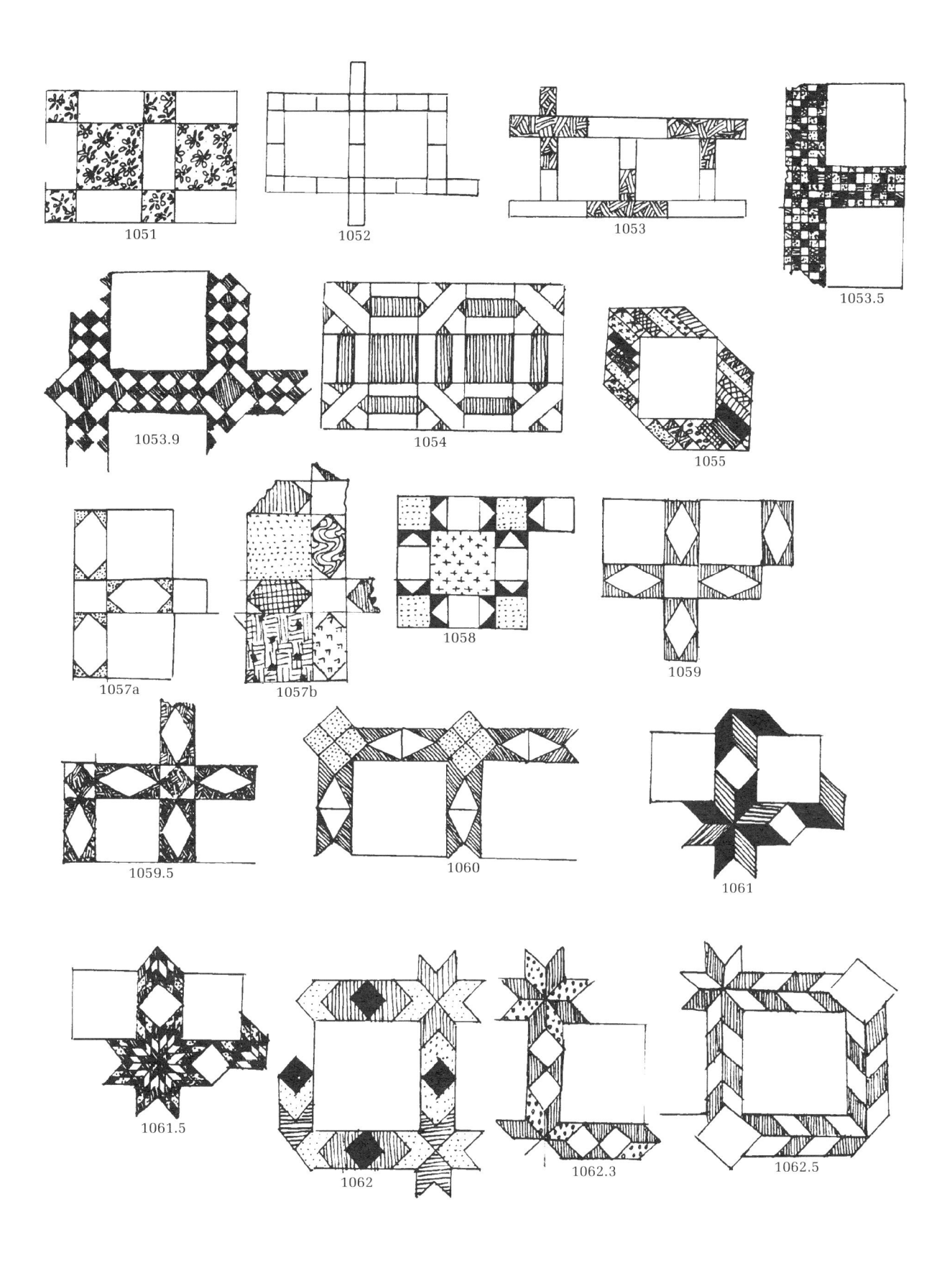

*Plain Block/Pieced Sashing (1051 – 1062.5)*

1051

1052

1053

1053.5

1053.9

1054

1055

1057a

1057b

1058

1059

1059.5

1060

1061

1061.5

1062

1062.3

1062.5

149

Pattern Category 7: *Sash & Block*

PLAIN BLOCK/
PIECED SASHING

| | | |
|---|---|---|
| | 1062.7 | BRAIDED BORDER – Nancy Page |
| | 1063 | CRAZY PATCH STAR – Grandmother Clark Bk. 21, 1931 |
| | 1065 | CENTURY QUILT – Danner/Ericson Bk. 5, 1970 |
| | 1065.3 | THE PENNSYLVANIAN – Rural New Yorker 4/6/46 |
| | 1065.7 | FEATHER STAR – Nancy Cabot |
| | 1066 | CRADLE QUILT – attributed to Hearth and Home by Wilma Smith<br>FLYING GEESE AND LEMOYNE STARS – Quilt Engagement Calendar 1982. *See 1075.2.* |
| | 1067 | A KENTUCKY QUILT – Lockport Batting |
| | 1068 | SAWTOOTH SQUARES – Orlofsky |

PIECED BLOCK/
PIECED SASHING

| | | |
|---|---|---|
| | 1070 | CHILDREN'S DELIGHT – LAC #319 |
| | 1070.5 | CROSS BAR AND SQUARE – Comfort |
| | 1071 | STORM AT SEA – Coats and Clark. *See 2185.* |
| | 1071.3 | NINE PATCH – Grandma Dexter |
| | 1072 | COMPASS AND CHAIN – KC Star 11/27/35. *See 3735.* |
| | 1072.5 | STREETS OF NEW YORK – attributed to Good Housekeeping 1/30 by Khin |
| | 1073 | A THREE IN ONE QUILT PATTERN – KC Star 12/15/48. *See 3735.* |
| | 1073.5 | FIELD AND STREAM – by Shelly Wolff in LCPQ #19, 1980. *See 2880.* |

*NOTE: Any eight pointed star can be constructed as a Sash and Block Design. If you can't find your star pattern here, it may be indexed as a block in Pattern Categories 11 or 22.*

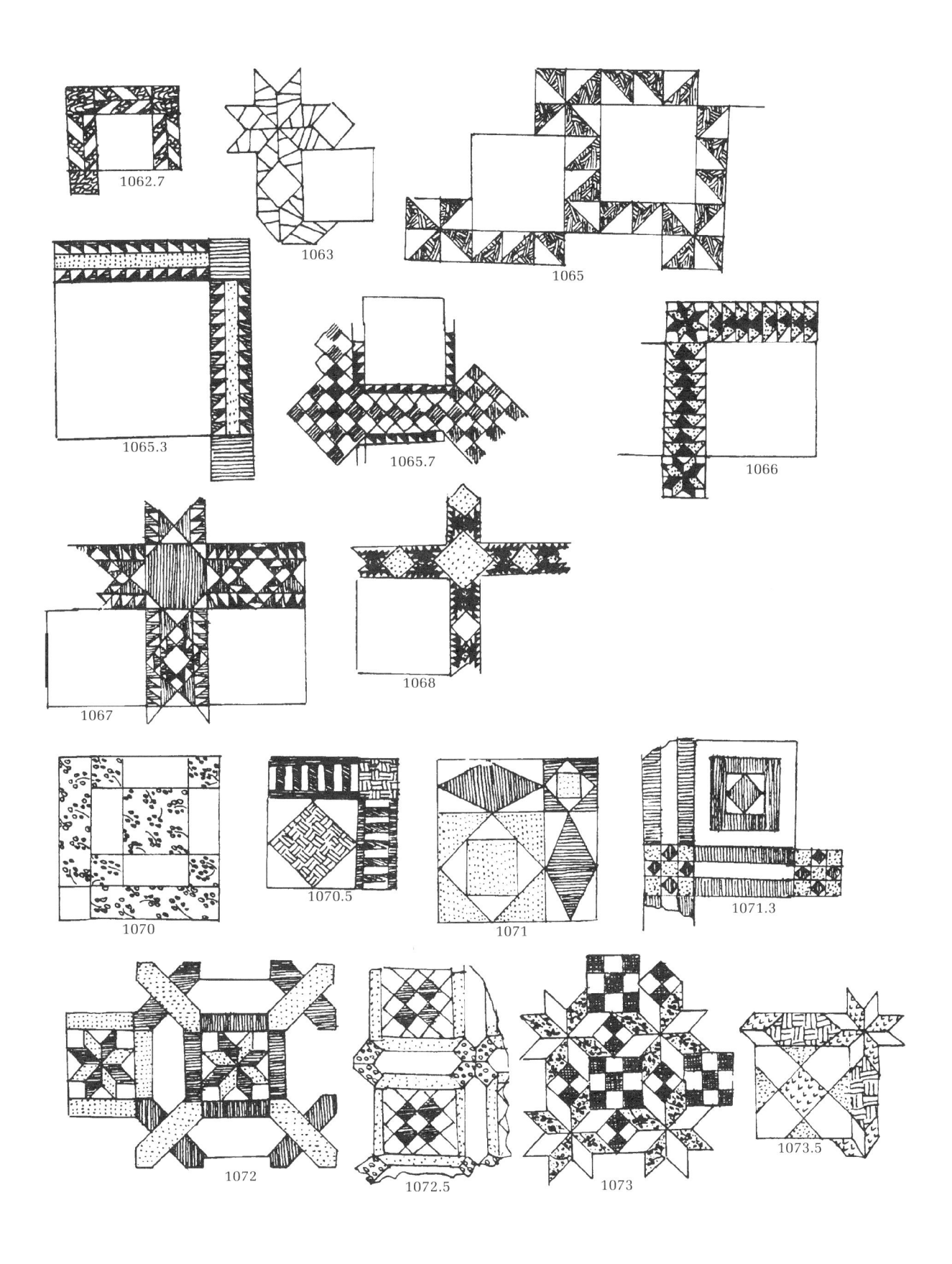

*Plain Block/Pieced Sashing, Pieced Block/Pieced Sashing (1062.7 – 1073.5)*

1062.7

1063

1065

1065.3

1065.7

1066

1067

1068

1070

1070.5

1071

1071.3

1072

1072.5

1073

1073.5

151

# Pattern Category 7: *Sash & Block*

PIECED BLOCK/
PIECED SASHING

| | | |
|---|---|---|
| | 1074 | TANGLED COBWEBS – Home Art #319, 1933 |
| | 1075 | SPIDER WEB – Mrs. Danner Bk. 2, 1934 |
| | | WILD GOOSE CHASE – Holstein |
| | 1075.2 | FOX AND GEESE – Clara Stone. *See 1066.* |
| | 1076 | SUNRISE – Nancy Cabot. *See 2677 & 3281.* |
| | | ROCKY MOUNTAIN ROAD – Hall |
| | 1076.5 | SPRINGTIME IN THE ROCKIES – Capper's Weekly 3/21/31 |
| | 1077 | CROWN OF THORNS – Hall |
| | | ROCKY MOUNTAIN ROAD – Hall |
| | | NEW YORK BEAUTY – Mountain Mist |
| | 1079 | ROCKY MOUNTAIN – Prudence Penny, Seattle Post Intelligencer |
| | | NEW YORK BEAUTY – Shelburne |
| | | SPLIT RAIL – Quilt Engagement Calendar 1978 |
| | | EARLIEST EXAMPLE: of designs #1076 to 1083 I've yet found is dated 1849 in Quilt Engagement Calendar 1978, Pl. 38 |
| | 1080 | CROWN OF THORNS – Prudence Penny, Seattle Post Intelligencer |
| | 1081 | SUNRISE – Modern Priscilla |
| | | SUNRISE IN THE PINES – Pioneer Quilts, Catalog by the Daughters of Utah Pioneers 1979 |
| | 1081.5 | SPICE PINK – QNM #42, 1973 |
| | 1082 | BEAUTY EVERLASTING – QNM #60, 1974 |
| | 1083 | ROCKY MOUNTAIN – Ladies' Home Journal 7/09 |
| | | THE GREAT DIVIDE – Ladies' Home Journal 7/09 |
| | 1085 | THE LADY FINGER – Ladies' Home Journal 2/12 |
| | | FANNY'S FAVORITE – Capper's Weekly 1/1/30 |
| | | WHIG'S DEFEAT – Peto in Hobbies Magazine 1941 |
| | | DEMOCRAT'S FANCY – Peto in Hobbies Magazine 1941 |
| | | EARLIEST EXAMPLE: of any of the variations #1085-1087 I've yet found is in the collection of the Kansas City Museum, dated 1844. |
| | 1086 | LOTUS BLOSSOM – Mrs. Danner Bk. 1, 1934 |
| | | RICHMOND BEAUTY – Mrs. Danner Bk. 1, 1934 |
| | | THE LOTUS – Ladies' Home Journal 9/47 |
| | 1087 | GRANDMOTHER'S ENGAGEMENT RING – Mountain Mist |
| | | MISSOURI BEAUTY – McCall's Bicentennial Bk./Quilts 1975. *See 2529, 2680, & 4074 for other variations.* |

*Pieced Block/Pieced Sashing (1074 – 1087)*

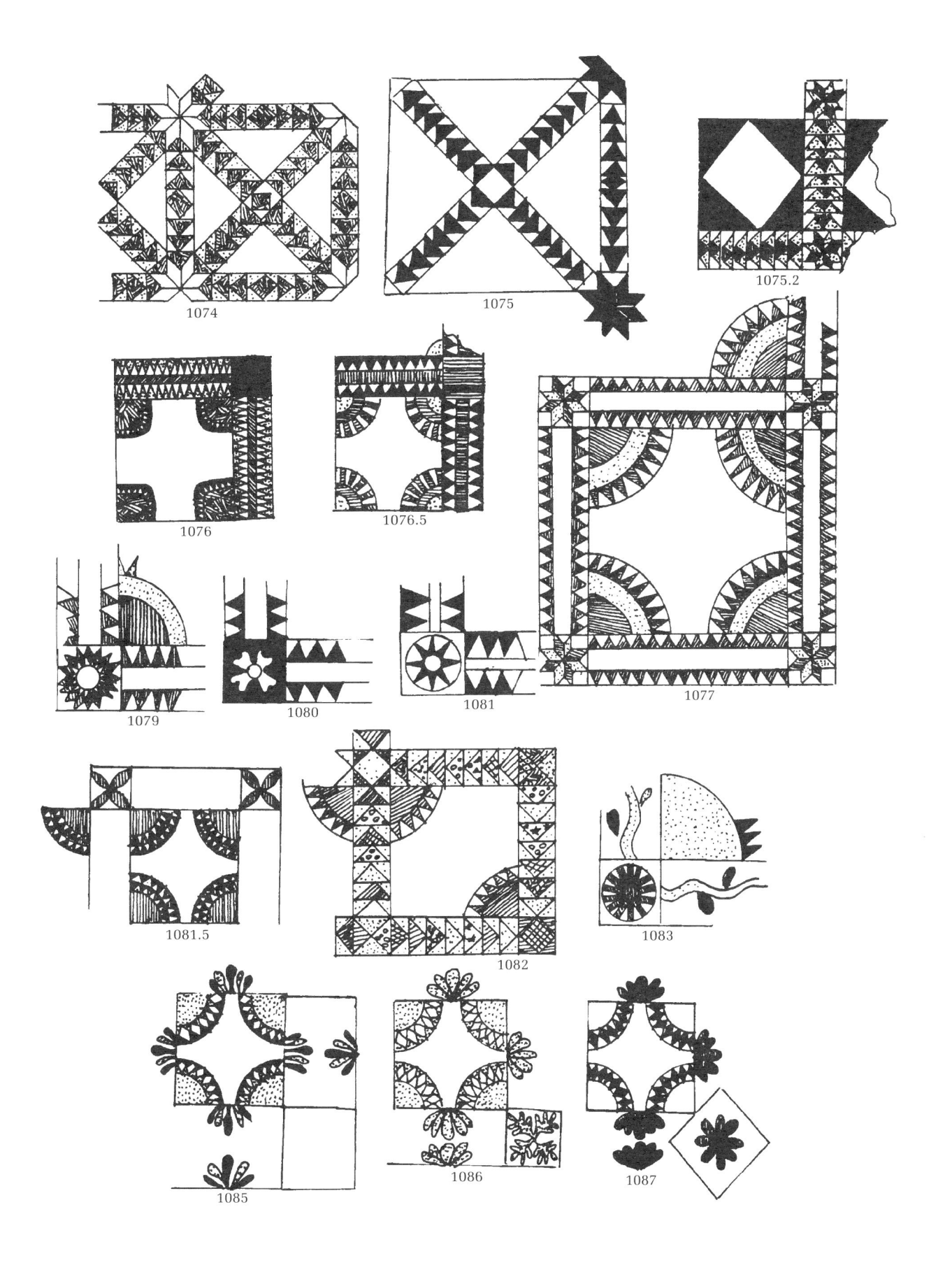

1074

1075

1075.2

1076

1076.5

1077

1079

1080

1081

1081.5

1082

1083

1085

1086

1087

153

# PATTERN CATEGORY 8

## Four Patch

**Patterns in Category 8 share these characteristics:**

- They are square blocks divided into four parts by horizontal and vertical seams.

- They are common because a set of four is a logical way to look at many repeats. Some patterns which appear as a FOUR PATCH in one source may appear as a single unit in another source. Consequently these patterns are classified under both FOUR PATCH and a second category. The Necktie pattern is a good example. It appears as a FOUR PATCH in #1429, and as a single unit classified as a SQUARE IN A SQUARE.

**Category 8 includes**
- Squares and Rectangles Only, 156
- Sixteen Squares, 158
- Thirty-six Squares, 162
- Thirty-four Squares, 162
- Block Is a Star, 170
- Misc. Pinwheel Types, 180
- Misc. Sawtooth Types, 180
- Asymmetrical Four Patch, 182
- Unequal Four Patch, 184
- Misc. Four Patch, 184
- Four Patch with Curves, 194
- Blocks with Specific Construction, 155, 172, 182

# KEY TO PATTERN CATEGORY 8: FOUR PATCH

| | |
|---|---:|
| 1. If block has curved pieces, | *continue with Number 26 below* |
| 2. If block has no curved pieces, | *continue with Number 3 below* |
| 3. If each of the four sections is of equal size, | *continue with Number 5 below* |
| 4. If the four sections are not of equal size, | *Turn to pg. 184* |
| 5. If block has squares and rectangles only, | *Turn to pg. 156* |
| 6. If block has triangles, diamonds and other shapes, | *Go to Number 7 below* |
| 7. Go through the list below in order, choosing the first applicable description, | |
| 8. If block is gridded into 36 squares by major seams, | *turn to pg. 162* |
| 9. If the blocks are gridded into 64 squares by major seams, | *turn to pg. 162* |
| 10. If block has a square in each patch ⊠, | *turn to pg. 164* |
| 11. If block has a ◩ in each patch, | *turn to pg. 164* |
| 12. If block is constructed like this ⊡, | *turn to pg. 166* |
| 13. If block is gridded into 16 squares by major seams, | *turn to pg. 158* |
| 14. If block is a star, | *turn to pg. 170* |
| 15. If block is of this construction ✸, | *turn to pg. 172* |
| 16. If block is of this construction ✕, | *turn to pg. 172* |
| 17. If block is of this construction ◳, | *turn to pg. 178* |
| 18. If block is of this construction ◪, | *turn to pg. 178* |
| 19. If block is of this construction ▦, | *turn to pg. 178* |
| 20. Miscellaneous Pinwheel Types, | *turn to pg. 180* |
| 21. Miscellaneous Sawtooth Types, | *turn to pg. 180* |
| 22. If block has this piece ▱, | *turn to pg. 182* |
| 23. If block is of this construction ◈, | *turn to pg. 182* |
| 24. Asymmetrical Four Patch (all patches are not same or mirror image), | *turn to pg. 182* |
| 25. If block doesn't fit in any prior category, | *turn to pg. 186* |
| 26. If block has this piece ◜, | *turn to pg. 190* |
| 27. If block has curves, | *turn to pg. 194* |

# Pattern Category 8: *Four Patch*

SQUARES AND RECTANGLES ONLY

**1101**    FOUR PATCH – Hall. *See 1007, 1010 & 2276.*
CHECKERBOARD – Gutcheon

**1102a**    MOSAIC #20 – LAC #348

**1102b**    SQUARES WITHIN SQUARES – Nancy Cabot. *See 1009, 1829, & 2382.*

*Each of the above patterns can also be found in ONE PATCH-SQUARE, pg. 285.*

**1103a**    FOUR PATCH – Hall

**1103b**    CARMEN'S BLOCK – Nancy Page

**1103c**    AUTUMN TINTS – Hall (in earth colors). *See 1117, 1104.5, 1025, & 2381.*

**1104**    SQUARES UPON SQUARES – Farm Journal

**1104.5**    WORLD'S FAIR BLOCK – LAC #66. *1104.5 & 1103 are identical when set all over.*

**1105**    CARRIE NATION QUILT – KC Star 1940

**1106**    FOUR PATCH – Hinson QM

**1107**    THE RED CROSS – KC Star 1934. *See 1601.*

**1110**    ENDLESS STAIRS – Hearth & Home, Comfort
LONDON STAIRS – KC Star 1934
ENDLESS STAIR – Farm Journal, Nancy Cabot 1934
WINDING STAIRWAY – Evangeline's

**1111a**    ROMAN SQUARE – Orlofsky (random colors)
THREE BY THREE – Country Gentleman 1948
FENCE POSTS – Orlofsky

**1111b**    INTERLOCKED SQUARES – KC Star 1932
FOUR PART STRIP BLOCK – KC Star

**1111c**    ZIG ZAG – Shelburne (set on an angle)
ROMAN STRIPE ZIG ZAG – Gutcheon PPP. *See 1821.2.*

**1111d**    TRICOLOR BLOCK – Nancy Cabot
SPIRIT OF ST. LOUIS – Nancy Cabot 1934, Farm Journal red, white, blue

**1112a**    MODERN DESIGN – OCS Bk. 116 (random)

**1112b**    MODERN BLOCKS – OCS Bk. 116

**1112c**    UP AND DOWN BLOCKS – OCS Bk. 116

**1112d**    COLT'S CORRAL – Prudence Penny
FIVE STRIPES – LAC. *See 1620.*

**1113**    COUNTRY CHARM – OCS Bk. 116

**1114**    LOG CABIN – Denver Art Museum

**1116**    CALIFORNIA – Nancy Page

*Squares and Rectangles Only (1101 – 1116)*

1101

1102a

1102b

1103a

1103b

1103c

1104

1104.5

1105

1106

1107

1110

1111a

1111b

1111c

1111d

1112a

1112b

1112c

1112d

1113

1114

1116

157

# Pattern Category 8: *Four Patch*

| | | |
|---|---|---|
| SQUARES AND RECTANGLES ONLY | **1117** | **Tam's Patch** – Gutcheon PPP. *See 1367.* |
| | **1118** | **Swastika** – Grandmother Clark Bk. 21, 1931 |
| | **1119** | **One Dozen Napkins** – Nancy Cabot. *See 1812.* |
| SIXTEEN SQUARES | **1121** | **Pinwheel** – Finley<br>**Paper Pinwheels** – Nancy Page |
| | **1122** | **The Anvil** – Source Unknown. *See 1314 & 2645.* |
| | **1123a** | **Crockett Cabin Quilt** – Marshall |
| | **1123b** | **Road to Oklahoma** – Hall |
| | **1123c** | **The Arkansas Cross Roads** – KC Star 1941. *See 207, 2086, 2644, & 4208.* |
| | **1124** | **Wild Duck** – Nancy Page |
| | **1125** | **Nelson's Victory** – Finley |
| | **1126** | **Windmill** – OCS Bk. 116 |
| | **1127** | **X Quartet** – Woman's World<br>**Flying X** – KC Star<br>**Double Quartet** – Capper's 1927 |
| | **1128a** | **Clay's Choice** – Finley<br>**Harry's Star** – Finley<br>**Henry of the West** – Finley<br>**Star of the West** – Finley<br>**Clay's Star** – McKim 101<br>**Clay's Favorite** – Nancy Cabot 1937<br>**Beauty Patch** – OCS Bk. 116 |
| | **1128b** | **Blocks and Pinwheels** – OCS Bk. 116. *See 1347.* |
| | **1129a** | **Year's Favorite** – Farm Journal |
| | **1129b** | **Pinwheels** – OCS Bk. 116 |
| | **1129.5** | **Mr. Roosevelt's Necktie** – Source Unknown |
| | **1130a** | **Yankee Puzzle** – LAC #28 |
| | **1130b** | **Flyfoot** – Finley<br>**Devil's Puzzle** – Finley<br>**Swastika** – Finley<br>**Indian Emblem** – KC Star<br>**Winding Blades** – KC Star 1943<br>**Whirligig** – Household Journal<br>**Devil's Dark Horse** – Source Unknown<br>**Pure Symbol of Right Doctrine** – Hall<br>**Heart's Seal** – Hall<br>**Favorite of the Peruvians** – Hall<br>**Chinese 10, 000 Perfections** – Hall<br>**Battle Ax of Thor** – Hall<br>**Mound Builders** – Hall<br>**Catch Me If You Can** – Hall<br>**Wind Power of the Osages** – Hall<br>**Spider** – Famous Features Bk. Q105. *See 1336, 1339, & 1169.* |
| | **1131** | **Ladies' Wreath** – LAC #322 |
| | **1132** | **Mosaic #17** – LAC<br>**Mosaic #10** – Nancy Cabot. *See 113, 1311, & 3150.*<br>**Ann and Andy** – Source Unknown<br>**Triangle Tiles** – Needlecraft Supply 1930's |
| | **1133** | **Hopscotch** – attributed to Nancy Cabot, Nancy's. *See 213, 214, 480, 1371, & 3150.* |

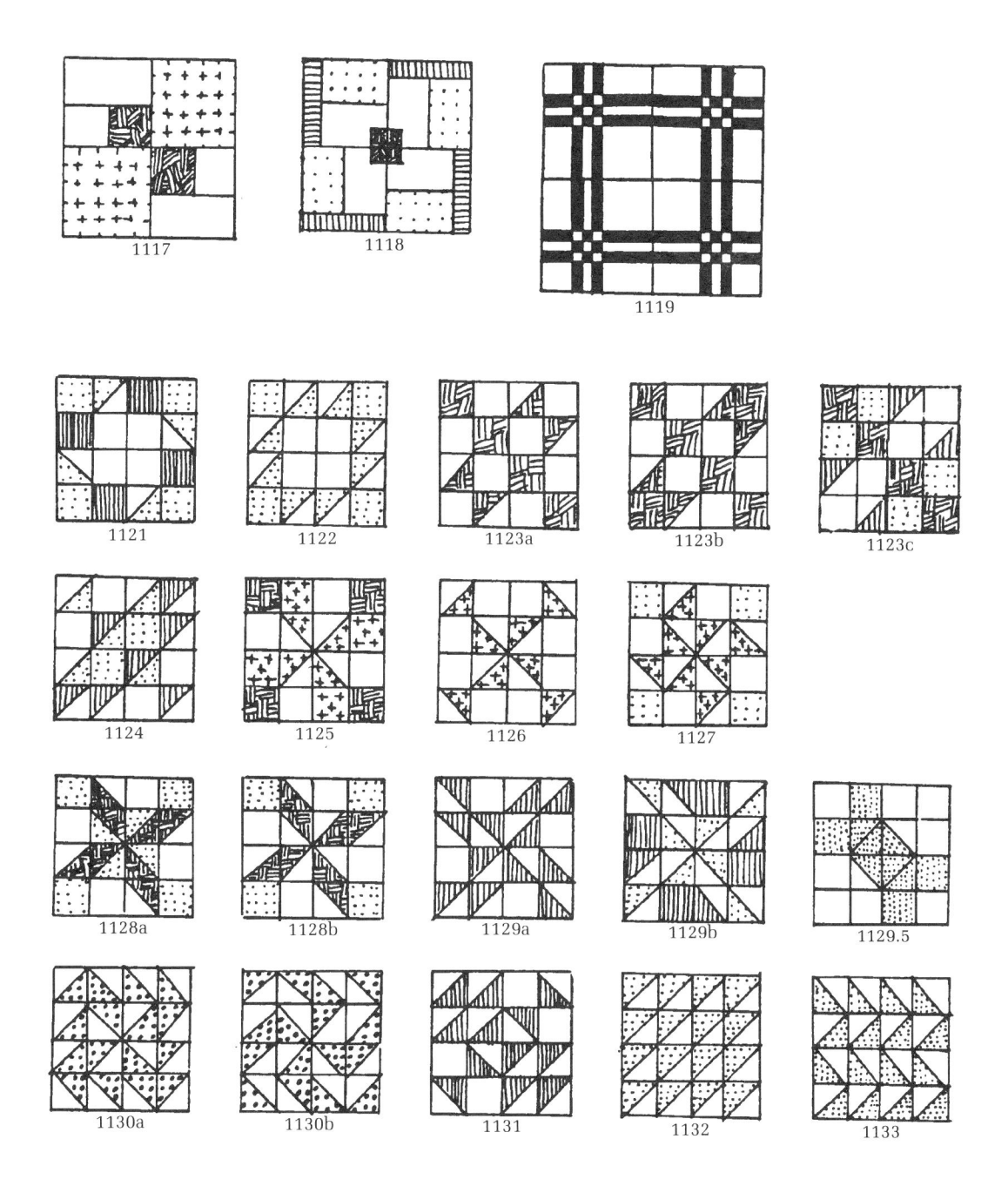

*Squares and Rectangles Only, Sixteen Squares (1117 – 1133)*

159

## Pattern Category 8: *Four Patch*

SIXTEEN SQUARES

1136a   **SAW TOOTHED STAR** – Golden Hands #10. *See 2104, 2138, 2155, & 1710.*
        **SINGLE STAR** – Golden Hands #10

1136b   **TWO PATCH QUILT** – OCS Bk. 116

1137   **FREE TRADE** – KC Star 1933. *See 2169.*

1138   **RIBBON STAR** – Source Unknown *See 2141.*

1139   **CHISHOLM TRAIL** – KC Star

1140a   **UNNAMED** – Dakota Farmer 1926
        **BARBARA FRIETSCHIE** – Grandmother Clark 1932

1140b   **THE COLORADO QUILT** – KC Star 1941

1140c   **PIECED STAR** – Famous Features Q109. *See 1249.1, 2144, & 2145.*

1141a   **ANNA'S CHOICE QUILT** – KC Star 1941

1141b   **MARGARET'S CHOICE** – unknown clipping, Hearth and Home?

1142a   **FRIENDLY HAND** – Comfort ca. 1920
        **INDIANA PUZZLE** – KC Star 1930
        **MONKEY WRENCH** – Aunt Martha, Mrs. Danner 1934
        **CHINESE COIN** – Aunt Martha
        **INDIAN PUZZLE** – Aunt Martha

1142b   **MILKY WAY** – LAC

1142c   **PINWHEELS** – Nancy Cabot 1933
        **CROSSES AND LOSSES** – QNM #54. *See 1763.*

1143   **STATE HOUSE** – Franks, Nancy Cabot 1937. *See 1312.*
        **DOUBLE FOUR PATCH** – Household Journal
        **NEW FOUR PATCH** – Aunt Jane Household Journal 1914

1144   **SUNNY LANES** – Nancy Page

1145   **LADY OF THE WHITE HOUSE** – Little 'n Big 1965

1146   **LADY IN THE WHITE HOUSE** – Famous Features/Obenchain
        **WHITE HOUSE** – Nancy Cabot 1937

1147   **UNNAMED** – QNM #94

1148   **CROSS ROADS** – attributed to Nancy Cabot, Nancy's

1149   **OLD MAID'S PUZZLE** – Farm Journal. *See 1317.*

1150   **BRIDLE PATH** – KC Star 1935

1151   **FOUR BUDS** – Progressive Farmer 1949

1152   **COLUMBIA PUZZLE** – LAC #31

1152.3   **NECKTIE** – KC Star 1932. *See 1376, 1429, 1712, 1899, & 3608.*

1152.7   **SHOOTING STAR** – Source Unknown

1152.8   **UTAH STAR** – Source Unknown

*Sixteen Squares (1136a – 1152.8)*

Pattern Category 8: *Four Patch*

THIRTY-SIX SQUARES
 **1153** Jacob's Ladder – Bureau Farmer 1930 & Finley
    Stepping Stones – Finley
    Road To California – Capper's 1930. *See 1695.*

 **1154** Oklahoma Twister – Aunt Kate

 **1155** Spinning Arrows – Nancy Cabot 1936

 **1156** Lightning in the Hills – Nancy Cabot

 **1157** Kissing Lanes – attributed to Nancy Cabot, Nancy's, but doubtful.
    Lover's Lane – KC Star 1934. *See 1769.*

 **1158** Unnamed – Woman's Circle 1963
    Flower Garden Path – QNM #72 (flower garden prints)

 **1159** Keyhole – Aunt Kate

 **1160** Ribbon Quilt – Nancy Page. *See 1657.*

SIXTY-FOUR SQUARES
 **1161** Aunt Em's Pattern – Heath

 **1162** Memory's Chain – Farm Journal

 **1163** Chain Links Quilt – attributed to Nancy Cabot, Nancy's

 **1164** Arrow Crown – Heath

 **1165** Flowering Cross – Heath

 **1166** Divided Cross – Heath

 **1167** Gothic Pattern – Heath

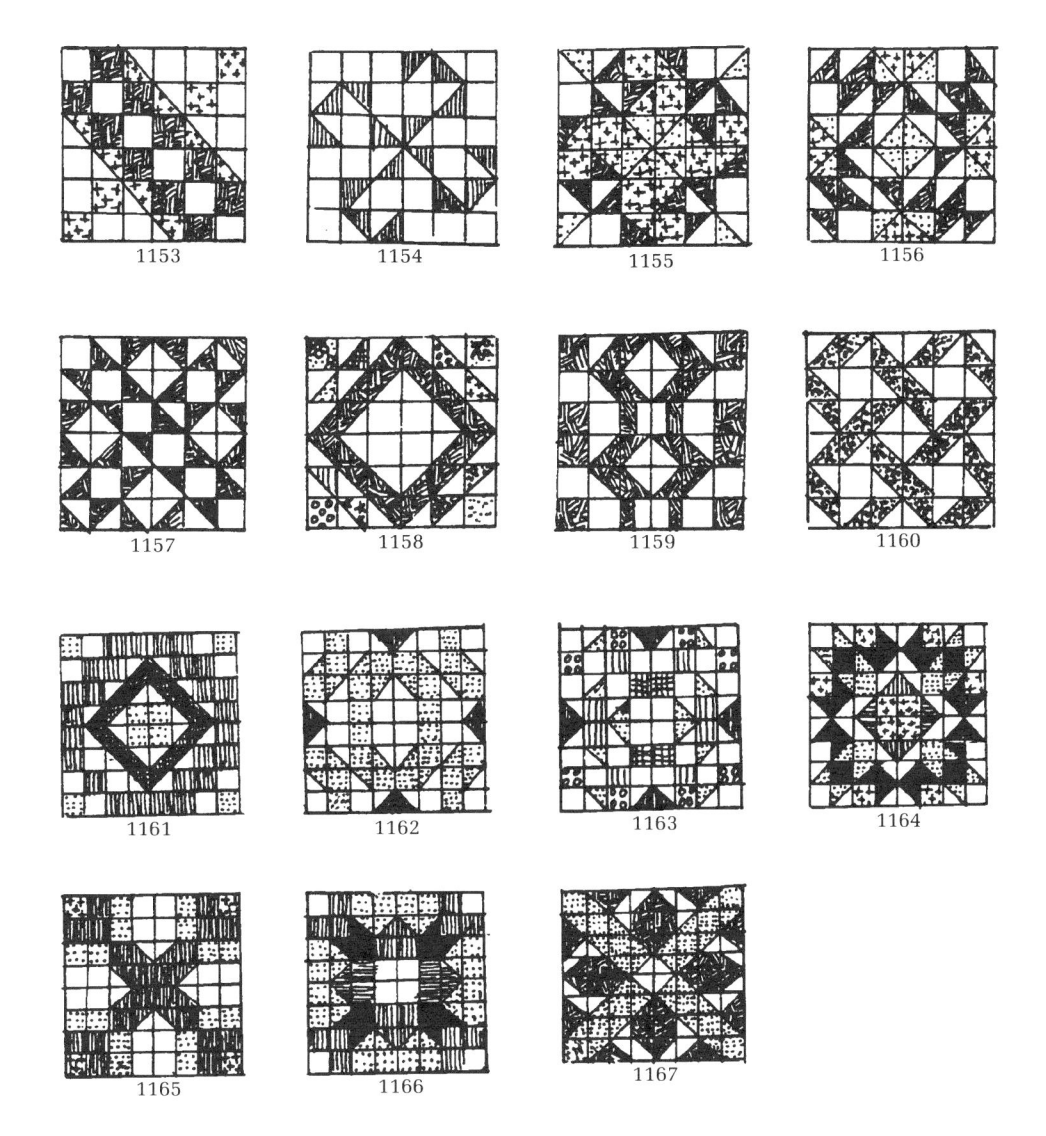

*Thirty-six Squares, Sixty-four Squares (1153 – 1167)*

1153
1154
1155
1156
1157
1158
1159
1160
1161
1162
1163
1164
1165
1166
1167

# Pattern Category 8: *Four Patch*

BLOCKS WITH A SQUARE IN EACH PATCH

| | 1171a | BROKEN SASH – Gammel. *See 2775.* |
|---|---|---|
| | 1171b | UNNAMED – Hectlinger ca. 1870<br>ALAMANIZER – Nancy Cabot<br>EIGHT POINT ALL OVER – QNM #76<br>SHOO FLY – Holstein.<br>TRIANGLES AND SQUARES – KC Star 1952. *See 2375.* |
| | 1172 | YOKAHAMA BANNER – Nancy Cabot 1937. *See 2311 & 2789.*<br>WHIRLING SQUARES – Nancy Page |
| | 1173 | ARROWHEAD PUZZLE – Aunt Martha Bk. 3614. *See 2311, & 2789.* |
| | 1174 | CHUCK-A-LUCK – Nancy Cabot 1937. *See 2779.* |
| | 1175 | THE H SQUARE QUILT – KC Star 1941. *See 2780.* |
| | 1176a | OLD TIPPECANOE – LAC #194<br>BROKEN DISHES – McKim 101. *See 1193.* |
| | 1176b | AN ENVELOPE MOTIF – KC Star 1942 |
| | 1176c | THE FOUR PATCH FOX AND GEESE – KC Star 1940 |
| | 1176d | TRIANGLE BEAUTY – OCS Bk. 116 |
| | 1176e | PORT AND STARBOARD – Nancy Cabot 1937. *See 2142, 2143, 2784, 2785, 2786, 2787, 2788, & 2898.* |
| | 1177 | OPEN WINDOW – Little 'n Big |
| | 1178 | DIAMOND STRIPE – Heath |
| | 1179 | SPOOL AND BOBBIN – Nancy Cabot 1936. |
| | 1180 | THIS AND THAT – Source Unknown<br>UNNAMED – Bishop. *See 2792.* |

BLOCKS CONTAINING THIS CONSTRUCTION:

| | 1181 | LATTICE – Nancy Page<br>A QUILT OF VARIETY – KC Star 1938<br>THE QUINT FIVE QUILT – KC Star 1941. *See 1187 & 3250.* |
|---|---|---|
| | 1182 | MANY ROADS TO THE WHITE HOUSE – KC Star 1955. *See 3251.* |
| | 1183a | DEVIL'S PUZZLE – LAC #24 |
| | 1183b | FLY FOOT – Hall |
| | 1184 | GOOD FORTUNE – Clara Stone<br>CROSS BARS – Nancy Page. *See 2883.* |
| | 1185 | WINDMILL – Bureau Farmer 1930. *See 2799.* |
| | 1186 | INDIAN HATCHETS – LAC #397. *See 3250.* |
| | 1187a | SIGNATURES FOR GOLDEN MEMORIES – KC Star 1961<br>PATHS TO PIECE – Household Magazine<br>FRIENDSHIP – LCPQ 8. *See 1181 & 3250.* |
| | 1187b | TRIANGLE OF SQUARES – attributed to Nancy Cabot – Nancy's |
| | 1188 | LEFT AND RIGHT – Nancy Cabot 1935. *See 1189.* |
| | 1189 | BEG AND BORROW – Nancy Cabot. *See 1188.* |
| | 1190 | GARRET WINDOWS – Nancy Cabot 1938. *See 3256, 1687, & 3023.* |
| | 1191 | NEW JERSEY – Nancy Page |
| | 1192 | A STRIPED-PLAIN QUILT – KC Star 1944 |

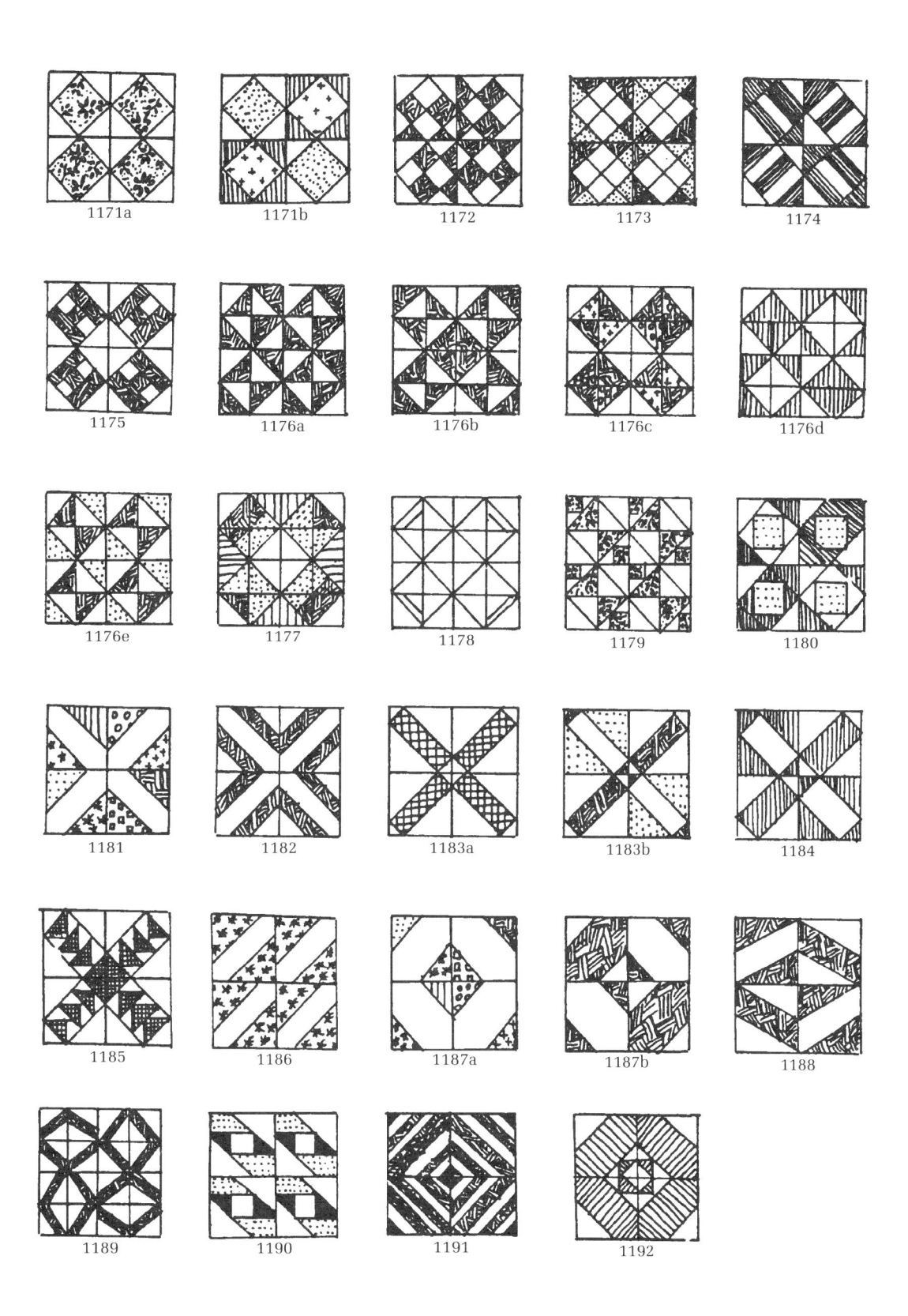

*Blocks with a Square in Each Patch, Blocks with Specific Construction (1171a – 1192)*

165

# Pattern Category 8: *Four Patch*

BLOCKS OF THIS CONSTRUCTION:

| | | |
|---|---|---|
| **1193a** | | **A Simple Quilt Block** – Orange Judd Farmer 1903<br>**Broken Dishes** – McKim. *See 1176, 1009, 1873, 2034, & 2301.*<br>**The Double Square** – KC Star |
| **1193b** | | **Small Triangles Quilt** – KC Star 1945 |
| **1193c** | | **Pretty Triangles** – OCS Bk. 116 |
| **1193d** | | **Triangle Combination** – OCS Bk. 116 |
| **1194** | | **Spiritus Mundi** – Gutcheon QDW |
| **1195a** | | **Big Dipper** – LAC<br>**Yankee Puzzle** – Finley<br>**Hour Glass** – KC Star 1932<br>**Envelope Quilt** – KC Star 1943<br>**The Whirling Blade** – KC Star 1944<br>**Bow Ties** – Nancy Cabot<br>**Pork and Beans** – Evangeline's. *See 2301.* |
| **1195b** | | **Electric Fan** – Clara Stone<br>**Pinwheel** – OCS Brooks. *See 1210.5.* |
| **1196** | | **Storm Signal** – Nancy Cabot 1937<br>**Hail Storm** – Nancy Cabot 1935<br>**Hail Stone** – Nancy Cabot? |
| **1197** | | **Four Knaves** – Nancy Cabot 1938 |
| **1198** | | **Windmill** – Nancy Page |
| **1199** | | **Windmill** – LAC #127 |
| **1200** | | **Pinwheels and Squares** – Nancy Cabot 1937. *Through an error 1200 & 1202 are identical.* |
| **1201** | | **Peace and Plenty** – Farm Journal |
| **1202a** | | **Pinwheel** – Grandmother Clark 1930<br>**Pinwheel Quilt** – OCS Bk. 116 |
| **1202b** | | **Shoo Fly** – OCS Bk. 116 |
| **1202c** | | **Simplicity** – Hearth & Home |
| **1202d** | | **Milly's Favorite** – American Woman 1911. *See 1200, 1262, 1691, & 2175.* |
| **1203** | | **Windmill** – Farm Journal |
| **1204a** | | **Depression** – KC Star 1937 |
| **1204b** | | **Magic Triangles** – OCS Bk. 116. *See 2123 & 2124.* |
| **1205** | | **Missouri Windmills** – QNM #41 |
| **1206a** | | **Corn and Beans** – LAC #100 (must be green and yellow, says Hall)<br>**Hen and Chicks** – Grandmother Clark 1931<br>**Ducks and Ducklings** – Hall<br>**Hen and Chickens** – Hall<br>**Shoo Fly** – Hall<br>**Handy Andy** – Hall |
| **1206b** | | **Triangle** – Carlie Sexton. *See 2483, 2486, & 3162.* |
| **1207** | | **Vines at the Window** – Nancy Cabot 1937 |
| **1208** | | **Linton** – LAC<br>**Sun and Shade** – Nancy Page. *See 1276.* |
| **1209** | | **London Square** – Famous Features Bk. 111. *See 1277 & 3164.* |
| **1210** | | **Windmill** – Bacon |
| **1210.5** | | **Reverse X** – Grandmother Clark Bk. 20, 1931. *See 1195 & 2301.* |

*Blocks with Specific Construction (1193a – 1210.5)*

167

## Pattern Category 8: *Four Patch*

BLOCKS OF THIS CONSTRUCTION:

| | | |
|---|---|---|
| | 1211 | BALKAN PUZZLE – Capper's 1927. *See 2476.* |
| | 1212 | BLOCKADE – KC Star 1938 |
| | | A FOUR CORNER PUZZLE – KC Star 1943 |
| | 1213 | HAZY DAISY – Nancy Cabot 1937 |
| | 1214 | MILL AND STARS – Nancy Cabot. *See 2324.* |
| | 1215 | CHINESE LANTERNS – attributed to Nancy Cabot, Nancy's |
| | 1216 | PERPETUAL MOTION – Nancy Cabot 1936 |
| | 1217 | STAR OF SPRING – OCS Wheeler |
| | 1218 | NIGHT AND DAY – Nancy Cabot 1934 |
| | | WHITE CROSS – Needlecraft Supply ca. 1938 |
| | 1219 | MOSAIC, NO. 4 – LAC #332 |
| | 1220 | THE SCOTTISH CROSS – KC Star 1945 |
| | 1221 | UNNAMED – Farm and Fireside 1904 |
| | | LADIES' AID BLOCK – Nancy Cabot 1938 |
| | 1222 | BLACKS AND WHITES – Nancy Cabot 1936 |
| | 1223 | UNNAMED (#7222) – OCS |
| | | FIVE PATCH – LCPQ 9 |
| | 1224 | THE JIG JOG PUZZLE – KC Star 1938 |
| | 1225 | SMALL BUSINESS – Gutcheon PPP |
| | 1226 | KANKAKEE CHECKERS – Nancy Cabot 1935 |
| | 1227 | GOLDEN STAIRS – OCS Wheeler 1933 |
| | 1228 | MERRIE ENGLAND – Nancy Cabot 1935 |
| | 1229 | PETER'S QUILT – designed by Nancy Crow, in Dubois |
| | 1230 | CROSSES – designed by Nancy Crow, in Dubois |
| | 1231 | FLYING FISH – Nancy Cabot 1937 |
| | 1232 | OHIO – Hearth & Home |
| | | OHIO STAR – Capper's Weekly |
| | | STATE OF OHIO – Household Magazine |

*Blocks with Specific Construction (1211 – 1232)*

169

# Pattern Category 8: *Four Patch*

BLOCK IS A STAR

| | | |
|---|---|---|
| | 1235 | STAR AND DOT – Comfort 1910<br>TELSTAR – QNM #45 |
| | 1236 | BLAZING STAR – Hinson QM. *See 4213.* |
| | 1237a | EIGHT POINTED STAR – LAC #450<br>MARINER'S COMPASS – Home Art |
| | 1237b | ST. LOUIS – Carlie Sexton 1930<br>MOTHER'S DELIGHT – Carlie Sexton 1930<br>BLAZING STAR – Hall<br>FOUR POINTED STAR – Hall |
| | 1237c | NORTHERN LIGHTS – Nancy Page<br>FLAMING STAR – Nancy Page |
| | 1238 | BLAZING STAR – Nancy Cabot 1933 |
| | 1239 | AUTUMN STARS – Progressive Farmer<br>GOLDEN CHAINS – Nancy Cabot 1937 |
| | 1240 | OPTICAL ILLUSION – Farm Journal |
| | 1241 | RIVIERA – Nancy Cabot 1938 |
| | 1242 | NORTH STAR – OCS Wheeler |
| | 1243 | EMERALD BLOCK – Nancy Cabot 1936 |
| | 1244 | TANGLED STARS – OCS (possibly) |
| | 1245 | FOUR BLOCK STAR – Aunt Kate 1966 |
| | 1246 | FOUR POINTS – LAC #306<br>STAR KITES – Nancy Cabot<br>SNOWBALL – Hall<br>JOB'S TROUBLES – Hall<br>KITE – Hall. *See 445.9, 1214, 2324, 3870, 3891, & 3892.* |
| | 1247 | UNNAMED – Aunt Martha 1933 |
| | 1248 | SHOOTING STARS – Nancy Cabot 1934 |
| | 1249 | NEW STAR – Aunt Kate's 1964 |

*Any of the following stars may also appear as a Nine X, #2975 to 2989*

| | | |
|---|---|---|
| | 1250 | MOUNTAIN STAR – QNM #1973<br>STARS AND STRIPES – LCPQ 9, 1978 |
| | 1251 | CROSSED CANOES – LAC #89<br>SANTA FE QUILT – Comfort<br>INDIAN CANOES – KC Star 1933<br>THE DRAGON FLY – KC Star<br>TWINKLING STAR – Grandmother's Quilt Bk. 48-7<br>TIPPECANOE – Gutcheon. *See 413, 1252, 1259, 1260, & 2976.* |
| | 1252 | SUGAR CONE – James. *See 1260.* |
| | 1253 | PINE BURR – Nancy Page. *See 415.27 & 2984.* |
| | 1254 | BUCKEYE BEAUTY – Nancy Cabot. *Actually published as 2987.* |
| | 1255 | STAR OF MANY POINTS – Nancy Cabot 1933. *See 2988.* |
| | 1256 | JULY'S SUMMER SKY – Evelyn Brown |
| | 1257 | THE MILKMAID'S STAR – KC Star 1948 |
| | 1258 | BLACK & WHITE – OCS Bk. 116<br>BAMBOO QUILT – OCS Bk. 116<br>DIAMONDS GALORE – OCS Bk. 116. *See 415.21, 3055, 3056, & 3872.* |
| | 1259 | AMETHYST – KC Star 1931<br>GOLDEN WEDDING QUILT – Nancy Page.<br>DIAMOND STAR – Oklahoma Farmer Stockman 1930. *See 413, 413.1, 1251, 1252, 2975, 2976, 3873, 3874, & 3945.* |

170

*Block Is a Star (1235 – 1259)*

171

# Pattern Category 8: *Four Patch*

BLOCKS OF THIS CONSTRUCTION:

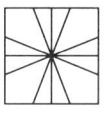

BLOCKS OF THIS CONSTRUCTION:

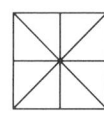

*When set all over these patterns are identical to blocks in previous sections.*

| | |
|---|---|
| 1260a & b | CONNECTICUT – Hearth & Home<br>SHOEMAKER'S PUZZLE – Hearth & Home. *See 1251, 1252, 413, & 27.* |
| 1260b | BLOCK ISLAND PUZZLE – QNM #66. *See 1251.* |
| 1261 | PLAIN SAILING – Comfort. |
| 1262a | MOSAIC #9 – LAC #337<br>WINDMILL – Ohio Farmer 1898<br>WATER WHEEL – Finley<br>WATERMILL – Finley<br>MILLWHEEL – Finley<br>SUGARBOWL – Household Journal, Dakota Farmer 1929<br>OLD CROW – Woman's World 1931<br>FLY – Hall<br>KATHY'S RAMBLE – Hall<br>CROW'S FOOT – Hall<br>FAN MILL – Hall<br>PINWHEEL – Famous Features Bk. 105<br>FOUR LEAF CLOVER – Farm Journal<br>BROKEN WHEEL – Dakota Farmer 1929<br>CORN DESIGN – Dakota Farmer 1929 |
| 1262b | THE GAY PINWHEEL – Famous Features Bk. 107. *See 1202, 1691, 1708, 2036, 2175, & 3150.* |
| 1264 | PINWHEELS – Hall<br>FLASHING WINDMILLS – Nancy Cabot 1938 |
| 1265a | THE SPINNER – Nancy Page |
| 1265b | BRAVE WORLD – Farm Journal 1944<br>BROWN WORLD – attributed to Nancy Cabot, Nancy's, but unlikely. |
| 1266a | UNNAMED – Farm and Fireside 1904<br>TURNSTILE – LAC #519 |
| 1266b | WHIRLWIND – Spool Cotton (Coats & Clark) 1940 |
| 1266c | WINDMILL – McKim & Farm Journal<br>OLD WINDMILL – attributed to Nancy Cabot, Nancy's |
| 1266d | WHIRLWIND – McKim 101<br>PINWHEEL – McKim 101<br>MODERN ENVELOPE – KC Star 1945 |
| 1266e | WINDMILL – Grandmother Clark. *See 2314.*<br>WHIRLIGIG – KC Star 1950. *See 1345, 2314, 2406, & 3151.* |
| 1267 | DOUBLE PINWHEEL WHIRLS – QNM #40 |
| 1268 | JOHN'S PINWHEEL – Source Unknown |
| 1269 | DUTCH WINDMILL – LAC #520 |
| 1270 | KANSAS TROUBLES – LAC #210<br>GRAND RIGHT & LEFT – Farm Journal |
| 1271 | TRIANGLES – Woman's Day 1943 |
| 1272 | TAKING WING – Beth Gutcheon in QNM #107 |
| 1273 | ROSEBUD – LAC<br>HUMMINGBIRD – Comfort<br>MAPLE LEAF – Nancy Cabot 1936<br>BRIGHT STAR – Nancy Cabot 1934<br>CROW'S FOOT – Rural New Yorker 1931 |
| 1274 | PATCH AS PATCH CAN – Aunt Martha |
| 1275 | PATH THRU THE WOODS – Carlie Sexton. *See 1207 & 3163.*<br>LINTON PATHWAY – Rural New Yorker 1931 |
| 1276 | HILL AND HOLLOW – Nancy Cabot 1937. *See 1208.* |
| 1277 | DANGER SIGNAL – Nancy Page. *See 1209 & 3164.* |
| 1278 | WHEELS – Progressive Farmer, Johnson 1976 |
| 1279 | WHIRLIGIG – Farmer's Wife 1931<br>DOUBLE PINWHEEL – Nancy Cabot 1937 |
| 1280 | WHIRLING STAR – OCS Wheeler |
| 1281 | BEGINNER'S CHOICE – OCS Wheeler |

*Blocks with Specific Construction (1260a – 1281)*

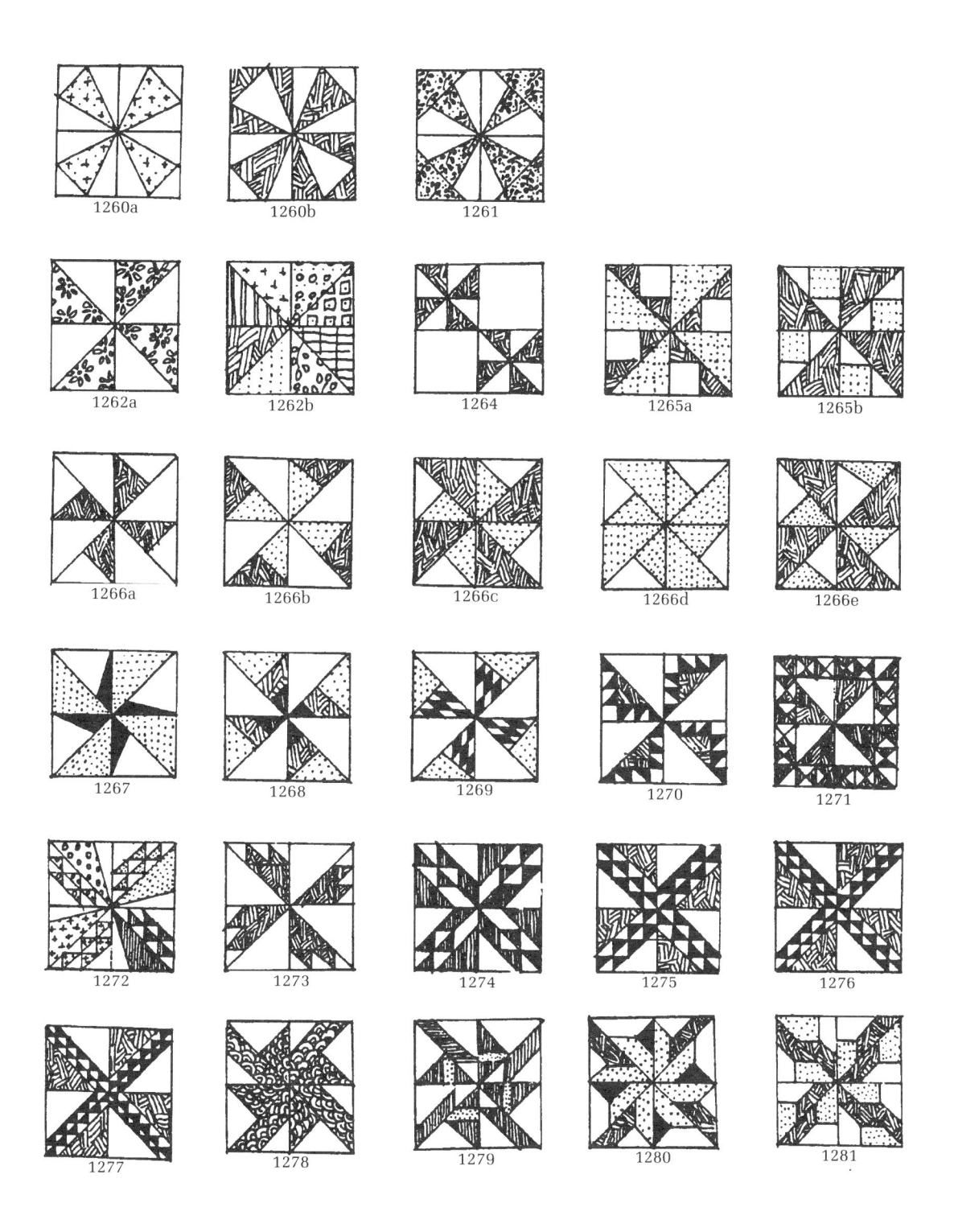

1260a  1260b  1261

1262a  1262b  1264  1265a  1265b

1266a  1266b  1266c  1266d  1266e

1267  1268  1269  1270  1271

1272  1273  1274  1275  1276

1277  1278  1279  1280  1281

173

## Pattern Category 8: *Four Patch*

BLOCKS OF THIS CONSTRUCTION:

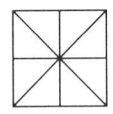

| | | |
|---|---|---|
| | 1282 | PIN WHEEL – Orange Judd Farmer 1899<br>STAR OF THE MILKY WAY – 1930<br>TWINKLE STAR – Capper's 1933<br>LEMOYNE STAR & WINDMILL – QEC 1977. *See 1291.* |
| | 1283 | SHASTA DAISY – OCS Wheeler |
| | 1284 | INDIAN ARROWHEAD – Aunt Martha Bk. 3540<br>HUNTER'S STAR – Hall. *See 3158.* |
| | 1285 | LITTLE PENGUINS – Nancy Cabot 1936 |
| | 1286 | GOOD LUCK TOKEN – Frank. *See 2319.* |
| | 1287 | END OF THE DAY – Farm Journal |
| | 1288 | BETTY'S DELIGHT – KC Star 1949. *See 1368.* |
| | 1289 | MARKET SQUARE – Nancy Cabot 1936 |
| | 1290 | KING'S X – Farm Journal<br>HIDE AND SEEK – Aunt Kate 1966 |
| | 1291 | SQUIRE SMITH'S CHOICE – Hearth and Home 1899, Farm & Fireside ca. 1900. *See 1282.* |
| | 1292 | GRETCHEN – KC Star 1932, Oklahoma Farmer Stockman<br>FEATHER BONE BLOCK – attributed to Nancy Cabot, Nancy's<br>OLD MAID'S QUILT – Oklahoma Farmer Stockman. *See 3159.* |
| | 1293 | DOUBLE WINDMILL – OCS |
| | 1294 | PINWHEEL – Grandmother Clark Bk. 21, 1931<br>FLYING KITE – KC Star 1937 |
| | 1295 | SPINNING COLOR WHEEL – QNM #56 |
| | 1296 | PINWHEEL PARADE – Aunt Kate 1966 |
| | 1297 | THE WHIRLING STAR – KC Star 1941<br>PATRIOTIC STAR – KC Star 1941 |
| | 1298 | STAR OF ERIN – Nancy Cabot 1936 |
| | 1299 | ROAD TO FORTUNE – OCS Wheeler<br>WHEEL OF FORTUNE – OCS Brooks<br>ROAD OF FORTUNE – Betty Jones<br>PINWHEEL QUILT – McCall's |
| | 1300 | FLYING SAUCER – QNM Catalog. *See 3599.* |
| | 1301 | LUCKY STAR – attributed to Nancy Cabot, Nancy's |
| | 1302 | MORNING STAR – OCS |
| | 1303 | STRING QUILT – Home Art. *See 2326.* |
| | 1304 | TARGET – Mountain Mist |
| | 1304.3 | DOUBLE STAR – OCS Wheeler |
| | 1304.5 | PALM – LAC #461<br>PALM LEAF – McKim & Grandmother Clark<br>HOSANNAH – McKim 101. *See 3174.* |

*Blocks with Specific Construction (1282 – 1304.5)*

1282  1283  1284  1285

1286  1287  1288  1289

1290  1291  1292

1293  1294  1295  1296

1297  1298  1299  1300  1301

1302  1303  1304  1304.3  1304.5

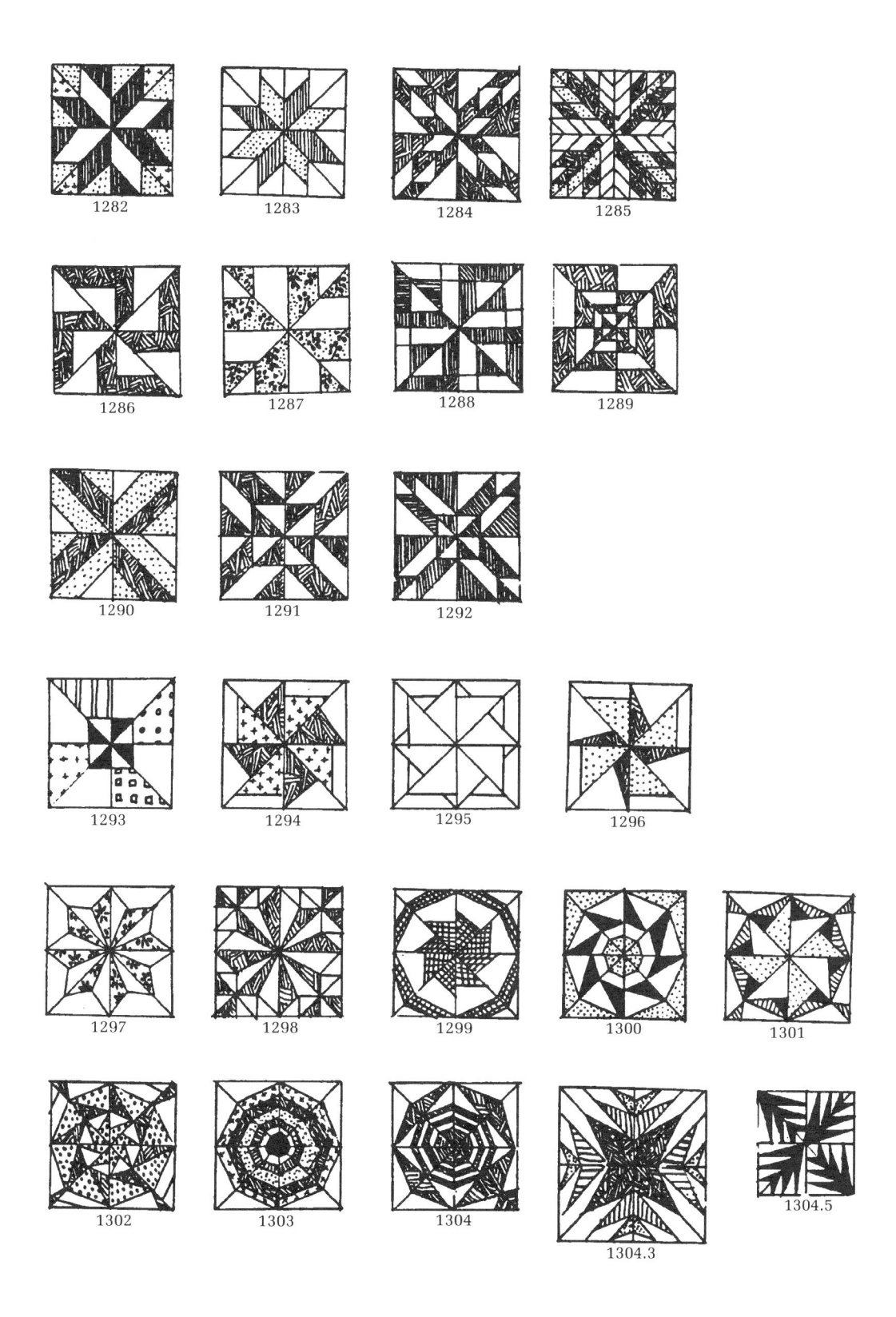

175

# Pattern Category 8: *Four Patch*

BLOCKS OF THIS CONSTRUCTION:

| 1305 | Turkey Giblets – Nancy Cabot 1938 |
|---|---|
| 1306 | Spider Web – OCS |
| 1307 | Spider Web – LCPQ #8 |
| 1308 | Four Winds – Nancy Cabot |
| 1309 | Star Points – Farm Journal |

BLOCKS OF THIS CONSTRUCTION:

| 1310a | Homeward Bound – Nancy Cabot 1937 |
|---|---|
| 1310b | Odds and Ends – LAC #102 (set with sashing as shown). *See 1821.5.* |
| 1311a | The Little Cedar Tree – KC Star 1940 |
| 1311b | Slanted Diamond – Famous Features Bk. Q 105. *See 113, 1132, 1692, & 1878.* |
| 1312 | Hour Glass – Wallace's Farmer 1929<br>Railroad Crossing – Finley<br>World's Fair – Farm & Fireside, Coats & Clark 1933<br>Jacob's Ladder – Grandmother Clark 1932<br>Double Four Patch – Household Journal<br>Railroad – Farm Journal, Nancy Cabot 1934<br>Going to Chicago – Nancy Page 1933<br>New Four Patch – Farm and Fireside 1884<br>Gay Scrap Quilt – OCS Wheeler<br>Buckeye Beauty – Clara Stone. *See 1143 & 2114.* |
| 1313 | Crosses and Losses – LAC #251<br>Fox and Geese – Hall<br>Bouncing Betty – Pictorial Review 1911 |
| 1314a | Old Maid's Puzzle – Nancy Cabot 1934 & 1936 |
| 1314b | The Anvil – Hall. *See 1122 & 2645.* |
| 1315 | Double X #3 – LAC #78. *See 2178.* |
| 1316a | Double X #2 – LAC #77<br>Fox and Geese – Finley<br>Crosses and Losses – Finley<br>Bow Tie Variation – Bishop and Safanda. *See 2052 & 2170.*<br>Goose and Goslings – Capper's |
| 1316b | Fireflies – James |
| 1316c | Triangle Weave – QNM #52 |
| 1317 | Old Maid's Puzzle – LAC #25. *See 1149.*<br>Hour Glass – Grandma Dexter<br>School Girl's Puzzle – Needlecraft Supply 1936 |
| 1318 | Double Cross – Hearth and Home |
| 1319 | Aircraft – attributed to Nancy Cabot, Nancy's<br>Dutchman's Puzzle – QNM Catalog |
| 1320 | Airplane – Household Magazine |
| 1321 | Flock of Geese – Finley |
| 1322 | Flying Birds – Finley<br>Birds in the Air – Finley<br>Flock of Geese – Finley<br>Flight of Swallows – Nancy Cabot 1937. *See 3161.* |
| 1323 | Hovering Hawks – Finley<br>Triple X – Finley |
| 1324 | Road to Heaven – James |
| 1325 | Picket Fence – Gutcheon QDW |

*Blocks with Specific Construction (1305 – 1325)*

1305
1306
1307
1308
1309
1310a
1310b
1311a
1311b
1312
1313
1314a
1314b
1315
1316a
1316b
1316c
1317
1318
1319
1320
1321
1322
1323
1324
1325

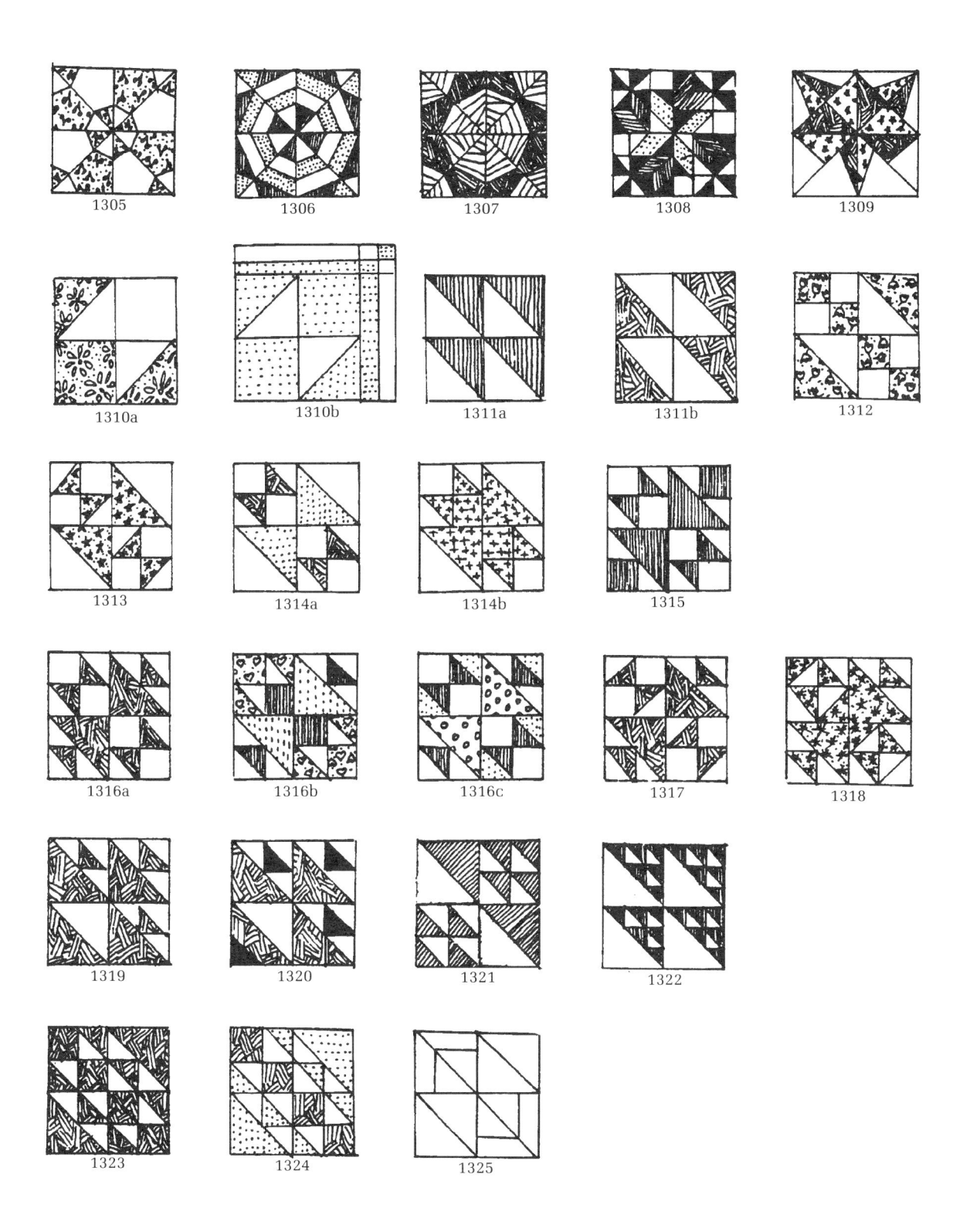

# Pattern Category 8: *Four Patch*

BLOCKS OF THIS CONSTRUCTION:

| | |
|---|---|
| **1326** | **Cotton Reels** – Golden Hands #10 |
| **1327** | **The Sickle** – KC Star 1936 |
| **1328** | **Unnamed** – Burhham |
| **1329** | **Autumn Leaves** – Nancy Cabot 1936 |
| **1330** | **English Ivy** – KC Star 1931 |
| | **The Clover Blossom** – Mrs. Danner 1934 |
| **1331** | **The Broken Branch** – KC Star |

BLOCKS OF THIS CONSTRUCTION:

| | |
|---|---|
| **1332** | **Susannah** – Gutcheon PPP. *See 2534 & 2535.* |
| **1333** | **Katherine Wheels** – Gutcheon QDW |
| **1334** | **Scrap Zig Zag** – attributed to Nancy Cabot, Nancy's, but unlikely |
| **1335** | **Louisiana** – Hearth & Home |
| **1336** | **Seesaw** – Gutcheon PPP |
| **1337** | **Next Door Neighbor** – Gutcheon PPP |
| **1338** | **Mosaic #12** – LAC #340 |
| | **Mosaic #9** – Nancy Cabot 1934. *See 2536.* |
| **1339a** | **Dutchman's Wheel** – Ohio Farmer 1898 |
| | **Wheel** – Ohio Farmer 1894 |
| | **Dutchman's Puzzle** – LAC #26 |
| | **Wild Goose Chase** – Gutcheon QDW |
| **1339b** | **Virginia Reel** – Workbasket. *See 1130 & 1346.* |
| | **Zig Zag** – Comfort |
| **1340** | **Return of the Swallows** – KC Star 1946 |
| **1341** | **Pinwheel** – OCS Brooks |
| **1342** | **Lady of the Lake** – Hearth & Home. *See 1146.* |
| **1343** | **Chinese Puzzle** – Grandmother Clark Bk. 21, 1931. *See 3199.* |

*Blocks with Specific Construction (1326 – 1343)*

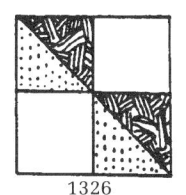

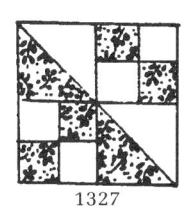

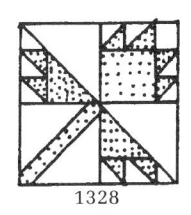

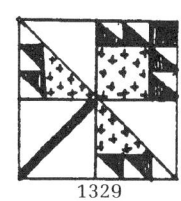

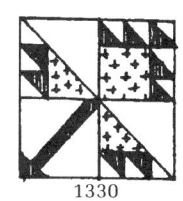

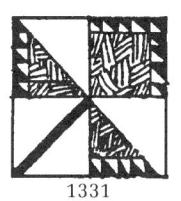

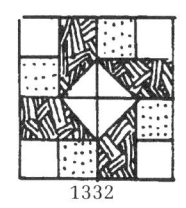

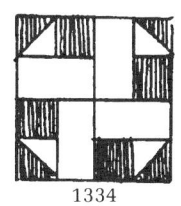

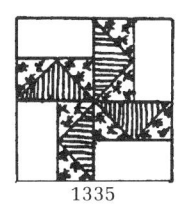

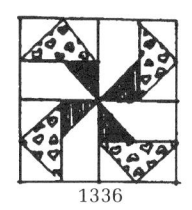

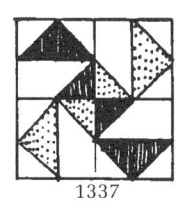

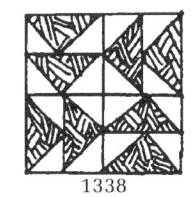

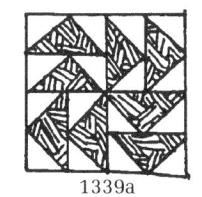

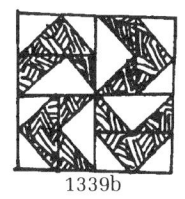

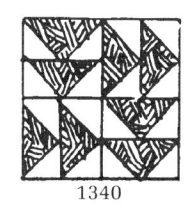

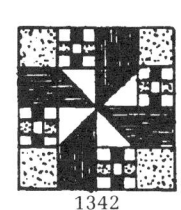

179

# Pattern Category 8: *Four Patch*

| | | |
|---|---|---|
| MISC. PINWHEEL TYPES | **1345** | CHURN DASH – Finley. *See 1266 & 2313.* |
| | **1346** | WHIRLIGIG DESIGN – Woman's World 1931. *See 1130 & 1339.* |
| | **1347** | SHOOTING STAR – LAC #16 |
| | | METEOR QUILT – Nancy Page. *See 1128.* |
| | **1348** | ROLLING PINWHEEL – LAC #253 |
| | **1349** | ROLLING PINWHEEL – Nancy Cabot |
| | **1350** | WHIRLING PINWHEELS – KC Star 1934 |
| | **1351a** | MRS. MORGAN'S CHOICE – LAC #255. *See 4030.* |
| | **1351b** | SPINNING WHEEL – Household Quilt Block Service |
| | **1352** | FLYING DUTCHMAN – LAC #247 |
| | | FLYING DUTCHMAN – Nancy Page (must be blue and white) |
| MISC. SAWTOOTH TYPES | **1353** | WAVES OF THE SEA – KC Star 1937 |
| | **1354** | BEAR'S PAW – LAC #162 |
| | | INDIAN TRAIL – KC Star 1931 |
| | | FOREST PATH – KC Star 1931 |
| | | RAMBLING ROAD – KC Star 1931 |
| | | NORTH WIND – KC Star 1931 |
| | | IRISH PUZZLE – KC Star 1931. *See 1363 & 2584.* |
| | **1355** | MERRY GO ROUND – McKim 101 |
| | | ETERNAL TRIANGLE – Hall |
| | **1356** | GRANDMOTHER'S PINWHEEL – Mrs. Danner 1970 |
| | **1357** | DELECTABLE MOUNTAINS – Burnham |
| | **1357.5** | WORLD'S FAIR PUZZLE – LAC #30 |
| | **1358** | LARGE STAR – Ladies' Home Journal 1896 |
| | | CROW'S FOOT – Nancy Page |
| | **1359** | TWELVE CROWNS – Farm Journal |
| | | WEDDING MARCH – Comfort |
| | | BRIDE'S PUZZLE – Prairie Farmer Bk. 1, 1931 |
| | **1360** | BLAZED TRAIL – Nancy Cabot 1937 |
| | **1361** | LOST SHIP – LAC #318. *See 1393.* |
| | **1362** | THE LOST SHIP – Finley |
| | | ROCKY GLEN – Finley |
| | **1363** | BARRISTER'S BLOCK – LAC #63 |
| | | LAWYER'S PUZZLE – Finley |
| | | THE SAW – Prudence Penny. When set all over 1363 & 1354 are identical. |
| | **1364** | NEW BARRISTER'S BLOCK – Nancy Cabot 1938 |
| | **1365** | FLAMINGOS IN FLIGHT – Nancy Cabot 1936 |

*Misc. Pinwheel Types, Misc. Sawtooth Types (1345 – 1365)*

# Pattern Category 8: *Four Patch*

BLOCKS OF THIS CONSTRUCTION:

| | | |
|---|---|---|
| | 1366 | NEW PATTERN – Peterson's Magazine 1857 |
| | | SHADOW BOX – Nebraska Collections |
| | | ATTIC WINDOWS – Holstein |
| | 1367 | UNNAMED – OCS Wheeler. *See 1117.* |
| | 1368 | UNNAMED – Burnham. *See 1288 & 2643.* |
| | 1369 | LUCKY CLOVER – Aunt Martha |
| | 1370 | DOMINO NET – Nancy Cabot 1937 |

BLOCKS OF THIS CONSTRUCTION:

| | | |
|---|---|---|
| | 1371a | A VICTORY QUILT – KC Star 1942 |
| | | ARROWHEAD QUILT – OCS Bk. 116 |
| | 1371b | BANNER QUILT – OCS Bk. 116 |
| | 1371c | HEDGEWORK – The Evangeline's. *See 213, 214, 480, & 1133.* |
| | 1372 | OZARK MOUNTAINS – Nancy Cabot 1936 |
| | 1373 | FLYING GEESE – Nancy Cabot 1935 |

ASYMMETRICAL FOUR PATCH

For other patterns similar to this category see TWO BLOCK PATTERNS, Two-Block, p. 138.

| | |
|---|---|
| 1376 | NECKTIE – Finley. *See 1429, 1152.3, 1712, 1899, & 2533.* |
| 1377 | HAYES CORNER – Gutcheon PPP |
| 1378 | INDIAN MAT – Nancy Cabot 1938 |
| 1379 | CROSSED CHAINS – Nancy Cabot 1938 |
| 1380 | THE SPRITE – Aunt Martha, Prize Winning Quilts 1933 |
| 1381 | FLUTTERBYE – QNM #97 |
| 1382 | CROSS AND CROWN – Finley |
| 1383 | NEW YORK – Hearth & Home |
| 1384 | SPANISH SQUARES – Nancy Cabot |
| 1385 | THE T QUILT PATTERN – KC Star 1939. *See 1662 & 2650.* |
| 1386 | SINGLE LILY – Nancy Cabot |
| 1387 | COLUMBUS – Hearth & Home. *See 768.2.* |

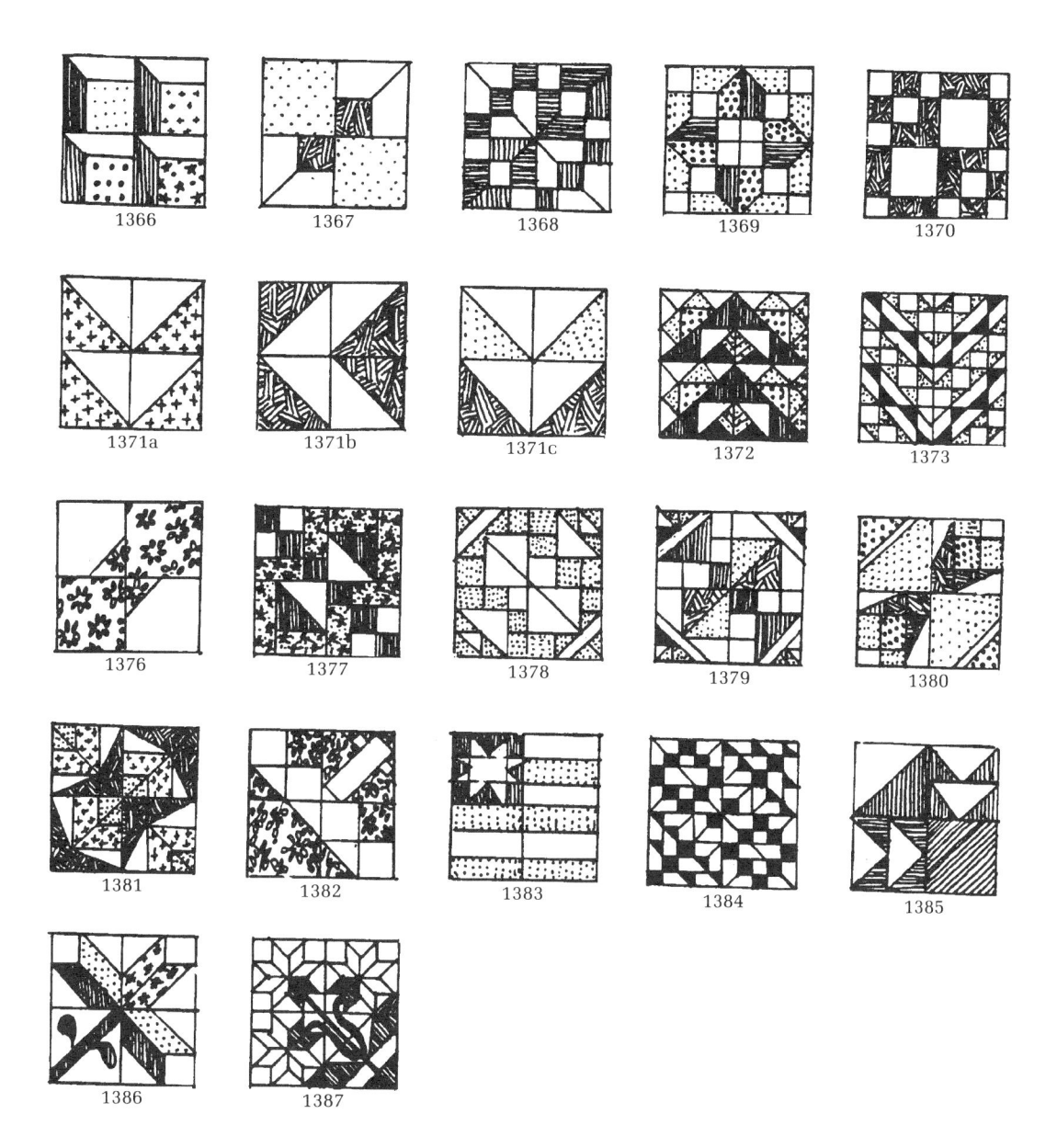

*Blocks with Specific Construction, Asymmetrical Four Patch (1366 – 1387)*

183

# Pattern Category 8: *Four Patch*

UNEQUAL FOUR PATCH

**1390** SCOTCH QUILT – OCS Bk. 3, 1968
BONNIE SCOTSMAN – Evelyn Brown

**1391** BIRDS IN THE AIR – Holstein

**1392** DOUBLE T – Nancy Page
MIXED T – Nancy Page. *See 1360.5, 1784, 3274, & 3275.*

**1393** SAIL BOAT BLOCK – McKim
WEST WIND – Nancy Page. *See 1361 & 1363.*

**1394** CACTUS FLOWER – KC Star 1931. *See 2057.*

**1395** TEXAS FLOWER – LAC #304

**1396** MAPLE LEAF – Wallace's Farmer 1928
THE APPLE LEAF – KC Star 1935

**1397** UNNAMED – Prudence Penny 1927
LILY OF THE FIELD – Hall

**1398** TREE OF LIFE – OCS Wheeler

*Many tree patterns are unequal Four Patches, but most are indexed as Trees under Realistic Designs, #801 – 860.*

**1399.2** PIECED BOUQUET – Nancy Cabot 1933. *See 1427 & 1977.*

**1399.4** NOSE-GAY – KC Star 1932. *See 1427 & 1977.*

**1399.6** BOUQUET IN A FAN – KC Star 1933

MISC. FOUR PATCH

**1400** ARKANSAS TRAVELER – LAC #205. *See 1407, 2350, & 2594.*

**1401** BORROW AND LEND – Evangeline's

**1402** FOUR H – KC Star 1940

**1403** T QUILT – LAC #369

**1404** FOUR E BLOCK – LAC #35

**1405** FOUR Z PATCH – LAC

**1406** SPINNING L – QNM #107

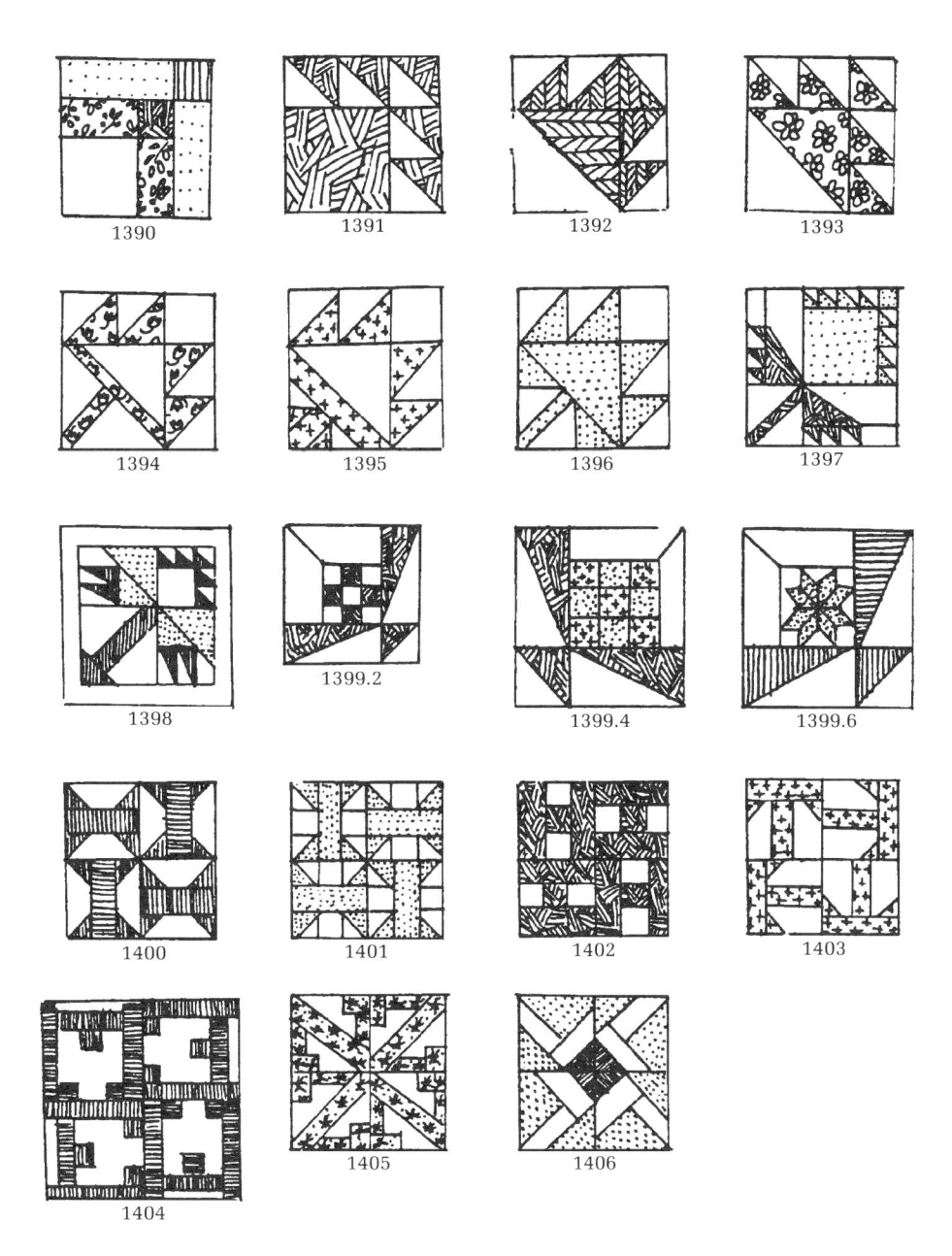

*Unequal Four Patch, Misc. Four Patch (1390 – 1406)*

185

# Pattern Category 8: *Four Patch*

MISC. FOUR PATCH

| | | |
|---|---|---|
| | 1407a | FRED'S SPOOL – Clara Stone |
| | | SPOOL – McKim 101. *See 1400, 2350, 2594, 4032, & 4104.* |
| | 1407b | LATTICE SQUARE – Nancy Cabot |
| | 1408 | THE BAT – Aunt Martha 1933 |
| | | THE BAT'S BLOCK – Nancy Cabot 1937 |
| | 1409 | THIRTEEN SQUARES – Farm Journal |
| | | THIRTEEN SQUARED – Farm Journal |
| | 1410 | HOPSCOTCH – QNM #70 |
| | 1411 | KANSAS – Hearth & Home |
| | 1412 | CITY BLOCKS – QNM #94 |
| | 1413 | ROLLING PINWHEEL – Gutcheon QDW |
| | 1414 | BLACKFORD'S BEAUTY – Nancy Cabot |
| | | THE ARROWHEAD – Farmer's Wife ca. 1920. *See 1983.* |
| | 1415 | RED AND WHITE CROSS – Nancy Cabot |
| | 1416 | BROKEN RAINBOWS – Nancy Cabot 1937 |
| | 1417 | HONEYCOMB – LAC #197 |
| | 1418 | BIRDS AND KITES – Nancy Cabot |
| | 1419 | UNNAMED – QNM #73 |
| | 1420 | WINDMILL – Aunt Martha |
| | 1421 | KALEIDOSCOPE – Farm Journal. *See 2561.* |
| | 1422 | THE CHIEFTAIN – Nancy Cabot |
| | 1423 | BOW KNOTS – Nancy Cabot |
| | 1424 | WINDING TRAIL – Nancy Cabot |
| | 1425 | DAY AND NIGHT – OCS |
| | 1426 | WINGED SQUARE – Nancy Cabot. *See 2546.* |

*Misc. Four Patch (1407a – 1426)*

1407a
1407b
1408
1409
1410
1411
1412
1413
1414
1415
1416
1417
1418
1419
1420
1421
1422
1423
1424
1425
1426

187

Pattern Category 8: *Four Patch*

| | | |
|---|---|---|
| MISC. FOUR PATCH | **1427** | **The Quilt Without a Name** – KC Star 1937. *See 1399.2, 1399.4, & 1977.* |
| | **1428** | **Calico Mosaic** – Nancy Cabot |
| | **1429a** | **Magic Circle** – LAC #384<br>**Magical Circle** – Nancy Cabot<br>**True Lover's Knot** – Aunt Martha Bk. 3333<br>**Dumbell Block** – Nancy Cabot |
| | **1429b** | **True Lover's Knot** – LAC #262. *See 1376, 1152.3, 1712, 1899, 2533, & 3608.* |
| | **1430** | **Victorian Maze** – Nancy Cabot. *See 438 & 4110.* |
| | **1431** | **Inspiration Patch** – Aunt Martha |
| | **1432** | **Michael's Joke** – Evelyn Brown |
| | **1433** | **Constellation** – Heath |
| | **1434** | **The Alta-Plane** – QNM #97 |
| | **1435** | **Star and Mill Block** – Nancy Cabot |
| | **1436** | **Constellation** – Nancy Cabot |
| | **1437** | **Double Tulip** – Source Unknown |
| | **1438** | **Blue Boutonnieres** – Nancy Cabot<br>**Turkey Tracks** – attributed to Nancy Cabot, Nancy's |
| | **1439** | **Broad Arrow** – Farm Journal |
| | **1440** | **Maple Leaf Design** – Ladies' Home Journal 1900<br>**Broad Arrows** – Farm Journal, Nancy Cabot<br>**Arabic Latticework** – QNM #86<br>**Fig Leaf** – QNM #86 |
| | **1441** | **Le Jet** – M. McLean in QNM #97 |
| | **1442** | **Silver Maple** – Prudence Penny 1932 |
| | **1443** | **Old Indian Trail** – KC Star 1943 |
| | **1444** | **Old Indian Trail** – KC Star 1943 |

*Misc. Four Patch (1427 – 1444)*

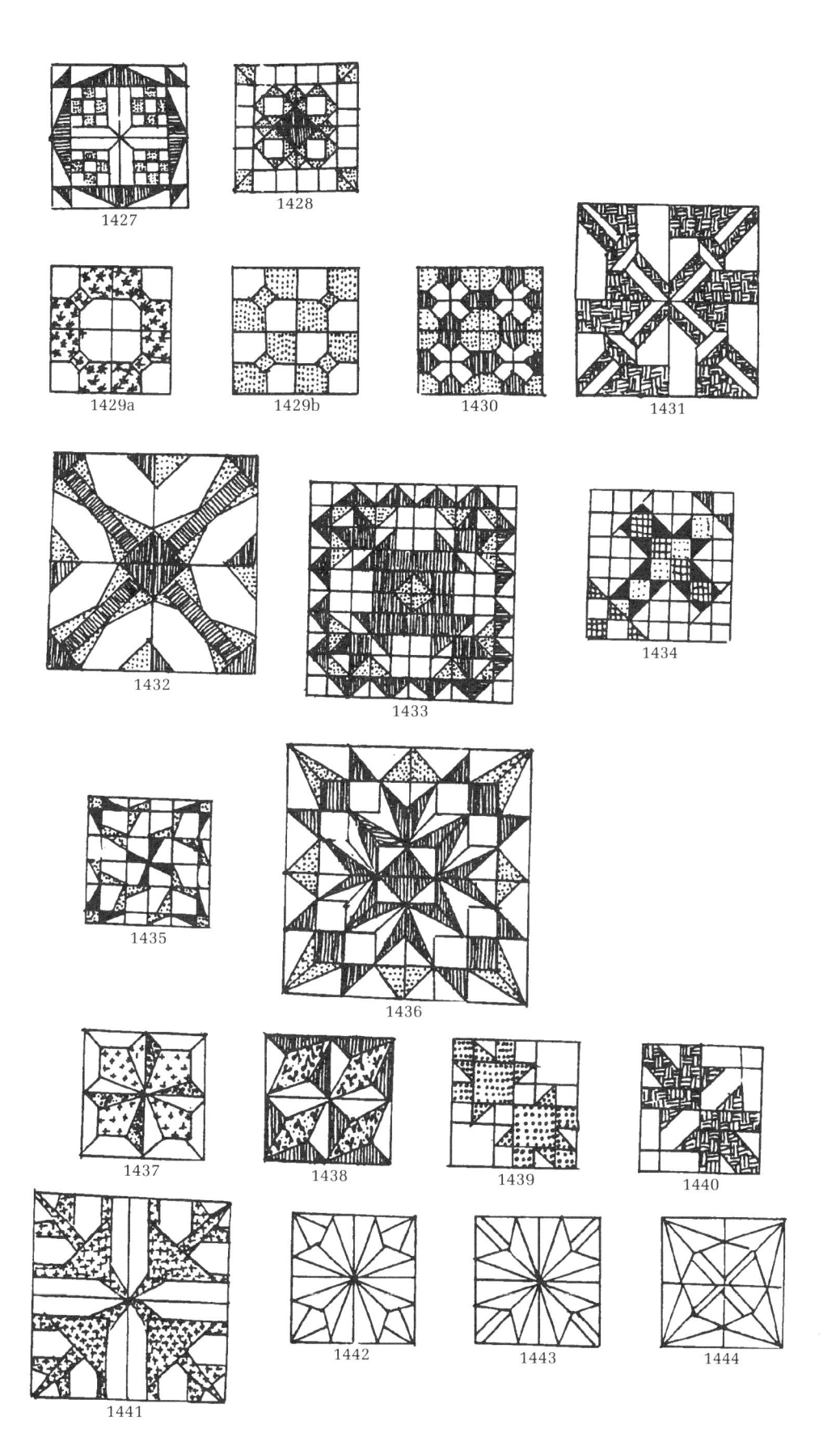

189

## Pattern Category 8: *Four Patch*

BLOCKS OF THIS CONSTRUCTION:

| | | |
|---|---|---|
| | 1450 | INDIANA PUZZLE – Carlie Sexton 1930<br>ROB PETER TO PAY PAUL – Hall<br>SNOWBALL – OCS Wheeler<br>STEEPLECHASE – Denver Art Museum. *See 2671.* |
| | 1451 | POLKA DOTS – Aunt Martha Bk. 3500, 1958. *See 2671.* |
| | 1452 | MILLWHEEL – McKim<br>SNOWBALL – Nancy Cabot 1933. *See 1517 & 2671.* |
| | 1453 | SNOWBALL – LAC #104. *See 2671.* |
| | 1454 | DIRTY WINDOWS – attributed to Nancy Cabot, Nancy's<br>SNOWY WINDOWS – QNM #104 |
| | 1455 | CHAIN QUILT – KC Star 1942 |
| | 1456 | MUSHROOMS – Farm Journal |
| | 1457 | SEA SHELLS – OCS Bk. 3, 1968 |
| | 1458 | THE DOVE – attributed to KC Star by QNM (alternated with plain blocks) |
| | 1459 | VINE OF FRIENDSHIP – Aunt Martha 1932<br>DIAGONAL STRIPES – Aunt Martha 1958<br>FALLING TIMBERS – Hinson<br>SNAKE TRAIL – QNM #104<br>DOVE – QNM #104 |
| | 1460 | GHOST WALK – attributed to Nancy Cabot, Nancy's. *See 1007.* |
| | 1461a | WANDERER'S PATH IN THE WILDERNESS – Farm and Home 1888<br>CRAZY QUILT – The Woman's Century<br>DRUNKARD'S PATH – LAC #46<br>WONDER OF THE WORLD – LAC<br>ROBBING PETER TO PAY PAUL – Finley<br>SOLOMON'S PUZZLE – Woman's World 1931<br>DRUNKARD'S TRAIL – Woman's World<br>OLD MAID'S PUZZLE – The Country Home 1933<br>ENDLESS TRAIL – Nancy Page 1934<br>CROOKED PATH – Nancy Page 1934<br>COUNTRY COUSIN – attributed to Nancy Cabot, Nancy's<br>WORLD'S WONDER – Nancy Cabot<br>BOSTON TRAIL – attributed to Nancy Cabot, Nancy's<br>THE PUMPKIN VINE – Orlofsky |
| | 1461b | OREGON TRAIL – Carlie Sexton<br>ROCKY ROAD TO DUBLIN – Hall<br>COUNTRY HUSBAND – Hall<br>THE ROAD TO CALIFORNIA – Workbasket |
| | 1461c | DRUNKARD'S TRAIL – Grandmother Clark Bk. 19<br>ROCKY ROAD TO DUBLIN – Grandmother Clark Bk. 19. *See 1039, 1040, & 3020.* |
| | 1462 | OREGON TRAIL – Carlie Sexton 1930<br>SOLOMON'S PUZZLE – Carlie Sexton 1930 |
| | 1463 | UNNAMED – Robertson (diamonds are appliquéd) |
| | 1464 | OLD MAID'S PUZZLE – Ohio Farmer 1896<br>SUNSHINE AND SHADOW – QNM #104 |

*Blocks with Specific Construction (1450 – 1464)*

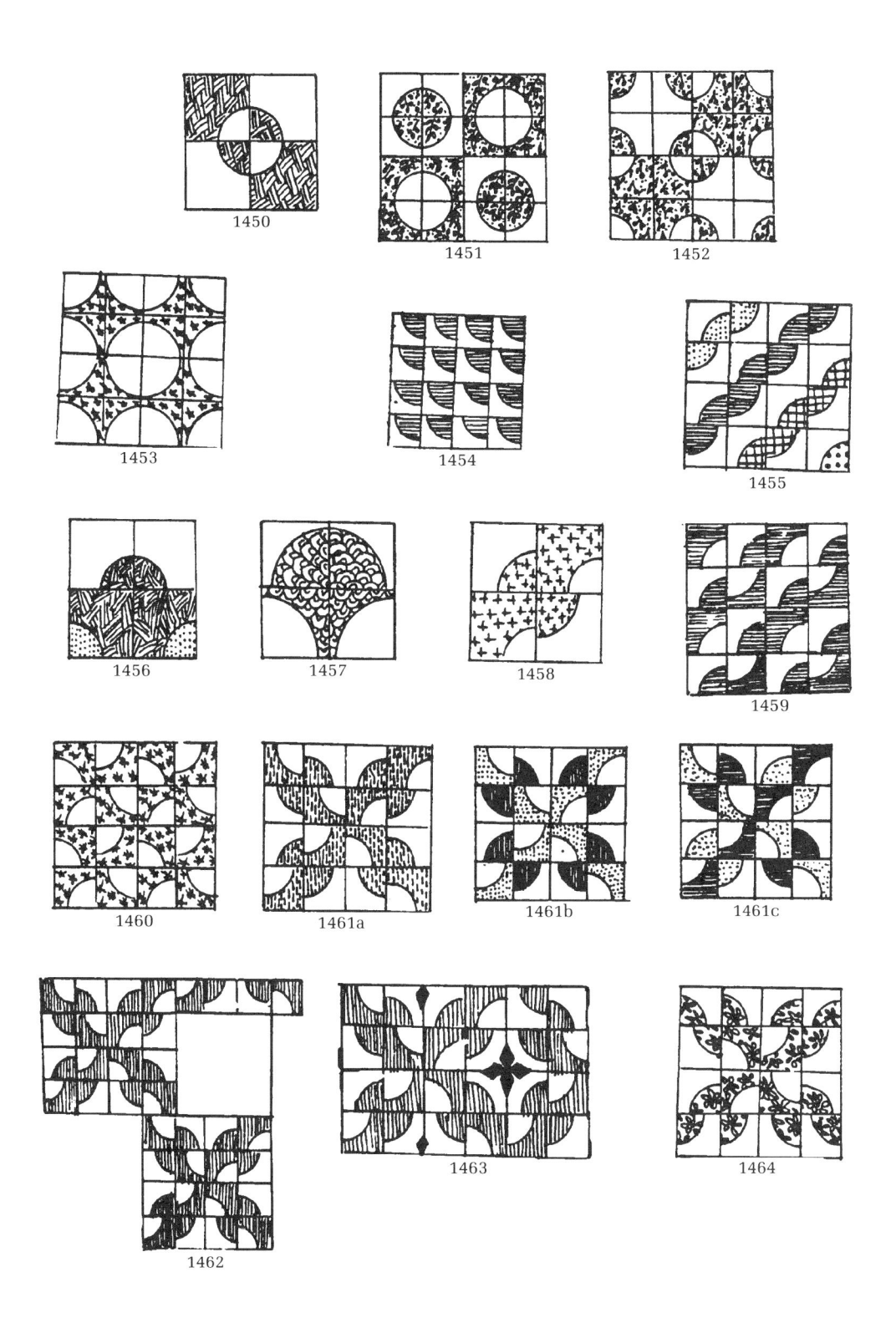

1450
1451
1452
1453
1454
1455
1456
1457
1458
1459
1460
1461a
1461b
1461c
1462
1463
1464

# Pattern Category 8: *Four Patch*

BLOCKS OF THIS
CONSTRUCTION:

| | | |
|---|---|---|
| **1465** | **Falling Timbers** – Aunt Martha 1932 | |
| **1466a** | **Fool's Puzzle** – Hall | |
| **1466b** | **Fool's Puzzle** – LAC #29 (2 colors) | |
| | **Arkansas Troubles** – Workbasket (3 colors) | |
| **1466c** | **Wonder of the World** – Capper's, Famous Features Bk. Q109 (2 colors) | |
| | **I Wish You Well** – Clarke (3 colors) | |
| | **Tumbleweed** – QNM #104 (2 colors, reversed shading) | |
| **1467** | **'Round the World** – Capper's | |
| | **Around the World** – Hall | |
| **1468** | **King Tut's Crown** – Prairie Farmer 1931 | |
| | **Cleopatra's Puzzle** – Nancy Cabot 1933 | |
| **1469** | **Nonesuch** – Aunt Martha | |
| | **Love Ring** – Hall | |
| | **The Jig Saw Puzzle** – KC Star 1940 | |
| | **Ozark Puzzle** – LCPQ 8 | |
| **1470** | **Chain Links** – Aunt Martha 1958 | |
| **1471** | **Around the World** – Holstein | |
| **1472** | **Rob Peter to Pay Paul** – Hinson QM | |
| **1473** | **Quilter's Delight** – Nancy Cabot | |
| **1474** | **Pictures in the Stairwell** – KC Star | |
| **1475** | **Oklahoma Dogwood** – Mountain Mist. *See 1037.* | |
| **1476** | **Windflower** – OCS Wheeler | |
| **1477** | **The Road Home** – Nancy Cabot | |
| **1478** | **Unnamed** – OCS Wheeler | |
| **1479** | **Turtle on a Quilt** – KC Star 1943 | |
| | **The Terrapin** – KC Star 1949 | |
| **1480** | **Time and Energy** – QNM #109 | |
| **1481** | **The Winding Trail** – Winthrop 1938 | |

*Many fan patterns could be indexed here but most are found under FANS, page 396.*

*Blocks with Specific Construction (1465 – 1481)*

193

# Pattern Category 8: *Four Patch*

FOUR PATCH
WITH CURVES

**1482**    Fair Play – LAC #454
Quarter Turn – Woman's World 1907
The Pig Pen – KC Star 1939
Wedding Ring – Dakota Farmer 1927

**1483**    Scrap Happy – OCS

**1484**    Moon and Stars – LAC #183

**1485**    Grandma's Red and White Quilt – Hinson

**1486**    The Formal Flower Bed – KC Star 1943

**1487**    Mill Wheel – OCS Brooks
Wagon Wheel Quilt – American Agriculturalist 1961

**1488**    The Electric Fan – KC Star 1938

**1489**    Pride of the Prairie – OCS Wheeler

**1490**    Evelyne's Whirling Dust Storm – KC Star 1943

**1491**    The Compass Quilt – KC Star 1930

**1492**    Old Maid Combination – LAC #214

**1493**    Square and Compass – Capper's, Home Art, McKim 101, Doyle. *See 2366, & 3188.*

**1494**    Merry Go Round – OCS Brooks

**1495**    Four Patch – OCS Wheeler
Southern Moon – OCS

**1496a**    Greek Square – LAC #328

**1496b**    Lansing – Hearth & Home. *See 2514.*

**1497**    Sunshine and Stained Glass – Progressive Farmer, Johnson 1976

**1498**    Love in a Tangle – KC Star
Pinwheel – Bruce Johnson. *See 1499.*

**1499**    Snowball – The Household Journal ca. 1920
Windmill Design – The Farmer's Wife ca. 1930.
*1499 and 1498 are identical if set all-over.*

*Four Patch with Curves (1482 – 1499)*

1482　1483　1484　1485

1486　1487　1488

1489　1490　1491　1492　1493

1494　1495　1496a　1496b

1497　1498　1499

195

# Pattern Category 8: *Four Patch*

FOUR PATCH
WITH CURVES

**1500**  HEARTS & GIZZARDS – Finley
PIERROT'S POM POM – Finley
SNOWBALL – Household Journal & Holland's Magazine, Dallas, ca. 1933
TENNESSEE SNOWBALL – Woman's World
SPRINGTIME BLOSSOMS – Mrs. Danner 1934
WINDMILL – OCS Brooks
DUTCH WINDMILL – OCS Wheeler, Capper's, Nancy Page
DUTCH ROSE – Home Art, Nancy Cabot
LOVER'S KNOT – Nancy Page, Aunt Martha
HEARTS & FLOWERS – Spool Cotton Bk. 160
MORNING GLORY – Aunt Martha
WHEEL OF FORTUNE – Ickis. *See 3189.*
PRIMROSE – The Farmer's Wife 1932

**1501**  MARTHA'S CHOICE – Nancy Cabot 1934
VIRGINIA'S CHOICE – Nancy Cabot

**1502**  SPRINGTIME BLOSSOMS – Hinson QM

**1503a**  HEARTS AND GIZZARDS – LAC #125
HEARTS – Needlecraft Supply ca. 1937
PIERROT'S POM POM – Hall
AUNT JERUSHA – attributed to Nancy Cabot, Nancy's

**1503b**  FRIENDSHIP QUILT – QNM #42

**1504a**  BASEBALL – LAC #179
CIRCLE DESIGN – Grandmother Clark Bk. 20, 1931

**1504b**  MARBLE – KC Star 1934

**1504c**  THE SILK PATCH QUILT – American Farmer 1896
STEEPLECHASE – Finley
BOW AND ARROWS – Finley

**1505**  BOSTON PUZZLE – LAC #249. *1504 & 1505 are identical when set all over.*
THE WINDING BLADE – KC Star 1937. *See 3349.*

**1506**  NEW MOON – attributed to Nancy Cabot, Nancy's, but doubtful. *See 4057.*

**1507**  SNOWBALL – QW 1979 (centers are white)
FIREBALL – QW 1979 (centers are red)

**1508**  PULLMAN PUZZLE – LAC #23
ROMAN PAVEMENTS – Nancy Cabot
BASEBALL – Hall
SNOWBALL – Hall

**1509**  YULETIDE – Aunt Kate

**1510**  BRIDLE PATH STAR – Aunt Kate 1966

**1511**  VEGETABLE SOUP – QNM #44

**1512**  WINDING WAYS – LAC #463
NASHVILLE – Hearth & Home
WHEEL OF MYSTERY – KC Star 1931, Grandmother Clark 1932
ROBBING PETER TO PAY PAUL – Hinson QM

**1513**  ELECTRIC FANS – Gutcheon PPP

*Four Patch with Curves (1500 – 1513)*

1500
1501
1502
1503a
1503b
1504a
1504b
1504c
1505
1506
1507
1508
1509
1510
1511
1512
1513

# Pattern Category 8: *Four Patch*

FOUR PATCH
WITH CURVES

| | | |
|---|---|---|
| | 1514 | **Sunshine and Shadow** – Nancy Cabot 1937<br>**Wonder of the World** – Nancy Cabot |
| | 1515 | **Snowball Wreath** – OCS Wheeler |
| | 1516 | **Biloxi** – Scribner's Magazine 1894<br>**Winding Walk** – LAC #409<br>**Fox Chase** – Hearth & Home 1902 *See QNM #110 for the history of this pattern.* |
| | 1516.5 | **The World's Fair** – LAC #134 |
| | 1517 | **Maltese Cross** – Delineator 1906<br>**Snowball** – Nancy Cabot. *See 1452* |
| | 1518 | **Snowball** – Nancy Cabot. *See 2656 & 305.8.* |
| | 1519a | **Pincushion** – LAC #133 *See 1527. See Cathedral Window, pg. 79.*<br>**Pincushion and Cucumbers** – Hearth and Home |
| | 1519b | **Rob Peter and Pay Paul** – McKim 101<br>**Orange Peel** – McKim 101<br>**Dolly Madison's Workbox** – McKim 101<br>**Love Ring** – KC Star 1931<br>**Sugar Bowl** – Nancy Page<br>**Mary's Choice** – Rural New Yorker 1933 |
| | 1519c | **Turn About Quilt** – OCS Brooks. *See 2683.* |
| | 1520 | **Dolly Madison's Workbox** – Carlie Sexton<br>**Robbing Peter to Pay Paul** – Hall<br>**Steeplechase** – Colby<br>**Peter and Paul** – Colby. *See 4075.*<br>**Mutual Benefit** – Clara Stone |
| | 1521 | **Everglades** – Nancy Cabot. *See 2687.* |
| | 1522 | **Light and Dark** – Aunt Kate 1964. (centers are appliqué) |
| | 1523 | **London Bridge** – Aunt Kate 1963 |
| | 1524 | **Melon Patch** – Woman's World. *See 1527.* |
| | 1525 | **Grist Mill** – Nancy Cabot |
| | 1526 | **Magic Circle** – Needlecraft |
| | 1527a | **Orange Peel** – LAC #107<br>**Lafayette Orange Peel** – McKim 101<br>**Save a Piece (Scraps)** – Holland's Magazine, Dallas 1933 |
| | 1527b | **Melon Patch** – Finley<br>**Flower Petals** – Woman's World. *See 1519. 1524 & 1527 are identical when set all over. See 1791.* |
| | 1528 | **Spring Beauty** – Heath |
| | 1529 | **Bay Leaf** – Aunt Martha ca. 1930 |
| | 1530 | **Rob Peter to Pay Paul** – Wallace's Farmer 1928<br>**The Melon Patch** – KC Star 1935 |
| | 1531 | **Whale Block** – LAC #490 |
| | 1532 | **Rose Dream** – KC Star 1930 & Aunt Martha<br>**Endless Chain** – Nancy Cabot 1933<br>**True Lover's Knot** – Home Art & Mrs. Danner 1934<br>**Broken Square** – KC Star 1938. *See 3090.*<br>**Martha** – Oklahoma Farmer Stockman 1932<br>**Lover's Knot** – Capper's 1930<br>**Lover's Bowtie** – Franks |

*Four Patch with Curves (1514 – 1532)*

1514
1515
1516
1516.5
1517
1518
1519a
1519b
1519c
1520
1521
1522
1523
1524
1525
1526
1527a
1527b
1528
1529
1530
1531
1532

199

Pattern Category 8: *Four Patch*

FOUR PATCH WITH CURVES

| | | |
|---|---|---|
| | 1533 | Winner's Circle – QNM #90 |
| | 1534 | Job's Tears – KC Star 1932. *See 3079.* |
| | 1535 | Twist and Turn – OCS Brooks |
| | | Summer and Winter – OCS |
| | 1536 | Carolina Favorite – OCS Wheeler |
| | 1537 | America's Pride – OCS Wheeler |
| | 1538 | Illinois Star – Aunt Kate 1965 (center leaves green, corn cobs yellow checks) |
| | 1539 | Old Missouri – KC Star |
| | 1540 | Snowball Flower – OCS |
| | 1541 | Foundation Rose – Grandmother's Bk. 6.6 |
| | 1542 | Dahlia – OCS Wheeler |
| | 1543 | Cubic Measure – Nancy Cabot. *See 2362.* |
| | 1544 | Waving Plumes – OCS Wheeler |
| | 1545 | Alice's Tulips – QNM93 |
| | 1546 | Bird of Paradise – Aunt Martha. *See 3098.* |
| | 1547 | Bride's Quilt – OCS |
| | | Heart Quilt – OCS |
| | 1548 | Oklahoma – Hearth & Home |
| | 1549 | Compass Point – Capper's 1955 |
| | 1550 | Twist and Turn – OCS Wheeler |
| | 1551 | Wedgewood Tiles – Nancy Cabot 1937, Frank's |
| | 1552 | Diamond Head – Nancy Cabot |
| | 1553 | Unnamed – QNM #103 |
| | 1554 | Tangled Trails – Nancy Cabot 1936 |
| | 1555 | Thirteenth Summer – Evelyn Brown |

*Four Patch with Curves (1533 – 1555)*

# PATTERN CATEGORY 9

## Equal Nine Patch

**Patterns in Category 9 share these characteristics:**

- The block is divided by two horizontal and two vertical seams to form a grid.

- The grid divides the block into nine equal squares or nine squares and rectangles.

**Category 9 includes:**

- Block is Squares and/or Rectangles, 204
- Stars with Specific Construction, 206
- Blocks with Specific Construction, 208
- Blocks with Specific Patch Unpieced, 216
- Blocks with Specific Construction, 218
- Asymmetrical Blocks, 218
- Misc. Equal Nine Patch Blocks, 220
- Nine Patch Blocks with Curves, 224

# KEY TO PATTERN CATEGORY 9: EQUAL NINE PATCH

### STEP 1
If the pattern is a star composed of small triangles and/or edged with small triangles,     ***turn to p. 276, Feathered Star***

If the pattern is not a Feathered Star,     ***continue with STEP 2 below***

### STEP 2
If the block is divided by the grid of seams into nine squares of equal size,     ***continue with STEP 4 below***

If the grid divides the block into squares and rectangles,     ***continue with STEP 3 below***

### STEP 3
If the block is divided by the grid of seams into a pattern in which the center is a small square,     ***turn to p. 227, Key to Unequal Nine Patch with small center square***

If the grid divides the block into a pattern in which the center is a large square,     ***turn to p. 253, Key to Unequal Nine Patch with large center square***

### STEP 4
If the block has curved seams,     ***turn to p. 224***

If the block has all straight seams,     ***continue with STEP 5 below***

### STEP 5
Go through the following list of characteristics in order. Choose the first statement which describes the pattern and turn to the page indicated.

### STEP 6
If the block is made of square and rectangular pieces only,     ***turn to p. 204***

### STEP 7
If the block is a star of this construction,     ***turn to p. 206***

### STEP 8
If the block is a star of this construction,     ***turn to p. 206***

### STEP 9
If the block is of this construction,     ***turn to p. 208***

### STEP 10
If the block is of this construction,     ***turn to p. 212***

### STEP 11
If the block is of this construction,     ***turn to p. 212***

### STEP 12
If the blocks have these unshaded patches unpieced,     ***turn to p. 216***

### STEP 13
If the blocks have these unshaded patches unpieced,     ***turn to p. 216***

### STEP 14
If the block is of this construction,     ***turn to p. 218***

### STEP 15
If the four corner patches are not identical or mirror images of each other,     ***turn to p. 218***

### STEP 16
If the block is of another construction,     ***turn to p. 220***

# Pattern Category 9: *Equal Nine Patch*

BLOCK IS SQUARES AND/OR RECTANGLES

| | | |
|---|---|---|
| | 1601a | **NINE PATCH** – Ohio Farmer 1896 |
| | | **CHECKERBOARD DESIGN** – Woman's World 1931. *See 1828 & 2385.* |
| | 1601b | **ALBUM QUILT** – Country Gentleman |
| | | **NINE PATCH** – Ickis |
| | 1601c | **PATIENCE NINE PATCH** – Gutcheon PPP |
| | | **EASY QUILT** – OCS Bk. 116 |
| | 1601d | **DOUBLE NINE PATCH** – OCS Bk 116. *See 1101, 1107, & 1001-1006.* |
| | 1602 | **THRIFTY** – KC Star 1939 |
| | 1603 | **PUSS IN THE CORNER** – Nancy Cabot, KC Star 1932. |
| | | **PUSSY IN THE CORNER** – Grandmother Clark 1931 |
| | 1604 | **DOUBLE NINE PATCH** – McKim |
| | | **DUTCH NINE PATCH** – McKim |
| | 1605 | **NINE PATCH CHAIN** – Gutcheon PPP |
| | 1606a | **DOUBLE NINE PATCH** – Webster |
| | | **FUNDAMENTAL NINE PATCH** – QNM 1973 |
| | | **SINGLE IRISH CHAIN** – Mountain Mist |
| | | **GOLDEN STEPS** – OCS |
| | | All set with alternate plain blocks. |
| | 1606b | **IRISH CHAIN** – Univ. of Kansas. Set with strips between blocks. |
| | 1607 | **NINE PATCH VARIATION** – Famous Features |
| | 1608 | **ILLINOIS ROAD** – Nancy Cabot 1935. *See 1102 & 1615.* |
| | 1611 | **FIVE PATCH** – LAC #82 |
| | | **GLORIFIED NINE PATCH** – Evelyn Brown |
| | 1612 | **BUILDING BLOCKS** – Household Magazine 1929 |
| | 1613 | **PUSS IN THE CORNER** – Hall. *See 2020.* |
| | 1614 | **PUSS IN THE CORNER** – Webster. *See 2021.* |
| | 1615 | **ILLINOIS ROAD** – Nancy Cabot 1933. *See 1608.* |
| | 1616 | **SQUARED CHAIN** – QNM 1976. |
| | 1617 | **ANTIQUE TILE BLOCK** – Nancy Cabot 1938. |
| | 1618 | **VIRGINIA WORM FENCE** – Clara Stone. *See 1110.* |
| | 1619 | **THE ROMAN SQUARE** – Wooster |
| | | **BEGGAR'S BLOCKS** – Wooster |
| | | **CATS AND MICE** – Wooster |
| | 1620 | **COLT'S CORRAL** – Prudence Penny 1932. *See 1112.* |
| | 1621 | **INDEPENDENCE SQUARE** – Famous Features (Obenchain) (red, white, & blue) |

*Block is Squares and/or Rectangles (1601a – 1621)*

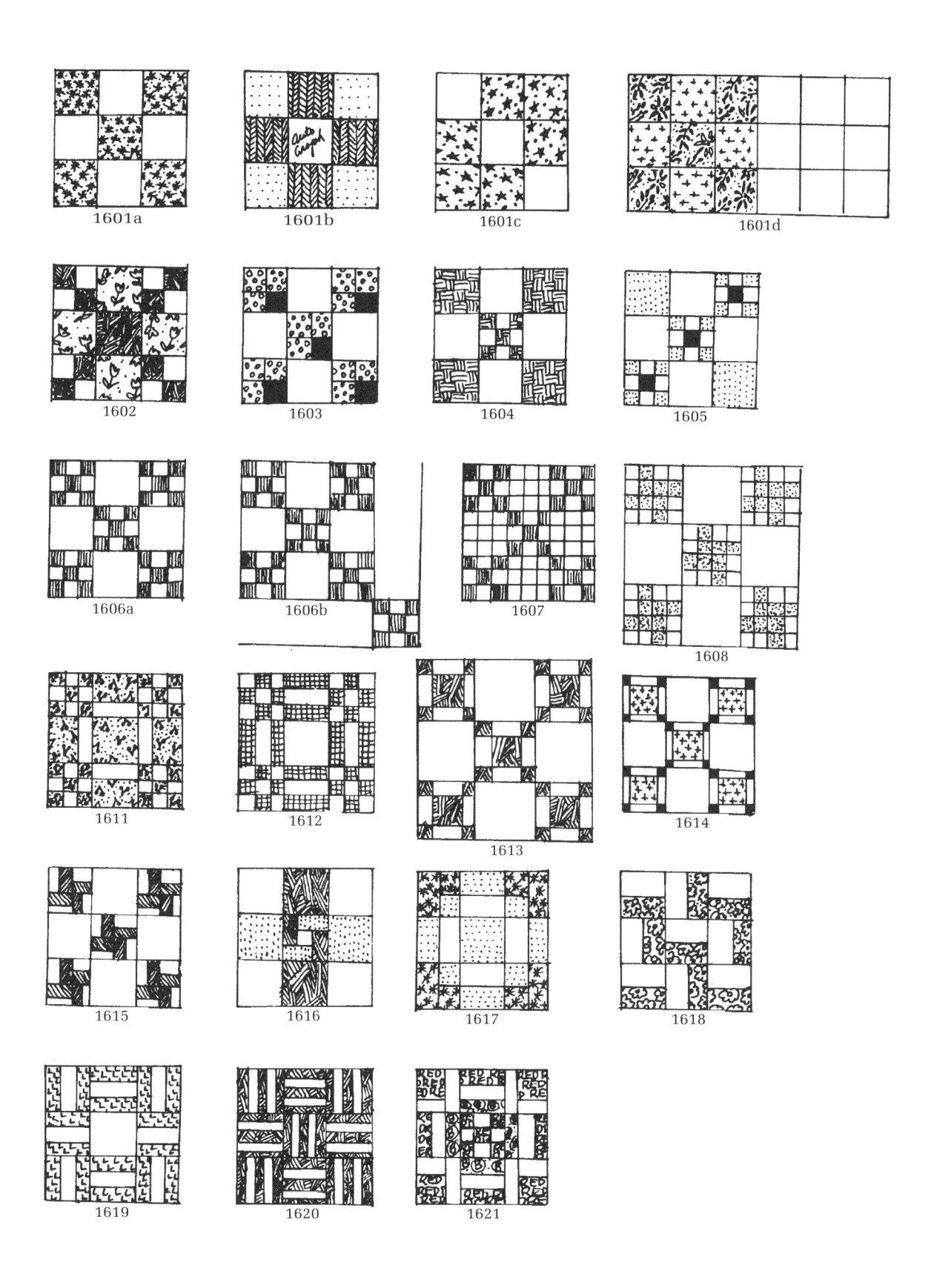

# Pattern Category 9: *Equal Nine Patch*

**STARS OF THIS CONSTRUCTION:**

| | | |
|---|---|---|
| | 1623 | SUN RAY'S QUILT – KC Star |
| | 1624 | THE EIGHT POINTED STAR – Needlecraft ca. 1918 |
| | 1625 | JUDY IN ARABIA – Gutcheon QDW |
| | 1626 | DORIS' DELIGHT – Farm Journal |
| | | ROAD TO PARADISE – Gutcheon QDW |
| | 1627a | GRANDMA'S STAR – Clara Stone |
| | | THE RAILROAD QUILT – Rural New Yorker 1934 |
| | | FIFTY-FOUR FORTY OR FIGHT – Finley (exact color combination not shown) |
| | 1627b | GARDEN WALK – KC Star 1940 |
| | | GARDEN PATCH – Grandma Dexter |
| | | TEXAS – Nancy Page |
| | 1627c | BIRD OF PARADISE – Quilt World 1976 |
| | 1629 | DOVE AT THE WINDOW – KC Star 1945 |

**STARS OF THIS CONSTRUCTION:**

| | | |
|---|---|---|
| | 1631a | MOSAIC PW #1 – Dictionary of Needlework |
| | 1631b | OHIO STAR – Nancy Cabot, Famous Features, Hall |
| | 1631c | EIGHT POINT DESIGN – LAC |
| | | LONE STAR – Hall |
| | | STAR DESIGN – Woman's World 1931 |
| | | TEXAS STAR – Hall |
| | | TIPPECANOE AND TYLER TOO – Hinson QC |
| | | TEXAS – Hinson QC |
| | | EASTERN STAR – Hinson QC |
| | | EIGHT POINT STAR – Hinson QC |
| | | SHOOFLY – Hinson QC |
| | | STAR – Vote |
| | 1631d | VARIABLE STAR – Finley |
| | | TEXAS – Finley |
| | | STAR SPANGLED – McCall's Magazine ca. 1930 |
| | | WESTERN STAR – Nancy Page |
| | | STAR OF THE WEST – NANCY Page |
| | | HENRY OF THE WEST – Nancy Page |
| | | STAR OF HOPE – Nancy Page |
| | | LONE STAR – Finley |
| | 1631e | FLYING CROW – Farm Journal. *See 2820.* |
| | 1632a | THE FOUR-X QUILT – Mrs. Danner 1970 |
| | 1632b | SWAMP ANGEL – Nancy Cabot |
| | 1633 | STAR X – Grandma Dexter |
| | | THE SILENT STAR – KC Star 1940 |
| | 1634 | MOSAIC – Nancy Page |
| | 1635 | MYSTERY FLOWER GARDEN – Aunt Martha |
| | 1636 | AUNT DINAH – Successful Farming 1946 (possibly OCS) |
| | 1637 | FOUR CORNERS – Grandma Dexter |
| | 1638 | TREASURE CHEST – OCS/Brooks. *See 2826.* |
| | | JACKNIFE – Gammel and Heard. |
| | 1639 | PHOENIX – Hearth & Home |
| | 1640 | DOLLEY MADISON'S STAR – Chicago Tribune 1975 |
| | 1641 | COMBINATION STAR – LAC |
| | | ORNATE STAR – Grandmother Clark |

*Stars with Specific Construction (1623 – 1641)*

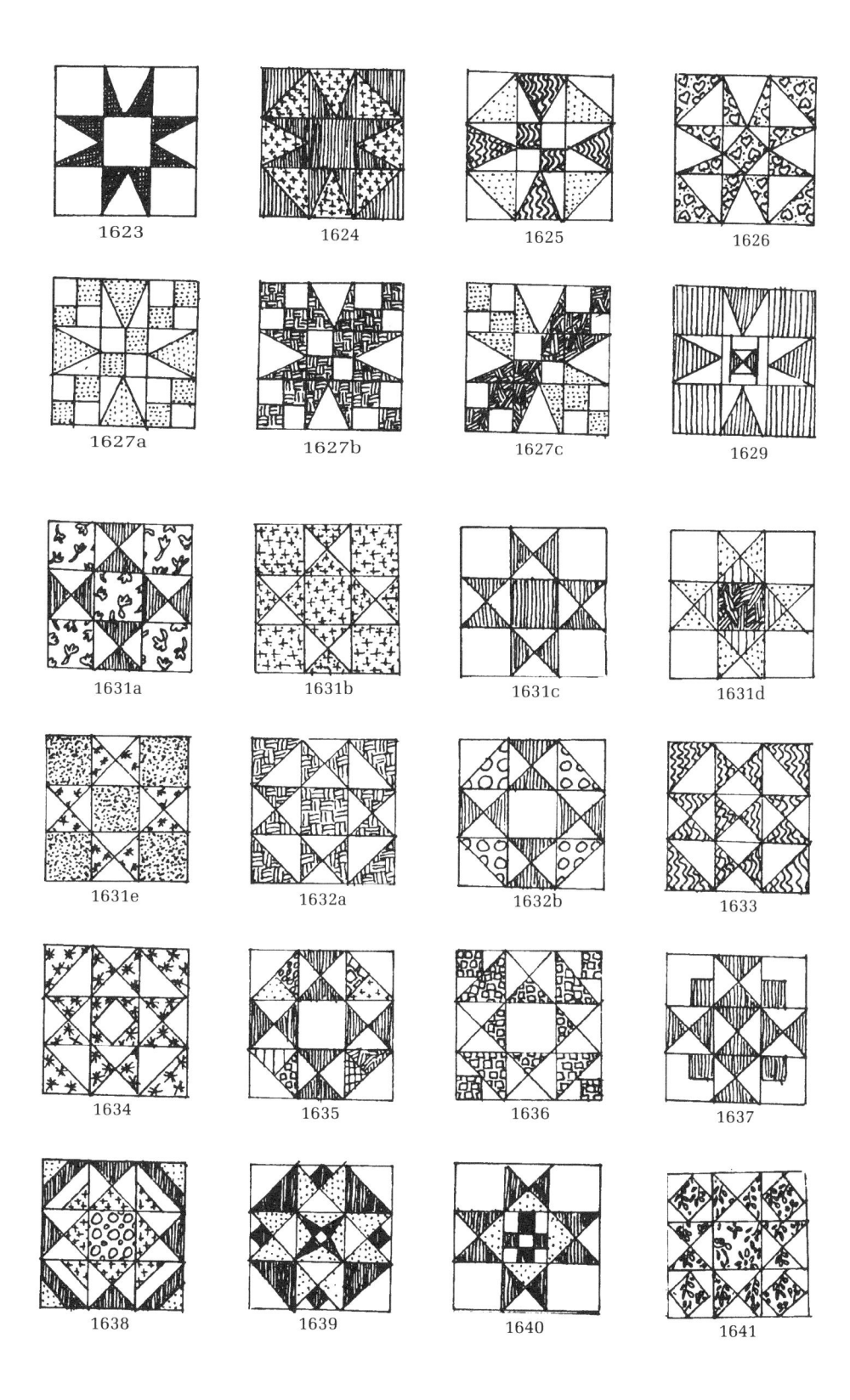

1623  1624  1625  1626

1627a  1627b  1627c  1629

1631a  1631b  1631c  1631d

1631e  1632a  1632b  1633

1634  1635  1636  1637

1638  1639  1640  1641

# Pattern Category 9: *Equal Nine Patch*

**STARS OF THIS CONSTRUCTION:**

**BLOCKS OF THIS CONSTRUCTION:**

**1642**    OLD SNOWFLAKE – Nancy Cabot

**1643**    TANGLED ARROWS – Aunt Kate 1966

**1645**    SHOO FLY – LAC #276
THE EIGHT-CORNERED BOX – The American Farmer 1896
FENCE ROW – KC Star 1931 (Set on diagonal in a zigzag set)
FIFTY-FOUR FORTY OR FIGHT – Nancy Cabot (set with strips and squares)
SIMPLICITY – OCS Bk. 116. *See 1847, 1936, & 2032.*

**1646a**    DOUBLE MONKEY WRENCH – Finley
CHURN DASH – McKim 101
OLD MILL DESIGN – The Farmer's Wife
HENS AND CHICKENS – Wallace's Farmer 1928
DOUBLE T – Hearth and Home
SHOO FLY – Nancy Cabot
SHERMAN'S MARCH – Capper's/Famous Feature
MONKEY WRENCH – Ickis
LOVE KNOT – Hall
HOLE-IN-THE-BARN-DOOR – Hall
PUSS-IN-THE-CORNER – Hall
SHOO-FLY – Hall
LINCOLN'S PLATFORM – Hall
INDIAN HAMMER – Rural New Yorker 1932
QUAIL'S NEST – Mrs. Danner 1975
BROKEN PLATE – attributed to Nancy Cabot, Nancy's
JOAN'S DOLL QUILT – Nancy Page (colors reversed)
FISHERMAN'S REEL – Little 'n Big 1965
PICTURE FRAME – Little 'n Big 1965
LUDLOW'S FAVORITE – Little 'n Big 1965

**1646b**    GRECIAN DESIGNS – LAC
GRECIAN SQUARE – Woman's World
GRECIAN – Woman's World
GREEK SQUARE – Nancy Cabot

**1646c**    GREEK CROSS – McKim

**1646d**    DRAGON'S HEAD – Woman's World. *See 1850.*

**1647**    CROW'S NEST – KC Star 1933
ATTIC WINDOW – Nancy Page

**1648**    FRIENDSHIP QUILT – KC Star 1934

**1649**    NEW WATERWHEEL – Nancy Cabot

**1650**    STILES AND PATHS – Capper's
PATH AND STILES – Nancy Cabot
SHOO FLY – LAC
FAR WEST – attributed to Nancy Cabot, Nancy's

**1651**    SQUARED CHAIN – QNM 1976

**1652**    SAW TOOTH PATCHWORK – LAC #271
MRS. BROWN'S CHOICE – Needlecraft Supply 1938
ANOTHER SAWTOOTH – Gutcheon PPP

**1653**    FIVE SPOT – Nancy Cabot

**1654**    RICHMOND – Hearth & Home
AUNT VINA'S FAVORITE – Aunt Martha
PIN WHEEL – KC Star 1930
BUTTERFLY – Nancy Cabot
LUCY'S FOUR AND NINE – Meeker

**1655**    CROSS AND CHAINS – Nancy Cabot 1938

**1656**    TRUE BLUE – Hearth and Home
PRAIRIE QUEEN – Finley

**1657**    RIBBON QUILT – Nancy Page. *See 1160.*

**1658**    MOSAIC #8 – LAC #336
LONDON ROADS – Nancy Page (set all over)

**1659**    ALBUM – QNM (Heirloom Plastics Catalog)

**1660**    CEDARS OF LEBANON – Hearth and Home
NEW ALBUM – KC Star 1934
AVA'S FRIENDSHIP QUILT – DuBois

*Blocks with Specific Construction (1642 – 1660)*

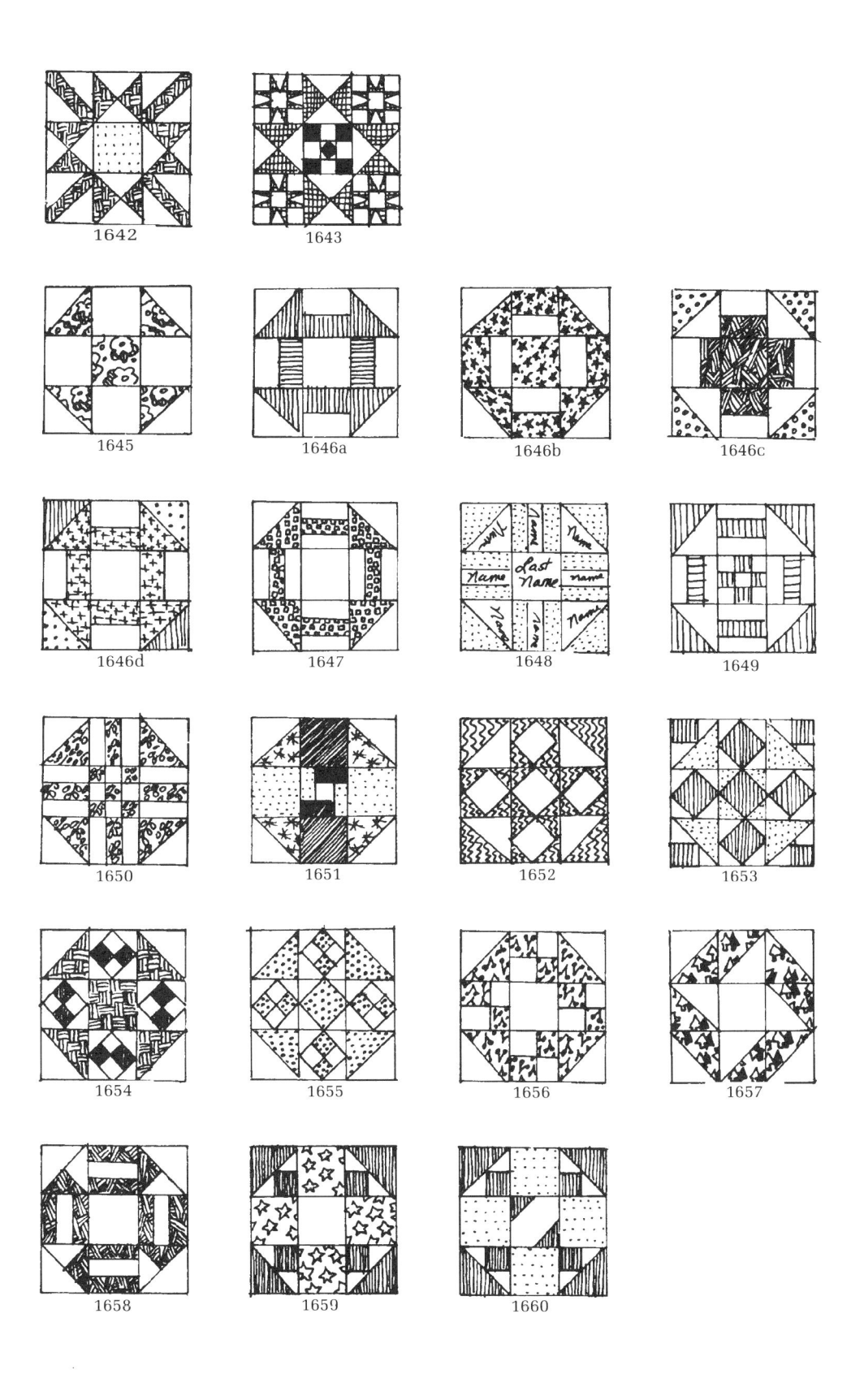

1642
1643
1645
1646a
1646b
1646c
1646d
1647
1648
1649
1650
1651
1652
1653
1654
1655
1656
1657
1658
1659
1660

209

# Pattern Category 9: *Equal Nine Patch*

BLOCKS OF THIS CONSTRUCTION:

| | | |
|---|---|---|
| **1661** | **BIG T** – attributed to Nancy Cabot, Nancy's, but unlikely |
| **1662a** | **FRIENDSHIP QUILT** – Capper's/Famous Features |
| **1662b** | **CAPITAL T** – LAC #84 |
| | **DOUBLE T** – Nancy Page |
| | **CUT THE CORNERS** – On a quilt ca. 1910 |
| **1662c** | **CAPITAL T** – Household Magazine |
| **1662d** | **DOUBLE T** – Nancy Page |
| | **FOUR T SQUARE** – Nancy Cabot. *See 1385.* |
| **1663** | **CUPS AND SAUCERS** – KC Star 1936 |
| **1664** | **ILLINOIS** – Hearth & Home |
| **1665** | **IMPERIAL T** – LAC #88 |
| | **CAPITAL T** – Hall |
| | **TEA FOR FOUR** – Nancy Page. *See 1385 & 2650.* |
| | **BIG T** – Dakota Farmer 1927 |
| **1666** | **WCTUNION** – LAC #161 (in green & white) |
| | **WCTU PATCH** – Hall (in blue & white) |
| | **WCTU** – Household Journal |
| | **MONTGOMERY** – Hearth & Home |
| | **CELESTIAL PROBLEM** – Nancy Cabot 1935 |
| **1667** | **NEW CROSS & CROWN** – Clara Stone |
| **1668** | **SUMMER WINDS** – Nancy Page |
| **1669** | **PUSS IN THE CORNER** – Nancy Page |
| **1670** | **BROKEN WINDOWS** – KC Star 1937 |
| **1671** | **JOSEPH'S COAT** – Finley |
| | **SCRAPBAG** – Finley |
| **1672** | **MOLLIE'S CHOICE** – LAC #315 |
| **1673** | **MISSOURI PUZZLE** – Clara Stone. *See 1817.* |
| **1674** | **CROW'S NEST** – Gutcheon QDW |
| | **CARD TRICK** – Gutcheon in McCall's |
| **1675a** | **THE LETTER X** – LAC #279 |
| **1675b** | **FLYING X** – Finley |
| **1677a** | **FIRESIDE VISITOR** – Clara Stone |
| | **ROPE AND ANCHOR** – KC Star 1937 |
| | **AT THE SQUARE** – Nancy Page |
| | **ARROW** – Aunt Martha |
| | **COLORADO'S ARROWHEAD** – Workbasket 1935 |
| | **BETTY'S CHOICE** – Needlecraft Supply ca. 1938 |
| **1677b** | **LONDON ROADS** – LAC #238 |
| **1678** | **CHAIN AND HOURGLASS** – Nancy Page |
| **1679** | **CREOLE PUZZLE** – Nancy Cabot 1938 |
| **1680** | **THE DANDY QUILT BLOCK** – The Woman's Century ca. 1910 |

*Blocks with Specific Construction (1661 – 1680)*

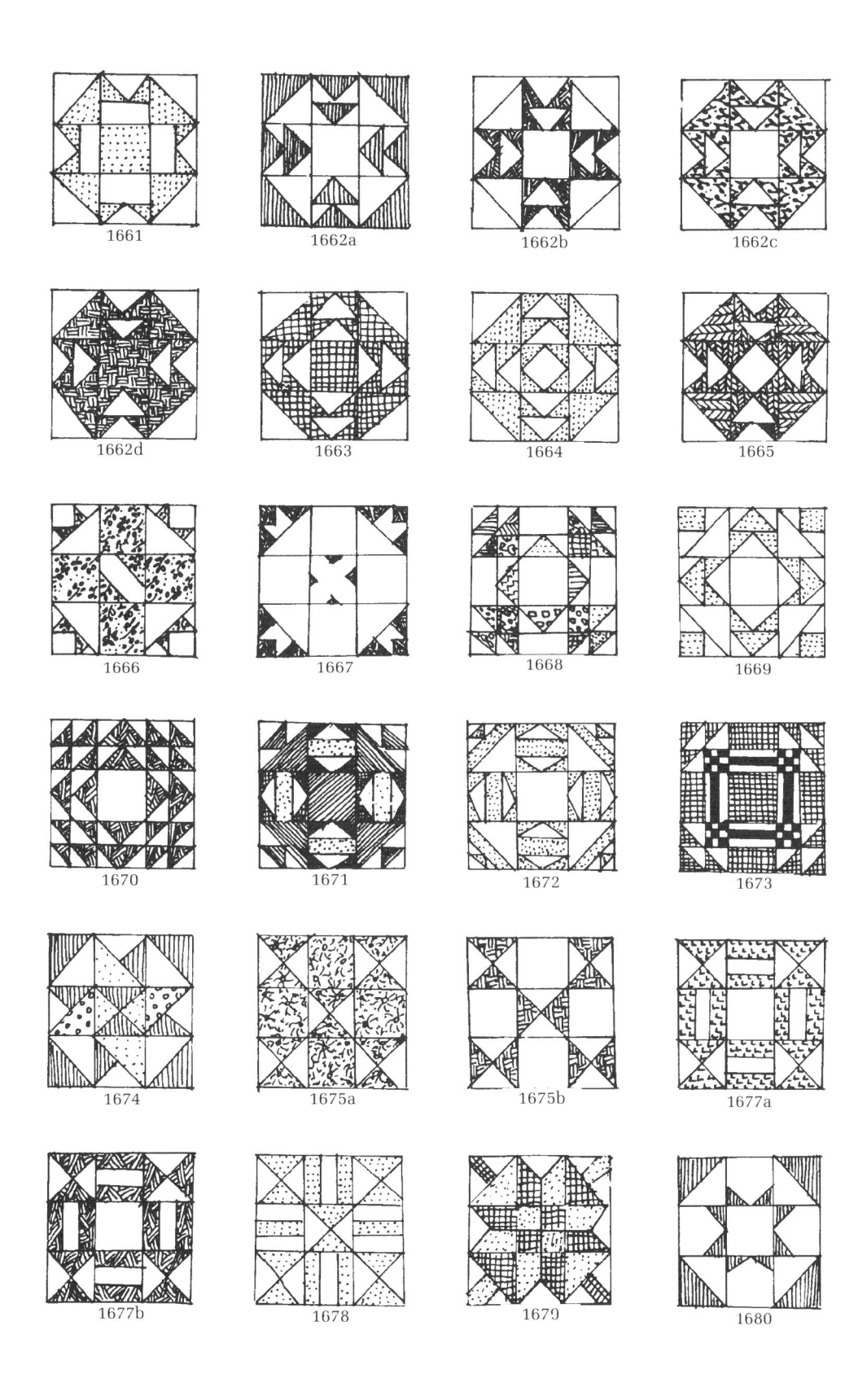

211

# Pattern Category 9: *Equal Nine Patch*

BLOCKS OF THIS CONSTRUCTION:

| | | |
|---|---|---|
| **1681a** | THE CALICO PUZZLE – KC Star 1930 | |
| **1681b** | THE SPOOL – Gammel | |
| **1682** | FARM FRIENDLINESS – Farm Journal | |
| **1683a** | ECCENTRIC STAR – Capper's/Famous Features | |
| **1683b** | ECCENTRIC STAR – attributed to Nancy Cabot, Nancy's. *See 2597.* | |
| **1684** | INDIANA PUZZLE – McKim's Parade of States | |
| **1685a** | PRACTICAL ORCHARD – LAC #141 | |
| **1685b** | HOUR GLASS #2 – Clara Stone. *See 1707.* | |
| **1686** | JEFFREY'S NINE PATCH – Gutcheon | |

BLOCKS OF THIS CONSTRUCTION:

**1687a** DOUBLE HOUR GLASS – Nancy Cabot 1933

**1687b** ATTIC WINDOW – Farm Journal. *See 3257.*

**1687c** CONTRARY WIFE QUILT – KC Star 1941

**1687d** ROAD TO CALIFORNIA – Gutcheon PPP (4 set in mirror image). *See 3023.*

**1688** SPLIT NINE PATCH – Hall. *See 1690 & 3258.*

**1689a** JACKS ON SIX – Ohio Farmers 1894
OLD MAID'S PUZZLE – American Farmer 1895
DOUBLE X #1 – LAC #76. *See 1692.*
THREE AND SIX – Nancy Cabot 1936
KINDERGARTEN BLOCK – Needlecraft Supply ca. 1938

**1689b** JACK AND SIX – Nancy Page
TENNESSEE – Nancy Page

**1690** SPLIT NINE PATCH – Capper's/Famous Feature. *See 1688.*

**1691** SPIDER – attributed to Nancy Cabot, Nancy's. *See 1202.*

**1692a** DOUBLE X – Capper's in Quilting: A New, Old Art

**1692b** WILD GEESE – Capper's in Quilting: A New, Old Art
ONE WAY – attributed to Nancy Cabot, Nancy's, but unlikely
TRIP TO THE ALTAR – Craft Horizons, 1968 (set all over, each block different)
GEOMETRIC PATCHWORK – University of Kansas, 1978 (set with a zigzag set)

**1692c** SLANTED DIAMONDS – attributed to Nancy Cabot, Nancy's, but unlikely. *See 113, 1132, 1311, & 3150.*

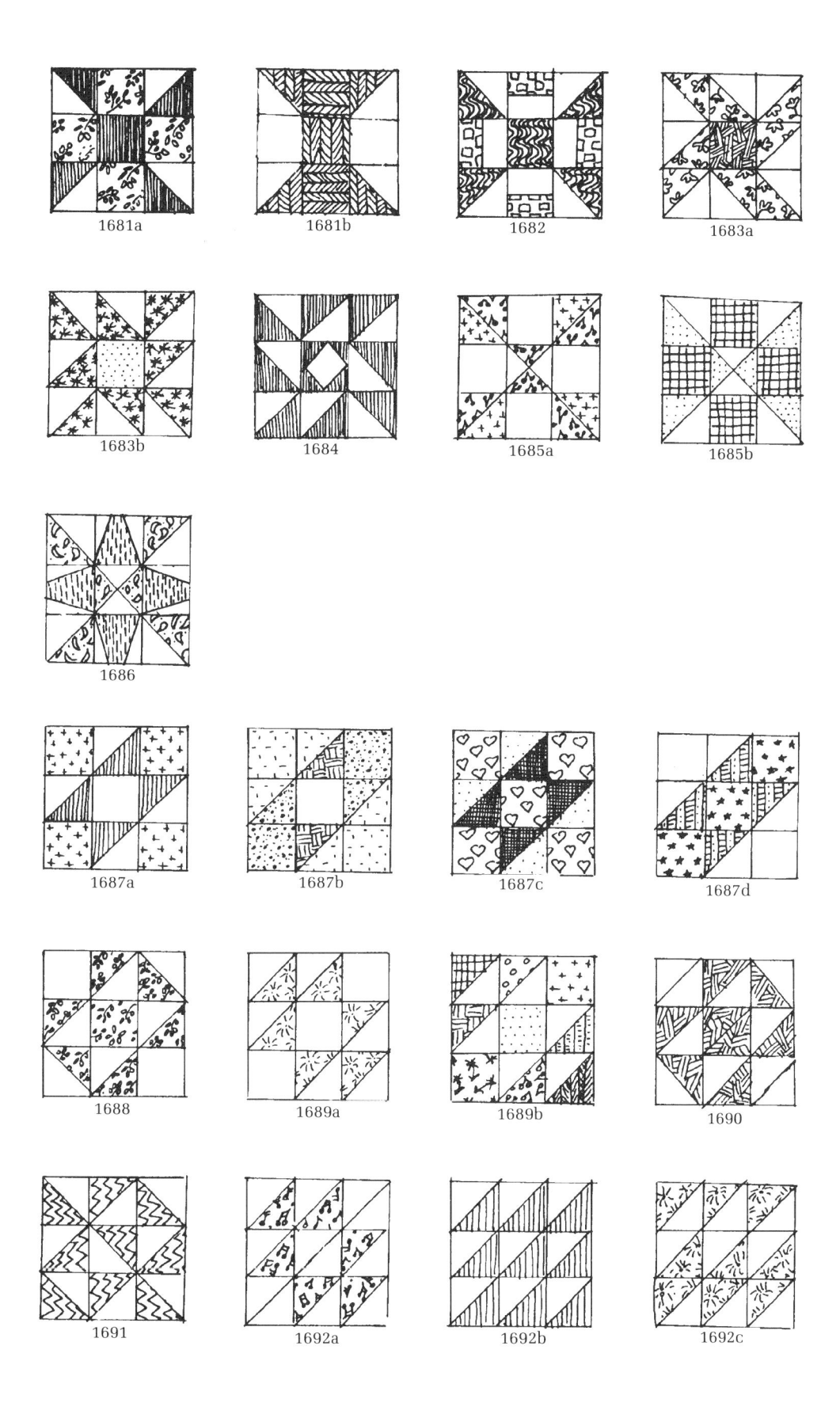

*Blocks with Specific Construction (1681a – 1692c)*

1681a  1681b  1682  1683a

1683b  1684  1685a  1685b

1686

1687a  1687b  1687c  1687d

1688  1689a  1689b  1690

1691  1692a  1692b  1692c

213

# Pattern Category 9: *Equal Nine Patch*

BLOCKS OF THIS CONSTRUCTION:

| | | |
|---|---|---|
| | **1693a** | HOME QUEEN – on a quilt ca. 1910<br>ROCKY ROAD TO CALIFORNIA – LAC #237 |
| | **1693b** | THE BROKEN SUGAR BOWL – KC Star 1942<br>ROAD TO THE WHITE HOUSE – Farm Journal |
| | **1694** | STEPS TO THE ALTAR – Jane Allen, Illinois State Register 1932 |
| | **1695a** | THE RAILROAD – LAC #207<br>JACOB'S LADDER – Webster<br>GOLDEN STAIRS – Nancy Cabot 1936<br>ROAD TO CALIFORNIA – McKim, 101 Quilt Patterns<br>OFF TO SAN FRANCISCO – Nancy Page<br>GOING TO CHICAGO – Nancy Page<br>SUSIE'S FANCY – Source Unknown |
| | **1695b** | JACOB'S LADDER – McKim<br>STEPPING STONES – Finley<br>THE TAIL OF BENJAMIN'S KITE – Finley<br>TRAIL OF THE COVERED WAGON – Finley<br>WAGON TRACKS – Finley<br>UNDERGROUND RAILROAD – Finley<br>DOUBLE HOUR GLASS – Grandmother Clark 1931 |
| | **1695c** | WAGON TRACKS – McKim's Parade of the States<br>PACIFIC RAIL ROAD – Nancy Cabot 1936 |
| | **1695d** | FOOT PRINTS IN THE SANDS OF TIME – Drover's Journal |
| | **1695e** | BLUE CHAINS – Nancy Cabot 1936 |
| | **1696** | ROCKY ROAD TO DUBLIN – Nancy Cabot 1933 |
| | **1697** | QUEEN'S PETTICOAT – Needlecraft for Today 1979 (set all over, mirror image) |
| | **1698** | DUBLIN STEPS – Grandma Dexter |
| | **1699** | FLYING SHUTTLES – Nancy Cabot 1937 |
| | **1700** | HARRISON – Dakota Farmer 1929<br>DOVE AT THE WINDOW – Comfort<br>WANDERING LOVER – Hearth and Home 1895<br>HARRISON ROSE – Rural New Yorker 1930<br>CAT'S CRADLE – KC Star 1934<br>THE HARRISON QUILT – Famous Features<br>FLYING BIRDS – Nancy Page<br>HOUR GLASS – Nancy Page<br>DOUBLE PYRAMIDS – Mrs. Danner Bk. 7 |
| | **1701** | WANDERING LOVER – On a quilt ca. 1910<br>DOUBLE HOUR GLASS – Aunt Martha |
| | **1702** | DOUBLE PYRAMID – KC Star 1933 |
| | **1703** | CUT GLASS DISH – LAC<br>WINGED SQUARE – Finley<br>GOLDEN GATES – Finley<br>PRISM BLOCK – Needlecraft Supply ca. 1937 |
| | **1704** | AIR CASTLE – LAC #101<br>TOWERS OF CAMELOT – Nancy Cabot 1937 |

*Blocks with Specific Construction (1693a – 1704)*

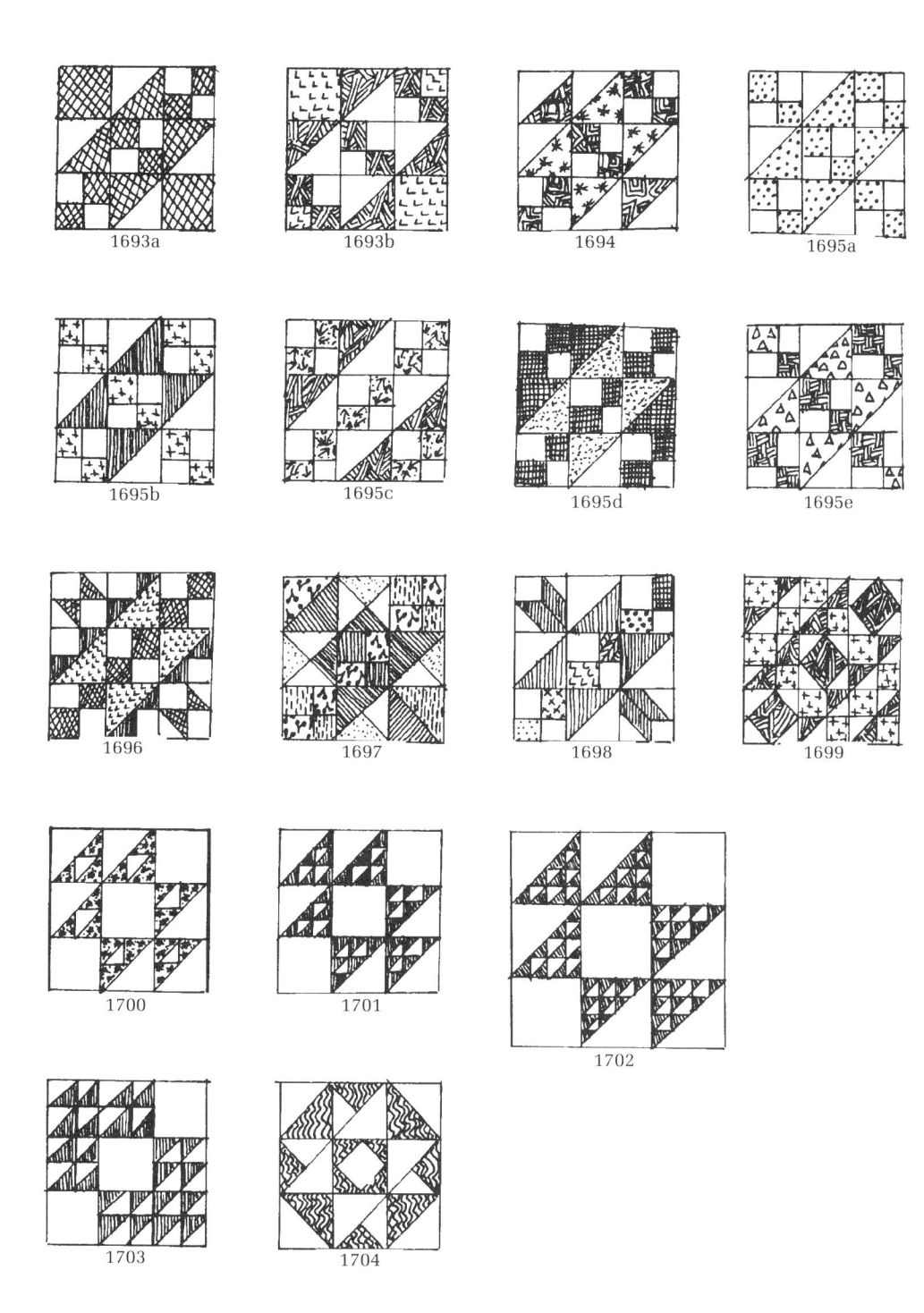

215

# Pattern Category 9: *Equal Nine Patch*

| | | |
|---|---|---|
| BLOCKS WITH THESE UNSHADED PATCHES UNPIECED | **1705** | HOUR GLASS – Finley |
| | **1706** | NINE PATCH STRAIGHT FURROW – Holstein<br>NINE PATCH VARIATION – Holstein<br>PERKIOMEN VALLEY – Nancy Roan in *Quilt Making in Goschenhoppen* Oral Tradition, Lewisburg, PA, 1986 |
| | **1707** | PRACTICAL ORCHARD – Nancy Cabot 1934. *See 1685.* |
| | **1708** | FLUTTER WHEEL – LAC #39<br>WINDMILL – Ladies' Home Journal 1903<br>PIN WHEELS – McKim 101. *See 1262.*<br>CLOVER LEAF – Dakota Farmer 1927 |
| | **1709** | WINDMILL – Good Housekeeping Bk. of Needlecraft |
| | **1710** | CLUSTER OF STARS – LAC #393<br>LONE STAR – Bruce Johnson. *See 2138.* |
| | **1711** | STAR IN A NINE PATCH – Prudence Penny. *See 3735.* |
| | **1712** | JOSEPH'S NECKTIE – LAC #43. *See 1376 & 1429.* |
| | **1713** | SAGE BUD – KC Star 1930<br>MEXICAN STAR – Hinson. *See 1889.* |
| | **1714** | ECONOMY NINE PATCH – Mrs. Danner Bk. 7. *See 2376.* |
| | **1715** | STAR CHAIN – QNM #43, 1973 |
| BLOCK WITH THESE UNSHADED PATCHES UNPIECED | **1716** | TRIPLET – KC Star 1933 |
| | **1717** | SIMPLEX STAR – Hearth and Home<br>THE PIN WHEEL – KC Star 1953<br>THE LOST GOSLIN' – KC Star 1939 |
| | **1718** | NINE PATCH T – Mrs. Danner Bk. 7 |
| | **1719** | LADIES' AID ALBUM – KC Star 1938 |
| | **1720** | THE 1941 NINE PATCH – KC Star 1941 |
| | **1721** | PRESIDENT CARTER – Quilt World Sept/Oct, 1977 |
| | **1722** | STAR A – LAC #399<br>AN A STAR – Nancy Cabot 1935 |
| | **1723** | FLAG IN, FLAG OUT – KC Star 1939 |
| | **1724** | MALTESE CROSS BLOCK – Nancy Cabot 1936 |
| | **1725** | SANTA FE BLOCK – LAC #467 |
| | **1726** | SANTA FE TRAIL – Nancy Cabot 1934 |

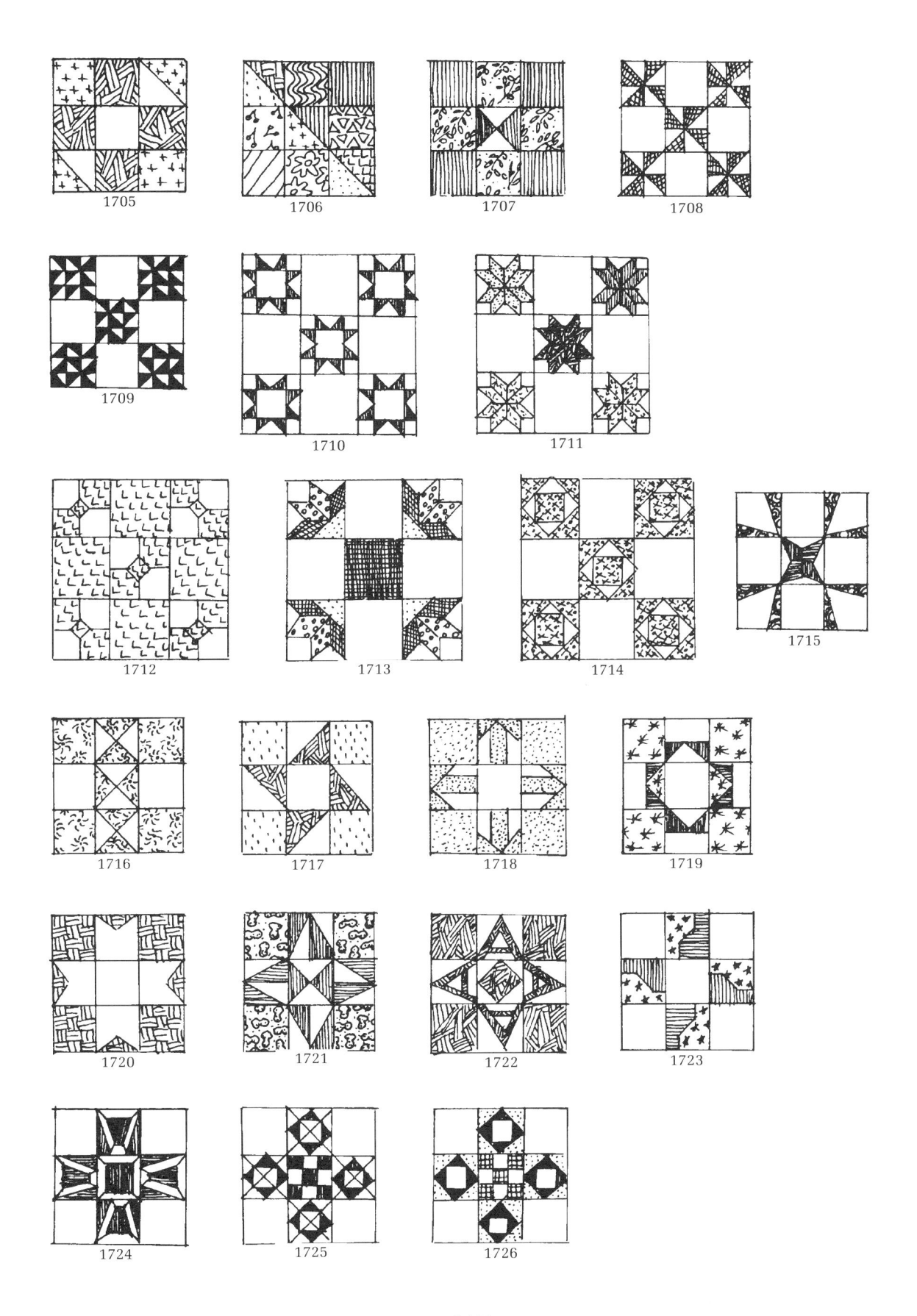

*Blocks with Specific Patches Unpieced (1705 – 1726)*

1705 1706 1707 1708
1709 1710 1711
1712 1713 1714 1715
1716 1717 1718 1719
1720 1721 1722 1723
1724 1725 1726

217

# Pattern Category 9: *Equal Nine Patch*

BLOCKS OF THIS CON-
STRUCTION:

| | 1727a | ROLLING STONE – LAC #216
WEDDING RING – Dakota Farmer 1927
LETTER O – Dakota Farmer 1921 |
|---|---|---|
| | 1727b | SQUIRREL IN A CAGE – KC Star 1935
SINGLE WEDDING RING – Comfort or Household Magazine
WHEEL – Hall
ANDERSON – attributed to Nancy Cabot, Nancy's, but unlikely
JOHNNIE-ROUND-THE-CORNER – QNM #61, 1974
BLOCK CIRCLE – QNM #61, 1974 |
| | 1727c | NEW HAMPSHIRE'S GRANITE ROCK – Workbasket 1935
KITTY CORNER – On a quilt ca. 1910 |
| | 1727d | BROKEN WHEEL – Clara Stone
PEEK-A-BOO – Joseph Doyle
MRS. MILLER'S FAVORITE – Needlecraft Supply ca. 1930 |
| | 1728 | KITTY CORNER – Finley
PUSS IN THE CORNER – Finley
TIC TAC TOE – Finley |
| | 1729 | BLOCKHOUSE – Nancy Cabot 1936 |
| | 1730 | PEEKABOO – Woman's World 1531 |
| | 1731 | ROLLING SQUARES – Nancy Cabot |
| | 1732a | EIGHT-POINT ALLOVER – Source Unknown
KANSAS STAR – KC Star 1932 |
| | 1732b | MONTPELIER – Hearth & Home. *See 1171 & 2375.* |
| | 1733 | MOTHER'S DREAM – Nancy Page, Aunt Martha
GRANDMOTHER'S DREAM – Mahler
TURKEY IN THE STRAW – Farm Journal 1937 |
| ASYMMETRICAL BLOCKS | 1734 | TEA LEAF – Modern Priscilla 1928
TEA LEAVES – Nancy Cabot 1937
BEAR TRACKS – Nancy Cabot 1937
DUCK'S FOOT IN THE MUD – Nancy Cabot 1937
MAPLE LEAF QUILT – NNT 1971. *See 1885 & 1886.* |
| | 1735 | MAPLE LEAF – Clara Stone
MAGNOLIA LEAF – Clara Stone. *See 1887.*
ALBUM – Comfort |
| | 1736 | AUTUMN LEAF – OCS Wheeler. *See 2224.*
POPLAR LEAF – Comfort |
| | 1737 | TEA LEAVES – Webster. *See 1944.* |
| | 1738 | DARTING BIRDS – Nancy Page |
| | 1739 | TASSAL PLANT – LAC #389 |
| | 1740 | MAPLE LEAF – Aunt Martha |
| | 1741 | TRIPLE ROSE – Aunt Martha 1963 |

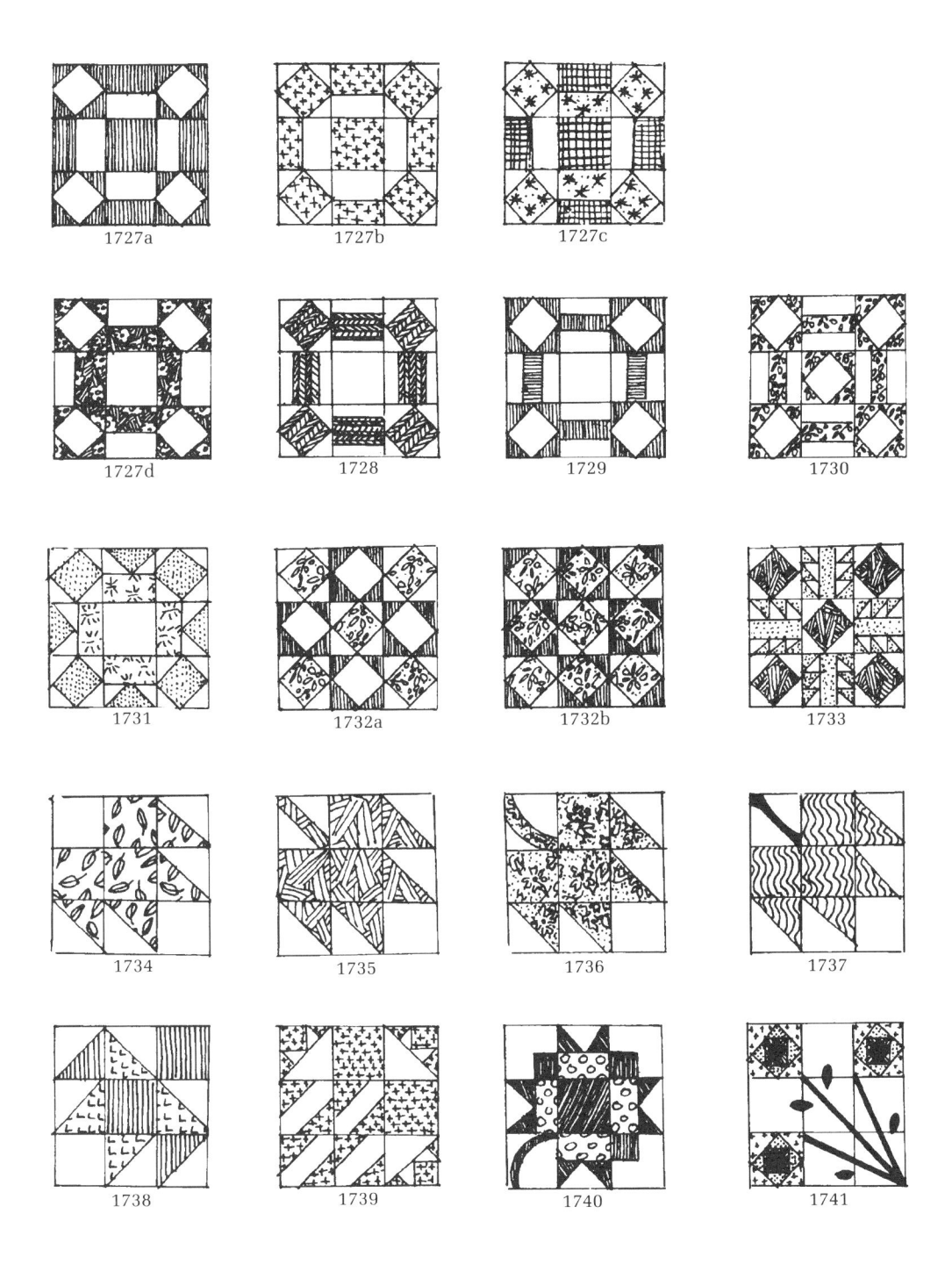

*Blocks with Specific Construction, Asymmetrical Blocks (1727a – 1741)*

| 1727a | 1727b | 1727c |
| 1727d | 1728 | 1729 | 1730 |
| 1731 | 1732a | 1732b | 1733 |
| 1734 | 1735 | 1736 | 1737 |
| 1738 | 1739 | 1740 | 1741 |

# Pattern Category 9: *Equal Nine Patch*

MISC. EQUAL NINE PATCH BLOCKS

| | | |
|---|---|---|
| | 1745a | HANDWEAVE – LAC #526 |
| | 1745b | CITY STREETS – Nancy Cabot 1937 |
| | 1746 | INTERWOVEN – Nancy Page |
| | | HAND WEAVE – Nancy Page |
| | | HANDWOVEN – Nancy Page |
| | | STRIPS AND SQUARES – Nancy Page |
| | | OVER AND UNDER – Nancy Page |
| | | HANDCRAFT – Nancy Cabot 1934 |
| | 1747 | BISHOP HILL – Nancy Cabot 1935 |
| | 1748 | TEXAS TREASURE – Nancy Page |
| | 1749 | MISSISSIPPI – Hearth & Home |
| | 1750 | BROKEN PATHS – Aunt Kate 1966. *See 3250.* |
| | 1751 | NONSUCH – LAC #363. *See 3250.* |
| | 1752 | EAST TO EDEN – Gutcheon QDW. *See 3250.* |
| | 1753 | CROSS ROADS – Nancy Page 1935. *See 2192.* |
| | 1754 | TANGLED GARTER – LAC #124 |
| | | CROSSROADS – Nancy Page |
| | | SUN DIAL – Nancy Cabot 1936. *See 1054.* |
| | | GARDEN MAZE – Nancy Cabot 1936 |
| | 1755 | PRAIRIE FLOWER – attributed to Nancy Cabot |
| | 1756 | A PATCHWORK CUSHION TOP – KC Star 1943 |
| | 1757 | FLYING LEAVES – Nancy Cabot 1936 |
| | 1758a | HOMESPUN – Nancy Page |
| | 1758b | BEGGAR BLOCK – LAC #68 |
| | | OVER AND UNDER QUILT DESIGN – Nancy Page |
| | 1758c | BEGGAR'S BLOCKS – Finley |
| | | CATS AND MICE – Finley |
| | | SPOOL AND BOBBIN – Nancy Cabot 1936 |
| | 1759 | BEGGAR'S BLOCKS – Nancy Page |
| | 1760 | WATER MILL – Grandmother Clark |

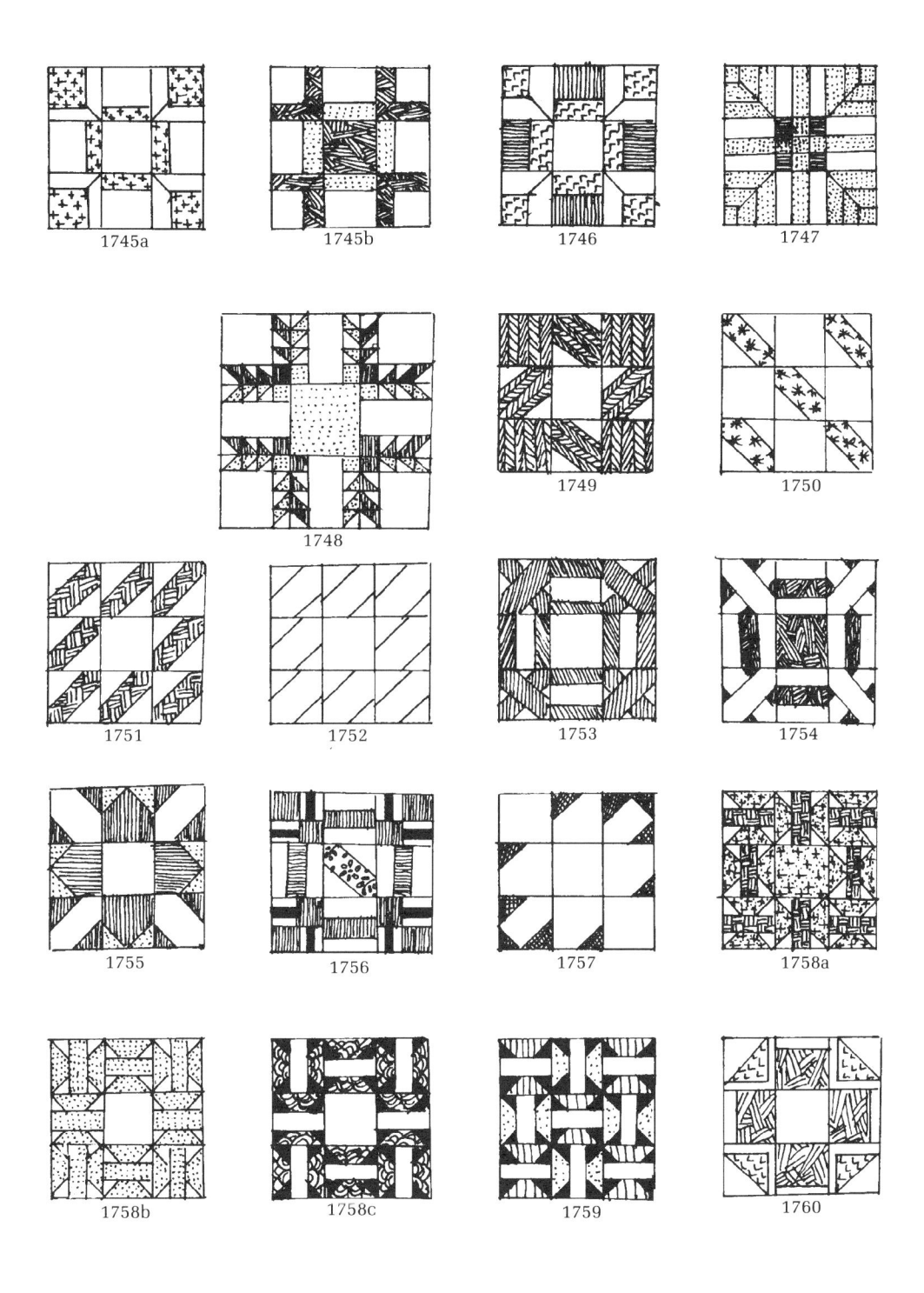

*Misc. Equal Nine Patch Blocks  (1745a – 1760)*

1745a   1745b   1746   1747

1748   1749   1750

1751   1752   1753   1754

1755   1756   1757   1758a

1758b   1758c   1759   1760

221

Pattern Category 9: *Equal Nine Patch*

MISC. EQUAL NINE PATCH BLOCKS

| | | |
|---|---|---|
| | 1761 | PROOF THROUGH THE NIGHT – J. Gutcheon, QNM 1977 |
| | 1762 | WAMPUM BLOCK – Nancy Cabot 1938 |
| | 1763a | SWASTIKA – Household Journal<br>SQUARE AND HALF SQUARE – KC Star 1933 |
| | 1763b | WATER WHEEL – Farm Journal |
| | 1763c | CHINESE COIN – Aunt Martha (set with bars and squares) |
| | 1763d | WATER WHEEL – Nancy Cabot. *See 1142.* |
| | 1764 | THE CHEESEBOX QUILT – Country Gentleman 1932 |
| | 1765 | CROSS PATCH – Aunt Kate 1966 |
| | 1766 | MRS. DEWEY'S CHOICE – Hearth & Home ca. 1890, Clara Stone. *See 2880 & 2099.* |
| | 1767 | SWING-IN-THE-CENTER – Clara Stone. *See 2881.* |
| | 1768 | WYOMING VALLEY BLOCK – Nancy Cabot |
| | 1769 | INDIAN PUZZLE – Nancy Cabot 1936. *See 1157.* |
| | 1770 | AMISH STAR – Dubois |
| | 1771 | ROBBING PETER TO PAY PAUL – LAC #154<br>ARIZONA – Nancy Page |
| | 1772 | MEMORY – Clara Stone |
| | 1773 | SQUASH BLOSSOM – Quilt World April, 1980 |
| | 1774 | THUNDER AND LIGHTNING – attributed to Nancy Cabot, Nancy's |
| | 1775 | VIRGINIA – Hearth & Home<br>MORNING STAR – LAC #7<br>ROSEBUD – Nancy Cabot 1934 |
| | 1776 | COLUMBIAN STAR – LAC #50 |
| | 1777 | CHICAGO STAR – LAC #22 |

*Misc. Equal Nine Patch Blocks (1761 – 1777)*

1761
1762
1763a
1763b
1763c
1763d
1764
1765
1766
1767
1768
1769
1770
1771
1772
1773
1774
1775
1776
1777

223

Pattern Category 9: *Equal Nine Patch*

| | | |
|---|---|---|
| MISC. EQUAL NINE PATCH BLOCKS | **1778** | ALICE'S FAVORITE – Hinson QM. *See 2541.* |
| | **1779** | PROSPERITY BLOCK – Nancy Cabot 1933<br>PROSPERITY QUILT – Prairie Farmer Bk. 1, 1931. *See 3609 & 4049.* |
| | **1780** | WEATHERVANE – McKim, Woman's World. *See 4033.* |
| | **1781** | GUIDING STAR – KC Star 1933 |
| | **1782** | MONA'S CHOICE – KC Star 1940 |
| | **1783** | THE STAR SPANGLED BANNER – KC Star 1941 |
| | **1784** | TWENTY T'S – Nancy Page<br>TWENTY TEES – Nancy Page. *See 1392, 3274, & 3275.* |
| NINE PATCH BLOCKS WITH CURVES | **1790** | PLANE THINKING – QNM #98, 1978 |
| | **1791** | UNNAMED – Robertson, set with alternate plain blocks. *See 1527.* |
| | **1792** | LOCK AND CHAIN – LAC #452<br>AMETHYST CHAIN – attributed to Nancy Cabot |
| | **1793** | MAGNOLIA BUD – Hinson QM |
| | **1794** | BLUEBELL – KC Star 1940 |
| | **1795** | QUEEN'S PRIDE – OCS Wheeler. *See 2222.* |
| | **1796** | WHEEL OF TIME – probably Comfort Magazine. *See 3314 & 4097.* |
| | **1797** | FAN AND RING – KC Star 1940<br>FANS AND A RING – KC Star 1948. *See 3305.* |

*Misc. Equal Nine Patch Blocks, Nine Patch Blocks with Curves (1778 – 1797)*

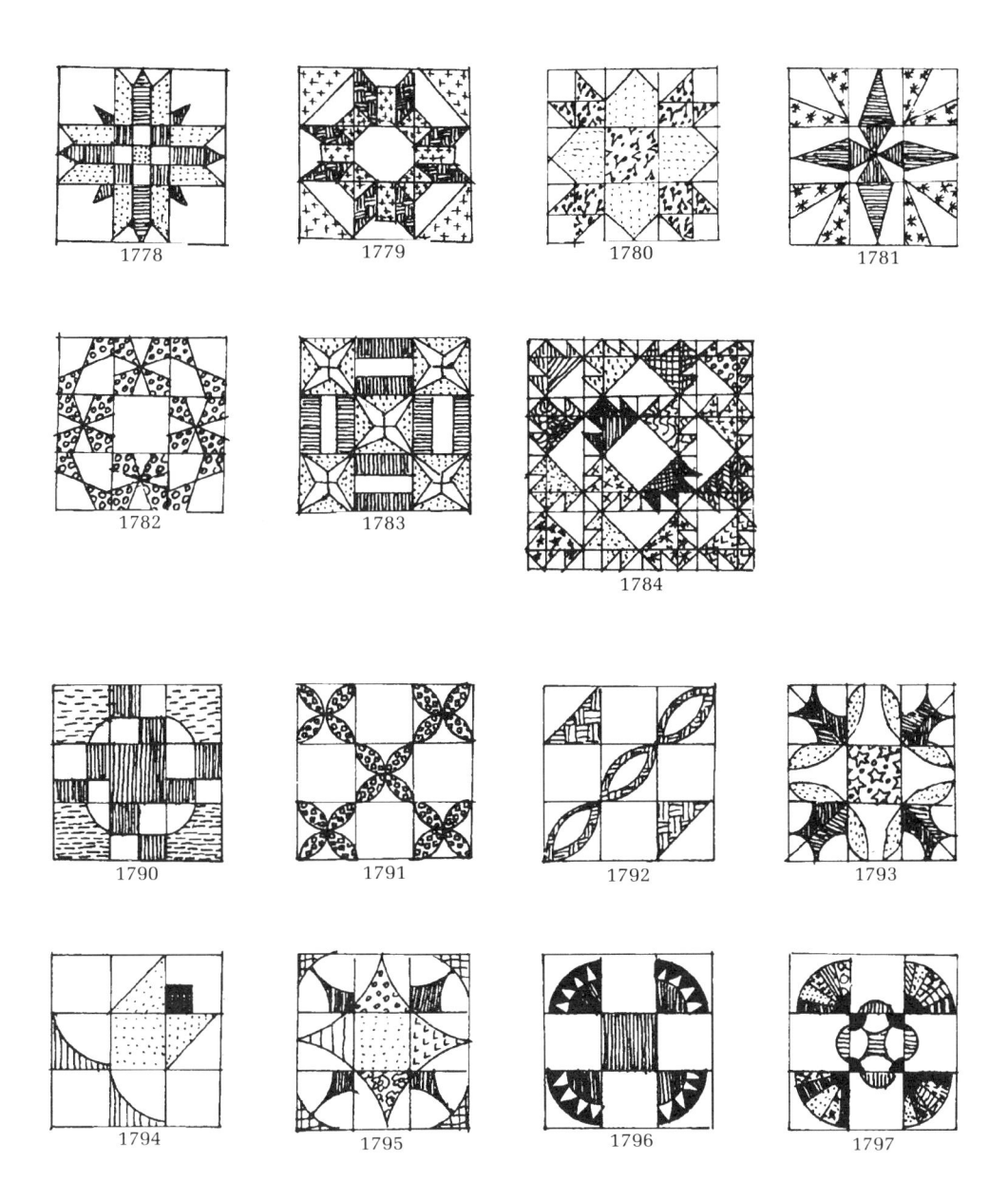

1778   1779   1780   1781

1782   1783   1784

1790   1791   1792   1793

1794   1795   1796   1797

# PATTERN CATEGORY 10

## Unequal Nine Patch with Small Center Square

**Patterns in Category 10 share these characteristics:**

- The block is divided by two horizontal and two vertical seams that form a grid.

- The grid divides the block into nine sections, some of which are squares and some of which are rectangles.

- The center square in the block is relatively small.

**Category 10 includes:**

- Blocks with Twenty-Five Squares, 228
- Blocks with Squares & Rectangles, 232
- Blocks of Specific Construction, 234
- Blocks with Unpieced Bars, 238
- Other Types of Blocks, 244
- Blocks with Curves, 250

**KEY TO PATTERN CATEGORY 10: UNEQUAL NINE PATCH WITH SMALL CENTER SQUARE**

If the block has curved seams, *turn to p. 250*

If the block is made of 25 equal squares , *turn to p. 228*

If the block is made of squares and rectangles only , *turn to p. 232*

If the block is of this construction , *turn to p. 234*

If the block is constructed with unpieced bars such as these , *turn to p. 238*

If the block is of another type of construction, *turn to p. 244*

# Pattern Category 10: *Unequal Nine Patch with Small Center Square*

| | | |
|---|---|---|
| TWENTY-FIVE SQUARES | **1801** | STATE OF GEORGIA – Workbasket 1935 |
| | **1802a** | 4X STAR – LAC #163<br>CHURN-DASHER – Hearth and Home<br>FIVE PATCH STAR – Gutcheon PPP |
| | **1802b** | NEW ENGLAND BLOCK – Needlecraft Supply ca. 1930<br>GREEK CROSS – KC Star 1954. *See 1930, 2129, 3034, 3229, & 3230.* |
| | **1802c** | FATHER'S CHOICE – James |
| | **1803** | DEWEY DREAM QUILT – Orange Judd Farmer 1899 |
| | **1804** | ROUND THE CORNER – Nancy Page<br>JOHNNY ROUND THE CORNER – Nancy Page |
| | **1805** | WISHING RING – Mrs. Danner 1934 |
| | **1806a** | WEDDING RING – LAC #48<br>ROLLING STONE – Farmer's Wife 1920<br>NEST AND FLEDGLING – KC Star 1933 |
| | **1806b** | ODD SCRAPS PATCHWORK – LAC #159<br>MILL WHEEL – Nancy Page<br>ENGLISH WEDDING RING – Nancy Page<br>VICE PRESIDENT'S BLOCK – attributed to Nancy Cabot<br>OLD FASHIONED WEDDING RING – The Country Gentleman ca. 1950 |
| | **1806c** | CHRISTMAS STAR – The Oklahoma Farmer Stockman |
| | **1806d** | CROWN OF THORNS – Capper's<br>GEORGETOWN CIRCLE – Hall<br>MEMORY WREATH – Hall<br>CROWN AND THORNS – Ickis |
| | **1806e** | WEDDING RING – KC Star 1930<br>OLD ENGLISH WEDDING RING – KC Star |
| | **1806f** | WEDDING RING – Gutcheon |
| | **1807a** | STRENGTH IN UNION – Nancy Cabot 1938 |
| | **1807b** | STRENGTH IN UNION – Famous Features (Bicentennial Quilts). *See 3150.* |
| | **1808** | BATON ROUGE SQUARE – Nancy Cabot 1936 |
| | **1809** | KING'S CROWN – Nancy Cabot |
| | **1810** | QUEEN CHARLOTTE'S CROWN – (Nancy Cabot) Grandmother's Quilt Bk. 11-5<br>QUEEN'S CROWN – (Nancy Cabot). *See 4134.* |

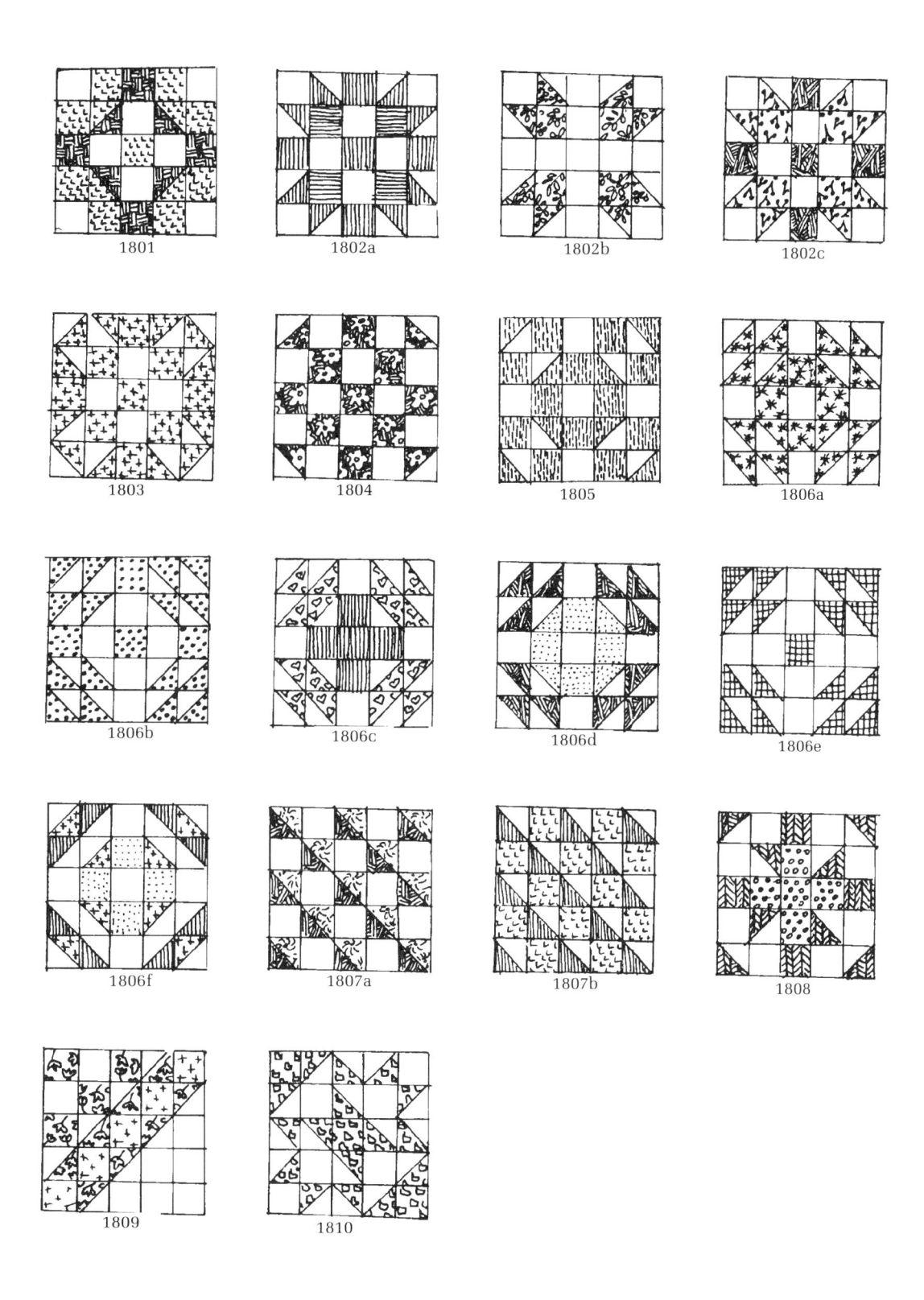

*Twenty-Five Squares (1801 – 1810)*

1801　　　1802a　　　1802b　　　1802c

1803　　　1804　　　1805　　　1806a

1806b　　　1806c　　　1806d　　　1806e

1806f　　　1807a　　　1807b　　　1808

1809　　　1810

229

# Pattern Category 10: *Unequal Nine Patch with Small Center Square*

TWENTY-FIVE SQUARES

| | | |
|---|---|---|
| | 1811 | SINGLE CHAIN AND KNOT – Nancy Cabot 1937 |
| | 1812a | ALBUM QUILT – LAC #267 |
| | 1812b | THE ALBUM PATTERN – Capper's<br>SOUTH CAROLINA'S ALBUM BLOCK – Workbasket 1935. *See 1119.* |
| | 1813 | ALBUM PATCH – Hall |
| | 1814 | UNNAMED – Bishop and Safanda |
| | 1815a | GOOSE IN THE POND – LAC #202<br>UNIQUE NINE PATCH – Wallace's Farmer 1928<br>YOUNG MAN'S FANCY – Finley<br>PATCHWORK FANTASY – Household Magazine 1929<br>GENTLEMAN'S FANCY – Modern Priscilla<br>GEOMETRIC GARDEN – Grandma Dexter<br>SCRAP BAG – KC Star 1935 (shading reversed)<br>MRS. WOLF'S RED BEAUTY – Mrs. Danner 1970<br>UNNAMED – Comfort 1923 |
| | 1815b | BACHELOR'S PUZZLE – Nebraska Collections |
| | 1816 | UNNAMED – Comfort 1923 (Note error in shading) |
| | 1817a | NEW MEXICO – Hearth & Home<br>MEXICAN BLOCK – Country Gentleman 1937<br>THE MISSOURI PUZZLE – Mrs. Danner 1970. *See 1673.* |
| | 1817b | MISSOURI PUZZLE – KC Star 1930 |
| | 1817c | BALANCE – Nancy Page |
| | 1817d | THE (NEW) MEXICAN STAR – Workbasket 1935 |
| | 1818 | QUEEN'S CROWN – Nancy Cabot 1933 |
| | 1819 | PROVIDENCE – Nancy Cabot. *See 2920.* |
| | 1820 | HANDY ANDY – LAC #254<br>FOOT STOOL – attributed to Nancy Cabot, Nancy's<br>MRS. JONES' FAVORITE – Needlecraft Supply ca. 1937 |
| | 1820.5 | CLOWN – LAC #524. *See 2301.* |
| | 1821a | CLOWN'S CHOICE – Hall |
| | 1821b | ACROBATS – attributed to Nancy Cabot, Nancy's, but unlikely |
| | 1822 | GAME COCKS – Nancy Cabot 1936 |
| | 1823 | THE OZARK TRAIL – KC Star 1935 |
| | 1824 | TRIANGLE PUZZLE – Grandma Dexter |
| | 1825 | PIGEON TOES – Gutcheon PPP |

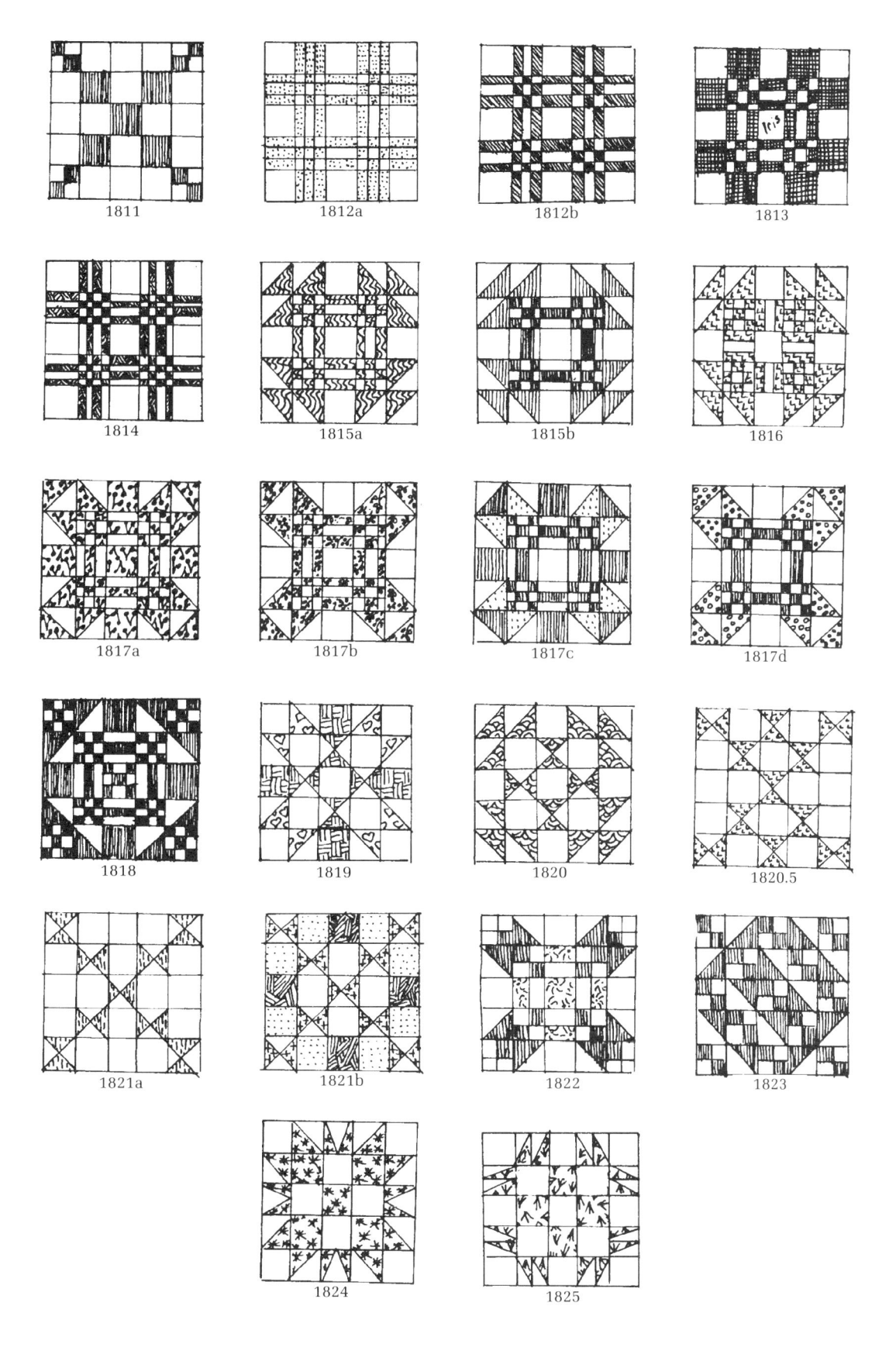

*Twenty-Five Squares (1811 – 1825)*

231

# Pattern Category 10: *Unequal Nine Patch with Small Center Square*

PATCHES ARE SQUARES & RECTANGLES

**1826a**    THE DOUBLE V – KC Star 1940

**1826b**    THE DOUBLE R – attributed to Nancy Cabot, Nancy's. *See 1838.5 & 3211.*

**1827**    PLAID – Hinson QC

**1828**    TONGANOXIE NINE PATCH – Hall. *See 1601.*

**1829**    COUNTRY LANES – Mountain Mist. *See 1102.*
CROSS IN THE SQUARE – Bishop and Safanda

**1830**    STRIP SQUARES – LAC #226
STRIPES AND SQUARES – Nancy Cabot

**1831**    TRUE LOVER'S KNOT – Hall
SASSAFRAS LEAF – Hall
HAND – Hall
CALIFORNIA OAK LEAF – Hall

**1832**    MONA AND MONETTE – Nancy Page

**1833**    TICK TACK TOE – LAC #227

**1834**    DIAGONAL PATHS – Nancy Cabot 1936
THREE STEPS – Nancy Cabot

**1835**    KING'S HIWAY – Nancy Page

**1836**    CHARIOT WHEEL – Nancy Cabot 1935
QUILTER'S DELIGHT – Nancy Cabot 1937

**1837**    MOUNTAIN HOMESPUN – Nancy Cabot 1935

**1838**    GOLDEN GATE – QNM #77, 1976

**1839**    IRISH CHAIN – Prudence Penny

**1840**    GOLDEN GLOW – Hall

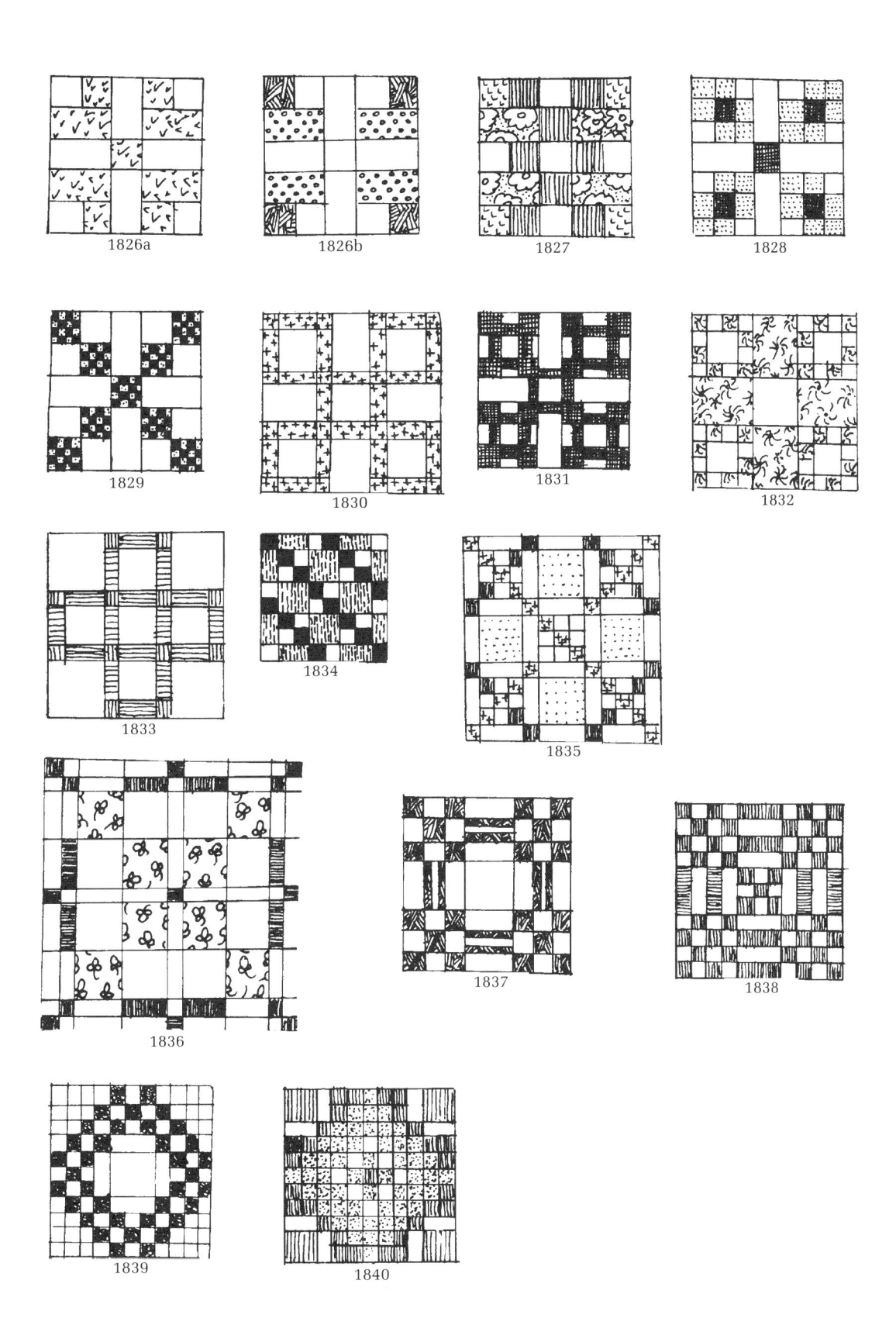

*Patches Are Squares & Rectangles (1826a – 1840)*

1826a 1826b 1827 1828

1829 1830 1831 1832

1833 1834 1835

1836 1837 1838

1839 1840

# Pattern Category 10: *Unequal Nine Patch with Vertical Rectangle*

| | | |
|---|---|---|
| PATCHES ARE SQUARES & RECTANGLES | **1842** | **SAVE ALL** – Aunt Martha |
| | **1843** | **HAPPY MEMORIES** – QNM #42, 1973 |
| | **1844** | **PINEAPPLE** – Woman's World 1931 |
| | **1845** | **PINEAPPLE SQUARES** – Nancy Cabot 1937 |
| BLOCKS OF THIS CONSTRUCTION: | **1847** | **GRANDMOTHER'S CHOICE** – Mrs. Danner 1975 |
| | | **SHOOFLY VARIATION** – Bishop and Safanda. *See 1645 & 1806.5.* |
| | **1848** | **TEXAS PUZZLE** – Aunt Kate 1965 |
| | **1849** | **DIAMOND PANES** – Nancy Cabot 1938 |
| | **1850** | **DOUBLE WRENCH** – Farm and Fireside 1884 |
| | | **WRENCH** – Ohio Farmer 1896 |
| | | **MONKEY WRENCH** – Ohio Farmer 1898 |
| | | **SQUARE TRIANGLES** – Ohio Farmer 1911 |
| | | **MALTESE CROSS** – Pictorial Review 1913 |
| | | **BRIDE'S KNOT** – Orange Judd Farmer 1913 |
| | | **T QUARTET** – Farm and Fireside |
| | | **T DESIGN** – Farm and Fireside |
| | | **HENS AND CHICKENS** – Wallace's Farmer 1928 |
| | | **TRUE LOVER'S KNOT** – Wallace's Farmer 1928 |
| | | **THE BROAD AXE** – Wallace's Farmer 1928 |
| | | **HONEY DISH** – Source Unknown |
| | | **BEAR PAW DESIGN** – Comfort |
| | | **AEROPLANE** – Woman's World 1931 |
| | | **DRAGON'S HEAD** – Woman's World |
| | | **AIRPLANE** – The Household Journal |
| | | **CHURN DASH** – Hall |
| | | **THE CROW'S NEST** – KC Star 1932 |
| | | **FRENCH 4's** – Nancy Page |
| | | **PIONEER PATCH** – Capper's/Famous Features |
| | | **ALASKA HOMESTEAD** – Rodgers |
| | | **HOLE IN THE BARN DOOR** – Bishop and Safanda. *See 1646.* |
| | **1851** | **GREEK CROSS** – Capper's |
| | **1852** | **GOSHEN STAR** – Clara Stone |
| | **1853** | **WALLS OF JERICHO** – Nancy Cabot 1935 |
| | **1854** | **HARMONY SQUARE** – Nancy Cabot 1937 |

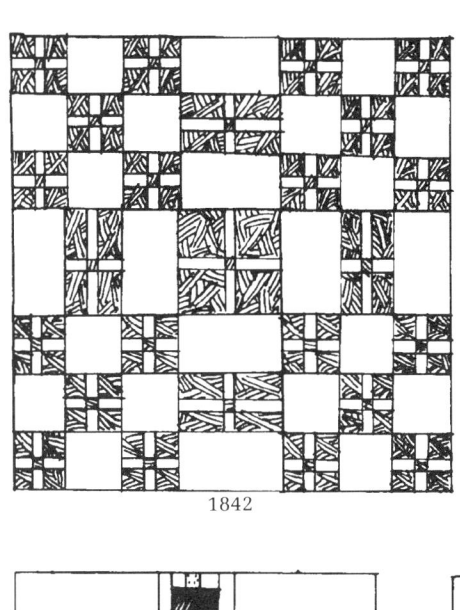

*Patches Are Squares & Rectangles, Blocks with Specific Construction (1842 – 1854)*

1842

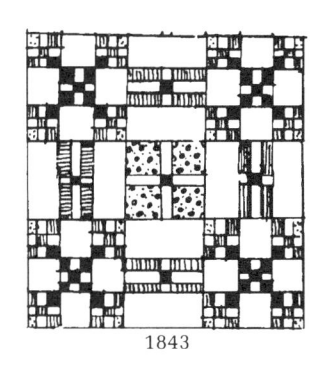

1843

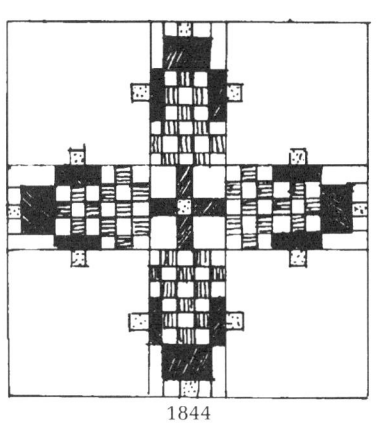

1844

1845

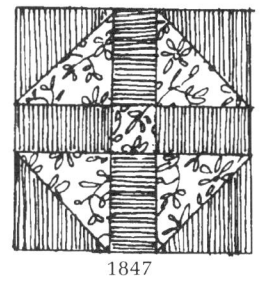

1847

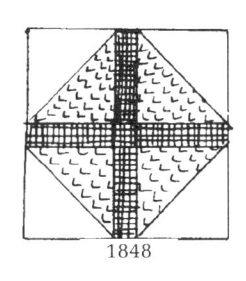

1848

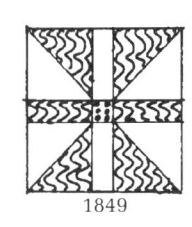

1849

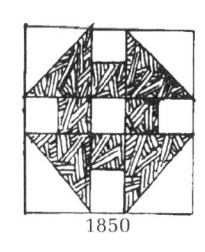

1850

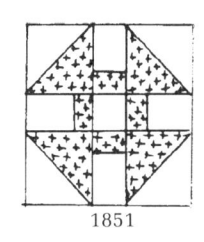

1851

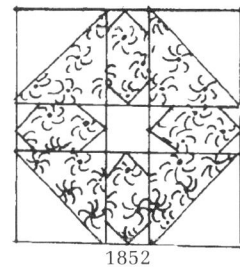

1852

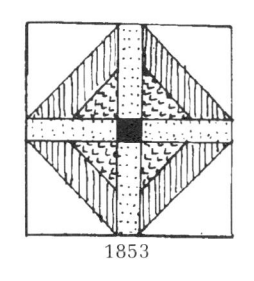

1853

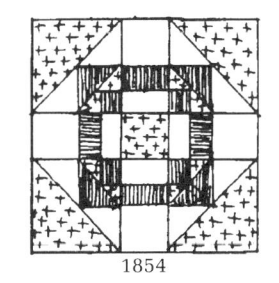

1854

235

# Pattern Category 10: *Unequal Nine Patch with Small Center Square*

BLOCKS OF THIS CONSTRUCTION:

| | | |
|---|---|---|
| | 1855a | GRANDMOTHER'S CHOICE – LAC #129 |
| | 1855b | DUCK'S FOOT – Hearth and Home<br>PATTERN WITHOUT A NAME – attributed to Nancy Cabot, Nancy's. |
| | 1855c | FRENCH PATCHWORK – Needlecraft Supply ca. 1937<br>CROSS WITHIN A CROSS – Haders. *See 1806.5 & 2465.* |
| | 1856 | CRAZY ANN – Finley<br>FOLLOW THE LEADER – Finley<br>TWIST AND TURN – Finley. *See 3238.* |
| | 1857 | PINWHEEL SQUARE – LAC #231 |
| | 1858 | SPINNING TOPS – Nancy Cabot 1937 |
| | 1859a | DUCKS AND DUCKLINGS – Finley<br>HEN AND CHICKENS – Finley<br>CORN AND BEANS – Finley |
| | 1859b | WILD GOOSE CHASE – The Farmer's Wife & Carlie Sexton 1928<br>DUCKLINGS – KC Star 1932<br>FOX AND GEESE – Nancy Cabot 1933<br>DUCK AND DUCKLINGS – Hall<br>HEN AND CHICKENS – Hall<br>CORN AND BEANS – Hall<br>HANDY ANDY – Hall<br>SHOO – FLY – Hall |
| | 1859c | WILD GOOSE CHASE – OCS/Wheeler |
| | 1859d | WHIRLING FIVE PATCH – KC Star 1941 |
| | 1860a | MRS. KELLER'S NINE PATCH – Hall |
| | 1860b | DUCK AND DUCKLINGS – LAC #245<br>AUNT KATE'S CHOICE – Needlecraft Supply ca. 1937 |
| | 1860c | MONKEY WRENCH – Nancy Cabot 1936 |
| | 1861 | RED CROSS – Clara Stone |
| | 1862 | GRANDMA'S FAVORITE – Clara Stone<br>GRANDMA'S CHOICE – Nancy Cabot 1935<br>HONEY'S CHOICE – Evangeline's |
| | 1863a | CROSS AND CROWN – LAC #151<br>BOUQUET'S QUILT – Nancy Page<br>TULIP WREATH – Pennsylvania Farmer |
| | 1863b | GOOSE TRACKS – Rural New Yorker 1932. *See 1665.8.*<br>SIGNAL – Woman's World |
| | 1864 | CROSS AND CROWN – KC Star 1929 |
| | 1865 | TULIPS – Aunt Martha |
| | 1866 | THE WHITE SQUARE QUILT – KC Star 1939 |
| | 1867 | SQUARE DANCE – James |
| | 1868 | FLYING GEESE – OCS/Wheeler |
| | 1869 | WEDDING RING – Bureau Farmer 1930 |
| | 1870 | FOUR CLOWNS – Nancy Cabot 1937 |
| | 1871 | CROSS AND CROWN – Country Gentleman 1930. *See 3185.* |
| | 1872 | MEDIEVAL WALLS – Nancy Cabot 1936<br>MEDIEVAL MOSAIC – Nancy Cabot 1936 |

*Blocks with Specific Construction (1855a – 1872)*

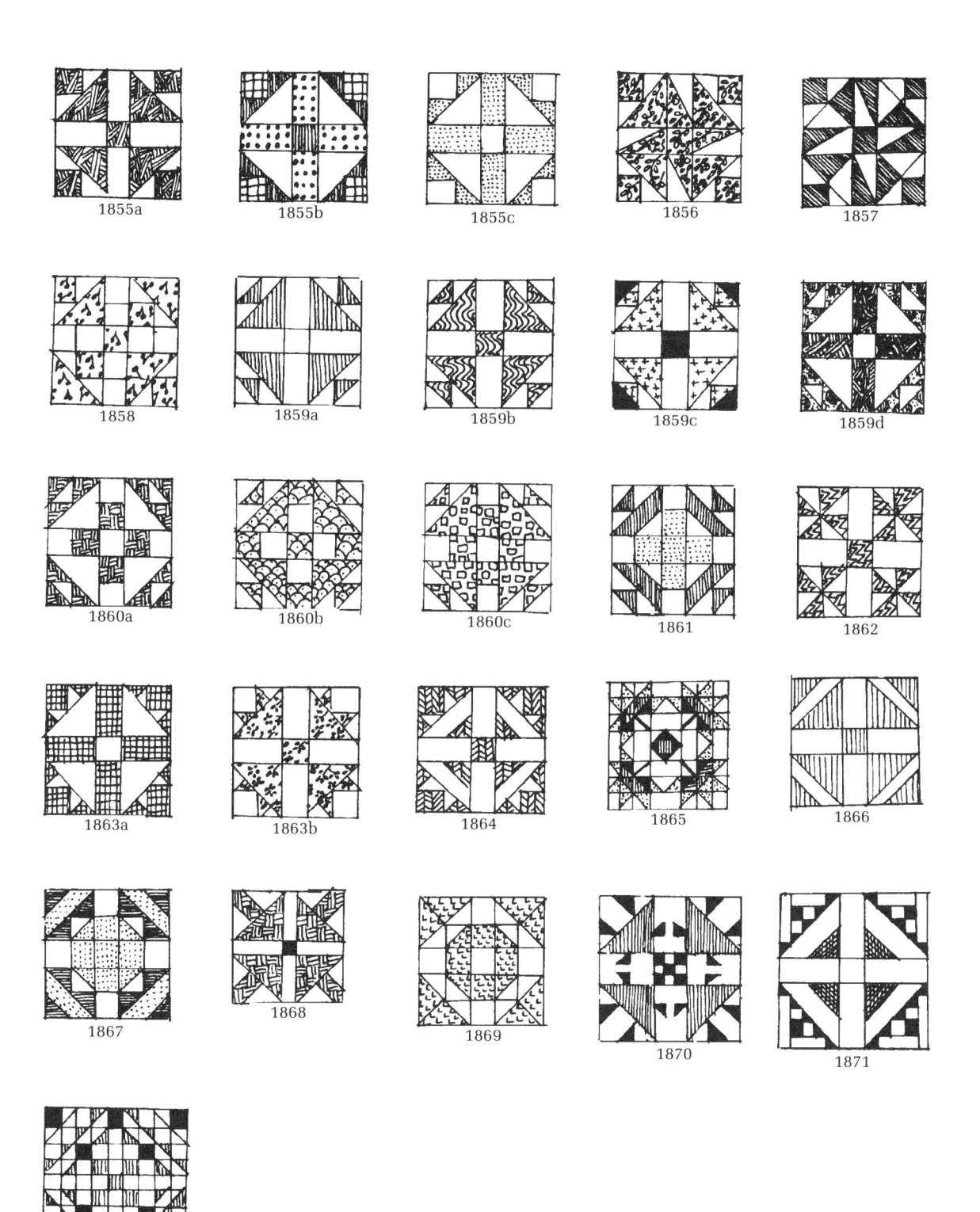

1855a  1855b  1855c  1856  1857

1858  1859a  1859b  1859c  1859d

1860a  1860b  1860c  1861  1862

1863a  1863b  1864  1865  1866

1867  1868  1869  1870  1871

1872

237

# Pattern Category 10: *Unequal Nine Patch with Small Center Square*

BLOCKS WITH
UNPIECED BARS

**1873**    Economy – KC Star 1933. *See 2375 & 3229.*
Garden of Eden – Nancy Cabot (no set indicated) 1934

**1874**    Red Cross – LAC #392. *See 1193.*

**1875**    Jack in the Box – James

**1876a**    Alpine Cross – Nancy Cabot 1936

**1876b**    Wheel of Chance – Nancy Cabot 1935

**1877**    Jack in the Box – McKim 101
Whirligig – Hall. *See 1960.*

**1878**    Handy Andy – Finley. *See 1311.*

**1879**    Bear's Foot – LAC #351
Bear's Paw – Finley
Duck's Foot in the Mud – Finley
Hand of Friendship – Finley
Tea Leaf Design – The Farmer's Wife
The Best Friend – Finley in Country Gentleman 1931
Cat's Paw – Nancy Page
Batsche – Graeff
Small Hand – Graeff
Illinois Turkey Track – Mrs. Danner 1958. *See 1311, 1885, & 1945.*

**1880**    Dove in the Window – LAC #215. *See 1546 & 1946.*

**1881**    Premium Star – LAC #14

**1882**    Hens and Chickens – LAC #385
Surprise Package – James

**1883**    Turkey Tracks – LAC #150
Resolutions – Nancy Page

**1884**    Rosebud – Aunt Martha
Tea Rose – Famous Features

**1885**    Bear's Paw – Grandmother Clark 1932
The Best Friend – Grandmother Clark 1932. *See 1734, 1875, & 1945.*

**1886**    Autumn Tints – attributed to Nancy Cabot. *See 1734.*

**1887**    Maple Leaf – KC Star 1930
Autumn Leaves – McKim, Parade of States
Autumn Leaf – Hall. *See 1735.*

*Blocks with Unpieced Bars (1873 – 1887)*

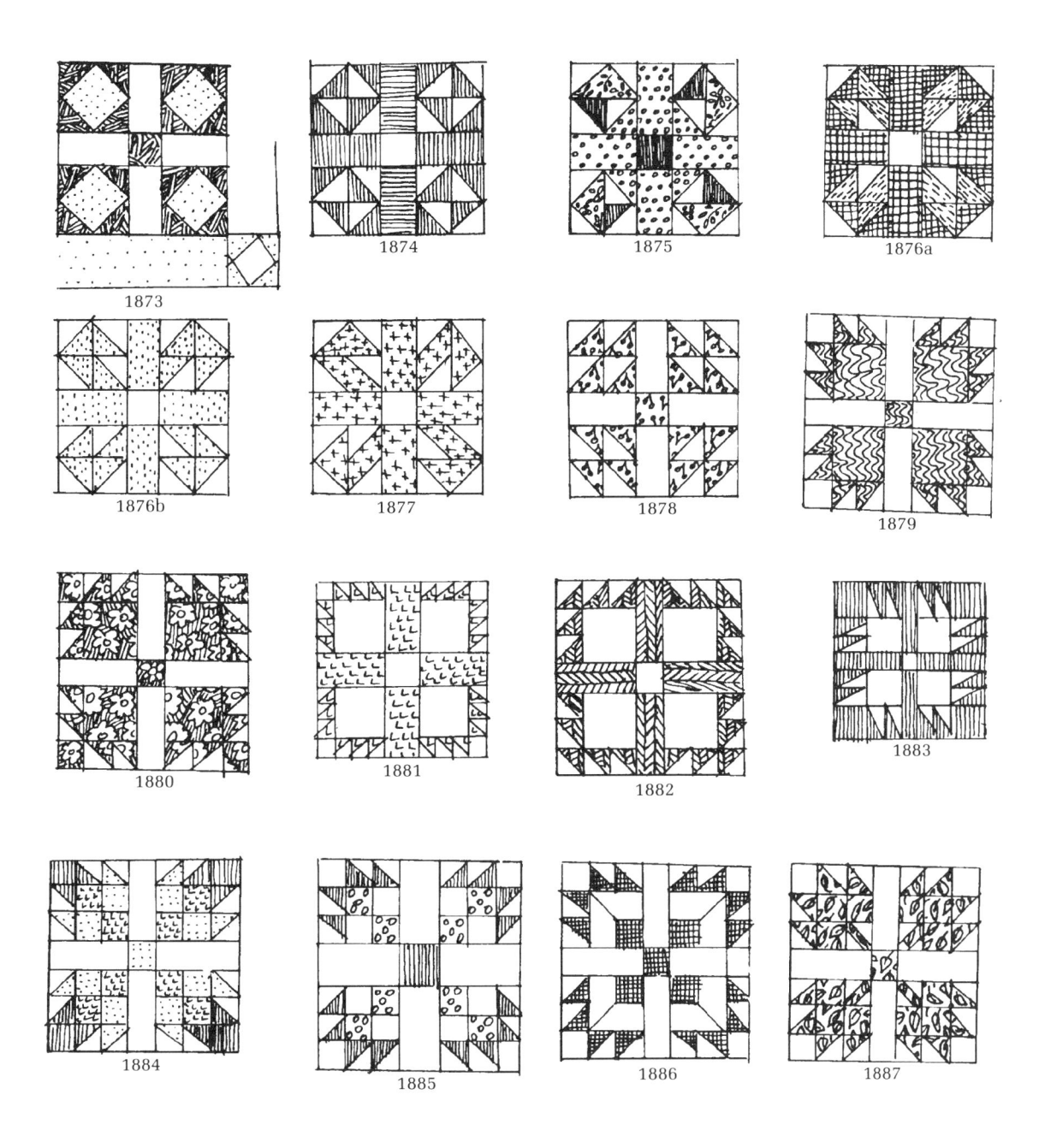

1873
1874
1875
1876a
1876b
1877
1878
1879
1880
1881
1882
1883
1884
1885
1886
1887

# Pattern Category 10: *Unequal Nine Patch with Small Center Square*

BLOCKS WITH
UNPIECED BARS

**1889a** GOOSE TRACKS – LAC #156
PRIDE OF ITALY – McKim 101 (red, white, & green)
ITALIAN BEAUTY – McKim 101
BLUE BIRDS FLYING – Household Magazine 1933

**1889b** DOVE AT THE CROSSROADS – Clara Stone
LILY POND – Nancy Cabot
SAGE BUD – The Family 1913

**1889c** THE CROSSROADS – Farmer's Wife
DOVE IN THE WINDOW – KC Star 1936
DUCK PADDLE – Household Journal
FANCY FLOWERS – Grandmother Clark Bk. 20
LILY CORNERS – Progressive Farmer (Hill)
CROW'S FOOT – Lithgow. *See 1713.*

**1890** THE SAGE BUD OF WYOMING – Workbasket. *See 1713.*

**1891** CROSS AND CROWN – QEC 1978

**1892** FANNY'S FAN – LAC #131
MODERN TULIP – Grandmother Clark, Grandma Dexter

**1893** BUTTERFLY AT THE CROSS – Clara Stone
SIMPLE SUE – Oklahoma Farmer Stockman
ALGONQUIN CHARM – Nancy Cabot

**1894** FLY AWAY FEATHERS – attributed to Nancy Cabot, Nancy's

**1895** THE E-Z QUILT – KC Star 1940

**1896** OLD FASHION QUILT – Oklahoma Farmer Stockman

**1897** CANDLEGLOW – attributed to Nancy Cabot, Nancy's

**1898** NEVADA – Workbasket. *See 3232.*

**1899** CARRIE'S CHOICE – Clara Stone. *See 1152.3, 1376, 1429, 1712, 1900, & 2533.*

**1900** MIDGET NECKTIE – KC Star 1937. *See 1152.3, 1376, 1429, 1712, 1899, & 2533.*

**1901** THE RED CROSS QUILT – KC Star 194

**1902** SQUARES AND SQUARE – Nancy Page

**1903** STONE MASON'S PUZZLE – LAC #457
CITY STREETS – Nancy Page

**1904** CROSSED SQUARE – Household Journal

**1905** BOWKNOT – Finley
FARMER'S PUZZLE – Finley

**1906** BOWKNOT – Nancy Cabot 1933

*Blocks with Unpieced Bars (1889a – 1906)*

| 1889a | 1889b | 1889c | 1890 |
| 1891 | 1892 | 1893 | 1894 |
| 1895 | 1896 | 1897 | 1898 |
| 1899 | 1900 | 1901 | 1902 |
| 1903 | 1904 | 1905 | 1906 |

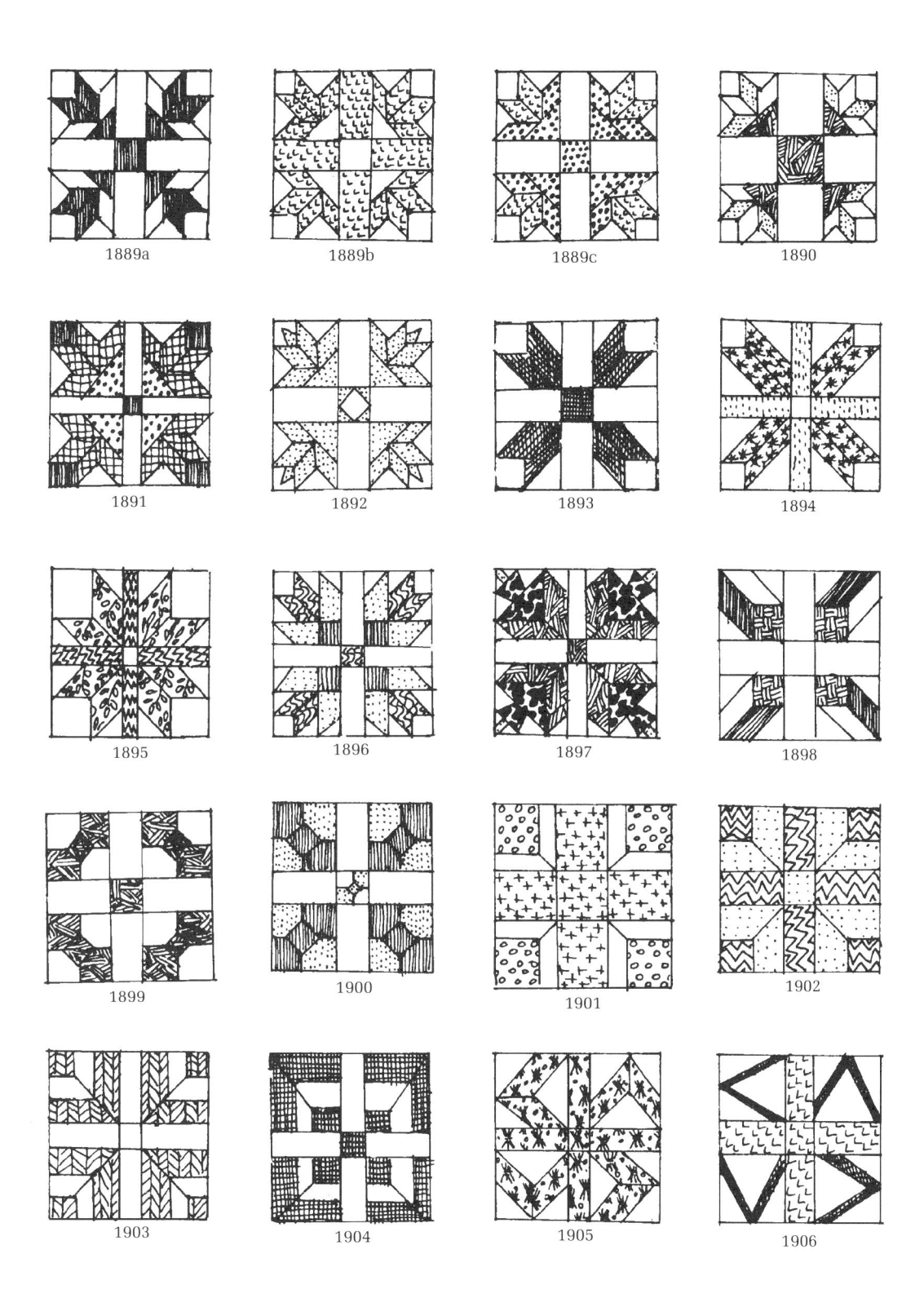

# Pattern Category 10: *Unequal Nine Patch with Small Center Square*

BLOCKS WITH
UNPIECED BARS

**1907**    BACHELOR'S PUZZLE – LAC #34
THE SEASONS – Nancy Cabot 1937
JOY'S DELIGHT – Needlecraft Supply ca. 1938
MRS. ANDERSON'S FAVORITE – Needlecraft Supply ca. 1938

**1908**    WIDOWER'S CHOICE – LAC #248

**1909**    LEAP FROG – LAC #256

**1910**    LEAP FROG – Gutcheon PPP

**1911**    BUFFALO RIDGE – attributed to Nancy Cabot, Nancy's
GRANDMOTHER'S FANCY – Comfort

**1912**    BUFFALO RIDGE QUILT – Marshall
COUNTRY ROADS – Quilt World February 1979. *See 3257.*

**1913**    OLD MAID'S PUZZLE – Comfort

**1914**    THE PRESIDENTIAL ARMCHAIR – Goodspeed, QMT 2

**1915a**    CROSSES AND STAR – LAC #112

**1915b**    STAR AND CROSS – Finley

**1916**    NEW STAR – LAC #17
HEAVENLY PUZZLE – Nancy Cabot 1935

**1917**    LADIES' DELIGHT – LAC #126. *See 1994.*

**1918**    OLD STAR – LAC #258
ROMAN ROADS – Nancy Cabot 1935

**1919**    CROSS AND STAR – Clara Stone

**1920**    BOUQUET– OCS/Wheeler

**1921**    ABE LINCOLN'S PLATFORM – Heard. *See 1935.*

**1922**    EASTERTIDE QUILT – Capper's Weekly 1933

**1923**    STARS OVER TENNESSEE – Aunt Kate 1966

**1924**    BIRDS IN A SQUARE – Evelyn Brown

**1925**    WIND STAR FOR NEW HAMPSHIRE – Aunt Kate 1966

**1926**    RHODE ISLAND MAPLE LEAF STAR – Aunt Kate 1966

*Blocks with Unpieced Bars (1907 – 1926)*

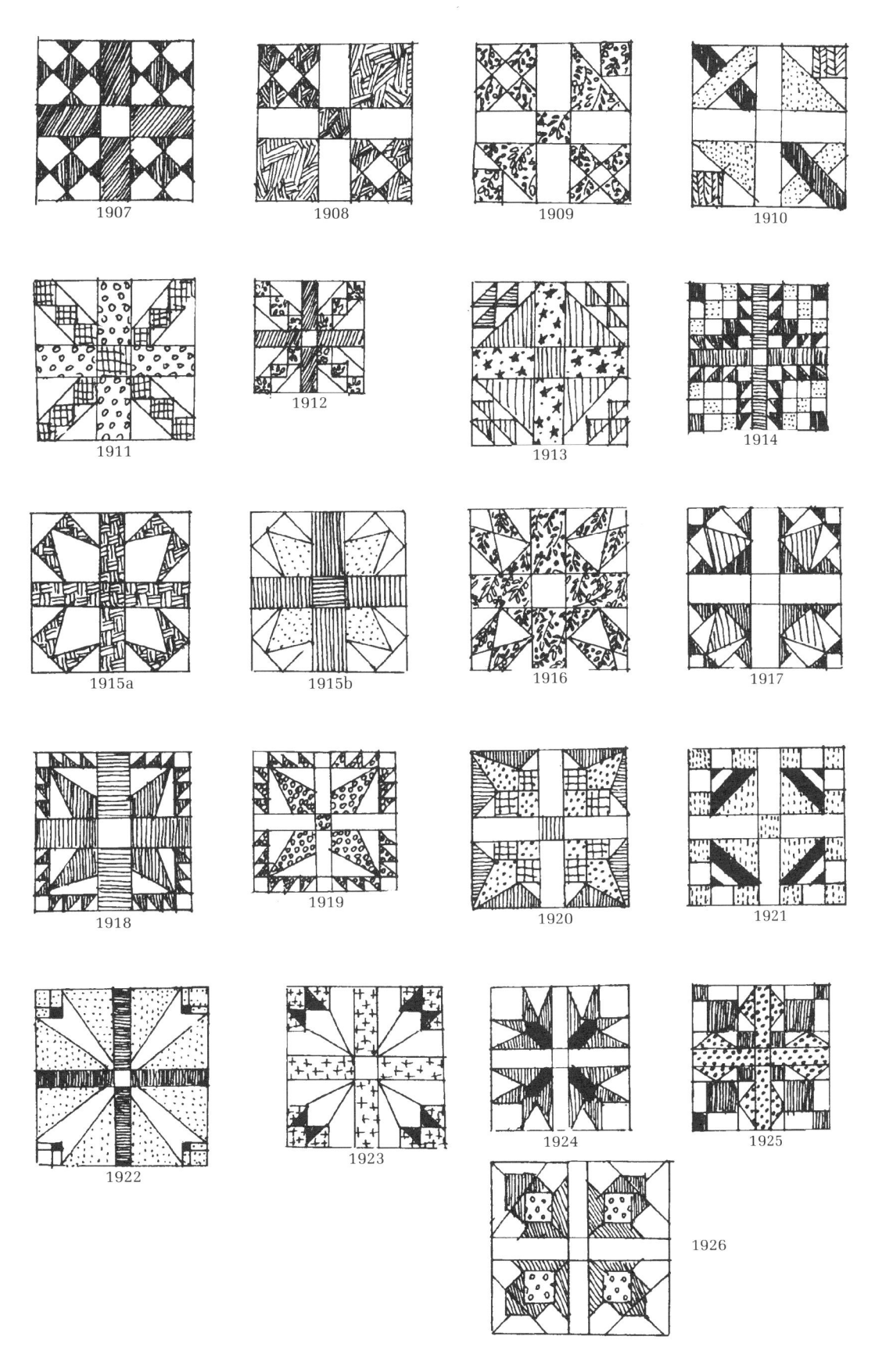

1907  1908  1909  1910
1911  1912  1913  1914
1915a  1915b  1916  1917
1918  1919  1920  1921
1922  1923  1924  1925
1926

# Pattern Category 10: *Unequal Nine Patch with Small Center Square*

| | | |
|---|---|---|
| OTHER TYPES OF BLOCKS | **1930** | **Sister's Choice** – LAC #257. *See 1802, 2129, 3034, 3230, & 3231.*<br>**Star and Cross** – OCS |
| | **1931** | **Crazy House** – LAC #516<br>**Z Cross** – Gutcheon PPP |
| | **1932** | **Home Circle** – Comfort?<br>**Mrs. Anderson's Quilt** – Mrs. Danner 1958<br>**Rolling Square** – Mrs. Danner 1958<br>**Garden of Eden** – Mrs. Danner 1958 |
| | **1933** | **Tete a Tete** – Nancy Cabot 1937<br>**Tote a Tote** – attributed to Nancy Cabot, Nancy's |
| | **1934** | **Propeller** – LAC #506<br>**Broken Arrows** – Quilt World October 1979 |
| | **1935** | **Lincoln's Platform** – LAC #147. *See 1921.*<br>**Three in a Corner** – Vickery Publications |
| | **1936** | **Greek Cross** – Clara Stone. *See 1645.* |
| | **1937** | **Table for Four** – Nancy Page |
| | **1938** | **Watermill** – Grandmother Clark |
| | **1939** | **Fanny's Favorite** – LAC #464<br>**Diamond Ring** – Clara Stone<br>**My Favorite** – Nancy Cabot 1933<br>**Old Favorite** – Nancy Cabot<br>**Grandma's Choice** – Needlecraft Supply ca. 1938 |
| | **1940** | **Spider's Den** – LAC #190 |
| | **1941** | **Nebraska** – Hearth & Home |
| | **1942** | **Cubes and Bars** – Aunt Martha 1933 |
| | **1943** | **Nebraska** – Nancy Cabot 1933 |
| | **1944** | **The Vermont Maple Leaf** – Workbasket 1935. *See 1737.* |
| | **1945** | **Ducks Foot in the Mud** – Nancy Cabot 1935<br>**Chinese Block Pattern** – Hechtlinger. *See 1879 & 1884.* |
| | **1946** | **Doves in the Window** – Nancy Cabot 1935. *See 1880.*<br>**Four Birds** – Nancy Cabot 1935 |
| | **1947** | **Unnamed** – Quilt World August 1979 |
| | **1948** | **Prickly Pear** – KC Star 1931 |

*Other Types of Blocks (1930 – 1948)*

245

# Pattern Category 10: *Unequal Nine Patch with Small Center Square*

OTHER TYPES OF BLOCKS

**1949**    THE CONTINENTAL – QNM #104, 1978. Designed by Twyla Dell to commemorate 1st Continental Quilting Congress.

**1950**    DAVID & GOLIATH – Finley
FOUR DARTS – Finley
BULL'S EYE – Finley
FLYING DARTS – Finley
DOE AND DARTS – Finley

**1951**    TUMBLING BLOCKS – Comfort
ROCKY MOUNTAIN CHAIN – Hearth and Home

**1951.5**    MINERAL WELLS – Nancy Page

**1952a**    DEVILS CLAWS – LAC #142
IDAHO BEAUTY – Clara Stone
CORNER STAR – Carlie Sexton 1930
CROSS PLAINS – Clara Stone
BRIGHT STARS – Nancy Cabot 1936
THE CROWFOOT – Mrs. Danner

**1952b**    DEVIL'S CLAWS – Nancy Cabot 1934

**1953**    CATHEDRAL WINDOW – Nancy Cabot 1933

**1954**    INTERWOVEN PUZZLE – Capper's 1933

**1955**    MEETING HOUSE SQUARE – Nancy Cabot 1935

**1956**    SCOTCH HEATHER – Nancy Cabot 1936

**1957**    MARYLAND – Hearth & Home

**1957.5**    GEORGIA – Hearth and Home

**1958**    WASHINGTON STAR – Aunt Kate 1966

**1959**    FLYING X – Nancy Cabot 1938. *See 1171 & 2301.*

**1960**    WHEEL OF FORTUNE – Nancy Cabot. *See 1876 & 1877.*

**1961**    CHAIN AND BAR – Clara Stone

**1962**    WOODLAND PATH – Nancy Cabot 1934

**1963**    ROAD TO CALIFORNIA – LAC #234
STEPPING STONES – Nancy Page
CROSSSROADS – Needlecraft Supply ca. 1938

**1964**    JACOB'S LADDER – Grandma Dexter

**1965**    FIELDS AND FENCES – Nancy Cabot 1938

**1966**    THE SQUARE DEAL – KC Star

**1967**    FLYING GEESE – James

*Other Types of Blocks (1949 – 1967)*

1949
1950
1951
1951.5
1952a
1952b
1953
1954
1955
1956
1957
1957.5
1958
1959
1960
1961
1962
1963
1964
1965
1966
1967

# Pattern Category 10: *Unequal Nine Patch with Small Center Square*

OTHER TYPES OF BLOCKS

**1968**    LONE X – Prudence Penny

**1969**    UNNAMED – OCS/Wheeler

**1970**    SPOOL BLOCK – attributed to Nancy Cabot 1938. *See 3031.*

**1971**    SUNBEAM – Woman's World

**1972**    ANNAPOLIS – Frank, Nancy Cabot 1937

**1973**    MY COUNTRY – KC Star 1955

**1974**    FAR WEST – Nancy Cabot 1937

**1975**    MILLER'S DAUGHTER – Nancy Cabot 1937. *See 1802, 1930, 3034, & 3231.*

**1976**    NOSE GAY – Nancy Cabot 1933
STEPPING STONES – Grandma Dexter

**1977**    WAVERLY STAR – Mitchell. *See 1399.2 & 1427.*

**1978**    MAGNOLIA BUD – Nancy Cabot 1934
PINK MAGNOLIAS – Nancy Cabot 1936. *See 2208.*

**1979**    MINNESOTA – Hearth & Home

**1980**    CALIFORNIA SNOWFLAKE – QNM #57

**1981**    THE ARMY STAR – KC Star 1943

**1982**    STAR AND STRIPE – Nancy Cabot 1938

**1983a**    BLACKFORD'S BEAUTY – LAC #388
BLACK BEAUTY – Nancy Cabot 1933
THE HUNT – Farm Journal
MRS. SMITH'S FAVORITE – Needlecraft Supply ca. 1930

**1983b**    GOOD CHEER – Clara Stone
STEPPING STONES – KC Star 1931. *See 1414.*

**1984**    ARROW POINTS – Nancy Page

**1985**    ARROWHEAD – KC Star 1936
THE ARROWHEAD QUILT – Home Art

**1986**    ARROWHEADS – McKim, Parade of States

**1987**    THE WINGED 9 PATCH – KC Star 1940

**1988**    RUBY ROADS – Nancy Cabot 1936

**1989**    FRIENDSHIP STAR – OCS/Wheeler

*Other Types of Blocks (1968 – 1989)*

# Pattern Category 10: *Unequal Nine Patch with Small Center Square*

| | | |
|---|---|---|
| OTHER TYPES OF BLOCKS | **1990** | SAILING DARTS – Aunt Kate 1965 |
| | **1991** | OUR COUNTRY – KC Star 1939 |
| | **1992** | SUNBURST – OCS/Wheeler |
| | **1993** | SCHOENROCK CROSS – Nancy Cabot 1937 |
| | **1994** | LADIES' DELIGHT – Nancy Cabot 1934. *See 1917.* |
| | **1995** | QUILTER'S DELIGHT – Nancy Cabot 1936 |
| | **1996** | PICKET AND POSTS – Aunt Kate 1966 |
| BLOCKS WITH CURVES | **2001** | AROUND THE WORLD – OCS, KC Star 1940. *See 3572.* |
| | **2002** | LADIES' FANCY – Farm and Fireside 1884. *See 3306.* |
| | **2003** | FREDONIA CROSS – Mrs. Danner 1970. *See 3314.* |
| | **2004** | THE BANNER QUILT – Orange Judd Farmer 1899. Center appliqué. |
| | **2005** | STAR AND CROSS – Nancy Cabot 1933 |
| | **2006** | NOCTURNE – Nancy Cabot 1934 |
| | **2007** | SACRAMENTO – Hearth & Home<br>SACRAMENTO CITY – Nancy Cabot 1938 |
| | **2008** | MORNING STAR – attributed to Nancy Cabot, Nancy's |
| | **2009** | PURITAN MAIDEN – Nancy Cabot 1935 |
| | **2009.5** | MAYFLOWER – OCS/Wheeler |
| | **2010** | AUTUMN LEAF – LAC #502. *See 1736, 1887, & 2224.* |
| | **2011** | AUTUMN LEAF – Hinson QM |
| | **2012** | DELAWARE – Hearth & Home |
| | **2013** | WORLD'S FAIR QUILT – Hinson QM. *See 1516.5.* |
| | **2014** | WORLD'S FAIR – Hall. *See 1516.5.* |

*Other Types of Blocks, Blocks with Curves (1990 – 2014)*

251

# PATTERN CATEGORY 11

## Unequal Nine Patch with Large Center Square

**Patterns in Category 11 share these characteristics:**

- The block is divided by two horizontal and two vertical seams which form a grid.

- The grid divides the block into nine sections, some of which are squares and some of which are rectangles.

- The center square in the block is relatively large.

**Category 11 includes:**

- Blocks with Unpieced Corners, 254

- Blocks with Squares and Rectangles in the Corners, 262

- Blocks with Specific Construction, 264

- Other Types, 270

- Blocks with Curved Seams, 274

- Feathered Stars, 276

### KEY TO PATTERN CATEGORY 11: UNEQUAL NINE PATCH WITH LARGE CENTER SQUARE

If the block is a Feathered Star, **turn to p. 276**

If the block has curved seams, **turn to p. 274**

If the block is a star of this construction , **turn to p. 266**

If the block is constructed with unpieced corner squares, **turn to p. 254**

If the block is constructed with squares and rectangles in the corners, **turn to p. 262**

If the block is of this construction , **turn to p. 264**

If the block is of another type of construction, **turn to p. 270**

# Pattern Category 11: *Unequal Nine Patch with Large Center Square*

BLOCKS WITH
UNPIECED CORNERS

2020    A PLAIN BLOCK – Ladies' Home Journal 1896
NINE PATCH – LAC #83
SHEEPFOLD QUILT – KC Star 1931, McKim, Parade of States
IRISH CHAIN – Shelburne (alternate plain blocks). *See 1613.*

2021    COUNTERPANE – Nancy Cabot 1934, Farm Journal. *See 1614.*

2022    LIGHT AND SHADOWS – Nancy Cabot

2023    PENNSYLVANIA – Nancy Page
THE SIMPLE CROSS – Marshall
SINGLE IRISH CHAIN – Nancy Cabot 1933 (alternate plain blocks)
CRISS CROSS QUILT – Nancy Page (alternate plain blocks)

2024    ALABAMA – Hearth & Home

2025    SQUARES AND OBLONGS – Capper's 1927
GEOMETRIC BLOCK – Capper's 1927

2026    ON THE SQUARE – Hearth & Home
NEW IRISH CHAIN – The American Woman ca. 1910

2027    STEPS TO THE LIGHT HOUSE – Nancy Page
WHITE HOUSE STEPS – Nancy Cabot

2028    DOUBLE IRISH CHAIN – Coats and Clark's

2029    DOUBLE SQUARE – adapted from Holstein, QNM #71

2030    RED CROSS – Nancy Page

2031    THE COMFORT QUILT – KC Star 1940

2032    PHILADELPHIA PAVEMENT – Finley
PHILADELPHIA BLOCK – Nancy Cabot. *See 1645.*

2033    NEW ALBUM – LAC #36. *See 2375*

2034    FAIR AND SQUARE – KC Star 1938. *See 1193.*

2035    COXEY'S CAMP – LAC #95
COXEY'S ARMY – Nancy Cabot

2036    FOREST PATHS – Farm Journal. *See 1262.*

2037    YOUNG MAN'S FANCY – OCS/Wheeler. *See as a Nine X.*

2038    PINWHEEL SKEW – Gutcheon

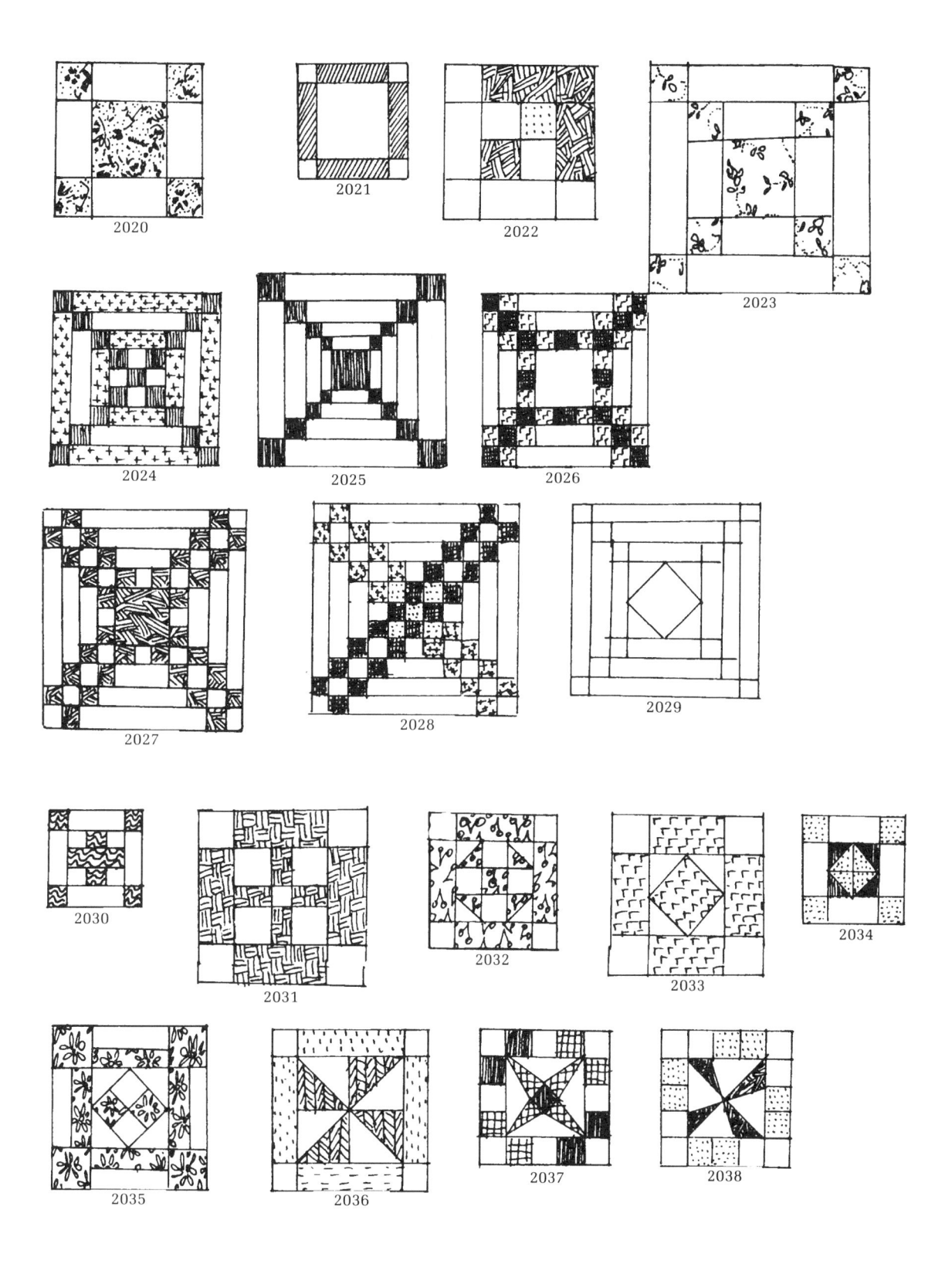

*Blocks with Unpieced Corners (2020 – 2038)*

# Pattern Category 11: *Unequal Nine Patch with Large Center Square*

BLOCKS WITH
UNPIECED CORNERS

**2039**    KING'S CROWN – KC Star 1931. *See 2392.*

**2040**    THE SIGNATURE FRIENDSHIP QUILT – KC Star 1953

**2041**    TRIANGLE SQUARES – Grandma Dexter Bk. 36a

**2042**    SUMMER'S DREAM – Orange Judd Farmer 8/2/02

**2043**    AROUND THE CORNER – Nancy Cabot 1936

**2044a**    HULL'S VICTORY – Clara Stone

**2044b**    TEMPLE COURT – from an old clipping, QNM 1973

**2045**    UNCLE SAM'S HOUR GLASS – Clara Stone

**2046**    SQUARE AND STAR – LAC #263
         SQUARES AND TRIANGLES – KC Star

**2047**    NAMELESS – Clara Stone

**2048**    CROWN OF THORNS – Finley
         GEORGETOWN CIRCLE – Finley
         GEORGETOWN PUZZLE – Nancy Cabot
         MEMORY WREATH – Hall
         MEMORY FRUIT – attributed to Nancy Cabot, Nancy's. *See 2462.*

**2049**    INDEPENDENCE SQUARE – Nancy Cabot 1938

**2050**    INDIAN – Nancy Page

**2051**    WILD GOOSE CHASE – Holstein

**2052**    INDIAN PLUMES – Hinson QC

**2053**    MASSACHUSETTS – Hearth & Home

**2054a**    KING'S CROWN – Nancy Page
         CROWN – Woman's Day 1949

**2054b**    MOSAIC – Woman's World 1931

**2055**    SUNSHINE – LAC #121

**2056**    AN EFFECTIVE SQUARE – Ladies' Home Journal 1899
         UNION – LAC #160
         FOUR CROWNS – KC Star 1933
         UNION BLOCK – Nancy Cabot
         UNION SQUARE – Hall, Capper's?

**2057**    AN ORIGINAL DESIGN – Sears 1934
         THE ORIGINAL – Nancy Cabot

*Blocks with Unpieced Corners (2039 – 2057)*

257

# Pattern Category 11: *Unequal Nine Patch with Large Center Square*

BLOCKS WITH
UNPIECED CORNERS

**2058a**    LILY QUILT PATTERN – LAC #365
DES MOINES – Hearth & Home
BOTCH HANDLE – Bishop & Safanda

**2058b**    CLUSTER OF LILIES – KC Star 1934
POND LILY – Needlecraft Supply ca. 1938

**2059**    THE CORNER STAR – KC Star 1939. *See 1952.*

**2060**    AUTUMN LEAF – Rural New Yorker 1931

**2061**    ARIZONA'S CACTUS FLOWER – Workbasket. *See 1394.*

**2062**    SPRING HAS COME – Nancy Page

**2063**    CHIMNEY SWEEP – Coats and Clark 1945
MALTESE CROSS – Bacon. *See as a Nine X.*

**2064**    BROKEN DISHES – Nancy Cabot

**2065**    BROKEN DISHES – Needlecraft Magazine February, 1930
THE CHINESE BLOCK QUILT – KC Star 1938

**2066**    LOVE IN A TANGLE – attributed to Nancy Cabot, Nancy's

**2067**    LOVE ENTANGLED – Denver Art Museum

**2068**    GOLGOTHA – Finley
THE THREE CROSSES – Finley
CROSS UPON CROSS – Finley

**2069**    CROSS AND CROWN – Spool Cotton 1942

**2070**    BEST OF ALL – Clara Stone
CHRISTMAS STAR – Workbasket 1950

**2071**    QUEEN VICTORIA'S CROWN – Prudence Penny

**2072**    BLIND MAN'S FANCY – LAC #201

**2073**    EDDYSTONE LIGHT – Nancy Cabot

**2074**    UNION STAR – Clara Stone

**2075**    THE OLD SPANISH TILE PATTERN – KC Star 1933

**2076**    STARS AND CUBES – The Household Management Journal, Batavia, IL

**2077**    COUNTY FAIR – Nancy Cabot
COUNTY FARM – Nancy Cabot

*Blocks with Unpieced Corners (2058a – 2077)*

2058a
2058b
2059
2060
2061
2062
2063
2064
2065
2066
2067
2068
2069
2070
2071
2072
2073
2074
2075
2076
2077

259

Pattern Category 11: *Unequal Nine Patch with Large Center Square*

BLOCKS WITH
UNPIECED CORNERS

| | | |
|---|---|---|
| **2078** | **PEACEFUL HOURS** – Farm Journal |
| **2079** | **ENIGMA STAR** – Hall |
| **2080** | **CHARM STAR** – Aunt Martha |
| **2081** | **THE RATCHET WHEEL** – KC Star 1947 |
| **2082** | **PRISCILLA'S DREAM** – Detroit News ca. 1938 |
| **2083** | **ARKANSAS** – Hearth & Home |
| **2084** | **THE AIRPORT** – KC Star 1936 |
| **2085** | **SQUARE DANCE** – QNM 1975 |
| **2086** | **ROAD TO OKLAHOMA CITY** – Gutcheon QDW. *See 1123, 2644, & 4208.* |
| **2087** | **DRAGONFLY** – Gutcheon QDW |
| **2088** | **ROLLING NINE PATCH** – Aunt Kate |
| **2089** | **JAM SESSION** – QNM 1979 |
| **2090** | **MISSOURI PUZZLE** – Hinson QC |
| **2091** | **SNAIL'S TRAIL** – Nancy Cabot. *See 7397.* |
| **2092** | **SQUARE WITHIN SQUARES** – Heirloom Plastics (QNM) |

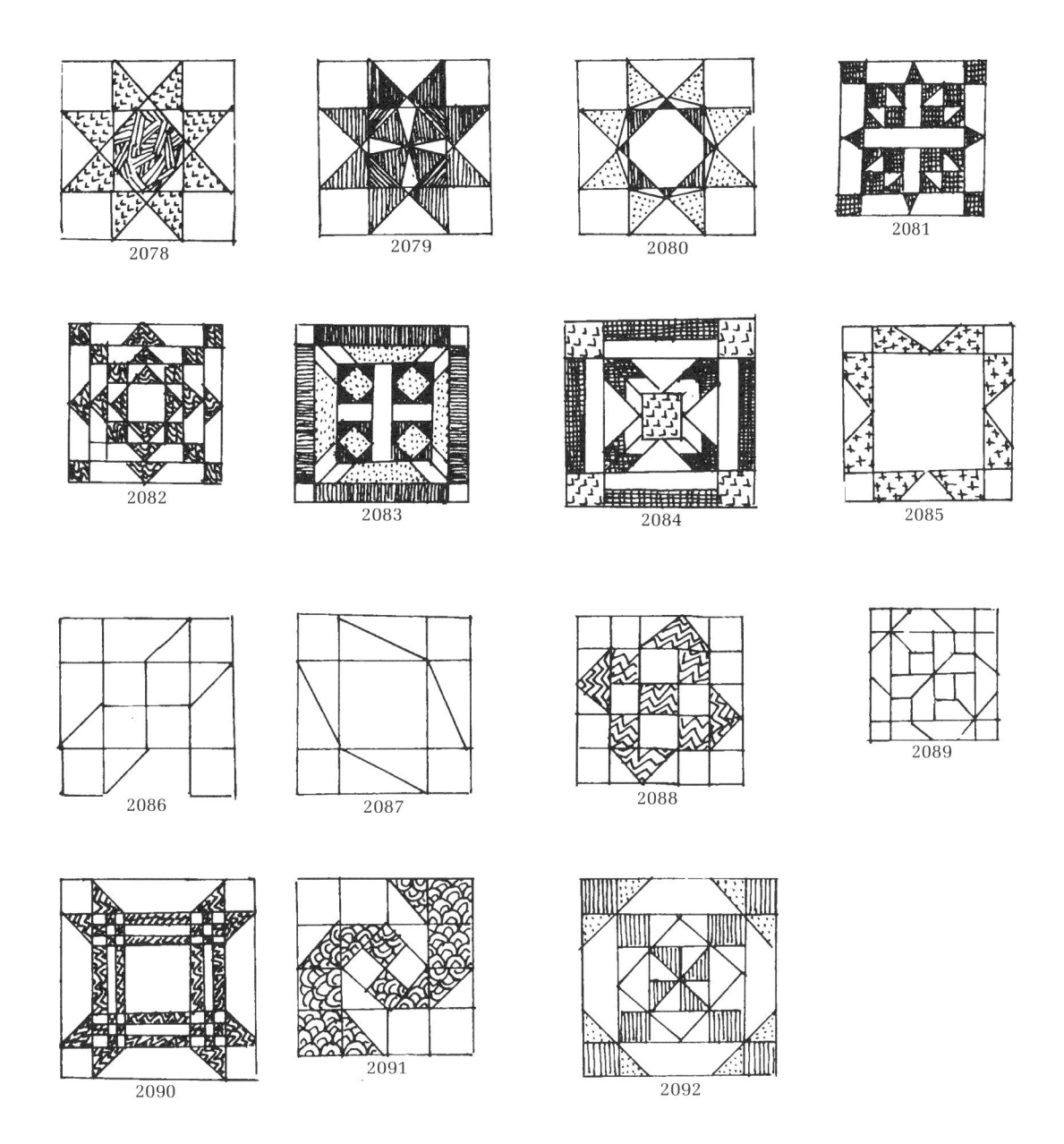

*Blocks with Unpieced Corners (2078 – 2092)*

2078  2079  2080  2081

2082  2083  2084  2085

2086  2087  2088  2089

2090  2091  2092

261

# Pattern Category 11: *Unequal Nine Patch with Large Center Squares*

BLOCKS WITH SQUARES AND RECTANGLES IN THE CORNERS

2095    THE ROSEBUD – KC Star 1942

2096    THE HEN AND HER CHICKS – KC Star 1947. *See 1612.*

2097    TRUE LOVER'S KNOT – Woman's World 1931. *See 1612.*

2098a    AN ODD PATCHWORK – LAC #285
BEAUREGARD'S SURROUNDINGS – Ohio Farmer ca. 1890
BURGOYNE SURROUNDED – Household Magazine ca. 1930
BURGOYNE'S PUZZLE – Home Art
COVERLET QUILT – Capper's

2098b    THE ROAD TO CALIFORNIA – Finley
WHEEL OF FORTUNE – Finley

2098c    HOMESPUN – Mountain Mist

2098d    BURGOYNE'S QUILT – McKim (colors: red, white, & blue, in set **b**)

2098e    BURGOYNE SURROUNDED – Capper's 1930 (block **a** with this set)

2099    MISSOURI PUZZLE – LAC #522. *See 1766 & 2080.*

2100    CROSS OF TEMPERANCE – Nancy Cabot? *See 2080.*
CROSS OF TENNESSEE – Nancy Cabot 1935

2101    TULIP TILE – Aunt Kate

2102    PETIT PARK – QNM 1973 (elephant quilted)

2103    TRACY'S PUZZLE – Aunt Kate 1965

2104    MOTHER'S FANCY – LAC #104
MOTHER'S FANCY STAR – Hall. *See 2138.*
EVENING STAR – Oklahoma Farmer Stockman ca. 1930

2105    STAR LANE – LAC #403
STARRY LANE – Hall
PATCH QUILT DESIGN – attributed to Nancy Cabot, Nancy's

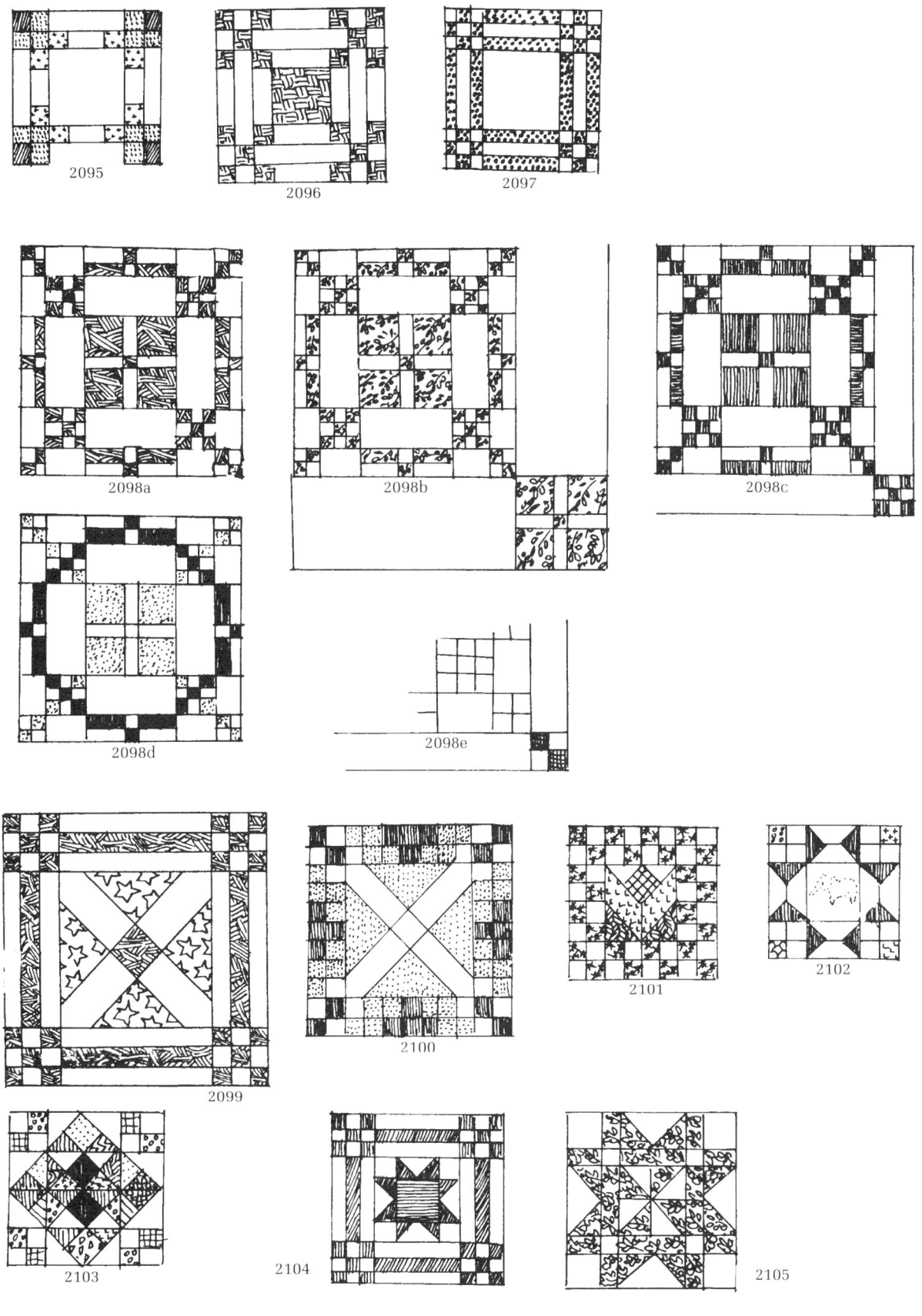

*Blocks with Squares and Rectangles in the Corners (2095 – 2105)*

2095

2096

2097

2098a

2098b

2098c

2098d

2098e

2099

2100

2101

2102

2103

2104

2105

263

# Pattern Category 11: *Unequal Nine Patch with Large Center Square*

BLOCKS OF THIS CONSTRUCTION:

| | | |
|---|---|---|
| | 2110 | PUSS IN THE CORNER – LAC #137 |
| | 2111 | PUSS IN THE CORNER – Nancy Cabot |
| | 2112 | EVERYBODY'S FAVORITE – Hearth & Home |
| | 2113 | CHEYENNE – Hearth & Home. *See 298.* |
| | 2114 | IRISH CHAIN – Mahler. *See 1143.5.* |
| | 2115 | YANKEE CHARM – Nancy Cabot 1933 |
| | 2116 | CHURN DASH – LAC #112<br>PICTURE FRAME – Clara Stone |
| | 2117 | ANN LEE'S BABY QUILT – attributed to Nancy Cabot, Nancy's |
| | 2118 | TRIANGLES & STRIPES – LAC #229<br>MAGIC BOX – Nancy Page |
| | 2119 | BURNHAM SQUARE – LAC #232<br>HOLE IN THE BARN DOOR – QNM 1977<br>STAR IN THE WINDOW – QNM 1977. *See 3992.* |
| | 2120 | THE DOUBLE ARROW – KC Star 1933 |
| | 2121 | THE CYPRESS – KC Star 1960 |
| | 2122 | CYPRESS – KC Star 1933 |
| | 2123 | MOSAIC #16 – LAC #344<br>CONNECTICUT – Nancy Page. *See 1204 & 2124.* |
| | 2124 | HOUR GLASS – Nancy Page<br>MOSAIC #12 – Nancy Cabot. *See 1204 & 2123.* |
| | 2125 | MOSAIC #8 – Nancy Cabot 1934 |
| | 2126 | GRANDMOTHER'S FAVORITE – KC Star 1932 (quilted sunflower) |
| | 2127 | FLOWER POT – Grandmother Clark 1932 (quilted sunflower) |
| | 2128 | DOUBLE X #4 – LAC #79 |
| | 2129 | FOOL'S SQUARE – KC Star. *See 1802, 1930, 3034, 3231.* |
| | 2130 | MOSAIC #1 – Nancy Cabot 1934. *See 3222 & 3223.* |
| | 2131 | HITHER & YON – Farm Journal<br>SPOOL – attributed to Nancy Cabot, Nancy's |
| | 2132 | FOX & GEESE – Farm Journal |

*Blocks with Specific Construction (2110 – 2132)*

265

# Pattern Category 11: *Unequal Nine Patch with Large Center Square*

BLOCKS OF THIS CONSTRUCTION:

| | | |
|---|---|---|
| | 2133 | FLAMING STAR – Nancy Cabot |
| | 2134 | STAR FLOWER – Grandma Dexter |
| | 2135 | JAPANESE POPPY – Nancy Cabot |
| | 2136 | AMETHYST CHAIN – Nancy Cabot (gold, amethyst & white) |
| | 2137 | SQUARE AND A HALF – LAC #246 |

BLOCKS OF THIS CONSTRUCTION:

2138a   EVENING STAR – LAC
CLUSTER OF STARS – Dubois. *See 1710.*

2138b   AUSTIN – Hearth & Home
OPTICAL SAWTOOTH – Dubois

2138c   SQUARE AND POINTS – KC Star 1933. *See 2104, 1249.3, 1631, & 2820.*

2138d   SAWTOOTH – Farm and Fireside 1884
NAMELESS STAR – Nancy Cabot
SAWTOOTH STAR – Dubois

2139   ALBUM QUILT – Mahler

2140   CORAL COURT FRIENDSHIP STAR – Aunt Kate 1964

2141a   VARIABLE STAR – Hall
UNNAMED – Farm and Fireside 1904

2141b   LONE STAR – Hall
TEXAS STAR – Hall
CRYSTAL STAR – KC Star 1934
JOINING STAR – Nancy Page 1934
STAR OF VIRGINIA – Wallace's Farmer 1928

2141c   OHIO STAR – Hall
THE COG BLOCK – KC Star 1955. *See 1138.*

2141d   EIGHT POINTED STAR – Farm Journal. *See 2578.*

2142   MOSAIC #19 – LAC #347
MOSAIC #7 – Nancy Cabot. *See 1176, 2784, & 2898.*

2143   WHEEL OF TIME – Clara Stone. *See 1176 & 2788.*

2144   OLD GREY GOOSE – Nancy Page. *See 1140 & 3221.*

2145   SARAH'S CHOICE – Clara Stone. *See 1140 & 2751.*

2146   STAR PUZZLE – LAC #10
PIECED STAR – McKim
PIERCED STAR – Dubois
BARBARA FRIETCHIE STAR – Peto. *See 1140 & 1249.5.*
WIND MILL QUILT – Wallace's Farmer 1928

*Blocks with Specific Construction (2133 – 2146)*

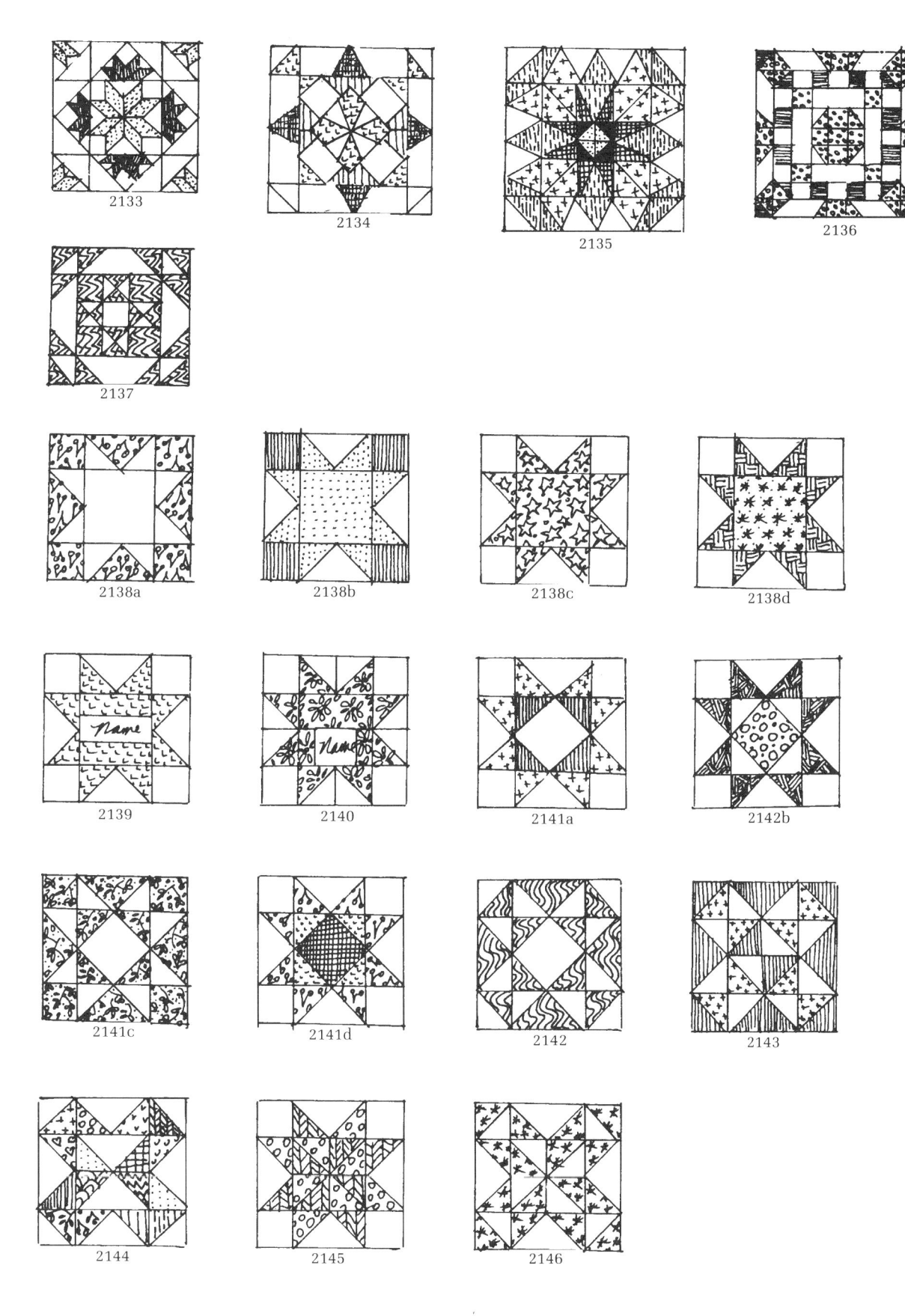

2133

2134

2135

2136

2137

2138a

2138b

2138c

2138d

2139

2140

2141a

2142b

2141c

2141d

2142

2143

2144

2145

2146

267

# Pattern Category 11: *Unequal Nine Patch with Large Center Square*

BLOCKS OF THIS CONSTRUCTION:

**2147** **Dewey's Victory** – Clara Stone
**Martha Washington Star** – Farmer's Wife 1926
**Martha Washington Design** – Farmer's Wife 1926
**Martha Washington** – Farmer's Wife 1926
**Octagonal Star** – Carlie Sexton 1928
**Queen Victoria** – Evangeline's

**2148** **Star & Pinwheels** – Nancy Cabot

**2149** **Flying Cloud** – Clara Stone
**Martha Washington's Star** – Peto 1949
**Solomon's Star** – attributed to Nancy Cabot, Nancy's

**2150** **Magic Cross Design** – Woman's World 1931

**2151** **White Hemstitch** – Grandma Dexter Bk. 36B

**2152** **Crown of Thorns** – Nancy Page

**2153** **Aunt Addie's Album** – Hearth & Home

**2154** **Missouri Star** – Nancy Cabot 1933

**2155** **Indian Star** – KC Star 1937. *See 1136.*

**2156** **Mrs. Lloyd's Favorite** – Clara Stone

**2157** **Grandmother's Quilt** – KC Star 1948

**2158** **Star Trek** – QNM 1974

**2159** **A Salute to the Colors** – KC Star 1942 (red, white, & blue)

**2160** **Cross and Square** – Nancy Cabot
**Home Treasure** – OCS

**2161** **The Star of Bethlehem** – KC Star 1937. *See 2823.*

**2162** **Unnamed** – Quilt World 1979

**2163** **Stockyard's Star For Nebraska** – Aunt Kate 1966

**2164** **The Twinkling Star** – Rural New Yorker ca. 1930

**2165** **The Twinkling Star** – Capper's, Nancy Cabot

**2166** **Aunt Rachel's Star** – Woman's Day 1942

*Blocks with Specific Construction (2147 – 2166)*

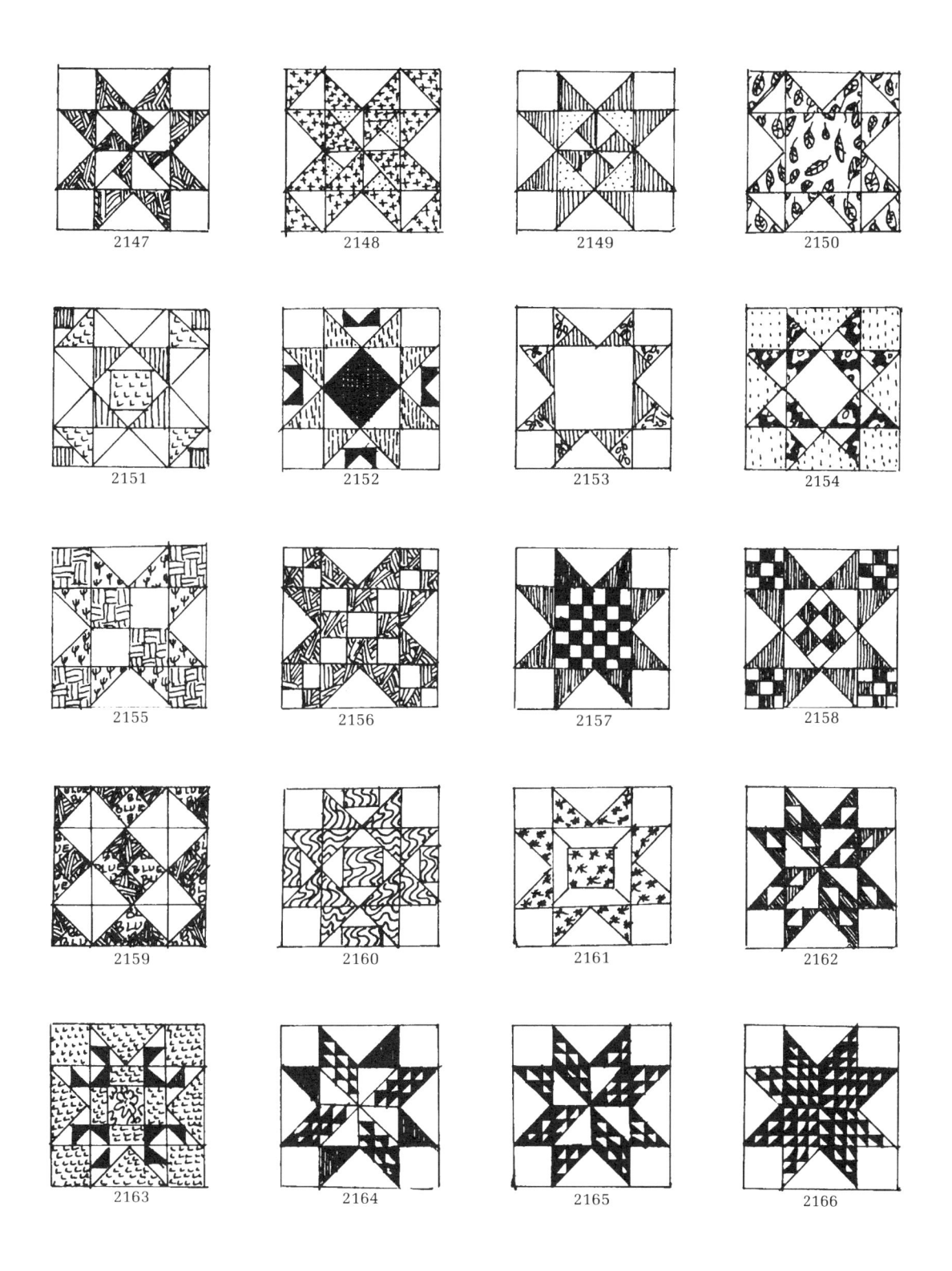

269

# Pattern Category 11: *Unequal Nine Patch with Large Center Square*

| | | |
|---|---|---|
| BLOCKS OF THIS CONSTRUCTION: | **2167** | **STARS AND SQUARES** – LAC #11<br>**RISING STAR** – Finley. *See 2826.* |
| | **2168** | **EIGHT HANDS AROUND** – LAC #149 |
| | **2169** | **FREE TRADE BLOCK** – Finley<br>**FREE TRADE PATCH** – Hall<br>**CORONATION** – Nancy Page 1937 |
| | **2170** | **ODD FELLOWS CHAIN** – LAC #61<br>**ODD FELLOWS MARCH** – Comfort 1918<br>**SAN DIEGO** – Nancy Page<br>**OLD MAID'S RAMBLE** – QEC 1978. *See 1316.* |
| | **2171** | **CASTLE GARDEN** – Nancy Cabot |
| | **2172** | **LEHIGH MAZE** – Nancy Cabot, Frank's |
| OTHER TYPES OF BLOCKS | **2175** | **OUR EDITOR** – Clara Stone. *See 1208.* |
| | **2176** | **A DESIGN FOR PATRIOTISM** – KC Star |
| | **2177** | **TWISTER** – James |
| | **2178** | **WHIRLING SQUARE** – attributed to Nancy Cabot, Nancy's. |
| | **2179** | **DOUBLE X** – Webster. *See 1316.* |
| | **2180** | **ROCKY MOUNTAIN PUZZLE** – Nancy Cabot 1933. |
| | **2181** | **GAY TWO PATCH QUILT** – OCS |
| | **2182** | **BEGINNER'S DELIGHT** – OCS |
| | **2183** | **FRAMED SQUARES** – Nancy Page |
| | **2184** | **WILD GOOSE CHASE** – Holstein |
| | **2185** | **SAWTOOTH** – Lithgow |
| | **2186a** | **JOHNNIE AROUND THE CORNER** – LAC #376 |
| | **2186b** | **THE BROKEN WHEEL** – KC Star 1943 |
| | **2187** | **STORM AT SEA** – KC Star 1932 |
| | **2188a** | **STORM AT SEA** – LAC #135. *See 1071.* |
| | **2188b** | **ROLLING STONE** – Finley |

*Blocks with Specific Construction, Other Types of Blocks (2167 – 2188b)*

271

# Pattern Category 11: *Unequal Nine Patch with Large Center Square*

| | | |
|---|---|---|
| OTHER TYPES OF BLOCKS | 2189 | FAIR AND SQUARE – KC Star 1938 |
| | 2190 | APRIL TULIPS – QNM 1980 |
| | 2191 | GIRL'S JOY – LAC #382<br>MAIDEN'S DELIGHT – Nancy Cabot |
| | 2192 | DUTCH PUZZLE – Aunt Martha. *See 1054 & 1753.* |
| | 2193 | VIRGINIA REEL – Clara Stone<br>TANGLED LINES – LAC #484 |
| | 2194 | HOBSON'S KISS – attributed to Nancy Cabot, Nancy's |
| | 2195 | MACKENZIE'S SQUARE – Nancy Cabot |
| | 2196 | COLUMBIAN PUZZLE – Clara Stone |
| | 2197 | COLUMBIA PUZZLE – LAC #31 |
| | 2198 | TULIP LADY FINGERS – LAC #394 |
| | 2199 | MONTANA MAZE – Nancy Cabot<br>MOUNTAIN MAZE – attributed to Nancy Cabot, Nancy's |
| | 2200 | GARDEN PATH – OCS/Wheeler |
| | 2201 | EASY WAYS – Farm Journal 1942. *See 1061.* |
| | 2202 | FIVE LILIES – Nancy Cabot<br>DOG TOOTH VIOLET – Lockport Batting |
| | 2203 | WILD IRIS – Prudence Penny |
| | 2204 | DESERT ROSE – Nancy Cabot |
| | 2205 | THE THORNY THICKET – KC Star 1942 |
| | 2206 | STARRY LANE – Famous Features |
| | 2207 | RIBBON SQUARE – LAC |
| | 2208 | MAGNOLIA BUD – KC Star 1932<br>PINK MAGNOLIA – attributed to Nancy Cabot, Nancy's. *See 1978.* |

*Other Types of Blocks (2189 – 2208)*

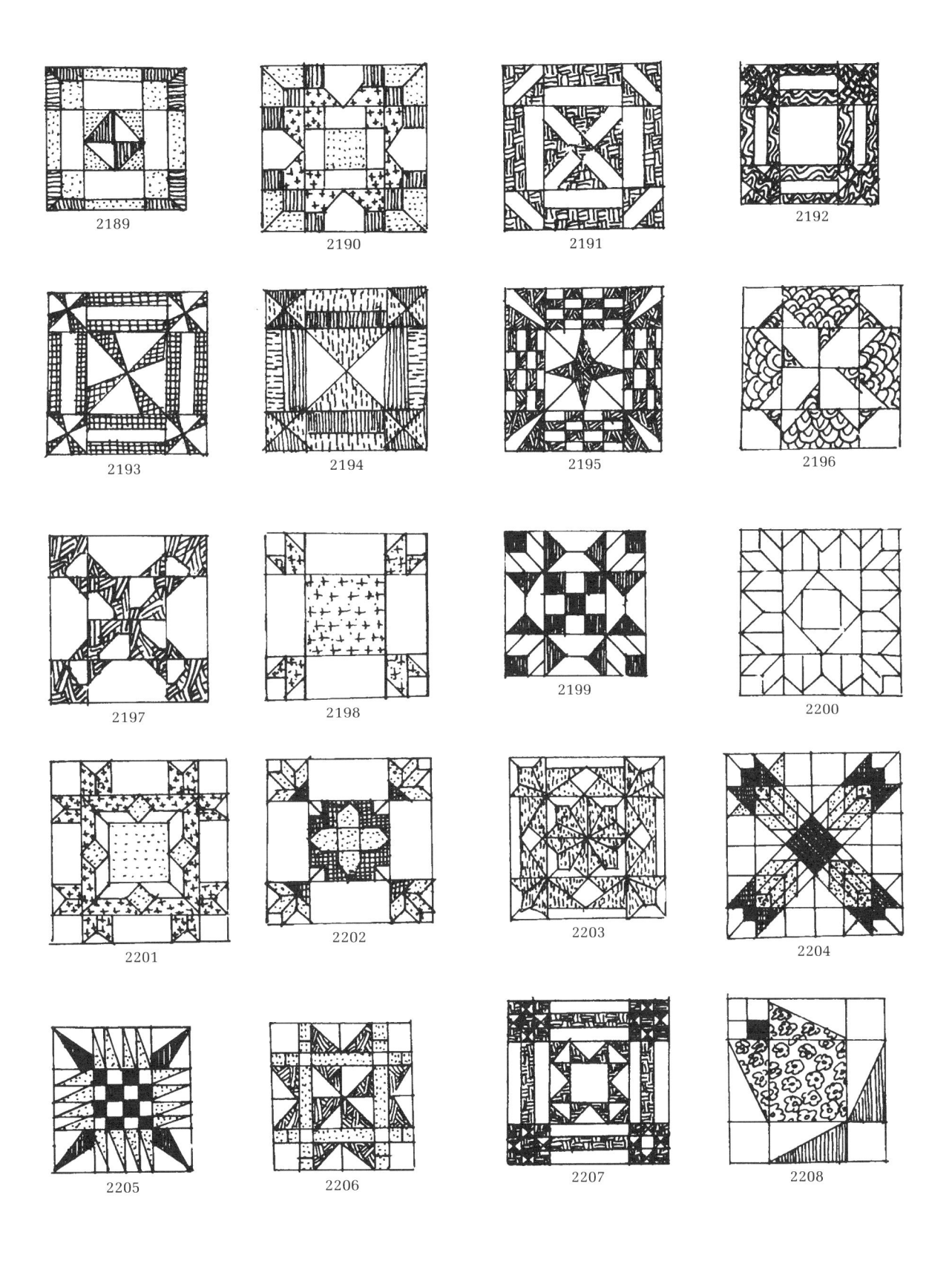

2189  2190  2191  2192
2193  2194  2195  2196
2197  2198  2199  2200
2201  2202  2203  2204
2205  2206  2207  2208

273

# Pattern Category 11: *Unequal Nine Patch with Large Center Square*

| | | |
|---|---|---|
| BLOCKS WITH CURVED SEAMS | **2210** | **Road to California** – Carlie Sexton (alternate plain blocks) |
| | **2211** | **End of the Century Patch Work** – Orange Judd Farmer 1899 (blue & green) |
| | **2212** | **Moon & Star** – Clara Stone |
| | **2213** | **Pinwheel** – Aunt Martha |
| | **2214** | **Pinwheel** – Hinson QM |
| | **2215** | **Hearts and Darts** – Aunt Kate ca. 1963 (hearts appliqué) |
| | **2216** | **Peony** – OCS/Wheeler |
| | **2217** | **Honey Bee** – McKim<br>**Blue Blazes** – Hall |
| | **2218** | **Birds in the Air** – Coats and Clark Spool Cotton 1942 |
| | **2219** | **Salal** – Prudence Penny |
| | **2220** | **Drunkard's Patchwork** – LAC. *See 1039, 1040, & 1461.* |
| | **2221** | **Queen's Crown** – LAC. *See 1510.* |
| | **2222** | **Queen's Pride** – Hinson QC. *See 1795.* |
| | **2223** | **Dogwood Blossom** – Capper's Weekly 1928<br>**Oklahoma Dogwood** – Mountain Mist. *See 1010 & 1037.* |
| | **2224** | **Autumn Leaf** – Finley. *See 1736, 1887, & 2010.* |
| | **2225** | **Old Maid's Puzzle** – Aunt Martha |
| | **2226** | **Circular Saw** – Hinson QM |
| | **2227** | **Unnamed** – Hinson QM |
| | **2228** | **Unnamed** – Hinson QM |

*Blocks with Curved Seams (2210 – 2228)*

2210  2211  2212  2213
2214  2215  2216  2217
2218  2219  2220  2221
2222  2223  2224  2225
2226  2227  2228

275

# Pattern Category 11: *Unequal Nine Patch with Large Center Square*

| | | |
|---|---|---|
| FEATHERED STARS | 2240 | THE KALEIDOSCOPE QUILT – KC Star 1930 |
| | 2241 | SANTA FE – Hearth & Home<br>DOLLY MADISON'S STAR – Finley<br>PRESIDENT'S BLOCK – Nancy Cabot |
| | 2242 | THE HOUR GLASS – Household Journal ca. 1920 |
| | 2243 | STAR DIAMOND – Ladies' Home Journal ca. 1920<br>TRIANGLE STAR – Household Journal ca. 1920 |
| | 2244a | ETOILE DE CHAMBLIE – Grandmother Clark |
| | 2244b | FEATHERED STAR OF BETHLEHEM – Capper's<br>FEATHER STAR – Carlie Sexton<br>STAR OF CHAMBLIE – Hall (red or green & white) |
| | 2245 | BLAZING STAR – Rural New Yorker 1930 (center dark)<br>STAR OF BETHLEHEM – Rural New Yorker 1930 (center light) |
| | 2246 | PINE CONE – KC Star 1935 |
| | 2247 | FEATHER EDGE STAR – KC Star 1934 |
| | 2248 | STAR OF BETHLEHEM – Capper's<br>RADIANT STAR – Aunt Martha<br>CHESTNUT BURR – Aunt Martha |
| | 2249 | FEATHER STAR – Hall<br>TWINKLING STAR – Hall<br>STAR OF BETHLEHEM – Hall<br>SAWTOOTH – Hall<br>CHESTNUT BURR – Hall |
| | 2250 | PIERRE – Hearth & Home (fence rail set) |
| | 2251 | FEATHER STAR – LAC |
| | 2252 | TWINKLING STAR – LAC<br>BLAZING STAR – Carlie Sexton<br>DIANA'S PRIDE – Capper's 1932<br>DINAH'S PRIDE – Little 'n Big |

*Feathered Stars (2240 – 2252)*

2240

2241

2242

2243

2244a

2244b

2245

2246

2247

2248

2249

2250

2251

2252

# Pattern Category 11: *Unequal Nine Patch with Large Center Square*

FEATHERED STARS
- **2253**    **UNNAMED** – Prudence Penny
- **2254**    **THE FEATHERED STAR** – Finley
- **2255**    **CALIFORNIA STAR PATTERN** – LAC
- **2256**    **CALIFORNIA STAR** – Aunt Kate 1965
- **2257**    **FEATHERED VARIABLE STAR** – QEC 1977
- **2258**    **OCTAGONAL STAR** – Safford & Bishop
- **2259**    **FEATHERED STAR** – Mountain Mist
- **2260**    **FEATHERED STAR** – Capper's  
               **FEATHER EDGE STAR** – McKim
- **2261**    **SUMMER SUN** – Nancy Cabot
- **2262**    **CALIFORNIA STAR** – Hall
- **2263**    **HALLEY'S COMET** – Aunt Mattie, Nancy Cabot

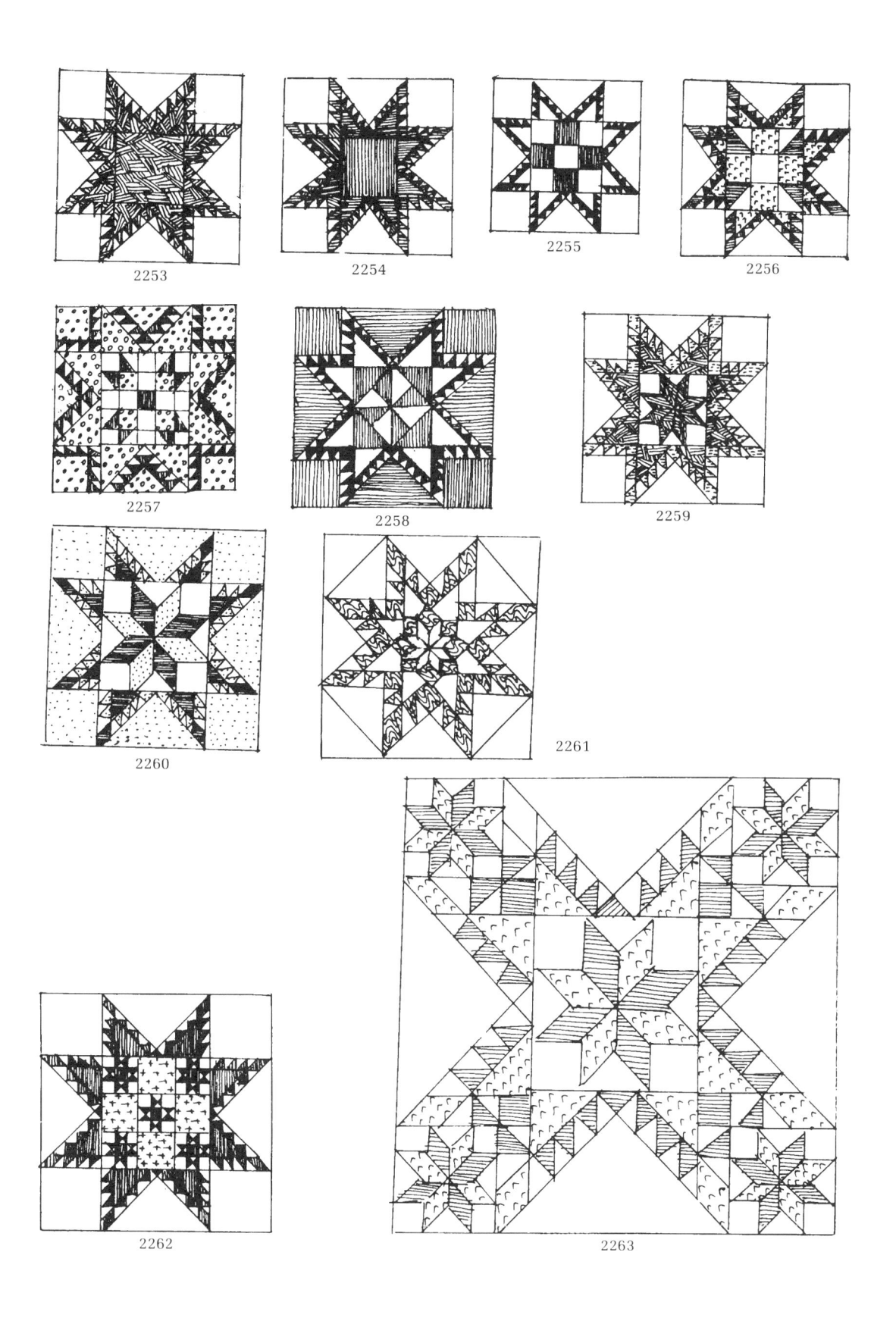

Feathered Stars (2253 – 2263)

2253

2254

2255

2256

2257

2258

2259

2260

2261

2262

2263

279

# Pattern Category 11: *Unequal Nine Patch with Large Center Square*

FEATHERED STARS

| | | |
|---|---|---|
| | **2265** | **MORNING STAR** – Nancy Cabot |
| | **2266** | **JOINING STAR** – LAC |
| | **2268** | **STAR SPANGLED BANNER** – Shelburne |
| | **2270** | **GOLDEN SPLENDOR** – Mrs. Danner 1934 (shades of yellow) |
| | | **STAR SPANGLED BANNER** – Mrs. Danner 1934 (red, white, & blue) |
| | **2271** | **PENNSYLVANIA MENNONITE FEATHER STAR** – QNM 1980 |
| | | **FEATHER STAR WITH BLAZING SUN CENTERS** – Safford & Bishop |

*A note about Feathered Stars:*

*Many of the Feathered Star patterns above do not really belong under NINE PATCH since they do not have 4 major seams which cross the block completely. But it seems that they have so much in common it would be easier to find them in one category, so I placed many of them here.*

*Also some of the stars in this category are constructed as SASH AND BLOCK rather than as a single block. See 1067 & 1068.*

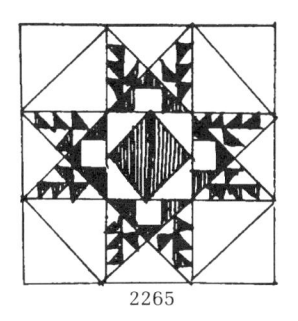

*Feathered Stars (2265 – 2271)*

2265

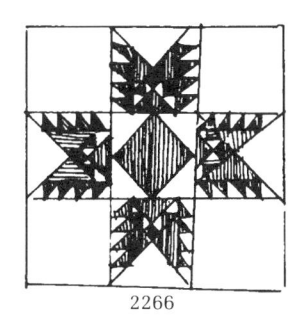

2266

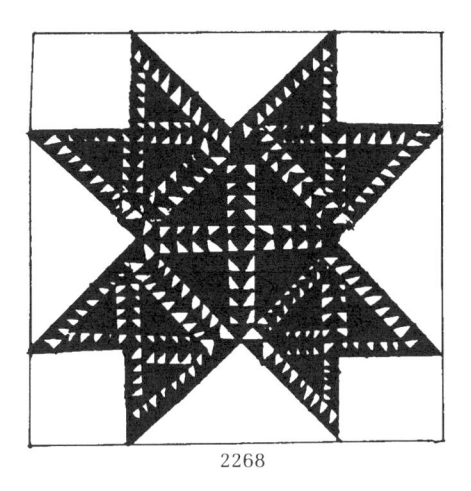

2268

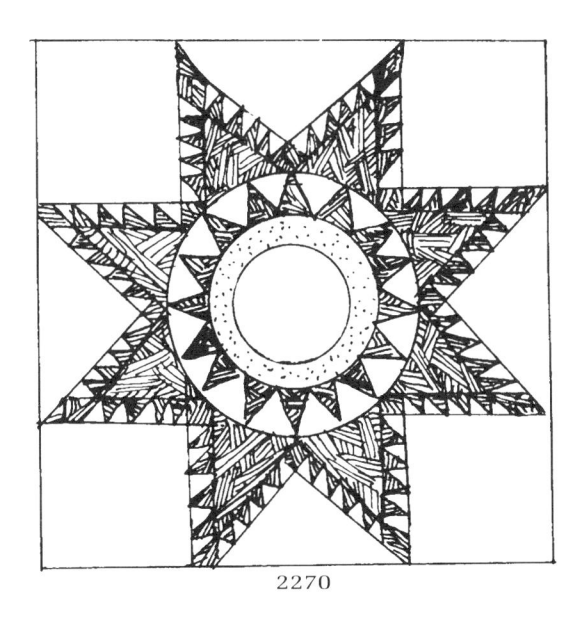

2270

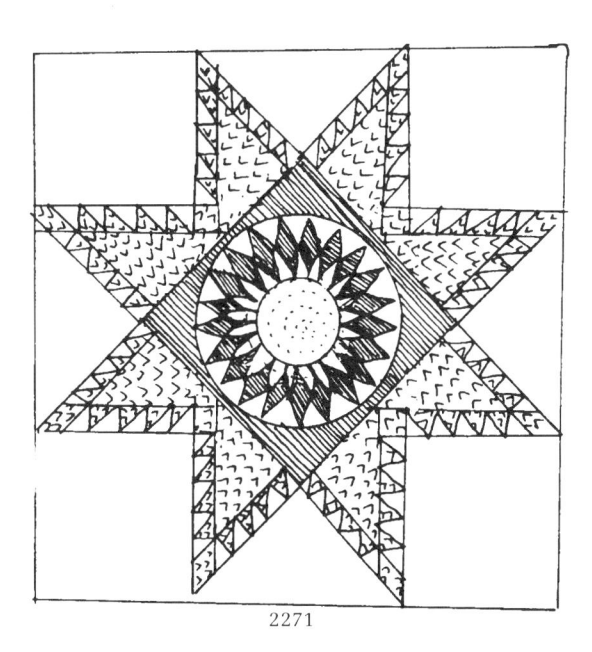

2271

# PATTERN CATEGORY 12

## One Patch – Square

**Patterns in Category 12 share these characteristics:**

- The block is made up of only squares.
- All of these squares are of equal size.

**Category 12 includes:**

- One Patch – Square Blocks, 284

## KEY TO PATTERN CATEGORY 12: ONE PATCH – SQUARE

If the block is made up of only squares and all of these are of equal size, **turn to p. 284**

# Pattern Category 12: *One Patch – Square*

ONE PATCH — SQUARE

**2276a**    **Postage Stamp** – Hall
**Hit or Miss** – Hinson QM
**Hairpin Catcher** – Hinson QM

**2276b**    **Check** – Dictionary of Needlework 1882
**Four Patch** – Hall
**Checkerboard** – Gutcheon. *See 1101.*

**2276c**    **Checkerboard** – Aunt Martha/Workbasket 1944

**2277**    *See 1601.*

**2278**    *See 1102.*
**Diagonal Square** – OCS Bk. 116

**2279**    **Building Blocks** – Nancy Cabot. *See 1013 – 1017.*

**2280a**    **Acanthus** – Attributed to Nancy Cabot, Nancy's

**2280b**    **Mosaic Rose** – Aunt Kate

**2280c**    **Leavenworth Nine Patch** – Hall

**2280d**    **Orchid Hemstitch** – Grandma Dexter (note embroidery)

**2281a**    **Crossword Puzzle** – Farm Journal

**2281b**    **Attic Stairs** – attributed to Nancy Cabot, Nancy's

**2281c**    **Tete a Tete** – Nancy Cabot

**2282a**    **Crosswords** – Farm Journal

**2282b**    **Bold Squares** – OCS Bk. 116

**2283a**    **Tahitian Postage Stamp** – Quilt World 1980

**2283b**    **Triple Irish Chain** – Capper's/Famous Features Bk. 112

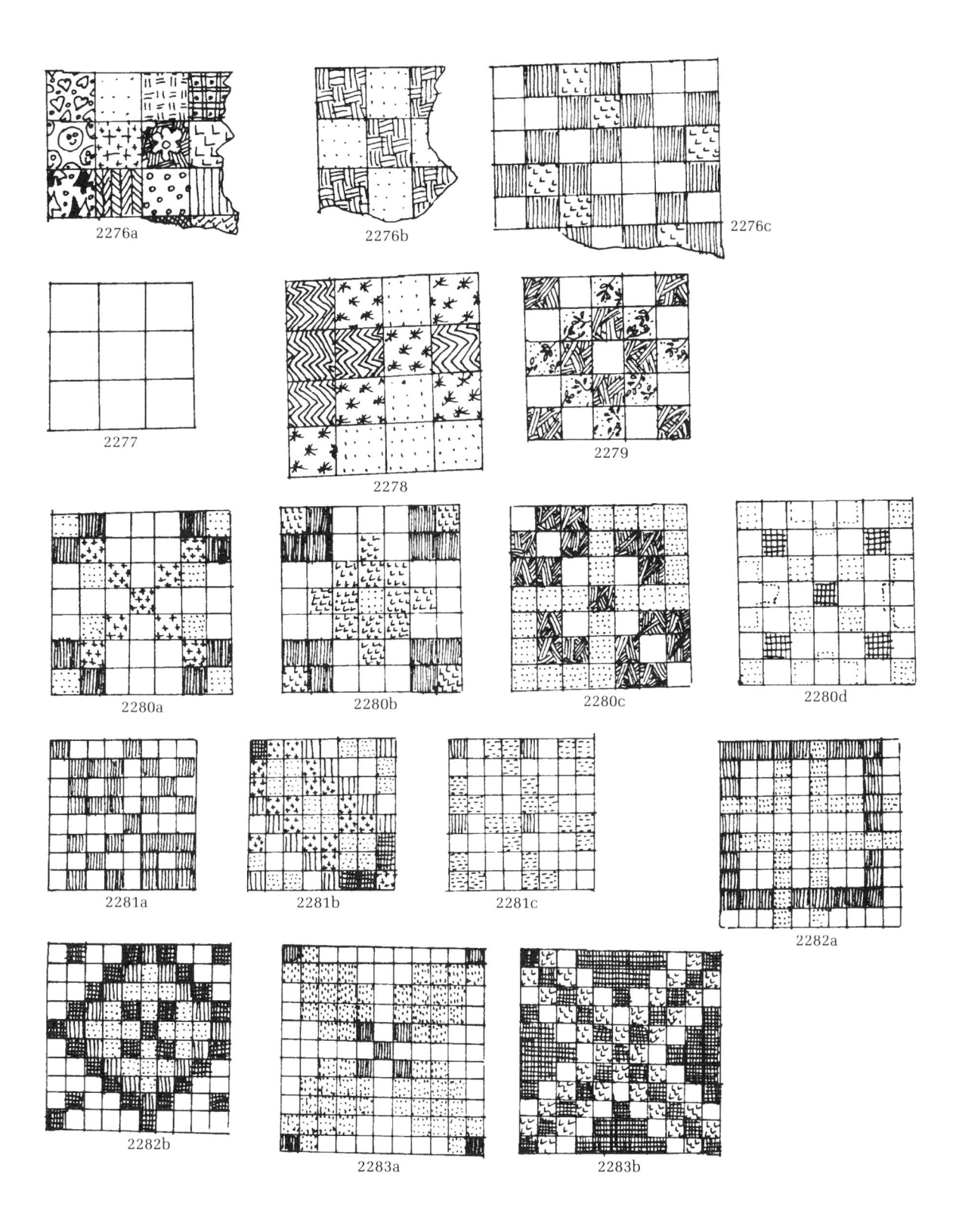

*One Patch – Square (2276a – 2283b)*

2276a
2276b
2276c
2277
2278
2279
2280a
2280b
2280c
2280d
2281a
2281b
2281c
2282a
2282b
2283a
2283b

285

Pattern Category 12: *One Patch – Square*

ONE PATCH — SQUARE

| | | |
|---|---|---|
| | **2284a** | **DOUBLE IRISH CHAIN** – OCS Wheeler |
| | **2284b** | **SUMMER GARDEN** – Nancy Cabot |
| | **2284c** | **STEPS TO THE GARDEN** – Nancy Cabot |
| | **2285a** | **BEAUTIFUL MOSAIC** – Farm Journal |
| | **2285b** | **CROSSWORD PUZZLE** – Hall |
| | **2286a** | Design is a block which is repeated |
| | | **MOSAIC BLOCK** – Rural New Yorker 1931 |
| | | **GRANDMA'S SQUARE** – Pforr |
| | | **TRIP AROUND THE WORLD** – Holstein |
| | **2286b** | Design is concentric squares over whole top; block does not repeat. |
| | | **SQUARES AROUND THE WORLD** – Mrs. Danner 1975 |
| | | **POSTAGE STAMP** – Mary McElwain |
| | | **A TRIP AROUND THE WORLD** – Holstein |
| | | **SUNSHINE AND SHADOW** – Holstein |
| | | **GRANDMA'S DREAM** – Holstein |
| | | **SUN AND SHADOW** – McCall's |
| | **2286c** | **THE WASHINGTON STAMP QUILT** – KC Star 1944 |
| | **2287** | **AUNT JEN'S STAMP QUILT** – Mrs. Danner 1958 |
| | **2288** | **STEPS TO THE ALTAR** – Mrs. Danner 1970 |

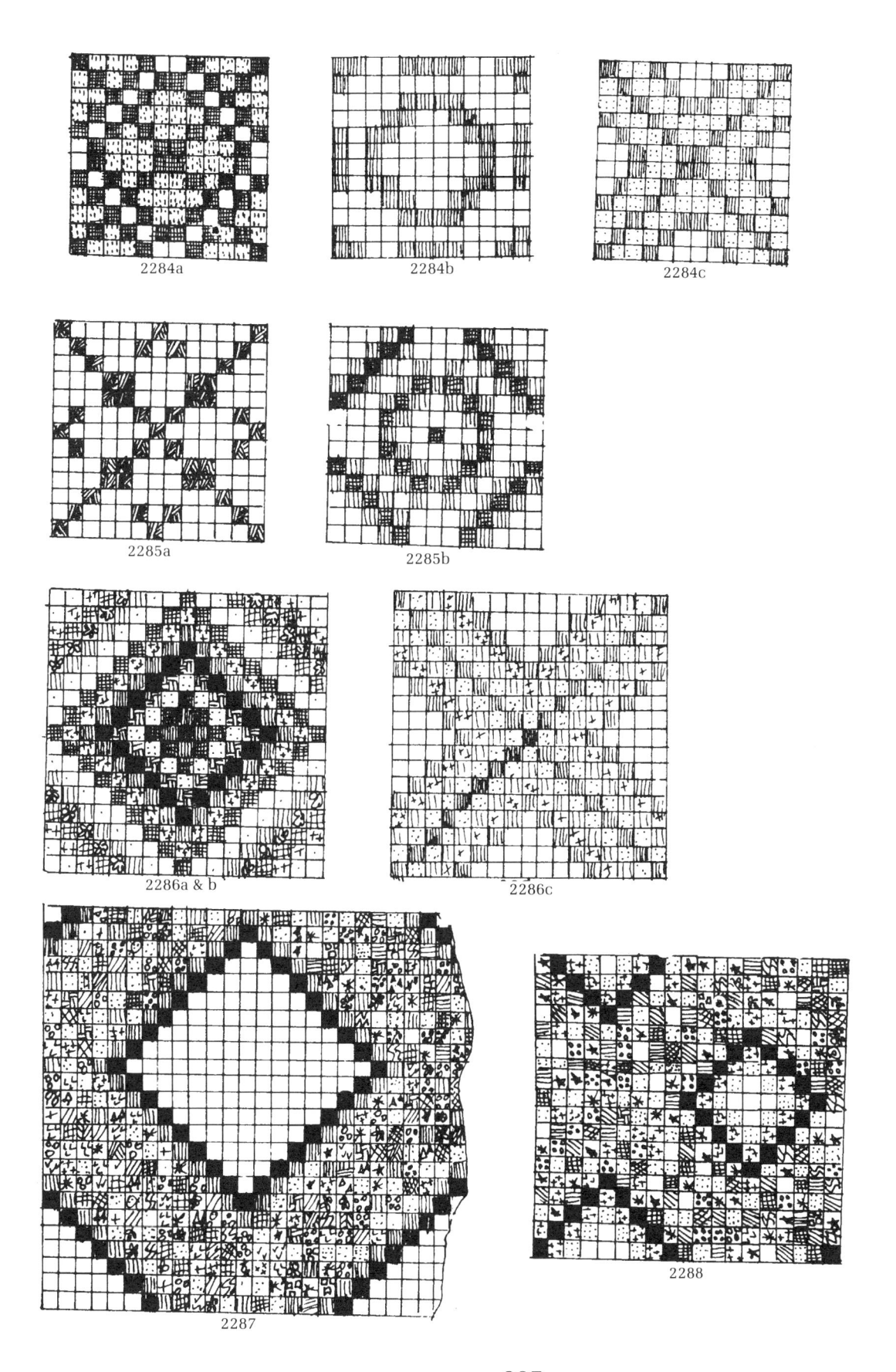

*One Patch – Square (2284a – 2288)*

2284a

2284b

2284c

2285a

2285b

2286a & b

2286c

2287

2288

# Pattern Category 12: *One Patch – Square*

ONE PATCH – SQUARE

**2289**    **RAINBOW QUILT** – Country Gentleman 1932
**SQUARES** – McCall's 1975

**2290**    **KITE'S TAIL** – Mills

**2291**    **MAGIC SQUARE** – OCS Bk. 116

**2292**    **SUGAR LOAF** – OCS Bk. 116

**2293**    **TRIP AROUND THE WORLD** – Aunt Martha & Home Art
**NINETY NINE TIMES AROUND THE WORLD** – Home Art
**POSTAGE STAMP** – KC Star 2/18/42
*This particular pattern has triangles many times to fill out the edges to make a square top; it is filed here for convenience.*
*For other similar blocks see: 2429 through 2431, 2814, & 2815.*
**RAINBOW** – McKim

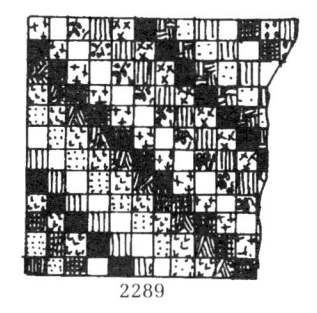

*One Patch – Square (2289 – 2293)*

2289

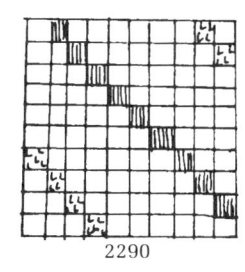

2290

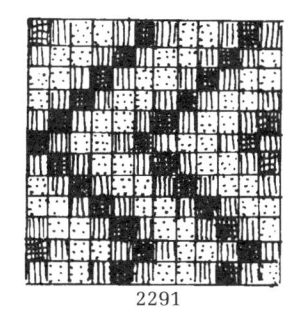

2291

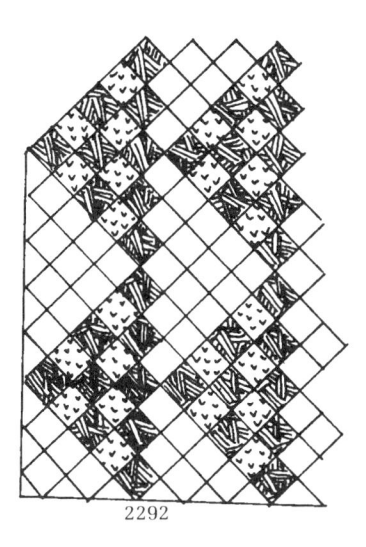

2292

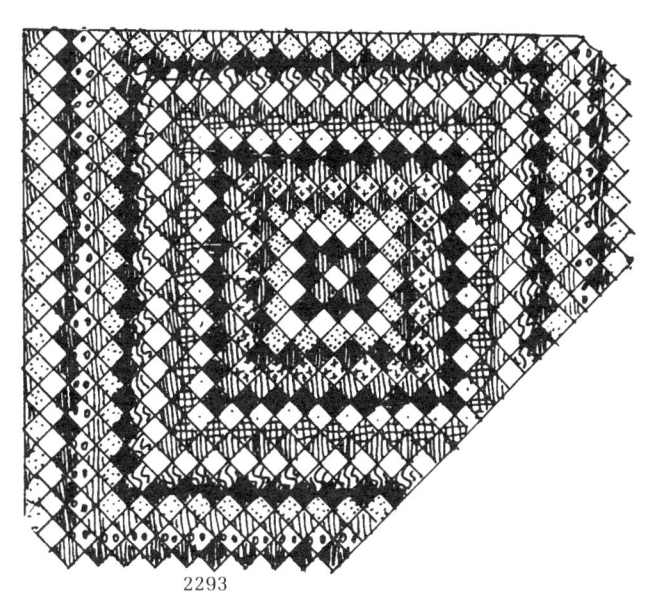

2293

289

# PATTERN CATEGORY 13

## Four X

**Patterns in Category 13 share this characteristic:**

- The block can be divided by two perpendicular lines extending from corner to corner

**Category 13 includes:**

- Four X with No Curves, 292
- Four X with Curves, 296

## KEY TO PATTERN CATEGORY 13: Four X

If the block has no curved seams, *turn to p. 292*

If the block has curved seams, *turn to p. 296*

# Pattern Category 13: *Four X*

FOUR X WITH NO CURVES

| | | |
|---|---|---|
| | 2301 | *See 1195, 1210.5, 1631, 1820.5, & 1959.* |
| | 2302 | *See 1173.* |
| | 2303 | COCK'S COMB – Nancy Cabot |
| | 2304 | BUCKWHEAT – Quilt World 10/79 |
| | 2305 | AUNT MELVERNIA'S CHAIN – attributed to Nancy Cabot, Nancy's MALVINA'S CHAIN – Quilt World 1979 |
| | 2306 | BOISE – Hearth and Home |
| | 2307 | UNNAMED – Ohio Farmer 1/27/1898 |
| | 2308 | UNNAMED – Hartman |
| | 2309 | GRANNY'S CHOICE – KC Star 12/29/48 |
| | 2310 | NEW HOUR GLASS – Clara Stone |
| | 2311 | SARAH'S FAVORITE – LAC #280<br>SALLY'S FAVORITE – Nancy Page |
| | 2312 | THE ARROWHEAD – KC Star 3/26/41. *See 172 & 2789.* |
| | 2313a | JEWEL STAR – Aunt Kate 1963 |
| | 2313b | JOHN F. KENNEDY STAR – Aunt Kate 1964 |
| | 2314 | TWIN SISTERS – LAC #213<br>WINDMILL – Grandma Dexter<br>WATER WHEEL – Ickis<br>PINWHEEL – Khin<br>WHIRLWIND – Khin. *See 1266, 1345 2406, & 1214.5.* |
| | 2315 | WINDMILL AND OUTLINE – McKim 101 (to alternate with embroidered blocks) |
| | 2316 | CRISS CROSS – Farm Journal |
| | 2317 | PATHFINDER – Nancy Cabot<br>PIONEER BLOCK – Nancy Cabot |
| | 2318 | MISSOURI'S GATEWAY STAR – Aunt Kate 2/66 |
| | 2319 | MOSAIC – LAC #18<br>SPINNING STARS – Nancy Page<br>MOSAIC #1 – Nancy Cabot<br>OLD POINSETTIA – Nancy Cabot |
| | 2320 | UNNAMED – Dakota Farmer 4/15/27 |
| | 2321 | GOOD LUCK – Nancy Cabot. *See 1286.* |
| | 2322 | CRAZY ANN – LAC #1650. *See 2487.* |

Four X with No Curves (2301 – 2322)

2301
2302
2303
2304
2305
2306
2307
2308
2309
2310
2311
2312
2313a
2313b
2314
2315
2316
2317
2318
2319
2320
2321
2322

293

# Pattern Category 13: *Four X*

FOUR X WITH
NO CURVES

| | | |
|---|---|---|
| | 2323 | TWIN DARTS – Farm Journal 2/45 |
| | 2324 | MILL AND STARS – Nancy Cabot. *See 1214, 1246, 445.9, and 3870.* |
| | 2325 | UNNAMED – Ruth Orr, Tulsa Daily World 1938 |
| | 2326 | STRING QUILT – McKim 101<br>BROKEN SPIDER WEB – Nancy Cabot |
| | 2327 | STRING QUILT – Capper's<br>RUBY'S STAR – Hectlinger |
| | 2328 | UNNAMED – OCS #548 |
| | 2329 | V BLOCK – QNM 1979 |
| | 2330 | JOB'S TROUBLES – LCPQ 1980 |
| | 2331 | STAR – Gutcheon PPP |
| | 2332 | THE EXPLODING STAR – Khin. *See 2612.* |
| | 2333 | CROSS AND DIAMOND STAR – Aunt Kate |
| | 2334 | WORLD'S FAIR (CHICAGO CENTURY OF PROGRESS) – OCS/LW |
| | 2337 | RAILROAD CROSSING – LAC #67 (set in groups of four) |
| | 2338a | OLD MAID'S RAMBLE – LAC<br>DOUBLE TRIANGLE – Rural New Yorker 2/13/32 |
| | 2338b | VERMONT – Nancy Page |
| | 2339 | OLD MAID'S RAMBLE – Woman's Day 4/65 |
| | 2340 | FLOCK OF BIRDS – Nancy Page. *See 2908.* |
| | 2341 | BIRDS IN AIR – Woman's Day ca. 1940<br>OCEAN WAVE – Wornan's Day ca. 1940 |

*There are several similar patterns indexed as Nine X. See 276 - 2800.*

Four X with No Curves (2323 – 2341)

295

# Pattern Category 13: *Four X*

| | | |
|---|---|---|
| FOUR X WITH NO CURVES | 2341.5 | THE RANGE'S PRIDE – Farm Journal |
| | 2342 | AUNT MARY'S DOUBLE IRISH CHAIN – Clara Stone |
| | 2343 | FULL BLOWN TULIP – OCS/Brooks |
| | 2344 | TWISTED RIBBONS – QNM #38, 1973 |
| | 2345 | WHEEL OF DESTINY – Farm Journal |
| | 2346 | STARRY PATH – OCS/ Brooks |
| | 2347 | SPINNING JENNY – Gutcheon PPP (one of a 2 Block Pattern) |
| | 2348 | ARKANSAS DIAMOND – Attributed to Nancy Cabot, Nancy's |
| | 2349 | LINDY'S PLANE – Nancy Cabot. *See 4165.* |
| | 2350 | LOVE KNOT – Marshall. *See 1407 & 2595.* |
| | 2351 | SPOOLS – LAC #398 |
| | 2352 | STARRY PATH – Farm Journal (set in groups of 4) |
| | 2353 | LETTER F – Clara Stone |
| | | FLORA'S FAVORITE – Clara Stone |
| | 2354 | CRAZY PIECES – Mountain Mist |
| | 2355 | ALASKA – Hearth and Home |
| | 2356 | POSY PLOT – Needlecraft Magazine 1934 |
| FOUR X WITH CURVES | 2360 | ROSE AND TRELLIS – OCS/Wheeler |
| | 2361 | HIDDEN FLOWER – OCS |
| | 2362 | PEONY – OCS/Brooks. *See 1543.* |
| | 2363 | TIC TAC TOE – QNM #66, 1975 |
| | 2364 | BOSTON – Hearth and Home |
| | 2365 | HERALD SQUARE – Nancy Cabot. *See 2943.* |
| | 2366 | SQUARE AND COMPASS – Nancy Cabot. *See 1493 & 3188.* |
| | 2367 | GRANDMOTHER'S PRIZE – OCS/Brooks 1939 |

*Four X with No Curves, Four X with Curves (2341.5 – 2367)*

297

# PATTERN CATEGORY 14

## Square in a Square

**Patterns in Category 14 share these characteristics:**

- There is a center square, which is either: a regular square or a "squeezed square."

- The center square is built up into a larger square with the addition of

    triangles

    strips

    or other shapes.

**Category 14 includes:**

- Unpieced Corners, 300
- Unpieced Center Square, 302
- Center Square Pieced of Squares and Rectangles, 302
- Specific Construction, 304
- Misc. Other Specific Construction, 308
- Curves, 250
- Blocks with Specific Construction, 314

## KEY TO PATTERN CATEGORY 14: SQUARE IN A SQUARE

**STEP 1**

| | |
|---|---:|
| If the block is of this construction ⬦, | *continue with STEP 3* |
| If the block is of this construction ⊠, | *turn to NINE X, p. 338* |
| If the block is of this construction ⊠ or this construction ⊞, | *turn to THREE PATCH, p. 386* |
| If the block is of this construction ⊠ or this construction ⊞, | *turn to NINE X, p. 338* |
| If the block is of this construction ⊞, | *turn to NINE X, p. 338* |
| If the block is not of the above construction, | *continue on to STEP 2* |

**STEP 2**

| | |
|---|---:|
| If the block is of this construction ⬦, | *turn to p. 314* |
| If the block is of this construction ⊠, | *turn to p. 316* |
| If the block is of this construction ⊠, | *turn to p. 316* |
| If the block is of this construction ⊞, | *turn to p. 318* |
| If the block is of this construction ⊡, | *turn to p. 320* |
| If the block is of this construction ⊡, | *turn to p. 322* |
| If the block is of this construction ⊚, | *turn to p. 324* |
| If the block is none of the above but has a square in the center ▫, | *turn to p. 324* |
| If the block is of this construction ⬦, | *turn to p. 326* |
| If the block is of this construction ⬦, | *turn to p. 326* |
| If the block is of this construction ⊡, or this construction ⊠, | *turn to p. 328* |

**STEP 3**

| | |
|---|---:|
| If the block has curved pieces ⬦, | *turn to p. 312* |
| If the block has unpieced corner triangles ⬦, | *turn to p. 300* |
| If the center square is unpieced ⬦, | *turn to p. 302* |
| If the center square is pieced only of squares and/or rectangles ⊠, | *turn to p. 302* |
| If the block is of this construction ⬦, | *turn to p. 304* |
| If the block has a nine patch in center square ⊞, | *turn to p. 306* |
| If the block is of this construction ⬦, | *turn to p. 332* |
| If the block is a miscellaneous Square in a Square ⬦, | *turn to p. 332* |

299

# Pattern Category 14: *Square in a Square*

BLOCKS WITH
UNPIECED CORNERS

**2375a**    TRIANGLE DESIGN – Woman's World 1931
BROKEN SASH – Nancy Cabot, Farm Journal
DUTCH TILE – Nancy Cabot
FRIENDSHIP ALBUM QUILT – Bruce Johnson
DIAMOND IN THE SQUARE – Bruce Johnson

**2375b**    PAVEMENT PATTERN – Hectlinger
ALAMANIZER – attributed to Nancy Cabot, Nancy's
SHOOFLY – Holstein. *See 1002, 1034, 1171, 1732, 1035, 1821.3, & 2033.*

**2376**    ECONOMY PATCH – Hall
HOUR GLASS – LAC
THRIFT BLOCK – Nancy Cabot
THIS AND THAT – KC Star 11/15/44. *See 1071, 2792, & 1714.*

**2377**    TWELVE TRIANGLES – Farm Journal
SHADOW BOXES – Khin. *See 2442.*

**2378**    SCRAP – Clara Stone
SQUARE ON SQUARE – Nancy Page

**2379a**    MOSAIC ROSE – Nancy Cabot

**2379b**    VIRGINIA REEL – Mountain Mist (alternate with plain blocks)
PIG'S TAIL – Mountain Mist (alternate with plain blocks)

**2380**    CRACKER – Woman's World 1931

**2381**    IMPROVED FOUR PATCH – Holstein. *See 1103.*

**2382**    COFFIN STAR – Hinson. *See 1102.*

**2383**    FRIDAY THE THIRTEENTH – KC Star 2/16/35

**2384**    LETTER H – LAC
"H" QUILT – KC Star 1/3/45
THE GATE – KC Star 1/3/45

**2385**    CROSS ROADS TO JERICO – Hearth and Home. *See 1061.*

**2386**    PATTERN WITHOUT A NAME – attributed to Nancy Cabot, Nancy's

**2387**    LOLA – Aunt Kate 1965 (corners specify striped fabric)

**2388**    VARIATION OF SAIL BOATS – Fadely

**2389**    BOWL OF FRUIT – Nancy Cabot

**2390**    MALTESE CROSS – LAC #272
IRON CROSS – Nancy Cabot
KING'S CROSS – attributed to Nancy Cabot, Nancy's. *See 2704.*

**2391**    SPINDLES AND STRIPES – KC Star 12/6/50 (striped fabric specified)

**2392**    THE WEDDING RING – Finley describes block but does not
picture it.
MEMORY WREATH – Finley (made of deceased's clothes with inscription)

**2393**    TUDOR ROSE – Nancy Cabot

**2394**    KING'S CROWN – Holstein

**2395**    "F" PATCHWORK – Orange Judd Farmer 3/17/1900

**2396**    DOUBLE ANCHOR – Little 'n Big 1964 (says "old design" but no source)
DOUBLE ANCHOR – attributed to Nancy Cabot, Nancy's

*Blocks with Unpieced Corners (2375a – 2396)*

| | | | |
|---|---|---|---|
| 2375a | 2375b | 2376 | 2377 |
| 2378 | 2379a | 2379b | 2380 |
| 2381 | 2382 | 2383 | 2384 |
| 2385 | 2386 | 2387 | 2388 |
| 2389 | 2390 | 2391 | 2392 |
| 2393 | 2394 | 2395 | 2396 |

301

# Pattern Category 14: *Square in a Square*

| | | |
|---|---|---|
| BLOCKS WITH UNPIECED CORNERS | 2397 | MONKEY WRENCH – McKim 101 (alternate with plain blocks, light & dark)<br>SNAIL'S TRAIL – McKim 101 (alternate with plain blocks, light & dark)<br>INDIANA PUZZLE – QNM #80, 1976 (alternate with plain blocks, light & dark). *See 2091.* |
| | 2398 | SNAIL'S TRAIL – LAC #504 (alternate with plain blocks, light & dark)<br>JOURNEY TO CALIFORNIA – KC Star 4/6/55<br>WHIRLIGIG QUILT – Country Gentleman<br>OCEAN WAVE – QNM #60, 1974 |
| | 2399 | SNAIL'S TRAIL – KC Star 11/29/35 (all-over) |
| | 2400 | NAUTILUS – Clara Stone |
| | 2401 | DELECTABLE MOUNTAINS – Pforr. *See 3985 & 3986.* |
| BLOCKS WITH UNPIECED CENTER SQUARE | 2403 | ART SQUARE – LAC #324<br>VILLAGE SQUARE – Nancy Cabot<br>DOTTIE'S CHOICE – Farm Journal |
| | 2404 | CAROL'S SCRAP TIME QUILT – Little 'n Big 10/64 |
| | 2105 | STAR PREMO – Clara Stone<br>DIADEM – Clara Stone |
| | 2406a | RIGHT AND LEFT – LAC #195. *See 1266, 1345, & 2314.* |
| | 2406b | SUGAR BOWL QUILT – Rural New Yorker 10/8/32, Nancy Cabot |
| | 2407 | DOVE OF PEACE – McKim (dove is quilted) |
| CENTER SQUARE PIECED OF SQUARES AND RECTANGLES | 2409 | LETTER L – The Farm News ca. 1923 |
| | 2410 | THE FRIENDSHIP QUILT – KC Star 8/17/38 |
| | 2411 | UTILITY BLOCK – Ohio Farmer 4/16/1896 |
| | 2412 | UNNAMED – Mahler |
| | 2413a | GRANDMOTHER'S PRIDE – Home Art |
| | 2413b | NINE PATCH CHECKERBOARD – Shelburne<br>OLD MAIL – The Woman's Century<br>THE QUEEN'S FAVORITE – Capper's 6/21/30<br>CHECKERBOARD – Gutcheon PPP. *See 2814.* |
| | 2414 | ODD FELLOW'S QUILT – Orange Judd Farmer<br>ALBUM – McKim. This is actually the only pattern with a name embroidered<br>COURTHOUSE SQUARE – Hall<br>ARBOR WINDOW – Grandmother Clark 1931<br>THE CROSS PATCH – Rural New Yorker 6/7/30 |
| | 2415 | MAYOR'S GARDEN – Nancy Cabot<br>MODERN BROKEN DISH – KC Star |

*Blocks with Unpieced Corners, Unpieced Center Square, Center Square Pieced of Squares and Rectangles (2397 – 2415)*

2397
2398
2399
2400

2401

2403
2404
2405
2406a

2406b
2407

2409
2410
2411
2412

2413a
2413b
2414
2415

# Pattern Category 14: *Square in a Square*

| | | |
|---|---|---|
| CENTER SQUARE PIECED OF SQUARES AND RECTANGLES | 2417 | **Union Square** – Nancy Cabot<br>**Beacon Light** – attributed to Nancy Cabot, Nancy's |
| | 2418 | **Oriental Puzzle** – attributed to Nancy Cabot, Nancy's |
| | 2419 | **The Pride of Ohio** – KC Star 6/28/39 |
| | 2420 | **Cabin Windows** – KC Star 4/17/40 |
| | 2421 | **Unnamed** – Ohio Farmer 9/20/1894<br>**Four-four Time** – Farm Journal |
| | 2422 | **Beacon Lights** – Nancy Page |
| | 2423 | **Four Points** – LAC<br>**Four Point** – Household Journal<br>**Lattice and Square** – Nancy Cabot. *See 2461.* |
| | 2424 | **Children of Israel** – Hall (corners are checked fabric) |
| | 2425 | **Children Israel** – Aunt Martha (corners are pieced) |
| | 2426 | **Country Checkers** – Progressive Farmer Johnson |
| | 2427A | **New Double Irish Chain** – Frank. *Same effect as 1013.* |
| | 2427B | **Yreka Square** – Nancy Cabot |
| | 2428 | **Windows and Doors** – Nancy Cabot<br>**Doors and Windows** – Nancy Cabot<br>**New Double Irish Chain** – attributed to Nancy Cabot, Nancy's |
| | 2429 | **Cobblestones** – Nancy Cabot<br>**Blue Heather** – Nancy Cabot<br>**Checkerboard Squares** – Bishop and Safanda. *See 2413 & 2314.* |
| | 2430 | **Chipyard** – Clarke<br>**Postage Stamp** – Clarke. *See 2293.* |
| BLOCKS OF THIS CONSTRUCTION: | 2433 | **Swallows in the Window** – KC Star 9/27/30 |
| | 2434 | **Mosaic #2** – LAC #330 |
| | 2435 | **Nine Patch Star** – Aunt Martha<br>**Long Nine Patch** – KC Star 6/12/40 |
| | 2436 | **Jewel** – Grandmother Clark 1931 |
| | 2438 | **The Broken Path** – KC Star 10/25/39 |
| | 2439 | **Duck and Ducklings** – Farm Journal and Nancy Cabot |
| | 2440 | **Pine Burr** – Hall |
| | 2441 | **King Solomon's Temple** – Clara Stone<br>**Solomon's Temple** – KC Star 11/17/36 |

*Center Square Pieced of Squares and Rectangles, Blocks with Specific Construction (2417 – 2441)*

305

# Pattern Category 14: *Square in a Square*

BLOCKS OF THIS CONSTRUCTION:

| | 2442 | UNNAMED – Bishop and Safanda |
|---|---|---|
| | 2443 | ECONOMY – Meeker. *See 2377.* |
| | 2444 | WIND BLOWN SQUARE – McKim 101 |
| | | WHIRLPOOLS – Nancy Page. *See 2476.* |
| | 2445 | MOSAIC #50 – LAC #333 |
| | 2446 | BROKEN BAND – The Farm News ca. 1920 |
| | 2447 | TOMBSTONE QUILT – attributed to Nancy Cabot, Nancy's |
| | 2448 | PYRAMIDS – Nancy Cabot |
| | 2449 | COLONIAL GARDEN – Progressisve Farmer |
| | 2450 | BOW BELLS – attributed to Nancy Cabot, Nancy's |
| | 2451 | OUR VILLAGE GREEN – Progressive Farmer 33/35. *See 283 & 2628.* |
| | 2452 | AUNT ANNA'S ALBUM BLOCK – Clara Stone |

BLOCKS OF THIS CONSTRUCTION:

| | 2453 | ROYAL STAR QUILT – LAC #462 |
|---|---|---|
| | 2454 | SKY ROCKET – McKim 101 |
| | | STARLIGHT – Nancy Page |
| | | JEWEL BOXES – Nancy Page |
| | | THE ALBUM – KC Star 6/15/37 |
| | 2455 | DOG TOOTH VIOLET – Nancy Cabot |
| | 2456 | INDIANAPOLIS – Hearth & Home |
| | 2457 | FOUR SQUARES – Nancy Cabot |
| | 2458 | CHINESE HOLIDAYS – Nancy Cabot |
| | 2459 | YELLOW CLOVER – Nancy Cabot |
| | 2460 | GRAPE VINES – Nancy Cabot |
| | 2461 | FORT SUMTER – Nancy Cabot. *See 2423.* |
| | 2462 | MEMORY BLOCKS – Nancy Cabot. *See 2048.* |
| | 2463 | SCOTCH PLAID – Carlie Sexton 1928 (plaid fabric) |
| | | SCOTCH SQUARES – Farm Journal & Nancy Cabot |
| | 2464 | MOSAIC #5 – LAC #335 |
| | | JACK IN THE PULPIT – Finley |
| | | TOAD IN THE PUDDLE – Finley |
| | | MOSAIC #2 – Nancy Cabot 1934 |

*Blocks with Specific Construction (2442 – 2464)*

2442  2443  2444  2445
2446  2447  2448  2449
2450  2451  2452
2453  2454  2455  2456
2457  2458  2459  2460
2461  2462  24663  2464

# Pattern Category 14: *Square in a Square*

BLOCKS OF THIS CONSTRUCTION:

| | 2465 | WORLD'S FAIR – Grandma Dexter |
|---|---|---|
| | 2466 | UNNAMED – Peterson's Magazine ca. 1880 |
| | 2467 | IOWA – Hearth and Home |

BLOCKS OF THIS CONSTRUCTION:

| | 2469 | MOSAIC #1 – LAC #329 |
|---|---|---|
| | | MOSAIC #3 – Nancy Cabot 1934 |
| | 2470 | MOSAIC #21 – LAC #349 |
| | | MOSAIC #6 – Nancy Cabot 1934 |
| | 2471 | GEM BLOCK – Woman's World 1931 |
| | | THE ROAD TO PARIS – Rural New Yorker 2/20/32 |
| | 2472 | DOUBLE SQUARES – LAC #225 |
| | | JACK IN THE PULPIT – Clara Stone |
| | | BROKEN DISHES – Needlecraft 1918 |
| | 2473 | THE DEWEY – Nancy Page (red, white, and blue) |
| | 2474 | MOTHER'S FAVORITE – Comfort |
| | 2475 | MOSAIC #6 – LAC #334 |
| | | MOSAIC #4 – Nancy Cabot 1934 |
| | | ZIG ZAG TILE QUILT – Nancy Page |
| | 2476 | BALKAN PUZZLE – Nancy Cabot |
| | | WINDBLOWN STAR – Nancy Cabot 1933. *See 1211.* |
| | 2477 | TWIN STARS – Aunt Kate 1963 |
| | 2478 | MISSISSIPPI STAR – Aunt Kate 1966 |
| | 2479 | THREE CHEERS – Farm Journal |
| | 2480 | ARRANT RED BIRDS – Nancy Cabot 1936 |
| | 2481 | MRS. CLEVELAND'S CHOICE – LAC #144 |
| | | COUNTY FAIR – Hall |
| | 2482 | STAR OF MANHATTAN – Aunt Kate 1964 |
| | 2483 | TRIANGLES – Khin. *See 206, 2486, & 3162.* |
| | 2484 | FRIENDSHIP'S CHAIN – Orange Judd Farmer 10/20/1900 |

MISC. BLOCKS OF THIS CONSTRUCTION:

| | 2486 | CORN AND BEANS – McKim 101. *See 1206, 2483, & 3162.* |
|---|---|---|
| | 2487 | CRAZY ANN – LAC 165 |
| | | PINWHEEL – Farm Journal. *See 2322.* |
| | 2488 | JAY WALKER – attributed to Nancy Cabot, Nancy's |
| | 2489 | CIRCLING SWALLOWS – OCS/Wheeler |

*Blocks with Specific Construction, Misc. Blocks with Specific Construction (2465 – 2489)*

# Pattern Category 14: *Square in a Square*

MISC. BLOCKS OF THIS CONSTRUCTION:

| | | |
|---|---|---|
| | 2490 | UNNAMED – OCS/Brooks |
| | 2491 | WHIRLING STAR – attributed to Nancy Cabot, Nancy's. *See 3924.* |
| | 2492 | ELLA'S STAR – Hearth and Home 1910<br>EXEA'S STAR – Clara Stone |
| | 2493 | ST. PAUL – Hearth and Home<br>LADY OF THE LAKE – Prairie Farmer ca. 1930. *See 2517.* |
| | 2494 | WINGED SQUARE – OCS/Wheeler |
| | 2495 | CROSS WITHIN A CROSS – LAC #3130. *See 1855.* |
| | 2496 | NIGHT AND DAY – Aunt Kate 1963 |
| | 2497 | SPINNING STARS – QNM 1976 |
| | 2498 | FOUR TRIANGLES – Farm Journal |
| | 2499 | SIGNS OF SPRING – Farm Journal |
| | 2500 | VICE PRESIDENT'S QUILT – LAC #298 |
| | 2501 | CENTURY OF PROGRESS – Gammell |
| | 2502 | THE RAINBOW SQUARE – Gammell |
| | 2503 | ANNAPOLIS – Hearth and Home |
| | 2504 | EIGHT DIAMONDS AND A STAR – Aunt Martha<br>ORIENTAL STAR – Nancy Cabot |
| | 2505 | KALEIDOSCOPE – Meeker |
| | 2506 | BRUNSWICK STAR – OCS/Wheeler |
| | 2507 | DIAMOND STAR – Aunt Martha |
| | 2508 | SKY ROCKET – Nancy Cabot. *See 3823.* |
| | 2509 | STAR AND CHAINS – LAC #6<br>ROLLING STAR – Hall<br>RING AROUND THE STAR – Hall |
| | 2510 | ALL HALLOWS – QNM 1975 |
| | 2511 | TRIPLE LINK CHAIN – Nancy Cabot |
| | 2512 | PYRAMIDS – Nancy Cabot |
| | 2513 | MAGNOLIA BLOCK – Nancy Cabot |

*Misc. Blocks with Specific Construction (2490 – 2513)*

311

Pattern Category 14: *Square in a Square*

BLOCKS WITH CURVES

| | 2514 | MOON AND SWASTIKA – Nancy Cabot. *See 1496.* |
|---|---|---|
| | 2515 | INDIANA – Hearth and Home<br>CIRCLE AND SQUARE – KC Star 1936<br>OIL FIELDS OF OKLAHOMA – KC Star |
| | 2516 | HONOLULU – Hearth and Home |
| | 2517 | LADY OF THE LAKE – Nancy Cabot 1933<br>GALAHAD'S SHIELD – Progressive Farmer. *See 2493.* |
| | 2518 | CRISS CROSS – OCS/Wheeler |
| | 2519 | PENELOPE'S FAVORITE – Nancy Cabot<br>PENN'S PUZZLE – Nancy Cabot |
| | 2520 | PENELOPE'S FAVORITE – Nancy Cabot 1934 |
| | 2521 | SQUARES AND CROSSES – Nancy Cabot |
| | 2522 | DAHLIA – Aunt Martha |
| | 2523 | QUATREFOILS – Frank's |
| | 2524 | MAINE – Hearth and Home<br>ARKANSAS – KC Star 12/9/33 |
| | 2525 | POSIES ROUND THE SQUARE – Needlecraft 7/34<br>DANDELION QUILT – QNM 1974 |
| | 2526 | THE POSEY QUILT – KC Star 6/8/29 |
| | 2527 | SPICE PINKS – Mrs. Danner 1934 |
| | 2528 | SWEETHEART GARDEN – Nancy Cabot |
| | 2529 | GRANDMOTHER'S ENGAGEMENT RING – Mountain Mist. *See 2680, 1085, & 4074.* |

*Blocks with Curves (2514 – 2529)*

2514  2515  2516  2517
2518  2519  2520  2521
2522  2523  2524  2525
2526  2527  2528  2529

# Pattern Category 14: *Square in a Square*

BLOCKS OF THIS
CONSTRUCTION:

2533   NECKTIE – LAC #119
       COLONIAL BOW TIE – Grandmother Clark, Grandma Dexter
       PEEKHOLE – Woman's World 1931. *See 1152.3, 1376, 1429, 1712, 1899, 1900, & 3608.*

2534   MR. ROOSEVELT'S NECKTIE – Clara Stone
       SUSANNAH – LAC #485
       OH SUSANNAH – Nancy Cabot. *See 1332 & 2535.*

2535   SUSANNAH – Gutcheon PPP. *See 1332 & 2534.*

2536   MOSAIC #5 – Nancy Cabot 1934
       WINGED ARROW – Nancy Page. *See 1338.*

2537   BACHELOR'S PUZZLE – KC Star 8/8/31
       THE PINWHEEL – KC Star 1938
       BUILDING BLOCKS – Grandma Dexter
       ROAD TO JERUSALEM – attributed to Nancy Cabot. *See 296.*

2538   STAR OF MANY POINTS – LAC
       MICHIGAN BEAUTY – Clara Stone
       ARROWHEAD STAR – KC Star 1931
       MODERN STAR – Grandmother Clark, Grandma Dexter
       MANY POINTED STAR – Nancy Cabot, Home Art
       BEECH MOUNTAIN QUILT – Marshall
       LAUREL WREATH – Grandmother Clark 1932 (appliquéd to a large square)

2539A  DIAMOND STAR – LAC #244
       A QUILT MOSAIC – KC Star 9/5/45

2539B  MOTHER'S CHOICE – Clara Stone
       DOVE AT THE WINDOWS – Mrs. Danner 1934
       FRINGED SQUARE – Nancy Cabot
       LAUREL WREATH – Capper's 1931, Prairie Farmer 1931

2539C  AUNT SUKEY'S PATCH – Aunt Jane/Household Journal 1914
       AUNT SUKEY'S PATTERN – Aunt Jane/Household Journal
       OPEN BOX – Nancy Page
       PAPER FLOWERS – Nancy Page

2540   SANDHILLS STAR – KC Star 1/18/39
       BLOSSOMING CACTUS – attributed to Nancy Cabot, Nancy's

2541   L QUILT – QNM 1980

2542   THE VILLAGE GREEN – Country Gentleman 7/30

2543   FOUR MILLS – Frank

2544   THE SPIDER WEB – KC Star 9/25/40

2545   OPTICAL ILLUSION – Little 'n Big 1965. *See 2605.*

2546   WINGED SQUARE – Progressive Farmer. *See 1426.*

2547   MICHIGAN – Hearth and Home

2548   PENNSYLVANIA – Hearth and Home

2549   FAIRY TALE – Aunt Kate 1964

2550   FRIENDSHIP RING – KC Star 12/3/41
       MEMORY QUILT – KC Star 12/3/41

2551   TULIP RING – Aunt Kate 1963

2552   CRAB APPLE BLOCK – Nancy Cabot

*Blocks with Specific Construction (2533 – 2552)*

Pattern Category 14: *Square in a Square*

BLOCKS OF THIS CONSTRUCTION:

| | 2554 | WORLD WITHOUT END – Mahler |
|---|---|---|
| | 2555 | ROSE TELLIS – Nancy Cabot |
| | 2556 | SHOOTING STAR – Nebraska Collections |
| | 2557 | COLONIAL PAVEMENT – OCS/Brooks |
| | 2558 | IRISH PLAID – attributed to Nancy Cabot, Nancy's |

BLOCKS OF THIS CONSTRUCTION:

| | 2560 | THE RADIO WINDMILL – KC Star 10/22/41<br>WINDMILL – Nancy Cabot |
|---|---|---|
| | 2561 | ARABIC LATTICE – LAC #413. *See 1421.* |
| | 2562 | WASHINGTON'S PUZZLE – LAC #32<br>CHECKERBOARD SKEW – Gutcheon PPP |
| | 2563 | DELAWARE CROSSPATCH – Nancy Cabot |
| | 2564 | UNNAMED – McCall's Book of Needlework Winter 1942/43 |
| | 2566 | DUCK CREEK PUZZLE – Nancy Cabot |
| | 2567 | QUEBEC – Nancy Cabot |
| | 2568 | THE TRIANGLE PUZZLE – LAC #33<br>TRIANGLE TRAILS – Nancy Cabot |
| | 2569 | SOUTHERN STAR – Grandma Dexter |

*Blocks with Specific Construction (2554 – 2569)*

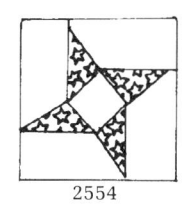

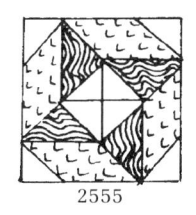

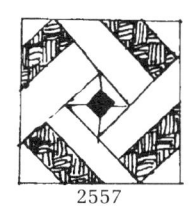

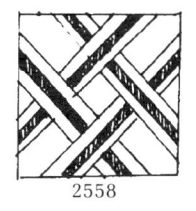

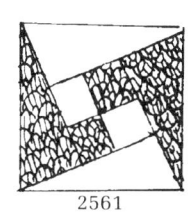

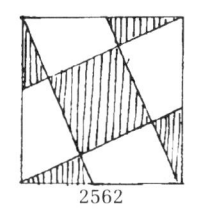

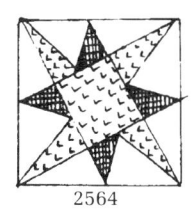

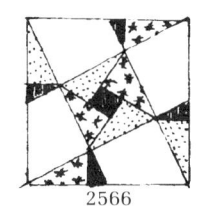

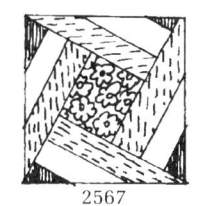

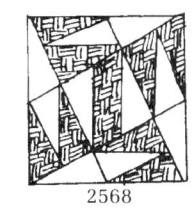

2554
2555
2556
2557
2558
2560
2561
2562
2563
2564
2566
2567
2568
2569

317

# Pattern Category 14: *Square in a Square*

BLOCKS OF THIS CONSTRUCTION:

| | | |
|---|---|---|
| | 2571 | BRIGHT HOPES – Farm Journal. *See 3210.* |
| | 2572 | WHITE HOUSE STEPS – LAC #221 |
| | 2573 | THE LOG PATCH – LAC #168 |
| | | AMERICAN LOG PATCHWORK – LAC #374 |
| | | COLONIAL BLOCK – Doyle (shaded as in #2572) |
| | | LOG CABIN – Finley. *See 3240.* |
| | | *The basic block can have 3 or more courses of logs. The shading arrangement is generally as shown or as in 2572.* |
| | | *There is much variety in the way the blocks are set together.* |
| | 2574 | LOG CABIN – Nebraska Collections |
| | 2576 | PIONEER BLOCK – Doyle |
| | | LOG CABIN – Finley |
| | 2577 | SWASTIKA PATCH – LAC #455 |
| | | SWASTIKA – Hall |
| | | THE PURE SYMBOL OF RIGHT DOCTRINE – Hall |
| | | HEART'S SEAL – Hall |
| | | CHINESE 10,000 PERFECTIONS – Hall |
| | | FAVORITE OF THE PERUVIANS – Hall |
| | | BATTLE AX OF THOR – Hall |
| | | MOUND BUILDERS – Hall |
| | | CATCH ME IF YOU CAN – Hall |
| | | WIND POWER OF THE OSAGES – Hall |
| | 2578 | STAR OF VIRGINIA – Wallace's Farmer 5/11/28. *See 2141.* |
| | 2579 | INTERLACED BLOCKS – LAC #326 |
| | | TRUE LOVER'S KNOT – Capper's 2/27/31 |
| | 2580 | CARPENTER'S SQUARE – LAC #395 |
| | 2581 | FLYING SQUARES – LAC #233 |
| | 2582 | UNNAMED – QNM 1975 |
| | 2583 | LACY LATTICE WORK – Farm Journal |
| | 2584 | IRISH PUZZLE – LAC #27 |
| | | INDIAN TRAIL – Finley |
| | | FOREST PATH – Finley |
| | | WINDING WALK – Finley |
| | | RAMBLING ROAD – Finley |
| | | RAMBLING ROSE – Finley |
| | | CLIMBING ROSE – Finley |
| | | OLD MAID'S RAMBLE – Finley |
| | | STORM AT SEA – Finley |
| | | FLYING DUTCHMAN – Finley |
| | | NORTH WIND – Finley |
| | | WEATHER VANE – Finley |
| | | TANGLED TARES – Finley |
| | | PRICKLY PEAR – Finley |
| | | KANSAS TROUBLES – Hall. *See 1354 & 1363.* |
| | 2585 | QUARTERED STAR – James |
| | 2586 | HOPE OF HARTFORD – Farm Journal 2/45 |
| | | DOUBLE STAR – attributed to Nancy Cabot, Nancy's |
| | 2587 | NEBRASKA WINDMILL – QNM 1977 |
| | 2588 | SPINNING JENNY – Nancy Cabot |
| | 2589 | FOUR SQUARE – Hearth and Home |
| | 2590 | WHIRLING SQUARE – Nancy Cabot |
| | 2591 | DYNAMETRY – Canada Quilts 1980 |

*Blocks with Specific Construction (2571 – 2591)*

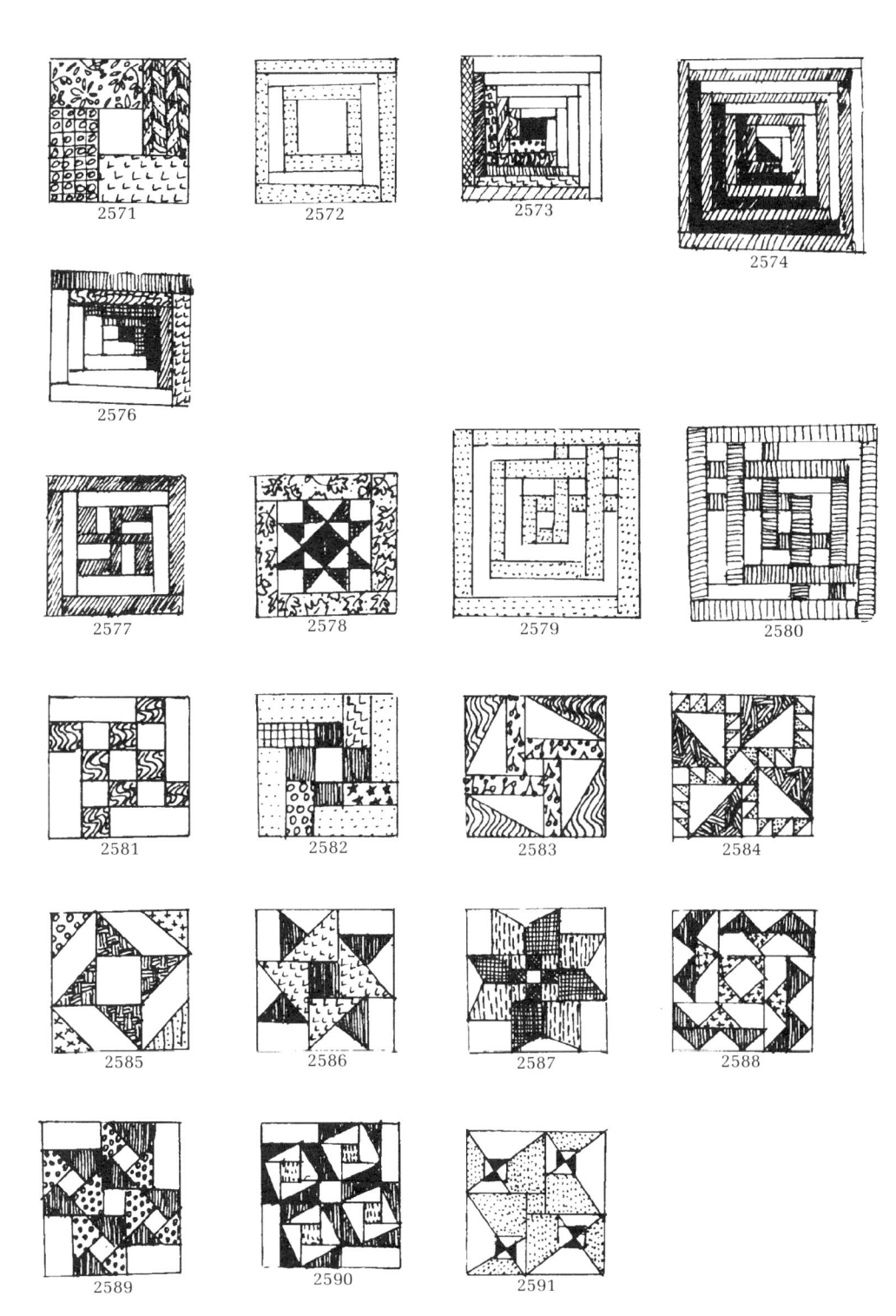

Pattern Category 14: *Square in a Square*

BLOCKS OF THIS CONSTRUCTION:

| | | |
|---|---|---|
| | 2594a | Spool – McKim 101 |
| | | Empty Spool – Nancy Cabot |
| | | Love Knot – Marshall |
| | 2594b | Gold Nuggets – Aunt Kate (center yellow). *See 1400, 1407, 2350, & 4104.* |
| | 2595 | The Diversion Quilt – KC Star 7/11/45 |
| | 2596 | Islam – Nancy Cabot |
| | 2597 | Box Quilt – LAC #351 |
| | | Eccentric Star – Grandmother Clark |
| | | Box Car Patch – Nancy Cabot |
| | | Open Book – Needlecraft Supply Co |
| | | Contrary Husband – KC Star 11/9/38 |
| | | Roads to Berlin – KC Star 8/13/44 |
| | | The Open Box – Gammell. *See 1683.* |
| | 2598 | Formal Garden – Farm Journal |
| | 2599 | Bacon Patch – attributed to Nancy Cabot, Nancy's |
| | 2600 | Double Windmill – Nancy Cabot |
| | 2601 | Slashed Album – LAC #37 |
| | | Diamond Point – Household Journal |
| | | Flying Bats – KC Star 1932/OCS–Wheeler |
| | | Around the Chimney – KC Star 1932 |
| | 2602 | Open Window – Nancy Cabot |
| | 2603 | Eccentric Star – Holstein |
| | 2604 | Captain's Wheel – Dunton |
| | 2605 | Star and Square – Ohio Farmer 1/18/1894 |
| | | Courtyard Square – Aunt Kate 1963. *See 1061, 1282, 2545, & 3735.* |
| | 2606 | White House Steps – OCS/Wheeler |
| | 2607 | Grandma's Hop-Scotch – KC Star 4/15/50 |
| | 2608 | Minnesota – Nancy Page |
| | | Depression – Nancy Page |
| | 2609 | The Star of Alamo – KC Star 11/12/41 |
| | 2610 | Grandmother's Cross – McKim 101 |
| | 2611 | Four Squares – Nancy Cabot |
| | 2612 | Exploding Stars – Khin. *See 2332.* |
| | 2613 | Carnival – Nancy Cabot |
| | 2614 | Star and Crown – OCS/Wheeler |
| | 2615 | Rustic Wheel – Nancy Cabot |
| | 2616 | Sentry's Pastime – Nancy Cabot |

*Blocks with Specific Construction (2594a – 2616)*

2594a  2594b  2595  2596
2597  2598  2599  2600
2601  2602  2603  2604
2605  2606  2607  2608
2609  2610  2611  2612
2613  2614  2615  2616

# Pattern Category 14: *Square in a Square*

BLOCKS OF THIS CONSTRUCTION:

| | | |
|---|---|---|
| | 2617a | MANILA QUILT DESIGN – Orange Judd Farmer 3/11/1899 |
| | 2617b | THE SQUARE DIAMOND – KC Star 1/27/37 |
| | 2618 | INTERLOCKED SQUARES – KC Star 1932 |
| | 2619 | KALEIDOSCOPE – QNM 1976 |
| | 2620 | SUNBEAM – McKim |
| | | SQUARED STAR – Home Art |
| | | WHIPPOORWILL – Nancy Cabot |
| | 2621 | MACAROON PATCHWORK – Peterson's Magazine |
| | 2622 | LOVE'S DREAM – Aunt Kate |
| | 2623 | ROSE – LCPQ 1980 |
| | 2624 | DOUBLE PINWHEEL – OCS/Wheeler |
| | 2625 | HONEYBEES IN THE GARDEN – QNM 1980. *See as a TWO BLOCK.* |

BLOCKS OF THIS CONSTRUCTION:

| | | |
|---|---|---|
| | 2626 | THE WISHING RING – KC Star |
| | 2627 | THE KITCHEN WOODBOX – KC Star 11/26/41 |
| | 2628 | OCEAN WAVE – McKim 101 |
| | | SAPPHIRE QUILT BLOCK – KC Star. *See 283 & 2451.* |
| | 2629 | BATON ROUGE – Hearth and Home |
| | | BATON ROUGE BLOCK – LAC #474 |
| | 2630 | A BEAUTY – Clara Stone |
| | 2631 | STATE FAIR – Nancy Cabot |
| | 2632 | HEARTS AND RINGS – QNM 1976 |

*Blocks with Specific Construction (2617a – 2632)*

2617a  2617b  2618  2619

2620  2621  2622  2623

2624  2625

2626  2627  2628  2629

2630  2631  2632

# Pattern Category 14: *Square in a Square*

BLOCKS OF THIS CONSTRUCTION:

*There is much variation in the Pineapple blocks; the shading, the number of bars, and the width of the bars can differ from example to example.*

2635    PINEAPPLE – LAC #92
MALTESE CROSS – Hall
WASHINGTON PAVEMENT – McKim 101
COLONIAL PINEAPPLE – Nancy Cabot 6/2/33
CHESTNUT BURR – Mrs. Danner 1934
CHURCH STEPS – Hall

2636    WASHINGTON PAVEMENT – OCS/Wheeler

2637    THE PINEAPPLE – OCS/Wheeler

2638    MALTESE CROSS – LAC #354
PINEAPPLE – Hall

2639    TREES IN THE PARK – Needlecraft 2/34

MISC. BLOCKS OF THIS CONSTRUCTION:

2642    SHADOW BOX – QNM 1974

2643    UNNAMED – OCS/Curtis. *See 1368 & 1288.*

2644    ROAD TO OKLAHOMA – LAC #2390. *See 1123 & 2086.*

2645    THE ANVIL – Finley. *See 1122 & 1314.*

2646    THE SWALLOW – Finley

2647    THE SWALLOW – Nancy Page

2648    SAWTOOTH – James

2649    CAPITAL T – Orange Judd Farmer 2/15/13

2650    THE T QUILT – Orange Judd Farmer 4/18/1896
T BLOCKS – Finley
FOUR T'S – Nancy Cabot. *See 1385 & 1665.*

2651    CONVENTIONAL ROSE – Farm Journal 2/45
CONFEDERATE ROSE – attributed to Nancy Cabot, Nancy's

2652    DAISY CHAIN – OCS/Wheeler

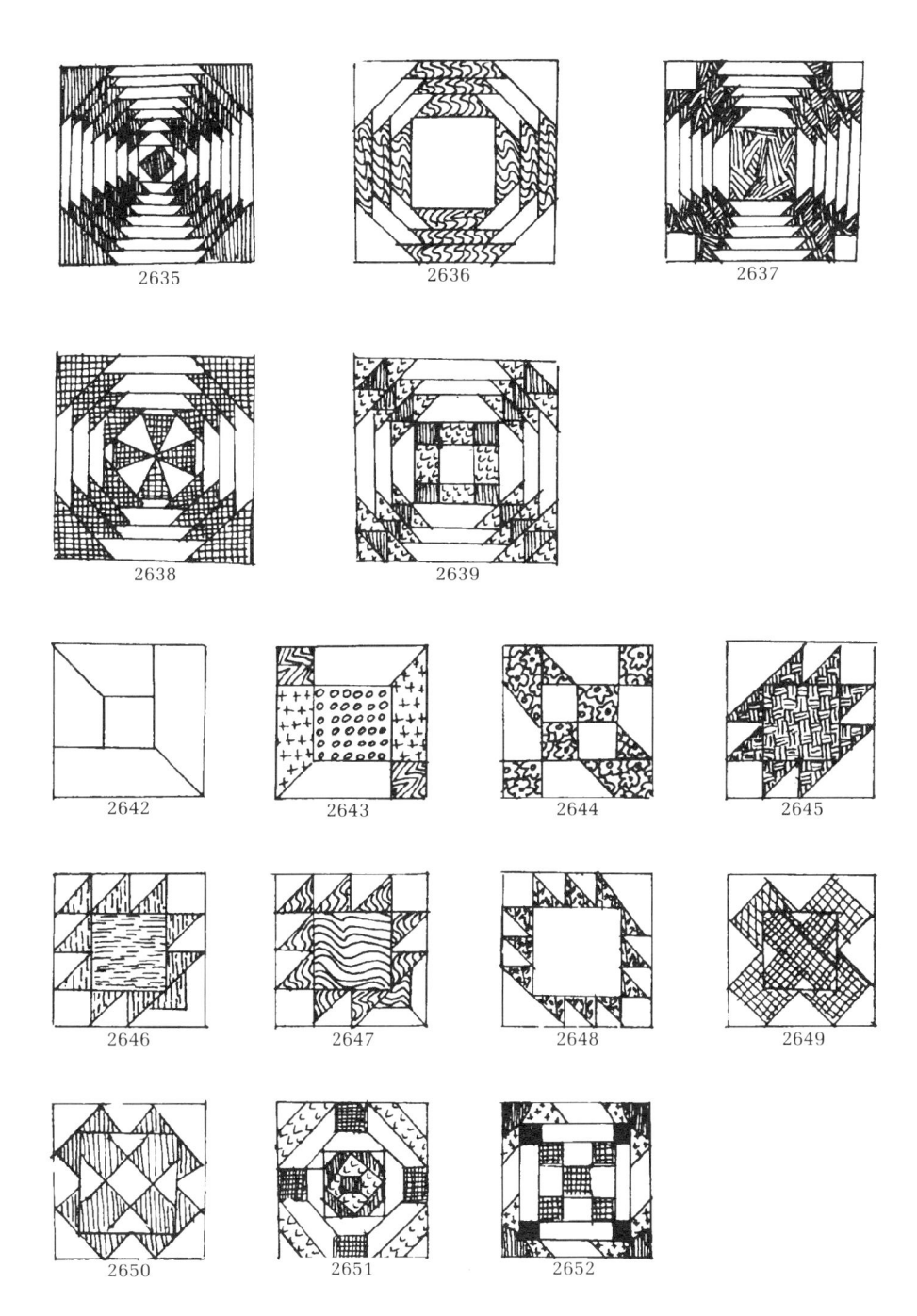

*Blocks with Specific Construction, Misc. Blocks with Specific Construction (2635 – 2652)*

325

Pattern Category 14: *Square in a Square*

BLOCKS OF THIS CONSTRUCTION:

| | | |
|---|---|---|
| | 2655 | WINDOWS AND DOORS – Clarke. *See 300, 1517, 1451, 1452, 1453, & 1041.* |
| | 2657 | THE KANSAS BEAUTY – KC Star 2/26/36 |
| | 2658 | BLEEDING HEART – Prudence Penny |
| | 2659 | THE ROSEBUD – KC Star 5/3/44 |
| | 2660 | TWIST – attributed to Nancy Cabot, Nancy's |
| | 2661 | PANELED ROSES – Nancy Cabot. *See 4065.* |
| | 2662 | SETTING SUN – Finley (set in a half drop repeat) <br> INDIAN SUMMER – Finley. *See 2677 & 3314.* |
| | 2663 | SUSPENSION BRIDGE – LAC #488 <br> BROKEN CIRCLE – Clara Stone. *See FANS, pg. 398.* <br> SUNFLOWER – KC Star <br> SUNBURST – Lithgow. *See 2678.* |
| | 2664 | WHEEL OF FORTUNE – Hall <br> BUGGY WHEEL – Hall. |
| | 2665 | HOME MAKER – Clara Stone |
| | 2666 | SATURN'S RINGS – Nancy Cabot <br> GRIST MILL – Little 'n Big 10/64 |
| | 2667 | MELON PATCH QUILT – OCS/Wheeler |
| | 2668 | BLEEDING HEART – LAC #501 <br> VIOLET BLOSSOMS – Nancy Cabot & Franks |
| | 2669 | BLAZING STAR – Evelyn Brown |
| | 2670 | EVERGREEN – Home Art |
| | 2671 | *See 1039, 1450, 1451, 1452, 1453, & 1517.* |

BLOCKS OF THIS CONSTRUCTION:

| | | |
|---|---|---|
| | 2672 | VIRGINIA SNOWBALL – Farmer's Wife <br> FOUR POINT – Aunt Martha <br> SNOWBALL – Nancy Cabot 5/18/33. *See 305.8 & 1518.* |
| | 2673 | A FRIENDSHIP QUILT – KC Star 5/2/45 |
| | 2674 | BLOCK AND RING QUILT – Aunt Martha <br> FRIENDSHIP – Little 'n Big 6/65 |
| | 2675 | COUNTRY CROSS ROADS – Ickis |

*Blocks with Specific Construction (2655 – 2675)*

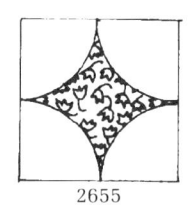

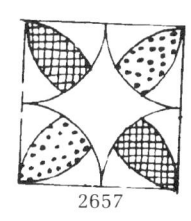

# Pattern Category 14: *Square in a Square*

**BLOCKS OF THIS CONSTRUCTION:**

| | | |
|---|---|---|
| | 2676 | DUKE'S DILEMMA – QNM 1978 |
| | 2677 | A RED, WHITE AND BLUE QUILT – Mrs. Danner. *See 2662 & 3314.* |
| | 2678 | SUNFLOWER – Aunt Martha. *See 2663.* |
| | 2679 | JUPITER'S MOONS – Nancy Cabot. |
| | 2680 | LADY FINGER – Ladies' Home Journal<br>LADY FINGER AND SUNFLOWERS – Hall<br>GRANDMOTHER'S ENGAGEMENT RING – Mountain Mist. *See 1085, 3480, & 4074.* |

*If you can't find your pattern here, look under Wedding Ring Types, page 58.*

**BLOCKS OF THIS CONSTRUCTION:**

| | | |
|---|---|---|
| | 2683 | PINCUSHION – LAC<br>ROB PETER AND PAY PAUL – McKim 101<br>ORANGE PEEL – McKim 101<br>TURN ABOUT QUILT – OCS/Brooks. *See 1519, 2684, 301, & 4076.* |
| | 2684 | NEW MOON – KC Star 9/14/55. *See 1519 & 2683.* |
| | 2685 | BUTTER AND EGGS – attributed to Nancy Cabot, Nancy's<br>DOLLY MADISON'S WORKBOX – McKim 101<br>ROBBING PETER TO PAY PAUL – Hall<br>STEEPLECHASE – Colby<br>PETER AND PAUL – Colby. *See 1520 & 4075.* |
| | 2686 | DOUBLE WEDDING RING – OCS/Wheeler. *See 3020.* |
| | 2687 | ELSIE'S FAVORITE – Clara Stone. *See 1521.* |
| | 2688 | RAINBOW SQUARE – OCS/Wheeler |
| | 2689 | GLORIFIED NINE PATCH – QNM (Heirloom Plastics Catalog)<br>IMPROVED NINE PATCH – Hinson QC. *See 306.* |
| | 2690 | CHIMNEY SWALLOW – Ohio Farmer 1/16/1896<br>ARAB TENT – Nancy Cabot 11/37 |
| | 2691A | CHIMNEY SWALLOWS – LAC 355 |
| | 2691B | CHIMNEY SWALLOWS – Clara Stone<br>CORONATION – Finley<br>KING'S CROWN – Finley<br>PRESIDENT'S QUILT – Finley<br>WASHINGTON'S OWN – Hall. *See 3914.* |
| | 2692 | PICKLE DISH – LAC #81 |

Blocks with Specific Construction (2676 – 2692)

2676

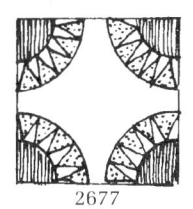

2677

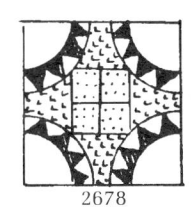

2678

2679

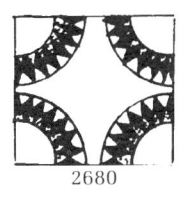

2680

2683

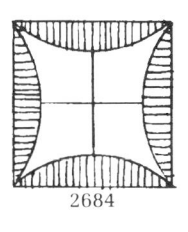

2684

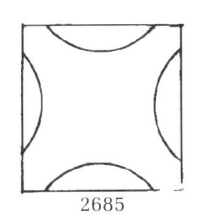

2685

2686

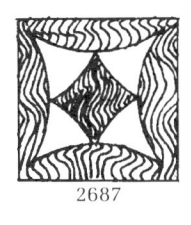

2687

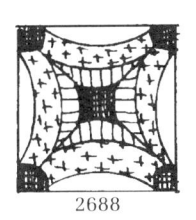

2688

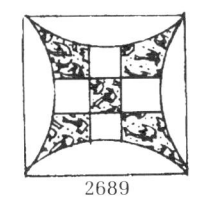

2689

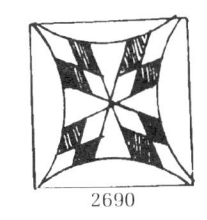

2690

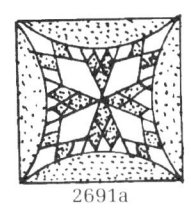

2691a

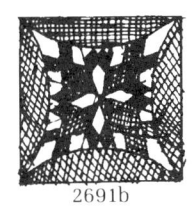

2691b

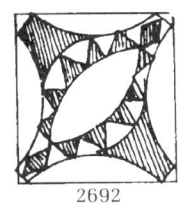

2692

329

# PATTERN CATEGORY 15

## Maltese Cross

PATTERN CATEGORY 15: MALTESE CROSS

**Patterns in Category 15 share these characteristics:**

- The block is divided by four intersecting diagonal seams into eight pie-shaped pieces.

**Category 15 includes:**

- Blocks With Specific Patches Unpieced, 332
- Blocks of Specific Construction, 334

## KEY TO PATTERN CATEGORY 15: MALTESE CROSS

If the block has this patch unpieced ▢, **turn to p. 332**

If the block has this patch unpieced ▢, **turn to p. 332**

If the block is of other construction (with all patches made up of smaller pieces), **turn to p. 334**

# Pattern Category 15: *Maltese Cross*

BLOCKS WITH THIS PATCH UNPIECED

| | | |
|---|---|---|
| | 2701 | Unnamed – Godey's 1859<br>Light and Dark – KC Star 4/19/33 |
| | 2702 | Square Dance – OCS<br>Oklahoma's Square Dance – KC Star 10/30/57<br>Starry Night – Capper's/Famous Features<br>All Around the Star – attributed to Nancy Cabot<br>*See 415.2, 1249.5, & 1258.* |
| | 2703 | Electric Fan #2 – Clara Stone. *See 413, 1251, & 1260.* |
| | 2704 | Octagons – Nancy Page<br>Semi-octagon – Household Journal<br>Will of the Wisp – Farm Journal<br>The Windmill – KC Star 11/10/54<br>Kaleidoscope – Holstein. *See 413, 1251, 1260, & 239c.* |
| | 2705 | Star of the East – Farm Journal<br>Midnight Stars – attributed to Nancy Cabot, Nancy's |
| | 2706 | Unnamed – Capper's |
| | 2707 | Crazy Quilt – LAC |
| | 2708 | Arrowheads – Grandma Dexter (appliqué)<br>Arrowheads – Nancy Cabot 3/33 |
| | 2709 | The Ice Cream Cone – KC Star 9/13/39 |
| | 2710 | The Rosebud Quilt – KC Star 9/13/39 |
| | 2711 | The Rosebud Quilt – Oklahoma Farmer Stockman 1932 |
| | 2712 | Bull's Eye – Nancy Page |

BLOCKS WITH THIS PATCH UNPIECED

| | | |
|---|---|---|
| | 2715 | Four Petals – Farm Journal |
| | 2716 | Crazy Star – Grandma Dexter<br>Endless Chain – OCS/Wheeler |
| | 2717 | V Block – LAC #483<br>Victory Quilt – Georgette Pattern Co. 1945<br>Churchill Block – Evelyn Brown |
| | 2718 | The Pinwheel – Gammell |
| | 2719 | Key West Star – Gutcheon |
| | 2720 | Sunshiny Day – Farm Journal |
| | 2721 | Sugar Loaf – Hearth and Home |
| | 2722 | Ships a Sailing Quilt – Workbasket 2/47 |
| | 2723 | Spider Web – Holstein |
| | 2724 | Unnamed – OCS/Wheeler & Curtis |
| | 2725 | Unnamed – OCS/Wheeler |

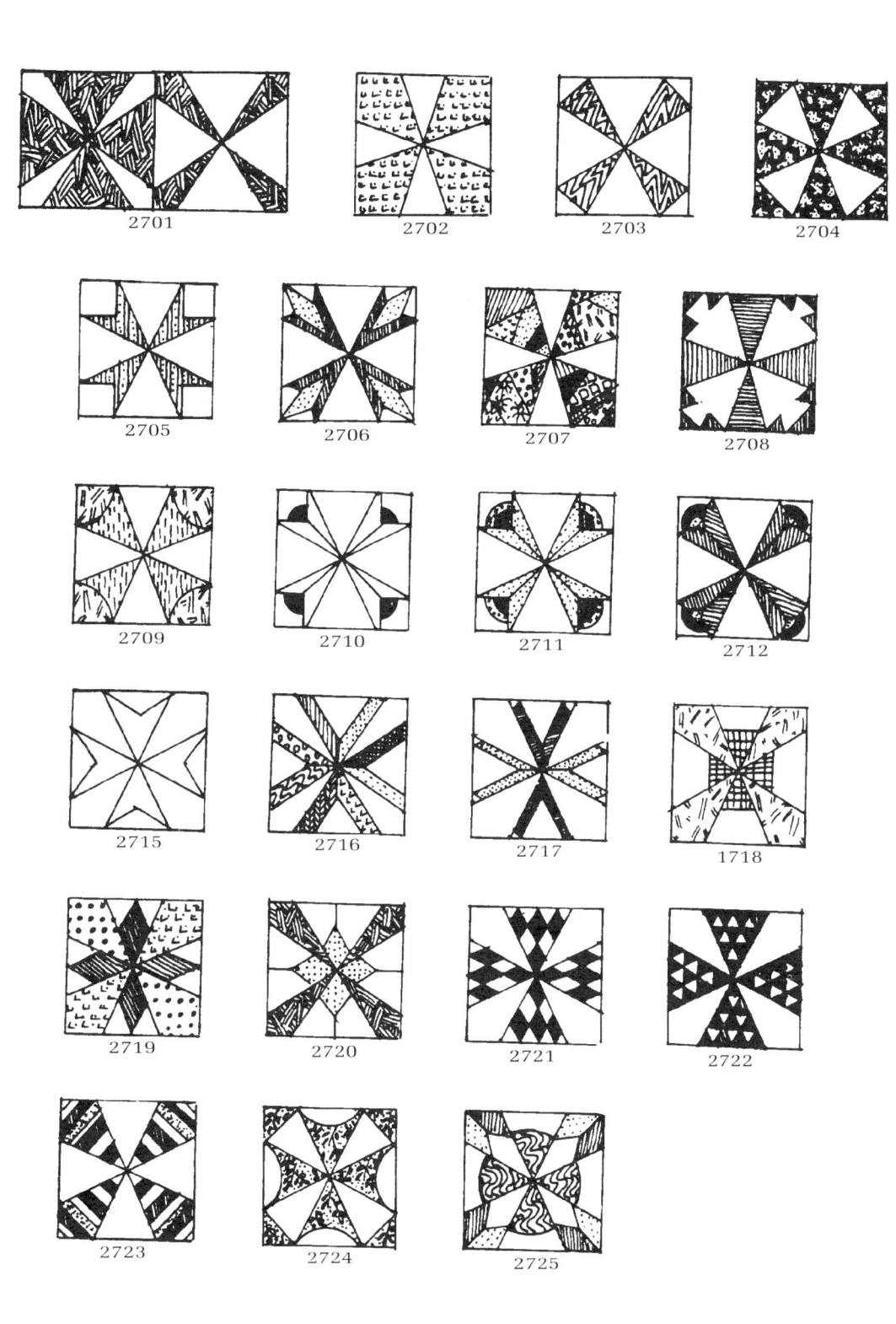

*Blocks with Specific Patch Unpieced (2701 – 2725)*

333

## Pattern Category 15: *Maltese Cross*

OTHER BLOCKS OF THIS CONSTRUCTION:

| | | |
|---|---|---|
| | 2726 | **Denver** – Hearth and Home<br>**Boston Pavement** – Farmer's Wife<br>**Spider Web** – McKim 101<br>**Mystic Maze** – Nancy Cabot 9/36 (alternate plain blocks)<br>**Merry Go Round** – Nancy Cabot<br>**Amazing Windmill** – Nancy Cabot<br>**Autumn Leaves** – Capper's 10/22/32 |
| | 2727 | **Spider Web** – Finley |
| | 2728 | **Mystic Maze** – Nancy Cabot 3/15/33<br>**Spider's Web** – Grandma Dexter |
| | 2729 | **Cobweb** – QEC 1978 |
| | 2730 | **Cobweb** – Bishop, New Discoveries |
| | 2731 | **Dakota Star** – Hearth and Home<br>**Key West Beauty** – LAC #482 |
| | 2732 | **Nine Patch Kaleidoscope** – Jinny Beyer |
| | 2733 | **Concord** – Hearth and Home |
| | 2734 | **Joseph's Coat** attributed to Noodle & Yarn 1966 by Khin |
| | 2736a | **Evening Star** – KC Star 11/28/31. *See 296.9 & 3585.* |
| | 2736b | **Kaleidoscope Quilt** – Capper's 3/1/30<br>**Morning Star** – KC Star 1931 |
| | 2737 | **St. Louis Star** – Clara Stone |
| | 2738 | **Verna Belle's Favorite** – KC Star 1937 |
| | 2739 | **Vermont** – Hearth and Home |
| | 2740 | **St. Louis Block** – LAC #491<br>**St. Louis Star** – Hall |
| | 2741 | **Golda, Gem Star** – QNM 1978 |
| | 2742 | **Broken Crystals** – Gammell |
| | 2743 | **Olympia** – Hearth and Home |
| | 2744 | **Illinois Star** – Prairie Farmer, Nancy Cabot, Workbasket 1935 |
| | 2745 | **Columbia** – Hearth and Home 10/15 |

*Blocks of Specific Construction (2726 – 2745)*

335

# Pattern Category 15: *Maltese Cross*

OTHER BLOCKS OF THIS CONSTRUCTION:

| | | |
|---|---|---|
| | 2746 | STAR OF FORTUNE – Capper's<br>STAR FLOWER – Capper's/Famous Features |
| | 2747 | HAWAII – Hearth and Home. *See 298.5.* |
| | 2748 | AERIAL BEACON – Nancy Cabot 4/18/38<br>LIGHTHOUSE BLOCK – Nancy Cabot 4/18/38 |
| | 2749 | SPIDER WEB – QNM 1977 |
| | 2750 | ARROW POINT – Prairie Farmer 1931 |
| | 2751 | ARROW OF PEACE – QNM 1978 |
| | 2752 | MICHIGAN STAR – Aunt Kate 1/66 |
| | 2753 | HATTIE'S CHOICE – Clara Stone |
| | 2754 | UNNAMED – Capper's |

MISC. MALTESE CROSS BLOCKS

| | | |
|---|---|---|
| | 2758 | JOSEPH'S COAT – OCS/Curtis. *See 301.* |
| | 2759 | THE FOUR LEAF CLOVER – KC Star 7/2/47 |
| | 2760 | ALABAMA BEAUTY – Nancy Cabot 6/6/33<br>TOBACCO LEAF – Pforr |
| | 2761 | WEDDING RING BOUQUET – Aunt Martha<br>FLORAL ELEGANCE – attributed to Aunt Sally's Quilt Chart in QNM 1973 |
| | 2764 | WINDING WAYS – LAC<br>NASHVILLE – Hearth and Home<br>FOUR LEAF CLOVER – Nancy Cabot<br>WHEEL OF MYSTERY – KC Star 1931, Grandmother Clark 1932<br>ROBBING PETER TO PAY PAUL – Hinson QM. *See 1512 & 2995.* |
| | 2765 | ARKANSAS CENTENNIAL – KC Star 1937 |
| | 2766 | THE RAINBOW – The Rural New Yorker 1/2/37<br>INDIAN RAID – Attributed to Nancy Cabot, Nancy's |

*Blocks of Specific Construction (2746 – 2766)*

# *P*ATTERN
## CATEGORY 16

## Nine X

**Patterns in Category 16 share these characteristics:**

- The blocks have a diagonal orientation within the square.

- The blocks are divided by diagonal seams to make eight or nine major shapes.

**Category 16 includes:**

- Blocks of Specific Construction, 340
- Misc. Nine X Blocks, 374

## KEY TO PATTERN CATEGORY 16: NINE X

**STEP 1**

If the block is intersected from corner
to corner by four diagonal seams forming an X ,                                    *continue with STEP 2 below*

If the block has an X appearance but does not
have four intersecting diagonal seams, corner to corner,                            *continue with STEP 3 below*

**STEP 2**

If seams form five squares, four in the corners and one of equal size in the center ⊠ ,    *turn to p. 340*

If seams form a large square in the center and small triangles on each side ⊠ ,    *turn to p. 344*

If seams form a square in the center, but the "arms" are longer
than wider, and the triangles on edges of block are large in proportion to the center square ⊠ ,   *turn to p. 350*

**STEP 3**

If the block is of this construction ⊠ ,                                            *turn to p. 358*

If the block is of this construction ⊠ ,                                            *turn to p. 358*

If the block is of this construction (a four pointed star or flower type) ⊠⊠⊠ ,    *turn to p. 360*

If the block is of this construction ⊞ ,                                            *turn to p. 362*

If the block is of this construction ⊠⊠ ,                                           *turn to p. 364*

If the block is of this construction ⊞⊞ ,                                           *turn to p. 364*

If the block is of this construction ⊠ ,                                            *turn to p. 366*

If the block is of this construction ⊠ (an X without a center square),              *turn to p. 368*

If the block is of this construction ⊠ ,                                            *turn to p. 368*

If the block is of this construction ⊠⊠ (with an octagon in center),                *turn to p. 368*

If the block is of this construction ⊠ ,                                            *turn to p. 370*

If the block is of this construction ⊠⊞ ,                                           *turn to p. 372*

If the block has an X appearance but fits no previous categories (Misc. Nine X blocks) ,   *turn to p. 374*

**STEP 4**

If you cannot find your block here, it might be classified as a WHEEL (Pattern Category 20), as a 4X (Pattern Category 2), or as a SQUARE IN A SQUARE (Pattern Category 3). The differences between these categories are sometimes subtle.

# Pattern Category 16: *Nine X*

BLOCKS OF THIS CONSTRUCTION:

| | | |
|---|---|---|
| | 2775a | MOSAIC #3 – LAC # 331 |
| | 2775b | UNNAMED – Orange Judd Farmer 1/18/1902 (embroidered detail) |
| | 2775c | DOUBLE CROSS – Orange Judd Farmer 2/15/13. *See 1171, 2375, 2776, 2883, & 3853.* |
| | 2776 | A RED, WHITE AND BLUE CRISS CROSS – KC Star 9/9/42 *See 1171 & 2375.* |
| | 2777 | GRECIAN SQUARE – Rural New Yorker 11/12/32 |
| | 2778 | THE HOUSE JACK BUILT – LAC #265<br>TRIPLE STRIPE – Grandma Dexter |
| | 2779 | AT THE DEPOT – Clara Stone<br>RAILROAD CROSSING – KC Star 8/21/35. *See 1174 & 2885* |
| | 2780 | 4 H CLUB QUILT – KC Star 1932. *See 1175.* |
| | 2781 | FIVE SQUARE – Farm Journal |
| | 2782 | TURKEY IN THE STRAW – Nancy Cabot<br>SWING IN THE CENTER – Nancy Cabot |
| | 2783 | JULY FOURTH – Nancy Page. (red, white, & blue) *See 2890.* |
| | 2784 | MOSAIC #15 – LAC #343<br>CASTLES IN SPAIN – attributed to Nancy Cabot, Nancy's. *See 1176 & 2142.* |
| | 2785 | MOSAIC #10 – LAC #338. *See 1176.* |
| | 2786 | MILL WHEEL – Nancy Cabot. *See 1176.* |
| | 2787 | NEXT DOOR NEIGHBOR – LAC #465<br>SQUARE UP – Hearth and Home. *See 1176.* |
| | 2788 | MOSAIC #11 – LAC #339. *See 1176 & 2143.* |
| | 2789 | GRANDMOTHER'S CROSS – KC Star 6/20/45. *See 1172 & 2311.* |
| | 2790 | EVA'S DELIGHT – clipping from unknown farm newspaper ca. 1930.<br>UNNAMED – Farm Journal 1928<br>OLD FASHIONED PIECED BLOCK – Nancy Cabot.<br>(small squares appliquéd) |
| | 2791 | OLD TIME BLOCK – Nancy Cabot |
| | 2792a | THE STAR AND BLOCK – LCPQ 1979 |
| | 2792b | PRIDE OF HOLLAND – Farm Journal. *See 2376.* |
| | 2793 | FEDERAL SQUARE – Nancy Cabot & R. Frank |
| | 2794 | ALBANY – Hearth and Home |

*Blocks of Specific Construction (2775a – 2794)*

341

# Pattern Category 16: *Nine X*

BLOCKS OF THIS CONSTRUCTION:

| | 2795 | **1904 Star** – Clara Stone |
|---|---|---|
| | 2796 | **Wild Goose** – McKim (syndicated column 1929) *See 2901 & 2902.* |
| | 2797 | **Toad in a Puddle** – LAC #150. *See 2911.* |
| | 2798 | **Rambler** – McKim (101) and Nancy Cabot 4/11/33<br>**Spring Beauty** – KC Star 2/20/32<br>**Crimson Rambler** – Little 'n Big 9/64. *See 2338.* |
| | 2799 | **Whirlwind** – unidentified printed pattern ca. 1930 |
| | 2800 | **Wild Goose Chase** – Nancy Cabot. *See 2906.* |
| | 2801 | **The Old Rugged Cross** – Ruby Hinson in Stitch and Sew 12/73 |
| | 2802 | **Cross Roads to Texas** – LAC #235<br>**Kentucky Cross Roads** – Prairie Farmer 1930<br>**Cross and Crown** – Nancy Page. *See 2914.* |
| | 2803 | **Another Double T** – Orange Judd Farmer 2/13/1896<br>**Boxed T's** – LAC #379<br>**Original Double T** – Prairie Farmer 1931 |
| | 2804 | **Secret Drawer** – KC Star 1930<br>**Spools** – Hall<br>**Arkansas Traveler** – Hall |
| | 2805 | **Hard Times Block** – Nancy Cabot |

*Blocks of Specific Construction (2795 – 2805)*

2795　2796　2797　2798
2799　2800　2801　2802
2803　2804　2805

# Pattern Category 16: *Nine X*

BLOCKS OF THIS CONSTRUCTION:

| | | |
|---|---|---|
| | 2810 | ST. JOHN PAVEMENT– Evangeline's |
| | 2811 | BOY'S NONSENSE – LAC #153 (original catalog)<br>NONSENSE – LAC #153 (revised catalog 1928)<br>BOY'S FANCY – Rural New Yorker 8/6/32<br>BOY'S PLAYMATE – Nancy Cabot |
| | 2812 | ALBUM – Ohio Farmer 12/6/1894<br>PUZZLE – McCall's ca. 1930<br>THE BASKET WEAVE FRIENDSHIP QUILT – KC Star<br>FRIENDSHIP QUILT – KC Star<br>FIVE CROSSES – McKendry |
| | 2813a | WASHINGTON SIDEWALK – LAC #175 |
| | 2813b | TENNALLYTOWN SQUARE – Nancy Cabot<br>WASHINGTON PAVEMENT – Walker 1932 |
| | 2813c | FRIENDSHIP CHAIN – Nancy Cabot 4/13/34<br>ALBUM – KC Star 10/30/35<br>CROSS PATCH– Woman's World 1931. *See 2806.* |
| | 2814 | ROMAN CROSS – LAC #364 |
| | 2815a | CHICAGO PAVEMENTS – Clara Stone |
| | 2815b | BASEMENT WINDOW – KC Star 1931<br>KATIE'S FAVORITE – attributed to Nancy Cabot, Nancy's |
| | 2815c | TINTED CHAINS – Nancy Cabot |
| | 2815d | THE GARDEN PATCH – Quilt World. *See 2413, 2429, 2430, 2815, 2816, & 2894.* |
| | 2816 | KATIE'S CHOICE – Farm Journal 2/45 (small nine patches in squares, or Farm Journal suggested that checked fabric could be substituted, in which case it is identical to 2803) |
| | 2817 | CROSS – Gutcheon |
| | 2818 | COURT HOUSE LAWN – Nancy Cabot. *See 2803, 2804, & 2805.* |
| | 2819 | LINCOLN – Hearth and Home<br>ALBUM – LAC #378 |
| | 2821 | DOMINO AND SQUARE – Hinson QC |
| | 2822 | WASHINGTON SIDEWALK – Famous Features |
| | 2823 | BRICK PAVEMENT – Nancy Cabot 6/9/38 |
| | 2824 | TAPESTRY – attributed to Nancy Cabot, Nancy's. *See 2293, 2413, 2429, 2430, 2805, & 2815.* |
| | 2825 | SCRAPBAG – Nancy Page<br>STEPS TO THE WHITEHOUSE – Nancy Page<br>PAISLEY SHAWL – Nancy Page. *See 2293, 2413, 2429, 2430, 2805, & 2814.* |
| | 2826 | TOP HAT – Nancy Cabot |
| | 2827 | LINCOLN'S HAT – Johnson, Prize Winning Quilts |

*Blocks of Specific Construction (2810 – 2827)*

2810
2811
2812
2813a
2813b
2813c
2814
2815a
2815b
2815c
2815d
2816
2817
2818
2819
2821
2822
2823
2824
2825
2826
2827

345

# Pattern Category 16: *Nine X*

BLOCKS OF THIS CONSTRUCTION:

| | | |
|---|---|---|
| | 2830 | AUNT ELIZA'S STAR – LAC #13<br>AUNT LOTTIE'S STAR – Nancy Cabot<br>TEXAS STAR – Dubois. *See 1631 & 2138.* |
| | 2831 | RIGHT HAND OF FRIENDSHIP – Hearth and Home<br>COUNTRY FARM – QNM 1979. *See as a DIAMOND.* |
| | 2832 | ANOTHER STAR – Gutcheon PPP |
| | 2833 | FRIENDSHIP STAR – Hearth and Home<br>BRACED STAR – LAC #486<br>ELIZA'S STAR – Rural New Yorker 1/4/36. *See 2822 & 2161.* |
| | 2834 | CARSON CITY – Hearth and Home<br>CARD BASKET – Ohio Farmer 1/11 |
| | 2835 | STAR X – attributed to Nancy Cabot, Nancy's. *See 1633.* |
| | 2836 | RHODE ISLAND – Hearth and Home. *See 2167.* |
| | 2837 | NIGHT & NOON – McCall's Book of Quilt. *See 1638.* |
| | 2838 | UNNAMED – Ohio Farmer 4/5/1894<br>GENTLEMAN'S FANCY – LAC #208<br>MARY'S BLOCK – Nancy Cabot<br>TWENTY-FOUR TRIANGLES – Farm Journal |
| | 2839a | PERSHING – Nancy Page |
| | 2839b | BOXES – Gutcheon PPP<br>HANDY ANDY – Gutcheon PPP |
| | 2840 | LAND'S END – QNM 1974 |
| | 2841 | JEFFERSON CITY – Hearth and Home |
| | 2842 | SCRAP BAG SQUARES – QNM 1976 |
| | 2843 | LATTICE WEAVE – Aunt Kate 4/65 |
| | 2844 | GUTHRIE – Hearth and Home |
| | 2845 | BLUE FIELDS – Nancy Cabot |
| | 2846 | JACK'S DELIGHT – Clara Stone |
| | 2847 | NAVAJO – LAC #513<br>INDIAN MATS – Nancy Cabot |
| | 2848 | ZIG ZAG – Mountain Mist |

Blocks of Specific Construction (2830 – 2848)

2830  2831  2832  2833
2834  2835  2836  2837
2838  2839a  2839b  2840
2841  2842  2843  2844
2845  2846  2847  2848

347

# Pattern Category 16: *Nine X*

BLOCKS OF THIS CONSTRUCTION:

| | 2849 | INDIAN MAZE – Nancy Cabot |
|---|---|---|
| | 2850 | MEMORY BLOCKS – LAC #87<br>ALBUM – Mrs. Danner, Bk. 5, 1970 |
| | 2851 | LIGHTHOUSE – Nancy Cabot |
| | 2852a | WHEEL OF FORTUNE – LAC #40 |
| | 2852b | BUTTONS AND BOWS – Mrs. Danner, Bk. 5, 1970<br>(note set with bows) |
| | 2852c | RISING SUN – Dakota Farmer 9/15/26<br>WHEEL OF LUCK – Nancy Cabot<br>WHEEL OF FORTUNE – Rural New Yorker 12/20/30<br>View c has no set indicated. *See 2854 & 291.* |
| | 2854 | THE WHEEL OF FORTUNE – Nancy Cabot. *See 2853 & 291.* |
| | 2855 | DINAH'S CHOICE – Hearth and Home |
| | 2856 | UNNAMED – OCS/LW (rick rack appliquéd to seams) |
| | 2857 | FOUR SQUARES – Oklahoma Farmer Stockman 11/25/22. |
| | 2858 | CIRCLE FOUR – Hearth and Home<br>PHARLEMIA'S FAVORITE – Hearth and Home |
| | 2859 | CHARLESTON – Hearth and Home |
| | 2860 | WASHINGTON – Hearth and Home |
| | 2861 | HOPES AND WISHES – QNM 1975 |
| | 2862 | LENA'S CHOICE – Clara Stone |
| | 2863 | TURNABOUT T – KC Star 12/6/30. |
| | 2864 | SUNDANCE – Meeker |
| | 2865 | AIMEE'S CHOICE – Hearth and Home |
| | 2866 | STAR OF MYSTERY – QNM 10/74 |
| | 2867 | THOUSAND ISLANDS – Nancy Cabot |
| | 2868 | LIGHTNING IN THE HILLS – attributed to Nancy Cabot, QNM 3/81. *See 1156.* |

*Blocks of Specific Construction (2849 – 2868)*

349

# Pattern Category 16: *Nine X*

**BLOCKS OF THIS CONSTRUCTION:**

| | | |
|---|---|---|
| | 2869 | HILL AND CRAG – Nancy Cabot |
| | 2870 | INDIAN SQUARES – Nancy Cabot |
| | 2871 | CHURCH WINDOWS – Nancy Cabot |
| | 2874 | BASEBALL – Little 'n Big 8/64 |
| | 2875 | UNNAMED – Bacon |
| | 2876 | EAST AND WEST – Hearth and Home |
| | | THE BROKEN STONE – KC Star |

**OTHER BLOCKS OF THIS CONSTRUCTION:**

2880    SNOWFLAKE – LAC #277
THE MOUNTAIN PEAK – KC Star 7/7/43
OLD ITALIAN DESIGN – Farm Journal
MAUD'S ALBUM QUILT – Nancy Page (name embroidered)
CROSS STITCH – Nancy Cabot
SNOW BLOCK – attributed to Nancy Cabot, Nancy's. *See 2099, 2100, & 2881.*

2881    OLD ITALIAN BLOCK – attributed to Nancy Cabot, Nancy's. *See 1766 & 2880.*

2882    AUTOGRAPH PATCH – Hinson QM

2883    CROSS ROADS – NNT 1974 (counterchange coloration). *See 1183 & 2775.*

2884    CRISS CROSS – Grandmother Clark Bk. 21, 1931

2885    AUTOGRAPH QUILT – KC Star 8/6/32. *See 2779.*

2886    MARY TENNY GRAY TRAVEL CLUB PATCH – Hall

2887    THE X – KC Star 7/10/40

2888    ENDLESS SQUARES – Nancy Cabot

2889    WHIRLING L – QNM 101, 1978

2890    GARDEN PATHS – Nancy Cabot

2891    DOMINO AND SQUARE – LAC #278
DOMINO AND SQUARES – Nancy Cabot

*Blocks of Specific Construction (2869 – 2891)*

2869  2870  2871

2874  2875  2876

2880  2881  2882  2883

2884  2885  2886  2887

2888  2889  2890  2891

351

# Pattern Category 16: *Nine X*

OTHER BLOCKS OF THIS CONSTRUCTION:

| | | |
|---|---|---|
| | 2892 | BROKEN IRISH CHAIN – Nancy Cabot |
| | 2893 | CROSSED SQUARES – Nancy Cabot |
| | 2894 | RED CROSS – Coats and Clark. *See 2143, 2429, 2430, & 2812–2815.* |
| | 2895 | FRIENDSHIP QUILT – KC Star 9/21/38 |
| | 2896 | STAR OF DESTINY – Hearth and Home 7/1899. *See 2783 & 2787.* |
| | 2897 | UNNAMED – Orange Judd Farmer 2/12/1898<br>COMPLETED SQUARE – Hearth and Home<br>ODD FELLOW'S CROSS – Ickis |
| | 2898 | MAGIC CROSS – Nancy Cabot. *See 2142, 1176, & 2784.* |
| | 2899 | CENTENNIAL – LAC #158<br>AUTOGRAPH QUILT BLOCK – Hearth and Home |
| | 2900 | AUNT NANCY'S FAVORITE – Hearth and Home |
| | 2901a | DOUBLE T – McKim 101. *See 2796.* |
| | 2901b | EIGHT POINTED STAR – Nancy Cabot<br>NORTHUMBERLAND STAR – Gutcheon PPP |
| | 2901.5 | BROKEN STAR – Nancy Cabot |
| | 2902 | ODD FELLOWS – LAC #269<br>ODD FELLOWS CROSS – Nancy Cabot 9/25/34<br>ODD FELLOWS PATCH – Hall<br>BALTIMORE BELLE – Clara Stone<br>AN EFFECTIVE SQUARE – Hearth and Home<br>FLYING GEESE – Oklahoma Farmer Stockman 1/15/29. *See 1185 & 2799.* |
| | 2903 | ODD FELLOW'S CROSS – Finley<br>OZARK TRAILS – KC Star 1933 |
| | 2904 | UNNAMED – Oklahoma Farmer Stockman 7/1/31 |
| | 2905a | WILD GOOSE CHASE – Hearth and Home, McKim 101 |
| | 2905b | **(not illustrated)** OLD MEXICO – Mountain Mist (2905b is four blocks of block 2905a set together) |
| | 2906 | WILD GOOSE CHASE – Woman's World. *See 2800.* |
| | 2907 | WILD GOOSE CHASE – Capper's/Famous Features |
| | 2908 | PENNSYLVANIA PINEAPPLE – Workbasket. *See 2340.* |
| | 2909 | SPOKANE – Nancy Page |

*Blocks of Specific Construction (2892 – 2909)*

353

# Pattern Category 16: *Nine X*

OTHER BLOCKS OF THIS CONSTRUCTION:

| | | |
|---|---|---|
| | 2910 | BROKEN HEART – Prairie Farmer 1931 |
| | 2911 | GOOSE IN THE POND – Mahler. *See 2797.* |
| | 2912 | BALTIMORE BELLE – Clara Stone<br>WILD GOOSE CHASE – Household Journal |
| | 2913 | THE NORTH CAROLINA BEAUTY – Workbasket 1935<br>WILD GOOSE CHASE – Workbasket 1935 |
| | 2914 | KENTUCKY CROSSROADS – Nancy Cabot. *See 2802.* |
| | 2915 | LONE STAR – OCS Books |
| | 2916 | CATS AND MICE – LAC #317 |
| | 2917 | AUGUSTA – Hearth and Home |
| | 2918 | LONE STAR – OCS/Wheeler |
| | 2919 | BRIGHT SIDE – Hearth and Home |
| | 2920 | PROVIDENCE – Hearth and Home<br>PROVIDENCE QUILT BLOCK – LAC #478. *See 1818.* |
| | 2921 | THE PROVIDENCE STAR – Workbasket 1935 |
| | 2922 | JOSEPH'S COAT – LAC #146<br>LEWIS AND CLARK – Clara Stone<br>MRS. THOMAS – Nancy Page |
| | 2923 | YELLOW LILIES – Nancy Cabot |
| | 2924 | HEATHER SQUARE – Nancy Cabot 3/20/37 |
| | 2925 | ROSEMARY – Dakota Farmer 4/15/27 and Hearth and Home |
| | 2926 | CRISS CROSS – Hearth and Home |
| | 2927 | HOME TREASURE – LAC #114 |
| | 2928 | WATERWHEEL – Marshall (small squares appliquéd) |
| | 2929 | SOUTH CAROLINA – Hearth and Home |

*Blocks of Specific Construction (2910 – 2929)*

355

# Pattern Category 16: *Nine X*

BLOCKS OF THIS CONSTRUCTION:

2930 **Rain or Shine** – attributed to Nancy Cabot, Nancy's

2931 **Sunbeam Crossroad** – Nancy Cabot

2932 **Railroad Crossing** – QNM 94, 1977

2933 **Swing in the Center** – OCS/Wheeler

2934 **Joy Bells** – Hearth and Home
**Swing in the Center** – Finley
**Eight Hands Around** – Finley. *See 1767 & 2935.*

2935 **Swing in the Center** – LAC #252
**Mrs. Roosevelt's Favorite** – Clara Stone
**Dumbell Block** – Progressive Farmer
**Swinging in The Center** – Nancy Cabot
**Roman Pavement** – Nancy Cabot. *See 1767 & 2934.*

2936 **Chrysanthemum** – OCS/Wheeler

2937 **Mexican Star** – McKim 101
**Panama Block** – Nancy Cabot
**Mexican Rose** – Ickis

2938 **Star and Cross** – LAC #284
**North Star** – Lockport Batting
**Shining Hour** – Farm Journal 2/44

2939 **Railroad Crossing** – Nancy Cabot

2940 **Primrose Path** – OCS/Wheeler

2941 **Alice's Favorite** – Mrs. Danner 1934
**Ragged Robin** – OCS/Brooks. *See 177.*

2942 **Idle Hours** – Farm Journal 1937

2943 **Dover** – Hearth and Home
**Dover Quilt Block** – LAC #470. *See 2365.*

2944 **Grandmother's Brooch of Love** – Progressive Farmer, Johnson

2945 **Hazel Valley Cross Roads** – KC Star 1934

2946 **Cross Roads to Bachelor's Hall** – Clara Stone
**Cross Roads** – KC Star 1931, Capper's
**Wagon Wheels** – KC Star 5/28/41

2947 **Cross Roads** – Home Art

2948 **Cupid's Own** – QNM 99, 1978 (hearts appliquéd)

*Blocks of Specific Construction (2930 – 2948)*

357

# Pattern Category 16: *Nine X*

BLOCKS OF THIS CONSTRUCTION:

| | | |
|---|---|---|
| | 2951 | T Square – Clara Stone. *See 3261.* |
| | 2952 | New Jersey – Hearth and Home |
| | 2953 | Cross of Geneva – Nancy Cabot |
| | 2954 | Star and Cross – Nancy Cabot |
| | 2955 | Cart Wheel – Grandmother Clark |
| | 2956 | An Heirloom Quilt – OCS/Wheeler |
| | 2957 | Broken Squares – Grandmother Clark 1931, Bk. 21 |

BLOCKS OF THIS CONSTRUCTION:

| | | |
|---|---|---|
| | 2960 | Tallahassee Quilt Block – LAC #469 |
| | 2961 | Little Boy's Breeches – KC Star |
| | 2962 | State of North Carolina – Hearth and Home<br>Star of North Carolina – LAC #473 |
| | 2963 | Lover's Knot – OCS/Brooks |
| | 2964 | Album Flower – OCS/Wheeler |
| | 2965 | Holland Mill – Nancy Cabot. *See 2966.* |
| | 2966 | Dutch Mill – LAC #451. *See 2965.* |
| | 2967 | Saracen Chain – Meeker |
| | 2968 | Wisconsin – Hearth and Home |
| | 2969 | Greek Cross – LAC #173<br>Maltese Cross – Nancy Cabot<br>Cross Patch – attributed to Nancy Cabot, Nancy's |
| | 2970 | Work-basket – Hearth and Home |

*Blocks of Specific Construction (2951 – 2970)*

2951  2952  2953  2954
2955  2956  2957
2960  2961  2962  2963
2964  2965  2966  2967
2968  2969  2970

359

# Pattern Category 16: *Nine X*

BLOCKS OF THIS CONSTRUCTION:

| | | |
|---|---|---|
| | **2972** | **Dogwood** – OCS/Wheeler |
| | **2973** | **Full Blown Tulip** – OCS/Wheeler |
| | | **Cowboy's Star** – Capper's |

BLOCKS OF THIS CONSTRUCTION:

| | | |
|---|---|---|
| | **2975a** | **The Priscilla** – LAC #199 |
| | | **Amethyst** – KC Star 2/7/31 |
| | | **Star and Diamond** – Needlecraft 1932 |
| | | **Diamond Star** – Khin |
| | **2975b** | **World without End** – Finley. *See 413, 1252, 1259, & 2976.* |
| | **2976** | **Massachusetts Priscilla** – Workbasket 1935. *See 1251 & 2975.* |
| | **2977** | **Forgotten Star** – Khin |
| | **2978** | **Geometric Star** – Hall |
| | **2979** | **Rocky Road to Kansas** – LAC #236 |
| | **2980** | **Kite** – Clara Stone |
| | **2981** | **Scroll Work** – Aunt Martha |
| | **2982** | **Texas Ranger** – American Woman Magazine 1902 |
| | | **Iowa Star** – LAC #468. *See 2983.* |
| | **2983** | **Signal Lights** – Nancy Page, KC Star 1942 |
| | **2984** | **Lost Children** – attributed to Clara Stone by QNM. *See 1253 & 415.27.* |
| | **2985** | **Forgotten Star** – Prudence Penny |
| | **2986** | **The Shining Star** – Marshall |
| | **2987** | **Rockingham's Beauty** – LAC #203 |
| | | **Buckeye Beauty** – Nancy Cabot 1933. *See 1254.* |
| | **2988** | **Harlequin Star** – Peto. *See 1255.* |
| | **2989** | **Lucky Star** – OCS/Wheeler |

*Blocks of Specific Construction (2972 – 2989)*

2972

2973

2975a

2975b

2976

2977

2978

2979

2980

2981

2982

2983

2984

2985

2986

2987

2988

2989

# Pattern Category 16: *Nine X*

BLOCKS OF THIS CONSTRUCTION:

| | | |
|---|---|---|
| | 2991 | THE MAYFLOWER QUILT – Mrs. Danner, Bk. 5, 1970 |
| | 2992 | THE DOUBLE PINEAPPLE – Rural New Yorker 11/21/31 |
| | 2993 | PHILLIPINES – LAC #404 |
| | 2994 | BUTTERFLY BUSH – Nancy Cabot |
| | 2995 | THE GREAT CIRCLE QUILT – Aunt Martha/Workbasket. *See 2764.* |
| | 2996 | PINEAPPLE CACTUS – KC Star 1932. *See 4073.* |
| | 2998 | MORNING GLORY – OCS/Wheeler |
| | 2999 | LOST PARADISE – KC Star 10/11/31 |
| | 3000 | RADIANT STAR – OCS |
| | 3001 | PHILADELPHIA PATCH – LAC #492 |
| | 3002 | PINE BURR – Clara Stone |
| | 3003 | PINE CONES – Nancy Cabot |

BLOCKS OF THIS CONSTRUCTION:

| | | |
|---|---|---|
| | 3005 | MALTESE CROSS – Nancy Page |
| | 3006 | FANFARE – Better Homes and Gardens 2/76 |
| | 3007 | DIAMOND STAR – Nancy Cabot |
| | 3008 | PINWHEEL – OCS/Brooks |
| | 3009 | POINSETTIA – OCS/Wheeler |
| | 3010 | LOVER'S KNOT – OCS/Wheeler |
| | 3011 | M W BLOCK – QNM 108, 1978 |
| | 3012 | ROYAL GEMS – Aunt Kate |

*Blocks of Specific Construction (2991 – 3012)*

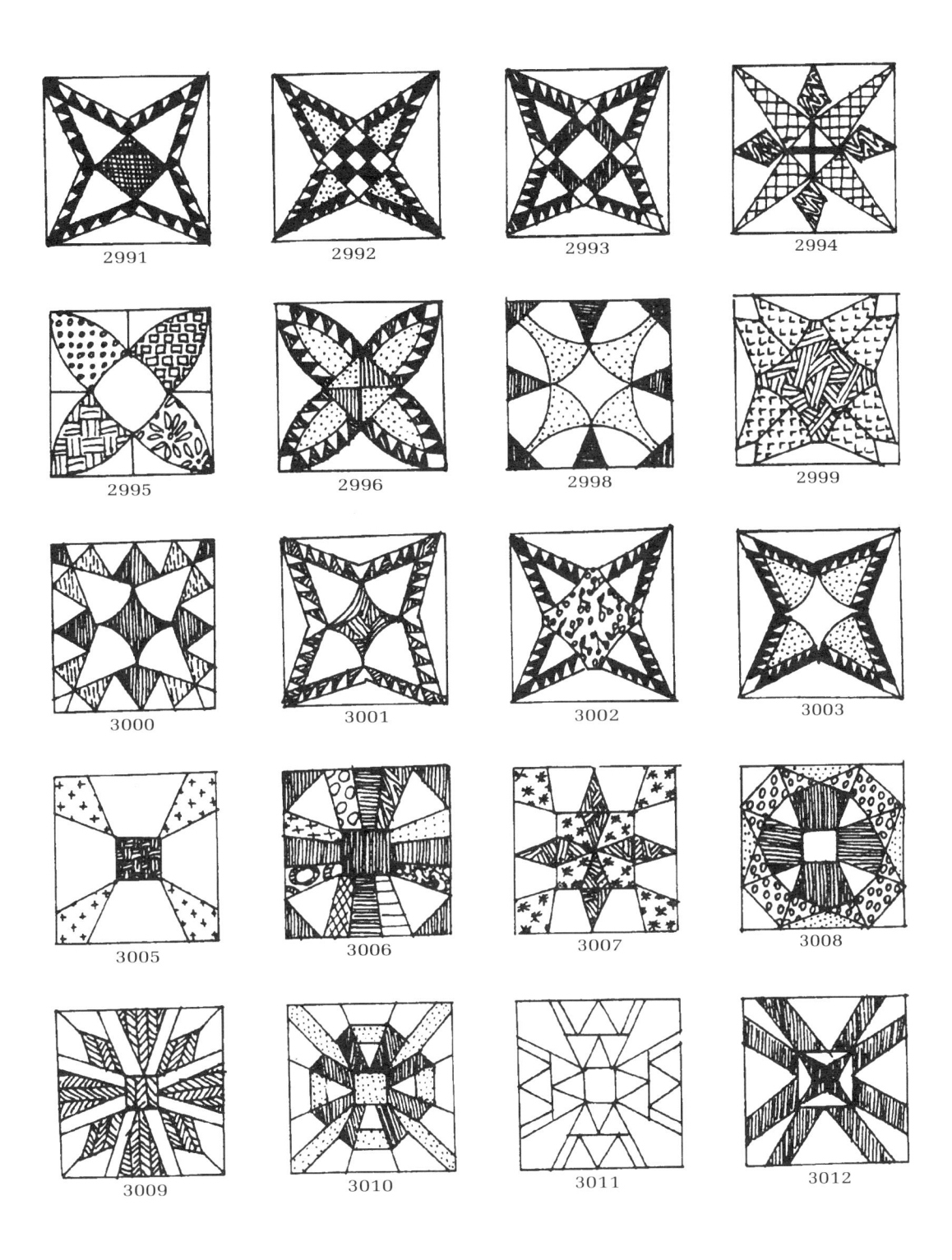

363

# Pattern Category 16: *Nine X*

BLOCKS OF THIS CONSTRUCTION:

| 3013 | BUCK 'N WING – Pforr |
| 3014 | SUNSET STAR – OCS/Wheeler |
| 3015 | PRISCILLA'S PRIZE – OCS/Wheeler |

BLOCKS OF THIS CONSTRUCTION:

| 3017 | DOUBLE Z – Nancy Cabot. *See as a THREE PATCH.* |
| 3018 | NINE PATCH STAR – Hearth and Home |
| 3019 | PIECED FLOWER – Quilt World 2/80 |
| 3020 | JAMESTOWN SQUARE – Nancy Cabot |
| 3021 | FLOWERING NINE PATCH – Khin |
| 3022 | FOX AND GEESE – Ohio Farmer 2/24/1898 |
| 3023 | STAR PATTERN – American Needlewoman 1926. *See 1687.* |
| 3024 | HAPPY HUNTING GROUND – KC Star 10/10/36 |
| 3025 | SHASTA DAISY – OCS/Brooks |
| 3026 | ALABAMA RAMBLER – Nancy Cabot |
| 3027 | PERSIAN – LAC #525<br>PERSIAN STAR – Hall |

BLOCKS OF THIS CONSTRUCTION:

| 3030 | GARDEN MAZE – Nancy Cabot. *See 1054.* |
| 3031 | LINOLEUM – Nancy Page<br>VIOLET'S DREAM – Aunt Kate 2/65 |
| 3032 | KING DAVID'S CROWN – Hall |
| 3033 | CHAIN OF DIAMONDS – Hinson QM |

*Blocks of Specific Construction (3013 – 3033)*

3013　　3014　　3015

3017　　3018　　3019　　3020

3021　　3022　　3023　　3024

3025　　3026　　3027

3030　　3031　　3032　　3033

# Pattern Category 16: *Nine X*

BLOCKS OF THIS CONSTRUCTION:

| | | |
|---|---|---|
| | **3034a** | **Farmer's Daughter** – Clara Stone<br>**Rolling Stone** – Doyle<br>**Jack's Blocks** – Grandmother Clark<br>**Corner Posts** – KC Star 1932<br>**Flying Birds** – Nancy Cabot |
| | **3034b** | **Farmer's Daughter** – LAC 419<br>**Two Crosses** – Nancy Cabot. *See 1802 & 1930 – 2129.* |
| | **3035** | **The Airplanes** – Gammell |
| | **3036** | **Jim Dandy** – Nancy Cabot |
| | **3037** | **Annapolis Patch** – LAC #471 |
| | **3038** | **Klondike Star** – Clara Stone |
| | **3039** | **Granny's Favorite** – Nancy Cabot |
| | **3040** | **New Star of North Carolina** – Nancy Cabot. *See 3045 & 3046.* |
| | **3041** | **Space Ships** – QNM 48, 1973 |

BLOCKS OF THIS CONSTRUCTION:

| | | |
|---|---|---|
| | **3044** | **Skyrocket Design** – Woman's World<br>**Dogtooth Violet** – Nancy Cabot. *See 2454.* |
| | **3045** | **North Carolina Star** – Nancy Cabot<br>**Star of North Carolina** – Hall. *See 3040 & 3046.* |
| | **3046** | **Unnamed** – Aunt Martha 1931. *See 3040 & 3045.* |
| | **3047** | **Prairie Queen** – Household Magazine 3/37, OCS/Brooks |
| | **3048** | **Prudence's Star** – OCS/Wheeler |
| | **3049** | **Morning Star** – OCS |

*Blocks of Specific Construction (3034a – 3049)*

3034a    3034b    3035    3036

3037    3038    3039    3040

3041

3044    3045    3046    3047

3048    3049

367

# Pattern Category 16: *Nine X*

| | | |
|---|---|---|
| BLOCKS OF THIS CONSTRUCTION: | 3051 | MOTHER'S CHOICE – KC Star 12/4/46. *See 433.5.* |
| | 3052 | THE MAYFLOWER – LAC #200<br>HARD TIMES BLOCK – Nancy Cabot |
| | 3053 | REPEAT X – Farm Journal |
| | 3054 | VIRGINIA REEL – Gammell |
| | 3055 | THOUSAND STARS – KC Star. *See 2056.* |
| | 3056 | HUMMINGBIRD – Mary McElwain<br>DRAMATIC PATCH – OCS Bk. 116<br>ROCK GARDEN – Lithgow |
| | 3057 | FAIRY STAR – Nancy Cabot 11/16/33 |
| | 3058 | FLOWER BED – Johnson, Prize Winning Quilts |
| BLOCKS OF THIS CONSTRUCTION: | 3060 | COBBLESTONES – attributed to Nancy Cabot, Nancy's. *See 442.5.* |
| | 3061 | THE FOUR LEAF CLOVER – KC Star 10/29/41. *See 442.* |
| | 3062 | INDIAN MATS – Nancy Cabot |
| | 3063 | SIMPLE DESIGN – Nancy Cabot<br>FLOWER BED – Nancy Cabot |
| | 3064 | ANN'S SCRAP QUILT – OCS/Wheeler |
| | 3065 | MAGIC SQUARES – Nancy Cabot |
| BLOCKS OF THIS CONSTRUCTION: | 3066 | DOMINO – Vote |
| | 3067 | SADDLEBAG – Vote |
| | 3068 | THE DOUBLE CROSS QUILT – KC Star 9/7/38 |
| | 3069 | DARTS AND SQUARES – Farm Journal |

*Blocks of Specific Construction (3051 – 3069)*

3051 3052 3053 3054
3055 3056 3057 3058
3060 3061 3062 3063
3064 3065
3066 3067 3068 3069

# Pattern Category 16: *Nine X*

| BLOCKS OF THIS CONSTRUCTION: | 3070 | MIDSUMMER NIGHT – Nancy Cabot |
|---|---|---|
| | 3071 | LADIES CHAIN – Clara Stone |
| | 3072 | ALL KINDS – LAC #377<br>BEGGAR'S BLOCK – Household Journal<br>TURNSTILE – Nancy Page<br>CATS AND MICE – Hall |
| | 3073 | FARMER'S FIELDS – KC Star 4/5/39 |
| | 3074 | STARRY PAVEMENT – OCS/Wheeler |
| | 3075 | WEDGE AND CIRCLE – Clara Stone<br>ADAM'S REFUGE – Nancy Cabot. *See 3076.* |
| | 3076 | ENDLESS CHAIN – Rural New Yorker 3/14/31. *See 3075.* |
| | 3077 | THE WINDMILL – KC Star 8/7/35 |
| | 3078 | DUSTY MILLER – Finley |
| | 3079 | JOB'S TEARS – Finley<br>SLAVE CHAIN – Finley<br>TEXAS TEARS – Finley<br>ROCKY ROAD TO KANSAS – Finley<br>KANSAS TROUBLES – Finley<br>ENDLESS CHAIN – Finley |

| BLOCKS OF THIS CONSTRUCTION: | 3081 | FLOWERING SNOWBALL – Aunt Kate 7/65 |
|---|---|---|
| | 3082 | PAPA'S DELIGHT – Clara Stone |
| | 3083 | RALEIGH – Hearth and Home<br>TENNESSEE CIRCLES – Prairie Farmer, Bk. 1, 1931 |
| | 3084 | THE ROYAL – LAC #282<br>GRECIAN CROSS – Rural New Yorker 5/23/31<br>ROYAL CROSS – Hall |
| | 3085 | HUNTER'S HORNS – Gammell |
| | 3086 | BROKEN STONE – Aunt Martha 1931<br>LOVER'S QUARREL – Aunt Martha 1931<br>NEW WEDDING RING – Rural New Yorker 3/21/31 |
| | 3086.5 | FRIENDSHIP CIRCLE – OCS/Wheeler |

Blocks of Specific Construction (3070 – 3086.5)

3070
3071
3072
3073
3074
3075
3076
3077
3078
3079
3081
3082
3083
3084
3085
3086
3086.5

371

# Pattern Category 16: *Nine X*

BLOCKS OF THIS CONSTRUCTION:

| | | |
|---|---|---|
| | 3090 | IDAHO – Hearth and Home. *See 1532.* |
| | 3091 | MORNING STAR – Hinson QM |
| | 3092 | SPIRIT OF 1849 – Nancy Cabot |
| | 3093 | SUNSHINE AND SHADOW – Rural New Yorker 7/14/35 |
| | 3094 | THE PRESIDENT ROOSEVELT – KC Star 5/17/44 |
| | 3095 | OLA'S QUILT – KC Star 5/13/42 |
| | 3096 | BIRD OF PARADISE – Hall<br>FOUR BUDS QUILT – KC Star 10/1/41 |
| | 3097 | THE TULIP QUILT – KC Star 4/24/35 |
| | 3098 | TURKEY TRACKS – KC Star 1936 |
| | 3099 | THE SWALLOW – Rural New Yorker 4/10/37<br>BURR AND THISTLE – Rural New Yorker 4/10/37<br>BIBLE TULIP – attributed to Nancy Cabot, Nancy's |
| | 3100 | WANDERING FOOT – Gutcheon |
| | 3101 | PINCUSHION AND BURR – Woman's Home Companion 1911 |
| | 3102 | ROSEBUDS OF SPRING – KC Star |
| | 3103 | A CENTURY OLD TULIP PATTERN – KC Star 9/24/47<br>PIECED TULIP – KC Star 9/24/47 |
| | 3104 | SQUARES AND LILY – Woman's World |
| | 3105 | MRS. EWER'S TULIP – Hall |
| | 3106 | EIGHT HANDS AROUND – attributed to Nancy Cabot, Nancy's |
| | 3107 | SWALLOW'S NEST – Clara Stone<br>SINGING CORNERS – LAC #401<br>FLYING SWALLOWS – KC Star 1933 |
| | 3108 | DUTCH TULIPS – Grandma Dexter (shown as appliqué) |
| | 3109 | TURKEY TRACKS – Finley (appliqué)<br>WANDERING FOOT – Finley (appliqué)<br>IRIS LEAF – KC Star 1931 (pieced) (green & white) |

*Blocks of Specific Construction (3090 – 3109)*

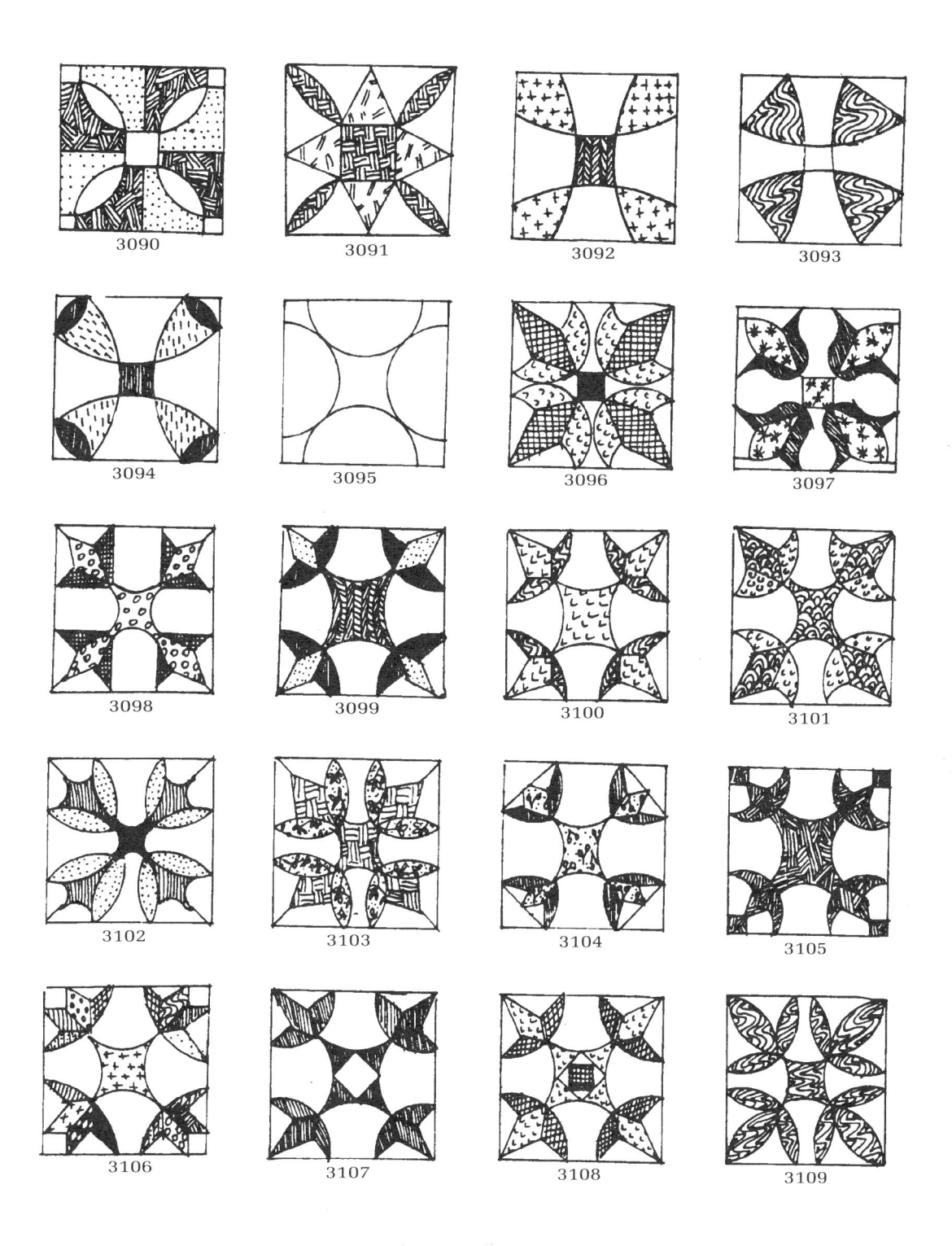

3090  3091  3092  3093
3094  3095  3096  3097
3098  3099  3100  3101
3102  3103  3104  3105
3106  3107  3108  3109

# Pattern Category 16: *Nine X*

| | | |
|---|---|---|
| BLOCKS OF THIS CONSTRUCTION: | 3110 | HICKORY LEAF – LAC #70 (1898 edition), McKim<br>JOB'S PATIENCE – Country Life 2/23<br>ORANGE PEEL – Carlie Sexton in Country Gentleman 7/26<br>THE REEL – Finley<br>COMPASS – Carlie Sexton<br>IRISH CHAIN – Hearth and Home, Grandmother Clark<br>ORDER #11 – McKim<br>ORANGE SLICES – Shelburne<br>OAK LEAF – Gutcheon PPP |
| | 3111 | TEXAS POINTER – KC Star 1934 |
| | 3112 | SUMMER FANCY – OCS/Wheeler<br>RAINBOW BLOCK – Nancy Cabot 9/7/34<br>INDIAN RAID – attributed to Nancy Cabot, Nancy's |
| | 3113 | GARDEN BLOOM – OCS/Wheeler |
| MISC. NINE X BLOCKS: | 3114 | FOUR TULIPS – LAC #453 |
| | 3115 | PATHFINDER – Successful Farming 1946 |
| | 3116 | SUE'S DELIGHT – Farm Journal |
| | 3117 | SAPPHIRE NET – Nancy Cabot |
| | 3119 | FOUR QUEENS – Nancy Cabot |
| | 3120 | UNNAMED – OCS/Wheeler |
| | 3121 | STAR AND TRIANGLES – Grandma Dexter |
| | 3122 | FIRECRACKERS AND ROCKETS – Farm Journal |
| | 3123 | CALIFORNIA – Hearth and Home<br>CHIMNEY – Capper's |
| | 3124 | A DANDY – Clara Stone |
| | 3125 | MOTHER'S OWN – Clara Stone<br>FORKS – Oklahoma Farmer Stockman 11/25/22 |
| | 3126 | ST. ELMO'S CROSS – Nancy Cabot |
| | 3127 | FOUR VASES – KC Star |
| | 3128 | GARDEN BEAUTY – OCS/Wheeler |
| | 3129 | ROSE WINDOWS – OCS/Wheeler |
| | 3130 | SPRINGTIME – OCS/Wheeler |

*Blocks of Specific Construction (3110 – 3130)*

3110  3111  3112  3113
3114  3115  3116  3117
3119  3120  3121  3122
3123  3124  3125  3126
3127  3128  3129  3130

375

# Pattern Category 16: *Nine X*

| MISC. NINE X BLOCKS | 3131 | DOUBLE POPPY – Nancy Cabot |
|---|---|---|
|  |  | MODERNIZED POPPY – Nancy Cabot |
|  | 3132 | FLOWER OF SPRING – OCS/Wheeler |
|  | 3133 | BACHELOR'S PUZZLE – Grandma Dexter |
|  | 3134 | CLAWS – Nancy Cabot |

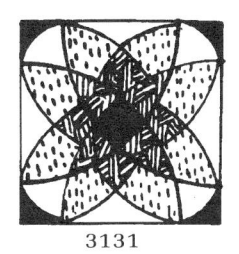

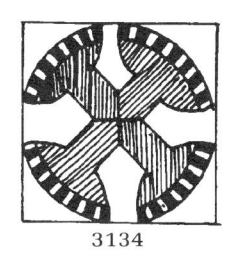

*Misc. Nine X Blocks (3131 – 3134)*

3131  3132  3133  3134

# PATTERN CATEGORY 17

## Two Patch Patterns

**Patterns in Category 17 share these characteristics:**

- They can be divided into two major areas by one seam.
- The areas can be equal or of unequal size.
- The seams can be diagonal, horizontal or vertical.

**Category 17 includes:**

- Equal Diagonal Division, 380
- Unequal Diagonal Division, 384
- Horizontal or Vertical Division, 384

## KEY TO PATTERN CATEGORY 17: TWO PATCH

**STEP 1**

If the block is divided by a diagonal seam ◰ ,					***continue with STEP 2 below***

If the block is divided otherwise ▯▭ ,					***turn to p. 384***

**STEP 2**

If the block is divided unequally ◱ ,					***turn to p. 384***

If the block is divided equally ◰ ,					***turn to p. 380***

# Pattern Category 17: *Two Patch*

EQUAL DIAGONAL DIVISION

3150    OCEAN WAVES – LAC #182
       TENTS OF ARMAGEDDON – University of Kansas
       THOUSANDS OF TRIANGLES – McKendry. *See 113, 1132, 1133, & 1692.*

3151    *See 1256.*

3152    ROCKY MOUNTAIN – QNM #38, 1972
       WASTE NOT WANT NOT – QNM #38, 1972
       PIGEONS IN THE COOP – QNM #38, 1972
       SHADOW BOX – QNM #38, 1972

3153    SHADOWS – McCall's *Quilt It*
       RAINBOW BLOCK – Bishop & Safanda
       ROMAN STRIPES – Bishop & Safanda
       SHADOW QUILT – QNM #75, 1976

3154    UNNAMED – All About Patchwork, Golden Hands

3155    PETER'S QUILT – Nancy Crow in Dubois, The Wool Quilt

3156    RED, WHITE, AND BLUE – Farm Journal 2/45

3157    GOOD LUCK – Farm Journal

3158    INDIAN ARROWHEAD – Workbasket Vol. 9, #3, 1934. *See 1284.*

3159    OLD MAID'S RAMBLER – Orange Judd Farmer 9/13/03

3160    FLYING GOOSE – Little 'n Big 10/64. *See 1292.*

3161    BIRDS IN THE AIR – Finley
       FLYING BIRDS – Finley
       FLOCK OF GEESE – Finley

       BIRDS OF THE AIR – Mrs. Danner #7
       FLYING GEESE – attributed to Ickis by Khin. *See 1322.*

3162    SIMPLE DESIGN – Hearth and Home
       CORN AND BEANS – Hearth and Home, Comfort
       NORTHWIND – Hinson QC. *See 1206, 2483, & 2486.*

3163    OCEAN WAVE – Ohio Farmer 4/5/1894. *See 1275.*

3164    LONDON SQUARE – attributed to Nancy Cabot, by Wilma Smith. *See 1209 & 1277.*
       CITY SQUARE – QNM (Quilts and Other Comforts, Catalog #6)

3165    STAR OF HOME – LAC #523
       RISING SUN – Aunt Martha

3166    SAW TOOTH – Woman's World
       LEND AND BORROW – Woman's World
       ROCKY GLEN – Woman's World
       INDIAN MEADOW – Woman's World
       THE LITTLE SAW TOOTH – Woman's World
       GEOMETRIC – Robertson. *See 3169.*

3167    SAWTOOTH – OCS Needlecraft *Museum Quilts*

3168    SAWTOOTH – Safford and Bishop
       KANSAS TROUBLES – Safford and Bishop

3169    MARYLAND BEAUTY – McKim, Patchwork Parade of States. *See 3166.*

3170    MARYLAND BEAUTY – Hinson QC

3171    ALLENTOWN – Pace

3172    SAIL BOAT – Hall

3173    THE ANVIL – Marshal

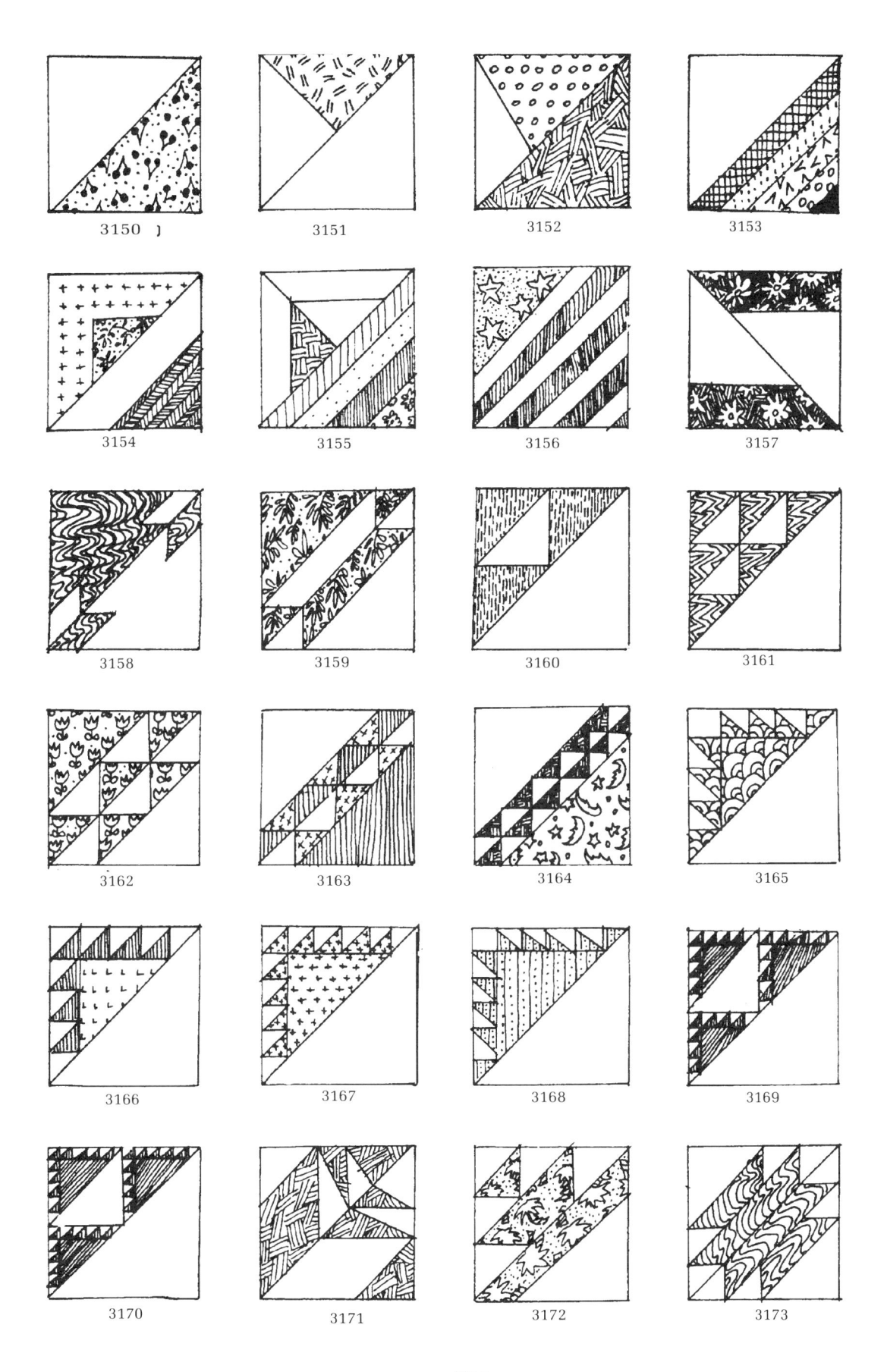

*Equal Diagonal Division (3150 – 3173)*

3150
3151
3152
3153
3154
3155
3156
3157
3158
3159
3160
3161
3162
3163
3164
3165
3166
3167
3168
3169
3170
3171
3172
3173

## Pattern Category 17: *Two Patch*

EQUAL DIAGONAL DIVISION

| | | |
|---|---|---|
| 3174 | THE PALM – Mountain Mist. *See 1304.5.* |
| 3175 | WINTER CACTUS QUILT – Michael James, QNM #107, 1978 |
| 3176 | WINTER CACTUS QUILT – Michael James, QNM #107, 1978 |
| 3177 | MODERN FLAME – Spool Cotton Co., Woman's Day 9/42 |
| 3178 | CHEVRONS – Aunt Kate 9/66 |
| 3179 | CHEVRONS – Spool Cotton Co., Woman's Day 8/42 (set in groups of 4) |
| 3180 | F BLOCK – QNM #105, 1978 (set in groups of 4) |
| 3181 | SHIP AT SEA – Dakota Farmer 11/15/27<br>SHIPS AT SEA – Farm Journal 1928 |
| 3182 | CLAY'S COMPROMISE – Nancy Cabot |
| 3183 | GRANDMA'S HOP SCOTCH QUILT – KC Star |
| 3184 | KING'S CROWN – LAC #362<br>OLD KING COLE'S CROWN – Hall |
| 3185 | JOHN'S FAVORITE – Clara Stone |
| 3186 | FLAT IRON PATCHWORK – Ohio Farmer 7/23/1896<br>STEPS TO THE ALTAR – LAC #206<br>DISH OF FRUIT – Rural New Yorker 9/13/30 |
| 3187 | STRAWBERRY BASKET – Grandmother Clark Bk. 21 |
| 3188 | LILLIAN'S FAVORITE – Clara Stone<br>MONKEY PUZZLE – Aunt Martha, Prize Winning Quilts. *See 1492, 1493, & 2366.* |
| 3189 | BORROW AND RETURN – Coats & Clark (set with alternate plain blocks). *See 1500.* |
| 3190 | PRIDE OF THE BRIDE – OCS Needlecraft, Alice Brooks |
| 3191 | BRIDE'S PRIZE – Laura Wheeler |
| 3192 | JACQUES IN THE BOAT – QNM #98 (blue & green) |

*Equal Diagonal Division (3174 – 3192)*

383

# Pattern Category 17: *Two Patch*

| | | |
|---|---|---|
| UNEQUAL DIAGONAL DIVISION | 3195 | ICE CREAM BOWL – LAC #97 |
| HORIZONTAL OR VERTICAL DIVISION | 3198 | COLLEGE CHAIN – Orange Judd Farmer 3/1/02 |
| | 3199 | CHINESE PUZZLE – Nancy Page. *See 1343.* |
| | 3200 | UNKNOWN – Meeker |
| | 3201 | TEA LEAF – Gutcheon PPP |
| | 3202 | CHINESE GONGS – Nancy Cabot 1937 |
| | 3203 | CHARM – LAC #96<br>DOUBLE TRIANGLE – Attributed to Nancy Cabot by Wilma Smith |
| | 3204 | LILIES – Quilt World 12/80 |
| | 3205 | BECKY'S NINE PATCH – Gutcheon PPP |

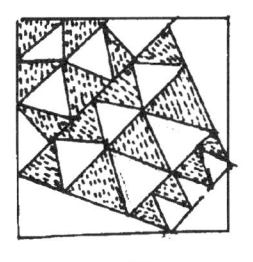

*Unequal Diagonal Division, Horizontal or Vertical Division (3195 – 3205)*

3195

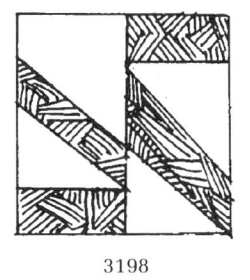

3198

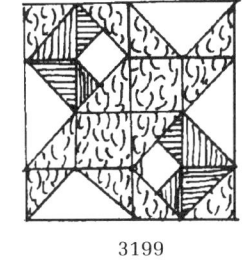

3199

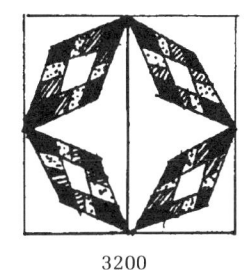

3200

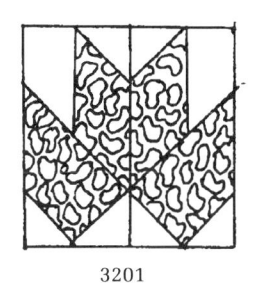

3201

3202

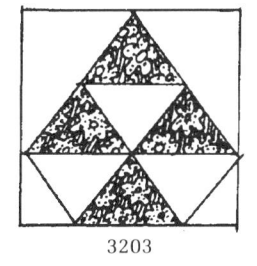

3203

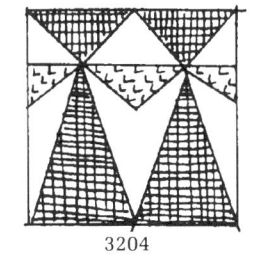

3204

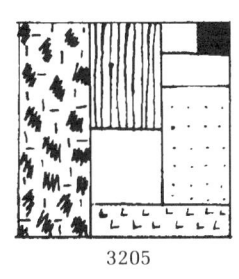

3205

# PATTERN CATEGORY 18

## Three Patch Patterns

**Patterns in Category 18 share these characteristics:**

- The block is divided into three major areas by two seams.

- These seams can run parallel or can intersect.

**Category 18 includes:**

- Horizontal or Vertical Division, 388
- Diagonal Division, 392
- Off–Center Diagonal Construction, 394
- Blocks of Specific Construction, 394

## KEY TO PATTERN CATEGORY 18: THREE PATCH

If seams run horizontally or vertically, *turn to p. 388*

If seams run diagonally and parallel, *turn to p. 392*

If seams meet, *turn to p. 394*

Pattern Category 18: *Three Patch*

HORIZONTAL OR VERTICAL DIVISION

3210   **Blocks in a Box** – LCPQ #16, 1979. *See 2571.*

3211   **Does Double Duty** – attributed to Nancy Cabot by Wilma Smith. *See 1826.*

3212   **The Crayon Box** – QNM #78, 1976

3213   **Missouri Corn Field** – Quilt World 10/81

3214   **Dewey Block** – Clara Stone

3215   **American Chain** – Orange Judd Farmer 7/7/1900

3216   **The Bobbin** – QNM 1973

3217   **Sylvia's Beige and Brown** – Evelyn Brown

3218   **American Homes** – Quilt World 12/81

3219   **Buzzard's Roost** – Khin

3220   **Old Maid's Puzzle** – Clara Stone
       **Brown Goose** – Finley (in brown)
       **Gray Goose** – Finley (in gray)
       **Devil's Claws** – Finley
       **Double Z** – Finley
       **Framed X** – Farm Journal
       **Old Gray Goose** – Nancy Cabot.

3221   **Double Z** – LAC #192. *See 1140 & 2144.*

3222   **Empire Star** – Hearth and Home
       **Star of the West** – Comfort. *See 2130.*

3223   **Mosaic #22** – LAC #350. *See 2130.*

3224   **Fool's Puzzle** – Comfort

3225   **Double Z** – LAC #360. *See 3017.*

3226   **Salt Lake City** – Hearth and Home. *See 3020.*

3227   **Diamond Stripe** – attributed to an old leaflet in Little 'n Big 7/65

3228   **Foot Bridge** – Clara Stone

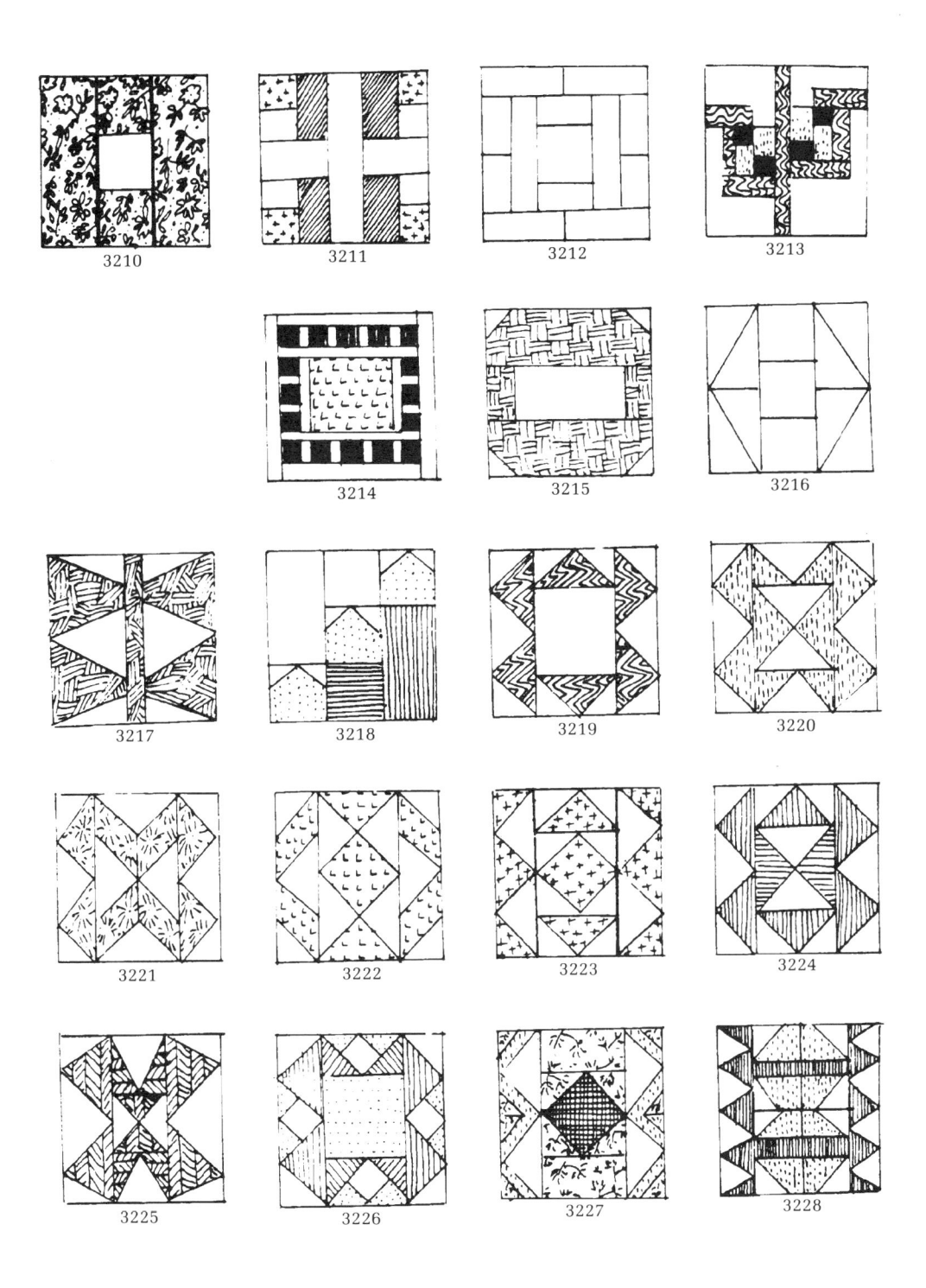

*Horizontal or Vertical Division (3210 – 3228)*

Pattern Category 18: *Three Patch*

HORIZONTAL OR
VERTICAL DIVISION

| | | |
|---|---|---|
| | 3229 | GARDEN OF EDEN – LAC #204. *See 1873 & 2375.* |
| | 3230 | FRIENDSHIP BLOCK – unknown clipping ca. 1907, copyright Currier Boye Co.<br>HEARTH AND HOME QUILT – Hearth and Home<br>A NAME ON EACH FRIENDSHIP BLOCK – LCS 10/10/55<br>STAR AND CROSS – OCS Needlecraft Museum Quilts. *See 1802, 1930, 1975, 3034, & 3231.* |
| | 3231 | GREEK CROSS – KC Star 7/7/54 |
| | 3231.5 | FOOL'S SQUARE – LAC. *See 1802, 1930, 3034, 2129, & 3230.* |
| | 3232 | GOLD BRICK – Aunt Martha. *See 1898.* |
| | 3233 | IDAHO STAR – Aunt Kate 9/65 |
| | 3234 | CROSS AND CROWN – Orange Judd Farmer 9/8/1900 |
| | 3235 | WEDDING RING – Dakota Farmer 2/15/27 |
| | 3236 | FIVE DIAMONDS – unknown clipping #K1515, might be Helen Kaufman. *See 1652.* |
| | 3237 | BIRD'S NEST – Ohio Farmer 12/6/1894 |
| | 3238 | CRAZY ANN – Gutcheon PPP. *See 1856.* |
| | 3239 | HOUR GLASS – LAC #196. *See 2376.* |
| | 3240 | LOG CABIN – McKim 101. *See 2573.* |
| | 3241 | FRENCH LOG CABIN – Anne Orr |
| | 3242 | OREGON – Hearth and Home |
| | 3243 | TWISTED RIBBON – QNM #76, 1976<br>KNAPP QUILT – QNM #76, 1976 |
| | 3244 | STARS AND STRIPES – Nancy Cabot |
| | 3245 | GOLDEN STAIRS – Aunt Martha |
| | 3246 | THE CHIEF – Lockport, McKim Patchwork Parade of States |
| | 3247 | STYLIZED EAGLE – Aunt Kate |

*Horizontal or Vertical Division (3229 – 3247)*

3229
3230
3231
3231.5
3232
3233
3234
3235
3236
3237
3238
3239
3240
3241
3242
3243
3244
3245
3246
3247

391

# Pattern Category 18: *Three Patch*

DIAGONAL DIVISION

| | | |
|---|---|---|
| | 3250 | The X quisite – LAC #281 (all over)<br>A Quilt of Variety – KC Star 1/19/38<br>Floating Star – QNM #49, 1973. *See 433, 1181, 1186, 1187, 1750, 1751, 1752, & 4103.* |
| | 3251 | Unnamed – KC Star 9/7/55. *See 1182.* |
| | 3252 | Unknown |
| | 3253 | Quilt in Light and Dark – KC Star 10/24/41. *See 2775, 1171, 2375, 2775, 2776, & 2883.* |
| | 3254 | The Friendship Name Chain – KC Star 4/5/44<br>Marcella's Friendship Quilt – QNM #77, 1976 |
| | 3255 | Autograph Quilt – Hearth and Home |
| | 3256 | Attic Window – American Needlewoman 4/26. *See 3257.* |
| | 3257 | Attic Windows – attributed to Nancy Cabot by Wilma Smith. *See 1190, 1912, 1023, & 3256.* |
| | 3258 | Hour Glass – OCS Needlecraft, Laura Wheeler. *See 1688.* |
| | 3259 | The Anvil – attributed to Nancy Cabot by Wilma Smith |
| | 3260 | Fair Play – Hearth and Home |
| | 3261 | Texas Tears – LAC #105<br>Crowned Cross – Finley<br>Cross and Crown – Finley<br>Double T – Nancy Cabot. *See 2951.* |
| | 3262 | The Coverlet – Aunt Martha. *See 2822 & 3264.* |
| | 3263 | Railroad Crossing – Doyle, Capper's Quilting: A New, Old Art |
| | 3264 | Paths to Peace – unknown clipping ca. 1930. *See 3262.* |
| | 3265 | Four Cross – Clara Stone |
| | 3266 | Chimney Sweep – Finley<br>Christian Cross – Shelburne. *See 2812, 2813, 2814, 2815, & 2818.* |
| | 3267 | Unnamed – Hinson |
| | 3268 | Log Cabin and Album Pattern – Comfort |
| | 3269 | Rocky Glen – LAC #171 |

*Diagonal Division (3250 – 3269)*

| | | | |
|---|---|---|---|
| 3250 | 3251 | 3252 | 3253 |
| 3254 | 3255 | 3256 | 3257 |
| 3258 | 3259 | 3260 | 3261 |
| 3262 | 3263 | 3264 | 3265 |
| 3266 | 3267 | 3268 | 3269 |

393

# Pattern Category 18: *Three Patch*

| | | |
|---|---|---|
| DIAGONAL DIVISION | 3270 | THE GOOSE TRACK – KC Star 10/25/44 |
| | 3271 | MRS. TAFT'S CHOICE – Happy Hours Magazine ca. 1900 |
| | 3272 | INDIAN DESIGN – Comfort, Hearth and Home |
| | 3273 | BISMARCK – Hearth and Home 1/16<br>PRIMROSE PATH – Finley |
| | 3274 | MIXED T – LAC #5. *See 1284, 1392, & 3275.* |
| | 3275 | T QUARTETTE – LAC #86<br>TETE A TETE – Hearth and Home. *See 1392, 1784, & 3274.* |
| | 3276 | THE BUILDER'S BLOCK QUILT – KC Star 3/31/43 |
| | 3277 | THE MAPLE LEAF – KC Star 5/28/37<br>AMBER LEAF – attributed to Nancy Cabot by Wilma Smith |
| | 3278 | TREE AND TRUTH – Walker 1932<br>WASHINGTON QUILT PATTERN – Walker 1932 |
| | 3279 | BROTHERS – Aunt Kate 1966 |
| | 3280 | OLD MISSOURI – KC Star 10/26/32. *See 1539.* |
| | 3281 | CONSTELLATION – Grandma Dexter. Set solid is similar to 1077 |
| | | |
| OFF-CENTER DIAGONAL CONSTRUCTION | 3284 | PUZZLE QUILT – Hartman |
| | 3285 | ABE LINCOLN LOG CABIN – Capper's 2/10/34 (a border) |
| | 3286 | OLD RAIL FENCE – Progressive Farmer 1976 |
| | | |
| BLOCKS OF THIS CONSTRUCTION | 3288 | AMBER WAVES – Gutcheon QDW |
| | 3289 | SWEET GUM LEAF – LAC #71 |
| | 3290 | SHOOTING STAR – Quilt World 4/80 |

*Diagonal Division, Off-Center Diagonal Construction, Blocks of Specific Construction (3270 – 3290)*

395

# PATTERN CATEGORY 19

## Fans

**Patterns in category 19 share these characteristics:**

- Pieces radiate out from a corner.
- Generally there is a quarter circle in that corner.
- Occasionally there is a fan in two corners of the block.

**Category 19 includes:**

- Fans with a Smooth Edge, 398
- Fans with Scalloped Edges, 400
- Fans with Other Edges, 400
- Blocks of Specific Construction, 400
- Double Fans, 402
- Miscellaneous Fans, 402
- Sets of Fans, 402

**KEY TO PATTERN CATEGORY 19: FANS**

**STEP 1**

If the pattern is a fan block, *continue with STEP 2 below*

If the pattern is a set for fan blocks, *turn to p. 402*


**STEP 2**

If the pattern has a single fan in one corner, *continue with STEP 3 below*

If the pattern has two fans in two different corners, *turn to Double Fans on p. 402*


**STEP 3**

If the fan has a scalloped edge, *turn to p. 400*

If the fan has a smooth edge, *turn to p. 398*

If the fan has another type of edge, *turn to p. 400*

If the block is of this construction, *turn to p. 400*

If the block is another fan type block, *turn to p. 402*

## Pattern Category 19: *Fans*

| | | |
|---|---|---|
| FANS WITH A SMOOTH EDGE | **3301** | This block is usually shown as a FOUR PATCH. *See 1007, 1039, 1040, 145, 1481, 1517, 2219–21, & 2671.* |
| | **3302** | SUNRISE, SUNSET – Good Housekeeping 3/78 |
| | **3302.5** | MOHAWK TRAIL – McKim, Nancy Cabot 1933, Grandma Dexter<br>PATH OF FANS – Pforr<br>CHINESE FAN – QNM<br>BABY BUNTING – QNM. *See 3369 for set.* |
| | **3303** | FAN QUADRILLE – attributed to Mountain Mist by Shogren |
| | **3304** | FAN OF FRIENDSHIP – OCS Needlecraft, Alice Brooks #6184 |
| | **3305** | GRANDMOTHER'S FAN – Doyle, Herrschner. *See 454.3.* |
| | **3306** | GRANDMOTHER'S FAN – McKim 101<br>FAN QUILT – KC Star 1935<br>FORMOSA FAN – Nancy Cabot. *See 2002 & 3310.* |
| | **3307** | FAN PATCHWORK – LAC #296<br>MARY'S FAN – Home Art<br>A FAN OF MANY COLORS – KC Star<br>GRANDMOTHER'S FAN – Shogren |
| | **3308** | ART DECO FANS – McCall's *Antique Quilts* |
| | **3309** | JAPANESE FAN – OCS Needlecraft, Laura Wheeler #645 |
| | **3310** | GRANDMOTHER'S FAN – McKim (edge appliqué braid). *See 3306.* |
| | **3311** | UNNAMED – Shogren |
| | **3312** | UNNAMED – Shogren |
| | **3313** | LATTICE FAN – Aunt Martha, Workbasket 1941, #09371 |
| | **3314** | CHINESE FAN – Nancy Cabot 1932. *See 1796, 2662, 2667, & 4068.* |
| | **3315** | RAINBOW QUILT DESIGN – Nancy Page. (Shows this but says it is set as 3374.)<br>FLO'S FAN – Shogren |
| | **3316** | IMPERIAL FAN – KC Star. *See 3371.* |
| | **3317** | FANCY FAN – Shogren<br>DIAMOND FAN – Shogren |
| | **3318** | THE FANCY FAN – Aunt Kate Vol 3, #5 |
| | **3319** | FLO'S FAN – Shogren |
| | **3320** | FAN – LAC #143 |
| | **3321** | FLO'S FAN – Hall |

*Fans with a Smooth Edge (3301 – 3321)*

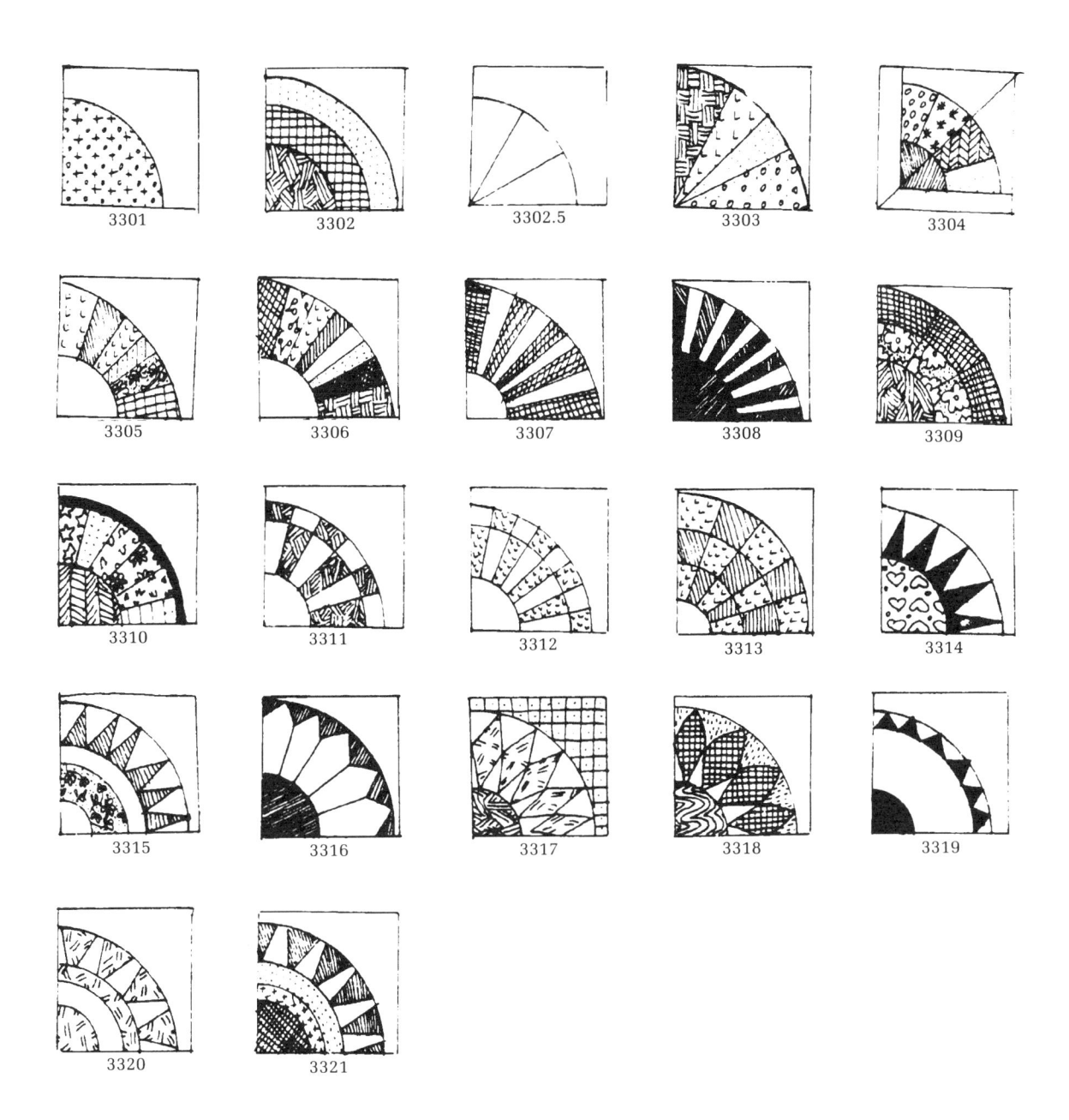

# Pattern Category 19: *Fans*

| | | |
|---|---|---|
| SCALLOPED EDGES | **3322** | **DAISY FAN** – Aunt Martha, Workbasket 1942 |
| | **3323** | **GRANDMOTHER'S FAN** – Shogren |
| | **3324** | **DRESDEN FAN** – LCPQ #19, 1980 |
| | **3325** | **GRANDMOTHER'S FAN** – OCS Needlecraft, Brooks <br> **ART DECO FANS** – Holstein |
| | **3326** | **UNNAMED** – OCS/Wheeler |
| | **3327** | **CALICO FAN** – Nancy Cabot 1936 |
| OTHER EDGES: | **3328** | **MARY'S FAN** – Grandmother Clark, Grandma Dexter <br> **MARY'S STAR** – Grandma Dexter 1932 |
| | **3329** | **JAPANESE FAN** – McKim. *See 3330.* |
| | **3330** | **GRANDMOTHER'S FAN** – Grandmother Clark Bk. 20, 1931. *See 3329.* |
| | **3331** | **FAN** – Shogren |
| | **3332** | **JAPANESE FAN** – Capper's 8/27/32 |
| | **3333** | **FANCY FAN** – Aunt Kate 1963 |
| | **3334** | **UNNAMED** – Shogren |
| | **3335** | **FRINGED ASTER** – Workbasket 1943 |
| | **3336** | **SUNSET GLOW QUILT** – Little 'n Big 4/65 <br> **SUNSET** – attributed to Nancy Cabot by Wilma Smith |
| | **3337** | **FLOWER OF THE WOODS** – OCS Needlecraft, Laura Wheeler #791 |
| | **3339** | **RISING SUN** – OCS Needlecraft, Alice Brooks #5346 |
| | **3340** | **MILADY'S FAN** – Aunt Martha |
| | **3341** | **GRANDMOTHER'S PRIDE** – OCS/Wheeler #1375 <br> **EMPRESS** – QNM #100, 1978 |
| | **3342** | **UNNAMED** – Shogren |
| | **3343** | **SUNRISE** – Marie Hartman |
| BLOCKS OF THIS CONSTRUCTION: | **3344** | **HARVEST SUN** – Holstein. *See 227.3.* |
| | **3345** | **REBECCA'S FAN** – KC Star 3/14/31 |
| | **3346** | **FRIENDSHIP FAN** – Nancy Cabot 1933 |
| | **3347** | **SUNSHINE** – Clara Stone <br> **FRIENDSHIP FAN** – Clara Stone |

*Scalloped Edges, Other Edges, Blocks with Specific Construction (3322 – 3347)*

401

# Pattern Category 19: *Fans*

| | | |
|---|---|---|
| DOUBLE FANS | 3349 | **GRANDMA'S FAVORITE** – Progressive Farmer (Johnson, 1971) (alternate blocks, mirror image). *See 1505.* |
| | 3350 | **THE RAINBOW QUILT** – KC Star<br>**THE DRUNKARD'S TRAIL** – KC Star 9/16/42 (shown like this but described as 3351). |
| | 3351 | **THE DRUNKARD'S TRAIL** – KC Star 9/16/42 (described like this but shown like 3350). |
| | 3352 | **RAILROAD AROUND ROCKY MOUNTAIN** – attributed to Comfort by Wilma Smith. Also in The Woman's Century ca. 1910<br>**RATTLESNAKE** – attributed to Nancy Cabot by Wilma Smith<br>**SNAKE TRAIL** – Clarke |
| | 3353 | **SNAKE IN THE HOLLOW** – QNM #100, 1978<br>**GYPSY TRAIL** – Meeker pg. 41 |
| | 3354 | **FAN CRAZY QUILT** – QNM #100, 1978 |
| | 3355 | **WHIRLING FANS** – OCS Needlecraft, Alice Brooks<br>**DOUBLE FANS** – Shogren |
| | 3356 | **RAINBOW** – Aunt Martha Prize Winning Quilts |
| MISC. FANS | 3357 | **THE SEA SHELL QUILT** – KC Star 7/28/48 (in OK & AR editions only) |
| | 3358 | **THE BLEEDING HEART** – Orange Judd Farmer 6/1/1898 |
| | 3359 | **FLOWER OF AUTUMN** – OCS/Wheeler |
| SETS FOR FANS | 3361 | **SPANISH FLEET** – Nancy Page 1935. |
| | 3362 | **UNNAMED FAN SET** – Dakota Farmer 3/1/26. *See 1455.* |
| | 3363 | **ALTERNATING FAN DESIGN** – John C. Michael Co. |
| | 3364 | **FAN QUADRILLE** – Mountain Mist |
| | 3365 | **UNNAMED** – OCS/Wheeler |
| | 3366 | **DRUNKARD'S PATH** – Ruby Hinson Duncan, Quilt World 10/80. *See 3315 & 1461.* |
| | 3367 | **UNNAMED** – Farmer's Wife. *See 3315.* |
| | 3368 | **A WINDING TRAIL** – Nancy Cabot |

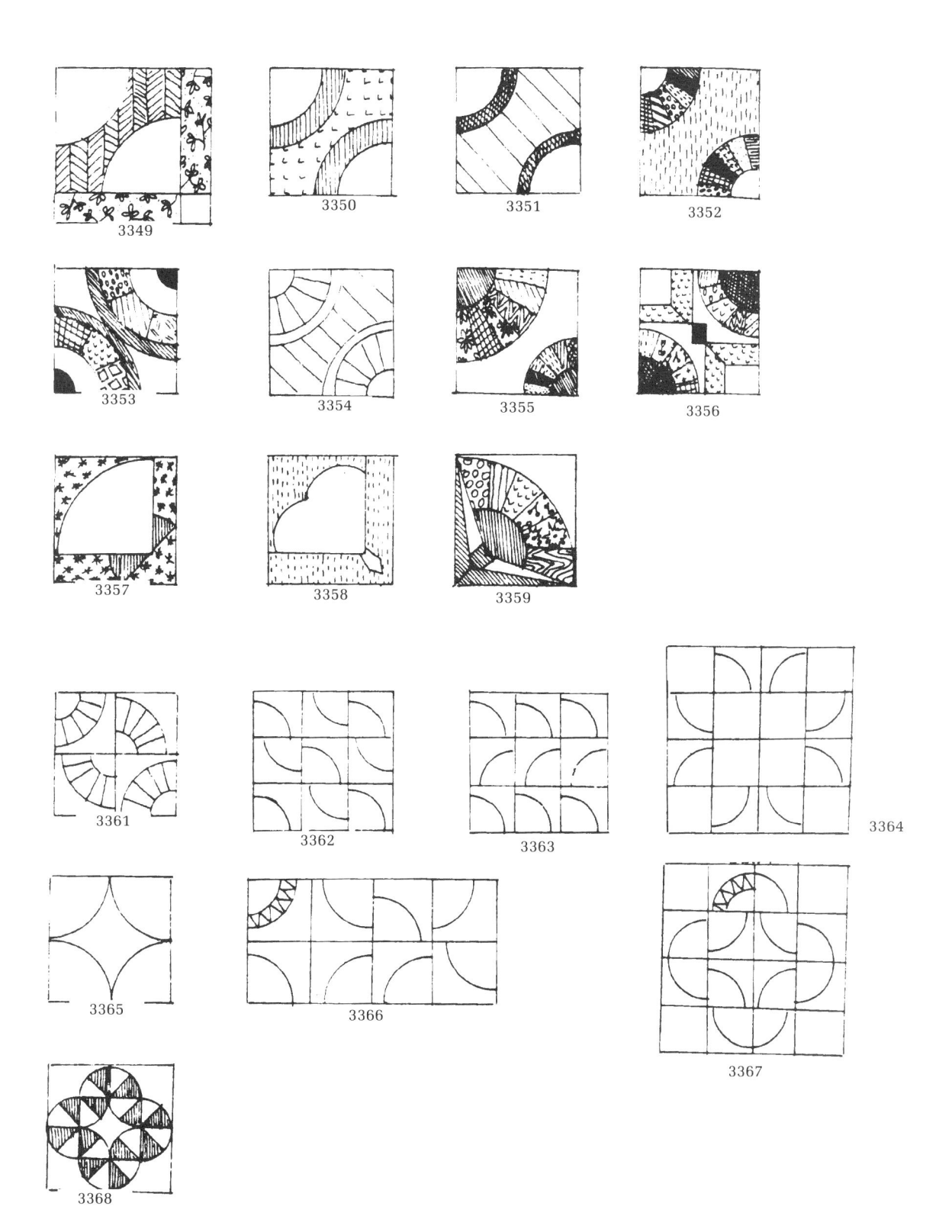

*Double Fans, Misc. Fans, Sets for Fans (3349 – 3368)*

403

# Pattern Category 19: *Fans*

SETS FOR FANS

**3369**    **Mohawk Trail** – McKim, Parade of States, Nancy Cabot 1933, Grandma Dexter
**Path of Fans** – Nancy Cabot
**Chinese Fan** – QNM
**Baby Bunting** – QNM

**3370**    **Baby Bunting** – LAC #493
**The Wanderer** – Comfort
**Broken Saw** – Comfort
**Chinese Fan** – Nancy Cabot. *See 3315.*

**3371**    **Imperial Fan** – KC Star. *See 3316.*

**3372**    **Rocky Road to Jerico** – Meeker pg. 41

**3373**    **Sunburst** – Needle and Brush, Butterick Pub. Co. Ltd., 1889
**Sunrise** – Nebraska Collections. *See 229.*

**3374**    **Rainbow** – LAC #130. *See 3315.*

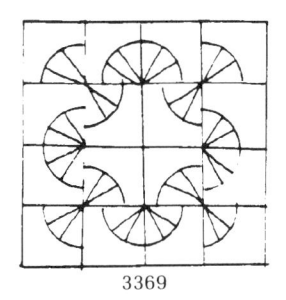

*Sets for Fans (3369 – 3374)*

3369

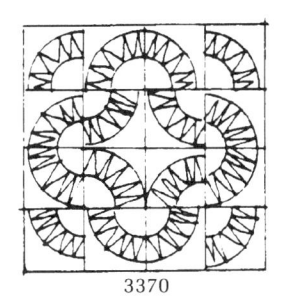

3370

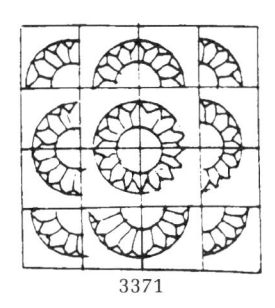

3371

3372

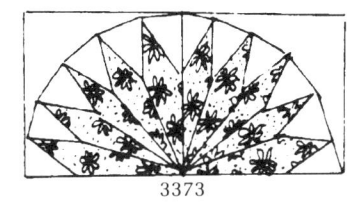

3373

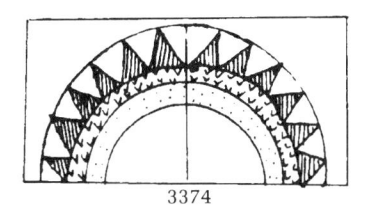

3374

405

# PATTERN CATEGORY 20

## Wheels

**Patterns in Category 20 share these characteristics:**

- Pieces radiate from the center.
- The center of the block has a circular appearance.
- Some wheel patterns are not actually pieced blocks but are circles appliquéd to a background.

**Category 20 includes:**

- Spokes, 408
- Spirals, 408
- Four Identical Radiating Petals, 410
- Six Identical Radiating Petals, 410
- Eight Identical Radiating Petals, 412
- More Than Eight Petals, 416
- Miscellaneous, 422
- Intersecting Curved Lines, 426
- Intersecting Straight Lines, 426
- Square in Center, 430
- Hexagon or Octagon in Center, 430
- Specific Shapes in Center, 434
- Odd Curved Shapes in Center, 438

**KEY TO PATTERN CATEGORY 20: WHEELS**

**STEP 1**

If seams intersect in center of the block , *go to STEP 5 below*

If there is a shape in the center of the block , *go to STEP 2 below*

**STEP 2**

If shape in the center is a circle, *go to STEP 3 below*

If shape in center is a square, *turn to p. 430*

If shape is an octagon or a hexagon, *turn to p. 430*

If shape is ⌑ or ◇ , *turn to p. 438*

**STEP 3**

If spokes radiate from circle in center; straight seams extend to edge of outer circle , *turn to p. 408*

If circle has spiral seams radiating from center , *turn to p. 408*

If petals radiate from center circle; seams do not all extend to edge of outer circle , *go to STEP 4 below*

If miscellaneous construction, *turn to p. 422*

**STEP 4**

Find the innermost circle. Count the number of identical petals touching that circle and choose below:

If four identical petals, *turn to p. 410*

If six identical petals, *turn to p. 410*

If eight identical petals, *turn to p. 412*

If more than eight identical petals, *turn to p. 416*

**STEP 5**

If seams which intersect are straight , *continue with STEP 6 below*

If seams which intersect in center are curved , *turn to p. 424*

**STEP 6**

If star in center of block , *see DIAMOND STAR (PATTERN CATEGORY 23)*

If seams do not form a star, *turn to p. 426*

# Pattern Category 20: *Wheels*

| | | |
|---|---|---|
| SPOKES | 3376 | ROUND TABLE – Clara Stone |
| | 3377 | CIRCLE WITHIN A CIRCLE – LAC #42<br>BIRD'S EYE VIEW – Clara Stone, Comfort |
| | 3378 | WHEEL OF FORTUNE – McKim |
| | 3379 | WHEEL OF FORTUNE – McKim, Woman's World 1928 |
| | 3380 | BABY ASTER – Aunt Martha |
| | 3381 | WAGON WHEELS CARRY ME HOME – KC Star 6/4/52<br>THE OLD FASHIONED WAGON WHEEL – KC Star 6/20/55 |
| | 3382 | WHEEL OF FORTUNE – Oklahoma Farmer Stockman |
| | 3383 | DOUBLE RAINBOW – OCS/Wheeler<br>(note dark prints on left; light on right) |
| | 3384 | WHEEL OF FORTUNE – Finley |
| | 3385 | CHINA PLATE – Herrschner's Quilts |
| | 3386 | TRUE LOVER'S BUGGY WHEELS – KC Star 2/1/30<br>WHEEL OF CHANCE – KC Star 2/1/30 |
| | 3387 | WHEEL OF FORTUNE – Webster |
| | 3388 | CHARIOT WHEEL – Clementine Paddleford, unknown publication ca. 1925 |
| SPIRALS | 3389 | FEATHERED STAR – OCS/Wheeler |
| | 3390 | RISING SUN – LAC #177<br>WAGON WHEEL – Hearth and Home<br>FLY WHEEL – Grandmother Clark Bk. 20, 1931<br>CIRCLE SAW – KC Star<br>WHEEL OF LIFE – Home Art<br>OKLAHOMA STAR – Lithgow |
| | 3391 | THE WHEEL OF FORTUNE – Hearth and Home |
| | 3392 | WINDBLOWN DAISY – Nancy Cabot 1933 |
| | 3393 | WHEEL OF TIME – Woman's World |
| | 3394 | PINWHEEL QUILT – Baltimore Museum |
| | 3395 | PARASOL BLOCK – Nancy Cabot |

*Spokes, Spirals (3376 – 3395)*

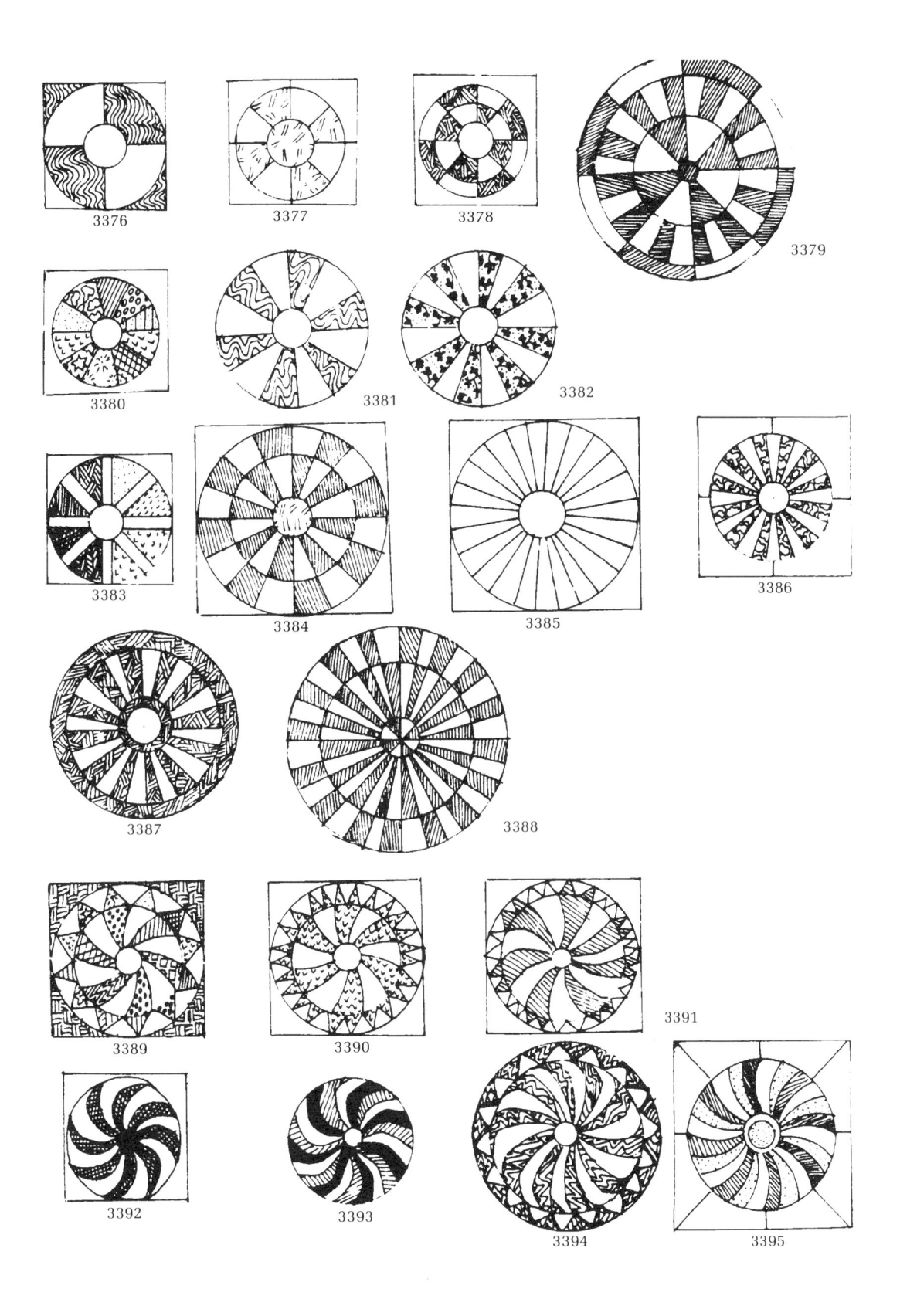

409

## Pattern Category 20: *Wheels*

| | | |
|---|---|---|
| FOUR IDENTICAL RADIATING PETALS | 3396 | THE CINCINNATI COG WHEEL – American Antiques Journal 3/47 |
| | 3397 | NECKTIE PATCHWORK – Woman's Day 8/53 (note embroidery) |
| | 3398 | LONELY STAR – Aunt Kate 1966 |
| | 3399 | CIRCLE STAR – Khin |
| | 3400 | THE EXPLOSION – Finley, Country Gentleman 1931<br>MARINER'S COMPASS – Finley, Country Gentleman<br>SUNBURST – Robertson<br>CHIPS AND WHETSTONES – Hall |
| | 3401 | SLASHED STAR – The Country Home Magazine 2/33 |
| | 3402 | SUNBURST – Webster<br>SUNRISE – Grandma Dexter<br>MARINER'S COMPASS – Oklahoma Farmer Stockman |
| | 3403 | SUNBURST – Nancy Cabot |
| | 3404 | MARINER'S COMPASS – QNM #121, 1980 |
| SIX IDENTICAL RADIATING PETALS | 3404.5 | MARINER'S COMPASS – Orlofsky<br>MARY STRICKLER'S QUILT – Orlofsky |
| | 3405 | UNNAMED – OCS Needlecraft/Alice Brooks #7381 |
| | 3406 | STAR OF MEXICO – Aunt Kate 5/66 |
| | 3407 | WYOMING – Hearth and Home |
| | 3408 | SOUTHERN STAR – Hearth and Home |
| | 3409 | CHIPS AND WHETSTONES – QNM #121, 1980 |
| | 3410 | SAMOAN POPPY – attributed to Nancy Cabot by Wilma Smith |

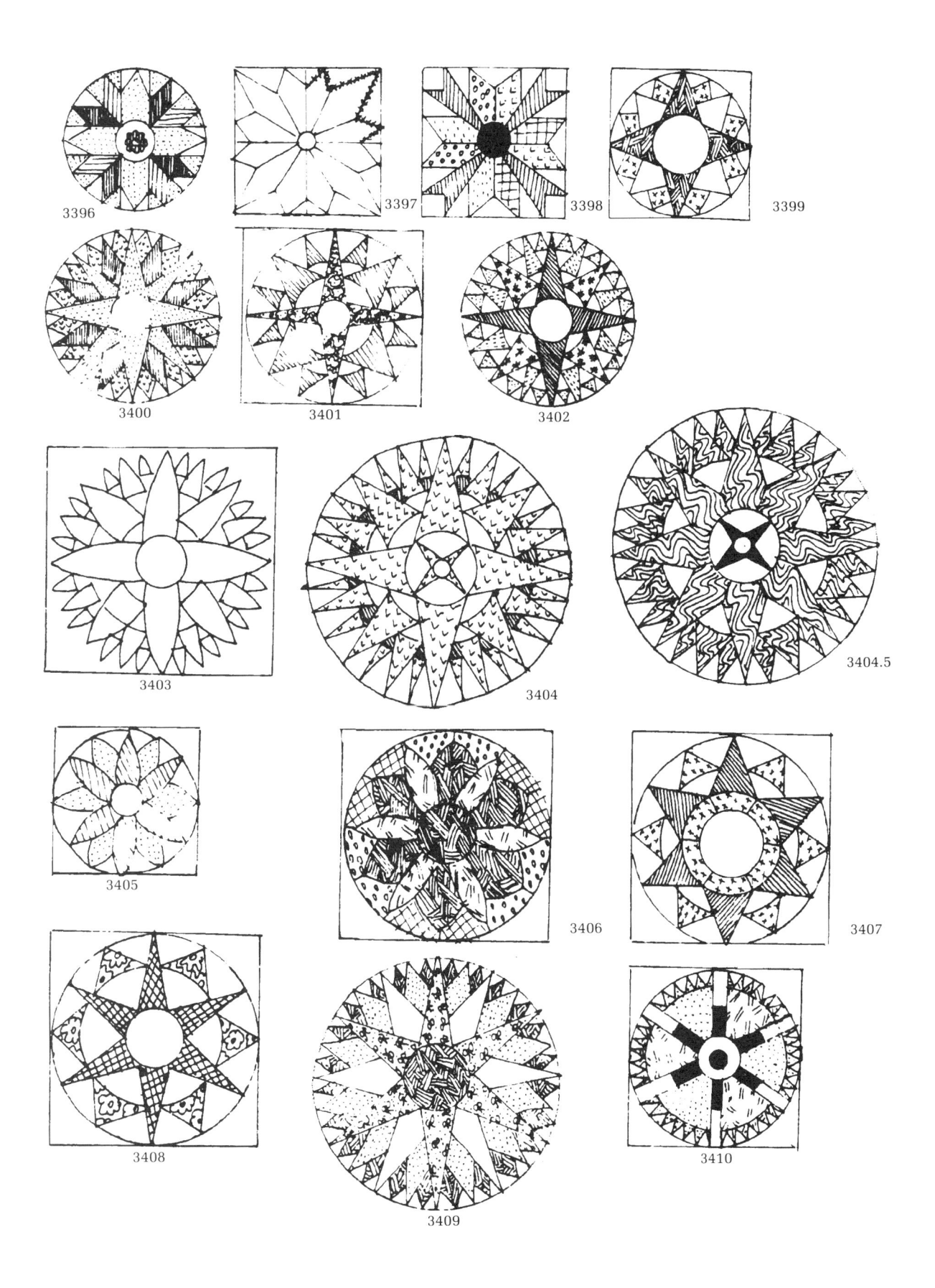

*Four and Six Identical Radiating Petals (3396 – 3410)*

3396
3397
3398
3399
3400
3401
3402
3403
3404
3404.5
3405
3406
3407
3408
3409
3410

411

## Pattern Category 20: *Wheels*

EIGHT IDENTICAL RADIATING PETALS

| | | |
|---|---|---|
| | 3411 | DRESDEN PLATE – Home Art. *See 3452, 3471, & 3488.* |
| | 3412 | THE OAK GROVE STAR – KC Star 6/21/39 |
| | 3413 | EIGHT POINTS IN A SQUARE – KC Star |
| | 3414 | SNOWFLAKE CONTINUITY – attributed to KC Star by Khin |
| | 3415 | EIGHT POINTED STAR – KC Star 3/34. *See 3542.* |
| | 3416 | MOTHER'S CHOICE QUILT – KC Star 2/5/41 (red, white, & blue) |
| | 3417 | CHARITY WHEEL – Hearth and Home |
| | 3418 | THE WHIRLING PINWHEEL – KC Star 9/22/43 |
| | 3419 | BLAZING STAR – Progressive Farmer 1971 |
| | 3420 | BLACK-EYED SUSAN – Capper's/Famous Features |
| | 3421 | FOUNDATION ROSE – Finley<br>CALICO ROSE – Famous Features, Rose Quilts. *See 1541.* |
| | 3422 | MOTHER'S FAVORITE – Grandma Dexter |
| | 3423 | STAR FLOWER – Grandmother Clark 1931<br>GOLDEN GLOW – Hall |
| | 3424 | STAR FLOWER – Helen Kaufman, Oklahoma Farmer Stockman 1/1/35 |
| | 3425 | SUNFLOWER – Capper's<br>STAR AND CROWN – Quilt World 4/80 |
| | 3425.5 | SUNFLOWER – McKim. *See 3448, 3457, 3480, 3484, 3486, & 3490.* |
| | 3426 | GOLDEN GLOW – KC Star 1932 (gold and white)<br>MISSOURI DAISY – KC Star 3/2/35 (petals gathered in both) |
| | 3427 | STAR FLOWER – Aunt Martha, Prize Winning Quilts<br>MISSOURI DAISY – Aunt Martha, Home Art<br>SUNFLOWER – Rural New Yorker 12/19/31 |
| | 3428 | STAR DAHLIA – LCPQ #19, 1980 |

Eight Identical Radiating Petals (3411 – 3428)

3411
3412
3413
3414
3415
3416
3417
3418
3419
3420
3421
3422
3423
3424
3425
3425.5
3426
3427
3428

413

# Pattern Category 20: *Wheels*

EIGHT IDENTICAL RADIATING PETALS

| | | |
|---|---|---|
| | 3429 | TEXAS DAISY – Della Harris |
| | 3430 | COGWHEELS – Nancy Cabot |
| | 3431 | WATER LILY – Aunt Martha Bk. 3450 |
| | 3432 | COURTYARD – Meeker |
| | 3433 | GEORGETOWN CIRCLE – Khin |
| | 3434 | SHEPHERD'S LIGHT – Workbasket, Aunt Martha<br>SHADOW STAR – Aunt Martha |
| | 3435 | FERRIS WHEEL – Hearth and Home |
| | 3436 | NELLY BLY – Farm Journal |
| | 3437 | THE GARDENER'S PRIZE – Aunt Martha, Workbasket |
| | 3438 | ROSE ALBUM – McKim, KC Star 6/19/30 |
| | 3439 | COG WHEEL – Grandmother Clark Bk. 20, 1931 |
| | 3440 | GARDEN SPOT – Progressive Farmer 1976 |
| | 3441 | RHODODENDRON STAR – QNM #62, 1975 |
| | 3442 | QUEEN'S DELIGHT – Hearth and Home |
| | 3443 | GEORGETOWN – Oklahoma Farmer Stockman 1/16/1896<br>GEORGETOWN CIRCLE – LAC #99 |
| | 3444 | MARINER'S COMPASS – QNM #121, 1980 |
| | 3445 | THE RISING SUN – Finley<br>MARINER'S COMPASS – Shelburne |

*Eight Identical Radiating Petals (3429 – 3445)*

3429
3430
3431
3432
3433
3434
3435
3436
3437
3438
3439
3440
3441
3442
3443
3444
3445

# Pattern Category 20: *Wheels*

MORE THAN EIGHT PETALS (NUMBER OF PETALS IN PARENTHESES)

3448   **Kansas Sunflower (9)** – Hall. *See 3425.5, 3457, 3480, 3484, 3486, & 3490.*

3449   **Sunflower (9)** – Clara Stone
**Sunburst** – Clara Stone

3450   **The Hex Stars (10)** – Mrs. Danner Bk. #7

3451   **Kansas Sunflower (12)** – Capper's 11/17/28. *See 3473, 3474, 3485, & 3489.*

3452   **The Dessert Plate (12)** – KC Star 6/23/54. *See 3411, 3471, & 3488.*

3453   **Sunflower (12)** – OCS/Curtis

3454   **Wheel of Fortune (12)** – OCS/Wheeler

3455   **The Cog Wheel Quilt (12)** – Rural New Yorker

3456   **The Sunburst Quilt (12)** – KC Star

3457   **A Striking Pattern (12)** – Hearth and Home. *See 3425.5, 3448, 3480, 3484, 3486, & 3490.*
**Noonday** – Finley

3458   **The Kansas Sunflower (12)** – McKim, Parade of States (inner petals gathered)

3459   **Kansas Sunflower (12)** – Nancy Cabot, Capper's 1948

3460   **Double Poppy (12)** – Nancy Cabot

3461   **Pyrotechnics (12)** – LAC #196
**Wheel** – Farm Journal
**Wheel of Fortune** – Robertson

3462   **Sunburst (12)** – Shelburne. *See 3467.*

3463   **Slashed Star (12)** – LAC #266
**Mariner's Compass** – QNM #121, 1980
**Sunrise Pattern** – Robertson (larger center circle)

3464   **Ray of Light (12)** – Jinny Beyer. *See 3995.*

*More Than Eight Petals (3448 – 3464)*

417

# Pattern Category 20: *Wheels*

MORE THAN EIGHT PETALS (NUMBER OF PETALS IN PARENTHESES)

**3465**    KING DAVID'S CROWN (12) – Hearth and Home

**3466**    SUNBURST (13) – University of Kansas. *See 3487.*

**3467**    MERRY GO ROUND (13) – Capper's 3/30/28, Home Art. *See 3462.*

**3468**    GIG PRONG (14) – Country Gentleman ca. 1941.

**3469**    SUNBURST (14) – Nebraska Collections

**3470**    SUNBURST (15) – Mrs. Danner Bk. #1, 1934

**3471a**    FRIENDSHIP RING (16) – Coats and Clark

**3471b**    FRIENDSHIP QUILT (16) – Oklahoma Farmer Stockman. *See 3411, 3452, & 3488.*

**3472**    ASTER (16) – Meeker

**3473**    SUNFLOWER (16) – Home Art
THE LANDON SUNFLOWER – KC Star 9/12/36 (yellow & brown)
*See 3451, 3474, 3485, & 3489.*

**3474**    THE CHINA ASTER (16) – Rural New Yorker 1930.
*See 3451, 3473, 3485, 3489, & 3543.*

**3475**    MERRY GO ROUND (16) – OCS/Wheeler
CHINESE WATERWHEEL – Nancy Cabot

**3476**    PINWHEEL (16) – Grandma Dexter

**3477**    TEXAS SUNFLOWER (16) – Nancy Cabot

**3478**    DRESDEN PLATE (16) – Hinson QC

**3479**    HOOSIER CIRCLES (16) – attributed to Nancy Cabot by Wilma Smith

**3480**    RISING SUN (16) – Clara Stone
KANSAS SUNFLOWER – Capper's, Household Mag. 1/15
RUSSIAN SUNFLOWER – KC Star 5/7/32
OKLAHOMA SUNBURST – KC Star 1933
A BRAVE SUNFLOWER – KC Star
NOONDAY – Shelburne
SUNBURST – Shelburne. *See 3425.5, 3448, 3457, 3464, 3486, 3490, & 3687.*

**3481**    SINGLE SUNFLOWER (16) – Hearth and Home, LAC #3
SUNFLOWER – Hall
BLAZING SUN – Hall
BLAZING STARS – Hall

*More than Eight Petals (3465 – 3481)*

# Pattern Category 20: *Wheels*

MORE THAN EIGHT PETALS (NUMBER OF PETALS IN PARENTHESES)

| | | |
|---|---|---|
| 3482 | **SUNFLOWER (16)** – Capper's 1/7/28, LAC #448 |
| 3483 | **SUNSET (15)** – Quilt World 2/81 |
| 3484 | **VALLEY FORGE QUILT (17)** – Country Gentleman 2/41 |
| | **GEORGE WASHINGTON QUILT** – Country Gentleman 2/41 |
| | *See 3425.5, 3448, 3457, 3480, 3486, & 3490.* |
| 3485 | **ASTER (18)** – Nancy Cabot 6/21/33. *See 3451, 3473, 3474, & 3489.* |
| 3486 | **SUNBURST (18)** – Shelburne. *See 3425.5, 3448, 3457, 3480, 3484, & 3490.* |
| 3487 | **THE SUN (18)** – Rural New Yorker ca. 1936. *See 3466.* |
| 3488a | **FRIENDSHIP RING (20)** – McKim 101 |
| | **DRESDEN PLATE** – McKim 101 |
| | **ASTER** – McKim 101 |
| 3488b | **GRANDMOTHER'S SUNBONNET (20)** – Prairie Farmer Bk. 1 |
| | **GRANDMOTHER'S SUNBURST** – Wallace's Farmer 10/12/28. |
| | *See 3411, 3452, & 3471.* |
| 3489 | **SUNFLOWER (20)** – Grandmother Clark, Grandma Dexter. *See 3451, 3473, 3474, 3485, & 3489.* |
| 3489.5 | **DRESDEN PLATE (20)** – Mountain Mist |
| 3490 | **CART WHEEL QUILT (21)** – Rural New Yorker 10/15/32 |
| | **DINNER PLATE** – Woman's Day 6/49. *See 3425.5, 3448, 3457, 3480, 3484, & 3486.* |
| 3491 | **SPIDER WEB (21)** – Ladies' Home Journal ca. 1920 |
| | **SUNBURST** – Ladies' Home Journal ca. 1920 |
| 3492 | **SUNFLOWER (24)** – Needlecraft Magazine 1931. *See 3544.* |
| 3493 | **SUNBURST (24)** – Grandmother Clark Bk. 21, Nancy Cabot |
| | **TROPICAL SUN** – Home Art |

*More than Eight Petals (3482 – 3493)*

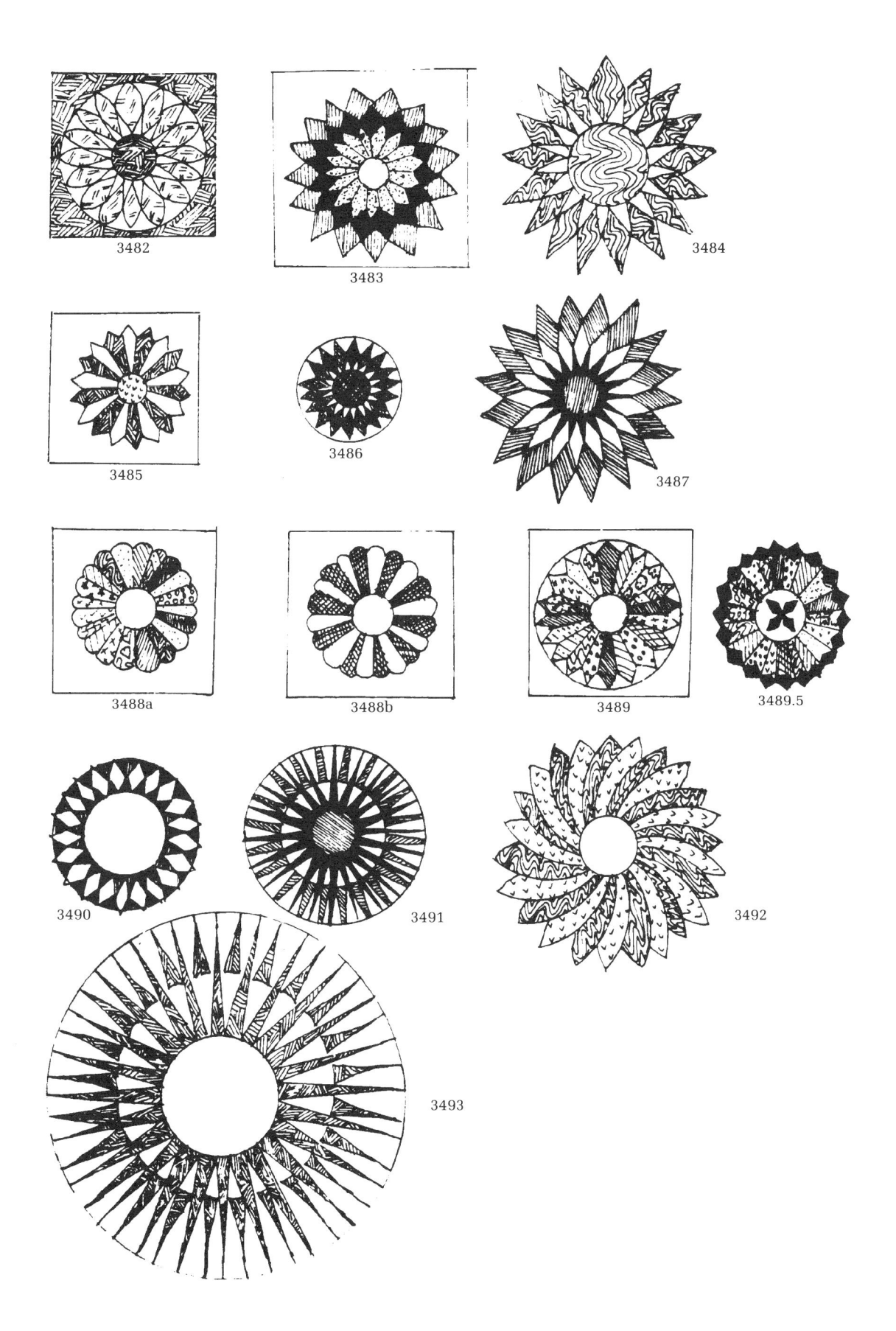

3482

3483

3484

3485

3486

3487

3488a

3488b

3489

3489.5

3490

3491

3492

3493

# Pattern Category 20: *Wheels*

MISC. WHEEL BLOCKS

| | | |
|---|---|---|
| | 3495 | NO NAME – Aunt Martha 1933 |
| | 3496 | THE THRIFTY WIFE – KC Star 5/10/39 |
| | 3497 | A DAINTY QUILT – Comfort |
| | 3498 | THE SPIDER WEB – KC Star 7/15/42<br>NORTHERN LIGHTS – attributed to Nancy Cabot by Wilma Smith |
| | 3499 | AIR SHIP PROPELLER – KC Star 1938<br>TEXAS TULIP – Nancy Cabot |
| | 3500 | TEXAS TULIP – Orbelo |
| | 3501 | NEVADA – Hearth and Home |
| | 3502 | ROSETTE – OCS/Wheeler |
| | 3503 | GRANDMA'S TULIPS – Aunt Martha, Prize Winning Designs. *See 3504.* |
| | 3504 | GRANDMOTHER'S TULIP – KC Star 12/16/36<br>BULL'S EYE – Nancy Page. *See 3503.* |
| | 3505 | BUCKEYE – Aunt Martha, Prize Winning Designs |
| | 3506 | MISSISSIPPI DAISY – Hearth and Home, Comfort<br>BRITCHES QUILT – Aunt Martha, Prize Winning Designs<br>THE BREECHES QUILT – Workbasket 1939<br>DUTCHMAN'S PUZZLE – Nancy Cabot<br>DUTCHMAN'S BREECHES – Progressive Farmer 1949 |
| | 3507 | SUN, MOON, AND STARS – Needlecraft Magazine 3/37 |
| | 3508 | GREEN CROSS – Nancy Cabot |
| | 3509 | ROUND ROBIN – Clara Stone |
| | 3510 | SQUARE AND CIRCLE – Clara Stone |
| | 3511 | THE FULL MOON – KC Star 10/14/42 |
| | 3512 | SAMOA – Hearth and Home |
| | 3513 | CHAINED STAR – OCS/Wheeler |
| | 3514 | RISING STAR – OCS/Wheeler |

*Misc. (3495 – 3514)*

3495　3496　3497　3498
3499　3500　3501　3502
3503　3504　3505　3506
3507　3508　3509　3510
3511　3512　3513　3514

423

# Pattern Category 20: *Wheels*

| | | |
|---|---|---|
| MISC. WHEEL BLOCKS | 3518 | **Ray** – attributed to Nancy Cabot by Wilma Smith |
| | 3519 | **Noon Day Splendor** – OCS Needlecraft/Laura Wheeler 689 |
| | 3520 | **Spider and the Fly** – attributed to Nancy Cabot by Wilma Smith |
| | 3521 | **Avalanche Lily** – Prudence Penny |
| | 3522 | **Letha's Electric Fan** – KC Star 1938 |
| | 3523 | **Primrose** – Capper's/Famous Features |
| | 3524 | **Compass** – LCPQ 16, 1979 |
| | 3525 | **Narcissus** – Oklahoma Farmer Stockman ca. 1925. *See 3539 & 3556.* |
| | 3526 | **Mexican Siesta** – Nancy Cabot <br> **Sombrero Applique** – Nancy Cabot |
| | 3527 | **Full Blown Rose** – Nancy Cabot 1937 |
| | | |
| CURVED SEAMS MEET IN CENTER | 3529 | **Airship** – Comfort |
| | 3530 | **Magnolia Blossom** – Oklahoma Farmer Stockman 9/15/30 |
| | 3531 | **Alabama Beauty** – Aunt Martha, Prize Winning Designs |
| | 3532 | **Peeled Orange** – Nancy Cabot. *See 451.* |
| | 3533 | **Star of West Virginia** – Hearth and Home |

*Misc. (3518 – 3533)*

| | | | |
|---|---|---|---|
| 3518 | 3519 | 3520 | 3521 |
| 3522 | 3523 | 3524 | 3525 |
| 3526 | 3527 | | |
| 3529 | 3530 | 3531 | 3532 |
| 3533 | | | |

425

# Pattern Category 20: *Wheels*

| | | |
|---|---|---|
| INTERSECTING CURVED LINES | **3535** | **Spinning Ball** – Hall |
| | **3536** | **Whirlwind** – Prudence Penny |
| | **3537** | **Spiral** – LCPQ #19, 1980 |
| | | **Spinning Ball** – LCPQ #19, 1980 |
| | | |
| INTERSECTING STRAIGHT LINES (NUMBER OF PIECES IN PARENTHESES) | **3538** | **Pilot Wheel (4)** – Grandmother Clark Bk. 21, 1931 |
| | **3539** | **Orange Peel (4)** – Grandma Dexter (appliqué). *See 3525 & 3555.* |
| | **3540** | **French Star (4)** – McKim 101 |
| | | **Flaming Sun** – Nancy Cabot |
| | | **Gleaming Sun** – attributed to Nancy Cabot by Wilma Smith |
| | **3541** | **The Sunflower (4)** – Country Gentleman 7/30 |
| | **3542** | **Star within Star (4)** – Nancy Cabot. *See 3415.* |
| | **3543** | **Friendship Daisy (4)** – Nancy Cabot. *See 3451, 3473, 3474, 3485, & 3489.* |
| | **3544** | **Circular Saw (4)** – Hearth and Home. *See 3492.* |
| | **3545** | **Sunburst (4)** – Orlofsky pg. 123 (original in a Garden Maze set) |
| | **3546** | **Spider Web (4)** – Khin. *See 246.* |
| | **3547** | **Four O'Clock Quilt (6)** – KC Star 3/18/42 |
| | **3548** | **Compass (6)** – Prudence Penny 12/4/32 |

*Intersecting Curved Lines, Intersecting Straight Lines (3535 – 3548)*

3535
3536
3537
3538
3539
3540
3541
3542
3543
3544
3545
3546
3547
3548

## Pattern Category 20: *Wheels*

INTERSECTING STRAIGHT LINES (NUMBER OF PIECES IN PARENTHESES)

| | | |
|---|---|---|
| | 3550 | PATCHWORK SOFA (8) – LAC #310 |
| | 3551 | OLD MILL WHEEL (8) – Aunt Kate ca. 1963 |
| | 3552 | THE JEWEL (8) – Aunt Martha Prize Winning Designs<br>HUMMINGBIRDS – Nancy Cabot |
| | 3553 | MY NOVA (8) – Hinson QC |
| | 3554 | STATE OF OKLAHOMA (8) – Hearth and Home |
| | 3555 | FERRIS WHEEL (8) – Aunt Martha Book 3175 |
| | 3556 | PAINTED SNOWBALL (8) – Nancy Cabot. *See 3525 & 3539.* |
| | 3557 | NOXALL (8) – Hearth and Home |
| | 3558 | THE AMERICAN WOMAN'S OWN QUILT BLOCK (8) – Hearth and Home |
| | 3559 | SUNFLOWER (8) – Robertson |
| | 3560 | MOUNTAIN PINK (10) – Aunt Martha Prize Winning Designs and Nancy Cabot 1933<br>BROKEN CROWN – KC Star 1933 |
| | 3561 | MOUNTAIN PINK (10) – Evelyn Brown |
| | 3562 | THE BUZZ SAW (12) – KC Star 11/4/41 |
| | 3563 | NOON DAY LILY (12) – Home Art |
| | 3564 | SUNFLOWER (12) – OCS/Wheeler |
| | 3565 | WYOMING PATCH (16) – LAC #494<br>TEXAS SUNFLOWER – Comfort |
| | 3566 | INDIAN PAINTBRUSH (16) – Prudence Penny |

*Intersecting Straight Lines (3550 – 3566)*

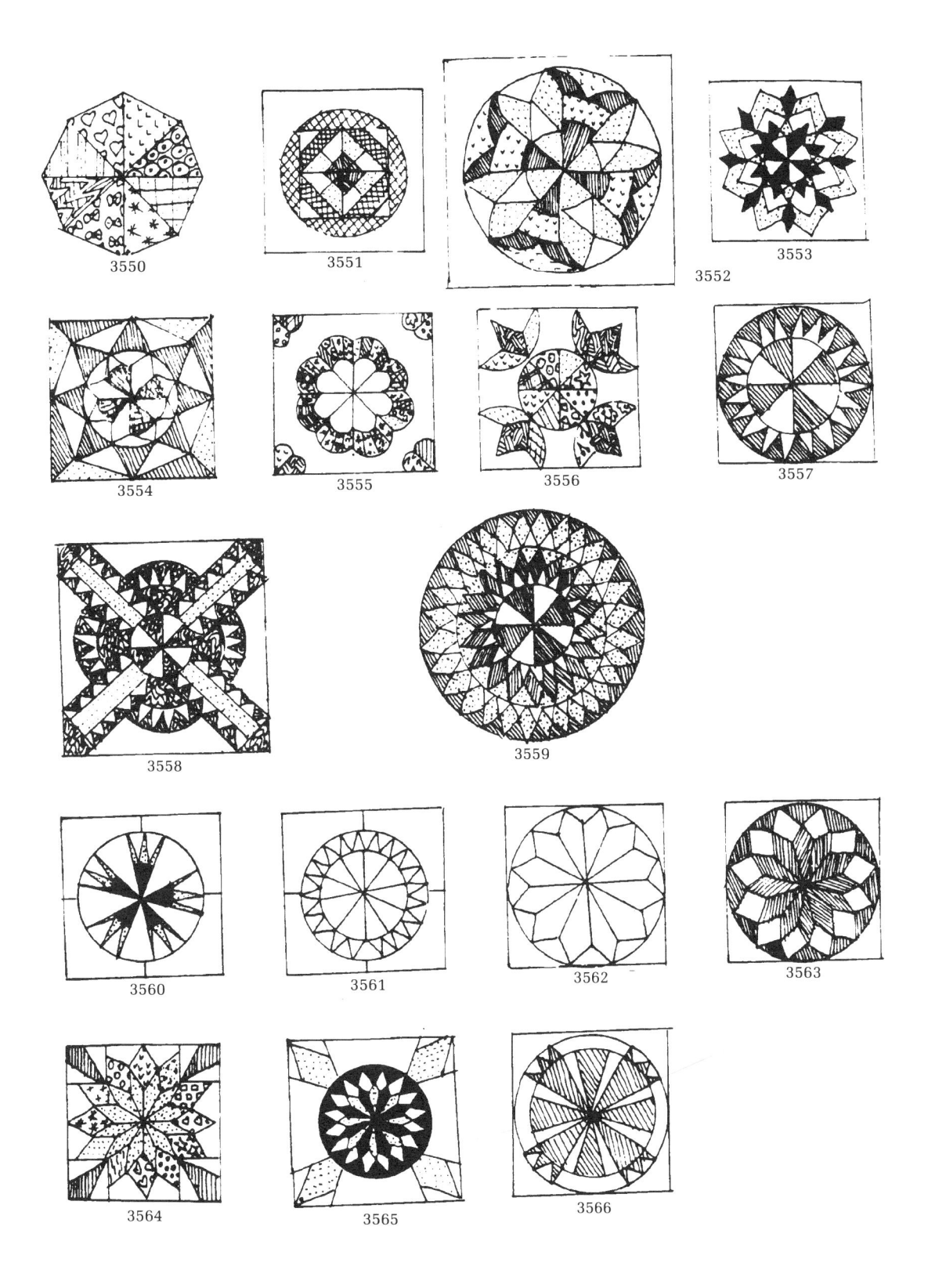

3550
3551
3552
3553
3554
3555
3556
3557
3558
3559
3560
3561
3562
3563
3564
3565
3566

# Pattern Category 20: *Wheels*

| | | |
|---|---|---|
| SQUARE IN CENTER | **3570** | UNNAMED – Holstein |
| | **3571** | SPOOL OF 1966 – Aunt Kate 12/66 |
| | **3572** | DOGWOOD BLOOM – Clara Stone. *See 2001.* |
| | **3573** | THE TULIP DESIGN – Household Magazine, Capper's 1/1915 |
| | **3574** | FOX AND GEESE – LAC #458 |
| | **3575** | ELGIN MAID – Grandma Dexter |
| | **3576** | TULIP WHEEL – Hinson QC |
| | **3577** | FORTUNE'S WHEEL – LAC #521 |
| | **3578** | CHIPS AND WHETSTONES – KC Star 9/19/31 |
| | | |
| HEXAGONS OR OCTAGONS IN CENTER | **3579** | OZARK SUNFLOWER – KC Star 8/4/37<br>THE PIECED SUNFLOWER – KC Star 5/3/47 |
| | **3580** | WAGON WHEEL – Quilt, KC Star |
| | **3581** | VENETIAN DESIGN – LAC #115<br>MOSAIC – Grandmother Clark |
| | **3582** | STAR OF SWEDEN – Comfort |
| | **3583** | THE CAR WHEEL – Quilt, KC Star 9/4/40 |
| | **3584** | RISING SUN – OCS/Wheeler |
| | **3585** | EVENING STAR – KC Star 1931 (described). *See 296.7, 296.9, & 2736.*<br>JUPITER STAR – KC Star 6/24/35<br>JUPITER OF MANY POINTS – KC Star |

*Square in Center, Hexagon or Octagon in Center (3570 – 3585)*

3570
3571
3572
3573
3574
3575
3576
3577
3578
3579
3580
3581
3582
3583
3584
3585

431

# Pattern Category 20: *Wheels*

| | | |
|---|---|---|
| HEXAGONS OR OCTAGONS IN CENTER | 3586 | **Album Blocks** – LAC #352<br>**Folded Stars** – Nancy Page<br>**Tricolor Star** – Nancy Cabot. *See 3587.* |
| | 3587 | **Missouri Daisy** – Aunt Martha. *See 3592.* |
| | 3588 | **Friendship Star** – KC Star 1933<br>**Alma's Choice** – attributed to Nancy Cabot by Wilma Smith |
| | 3589 | **Ring around the Rosy** – Hearth and Home 2/29 |
| | 3590 | **Ring around the Rosy** – Hearth and Home 6/1899 |
| | 3591 | **Cornflower** – QNM #61, 1974 |
| | 3592 | **Star of Texas** – Ladies' Home Journal 1912. Star is quilted in center. *See 3587.* |
| | 3593 | **LeMoyne Star** – Denver<br>**Lemon Star** – Denver |
| | 3594 | **A Sunflower Quilt** – Orange Judd Farmer 2/19/1900 |
| | 3595 | **Starry Crown** – Household Magazine, Capper's |
| | 3596 | **The Kansas Dust Storm** – KC Star 12/28/35 |
| | 3597 | **Friendship Garden** – OCS/Wheeler |
| | 3598 | **Queen of the May** – OCS/Wheeler |
| | 3599 | **Carnival Time** – Aunt Martha Bk. 3230. *See 1300.* |
| | 3600 | **Friendship Circle** – OCS/Wheeler |
| | 3601 | **Mariner's Compass** – QNM 121, 1980 |
| | 3602 | **Rolling Pinwheel** – Ickis |
| | 3603 | **Mariner's Compass** – QNM #121, 1980 |
| | 3604 | **Rising Sun** – Coats and Clark, Bk. 160 |
| | 3605 | **Feathered Star** – Mrs. Danner Bk. 2, 1934 |

*Hexagon or Octagon in Center (3586 – 3605)*

433

# Pattern Category 20: *Wheels*

HEXAGONS OR OCTAGONS IN CENTER

| | |
|---|---|
| 3606 | CALICO STAR – Nancy Cabot 1933 |
| 3607 | THE FOUR POINTER QUILT – Quilt World 6/77 |
| 3608 | BOW TIE QUILT – Aunt Martha Bk. 3333. *See 1152.3, 1376, 1429, & 2533.* |
| 3609 | JACKSON – Hearth and Home<br>MISS JACKSON – LAC #479<br>EMPTY SPOOLS – Nancy Page<br>WISCONSIN STAR – Detroit Free Press. *See 1779.* |
| 3610 | THE CASTLE WALL – KC Star 1931 |
| 3611 | DOGWOOD – Lockport |
| 3612 | THE ARDMORE – Oklahoma Farmer Stockman |
| 3613 | BROWN EYED SUSAN – Needlecraft Magazine 2/35 |

◇ OR ◇ IN CENTER

| | |
|---|---|
| 3620 | REMINISCENT OF THE WEDDING RING – KC Star 8/11/43 |
| 3621 | UNNAMED – Home Art |
| 3623 | PROGRESSIVE – Hearth and Home |
| 3624 | PETAL CIRCLE IN A SQUARE – KC Star 8/24/55 |
| 3625 | SPINNING WHEEL – Prudence Penny |
| 3626 | CIRCLE AND STAR – Hearth and Home 1/27 |
| 3627 | MY GRADUATION CLASS RING – KC Star 4/3/35 |
| 3628 | DRESDEN PLATE – McKendry<br>ASTER – McKendry |
| 3629 | FRIENDSHIP CIRCLE – Home Art<br>DRESDEN PLATE – Successful Farming |
| 3630 | BAY LEAF – Grandmother Clark (appliqué). *See 301, 1519, 2683, & 2684.* |
| 3631 | WANDERING FOOT – Hinson QC<br>TURKEY TRACKS – Hinson QC |
| 3632 | WESTERN ROSE – OCS/Wheeler |

*Hexagon or Octagon in Center, Specific Shapes in Center (3606 – 3632)*

3606　3607　3608　3609

3610　3611　3612　3613

3620　3621　3623　3624

3625　3626　3627　3628

3629　3630　3631　3632

435

# Pattern Category 20: *Wheels*

◇ OR ◇ IN CENTER

| | |
|---|---|
| 3633 | **Mississippi Oak Leaf** – Clara Stone<br>**Cactus Blossom Patch** – LAC #300 |
| 3634 | **Cactus Bloom** – Nancy Cabot 1934 |
| 3635 | **Devil's Footprints** – Nancy Cabot<br>**Milwaukee's Own** – LAC #489<br>**Mississippi Oak Leaves** – Nancy Cabot 1933 |
| 3636 | **Dutch Tulips** – KC Star 1931 |
| 3637 | **Unknown** – McKendry pg. 142 |
| 3638 | **Caesar's Crown** – LCPQ<br>**Grandmother's Quilt** – Aunt Martha, Prize Winning Designs (center shape rotated) |
| 3639 | **Whirling Wheel** – Household Magazine, Capper's 1933 |
| 3640 | **Strawberry** –LAC #212<br>**Full Blown Tulip** – McKim<br>**Pilot's Wheel** – KC Star<br>**Friendship Ring** – OCS/Wheeler<br>**Oriental Star** – Rural New Yorker 3/25/33. *See 3643 & 458.5.* |
| 3641 | **Strawberry** – Grandmother Clark 1932<br>**Full Blown Tulip** – Grandmother Clark 1932 |
| 3642 | **Star and Stirrups** – Pforr (Progressive Farmer) |
| 3643 | **Caesar's Crown** – Finley, plate 68. *See 3640.*<br>**Grecian Star** – Grandmother Clark Bk. 20, 1931<br>**Whirling Wheel** – Household |
| 3644 | **Victoria's Crown** – Grandmother Clark 1932 |
| 3645 | **The Sunflower** – LAC #73<br>**Queen of the May** – Clara Stone<br>**Chinese Star** – Grandmother Clark |
| 3646 | **Chinese Star** – Hall |
| 3647 | **Oriental Star** – Grandmother Clark, Grandma Dexter |
| 3648 | **Victoria's Crown** – Finley, Country Gentleman 1931 |
| 3649 | **King David's Crown** – Clara Stone |
| 3650 | **Indiana Farmer** – Nancy Cabot |
| 3651 | **Rose Album** – LAC #38 |
| 3652 | **Hands All Around** – Progressive Farmer 1935<br>**Grecian Star** – Progressive Farmer 1935<br>**Friendship Ring** – Progressive Farmer 1935<br>**Caesar's Crown** – Progressive Farmer 1935 |

*Specific Shapes in Center (3633 – 3652)*

3633  3634  3635  3636

3637  3638  3639  3640

3641  3642  3643  3644

3645  3646  3647  3648

3649  3650  3651  3652

437

# Pattern Category 20: *Wheels*

☐ OR ◇
IN CENTER

| | | |
|---|---|---|
| | 3653 | CALIFORNIA ROSE – LAC #184 |
| | | FULL BLOWN TULIP – Finley Plate 19 |
| | 3654 | A CROWN OF THORNS – KC Star |
| | 3655 | STAR OF BETHLEHEM – Comfort |
| | | STAR TULIP – Nancy Cabot |
| | 3656 | MARINER'S COMPASS – QNM #121, 1980 |
| | 3657 | COMPASS STAR QUILT – Betterton |
| | 3658 | MARINER'S COMPASS – McCall's Book of Quilts |

ODD CURVED SHAPE IN CENTER

| | | |
|---|---|---|
| | 3659 | FRENCH STAR – McKendry |
| | 3660 | COG WHEELS – LAC #41 |
| | | TOPEKA – Hearth and Home |
| | | PENNSYLVANIA WHEEL QUILT – Hearth and Home |
| | | HARVEST SUN – McKendry |
| | 3661 | GRANDMA'S FAVORITE COMPASS – Aunt Martha |
| | | SETTING SUN – Hall |
| | 3662 | ALBUM QUILT – OCS Needlecraft Museum Quilts |
| | 3663 | HOUR GLASS – Carlie Sexton 1928 |
| | 3664 | ELEPHANT FOOT – Aunt Martha, Prize Winning Designs |
| | 3665 | ARKANSAS STAR – KC Star 3/4/33 |
| | | MORNING SUN – KC Star 3/7/45 |
| | | BURSTING STAR – Home Art |
| | 3666 | QUEEN'S CROWN – OCS/Wheeler |
| | 3667 | ALCAZAR – Nancy Cabot |
| | | A YOUNG MAN'S INVENTION – KC Star 1936 |
| | 3668 | STARRY CROWN – Nancy Cabot |

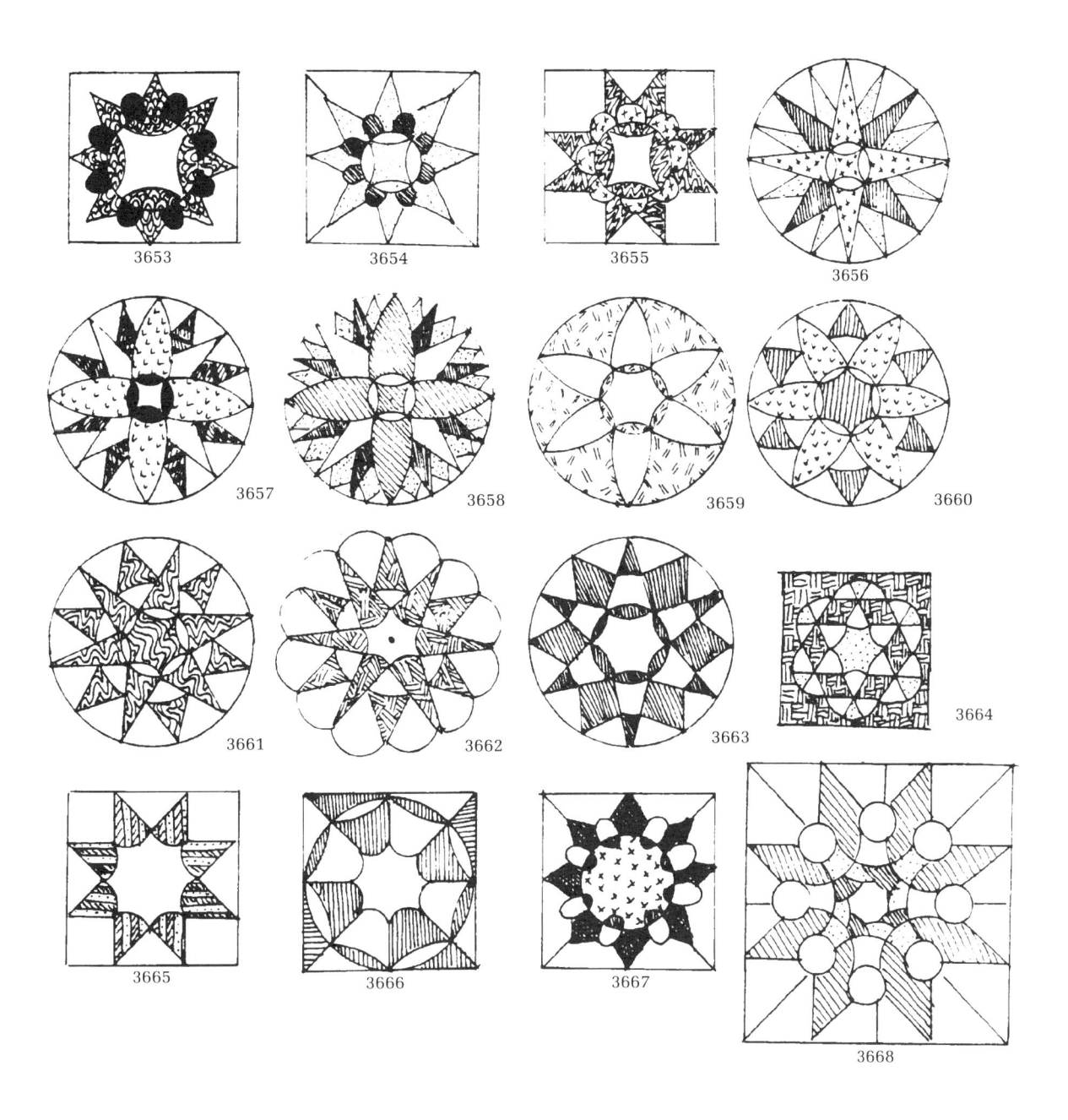

*Specific Shapes in Center, Odd Curved Shapes in Center (3653 – 3668)*

3653　3654　3655　3656
3657　3658　3659　3660
3661　3662　3663　3664
3665　3666　3667　3668

# PATTERN CATEGORY 21

## Five- and Six-Pointed Star Blocks

**Patterns in Category 21 share these characteristics:**

- The pattern does not fit a prior category.

- The pattern has the general appearance of a star.

- At least one star in the block is complete and symmetrical.

**Category 21 includes:**
- Five-Pointed Stars, 442
- Six-Pointed Stars, 444

## KEY TO PATTERN CATEGORY 21: FIVE- AND SIX-POINTED STAR BLOCKS

**STEP 1**

If star has five points, *turn to p. 442*

If star does not have five points, *continue with STEP 2 below*

**STEP 2**

If star has six radiating points, each a 60° diamond, *turn to p. 444*

If star has neither five nor six points, *see Eight-Pointed Stars* **(PATTERN CATEGORY 22)** *or Other Stars* **(PATTERN CATEGORY 23)**

# Pattern Category 21: *Five- & Six-Pointed Star Blocks*

FIVE-POINTED STARS

| | | |
|---|---|---|
| | 3675 | FIVE POINTED STAR – LAC #18<br>UNION STAR – attributed to Nancy Cabot, Nancy's |
| | 3676 | FIVE-POINT STAR – Hall |
| | 3677 | RED, WHITE AND BLUE QUILT – Orange Judd Farmer 12/17/1898 |
| | 3678 | STARFLOWER – Progressive Farmer, Johnson 1977 |
| | 3679 | STAR OF THE WEST – Ickis |
| | 3680 | UNION STAR – LAC #381<br>MOON AND STAR – Hearth and Home<br>THE 20TH CENTURY STAR – Clara Stone |
| | 3681 | STAR OF THE WEST – LAC #274 |
| | 3682 | TEXAS – Hearth and Home (note letters embroidered in the points) |
| | 3683 | EZEKIEL'S WHEEL – Aunt Kate 1966 |
| | 3684 | TEXAS BICENTENNIAL STAR – Progressive Farmer, Johnson 1977 |
| | 3685 | TEXAS RANGER'S BADGE – Orbelo |
| | 3686 | TEXAS REPUBLIC – Orbelo |
| | 3687 | STARS WITHIN STARS – Bacon. *See 3480.* |
| | 3688 | MOON FLOWER – Nancy Cabot |
| | 3689 | STAR AND CRESCENT – Clara Stone |

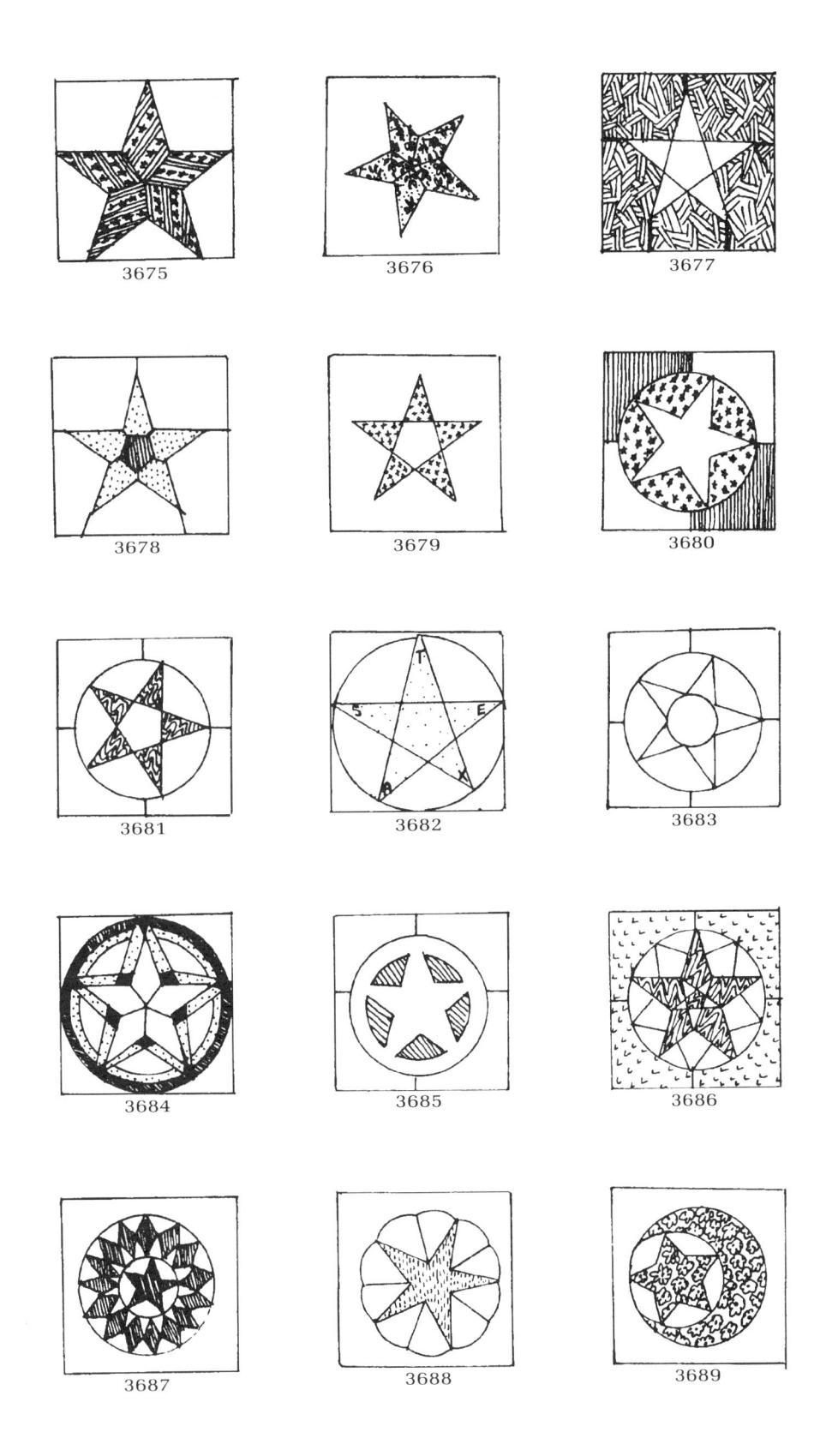

*Five-Pointed Stars (3675 – 3689)*

# Pattern Category 21: *Five- & Six-Pointed Star Blocks*

FIVE-POINTED STARS     **3690**     **UNNAMED** – The Clarion, Spring, 1982
Published by Museum of American Folk Art

SIX-POINTED STARS     In many cases these six-pointed stars are actually in blocks that are slightly rectangular.

         **3700**     **NOVEL STAR** – LAC #366
                         **MORNING STAR** – Joseph Doyle. *See 142 & 3701.*

         **3701**     **HEXAGONAL** – LAC
                         **BLOCK STAR** – Grandma Dexter
                         **A LITTLE GIRL'S STAR** – KC Star 8/15/50. *See 142 & 3700.*

         **3702**     **STAR OF THE EAST** – Country Home 2/33

         **3703**     **MEXICAN STAR** – Comfort

         **3704**     **BRUNSWICK STAR** – LAC #21
                         **ROLLING STAR** – Hall
                         **CHAINED STAR** – Hall. *See 441.*

         **3705**     **STAR OF THE EAST** – Wallace's Farmer 3/23/28

         **3706**     **STAR OF DIAMONDS** – Capper's 1932
                         **THE STAR** – Hearth and Home, Comfort

         **3707**     **LARGE STAR** – Helen Kaufman in Oklahoma Farmer Stockman 1/1/35

         **3708**     **THE COLUMBIA** – LAC #109
                         **COLUMBIA STAR** – Hall
                         **COLUMBIAN STAR** – Quilt World 6/79. *See 143.*

         **3709**     **TEXAS STAR** – Orbelo

*Five-Pointed Stars, Six-Pointed Stars (3690 – 3709)*

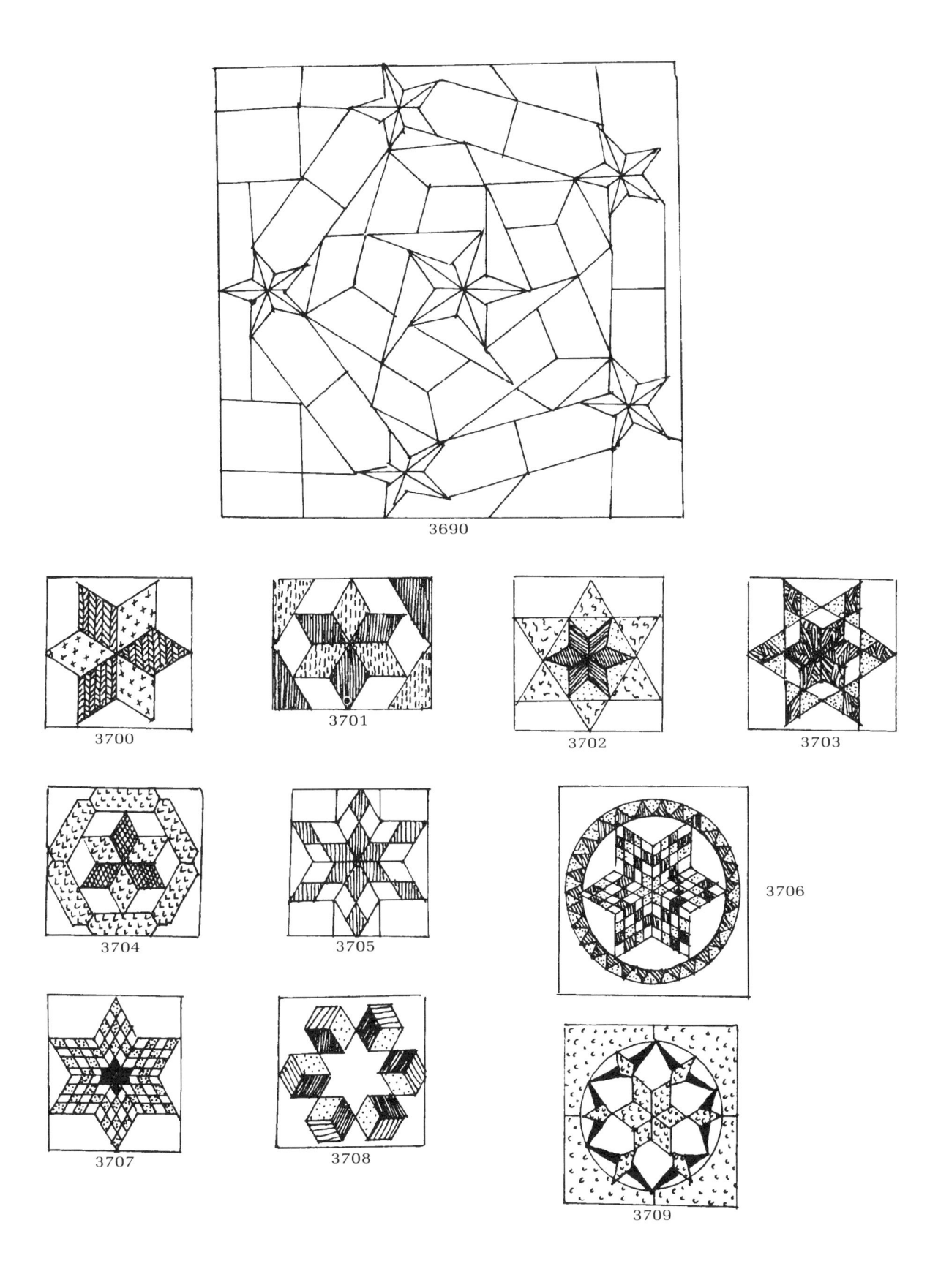

3690

3700
3701
3702
3703
3704
3705
3706
3707
3708
3709

445

# Pattern Category 21: *Five- & Six-Pointed Star Blocks*

SIX-POINTED STARS

**3710**    STAR AND PLANETS – Grandma Dexter, Grandmother Clark

**3711**    BUTTERCUP – Prudence Penny

**3712**    RAINBOW STAR QUILT – Home Art

**3713**    CENTURY OF PROGRESS – Nancy Cabot 1933

**3714**    CUBE WORK – LAC #228

**3715**    STAR OF BETHLEHEM – LAC
A PATTERN OF CHINESE ORIGIN – KC Star 12/30/42

**3716**    STAR OF THE EAST – Lockport Batting

**3717**    OLD COLONY STAR – Hall

**3718**    SIX POINT STRING QUILT – KC Star 2/21/40

**3719**    SYLVIA'S CHOICE – Clara Stone
SAVANNAH BEAUTIFUL STAR – LAC #487
SOUTHERN PLANTATION – attributed to Nancy Cabot by Nancy's

**3720**    SAVANNAH BEAUTIFUL STAR – Hall

**3721**    ROULETTE WHEEL STAR FOR NEVADA – Aunt Kate 4/66

**3722**    KENTUCKY – Hearth and Home

**3723**    SAWTOOTH PATTERN – Gammell
SIX-POINTED STAR – Gammell

**3724**    STAR OF BETHLEHEM – Hall

**3725**    SAM'S QUILT – Clara Stone

**3726**    WISCONSIN STAR – Aunt Kate 1966

*Six-Pointed Stars (3710 – 3726)*

3710
3711
3712
3713
3714
3715
3716
3717
3718
3719
3720
3721
3722
3723
3724
3725
3726

# Pattern Category 21: *Five- & Six-Pointed Star Blocks*

SIX-POINTED STARS

**3727**    **LATTICED STAR** – Meeker pg. 36 (appliqué lattice)

**3728**    **UNNAMED** – Safford and Bishop pg. 119

**3729**    **COLORADO** – Hearth and Home
**RISING SUN** – Hearth and Home
**RISING STAR** – Hearth and Home
**DOUBLE STAR** – Hall (reverse color scheme)

**3730**    **SAWTOOTH STAR** – Meeker pg. 35

**3731**    **OHIO STAR** – Aunt Kate 7/66

**3732**    **LACE FAN** – Aunt Martha

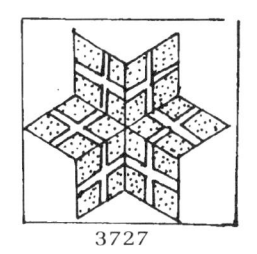

*Six-Pointed Stars (3727 – 3732)*

3727

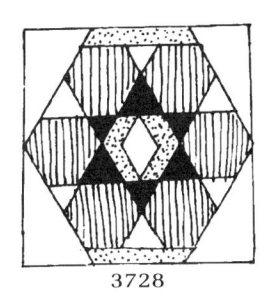

3728

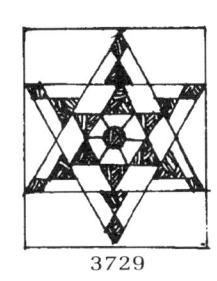

3729

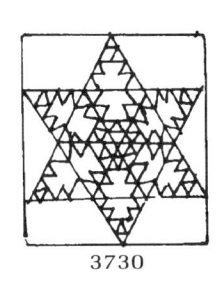

3730

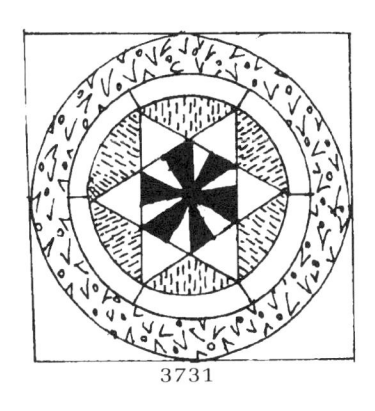

3731

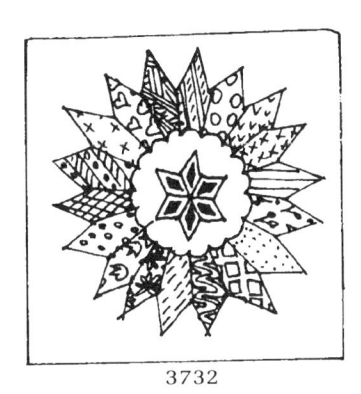

3732

# PATTERN CATEGORY 22

## Eight-Pointed/45° Diamond Stars

**Category 22 includes:**

- Single Stars, 452
- Star Off Center, 452
- Center Star If Made Up of Odd Pieces, 454
- Star Made Up of Many Diamonds, 456
- Star Surrounded by Parts of Other Stars, 460
- Star Inside Another Star, 462
- Stars Surrounded by Other Shapes, 464
- Stars with Points Oriented Up & Down, 468

**KEY TO CATEGORY 22: EIGHT-POINTED/45° STARS**

**STEP 1**

If the star is oriented in the center of the block, *continue with STEP 2 below*

If the star or stars are in the edge of the block, *turn to p. 452*

**STEP 2**

If the center star is positioned with the points up and down, *turn to p. 468*

If the center star is positioned with angles up and down in the block, *continue with STEP 3 below*

**STEP 3**

If the center star dominates the design, *continue with STEP 4 below*

If although there is a star in the center, that star is surrounded by other strong design elements, *continue with STEP 5 below*

**STEP 4**

If the points of the center star are made up of many diamonds, *turn to p. 456*

If the points of the center star are made up of only one diamond, *turn to p. 452*

If the points of the center star are made up of other shapes, *turn to p. 454*

**STEP 5**

If the star is inside another star, *turn to p. 462*

If the star is surrounded by parts of other stars made up of 45° diamonds and other shapes, *turn to p. 460*

If the star is surrounded by other shapes, *turn to p. 464*

451

# Pattern Category 22: *Eight-Pointed/45° Diamond Stars*

SINGLE STARS

**3735a**
- STAR – Ohio Farmer 11/29/1894
- EIGHT POINTED STAR – LAC #261
- EIGHT POINT STAR – McKim
- STAR BED QUILT – Hearth and Home
- SIMPLE STAR – Carlie Sexton 1928
- THE SOUTHERN STAR – KC Star
- VARIABLE STAR – QEC 1978
- TWINKLE, TWINKLE LITTLE STAR – KC Star 5/15/35, shows 4 set together

**3735b**
- PURITAN STAR QUILT – Joesph Doyle
- STAR OF LEMOYNE – Finley
- LEMON STAR – Finley
- DIAMOND DESIGN – Woman's World ca. 1930
- THE STAR – KC Star 8/8/36
- EASTERN STAR – McCall's ca. 1930
- IDAHO STAR – Nancy Cabot
- HANGING DIAMONDS – Denver Art Museum
- DIAMOND – Vote

**3735c** ARROW STAR – KC Star 1934

**3735d** COLUMNS – Gutcheon

**3735e** SUNLIGHT AND SHADOWS – KC Star 1/7/42
*See 1061, 1282, 1291, 2605, & 3736.*

STAR OFF CENTER

**3736a**
- FOUR STARS PATCHWORK – LAC #311
- THE FOUR STARS – Cappers, Hearth and Home
- OLD MAID'S PATIENCE – Nancy Cabot 6/24/33

**3736b** JACKSON STAR – KC Star 5/16/31

**3736c** THE MAPLE LEAF – Capper's 10/24/31. *See 3735.*

**3737** DIAMOND WEDDING BLOCK – Nancy Cabot, Progressive Farmer 9/50

**3738** GLITTERING STAR – Cappers (25 diamonds in each point). *See 3777.*

**3739** DIAMONDS IN THE CORNERS – KC Star

**3740** LAZY DAISY – KC Star 12/26/31

**3741** UNNAMED – Aunt Martha, Prize Winning Designs

**3742** THE LINCOLN QUILT – Anne Orr

**3743** MISSOURI – Hearth and Home

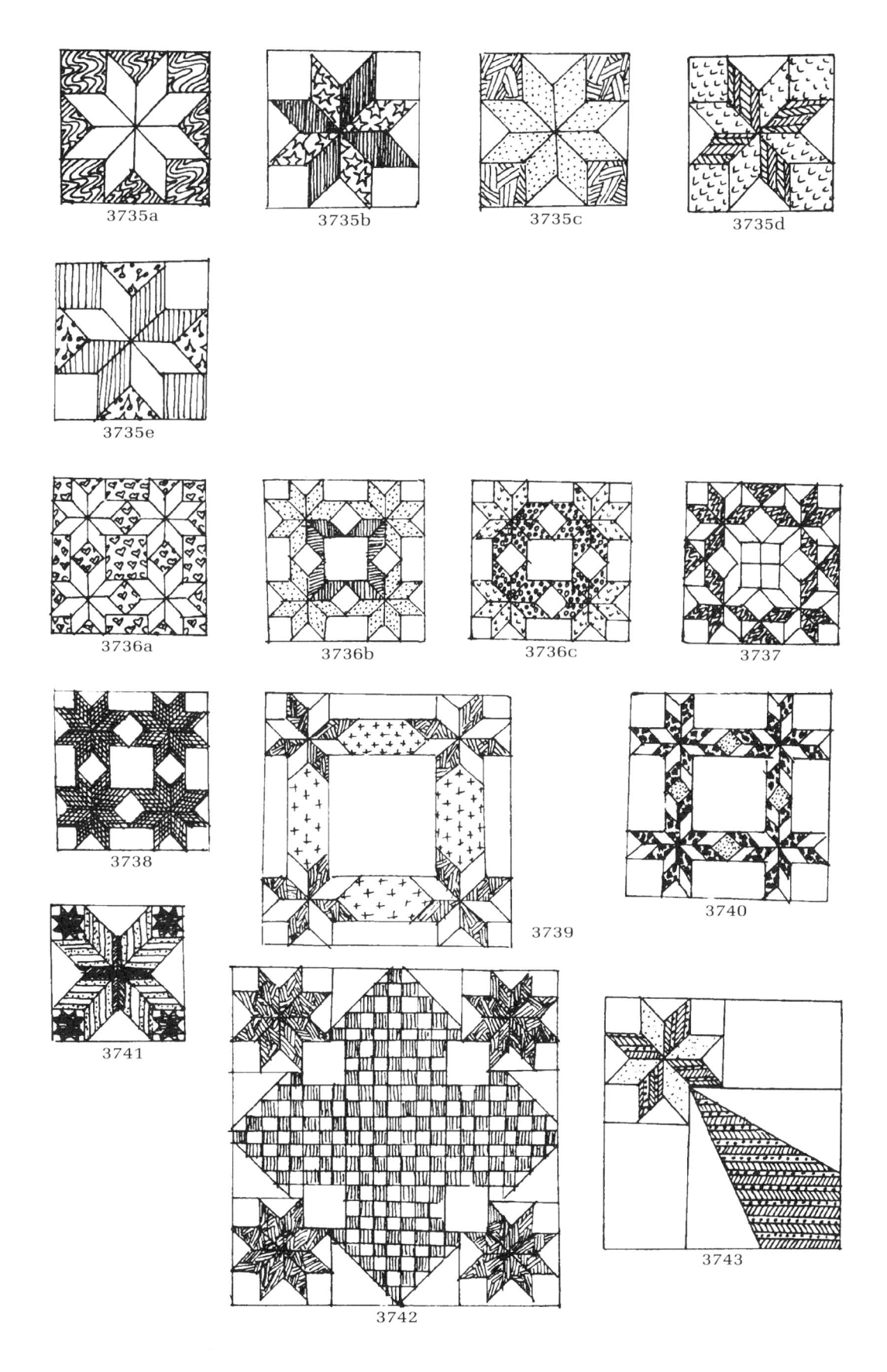

Single Stars, Star Off Center (3735a – 3743)

3735a
3735b
3735c
3735d
3735e
3736a
3736b
3736c
3737
3738
3739
3740
3741
3742
3743

453

# Pattern Category 22: *Eight-Pointed/45° Diamond Stars*

CENTER STAR IS MADE UP OF ODD PIECES

3745    STAR OF THE EAST – Rural New Yorker 3/12/32
NORTH STAR – Home Art
LEMOYNE STAR – Ickis
THE DIVIDED STAR – Danner 1958
LOUISIANA STAR – Aunt Kate 12/65
(in this pattern they used striped fabric
so the pattern was actually identical to 3735)

3746    SILVER AND GOLD – KC Star 1/3/31, Hearth and Home
GOLD AND SILVER – Nancy Cabot
WINTER STARS – Nancy Cabot

3747    TWINKLING STAR – Quilt World 4/80

3748    TENNESSEE – Hearth and Home
LIBERTY STAR – KC Star 1932 (red, white, & blue)
STARS OF STRIPES – Capper's 1941
STAR OF BETHLEHEM – Safford and Bishop

3749    FENCE ROW STAR – Hearth and Home
LOG CABIN STAR – Hearth and Home, Evangeline's

3750    TWO COLORS – Comfort

3751    DIAMOND STAR – Ohio Farmer 8/27/1896
PINWHEEL – Oklahoma Farmer Stockman 1930. *See 1140 & 2145.*

3752a    MOSAIC #13 – LAC #341

3752b    LUCKY PIECES – Nancy Page. *See 1140 & 2146.*

3753    HELENA – Hearth and Home
CAPITAL STAR – Hearth and Home

3754    SPIDERWEB STAR – Woodard & Greenstein

3755    LOG CABIN STAR – Hinson QC

3756    GRANDMA'S BROOCH – KC Star 6/24/35

3757    DIAMOND STAR – Hearth and Home
DIAMOND STAR #2 – Clara Stone

3758    FALLING STAR – Comfort, Finley
FLYING SWALLOW – LAC #503, Finley
FLYING SWALLOWS – Aunt Martha
FLYING STAR – Finley
CIRCLING SWALLOWS – Finley
THE WREATH – OCS/ Wheeler
FLYING BARN SWALLOWS – Nancy Cabot 2/27/35
WHIRLING STAR – KC Star 1/30/37

3759    SPINNING STAR – QNM #37, 1969

3760    SAILOR'S JOY – Clara Stone

3761    THE KING'S CROWN – LAC #181

3762    KING'S STAR – Nancy Cabot

3763    QUEEN'S STAR – Aunt Martha

## Center Star Made Up of Odd Pieces (3745 – 3763)

3745

3746

3747

3748

3749

3750

3751

3752a

3752b

3753

3754

3755

3756

3757

3758

3759

3760

3761

3762

3763

455

# Pattern Category 22: *Eight-Pointed/45° Diamond Stars*

STAR MADE UP OF MANY DIAMONDS

3765    FORMOSA TEA LEAF – KC Star 11/14/31

3766    FLYING BAT – LAC #44
DOVE IN THE WINDOW – Oklahoma Farmer Stockman
FLYING STAR – Home Art
DOVES – Home Art
POLARIS STAR  Hall
WITCHES STAR – Nancy Cabot

3767    DOVES AT THE WINDOW – Capper's 1930
THE DOVE – Della Harris
FOUR DOVES – Nancy Page 1934. *See 3772.*

3768    DOVE IN THE WINDOW – McKim
FOUR BIRDS – Woman's World
THE BLUE BIRDS – Rural New Yorker 1933
FOUR SWALLOWS – Rural New Yorker 1933
AIRPLANES – Farm Journal
BLUEBIRDS FOR HAPPINESS – Mountain Mist

3769    CONNECTICUT STAR – Farm Journal 1937

3770    KENTUCKY'S TWINKLING STAR – Good Housekeeping, 1979

3771    STAR OF VICTORY QUILT – Workbasket (small stars appliqué)

3772    BLAZING STAR – Joseph Doyle, Herrschner's, McKim
STAR OF THE EAST – Carlie Sexton
QUILT OF THE CENTURY – Capper's, ca. 1933
COMBINATION FEATHERED STAR – Aunt Martha 1933
THE BLAZING STAR OF MINNESOTA – Workbasket 1935
PATRIOTIC STAR – KC Star 5/9/36
LITTLE STAR – attributed to Nancy Cabot, Nancy's
RISING STAR – Nancy Page
STAR OF THE BLUEGRASS QUILT – Mountain Mist
MORNING STAR – KC Star 9/14/50
EASTERN STAR – Gutcheon PPP
UNKNOWN STAR – Alice Beyer

3773a    SHIPS WHEEL – Finley
HARVEST SUN – Finley
PRAIRIE STAR – Hall
STARS UPON STARS – Home Art

3773b    VIRGINIA STAR – Hall
STAR UPON STARS – Hall
VIRGINIA'S STAR – Ickis

3773c    STARS OF ALABAMA – Mountain Mist

3773d    STAR BOUQUET – Taylor Bedding

3773e    STAR OF HOPE – Clara Stone (note set). *See 3773 & 3780.*

3774    VIRGINIA STAR – McKim (corner stars appliqué)

3775    VIRGINIA STARS – Country Life 2/23

3776    THE LONE STAR – clipped from unknown paper, 1915

3777    STARS UPON STAR – LAC #211
MORNING STAR – Carlie Sexton
SUNBURST STAR – OCS/Wheeler
STAR OF BETHLEHEM – Ickis

3778    GLITTER STAR – Capper's 1929
RAINBOW STAR – Hall. *See 3738.*

3779    STARRY HEAVENS – KC Star 8/6/41 (appliqué). *See 3787.*

3780    PATTY'S STAR – Hall
NATIONAL STAR – Progressive Farmer, Pforr 1974

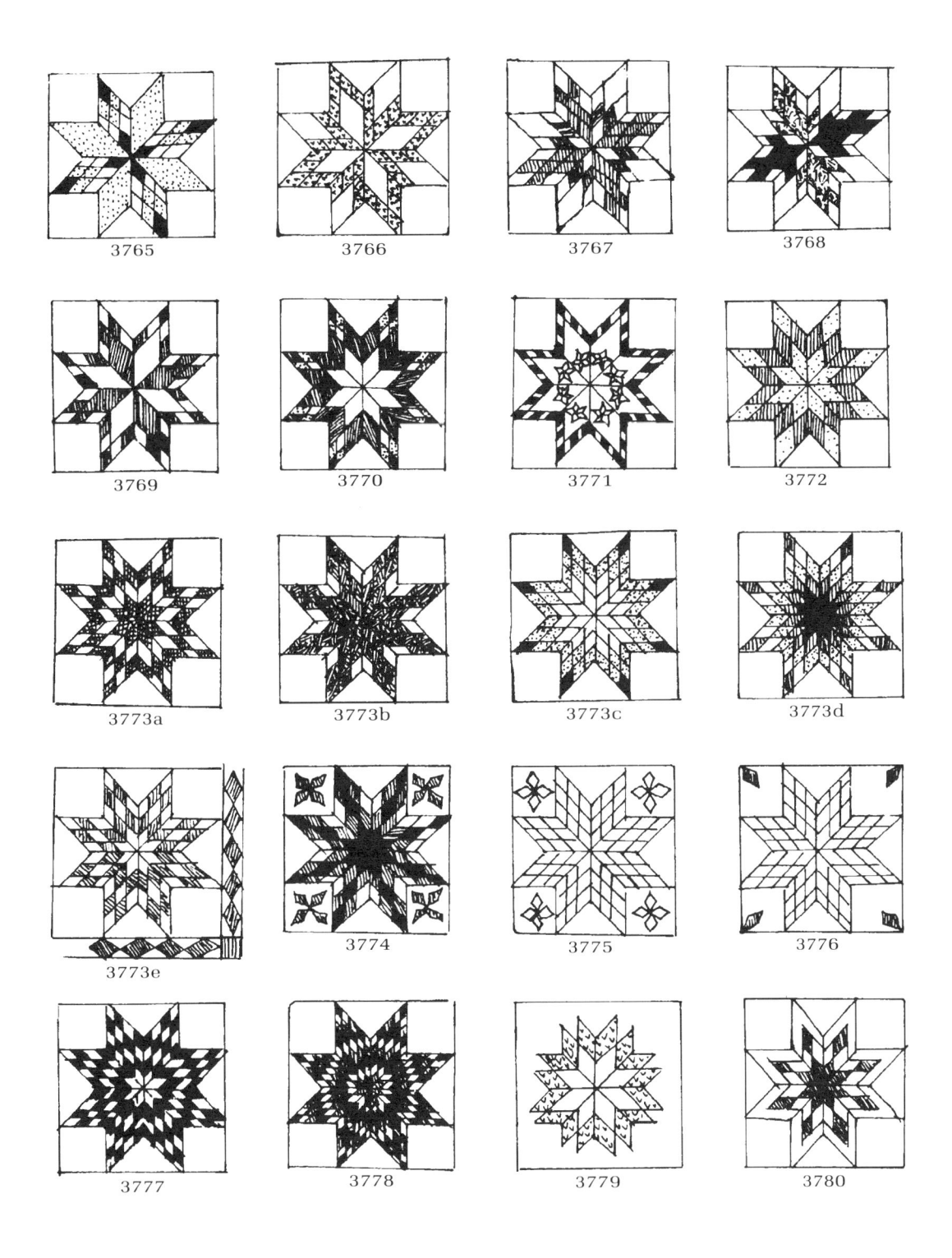

*Star Made Up of Many Diamonds (3765 – 3780)*

| | | | |
|---|---|---|---|
| 3765 | 3766 | 3767 | 3768 |
| 3769 | 3770 | 3771 | 3772 |
| 3773a | 3773b | 3773c | 3773d |
| 3773e | 3774 | 3775 | 3776 |
| 3777 | 3778 | 3779 | 3780 |

# Pattern Category 22: *Eight-Pointed/45° Diamond Stars*

STAR MADE UP OF MANY DIAMONDS

| | | |
|---|---|---|
| | 3781 | BLAZING STAR – LAC #372<br>HARVEST STAR – Danner/Ericson 1981 |
| | 3782 | SUNBURST AND MILLS – Nancy Cabot |
| | 3783 | BLAZING STAR OF KENTUCKY   Khin |
| | 3784 | DOUBLE STAR – Clara Stone<br>FISH TAILS – Nancy Page 1933 |
| | 3785 | A SWALLOW AT THE WINDOW – Capper's 5/24/30 |
| | 3786 | WANDERING JEW – Clara Stone<br>THE WINDING BLADES – KC Star 11/19/41 |
| | 3787 | CHIPS AND WHETSTONES – QEC 1981 pg. 50. *See 3773.* |
| | 3789 | CHRISTMAS STAR – KC Star 1931 |
| | 3790 | AUNT DINAH'S STAR – Home Art |
| | 3791 | RISING SUN – Dakota Farmer 9/15/26 |
| | 3792 | LOVE IN A MIST – Farm Journal |
| | 3793 | WOOD LILY – KC Star 1936<br>INDIAN HEAD – KC Star 1936<br>ST. ELMO'S FIRE – Nancy Cabot |
| | 3794 | MOSAIC – Farm Journal<br>MOORISH MOSAIC – Nancy Cabot<br>BURSTING STAR – Nancy Cabot |
| | 3794.5 | RING AROUND THE STAR – Workbasket 1937 |
| | 3794.7 | MY MOTHER'S STAR – Hall pg. 221 |

*Star Made Up of Many Diamonds (3781 – 3794.7)*

3781  3782  3783  3784

3785  3786  3787  3789

3790  3791  3792

3793  3794  3794.5

3794.7

459

# Pattern Category 22: *Eight-Pointed/45° Diamond Stars*

| | | |
|---|---|---|
| STAR SURROUNDED BY PARTS OF OTHER STARS | 3795 | ROLLING STAR – The Rural New Yorker 6/4/32 |
| | 3796 | STAR OF BETHLEHEM – Aunt Martha, Home Art <br> BETHLEHEM STAR – KC Star 5/18/38 <br> STAR OF THE MAGI – Nancy Cabot 2/24/37 <br> WINGED STAR – KC Star 5/18/38 <br> CHRISTMAS MEMORY QUILT – QNM 1972 <br> JEWELS IN A FRAME – Progressive Farmer, Pforr 1974 |
| | 3797 | PEGGY ANNE'S SPECIAL – KC Star 1936 (red, white, & blue) |
| | 3798 | WEST VIRGINIA – Hearth and Home <br> WEST VIRGINIA STAR – Workbasket 1935 |
| | 3799 | STAR – Ohio Farmer 1/23/96 <br> STARS AND CUBES – LAC #15 <br> YANKEE PRIDE – Finley <br> DOUBLE STAR – Hearth and Home <br> CUBES AND TILES – Nancy Cabot. *See 3800 & 3801.* |
| | 3800 | VICTORY STAR – Clara Stone. *See 3799 & 3801.* |
| | 3801 | ALL HANDS AROUND – Needlecraft 1930 <br> CAPTIVE BEAUTY – Aunt Martha <br> HEAVENLY STARS – Danner/Ericson 1934, Frank <br> STARS AND CUBES – Nancy Page |
| | 3802 | SNOW CRYSTALS – KC Star 12/13/30. *See 3795, 3800, & 3801.* |
| | 3803 | MY COUNTRY – Aunt Kate |
| | 3804 | BLAZING STAR – KC Star 1930 |
| | 3805a | ROLLING STAR – LAC #4 <br> CROSS AND CROWN – Oklahoma Farmer Stockman <br> BRUNSWICK STAR – Finley, Comfort <br> CHAINED STAR – Finley <br> VIRGINIA REEL – Danner/Ericson 1934 <br> ROLLING STONE – Grandma Dexter |
| | 3805b | PARALLELOGRAM – KC Star 5/30/45 <br> DESIGN FOR LIGHT AND DARK – Comfort (note embroidery) |
| | 3806 | LEMOYNE STAR – QNM 98, 1978 <br> (note small star pieced in squares) |

*Star Surrounded by Parts of Other Stars (3795 – 3806)*

3795

3796

3797

3798

3799

3800

3801

3802

3803

3804

3805a

3805b

3806

461

# Pattern Category 22: *Eight-Pointed/45° Diamond Stars*

| | | |
|---|---|---|
| STAR SURROUNDED BY PARTS OF OTHER STARS | 3807 | DUTCH ROSE – LAC #185<br>UNKNOWN STAR – Webster<br>OCTAGONAL STAR – Hearth and Home, Farm Journal, Comfort, Household Journal (in an octagonal block)<br>TRIPLE STAR – Household Journal<br>ORPHAN STAR – Home Art<br>ECCENTRIC STAR – Grandmother Clark, Grandma Dexter<br>STAR AND DIAMOND – Della Harris<br>MORNING STAR – Khin. *See 3808.* |
| | 3808 | STAR OF THE EAST – Danner/Ericson, 1934<br>CIRCLE SAW – KC Star. *See 3807.* |
| | 3809 | STAR OF BETHLEHEM – Clara Stone<br>BLACK DIAMOND – Clara Stone<br>STAR QUILT BLOCK – People's Popular Monthly, 8/15<br>DIADEM STAR – Hearth and Home 1928<br>DOUBLE STAR – Hearth and Home, KC Star 1929<br>DOUBLE STAR BED QUILT – Comfort<br>STAR OF BETHLEHEM – Comfort<br>CARPENTER'S WHEEL – Finley<br>LONE STAR OF PARADISE – KC Star 1933<br>TWINKLING STARS – Nancy Page<br>SUNFLOWER – Nancy Page<br>THE KNICKERBOCKER STAR – Workbasket 1935<br>STAR WITHIN A STAR – Hall. *See 3817.* |
| | 3810 | EIGHT POINTED BROKEN STAR – Bruce Johnson |
| | 3811a | BROKEN STAR – QEC 1978 |
| | 3811b | CARPENTER'S WHEEL – DuBois/Stars |
| | 3812 | DUTCH ROSE – Clara Stone<br>MOTHER'S CHOICE – Needlecraft 1918 |
| | 3613 | THE STARBRIGHT QUILT – Oklahoma Farmer Stockman 1/1/33 |
| | 3814 | POINSETTIAS – Quilters Newsletter #70, 1975 |
| | 3815 | NIGHT HEAVENS – Nancy Cabot |
| | 3816 | STAR FLOWERS – Nancy Cabot |
| | 3817 | BLACK DIAMOND – Needlecraft 10/30. *See 3809.* |
| | 3818 | PIN WHEEL STAR – LAC #75<br>STAR AND WREATH – Nancy Cabot |
| STAR INSIDE ANOTHER STAR | 3821 | ALL AMERICAN STAR – Aunt Martha |
| | 3822 | TENNESSEE STAR – Nancy Cabot |
| | 3823 | STAR SHOWER – Nancy Cabot. *See 2508.* |
| | 3824 | CALICO STARS – Evelyn Brown |

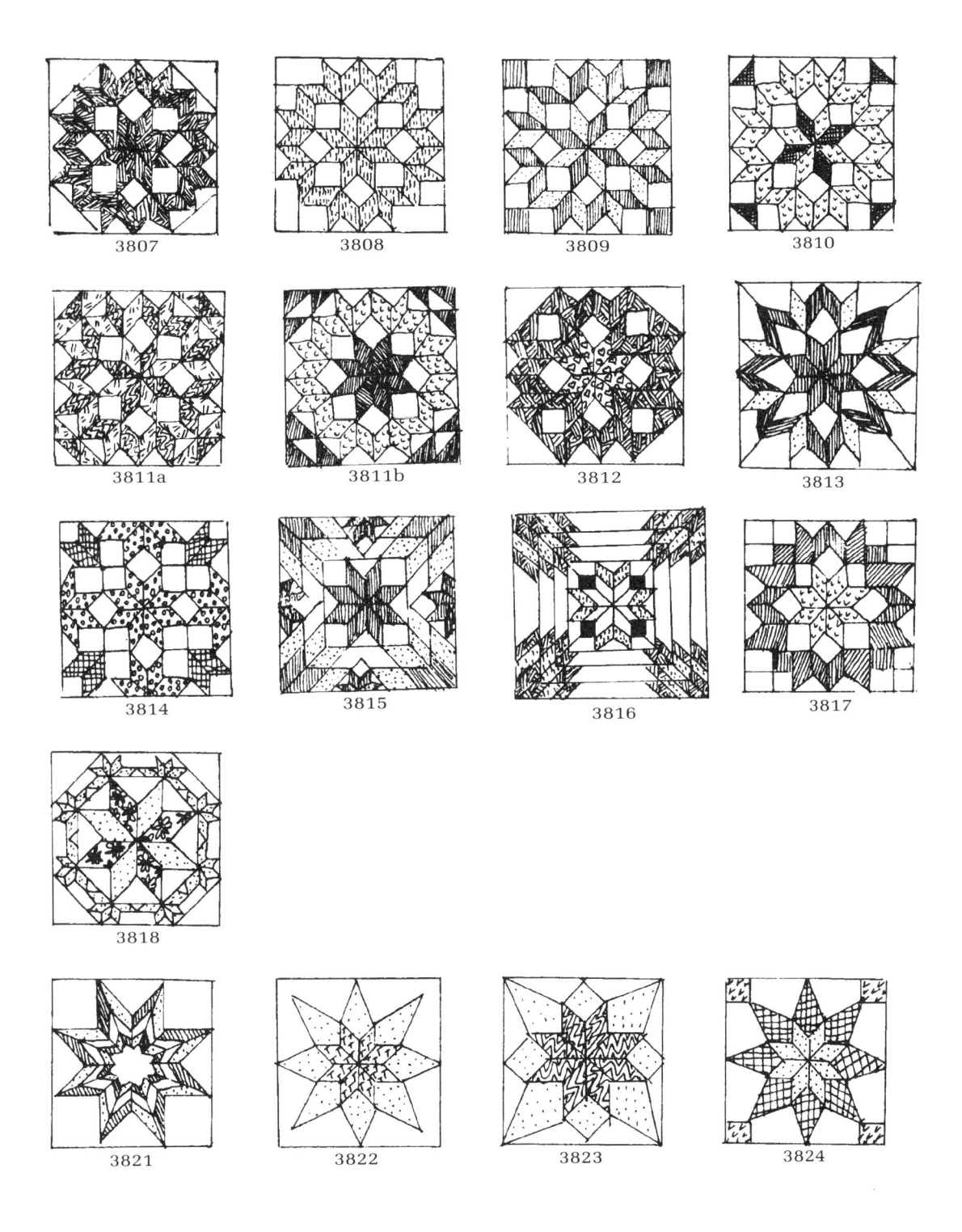

*Star Inside Another Star, Stars Surrounded by Parts of Other Stars (3807 – 3824)*

463

# Pattern Category 22: *Eight-Pointed/45° Diamond Stars*

| | | |
|---|---|---|
| STAR INSIDE ANOTHER STAR | 3825 | POLE STAR – Hearth and Home |
| | 3826 | THE TRIPLE STAR QUILT – Khin |
| STAR SURROUNDED BY OTHER SHAPES | 3828 | FISH – Clara Stone<br>WHIRLIGIG – Clara Stone<br>FISH BLOCK – McKim 101<br>GOLD FISH – KC Star 1931<br>TROUT AND BASS BLOCK – Nancy Cabot<br>AN AIRPLANE MOTIF – KC Star 4/2/47<br>FLYING FISH – KC Star 4/2/47<br>DOVE IN THE WINDOW – Tower Press<br>FISH CIRCLE – LCPQ #8<br>STARFISH – LCPQ #8<br>BASS AND TROUT – Quilt World V. 4, #4 |
| | 3829 | MISSOURI STAR – KC Star 5/24/30<br>SHINING STAR – Hall<br>STAR AND ARROW – Nancy Cabot |
| | 3830 | ST. LOUIS STAR – LAC #275<br>STAR OF ST. LOUIS – Nancy Cabot<br>VARIABLE STAR – Nancy Cabot |
| | 3831 | STAR NET – Nancy Cabot |
| | 3832 | UNNAMED – Godey's |
| | 3833 | GREEN MOUNTAIN STAR – Clara Stone<br>AUNT MARY'S STAR – Clara Stone |
| | 3834 | LUCINDA'S STAR – Hall |
| | 3835 | PIKE'S PEAK – Clara Stone<br>BRIDE'S FANCY – Clara Stone |
| | 3836 | TURTLE – Meeker pg. 43 |
| | 3837 | NEW STAR – Nancy Cabot 5/15/34 |
| | 3838 | NEW STAR – LAC #371<br>LEAVENWORTH STAR – Hall (inside star one color) |
| | 3839 | LAWRENCE STAR – Mitchell |
| | 3840 | WESTWARD HO – Nancy Cabot 3/21/36 |
| | 3841 | STAR OF '49 – Progressive Farmer 1949 |

*Star Inside Another Star, Star Surrounded by Other Shapes (3825 – 3841)*

465

# Pattern Category 22: *Eight-Pointed/45° Diamond Stars*

STAR SURROUNDED BY OTHER SHAPES

| | | |
|---|---|---|
| | **3842** | THE SPIDER WEB – KC Star 6/16/43 |
| | **3843** | SAWTOOTH – Nancy Cabot. *See 1074.* |
| | **3844** | SAWTEETH – Woman's World. *See 1075.* |
| | **3845** | UNNAMED – Nimble Needle Treasures, Fall 1973, QNM<br>FLIGHT OF THE WILD GOOSE – Meeker |
| | **3846** | PARTY PLATE QUILT – Workbasket 1943 |
| | **3847** | COMPASS – Aunt Martha<br>CALICO COMPASS – Nancy Cabot |
| | **3848** | COTTAGE TULIPS – KC Star 1931 |
| | **3849** | TEXAS STAR – Hall, pg. 231 |
| | **3850** | SLASHED STAR – Robertson |
| | **3851** | SUNBURST – Mountain Mist |

*Star Surrounded by Other Shapes (3842 – 3851)*

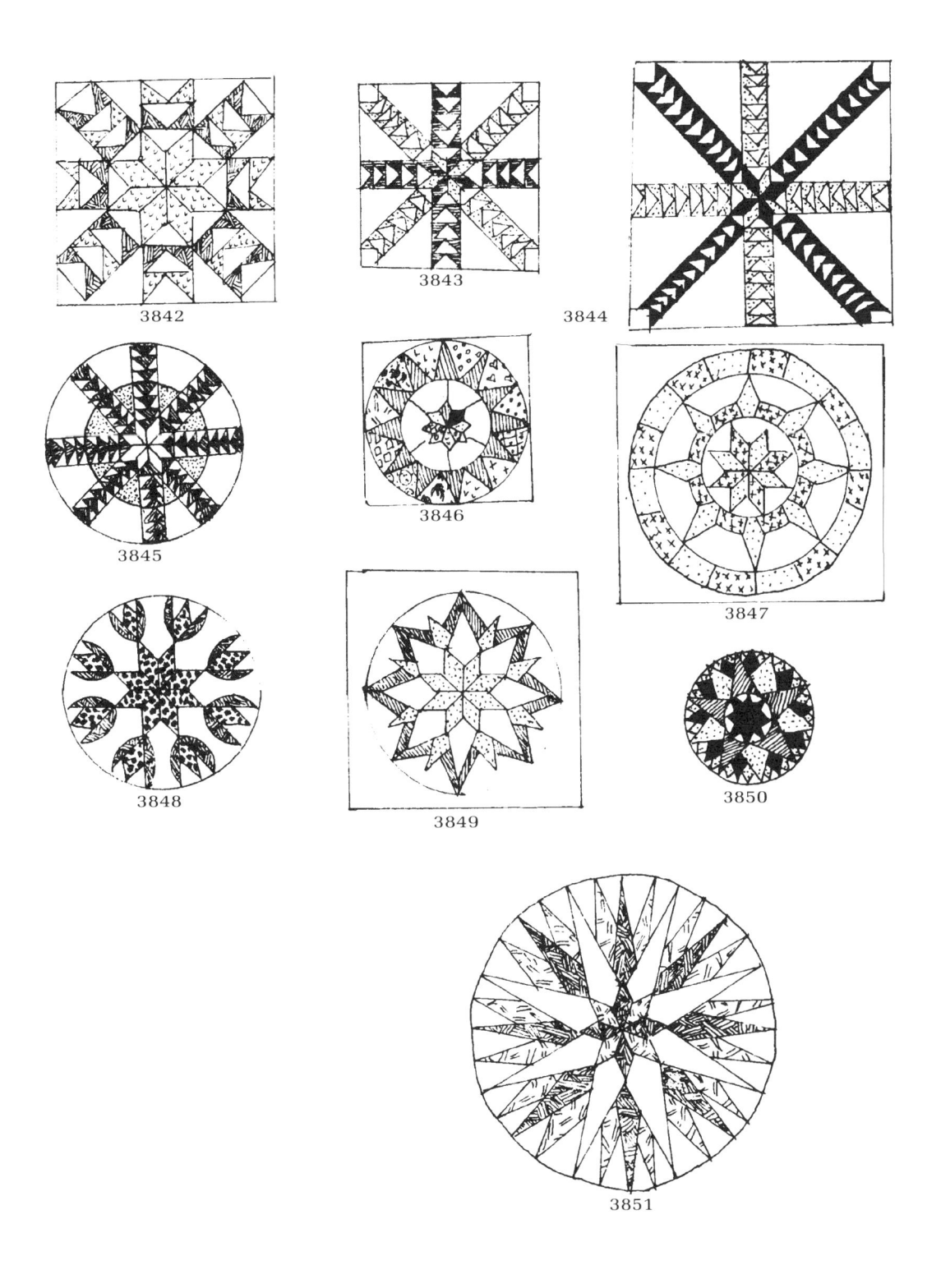

# Pattern Category 22: *Eight-Pointed/45° Diamond Stars*

STARS WITH POINTS ORIENTED UP & DOWN

| | | |
|---|---|---|
| | 3854 | ROYAL DIAMONDS – KC Star 6/30/48 |
| | 3855 | OCTAGON STAR – Comfort |
| | 3656 | OCTAGON STAR – Farm Journal |
| | 3857 | SITKA – Hearth and Home |
| | 3858 | THE STARLIGHT QUILT – Rural New Yorker, 1/20/34 |
| | | STARLIGHT – LAC #528 |
| | 3859 | WESTERN SPY – Clara Stone |
| | 3860 | NET OF STARS – Nancy Cabot |
| | 3861 | TWINKLING STARS – LAC #406 |
| | | STAR OF HOPE – KC Star 1932 |
| | | CELESTIAL SPHERE – Nancy Cabot |
| | 3862 | THE INLAY STAR – Hall, but not in her book, first published in QNM, 1977 |
| | 3863 | DIAMOND STAR – Nancy Cabot |
| | 3864 | UNNAMED – Godey's |
| | 3865 | ISLAND CREEK HUSTLER – Hearth and Home |
| | 3866 | PINWHEEL STAR – Woman's World |
| | | MODERN STAR – Hall |
| | 3867 | STARLIGHT – Nancy Cabot |

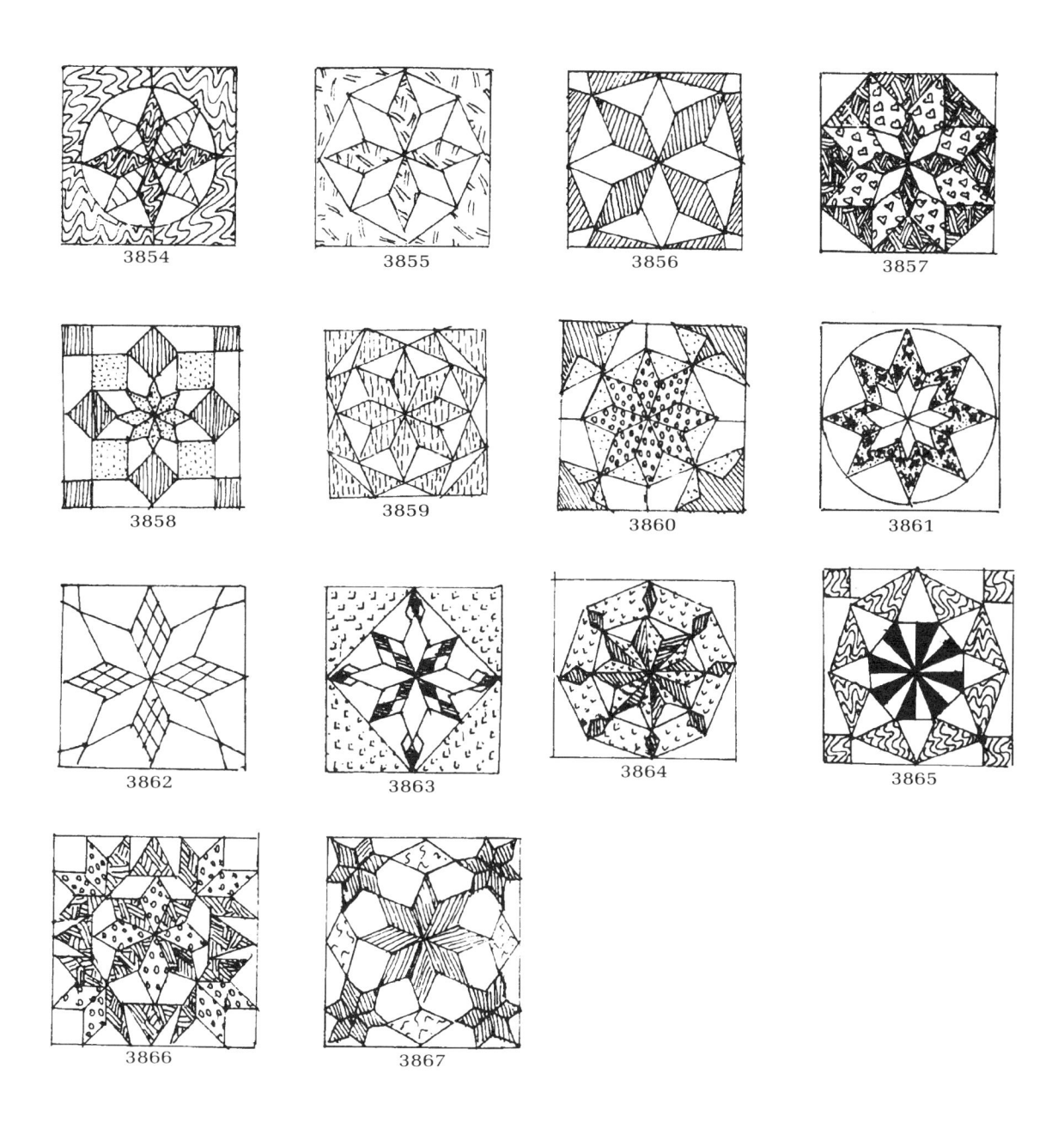

*Stars with Points Oriented Up & Down  (3854 – 3867)*

# Pattern Category 23

## Other Stars

**Category 23 includes:**

- Multiple Stars, 472
- Eight Equal/Wide Points, 472
- Wide Points Oriented Up & Down, 474
- Wide Points Oriented Left & Right, 474
- Odd Eight-Pointed Stars, 476
- Long Diamonds, 478
- Points Are Triangles or Other Shapes, 478

## KEY TO PATTERN CATEGORY 23: OTHER STARS

**STEP 1**

Points are Diamond-like ◇◇◊ ,                                          *continue with STEP 2 below*

Points are triangles or other shapes △ ,                               *turn to p. 478*

**STEP 2**

Points are diamond-like but wider than a 45° diamond or irregular ◇◇◊ , *continue with STEP 3 below*

Points are diamond-like but longer and narrower than a 45° diamond ◊ , *turn to p. 478*

**STEP 3**

Multiple stars are formed inside the block ⊠ ,                         *turn to p. 472*

Single star in center of block ✦ ,                                      *continue with STEP 4*

**STEP 4**

The star has eight points of generally equal size ✳ ,                  *turn to p. 472*

The star has four or eight points but four dominate in size ✦ ,        *continue with STEP 5*

**STEP 5**

The star has an orientation to the up and down axis ✦ ,                *turn to p. 474*

The star has an orientation to the diagonal, left and right axis ✦ ,   *turn to p. 474*

**STEP 6**

The star seems to have no dominant axis ✦ ,                            *turn to p. 476*

471

# Pattern Category 23: *Other Stars*

| | | |
|---|---|---|
| MULTIPLE STARS | **3870** | **MICHIGAN'S PONTIAC STAR** – Workbasket 1915 *See 1214, 1246, 2324, 3891, & 4459.* |
| | **3871** | **PONTIAC STAR** – Clara Stone |
| | **3872** | **SACRAMENTO** – Hearth and Home. *See 415.2, 1258, 3055, & 3056.* |
| | **3873** | **NORTH DAKOTA** – Hearth and Home <br> **THE WINDMILL** – Rural New Yorker, 4/19/32 <br> **WINDMILL STAR** – Grandmother Clark, Grandma Dexter <br> **THE WANDERING FLOWER** – KC Star 3/15/39 <br> **QUILT STAR** – Nancy Cabot <br> **CRAZY QUILT STAR** – Nancy Cabot <br> **CRAZY STAR QUILT** – attributed to Nancy Cabot, Nancy's <br> **AMETHYST** – Hall. *See 413, 413.1, 1251, 1252, 1259, 2975, 2976, 3874, & 3945.* |
| | **3874** | **KALEIDOSCOPIC PATCH** – LAC #386. *See 413, 413.1, 1251, 1252, 1259, 2975, 2976, & 3873.* |
| | **3875** | **GEOMETRICAL STAR** – Clara Stone |
| | **3876** | **4 STAR BLOCK** – Nancy Cabot |
| | **3877** | **NATIVITY STAR** – QNM #62, 12/74 |
| | | |
| STAR HAS EIGHT EQUAL/WIDE POINTS | **3880** | **THE PURPLE CROSS** – KC Star 1932 |
| | **3881** | **TENNESSEE MOUNTAIN LAUREL** – Elwood, Tennery, & Richardson |
| | **3882** | **ENIGMA** – LAC #400 <br> **NORTH STAR** – Nancy Page <br> **ST. LOUIS BLOCK** – Nancy Page |
| | **3883** | **WISHING STAR** – Workbasket, 1941 <br> **NEW STAR QUILT** – Workbasket, 1941 <br> **STAR OF ST. LOUIS** – Nancy Cabot |
| | **3884** | **DOUBLE STAR** – Home Art |
| | **3885** | **MISSIONARY BAPTIST** – Comfort |
| | **3886** | **PRINT AND PLAIN** – Farm Journal 2/45 |
| | **3887** | **HARRISBURG** – Hearth and Home |
| | **3888** | **PLAID STAR** – Khin |
| | **3889** | **DOUBLE STAR FLOWER** – Aunt Kate |
| | **3890** | **BLAZING STAR** – Grandma Dexter (appliqué star & edges) |

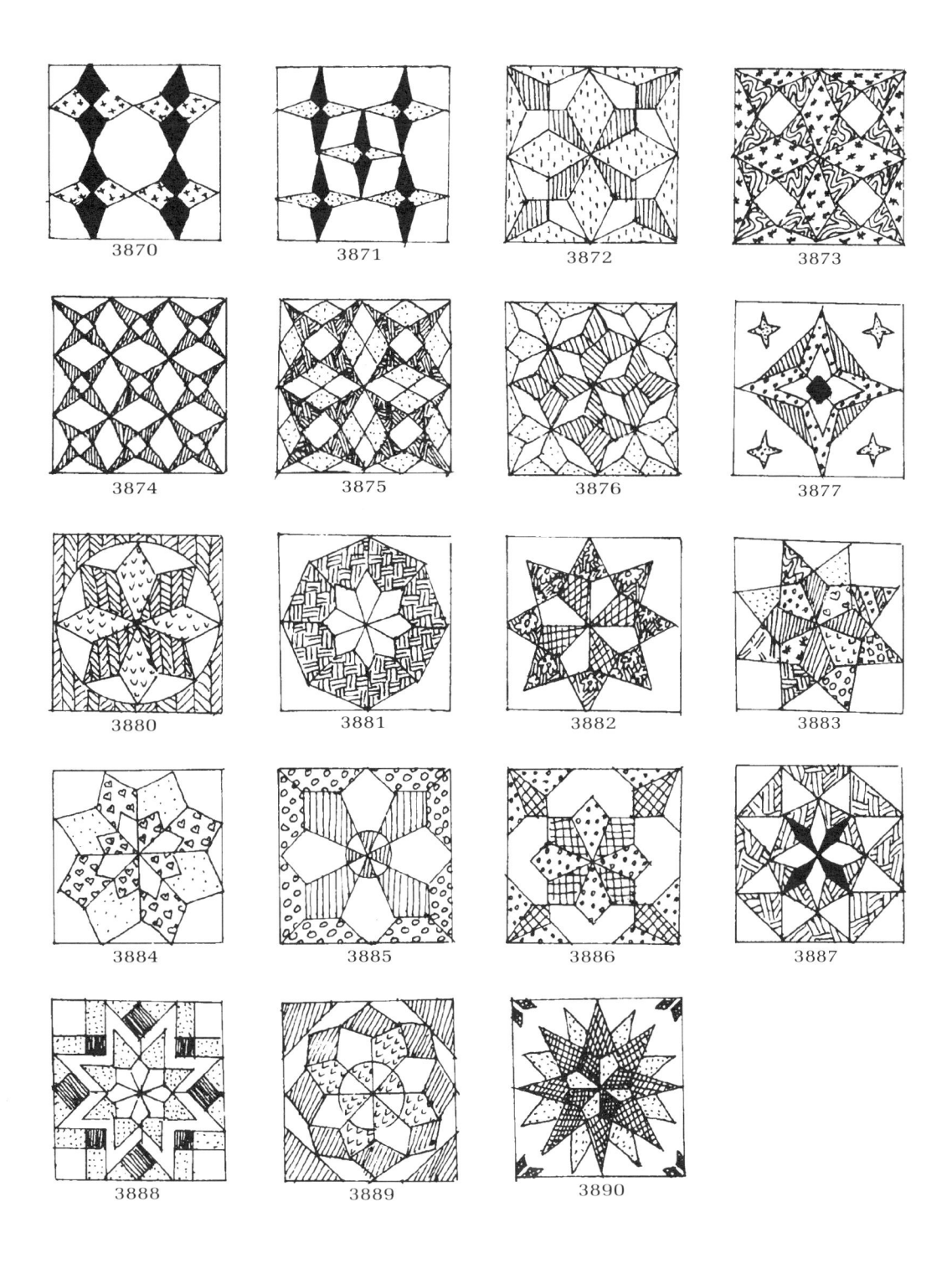

*Multiple Stars, Eight Equal/Wide Points  (3870 – 3890)*

| 3870 | 3871 | 3872 | 3873 |
| 3874 | 3875 | 3876 | 3877 |
| 3880 | 3881 | 3882 | 3883 |
| 3884 | 3885 | 3886 | 3887 |
| 3888 | 3889 | 3890 | |

# Pattern Category 23: *Other Stars*

| | | |
|---|---|---|
| WIDE POINTS ORIENTED UP & DOWN | 3891 | **Danish Stars** – KC Star 6/10/42. *See 445.9, 1214, 1246, 2324, 3970, 3871, & 3891.* |
| | 3892 | **The Kite Quilt** – KC Star 1931<br>**Arkansas Snow Flake** – KC Star 1935<br>**Arkansas Star** – KC Star 1935<br>**Star Kites** – Nancy Cabot (in a set of 4). *See 445.9.* |
| | 3893 | **Beautiful Star** – LAC<br>**Arrow Star** – Mills |
| | 3894 | **Oriental Star** – Nancy Cabot 8/10/33 |
| | 3895 | **Dervish Star** – Grandma Dexter (appliqué)<br>**Star of the Orient** – attributed to Nancy Cabot by Nancy's |
| | 3896 | **Home Again** – Farm Journal |
| | 3897 | **Four Leaf Clover** – Nancy Cabot |
| | 3898 | **Unnamed** – Godey's 1858 |
| | 3899 | **Twinkling Stars** – Comfort<br>**Four Pointed Star** – KC Star 2/13/37<br>**Time and Tide** – QNM #59, 1974 |
| | 3900 | **Byrd at the South Pole** – Nancy Cabot |
| | 3901 | **Peary's Expedition** – Nancy Cabot |
| | 3902 | **Star of the West** – Household Journal, Hearth and Home<br>**Star and Crescent** – Finley<br>**King's Crown** – Woman's World<br>**Compass** – Capper's 10/3/31<br>**The Four Winds** – KC Star<br>**Star of the Four Winds** – Ickis<br>**Star Crescent** – Khin<br>**Friendship Medley Quilt** – QUILT Fall 1980. *See 3903.* |
| | 3903 | **Lucky Star** – Nancy Page<br>**Four Winds** – Nancy Page<br>**Alaska Chinook** – Nancy Cabot. *See 3902.* |
| | 3904 | **Little Rock Block** – LAC #475<br>**Star of the Sea** – Nancy Cabot 3/22/33<br>**Sea Star** – Nancy Cabot<br>**Butterfly Block** – Nancy Cabot<br>**Arkansas Star** – attributed to Nancy Cabot, Nancy's |
| | 3905 | **Blue Heaven** – Nancy Cabot |
| | 3906 | **Blazing Star** – OCS/Brooks |
| WIDE POINTS ORIENTED LEFT & RIGHT | 3907 | **Florentine Diamond** – Clara Stone |
| | 3908 | **Diamond Solitaire** – Workbasket |
| | 3909 | **Arkansas Traveler** – Mills<br>**Travel Star** – Mills |
| | 3910 | **Diamond Chain** – Nancy Cabot<br>**Linked Diamonds** – Alice Beyer |

*Wide Points Oriented Up & Down, Wide Points Oriented Left & Right  (3891 – 3910)*

475

# Pattern Category 23: *Other Stars*

| | | |
|---|---|---|
| WIDE POINTS ORIENTED LEFT & RIGHT | 3911 | W‍HEEL OF F‍ATE – Clara Stone |
| | 3912 | T‍EDDY'S C‍HOICE – Clara Stone<br>C‍OWBOY'S S‍TAR – Finley<br>A‍RKANSAS T‍RAVELER – Finley<br>T‍RAVEL S‍TAR – Finley |
| | 3913 | C‍OWBOY'S S‍TAR – KC Star 6/8/32 |
| | 3914 | S‍WALLOW – Comfort |
| | 3915 | T‍HE K‍ITE – KC Star, 1937 (appliqué) |
| | 3916 | D‍RUCILLA'S D‍ELIGHT – QNM #104, 1978 |
| | 3917 | S‍HOOTING S‍TAR – Prudence Penny |
| | 3918 | C‍ASTOR & P‍OLLOX – Nancy Cabot |
| ODD EIGHT-POINTED STARS | 3920 | T‍HE L‍ONG P‍OINTED S‍TAR – KC Star 4/1/42<br>A‍PRIL S‍TAR – Attributed to Nancy Cabot by Nancy's |
| | 3921 | C‍OWBOY'S S‍TAR – Khin |
| | 3922 | G‍UIDING S‍TAR – Aunt Martha, 1941 |
| | 3923 | C‍ENTURY OF P‍ROGRESS – Farm Journal, ca. 1933<br>C‍OUNTER C‍HARM – Hearth and Home |
| | 3924 | D‍IAMOND – The Farm News, ca. 1920. *See 2491.* |
| | 3925 | W‍HIRLING S‍TAR – Grandma Dexter (partially appliquéd) |
| | 3926 | S‍TAR AND C‍ONE – Progressive Farmer. *See 3927.* |
| | 3927 | A D‍IAMOND F‍IELD – OCS/Curtis. *See 3926.* |
| | 3928 | A‍RAB T‍ENT – attributed to Nancy Cabot, Nancy's |
| | 3929 | U‍NNAMED – Peterson's Magazine |
| | 3930 | T‍WINKLING S‍TAR – Nancy Cabot |
| | 3931 | M‍ORNING S‍TAR – OCS/Wheeler |

*Wide Points Oriented Left & Right, Odd Eight-Pointed Stars (3911 – 3931)*

477

# Pattern Category 23: *Other Stars*

| | | |
|---|---|---|
| ODD EIGHT-POINTED STARS | 3932 | SPINNING STARS (1 OF 3 BLOCKS) – QNM #119, 2/80 |
| | 3933 | SPINNING STARS (1 OF 3 BLOCKS) – QNM #119, 2/80 |
| | 3934 | THE LOCKED STAR – Gammell |
| | 3935 | NINE PATCH STAR – QUILT Fall 1980 |
| | 3936 | UNNAMED – OCS/Wheeler |
| | 3937 | STAR OF THE NIGHT – Hearth and Home, Comfort |
| | 3938 | STATE OF NEBRASKA QUILT BLOCK #2 – Hearth and Home |
| | 3939 | PRAIRIE SUNRISE – Hearth and Home |
| | | |
| LONG DIAMONDS | 3940 | CROSS ROADS – Ohio Farmer, 2/24/1898 |
| | 3941 | CENTURY OF PROGRESS – Grandma Dexter, Capper's 1933 |
| | 3942 | GLOVE DESIGN – Aunt Martha |
| | | |
| POINTS ARE TRIANGLES OR OTHER SHAPES | 3945 | WINDMILL STAR – KC Star 1934 (appliqué) *See 413, 414, 1259, 2975, 3873, & 3950.* |
| | 3946 | IDAHO – Workbasket, 1935<br>THE GEM BLOCK – Workbasket<br>ARROWHEAD – Workbasket<br>SPARKLING JEWEL – Nancy Cabot |
| | 3947 | STAR – OCS/Wheeler<br>STAR OF THE EAST – OCS/Wheeler |
| | 3948 | THE JEWEL QUILT – KC Star 5/3/50 |
| | 3949 | ROSE IN SUMMER – OCS |
| | 3950 | NORTH STAR – KC Star 5/14/38<br>WHIRLING STAR – Khin. *See 413, 414, 1259, 2975, 3873, & 3945.* |
| | 3951 | THE EVENING STAR – KC Star |
| | 3952 | ARROWHEAD – Aunt Martha |

*Odd Eight-Pointed Stars, Long Diamonds, Points are Triangles or Other Shapes  (3932 – 3952)*

479

# Pattern Category 23: *Other Stars*

POINTS ARE TRIANGLES OR OTHER SHAPES

| | | |
|---|---|---|
| | **3953** | **Lover's Knot** – Grandma Dexter (pieced & appliquéd) |
| | **3954** | **Tennessee Star** – Clara Stone |
| | **3955** | **Tennessee Star** – Hall, Ickis |
| | **3956** | **Northumberland Star** – Clara Stone |
| | **3957** | **Flying Star** – Nancy Cabot |

*Points are Triangles or Other Shapes (3953 – 3957)*

3953

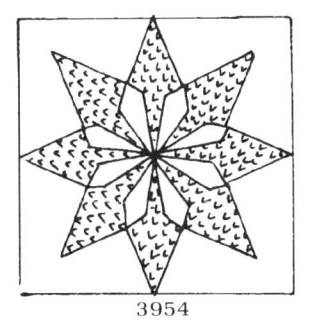

3954

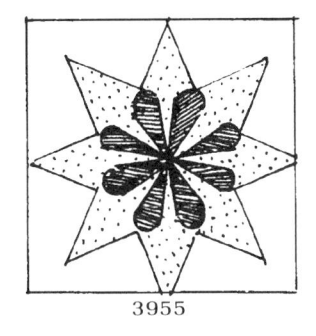

3955

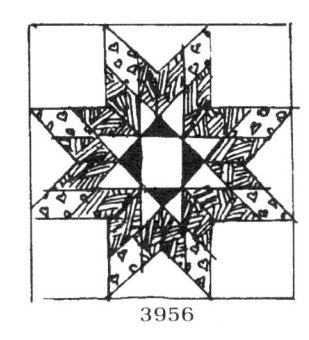

3956

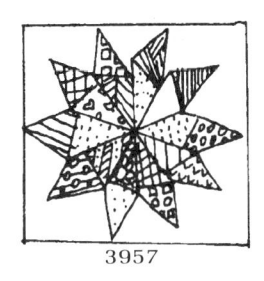

3957

481

# PATTERN CATEGORY 24

## Whole Top Designs

**Patterns in Category 24 share these characteristics:**

- The pattern repeat should be viewed in terms of the entire surface of the top.

- The patterns tend to be oriented to the center of the top with a radiating design, or concentric borders framing the center.

At one time I classified these patterns as Framed Medallions, but that term seemed too limiting, since many of the designs are not framed.

**KEY TO PATTERN CATEGORY 24: WHOLE TOP DESIGNS**

If the pattern repeat should be viewed in terms of the entire surface, *turn to p. 484*

# Pattern Category 24: *Whole Top Designs*

| | |
|---|---|
| **3974** | **Rainbow** – Holstein<br>**Joseph's Coat** – Holstein |
| **3975** | **Oblong** – Haders, Sunshine & Shadow |
| **3976** | **Center Diamond** – Bishop & Safanda |
| **3977** | **Center Diamond** – Bishop & Safanda |
| **3978** | **Philadelphia Pavement** – Carlie Sexton |
| **3979** | **Boston Commons** – Mountain Mist<br>**Going Around The Mountain** – Progressive Farmer, Pforr 1974 |
| **3980** | **Amish Checkerboard Diamond** – Woodard & Greenstein |
| **3981** | **Cross Purposes** – Mountain Mist |
| **3982** | **The Checkerboard** – Capper's 9/6/30 |
| **3983** | **Patriotic Quilt** – attributed to Peterson's Magazine (6/1861) by Ohio Farmer 10/27/1898 |
| **3984** | **Sawtooth** – Holstein |
| **3985** | **Red and White Quilt** – Hearth & Home<br>**Sawtooth** – Rural New Yorker 4/19/30<br>**Sawtooth Diamond** – Bishop & Safanda, Haders |
| **3986** | **Solomon's Temple** – LAC #193<br>**Delectable Mountains** – Danner/Ericson. *See 2401 & 3165.* |
| **3987** | **Delectable Mountains** – Finley (similar to 3986 with a star in the center) |

*Whole Top Designs (3974 – 3987)*

# Pattern Category 24: *Whole Top Designs*

| | |
|---|---|
| **3989** | **Rising Sun** – Aunt Martha. *See 3165.* |
| **3990** | **Delectable Mountains** – Hall |
| **3991** | **Path Through the Woods** – Danner/Ericson 1934 |
| **3992** | **Star in the Window** – QNM #97, 1977. *See 2119.* |
| **3993** | **Star in a Star** – QNM #76, 1975 |
| **3994** | **Daniel Boone Quilt** – ARC Publishing 7/64<br>*For similar quilts see pg. 282.* |
| **3995** | **Rising Sun** – Home Art |
| **3996** | **Rising Sun** – Orlofsky |

*Whole Top Designs (3989 – 3996)*

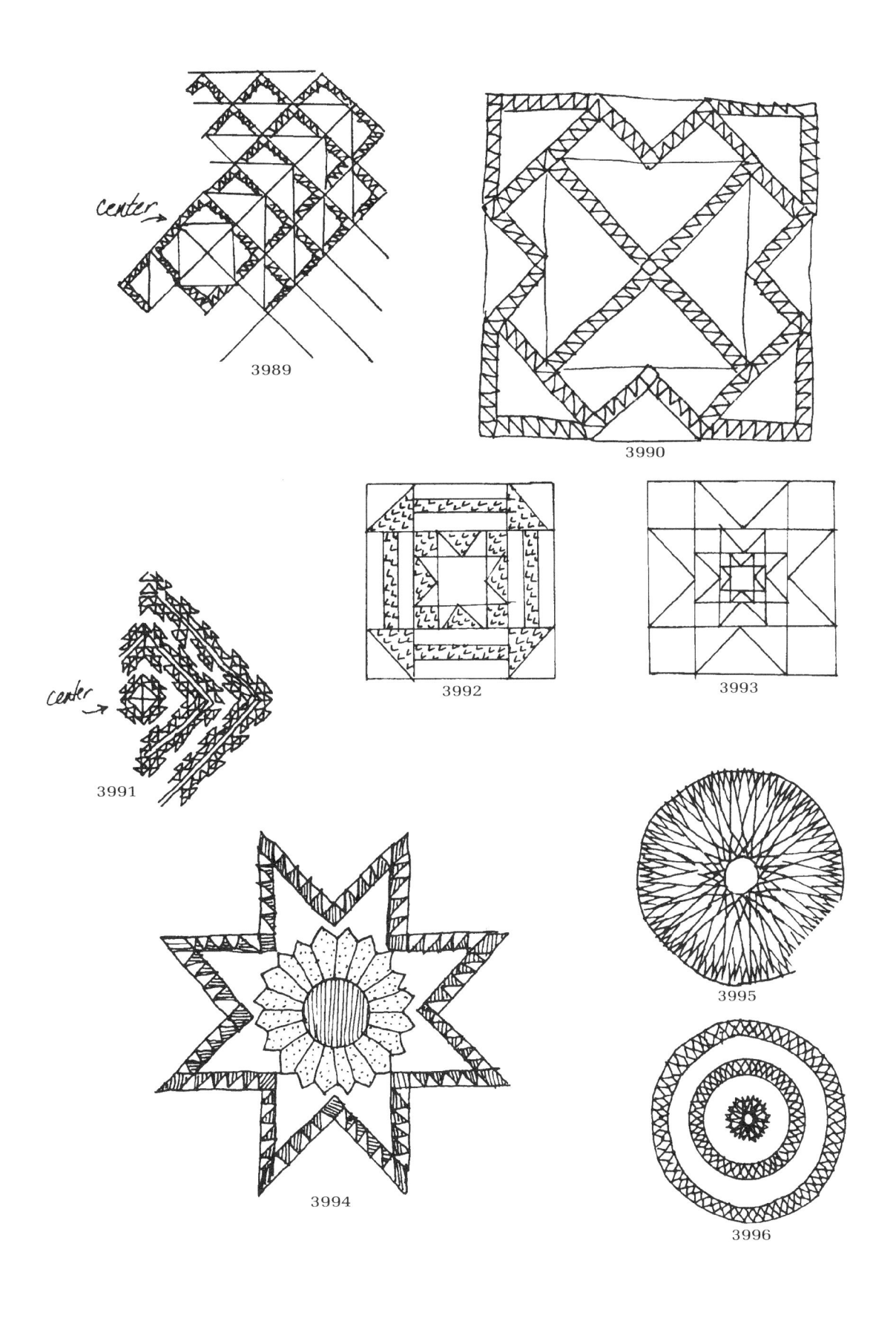

487

Pattern Category 24: *Whole Top Designs*

| 3997 | EVENING STAR – Home Art |
| 3998 | GIANT AMETHYST – Home Art |
| 3999 | THE ROYAL ASTER QUILT – Home Art |
| 4000 | STAR OF FRANCE – Home Art |
| 4001 | EASTERN STAR – Home Art |

*Whole Top Designs (3997 – 4001)*

3997

3998

3999

4000

4001

489

# Pattern Category 24: *Whole Top Designs*

| | |
|---|---|
| **4002** | THE D.A.R. QUILT – Home Art |
| **4003** | STAR OF THE EAST – Webster |
| | LONE STAR – Hall |
| | SILVER & GOLD – Ickis |
| **4004** | THE KALEIDOSCOPE QUILT – Home Art |
| **4005** | AN AESTHETIC QUILT – Hearth and Home |
| | LONE STAR – LAC #530, McKim, Sexton |
| | STAR OF THE EAST – McKim |
| | STAR OF BETHLEHEM – McKim, Finley |
| | BLAZING STAR – Rural New Yorker 9/10/30 |
| | RISING STAR – Rural New Yorker 9/10/30 |
| | PRIDE OF TEXAS – Home Art |
| | STAR OF STARS – Home Art |
| | RISING SUN – Bacon |
| | OVERALL STAR PATTERN – Bacon |
| **4006** | SUNBURST – Safford & Bishop |
| **4007** | GOLDEN DAHLIA – Home Art |

*Whole Top Designs (4002 – 4007)*

4002

4003

4004

4005

4006

4007

491

Pattern Category 24: *Whole Top Designs*

| | |
|---|---|
| **4007.5** | **Broken Star** – Capper's 6/15/25 |
| | **Blazing Star** – Rural New Yorker 11/14/31 |
| | **Diadem Star** – Rural New Yorker 11/14/31 |
| | **Star of Bethlehem** – Safford & Bishop |
| **4008** | **Bursting Cubes** – QEC 1979 |
| | **Expanding Star** – Meeker |
| **4009** | **Flying Swallows** – QNM #80, 6/76 |

Whole Top Designs (4007.5 – 4009)

4007.5

4008

4009

# Pattern Category 24: *Whole Top Designs*

| | |
|---|---|
| **4010** | SUMMER SUN – Peto, American Quilts & Coverlets |
| **4011** | THE MOORISH STAR QUILT – Home Art |
| **4012** | GORGEOUS CHRYSANTHEMUM QUILT – Home Art |
| **4013** | THE SIRIUS STAR QUILT – Home Art |
| **4014** | THE SUN BURST QUILT – Home Art |
| **4015** | THE GIANT DAHLIA QUILT – Home Art |

*Whole Top Designs (4010 – 4015)*

4010

4011

4012

4013

4014

4015

495

# Pattern Category 25

## Miscellaneous

**Patterns in Category 25 share this characteristic:**

- The pattern does not fit into any other category

**Category 25 includes:**

- With Diamonds, 498
- With Curves, 502
- With Six–Sided Pieces, 506
- Asymmetrical of Off–Center Blocks, 508
- With Octagon Shapes, 510
- Interlocking Horizontal & Verticals, 512
- Intersecting Lines in the Center, 512
- Square in the Center, 514
- Truly Miscellaneous, 518

## KEY TO PATTERN CATEGORY 25: MISCELLANEOUS BLOCKS

**STEP 1**

If the pattern contains at least two 60° or 45° diamonds, *turn to p. 498*

If the pattern does not contain two diamonds, *turn to p. 502*

**STEP 2**

If the pattern contains curved seams, *turn to p. 502*

If the pattern is all straight seams, *continue with STEP 3 below*

**STEP 3**

If the pattern has a six–sided shape in it ⬡⬡, *turn to p. 506*

If the pattern has no six–sided shapes, *continue with STEP 4 below*

**STEP 4**

If the Pattern is asymmetrical or off–center, *turn to p. 508*

If the pattern is four mirror images, *continue with STEP 5 below*

**STEP 5**

If the pattern has octagonal shapes in it, *turn to p. 510*

If the pattern consists of horizontal and vertical rectangles and squares, *turn to p. 512*

If the pattern has intersecting lines in the center ✕, *turn to p. 512*

If the pattern has a square in the center ☐◇, *turn to p. 514*

If the pattern is none of the above, *turn to p. 518*

# Pattern Category 25: *Miscellaneous*

WITH DIAMONDS      **4020**      **DIAMOND QUILT PATTERN** – Valley Farmer ca. 1915

                          **4021**      **SUGAR LOAF** – LAC #370. *See 204.*

                          **4022**      **WORK BOX** – LAC #358

                          **4023**      **PATIENCE CORNERS** – LAC #90
                                             **RIBBONS** – Gutcheon PPP

                          **4024**      **BACHELOR'S PUZZLE** – Oklahoma Farmer Stockman 9/15/31

                          **4025**      **GALAXY** – QNM #69, 1975
                                             **NIGHTWATCH** – QNM #69, 1975
                                             **CITY PARK** – QNM #69, 1975
                                             **CROSSROADS AMERICA 1976** – QNM #69, 1975 (red, white, & blue)
                                             **FLOWER FIELDS** – QNM #69, 1975
                                             **UNDER BLUE MOUNTAIN SKIES** – QNM #69, 1975

                          **4026**      **CUBE LATTICE** – LAC #412
                                             **CUBES AND TILE** – Nancy Cabot
                                             **IDLE MOMENTS** – Nancy Cabot

                          **4027**      **WEATHERVANE AND STEEPLE** – Nancy Cabot

                          **4028**      **KANSAS BEAUTY** – Clara Stone

                          **4029**      **GUAM** – Hearth and Home

                          **4030**      **MRS. MORGAN'S CHOICE** – Nancy Cabot

                          **4031**      **MAY TIME QUILT** – Workbasket 1947

                          **4032**      **SHADED TRAIL** – OCS/Wheeler, KC Star 6/17/35

                          **4033**      **WEATHERVANE** – Nancy Cabot. *See 1780.*

                          **4034**      **MRS. FAY'S FAVORITE FRIENDSHIP BLOCK** – Hearth and Home
                                             **MERRY KITE** – LAC #515

                          **4035**      **SPRINGFIELD** – Hearth and Home
                                             **SPRINGFIELD PATCH** – LAC #472

                          **4036**      **DANCING PINWHEELS** – Nancy Cabot

                          **4037**      **MOSAIC SQUARES** – Nancy Cabot

                          **4038**      **FRIENDSHIP STAR** – OCS/Wheeler

                          **4039**      **STAR AND CORONA** – Nancy Cabot

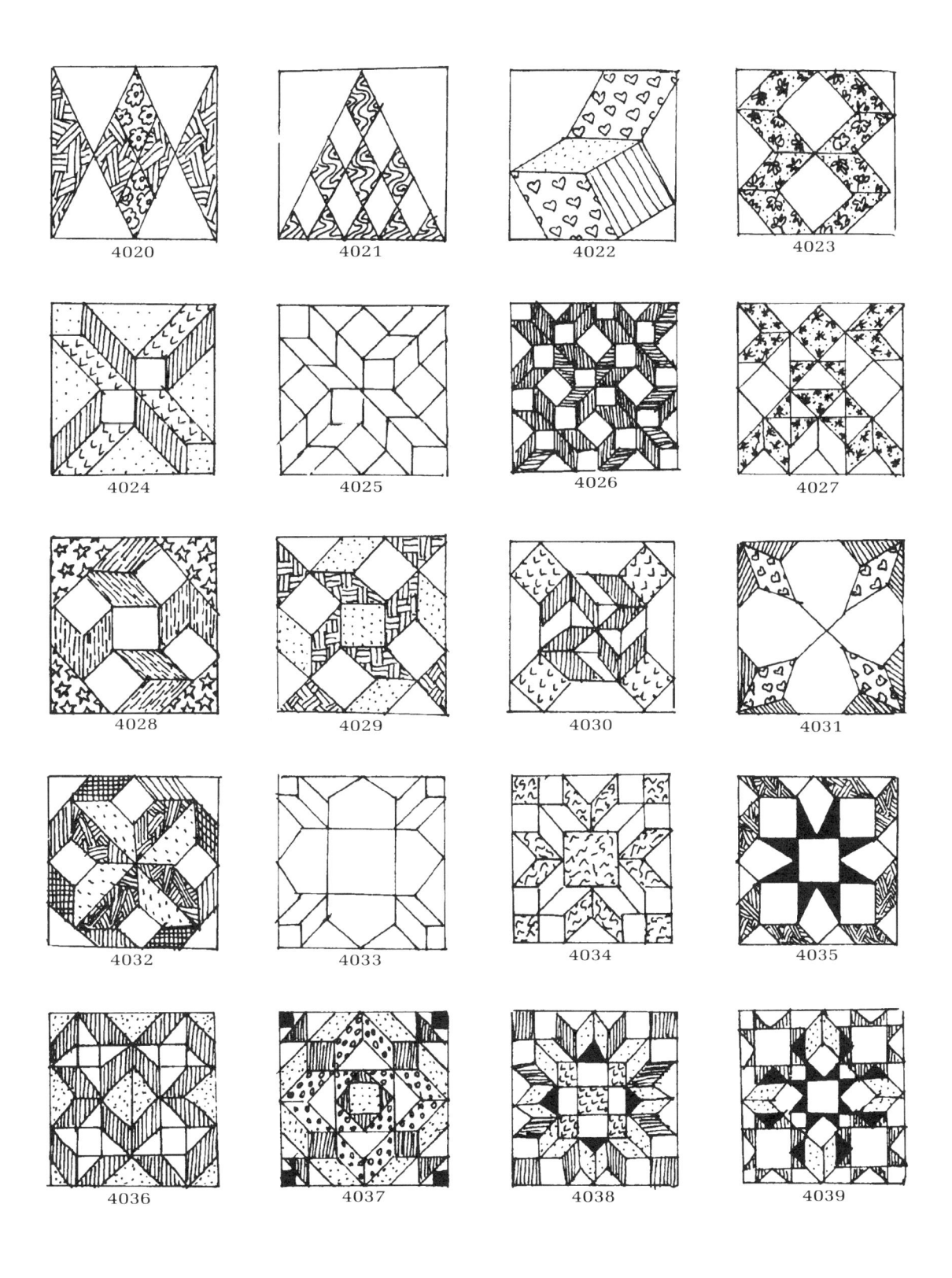

With Diamonds (4020 – 4039)

4020 4021 4022 4023
4024 4025 4026 4027
4028 4029 4030 4031
4032 4033 4034 4035
4036 4037 4038 4039

499

# Pattern Category 25: *Miscellaneous*

WITH DIAMONDS

| | | |
|---|---|---|
| | 4040 | STATE OF CALIFORNIA #2 – Hearth and Home. *See 725.* |
| | 4041 | LOTUS STAR – Grandma Dexter |
| | 4042 | MAPLE LEAF & ROSE – McKendry pg. 26c (center appliqué) |
| | 4043 | POINSETTIA – KC Star 12/5/31 (appliqué)<br>FLOWER OF CHRISTMAS – Hall |
| | 4044a | HANDS ALL ROUND – LAC #402<br>CENTER TABLE QUILT – Comfort<br>ALL HANDS ROUND – Carlie Sexton<br>WREATH OF LILIES – Cappers |
| | 4044b | OLD FASHIONED STAR QUILT – KC Star 12/12/56 |
| | 4045 | FRIENDSHIP KNOT – Finley<br>STARRY CROWN – Finley |
| | 4046 | FRIENDSHIP KNOT – KC Star 1/2/32 |
| | 4047 | FRIENDSHIP WREATH – Lockport Batting<br>FRIENDSHIP KNOT – OCS/Wheeler |
| | 4048 | STAR OF THE DECATHLON – QNM #98, 1978 |
| | 4049 | BASKET OF DIAMONDS – KC Star 1937 |
| | 4050 | STAR OVER THE MOUNTAIN – Ericson/Danner 1981 |
| | 4051 | CORNUCOPIA – Hinson QM. *See 4052.* |
| | 4052 | NOSE GAY QUILT – Rural New Yorker 1933<br>BRIDE'S BOUQUET – Rural New Yorker 1933<br>OLD FASHIONED NOSE GAY – OCS/Wheeler<br>THE NOSE GAYS – KC Star 2/6/37. *See 4051.* |
| | 4053 | COCKCOMB – Home Art |

## With Diamonds (4040 – 4053)

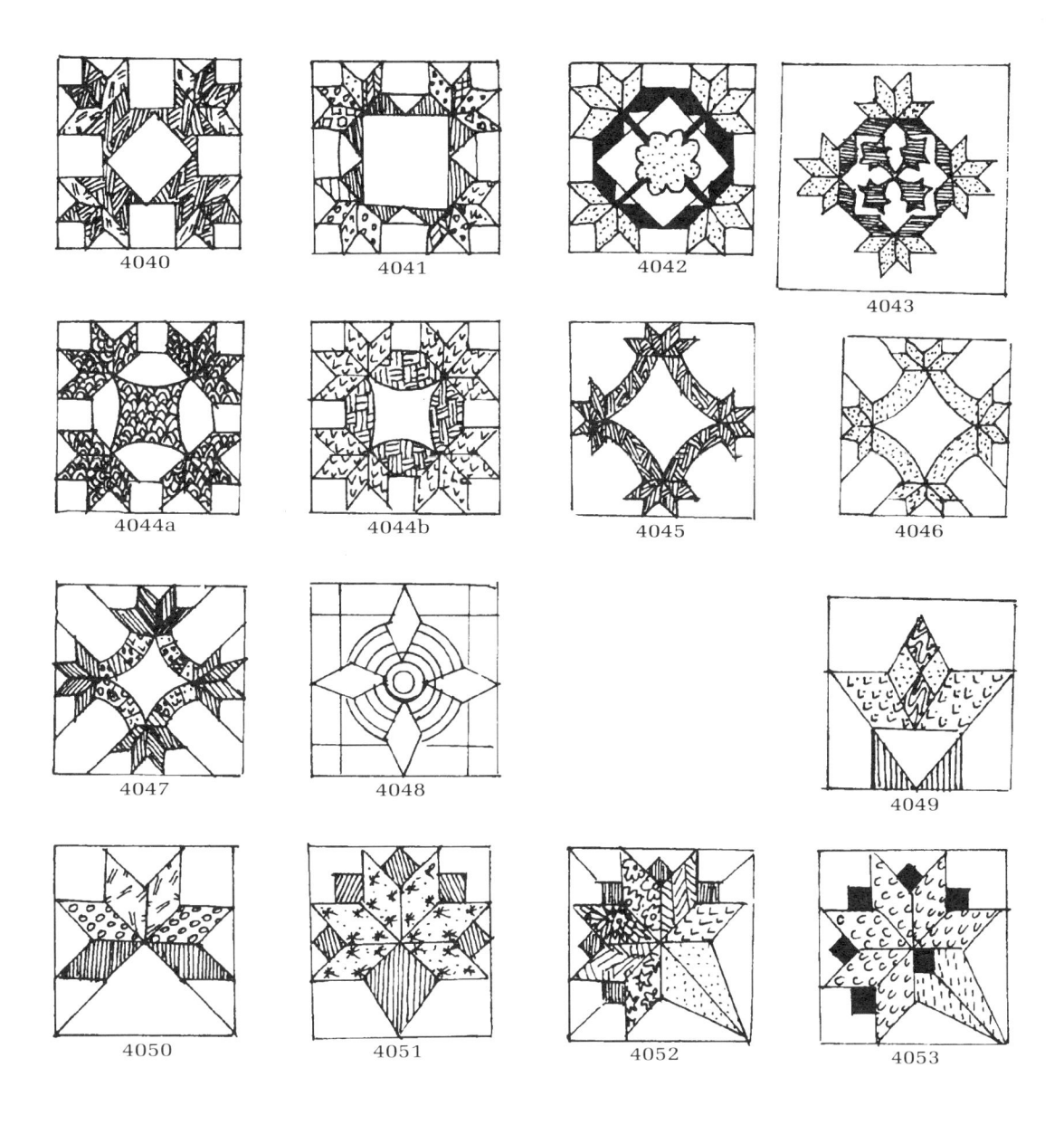

4040  4041  4042  4043

4044a  4044b  4045  4046

4047  4048  4049

4050  4051  4052  4053

# Pattern Category 25: *Miscellaneous*

WITH CURVES

| | | |
|---|---|---|
| | **4055** | **RED, WHITE AND BLUE** – Comfort |
| | **4056** | **SQUARED CIRCLE** – Household Journal |
| | **4057** | **SNOWBALL** – Nancy Page. *See 1506.* |
| | **4058** | **VICTORY** – Clara Stone |
| | **4059** | **BABE RUTH DIAMOND** – QNM #114 |
| | **4060** | **POINTS AND PETALS** – KC Star 1933 |
| | **4061** | **FLOWERING STAR** – attributed to Nancy Cabot, Nancy's |
| | **4062** | **RISING STAR** – OCS/Wheeler |
| | **4063** | **HALF MOON BLOCK** – Nancy Cabot<br>**MOON BLOCK** – Nancy Cabot |
| | **4064** | **JINX STAR** – KC Star 1934 |
| | **4065** | **TRENTON** – Hearth and Home<br>**TRENTON QUILT BLOCK** – LAC #475. *See 2661.* |
| | **4066** | **WINDOW SQUARES** – Grandmother Clark 1931 |
| | **4067** | **UNNAMED** – Aunt Martha |
| | **4068** | **THE CIRCULAR SAW** – KC Star 1/9/32<br>**THE ORIOLE WINDOW** – KC Star 1/9/32<br>**FOUR LITTLE FANS** – KC Star 1/9/32. *See 1796 & 3314.* |
| | **4069** | **OVER THE RAINBOW** – Aunt Kate |
| | **4070** | **LINKED SQUARES** – OCS/Wheeler |
| | **4071** | **HERO'S CROWN** – Hinson QM |
| | **4072** | **VALENTINE QUILT** – KC Star 2/10/34 |
| | **4073** | **COCKLEBURR** – LAC #505. *See 2996.* |

*With Curves (4055 – 4073)*

503

# Pattern Category 25: *Miscellaneous*

WITH CURVES

| | | |
|---|---|---|
| | 4074 | WHIG'S DEFEAT – Hall. *See 2529, 2680, & 1085.* |
| | 4075 | COMPASS – LAC #218. *See 1520 & 2685.*<br>CORN AND BEANS – Nancy Cabot |
| | 4076 | TREY'S QUILT – Hinson QM. *See 301, 1519, 2683, & 2684.* |
| | 4077 | UTAH – Hearth and Home |
| | 4078 | ANNA'S PRIDE – KC Star 8/5/36 |
| | 4079 | DAY LILY GARDEN – Aunt Kate |
| | 4080 | TULIP WHEEL – Grandma Dexter |
| | 4081 | HOUR GLASS – Nancy Cabot |
| | 4082 | FOUR LEAF CLOVER – Needlecraft 2/35 |
| | 4083 | FOUR LEAF CLOVER – Nancy Cabot |
| | 4084 | THE STOCKADE – Clara Stone |
| | 4085 | MISSOURI TROUBLE – Nancy Cabot |
| | 4086 | MODERN DAISY – Nancy Cabot 9/35 |
| | 4087 | PADUCAH PEONY – Nancy Cabot |
| | 4088 | FARMER'S WIFE – Carlie Sexton<br>ROLLING STAR QUILT – Nancy Cabot/Progressive Farmer 1931 |
| | 4089 | SWEET CLOVER – Capper's/Famous Features |
| | 4090 | OLD MILL WHEEL – Aunt Kate |
| | 4091 | HOMECOMING – QNM/Heirloom Plastic 1973 |
| | 4092 | MICHIGAN'S WATER WONDERLAND STAR – QNM #45, 1970 |

With Curves (4074 – 4092)

4074 4075 4076
4077 4078 4079 4080
4081 4082 4083 4084
4085 4086 4087 4088
4089 4090 4091 4092

# Pattern Category 25: *Miscellaneous*

| | | |
|---|---|---|
| WITH CURVES | **4093** | **QUILTER'S PRIDE** – OCS/Brooks |
| | **4094** | **POINTED OVALS** – KC Star<br>**LOVE'S CHAIN** – attributed to Nancy Cabot, Nancy's |
| | **4095** | **ARMS TO HEAVEN** – Nancy Cabot 8/35 |
| | **4096** | **GRANDMA'S FAN** – Progressive Farmer/Johnson 1977 |
| | **4097** | **QUEEN'S CROWN QUILT** – Orange Judd Farmer 1/20/1900 |
| | **4098** | **THE SUNRISE** – Progressive Farmer/Johnson 1977 |
| | **4099** | **PARAGON** – Hearth and Home |
| | | |
| WITH SIX-SIDED PIECES | **4101** | **GRANDMOTHER'S STAR** – Capper's 2/26/44 |
| | **4102** | **THE PYRAMIDS** – Progressive Farmer. *See 153.* |
| | **4103** | **THE COTTON BOLL QUILT** – KC Star 2/12/41. *See 433, 1181, 1187, 3250, 4106, 4104, & 4107.* |
| | **4104** | **GRANDMOTHER'S OWN** – LAC #166<br>**FOUR SQUARE** – Farm Journal, Nancy Cabot<br>**SHEPHERD'S CROSSING** – KC Star 6/24/42<br>*See 433, 1181, 1187, 1407, 3250, 4103, 2594, 4106, & 4107.* |
| | **4105** | **MORNING PATCH** – LAC #480 |
| | **4106** | **FIVE CROSS** – Clara Stone<br>**FIVE CROSSES** – Nancy Cabot<br>**LOVELY PATCHWORK** – attributed to Nancy Cabot, Nancy's<br>*See 433, 1184, 1187, 3250, 4104, 4106, & 4107.* |
| | **4107** | **GRANDMOTHER'S DREAM** – LAC #128. *See 433, 1181, 1187, 3250, 4104, & 4106.* |
| | **4108** | **BLUE BELL BLOCK** – Nancy Cabot |
| | **4109** | **DOGWOOD** – Prudence Penny |
| | **4110** | **NAUVOO LATTICE** – Nancy Cabot. *See 438 & 1430.* |
| | **4111** | **FRAMED CROSS** – Quilt World 2/81. *See 3225.* |
| | **4112** | **THE FLASHING STAR** – Aunt Kate 6/65 |

*With Curves, With Six-Sided Pieces (4093 – 4112)*

4093

4094

4095

4096

4097

4098

4099

4101

4102

4103

4104

4105

4106

4107

4108

4109

4110

4111

4112

# Pattern Category 25: *Miscellaneous*

ASYMMETRICAL OR OFF-CENTER BLOCKS

| | | |
|---|---|---|
| 4114 | | *See 1366.* |
| 4115 | | JEWEL – Dictionary of Needlework 1882 (Caulfeild) |
| 4116 | | ORIENTAL PUZZLE – Comfort |
| 4117 | | BECKY'S NINE PATCH – Gutcheon |
| 4118 | | CENTURY OF PROGRESS – Nancy Cabot ca. 1933 |
| 4119 | | MISSOURI RIVER VALLEY – Evelyn Brown 1978 |
| 4120 | | UNNAMED – Bishop & Safanda |
| 4121 | | NINE PATCH NOSE GAY – Mountain Mist (alternate with appliqué block) |
| 4122a | | GRANDMOTHER'S PUZZLE – Joseph Doyle |
| 4122b | | GRANDMOTHER PERCY'S PUZZLE – Hearth & Home |
| 4123 | | PATCHWORK BEDSPREAD – Hearth and Home |
| 4124 | | TENNESSEE MINE SHAFT – Elwood, Tennery, & Richardson |
| 4125 | | MAGNOLIA – OCS/Wheeler<br>SAWTOOTH – Mahler |
| 4126 | | LOTUS BLOCK – Nancy Cabot |
| 4127 | | GEESE IN FLIGHT – Nancy Cabot |
| 4128 | | SILK QUILT – QEC 1979 |
| 4129 | | SARGEANT'S CHEVRON – Farm Journal 2/44 |
| 4130 | | WATERED RIBBON & BORDER – LAC #157, 1897<br>RIBBON BORDER – LAC #157, 1929<br>BEACH AND BOOTS – Nancy Cabot |
| 4131 | | MARIGOLD GARDEN – QNM 1982 (alternate with 4132) |
| 4132 | | MARIGOLD GARDEN – QNM 1982 (with 4131) |

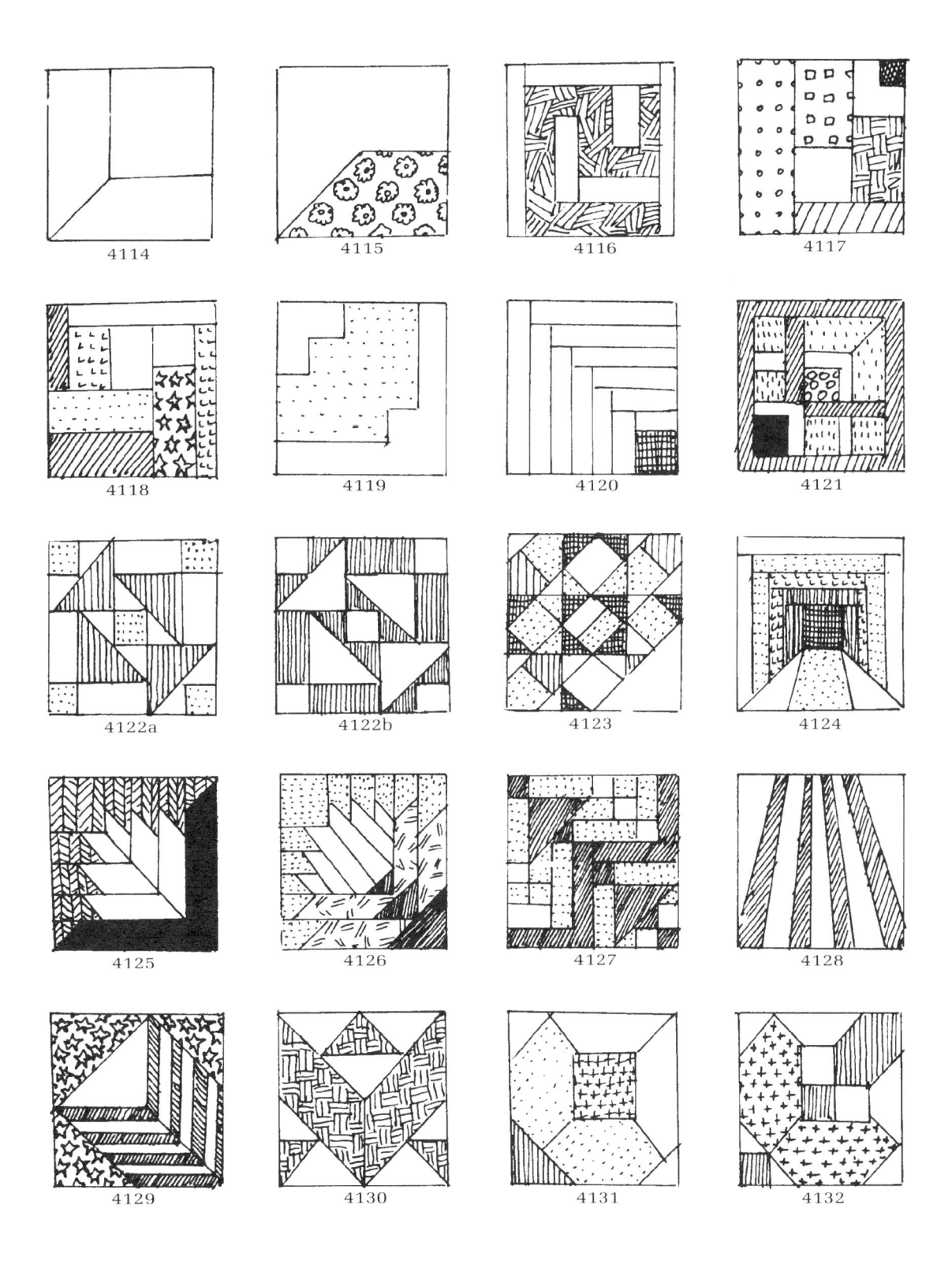

*Asymmetrical or Off-Center Blocks (4114 – 4132)*

509

# Pattern Category 25: *Miscellaneous*

| | | |
|---|---|---|
| ASYMMETRICAL OR OFF-CENTER BLOCKS | 4134 | QUEEN CHARLOTTE'S CROWN – Finley<br>INDIAN MEADOW – Finley<br>BASKET DESIGN – attributed to Nancy Cabot, Nancy's |
| | 4135 | DOUBLE BASKET – Household Journal ca. 1925 |
| | 4136 | FRIENDSHIP BOUQUET – OCS/Brooks |
| | 4137 | CRAZY QUILT BOUQUET – Nancy Cabot 10/24/33<br>CRAZY FLOWER PATCH – attributed to Nancy Cabot, Nancy's |
| | 4138 | QUEEN'S TREASURE – OCS |
| | 4139 | NORTHERN LIGHTS – Aunt Kate |
| WITH OCTAGONAL SHAPES | 4141 | ROB PETER TO PAY PAUL – Carlie Sexton<br>THE MARBLE FLOOR – KC Star 10/22/30.<br>HOUR GLASSES – Bacon. *See 442, 4142, & 414.*<br>OCTAGONS – Bacon<br>CALICO SNOWBALL – Evelyn Brown |
| | 4142 | SNOWBALLS – Nancy Cabot. *See 4421, 4141, & 4146.* |
| | 4143 | MEADOW FLOWER – OCS/Wheeler |
| | 4144 | SIMPLE DESIGN – LAC #321 |
| | 4145 | FORGET ME NOT – Aunt Martha (appliqué) |
| | 4146 | OCTAGONS – Nancy Cabot. *See 442, 4141, & 4142.* |
| | 4147 | OLD STAFFORDSHIRE – Nancy Cabot |
| | 4148 | CATALPA FLOWER – Nancy Cabot |
| | 4149 | NINE SNOWBALLS – Nancy Cabot 8/20/35 |
| | 4150 | HOUSEWIFE'S DREAM – Hearth and Home |
| | 4151 | WATERWHEELS – Nancy Cabot |
| | 4152 | BROKEN SAW BLADES – attributed to Nancy Cabot |

*Asymmetrical or Off-Center Blocks, With Octagonal Shapes (4134 – 4152)*

4134

4135

4136

4137

4138

4139

4141

4142

4143

4144

4145

4146

4147

4148

4149

4150

4151

4152

# Pattern Category 25: *Miscellaneous*

| | | |
|---|---|---|
| WITH OCTAGONAL SHAPES | 4153 | THE NEW 4-POINTER – KC Star 5/31/44 |
| | 4154 | NO NAME QUILT – LAC #169 |
| | 4155 | ALTAR STEPS – Prudence Penny ca. 1920 |
| | 4156 | UNNAMED – Safford & Bishop |
| | 4157 | UNFOLDING STAR – Nancy Cabot |
| | | |
| INTERLOCKING HORIZONTALS AND VERTICALS | 4159 | CARPENTER'S STAR – Meeker pg. 48 |
| | 4160 | BROKEN WINDMILLS – Nancy Cabot |
| | 4161 | HOMESPUN BLOCK – Nancy Cabot |
| | | |
| INTERSECTING LINES IN THE CENTER | 4162 | BELLE'S FAVORITE – Clara Stone |
| | 4163 | RAIL FENCE QUILT – McKim. *See 4216.* |
| | 4164 | CRAZY LOON – Nancy Cabot |
| | 4165 | TWISTING STAR – Hinson QM. *See 2349.* |
| | 4166 | PHILIPPINE ISLANDS – Hearth and Home |
| | 4167 | HARVEST HOME – Hearth and Home |
| | 4168 | HARTFORD – Hearth and Home |

*With Octagonal Shapes, Interlocking Horizontals & Verticals,
Intersecting Lines in the Center (4153 – 4168)*

4153  4154  4155  4156

4157

4159  4160  4161

4162  4163  4164

4165  4166  417  4168

513

# Pattern Category 25: *Miscellaneous*

| | | |
|---|---|---|
| INTERSECTING LINES IN THE CENTER | 4169 | SKYSCRAPERS – QNM #92, 1977 |
| | 4170 | FRIENDSHIP CHAIN – KC Star |
| | 4171 | RAZZLE DAZZLE – James in Handbook |
| | 4172 | FARMER'S WIFE – Hinson QM |
| | 4173 | ARABIC LATTICE – QNM #104, 1978 |
| | 4174 | FLY AWAY – QNM |
| | 4175 | NORTHERN LIGHTS – Nancy Cabot |
| | | |
| SQUARE IN THE CENTER | 4177 | SEMINOLE SQUARE – Nancy Cabot/Progressive Farmer 1949 |
| | 4178 | PEACH BLOW – Comfort/Clara Stone |
| | 4179 | THE CORNERSTONE – KC Star 1942 |
| | 4180 | QUATREFOILS – Nancy Cabot |
| | 4181 | THE STANLEY – Oklahoma Farmer Stockman 1/1/33 |
| | 4182 | FRIENDSHIP QUILT – Hearth and Home |
| | 4183 | STAR OF THE NIGHT – OCS/Wheeler |
| | 4184 | CROWS' FOOT – LAC #118<br>ARROWHEADS – Nancy Page |
| | 4185 | CORONATION BLOCK – Nancy Cabot |
| | 4186 | AUTUMN STAR – Nancy Cabot |
| | 4187 | DIAMOND PLAID BLOCK – Nancy Cabot |
| | 4188 | RUINS OF JERICHO – Nancy Cabot |

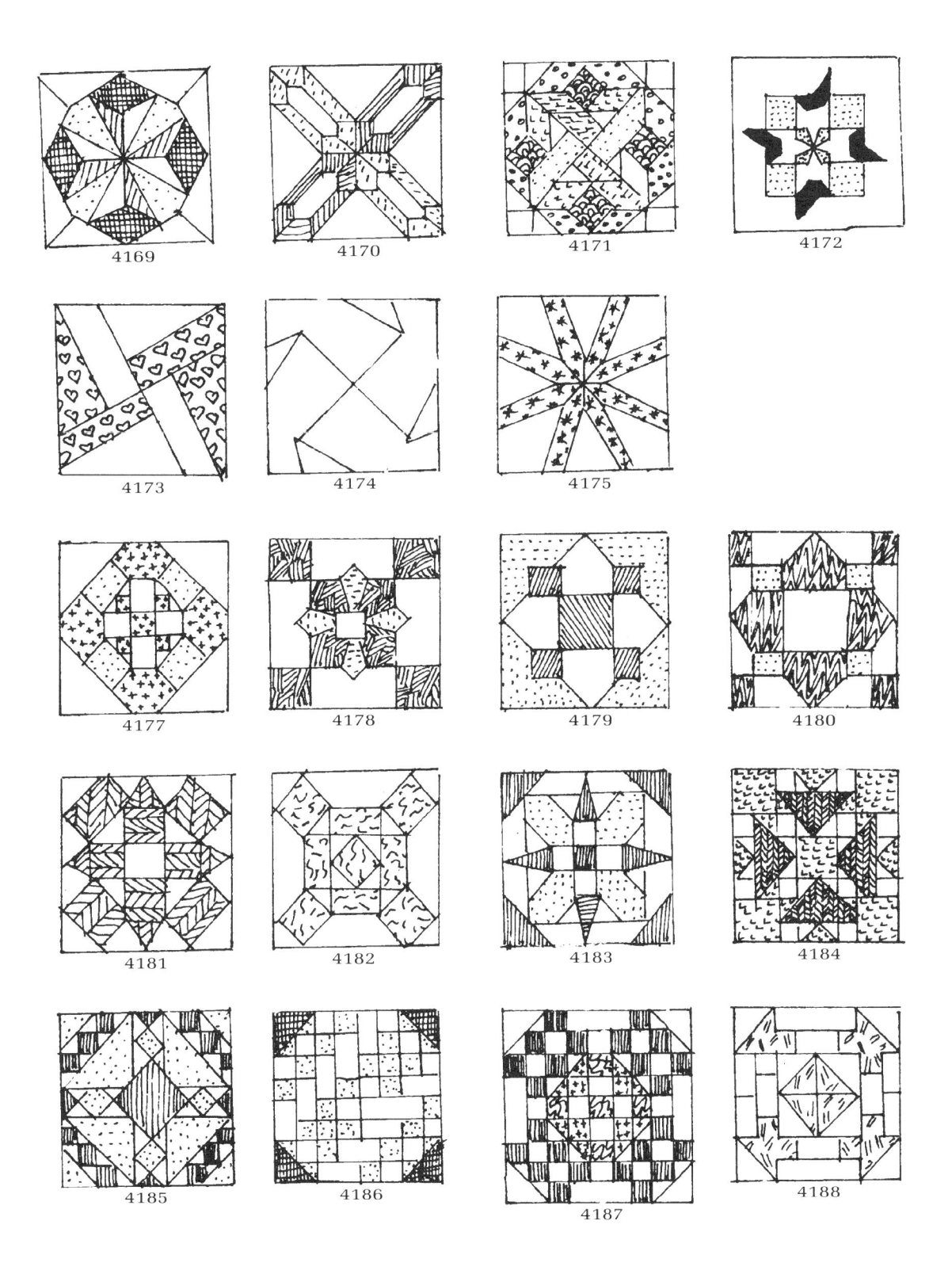

*Intersecting Lines in the Center, Square in the Center (4169 – 4188)*

4169  4170  4171  4172

4173  4174  4175

4177  4178  4179  4180

4181  4182  4183  4184

4185  4186  4187  4188

515

# Pattern Category 25: *Miscellaneous*

SQUARE IN THE CENTER

| | | |
|---|---|---|
| | 4189 | DOUBLE LINK – Aunt Martha<br>FRIENDSHIP QUILT – Oklahoma Farmer Stockman 1/1/35<br>FRIENDSHIP LINKS – Nancy Cabot |
| | 4190 | LUCKY KNOT – Nancy Cabot |
| | 4191 | THE FOUR CORNERS – Nancy Cabot |
| | 4192 | DOUBLE SQUARE – Grandma Dexter |
| | 4193 | GLORY VINE – Nancy Cabot |
| | 4194 | ROAD TO PARIS – Country Home 2/33 |
| | 4195 | PLAITED BLOCK – Nancy Cabot. *See 443.* |
| | 4196 | STAR FLOWER WREATH – OCS/Wheeler |
| | 4197 | THE NORTH STAR – KC Star 3/9/47 |
| | 4198 | BOX QUILT – Nancy Page |
| | 4199 | DIAMOND STAR – Mills |
| | 4200 | PATCHWORK POSY – Quilt World 10/80 |
| | 4201 | THE OWL QUILT – KC Star 1937 |
| | 4202 | DIAMOND KNOT – Nancy Cabot |
| | 4203 | WHIRLIGIG – Nancy Cabot |
| | 4204 | DOUBLE WINDMILL – Nancy Cabot |
| | 4205 | SPINNING HOUR GLASS – Nancy Cabot |
| | 4206 | DOUBLE ASTER – Nancy Cabot |
| | 4207 | PEONY AND FORGET ME NOTS – Nancy Cabot<br>PADUCAH PEONY – attributed to Nancy Cabot |
| | 4208 | KALEIDOSCOPE – Nancy Page (when set all over is similar to 1123, 2086, & 2644) |

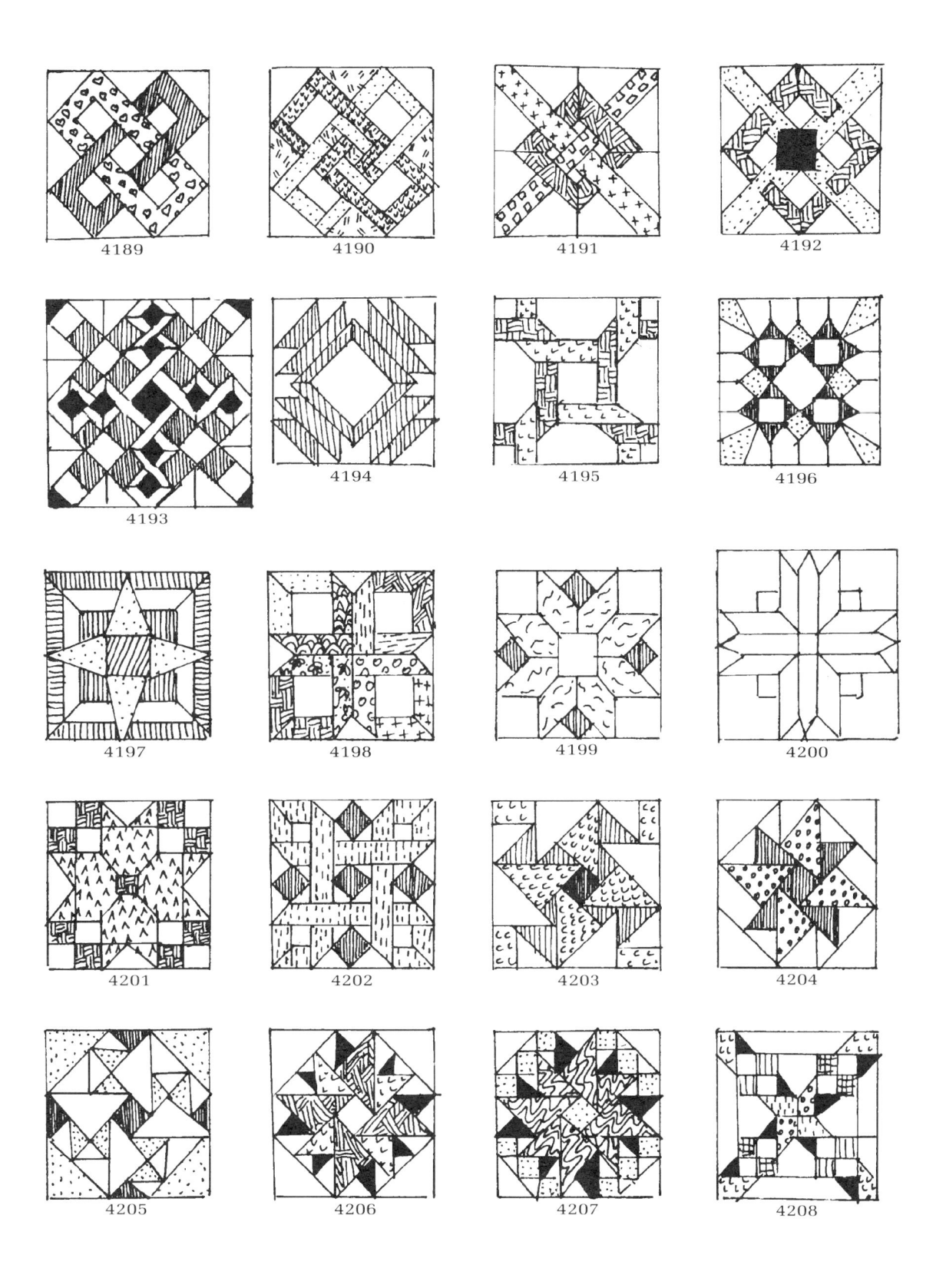

*Square in the Center (4189 – 4208)*

517

# Pattern Category 25: *Miscellaneous*

SQUARE IN THE CENTER      **4209**      OLD FASHION DAISY – Nancy Cabot 1/27/33

TRULY MISCELLANEOUS      **4211**      ROSE GARDEN – Nancy Cabot

**4212**      DIAMOND CROSS – KC Star 5/22/37

**4213**      DOUBLE STAR – Hearth and Home. *See 1236.*

**4214**      DOVE IN THE WNDOW – Finley. *See 295.*

**4215**      HOUR GLASS – Nancy Cabot

**4216**      ZIG-ZAG – Woman's World. *See 4163.*

*Square in the Center, Truly Misc. (4209 – 4216)*

4209

4211

4212

4213

4214

4215

4216

# References

Full entries for publications used for the development of this encyclopedia are included in this section. The names that are abbreviated in the book are listed under their abbreviations, so this section can also be used as a key to any abbreviations found in pattern source information.

ABC Publications. Published reprints and periodicals in the 1960s. SEE *Little 'n Big.*

*American Agriculturalist.* Periodical affiliated with the *Orange Judd Farmer* 1847-1918.

Aunt Ellen. SEE Aunt Martha.

Aunt Jane. SEE *Household Journal.*

*Aunt Kate's Quilting Bee.* Magazine published between July 1962 and July 1967. Editor Glenna Boyd, Vinta, OK.

Aunt Martha Studios. Booklets, kits and related items are still offered by Kansas City's Colonial Patterns Inc. that began, in the early 1930s when they were advertised in a syndicated column under various names including Aunt Ellen, Aunt Matilda, Betsy Ross, Royal Neighbor and Colonial Quilt. Aunt Martha was the most common name used. In 1935 Colonial Patterns began *The Workbasket* magazine duplicating many Aunt Martha designs. In 1949 Colonial Patterns and *Workbasket* split. Current address: Colonial Patterns, Inc. 340 W 5th St. Kansas City, MO 64105-1235. SEE *Workbasket.* Aunt Martha booklets: *A New & Easy Way to Make a Quilt* (ca. 1931 ), *Favorites Old and New* (#5511, ca. 1932), *Prize Winning Designs* (#300, ca. 1933), *Quilt Fair Comes to You* (#5514, ca. 1933), *Star Designs* (#9450, ca. 1942), *Quilt Designs, Old Favorites and New* (#3175), *Aunt Martha's Favorite Quilts* (#3230), *Quilts Modern and Colonial* (#3333), *Easy Quilts* (#3500), *Quilt Lover's Delight* (#3540), Quilts (#3614), *Bold & Beautiful Quilts* (#3778), *Patchwork Simplicity* (#3779) (also called *Patchwork, Plain & Simple), Quilts: Heirlooms of Tomorrow* (#3788).

Aunt Matilda. SEE Aunt Martha.

Aunt Mattie. A name used by Milwaukee Comfort Mills, Milwaukee, WI, in the 1930s.

Aunt Stella. A name associated with Burton/Land of Nod.

Bacon, Lenice Ingram. *American Patchwork Quilts.* Wm. Morrow & Co., New York, 1973.

Baltimore Museum of Art. *The Great American Cover-up: Counterpanes of the 18th and 19th Centuries.* Baltimore, MD, 1971. Catalog.

*Better Homes & Gardens.* Periodical published by Meredith Publishing Co., Des Moines, IA.

Betterton, Sheila. *Quilts & Coverlets from the American Museum in Britain.* Butler & Tanner, Ltd., London, 1978. Catalog.

Beyer, Alice. *Quilting.* South Park Recreation Dept., Chicago, 1934. Reprinted by East Bay Heritage Quilters. Sketches of Nancy Cabot patterns.

Beyer, Jinny. *Patchwork Patterns.* EPM Publications, McLean, VA, 1979.

Bishop, Robert. *The Knopf Collector's Guides to American Antiques, Quilts, Coverlets, Rugs & Samplers.* Knopf, New York, 1982.

Bishop, Robert & Patricia Coblentz. New *Discoveries in American Quilts.* E.P Dutton, New York, 1975

Bishop, Robert & Elizabeth Safanda. *A Gallery of Amish Quilts: Design Diversity from a Plain People.* E.P Dutton, New York, 1976.

Brooks, Alice. SEE OCS (Old Chelsea Station Needlecraft Service.)

Brown, Evelyn. *Tumbling Alley.* A periodical published from ca. 1970 to 1981. Also wrote and published *Quilting: Do It My Way.* Gainesville, FL, 1975.

*Bureau Farmer.* Periodical from the American Farm Bureau Federation from 1925-35.

Burnham, Dorothy. *Pieced Quilts of Ontario.* Royal Ontario Museum, Toronto, 1975. Catalog.

Cabot, Anne. SEE Famous Features.

Cabot, Nancy. Syndicated column written by Loretta Leitner Rising for the *Chicago Tribune* in *the* 1930s. There were hundreds of Cabot patterns that were sold mail-order and grouped in booklets. The same patterns were also sold by the Spinning Wheel syndicate and the *Progressive Farmer.* The Cabot column began in 1932 and continued through the decade. Patterns were reprinted in the 1960s and '70s by several small publishers but are currently out-of-print again as far as I know. Wilma Smith writing as "Nancy's" indexed the Cabot patterns. Many of those attributed to Cabot by various indexers are probably <u>NOT</u> actually from that source.

*Canada Quilts.* Periodical published from about 1970

*Capper's Weekly.* A periodical from Capper Publications, which has published the weekly newspaper since 1879. From 1927 through 1935 they offered a unique column authored by staff member Louise Fowler Roote, who wrote under the name Kate Marchbanks (the fictitious editor of the women's page, titled In the Heart of the Home.) Since 1935 they have offered various syndicated columns, particularly Famous Features (see entry), which incorporated some of Roote's designs. Other Capper publications that printed quilt patterns were the *Kansas Farmer, Capper's Farmer, Capper's Farm Press, The Mail & Breeze,* and *The Household Magazine* (see entry).

Caulfeild, Sophia Frances Anne & Blanche C. Saward. *The Dictionary of Needlework* Original copyright 1882, L. Upcott Gill, London. Reprinted by Arno Press, 1972.

## References

*Chicago Tribune.* SEE Nancy Cabot.

Clark, Grandmother. A series of booklets from the W.L.M. Clark Inc. of St. Louis that also published booklets on crocheting, tatting etc. and sold quilt kits. One other name occasionally used was Winifred Clark. They began publishing quilt patterns in the early 1930s, and continued selling stamped needlework items into the 1950s. There was no connection between Grandmother Clark and Coats & Clark thread company, an error I made in an earlier revision of these references. Grandmother Clark booklets: *Grandmother Clark's Patchwork Quilts* (#19, 1932) *Grandmother Clark's Patchwork Quilt Designs* (#20, 1931) *Grandmother Clark's Old Fashioned Quilt Designs* (#21, 1931) *Grandmother Clark's Quilting Designs* (#22) *Grandmother Clark's Authentic Early American Patchwork Quilts* (#23)

Clarke, Mary Washington. *Kentucky Quilts and Their Makers,* University Press of Kentucky, Lexington, KY, 1976.

Coats and Clark. The J & P Coats Company and the Clark Company were two independent thread manufacturers that merged in the mid-19th century. They continued to manufacture thread under their old names as well as under "Coats & Clark" and "Spool Cotton." Their pattern booklets: *Quilts* (#1145, S-22, 1945), *Heirloom Quilts* (#160).

Colby, Averil. *Patchwork,* Charles T. Branford, Co., Newton Centre, MA, 1958

Colby, Averil. *Patchwork Quilts,* Scribner's, New York, 1965.

Colonial Patterns, Inc. SEE Aunt Martha.

*Comfort.* Periodical published from 1888 to 1942 in Augusta, Maine by Gannet and Morse. *Comfort* published many patterns in *the* magazine, sold them mail-order and published at least one booklet: *Comfort's Applique and Patchwork: Revival of Old Time Patchwork (1921 or 1922).*

*Country Gentleman.* A periodical founded as *Gennessee Farmer* in the early 19th century. Became *Country Gentleman* in 1853; changed to *Better Farming* in 1955 and merged with *Farm Journal* that year. In the 1930s sold mail order patterns and published articles by Velma Mackey Paul and Florence LaGanke Harris, among others.

*Country Home.* Periodical that published patterns in the 1930s.

*Country Life.* Periodical that published patterns near the turn of the century.

*Dakota Farmer.* Periodical established in 1881 in Aberdeen, SD. In the late 1920s had a unique quilt column with readers sending in designs.

Danneman, Barbara. *Step By Step Quiltmaking.* Golden Press, Western Publishing Co., Racine, WI, 1974.

Danner, Scioto Imhoff. A mail-order pattern source known as Mrs. Danner's Quilts (established 1934) that was bought by Helen Ericson in 1970. Danner published four pamphlets and Ericson has added four more. All currently available from Mrs. Danner's Quilts, Box 650, Emporia, KS 66801.

Davison, Mildred. *American Quilts 1819-1948 from* the *Museum Collection,* The Art Institute of Chicago, 1959. Catalog.

DeGraw, Imelda. SEE Denver Art Museum.

Denver Art Museum has published two catalogs: DeGraw, Imelda. *Quilts and Coverlets,* 1974 and Dunham, Lydia Roberts. "Denver Art Museum Quilt Collection," *Denver Art Museum Winter Quarterly,* 1963.

*Detroit Free Press.* Periodical that published several syndicated columns in the 1920s and '30s but apparently also offered some unique patterns.

Detroit News/Public Service Bureau Home Newspaper. Unique pattern column in the mid 1930s by Marian Morris Goodman.

Dexter, Grandma. Series of booklets published in the early 1930s from the Virginia Snow Studios, a part of the Dexter Yarn and Thread Company and the Collingbourne Mills in Elgin, Illinois. Some syndicated column advertisements appeared (the one I have is from the *Missouri Farm Bureau News.)* Taylor Batting patterns are very similar (see entry). The Grandma Dexter booklets: *Grandma Dexter's Applique and Patchwork Quilt Designs* (#36) *Grandma Dexter's Applique and Patchwork Designs* (#36A) Grandma Dexter's New Applique and Patchwork Designs (#36B).

Doyle, Joseph. Newark, New Jersey company that printed at least two booklets offering mail-order patterns. *The Patchworker's Companion (1911) Patchwork and Quilt Making*

DuBois, Jean. Editor and publisher of LaPlata Press which published the following:

  *Bye Baby Bunting* (1979)

  *A Galaxy of Stars: America's Favorite Quilts* (1979)

  *The Wool Quilt* (1978).

Dunham, Lydia Roberts. SEE Denver Art Museum.

Dunton, William Rush, Jr., M.D. *Old Quilts.* Published by the author, Catonsville, MD, 1946.

Elwood, Judy, Joyce Tennery and Alice Richardson. *Tennessee Quilting: Designs Plus Patterns,* published by the authors, Oak Ridge, TN, 1982.

Ericson, Helen. SEE Scioto Danner.

*References*

Evangeline's. Pattern column, apparently unique to the St. John, New Brunswick *Maritime Farmer* in the 1920s and '30s.

Fadely, Jean. *Frameless Quilt Making for Beginners.* Published by the author. 1971.

Famous Features. A syndicated, mail-order source that still sells pattern booklets from a New York address. Some pattern collectors call them the Q Books since each number is preceded by a Q. They appear to have begun in the 1940s, probably an outgrowth of *Capper's Weekly* patterns (see entry). Mabel Obenchain is the author most commonly mentioned. Famous Feature booklets: *Flower Quilts* (#Q 101), *Grandmother's Patchwork Quilts* (#Q 102), *All Year Quilts* (#Q 103), *Young Folks Quilts* (#Q 104), *Covered Wagon Quilts* (#Q 105), *Bible Favorites* (#Q 106), *A B C Quilter* (#Q 107), *Centennial Quilts* (#Q 108), *Early American Quilts* (#Q 109), *Star Quilts* (#Q 110), *Round the World Quilts* (#Q 111), *One Piece Quilts* (#Q 112), *Blue Ribbon Quilts* (#Q 116), *Quilts on Parade* (also *Parade of Quilts) (#Q 117), *Grandmother's Flower Quilts* (# Q 118), *Bicentennial Quilts* (#Q 121), *White House Quilts* (#Q 124), *Rose Quilts* (#Q 125), *All Time Favorites* (#Q 126), *Keepsake Quilts* (#Q 130).

*Farm and Fireside.* Periodical published by Crowell, Springfield, Ohio. Patterns began in 1884.

*Farm and Home.* Periodical that printed patterns after the mid 1880s.

*Farm Journal* Periodical established in March, 1877 and still publishing. They have absorbed at least three other pattern sources (*Country Gentleman, The Farmers Wife* and *Household Journal.*) In the 20th century they have offered mail-order patterns and booklets. Some of the patterns are reproduced in Rachel Martens, Modern Patchwork, Countryside Press, Philadelphia, 1970.

*Farmer's Wife, The.* Periodical published in St. Paul, MN from the 19th century through 1939 when it merged with *Farm Journal* Booklets include: Lorene Dunnigan, *Quilts* (ca. 1930), Orrine Johnson and Eleanor C. Lewis, *The Farmer's Wife Book of Quilts* (1931), Orrine Johnson and Eleanor C. Lewis, *Farmer's Wife Quilts: A New Book of Patterns* (1932), *Farmer's Wife Book of Quilts IV* (1937).

Finley, Ruth. *Old Patchwork Quilts and the Women Who Made Them.* J.B. Lippincott, Philadelphia, PA, 1929. Reprinted by EPM, Box 490, McLean, VA, 22101, 1992.

Frank, Robert. Frank's Art Needlework of St. Louis was best known for its kits and stamped block sets, which they sold from about 1900 to 1980, but this is apparently another unrelated Frank. Robert Frank Needlework Supply Company of Kalamazoo, MI, published at least one booklet: *E-Z Patterns for Patchwork and Applique Quilts.*

Gammell, Alice. *Polly Prindle's Book of American Patchwork Quilts.* Grossett & Dunlap, New York, 1973. Reprinted by Dover Publications.

*Godey's Lady's Book.* Periodical published in Philadelphia from 1830 to 1898. Once in a long while they published a group of patchwork patterns, many of which were copied from English periodicals.

Golden Hands. Farnsworth, Ruth and Carol Collins, *Patchwork and Applique,* Golden Hands, Marshall Cavendish, London 1976, and Goodman, Liz and Stephanie Miller, *All About Patchwork: Golden Hands Special# 10,* Marshall Cavendish, London, 1973.

Goodspeed, Sally. *Quiltmaker's Time.* Books 1 & 2. In the 1970s this was a reprint source for Nancy Cabot patterns and some new designs.

*Good Housekeeping.* Periodical from the Hearst Corporation. Anne Orr was needlework editor in the early 20th century. SEE Anne Orr.

Graeff, Marie Knorr. *Pennsylvania German Quilts. Home Craft Course, Volume XIV.* Mrs. D. Naaman Kneiper, Kutztown, PA 1946.

Gutcheon, Beth. *The Perfect Patchwork Primer,* David McKay Co., Inc., New York, 1973.

Gutcheon, Beth and Jeffrey Gutcheon, *The Quilt Design Workbook,* Rawson Associates, New York, 1976.

Haders, Phyllis, *Sunshine & Shadow: The Amish and Their Quilts.* The Main Street Press, Clinton, NJ, 1976.

Haders, Phyllis, *The Warner Collector's Guide to American Quilts.* Main Street Press, Warner Books, New York, 1981.

Hall, Carrie A. and Rose G. Kretsinger, *The Romance of the Patchwork Quilt in America.* Caxton Printers, Caldwell, ID, 1935. Reprinted by Dover.

Harris, Della. Mail-order source for patterns from around 1930. Waco, Texas. Booklet included some McKim patterns and some unique.

Harris, Florence LaGanke. SEE Nancy Page.

Hartman, Marie. *Quilts, Quilts...* A booklet published by the author in Tampa, Florida, 1980.

Heard, Audrey and Beverly Pryor. *The Complete Guide to Quilting.* Creative Home Library (Better Homes and Gardens), Des Moines, IA, 1974.

*Hearth and Home.* Periodical published by Vickery and Hill Company in Augusta, Maine from 1885 to the 1930s. They offered

# References

their first mail order patterns in April, 1895. Needlework columns included "Useful and Fancy Work" by Mary E. Bradford and "Mutual Benefit Society" by Mrs. A.G. Spofford. Wilene Smith has evidence that several Vickery and Hill publications printed similar drawings and patterns, so accuracy in sources is a problem. Among the magazines from the same company: *American Woman, Fireside Visitor, Good Stories,* and *Happy Hours*. Smith suggests the name "Hearth and Home Group" as a term for this source. Clara Stone submitted a number of the patterns and they are also included in her booklet (see entry). Some *Hearth and Home* patterns are reprinted in the following: Bannister, Barbara & Edna Paris Ford, *The United States Patchwork Pattern Book,* Dover, NY, 1970. Bannister, Barbara & Edna Paris Ford, *State Capitals Quilt Blocks,* Dover, NY, 1977.

Heath, Thelma G. *How To Make a Really Different Quilt,* booklet published by the author, ca. 1940.

Hechtlinger, Adelaide. *American Quilts, Quilting, and Patchwork,* Harrisburg, PA: Stackpole Books, 1974.

Herrschner. Frederick Herrschner, Inc. is a mail-order source for kits and stamped blocks dating back to the early 20th century and still in business. One old booklet: *Quilts: Beautiful Designs for Applique, Embroidery: Authentic Reproductions for Patchwork.*

Hinson, Delores A. *Quilting Manual.* Hearthside Press, Inc. New York, 1966. Reprinted by Dover.

Hinson, Delores A. *A Quilter's Companion.* Arco, New York, 1973.

Holstein, Jonathan. *Abstract Design in American Quilts.* Whitney Museum of Art, New York, 1971.

Holstein, Jonathan. *American Pieced Quilts.* Viking Press, New York, 1973.

Holstein, Jonathan, *The Pieced Quilt.* The New York Graphic Society, Greenwich, CT, 1973.

Home Art Studios. A mail-order pattern source from Des Moines founded by H. VerMehren. Patterns appeared under the names Nancy Lee, Colonial Quilts, Bettina, Hope Winslow and others in periodicals during the 1930s. They can be confused with the Aunt Martha Studios since both used the name Colonial Quilts. Booklets included *Colonial Quilts* and *Master Quilting Album.*

*Household Journal.* Periodical published in Springfield, Ohio in the early 20th century by Crowell, which also published *Farm & Fireside*. Patterns were sold under the name Aunt Jane. *Household Journal* moved to Batavia, Illinois and was published as the *Household Management Journal.* Later absorbed by *Farm Journal.* Pamphlets include: *Aunt Jane's Quilt Pattern Book; Aunt Jane's Prize Winning Quilt Designs* (1914).

*Household Magazine.* Periodical published in Topeka by Capper's Publications. SEE *Capper's Weekly.*

Ickis, Marguerite. *The Standard Book of Quilt Making and Collecting.* Grey Stone Press, 1949. Reprinted by Dover, 1959.

James, Michael. *The Quiltmaker's Handbook: A Guide to Design and Construction.* Prentice Hall, Englewood Cliffs, New Jersey, 1978.

Johnson, Bruce. *A Child's Comfort: Baby and Doll Quilts in American Folk Art.* Harcourt, Brace, Jovanovich, New York, 1977.

Jones, Betty. SEE *Progressive Farmer.*

KC Star. *The Kansas City Star.* Patterns appeared in three periodicals *(Kansas City Star, Weekly Kansas City Star* and *Weekly Star Farmer)* from 1928 to 1960. Early patterns were McKim syndicated patterns but in the early 1930s began a unique column of traditional and new designs by staff members and readers. Reprints available from Groves Quilt Patterns, PO Box 5370, Kansas City, MO 64131.

Kaufman, Helen. Syndicated columnist. Patterns often numbered with a "K".

Khin, Yvonne. *The Collector's Dictionary of Quilt Names and Patterns.* Acropolis Books, Washington, DC, 1980.

LAC. Ladies Art Company. Founded in St. Louis by H.M. Brockstedt, it is credited as the first mail-order quilt pattern company. Exactly when they published their first catalog, *Diagrams of Quilt, Sofa, and Pin Cushion Patterns,* has not been determined, but an 1895 ad mentions 272 patterns. The 1906 edition included 450 designs. A second catalog, *Quilt Patterns: Patchwork and Appliqué,* was published in 1922 and revised again between 1928 and 1934 with patterns through 531. This last catalog was published until the company went out of business in the 1970s. Cuesta Benberry and Wilene Smith note that the number of the pattern can be used to date them. Appliqué designs from the 1920s were usually numbered in four digits. Following is an index of dates and numbers drawn from Wilene Smith's research, published as "Quilt History in Old Periodicals: A New Interpretation," *Uncoverings 1990,* Laurel Horton (ed.), The American Quilt Study Group, San Francisco, CA, 1991.

| LAC Pattern Number | Date Published |
| --- | --- |
| 1 - 272 | in print 1895 (may go back to 1889) |
| 273 - 400 | 1897 |
| 401 - 420 | 1901 |
| 421 - 450 | 1906 |

# References

451 - 500    1922
501 - 509    1928
511 - 530    1928 - 1934
531          1934.

*LCPQ. Lady's Circle Patchwork Quilts* is a periodical published from 1973 through the present. Editor: Karen O'Dowd. 111 E 35th St.. New York. NY. 10016.

*Ladies' Home Journal.* Periodical begun as *Ladies' Journal and Practical Housekeeper* in 1883. Has published patterns until the present. Marie Webster contributed a number of patterns in the first quarter of the century.

Lithgow, Marilyn. *Quiltmaking and Quiltmakers.* Funk & Wagnalls, NY, 1974.

*Little 'n Big.* Periodical published by ABC Publications from February, 1964 through March, 1966; reprinted old patterns and included some new designs. Betty Flack was editor.

Lockport Batting Company, Lockport, New York. In addition to selling supplies the company sold patterns during the 1930s and '40s. Lockport sold many Anne Orr designs (see entry). Booklets include: *Replicas of Famous Quilts, Old and New* (1942), *The Lockport Quilt Pattern Book.*

Mahler, Celine Blanchard. *Once Upon a Quilt.* Van Nostrand and Reinhold, NY, 1973.

Marchbanks, Kate. SEE *Capper's Weekly.*

*Maritime Farmer.* SEE Evangeline's.

Marshall, Martha. *Quilts of Appalachia: The Mountain Woman and Her Quilts.* Tri-City Printing Co., Bluff City, TN 37618, 1972.

McCall's Publishing Co. has been offering patterns throughout the twentieth century. To distinguish *between* older patterns offered through the magazine and a series of booklets, I have used the following: *McCall's Magazine.* Patterns were pictured in the magazine in the first half of the century. They could be mail-ordered. *McCall's* means the series of booklets with patterns included in them published from 1972 through 1975. The booklets were reprinted as *McCall's Book of Quilts,* Simon & Schuster/The McCall Pattern Co., NY, 1975.

McElwain, Mary A. The Mary McElwain Quilt Shop in Walworth, Wisconsin sold mail-order patterns in the 1930s, and some were included as premiums in batting. One booklet: *The Romance of Village Quilts,* 1936 (later reprinted by Rock River Cotton Co., Janesville, WI, ca. 1955.)

McKendry, Ruth. *Quilts and Other Bedcoverings in the Canadian Tradition.* Von Nostrand, Reinhold, Toronto, 1979.

McKim, Ruby Short. McKim Studios in Independence, Missouri was a mail-order source for patterns and she also syndicated a newspaper column with full-size patterns in the late 1920s and 30s. Booklets: *Designs Worth Doing,*
  Adventures in Needlecraft
  Adventures in Home Beautifying
  101 Patchwork Patterns (reprinted by Dover Publications, NY, 1962).

Meeker, L.K. *Quilt Patterns for the Collector.* Published by the author, Portland, OR, 1979.

Mills, Susan Winter, *Illustrated Index to Traditional American Quilt Patterns.* Arco Publishing, NY, 1980.

Mitchell, V. Jean. *Quilt Kansas.* Spencer Museum of Art, Lawrence, KS, 1978.

*Modern Priscilla.* Periodical begun in 1887 that offered mail-order patterns, primarily in the teens and twenties. Absorbed by *Needlecraft—The Home Arts Magazine* (see entry) in 1930.

Mountain Mist. The Stearns & Foster Co. began selling quilt batting in Cincinnati in 1846. It has offered mail-order patterns at least since the 1920s when it also began including a free pattern on the batting wrapper. Phoebe Edwards is one of the names used. Address: Stearns & Foster Co. Lockland, OH 45215. Booklets include *The Mountain Mist Blue Book of Quilts* (1935), *The Mountain Mist Album of Quilt Blocks* (1938), *The 1957 Mountain Mist Blue Book of Quilts, Anyone Can Quilt* (1975), *Stearns & Foster Quilt Pattern Designs and Needlecraft Supplies* (currently in print).

NNT = *Nimble Needle Treasures.* A periodical edited by Patricia Almy, Sapulpa, Oklahoma from 1969 through 1975.

Nebraska Collections refers to *Quilts from Nebraska Collections,* a catalog of an exhibit in 1975 organized by the Lincoln Quilters Guild and the University of Nebraska.

*Needlecraft Magazine* refers to a periodical published by the Vickery Publishing Company in Augusta, Maine, from 1909. It changed its name several times, among them: *Home-Arts/Needlecraft* and *Needlecraft: The Home Arts Magazine.* Absorbed *Modern Priscilla* in 1930 and ceased in 1943. Sold mail-order patterns throughout its history.

Needlecraft Supply, Chicago, was a mail-order house for patterns, kits and fabric. Booklet: *Patchwork Quilts and How to Make Them,* 1938.

OCS. SEE Old Chelsea Station Needlecraft Service.

*Ohio Farmer.* Periodical begun as the *Ohio Practical Farmer* around 1810, published by the Lawrence Publishing Co, Cleve-

# References

land. Patterns appeared on the woman's pages in the 1890s.

*Oklahoma Farmer Stockman.* A periodical published in Oklahoma City, which in the late 1920s and '30s had a unique column entitled Good Cheer Quilt Patterns.

Old Chelsea Station Needlecraft Service. A mail-order company begun in 1933 that continues to advertise in periodicals, although most of their quilt patterns are no longer offered. Names used were Alice Brooks, Laura Wheeler, and Carol Curtis. Mail orders were sent to Needlecraft Service at the Old Chelsea Station post office in New York, which is why collectors call this the Old Chelsea Station Needlecraft Company. Originally they offered single full-size patterns through the mail but in recent decades they have sold the following booklets: *Quilt Book #101, Museum Quilt Book #102, Quilts for Today's Living* #103, *Nifty Fifty Quilts* #116 (1974), *Stuff 'n Puff Quilts* #122, *Stitch 'n ' Patch Quilts* #123, *Petal Quilt Book* #125.

*Orange Judd Farmer.* The Western edition of the *American Agriculturalist,* a periodical begun around 1870, that offered patterns on the woman's page.

Orbelo, Beverly Ann. *A Texas Quilting Primer.* Corona Publishing Company, San Antonio, TX, 1980.

Orlofsky, Myron & Patsy Orlofsky. *Quilts in America.* McGraw Hill, NY, 1974, reprint Abbeville, 1992.

Orr, Anne. A designer of quilt and other needlework patterns in the early twentieth century and a needlework editor at *Good Housekeeping.* Anne Orr patterns were sold under her name, *Good Housekeeping's* name and the Lockport Batting Company's name.

Page, Nancy. A syndicated mail-order column written by Florence LaGanke Harris, which appeared in many periodicals in the late 1920s – '40s.

Penny, Prudence. The name for the column in the *Seattle Post-Intelligencer* in the 1920s and 30s. The author was Bernice Reddington. Some are syndicated columns (primarily McKim); others are unique, occasionally signed M. Buren. Booklet: *Old Time Quilts,* 1927.

*People's Popular Monthly. A* periodical published from 1896 to 1931, which absorbed *Ladies' Favorite Magazine in* 1908.

*Peterson's Magazine.* A periodical begun in 1842 as *Lady's World of Fashion.* In 1849 name changed. Merged with Argosy in 1894. Occasionally showed quilt patterns.

Peto, Florence. *American Quilts and Coverlets.* Chanticleer Press, Inc., NY, 1949.

Peto, Florence. *Historic Quilts.* American Historical Co., Inc., NY, 1939.

Pforr, Effie Chalmers. *Award Winning Quilts.* Oxmoor House, Progressive Farmer, Birmingham, AL, 1974.

*Prairie Farmer.* A periodical published in Chicago which sold mail-order patterns. Booklet: *Quilt Booklet #1,* edited by Lois Schenk, around 1931.

*Progressive Farmer.* Periodical published in Birmingham, Alabama since 1895. During the 1930s and 40s they sold mail-order patterns from The Spinning Wheel Company that were identical to Nancy Cabot patterns (see entry.) I have referred to most *Progressive Farmer* patterns as Nancy Cabot. They also used the name Betty Jones. Winners in a *PF* contest were published in Pforr (see entry.) Booklets: *Heirloom Quilts to Treasure,* 1931, *One Dozen Quilt Patterns, Progressive Farmer* by Sallie Hill, 1946.

Puckett, Marjorie and Gail Giberson. *Primarily Patchwork.* Orange Patchwork Publishers, Orange, CA, 1978.

QEC. SEE *Quilt Engagement Calendar.*

QNM. SEE *Quilters Newsletter Magazine.*

QW. SEE *Quilt World.*

*QUILT.* a periodical published since 1978 by Harris Publications, 1115 Broadway, *New York, NY* 10010.

*Quilt Engagement Calendar.* An annual desk calendar edited by Cyril Nelson from E.P. Dutton, published from 1975 to the present. Patterns for several quilts in Nelson, Cyril and Carter Houck, *The Quilt Engagement Calendar Treasury,* E.P. Dutton, NY, 1982.

*Quilt Close Up: Five Southern Views.* Catalog, Hunter Museum of Art, Chattanooga, TN.

*Quilt World.* Periodical published since 1976 by the House of White Birches, Box 337, Seabrook, NH 03874.

*Quilters Newsletter Magazine.* Periodical published since 1969 and edited by Bonnie Leman. Address: PO Box 394, Wheatridge, CO 80033. Includes a mail-order pattern service called Quilts and Other Comforts, once known as Heirloom Plastics.

Robertson, Elizabeth Wells. *American Quilts.* Studio Publications, NY, 1948.

Rodgers, Pauline Welton. 20 *Favorite Patchwork Quilts,* House of White Birches, Seabrook, New Hampshire, 1980.

*Rural New Yorker.* a periodical from Rural Publishing Co., New York. Begun in 1841, published through the mid-twentieth century. An apparently unique pattern column written by Mrs. R.E. Smith from 1930 through 1937. She mentioned once

# References

that the column was syndicated but I have not seen it elsewhere.

Safford, Carleton L. and Robert Bishop. *America's Quilts & Coverlets.* E.P. Dutton, NY, 1972.

Sears, Roebuck & Co. *Century of Progress in Quilt Making.* Chicago, 1934. Booklet featuring winners of their contest held in conjunction with the 1933 World's Fair.

Sexton, Carlie. Carlie Sexton Holmes ran a mail-order pattern company from Wheaton, Illinois in the late 1920s and 1930s. She also wrote for Meredith Corporation, publisher of *Successful Farming* and *Better Homes & Gardens.* Booklets, which were reprinted in the 1960s by Barbara Bannister, Alanson, MI: *Old Fashioned Quilts,* 1928 (Published by the author in Wheaton), *Yesterday's Quilts in Homes of Today,* 1928 (Meredith Publishing, Des Moines, IA), *How To Make A Quilt,* 1932 (published by the author in Wheaton).

Shelburne Museum. The catalog of the Shelburne's quilt collection was written by Lillian Baker Carlisle, *Pieced Work and Applique Quilts at Shelburne Museum,* Shelburne Museum, Shelburne, Vermont, 1957.

Shogren, Linda. Linda Shogren indexed patterns in the 1970's and named a few herself. Her indexes and compendiums are out of print.

Snow, Virginia. SEE Grandma Dexter.

Spinning Wheel. SEE Nancy Cabot and *Progressive Farmer.*

Spool Cotton. SEE Coats & Clark.

Stone, Clara. *Practical Needlework: Quilt Patterns, C.W.* Calkins & Co., Boston, MA, 1906. Booklet that was one of a series on needlework. Stone had contributed patterns to *Hearth and Home* (see entry) and this booklet included many published in the magazine.

*Successful Farming.* Periodical published by Meredith Corporation, Des Moines; began in 1902 and continued through the middle of this century. SEE Carlie Sexton.

Taylor Bedding Manufacturing Co., Taylor, Texas, sold betting and patterns. Booklets: *31 Quilt Designs by Taylor-Made* (ca. 1940). Patterns similar to Grandma Dexter (see entry.) *Barbara Taylor's Quilting for Fun & Profit.*

*Telegraphics.* Periodical from Baldwin City, Kansas which has published a unique column since 1976. Authors include Helen Ericson, Enola Gish, Betty Hagerman and Helen Storbeck.

University of Kansas. The art museum at the University in Lawrence, Kansas has published three catalogs: *One Hundred Years of American Quilt* (1973), *Quilters Choice* (1978), *American Patchwork Quilt* (1988).

Vote, Marjean. *Patchwork Pleasure: A Pattern Identification Guide.* Wallace Homestead, Des Moines, IA, 1960.

Walker Patterns. Syndicated mail-order patterns appearing as early as 1930. The drawings were signed Mary Evangeline Walker and the column was written by Lydia LeBaron Walker. The column in at least one paper was called "Concerning the Household" and discussed other things besides quilt designs.

*Wallace's Farmer.* Periodical published in Des Moines from 1874 through the middle of this century.

Webster, Marie D. *Quilts: Their Story And How To Make Them.* Tudor Publishing Co., New York, 1915. Webster wrote for the *Ladies Home Journal* and also sold patterns mail order from her home in Indiana.

Wheeler, Laura. SEE Old Chelsea Station Needlecraft Service.

Wilson, Erica. *Quilts of America,* Oxmoor House, Birmingham, Alabama, 1979.

Winthrop, Hettie. Syndicated column in the 1930s distributed by the Bell Syndicate.

*Woman's Circle.* Periodical that occasionally had patterns in the 1960s.

*Woman's Day.* Periodical that has included quilt patterns from the 1940s to the present. Some of the articles were reprinted in Rose Wilder Lane's *Woman's Day Book of American Needlework,* Simon & Schuster, New York, 1962.

*Woman's Home Companion.* Periodical that began in 1866 as *Ladies Home Companion* and changed its name in 1899.

*Woman's World.* Periodical published by the Manning Publishing Company, Chicago, in the 1920s and 30s. Patterns were sold mail order. Booklet: *The Patchwork Book, 1931.*

Woodard, Thomas K. and Blanche Greenstein. *Crib Quilts and Other Small Wonders,* E.P. Dutton, NY, 1981.

Wooster, Ann Sargent. *Quiltmaking: The Modern Approach to a Traditional Craft,* Drake, NY, 1972.

*Workbasket, The.* Periodical begun in 1935 as a leaflet by Colonial Patterns, Inc. (see Aunt Martha). It was affiliated with the Aunt Martha Studios (see entry) until 1949 when *Workbasket* and Colonial Patterns split and Modern Handcrafts began publishing *The Workbasket.* After 1950 the magazine rarely published quilt patterns. I have referred to most *Workbasket* patterns as Aunt Martha since they were the same.

# Index

The first index lists all pattern names alphabetically, and provides the pattern number that can be used for locating that design. The second index lists the types of patterns and indicates in which category these are classified in this book.

Indexes include:
- Pattern Name Index, p. 529
- Pattern Category Index, p. 551

| | |
|---|---|
| A Star, An | 1722 |
| Abe Lincoln Log Cabin | 3285 |
| Abe Lincoln's Log Cabin | 873 |
| Abe Lincoln's Platform | 1921 |
| Acanthus | 2280 |
| Acorn | 959 |
| Acrobats | 1821 |
| Adam's Refuge | 3075 |
| Aerial Beacon | 298 |
| Aeriel Beacon | 2748 |
| Aeroplane | 901 |
| Aeroplane | 902 |
| Aeroplane | 1858 |
| Aeroplanes | 901 |
| Aesthetic Quilt, An | 4005 |
| Aimeé's Choice | 2865 |
| Air Castle | 1704 |
| Air Ship Propeller | 3499 |
| Air Ways | 904 |
| Aircraft | 1319 |
| Aircraft Quilt, The | 902 |
| Airplane | 902 |
| Airplane | 907 |
| Airplane | 1320 |
| Airplane | 1850 |
| Airplane Quilt | 905 |
| Airplane, The | 903 |
| Airplane and Propeller | 908 |
| Airplane Motif, An | 3828 |
| Airplanes | 3768 |
| Airplanes, The | 3035 |
| Airport, The | 2084 |
| Airship | 3529 |
| Alabama | 2024 |
| Alabama Beauty | 2760 |
| Alabama Beauty | 3531 |
| Alabama Rambler | 3026 |
| Alamanizer | 2375 |
| Alaska | 2355 |
| Alaska Chinook | 3903 |
| Albany | 2794 |
| Album | 1659 |
| Album | 2414 |
| Album | 2812 |
| Album | 2813 |
| Album | 2819 |
| Album | 2850 |
| Album Blocks | 3586 |
| Album Flower | 2964 |
| Album House Quilt | 875 |
| Album Patch | 1813 |
| Album Pattern, The | 1812 |
| Album Quilt | 1601 |
| Album Quilt | 1812 |
| Album Quilt | 2139 |
| Album Quilt | 3662 |
| Album, The | 2454 |
| Alcazar | 3667 |
| Algonquin Charm | 1893 |
| Algonquin Trail | 1039 |
| Alice's Favorite | 1778 |
| Alice's Favorite | 2941 |
| Alice's Tulips | 1545 |
| All American Star | 3821 |
| All Around the Star | 2702 |
| All Hallows | 2510 |
| All Hands Around | 3801 |
| All Hands 'Round | 4044 |
| All Kinds | 3072 |
| All Over Pattern of Octagon, An | 442 |
| Allentown | 3171 |
| Alma's Choice | 3588 |
| Alpine Cross | 1876 |
| Alta Plane, The | 907 |
| Alta-Plane, The | 1434 |
| Altar Steps | 4155 |
| Alternating Fan Design | 3363 |
| Always Friends | 185 |
| American Woman's Own Quilt Block | 3558 |
| Amazing Windmill | 2726 |
| Amber Leaf | 3277 |
| Amber Waves | 3288 |
| America's Pride | 1537 |
| American Chain | 3215 |
| American Homes | 3218 |
| American Log Patchwork | 2573 |
| Amethyst | 1259 |
| Amethyst | 2975 |
| Amethyst | 3873 |
| Amethyst Chain | 1792 |
| Amethyst Chain | 2136 |
| Amish Checkerboard Diamond | 3980 |
| Amish Star | 1770 |
| Anchors Aweigh | 970 |
| Anderson | 1727 |
| Ann Lee's Baby Quilt | 2117 |
| Ann and Andy | 1132 |
| Ann's Scrap Quilt | 3064 |
| Anna Choice Quilt | 1141 |
| Anna's Basket | 713 |
| Anna's Pride | 4878 |
| Annapolis | 1972 |
| Annapolis | 2503 |
| Annapolis Patch | 3037 |
| Another Double T | 2803 |
| Another J | 984 |
| Another Sawtooth | 1652 |
| Another Star | 2832 |
| Antique Shop Tulip | 765 |
| Antique Tile Block | 1617 |
| Anvil | 2645 |
| Anvil, The | 1122 |
| Anvil, The | 1314 |
| Anvil, The | 3173 |
| Anvil, The | 3259 |
| Apple Leaf, The | 1396 |
| Apple Tree | 829 |
| April Tulips | 2190 |
| Arab Tent | 2690 |
| Arab Tent | 3928 |
| Arabian Star | 255 |
| Arabic Lattice | 2561 |
| Arabic Lattice | 4173 |
| Arabic Latticework | 1440 |
| Ararat | 226 |
| Arbor Window | 2414 |
| Ardmore, The | 3612 |
| Arizona | 1771 |
| Arizona's Cactus Flower | 2061 |
| Arkansas | 2083 |
| Arkansas | 2624 |
| Arkansas Centennial | 2765 |
| Arkansas Cross Roads, The | 1123 |
| Arkansas Diamond | 2348 |
| Arkansas Meadow Rose | 794 |
| Arkansas Snow Flake | 3892 |
| Arkansas Star | 3665 |
| Arkansas Star | 3892 |
| Arkansas Star | 3904 |
| Arkansas Traveler | 1400 |
| Arkansas Traveler | 2804 |
| Arkansas Traveler | 3909 |
| Arkansas Traveler | 3912 |
| Arkansas Troubles | 1466 |
| Arms To Heaven | 4095 |
| Army Star, The | 1981 |
| Around the Chimney | 2601 |
| Around the Corner | 2043 |
| Around the World | 302 |
| Around the World | 1467 |
| Around the World | 1471 |
| Around the World | 2001 |
| Arrant Red Birds | 2480 |
| Arrow | 1677 |
| Arrow Crown | 1164 |
| Arrow Point | 2750 |
| Arrow Points | 1984 |
| Arrow Star | 3735 |
| Arrow Star | 3893 |
| Arrow of Peace | 2751 |
| Arrowhead | 1985 |
| Arrowhead | 3946 |
| Arrowhead | 3952 |
| Arrowhead Puzzle | 1173 |
| Arrowhead Quilt | 1371 |
| Arrowhead Quilt, The | 1985 |
| Arrowhead Star | 2538 |
| Arrowhead, The | 1414 |
| Arrowhead, The | 2312 |
| Arrowheads | 204 |
| Arrowheads | 265 |
| Arrowheads | 479 |
| Arrowheads | 1986 |
| Arrowheads | 2708 |
| Arrowheads | 4184 |
| Art Deco Fans | 3308 |
| Art Deco Fans | 3325 |
| Art Square | 2403 |
| Aster | 756 |
| Aster | 3472 |
| Aster | 3485 |
| Aster | 3488 |
| Aster | 3628 |
| At the Depot | 2779 |
| At the Square | 1677 |
| Atlanta | 1023 |
| Attic Stairs | 2281 |
| Attic Stairs | 1044 |
| Attic Window | 1647 |
| Attic Window | 1687 |
| Attic Window | 3256 |
| Attic Windows | 468 |
| Attic Windows | 1366 |
| Attic Windows | 1357 |
| Augusta | 2917 |
| Aunt Addie's Album | 2153 |
| Aunt Anna's Album Block | 2452 |
| Aunt Dinah | 1636 |
| Aunt Dinah's Star | 3790 |
| Aunt Eliza's Star | 2830 |
| Aunt Em's Pattern | 1161 |
| Aunt Etta's Diamond Quilt | 427.5 |
| Aunt Jen's Stamp Quilt | 2287 |
| Aunt Jerusha | 1503 |
| Aunt Lottie's Star | 2830 |
| Aunt Lucinda's Block | 1053.9 |
| Aunt Lucinda's Double Irish Chain | 1053.9 |
| Aunt Martha's Rose | 428 |
| Aunt Mary's Double Irish Chain | 2342 |
| Aunt Mary's Star | 3833 |
| Aunt Melvernias's Chain | 2305 |
| Aunt Nancy's Favorite | 2900 |
| Aunt Patsy's Pet | 1001 |
| Aunt Patty's Favorite | 1001 |
| Aunt Rachel's Star | 2166 |
| Aunt Stella's Star | 143 |
| Aunt Sukey's Patch | 401 |
| Aunt Sukey's Patch | 2539 |
| Aunt Sukey's Pattern | 2539 |
| Aunt Vina's Favorites | 1654 |
| Austin | 2138 |
| Autograph Patch | 2882 |
| Autograph Quilt | 2885 |
| Autograph Quilt | 3255 |
| Autograph Quilt Block | 2899 |
| Autumn Leaf | 1736 |
| Autumn Leaf | 1887 |
| Autumn Leaf | 2010 |
| Autumn Leaf | 2011 |
| Autumn Leaf | 2060 |
| Autumn Leaf | 2224 |
| Autumn Leaves | 1329 |
| Autumn Leaves | 1887 |
| Autumn Leaves | 2726 |
| Autumn Star | 4186 |
| Autumn Stars | 1239 |
| Autumn Tints | 1103 |
| Autumn Tints | 1886 |
| Ava's Friendship Quilt | 1660 |
| Avalanche Lily | 3521 |
| Aztec | 228 |
| Babe Ruth Diamond | 4059 |
| Baby Aster | 3380 |
| Baby Basket | 651 |
| Baby Blocks | 415.34 |
| Baby Blocks | 426 |
| Baby Blocks and Stars | 142 |
| Baby Bunting | 706 |
| Baby Bunting | 3302.5 |
| Baby Bunting | 3369 |
| Baby Bunting | 3370 |
| Baby's Block | 142 |

529

Index


Bachelor's Puzzle ..... 1815
Bachelor's Puzzle ..... 1907
Bachelor's Puzzle ..... 2537
Bachelor's Puzzle ..... 3133
Bachelor's Puzzle ..... 4024
Bacon Patch ..... 2599
Badge of Friendship ..... 185
Bailey Nine Patch ..... 306
Balance ..... 1817
Balkan Puzzle ..... 1211
Balkan Puzzle ..... 2476
Balsam Fir ..... 832
Baltimore Belle ..... 2982
Baltimore Belle ..... 2912
Bamboo Quilt ..... 1258
Bamboo Spread ..... 457
Banner Quilt ..... 1371
Banner Quilt, The ..... 2004
Barbara Frietschie ..... 1140
Barbara Fritchie Star ..... 2146
Barn Bats ..... 4417
Barrister's Block ..... 1363
Bars ..... 475
Bars ..... 476.5
Bars ..... 477
Bars Variations ..... 483
Baseball ..... 1504
Baseball ..... 1508
Baseball ..... 2874
Basket ..... 650.2
Basket ..... 653.5
Basket ..... 658.5
Basket ..... 661
Basket ..... 669
Basket ..... 670
Basket ..... 673
Basket ..... 674
Basket ..... 682
Basket ..... 703
Basket ..... 707
Basket ..... 707.5
Basket Block ..... 664
Basket Design ..... 4134
Basket Design ..... 665.2
Basket Design ..... 671.5
Basket Flower ..... 690
Basket Lattice ..... 452
Basket Patch A ..... 656.2
Basket Quilt ..... 651
Basket Quilt ..... 657
Basket Quilt ..... 662
Basket Quilt ..... 704
Basket Quilt, The ..... 714
Basket Quilt in Triangles, A ..... 717
Basket, The ..... 659
Basket, The ..... 662
Basket, The ..... 672
Basket Weave Friendship Quilt ..... 2812
Basket Weave Three Patch ..... 134
Basket and Blossom ..... 691
Basket and Daisy ..... 1035.5
Basket and Flowers ..... 681
Basket and Iris ..... 677
Basket of Bright Flowers, A ..... 742
Basket of Chips ..... 712
Basket of Chips ..... 713
Basket of Diamonds ..... 220
Basket of Diamonds ..... 725
Basket of Diamonds ..... 4049
Basket of Flowers ..... 679
Basket of Flowers ..... 713
Basket of Flowers ..... 722.5
Basket of Flowers ..... 723
Basket of Flowers ..... 753.5
Basket of Lilies ..... 741
Basket of Lilies ..... 746
Basket of Lilies ..... 753.7
Basket of Oranges ..... 676
Basket of Scraps ..... 725.2
Basket of Scraps ..... 726
Basket of Scraps ..... 735
Basket of Triangles ..... 714
Basket of Tulips ..... 747
Basket with Handles ..... 655
Baskets ..... 662.5
Baskets ..... 667
Baskets Quilt ..... 678.5
Basketweave ..... 209.5
Bass and Trout ..... 3020
Bat, The ..... 1408
Bat Wings ..... 158
Bat's Block, The ..... 1408
Bat's Wings ..... 217.5
Baton Rouge ..... 2629
Baton Rouge Block ..... 2629
Baton Rouge Square ..... 1808
Batsche ..... 1879
Battle Ax of Thor ..... 1130
Battle Ax of Thor ..... 2577
Bay Leaf ..... 301
Bay Leaf ..... 1529
Bay Leaf ..... 3630
Bea's Basket ..... 718
Beach and Boats ..... 4130
Beacon Light ..... 2417
Beacon Lights ..... 2422
Bear's Foot ..... 1879
Bear's Paw ..... 1354
Bear's Paw ..... 1879
Bear's Paw ..... 1885
Beauregard's Surroundings ..... 2098
Beautiful Mosaic ..... 2285
Beautiful Star ..... 3893
Beauty, A ..... 2630
Beauty Everlasting ..... 1082
Beauty Patch ..... 1128
Beaver ..... 940.25
Becky's Nine Patch ..... 3205
Becky's Nine Patch ..... 4117
Bed of Peonies ..... 773.1
Bed of Roses ..... 192
Beech Mountain Quilt ..... 2538
Beg and Borrow ..... 1189
Beggar Block ..... 1758
Beggar's Block ..... 3072
Beggar's Blocks ..... 1619
Beggar's Blocks ..... 1758
Beggar's Blocks ..... 1759
Bell, The ..... 969
Belle's Favorite ..... 4162
Bellflower ..... 778
Berry Basket ..... 668
Best Friend, The ..... 1879
Best Friend, The ..... 1885
Best of All ..... 2070
Bethlehem Star ..... 3796
Batty's Basket ..... 704
Betty's Delight ..... 1288
Bible Tulip ..... 3099
Big Dipper ..... 1195
Big T ..... 1661
Biloxi ..... 1516
Bird Patchwork ..... 936
Bird at the Window ..... 726.5
Bird of Paradise ..... 1546
Bird of Paradise ..... 1627
Bird of Paradise ..... 3096
Bird's Eye View ..... 3377
Bird's Nest ..... 3237
Birds and Kites ..... 1418
Birds in Air ..... 2341
Birds in Flight ..... 480
Birds in a Square ..... 1924
Birds in the Air ..... 1322
Birds in the Air ..... 1391
Birds in the Air ..... 2218
Birds in the Air ..... 3161
Bisquit Quilt ..... 191
Bishop Hill ..... 1747
Bismarck ..... 3273
Black & White ..... 1258
Black Beauty ..... 305.7
Black Beauty ..... 1983
Black Diamond ..... 3809
Black Diamond ..... 3817
Black-eyed Susan ..... 3420
Blackford's Beauty ..... 1414
Blackford's Beauty ..... 1983
Blacks & Whites ..... 1222
Blazed Trail ..... 1360
Blazing Star ..... 415.3
Blazing Star ..... 1236
Blazing Star ..... 1237
Blazing Star ..... 1238
Blazing Star ..... 2245
Blazing Star ..... 2252
Blazing Star ..... 2669
Blazing Star ..... 3419
Blazing Star ..... 3772
Blazing Star ..... 3781
Blazing Star ..... 3804
Blazing Star ..... 3890
Blazing Star ..... 3906
Blazing Star ..... 4005
Blazing Star ..... 4007
Blazing Star of Kentucky ..... 3783
Blazing Star of Minnesota, The ..... 3772
Blazing Stars ..... 3481
Blazing Sun ..... 3481
Bleeding Heart ..... 2658
Bleeding Heart ..... 2668
Bleeding Heart, The ..... 3358
Blind Man's Fancy ..... 2072
Block Circle ..... 1727
Block Island Puzzle ..... 1260
Block Patchwork ..... 429
Block Pattern ..... 142
Block Star ..... 3701
Block Star ..... 1029
Block and Ring Quilt ..... 2674
Block and Star ..... 232.4
Blockade ..... 1212
Blockhouse ..... 1729
Blocks and Pinwheels ..... 1128
Blocks in a Box ..... 3210
Blossom Puffs ..... 171
Blossoming Cactus ..... 2540
Blue Bell Block ..... 4108
Blue Birds, The ..... 3768
Blue Birds of Happiness ..... 3768
Blue Blazes ..... 2217
Blue Boutonnieres ..... 1438
Blue Chains ..... 1695
Blue Eagle NRA ..... 226.71
Blue Fields ..... 2845
Blue Heather ..... 2429
Blue Heaven ..... 3905
Bluebell ..... 1794
Bluebirds ..... 934.6
Bluebonnet Beauty ..... 775.5
Bluet Quilt ..... 445.9
Board Meeting ..... 221
Bobbin, The ..... 3216
Boise ..... 2306
Bold Squares ..... 2282
Bon-Bon ..... 192
Bonnie Scotsman ..... 1390
Borrow and Lend ..... 1401
Borrow and Return ..... 3189
Boston ..... 2364
Boston Commons ..... 3979
Boston Corners ..... 141
Boston Corners ..... 231
Boston Pavement ..... 2726
Boston Puzzle ..... 1505
Boston Streets ..... 412.3
Boston Trail ..... 1461
Boston Trail ..... 1039
Botch Handle ..... 2058
Bouquet in a Fan ..... 1399.6
Bouquet's Quilt ..... 1963
Boutonniere ..... 424.8
Bow Bells ..... 2450
Bow Knots ..... 1423
Bow Tie Quilt ..... 3608
Bow Tie Variation ..... 1316
Bow Ties ..... 1195
Bow and Arrows ..... 1504
Bowknot ..... 1905
Bowknots ..... 1906
Bowknot and Rose ..... 1038
Bowl of Fruit ..... 2389
Box ..... 732
Box Car Patch ..... 2597
Box Patchwork ..... 142

# Index

| Entry | Number |
|---|---|
| Box Pattern | 142 |
| Box Quilt | 281 |
| Box Quilt | 427.4 |
| Box Quilt | 2597 |
| Box Quilt | 4198 |
| Box Upon Box | 142 |
| Boxed T's | 2803 |
| Boxes | 2839 |
| Boy's Fancy | 2811 |
| Boy's Nonsense | 2811 |
| Boy's Playmate | 2811 |
| Braced Star | 2833 |
| Braided Border | 1062.7 |
| Brave Sunflower, A | 3480 |
| Brave World | 1265 |
| Bread Basket | 657 |
| Breches Quilt, The | 3506 |
| Brick Crib Quilt | 133 |
| Brick Pavement | 2823 |
| Brick Pile | 412 |
| Brickwall | 132 |
| Brickwall One | 131 |
| Brickwork | 132 |
| Brickwork Quilt | 132 |
| Bridal Stairway | 1055 |
| Bride's Bouquet | 160 |
| Bride's Bouquet | 4052 |
| Bride's Fancy | 3835 |
| Bride's Prize | 3191 |
| Bride's Puzzle | 1359 |
| Bride's Quilt | 1547 |
| Bridge Quilt | 308 |
| Bridle Path | 1150 |
| Bridle Path Star | 1510 |
| Bright Hopes | 2571 |
| Bright Side | 2919 |
| Bright Star | 1273 |
| Bright Stars | 1952 |
| Brilliant Star | 262 |
| Britches Quilt | 3506 |
| Broad Arrow | 1439 |
| Broad Arrows | 1440 |
| Broad Axe, The | 1850 |
| Broken Arrows | 1934 |
| Broken Band | 2446 |
| Broken Branch, The | 1331 |
| Broken Circle | 2663 |
| Broken Crown | 3560 |
| Broken Crystals | 2742 |
| Broken Dishes | 1176 |
| Broken Dishes | 1193 |
| Broken Dishes | 2064 |
| Broken Dishes | 2472 |
| Broken Heart | 2910 |
| Broken Irish Chain | 2892 |
| Broken Path, The | 2438 |
| Broken Paths | 1750 |
| Broken Plate | 1646 |
| Broken Rainbows | 1416 |
| Broken Sash | 1171 |
| Broken Sash | 2375 |
| Broken Saw | 3370 |
| Broken Saw Baldes | 4152 |
| Broken Spider Web | 2326 |
| Broken Square | 1532 |
| Broken Squares | 2957 |
| Broken Star | 2981.5 |
| Broken Star | 3811 |
| Broken Star | 4007 |
| Broken Stone | 3086 |
| Broken Stone, The | 2876 |
| Broken Sugar Bowl, The | 714 |
| Broken Sugar Bowl, The | 1639 |
| Broken Wheel | 1727 |
| Broken Wheel, The | 2186 |
| Broken Windmills | 4160 |
| Broken Windows | 1670 |
| Brothers | 3279 |
| Brown Eyed Susan | 3613 |
| Brown Goose | 3220 |
| Brown World | 1265 |
| Brunswick Star | 441.2 |
| Brunswick Star | 2506 |
| Brunswick Star | 3704 |
| Brunswick Star | 3805 |
| Buck 'n Wing | 3013 |
| Buckeye | 3505 |
| Buckeye Beauty | 1254 |
| Buckeye Beauty | 1312 |
| Buckeye Beauty | 2987 |
| Buckeye Leaf | 857.09 |
| Buckwheat | 2304 |
| Buffalo | 94 |
| Buffalo Ridge | 1911 |
| Buffalo Ridge Quilt | 1912 |
| Bug Quilt | 218.3 |
| Buggy Wheel | 2664 |
| Builder's Blocks, The | 142 |
| Builder's Block Quilt, The | 3276 |
| Building Blocks | 142 |
| Building Blocks | 144 |
| Building blocks | 1612 |
| Building Blocks | 2279 |
| Building Blocks | 2537 |
| Bull's Eye | 1950 |
| Bull's Eye | 2712 |
| Bull's Eye | 3504 |
| Bun Quilt | 191 |
| Burgoyne Surrounded | 2098 |
| Burgoyne's Puzzle | 2098 |
| Burgoyne's Quilt | 2098 |
| Burnham Square | 2119 |
| Burr and Thistle | 3099 |
| Bursting Cubes | 4008 |
| Bursting Star | 3665 |
| Bursting Star | 3794 |
| Butter and Eggs | 2685 |
| Buttercup | 3711 |
| Butterfly | 1654 |
| Butterfly | 922 |
| Butterfly | 924 |
| Butterfly | 925 |
| Butterfly | 925.5 |
| Butterfly | 927.5 |
| Butterfly Block | 3904 |
| Butterfly Bush | 2994 |
| Butterfly Quilt | 145 |
| Butterfly Quilt | 224.2 |
| Butterfly Quilt | 929 |
| Butterfly Quilt #2 | 931 |
| Butterfly Quilt, The | 926 |
| Butterfly Quilt, The | 927 |
| Butterfly at the Cross | 1893 |
| Butterfly in Angles, A | 224 |
| Buttons and Bows | 2852 |
| Buzz Saw, The | 3562 |
| Buzzard's Roost | 3219 |
| Byrd at the South Pole | 3900 |
| Cabin Windows | 2420 |
| Cable | 425.6 |
| Cactus Basket | 725.5 |
| Cactus Basket | 729 |
| Cactus Basket | 730 |
| Cactus Basket | 731 |
| Cactus Bloom | 3634 |
| Cactus Blossom Patch | 3633 |
| Cactus Flower | 1394 |
| Cactus Flower | 758.5 |
| Cactus Pot | 700 |
| Cactus Rose | 857.033 |
| Cactus Rose | 857.04 |
| Caesar's Crown | 3638 |
| Caesar's Crown | 3643 |
| Caesar's Crown | 3652 |
| Cake Stand | 707 |
| Cake Stand | 711 |
| Calico Bush | 736 |
| Calico Cat | 937.5 |
| Calico Compass | 3847 |
| Calico Fan | 3327 |
| Calico Mosaic | 1428 |
| Calico Puzzle, The | 1682 |
| Calico Rose | 3421 |
| Calico Snowball | 4141 |
| Calico Star | 3603 |
| Calico Stars | 3824 |
| California | 1116 |
| California | 3123 |
| California Oak Leaf | 1831 |
| California Rose | 3653 |
| California Snowflake | 1980 |
| California Star | 2256 |
| California Star | 2262 |
| California Star Pattern | 2255 |
| Calla Lily Quilt | 792 |
| Camel | 939.5 |
| Canadian Conventional Star | 153 |
| Candleglow | 1897 |
| Capital Star | 3753 |
| Capital T | 1662 |
| Capital T | 1665 |
| Capital T | 2649 |
| Captain's Wheel | 2604 |
| Captive Beauty | 3801 |
| Car Wheel Quilt, The | 3583 |
| Card Basket | 2834 |
| Card Trick | 1674 |
| Carmen's Block | 1103 |
| Carnation | 779.5 |
| Carnival | 2613 |
| Carnival Time | 3599 |
| Carol's Scrap Time Quilt | 2404 |
| Carolina Favorite | 1536 |
| Carolina Lily | 743 |
| Carolina Lily | 768.2 |
| Caroline's Choice | 1026.5 |
| Carpenter's Square | 2580 |
| Carpenter's Star | 4159 |
| Carpenter's Wheel | 3809 |
| Carpenter's Wheel | 3811 |
| Carrie Nation Quilt | 1105 |
| Carrie's Choice | 1899 |
| Carson City | 2834 |
| Cart Wheel | 2955 |
| Cart Wheel Quilt | 3490 |
| Cascade Pride | 844 |
| Casement Window | 2815 |
| Castle | 891 |
| Castle Garden | 2171 |
| Castle Wall, The | 3610 |
| Castles in Spain | 2784 |
| Castor & Pollox | 3918 |
| Cat's Cradle | 1700 |
| Cat's Paw | 1879 |
| Catalpa Flower | 4148 |
| Catch Me If You Can | 1130 |
| Catch Me If You Can | 2577 |
| Cathedral Window | 301.5 |
| Cathedral Window | 460 |
| Cathedral Window | 1953 |
| Cats and Mice | 1619 |
| Cats and Mice | 1758 |
| Cats and Mice | 2916 |
| Cats and Mice | 3072 |
| Celestial Problem | 1666 |
| Celestial Sphere | 3861 |
| Centennial | 2899 |
| Centennial Maple | 857.01 |
| Centennial Tree | 810.5 |
| Centennial Tree | 815.3 |
| Center Diamond | 3976 |
| Center Diamond | 3977 |
| Center Table Quilt | 4044 |
| Century | 160 |
| Century Old Tulip Patter, A | 3103 |
| Century Quilt | 1065 |
| Century of Progress | 2501 |
| Century of Progress | 3713 |
| Century of Progress | 3923 |
| Century of Progress | 3941 |
| Century of Progress | 4118 |
| Chain Links | 212.2 |
| Chain Links | 1470 |
| Chain Links Quilt | 1163 |
| Chain Quilt | 1455 |
| Chain and Bar | 1961 |
| Chain and Hourglass | 1678 |
| Chain of Diamonds | 424 |
| Chain of Diamonds | 3033 |
| Chain of Diamonds Quilt | 1046 |
| Chained Five Patch | 1014 |
| Chained Lightning | 112 |
| Chained Star | 3513 |
| Chained Star | 3704 |
| Chained Star | 3805 |

531

# Index

| | |
|---|---|
| Chariot Wheel | 1836 |
| Chariot Wheel | 3388 |
| Charity Wheel | 3417 |
| Charleston | 2859 |
| Charm | 160 |
| Charm | 185 |
| Charm | 3203 |
| Charm Star | 2080 |
| Check | 2276 |
| Checkerboard | 1101 |
| Checkerboard | 2276 |
| Checkerboard | 2413 |
| Checkerboard Design | 1601 |
| Checkerboard Skew | 2562 |
| Checkerboard Skew | 1048 |
| Checkerboard Squares | 2429 |
| Checkerboard, The | 3982 |
| Checkered Star | 1021 |
| Checkers | 1051 |
| Cheesebox Quilt, The | 1764 |
| Cherry Basket | 664 |
| Cherry Basket | 668 |
| Cherry Basket | 670 |
| Cherry Basket | 685 |
| Cherry Tree Patchwork Design | 838 |
| Chestnut Burr | 2248 |
| Chestnut Burr | 2249 |
| Chestnut Burr | 2635 |
| Chevron | 160 |
| Chevrons | 3178 |
| Chevrons | 3179 |
| Cheyenne | 298 |
| Cheyenne | 2133 |
| Chicago Pavements | 2815 |
| Chicago Star | 1777 |
| Chicken | 936.7 |
| Chief, The | 3246 |
| Chieftain, The | 1422 |
| Children Israel | 2425 |
| Children of Israel | 2424 |
| Children's Delight | 1070 |
| Chimney | 3123 |
| Chimney Swallow | 2690 |
| Chimney Swallows | 2691 |
| Chimney Sweep | 2063 |
| Chimney Sweep | 3266 |
| China Aster, The | 3474 |
| China Plate | 3385 |
| Chinese 10,000 Perfections | 1130 |
| Chinese 10,000 Perfections | 2577 |
| Chinese Block Pattern | 1945 |
| Chinese Block Quilt, The | 2065 |
| Chinese Coin | 1142 |
| Chinese Coin | 1763 |
| Chinese Coins | 476 |
| Chinese Fan | 3302.5 |
| Chinese Fan | 3314 |
| Chinese Fan | 3369 |
| Chinese Fan | 3370 |
| Chinese Gongs | 3202 |
| Chinese Holidays | 2458 |
| Chinese Lantern | 957 |
| Chinese Lanterns | 1215 |
| Chinese Puzzle | 438 |
| Chinese Puzzle | 1343 |
| Chinese Puzzle | 3199 |
| Chinese Star | 3645 |
| Chinese Star | 3646 |
| Chinese Waterwheel | 3475 |
| Ching and Chow | 940.42 |
| Chip Basket | 713 |
| Chips and Whetstones | 3400 |
| Chips and Whetstones | 3409 |
| Chips and Whetstones | 3578 |
| Chips and Whetstones | 3787 |
| Chipyard | 2430 |
| Chisolm Trail | 1139 |
| Christian Cross | 2813 |
| Christian Cross | 3266 |
| Christmas Memory Quilt | 3796 |
| Christmas Star | 1806 |
| Christmas Star | 2070 |
| Christmas Star | 3789 |
| Christmas Tree | 809 |
| Christmas Tree | 823 |
| Christmas Tree | 824.5 |
| Christmas Tree | 834 |
| Christmas Tree Patch | 819 |
| Christmas Trees | 802 |
| Chrysanthemum | 2936 |
| Chrysthanthemum | 763.7 |
| Chuck a Luck | 1174 |
| Church Steps | 2635 |
| Church Windows | 171 |
| Church Windows | 433 |
| Church Windows | 2871 |
| Churchill Block | 2717 |
| Churn Dash | 1345 |
| Churn Dash | 1646 |
| Churn Dash | 1850 |
| Churn Dash | 2116 |
| Cincinnati Cog Wheel, The | 3396 |
| Circle Design | 1504 |
| Circle Four | 2858 |
| Circle Saw | 3390 |
| Circle Saw | 3808 |
| Circle Star | 3399 |
| Circle Upon Circle | 301 |
| Circle Upon Circle | 306 |
| Circle Upon Circle | 311 |
| Circle Within a Circle | 3377 |
| Circle and Square | 2515 |
| Circle and Star | 3625 |
| Circling Swallows | 2489 |
| Circling Swallows | 3758 |
| Circular Saw | 2226 |
| Circular Saw | 3544 |
| Circular Saw, The | 4068 |
| City Blocks | 1412 |
| City Park | 4025 |
| City Square | 3164 |
| City Streets | 1745 |
| Clamshell | 181 |
| Claws | 3134 |
| Clay's Choice | 1128 |
| Clay's Choice | 1347 |
| Clay's Compromise | 3182 |
| Clay's Favorite | 1128 |
| Clay's Star | 1128 |
| Cleopatra's Fan | 798.7 |
| Cleopatra's Puzzle | 1468 |
| Cleopatra's Puzzle | 1039 |
| Cleveland Lilies | 765.3 |
| Cleveland Tulip | 768.2 |
| Climbing Rose | 2584 |
| Clover Blossom, The | 1330 |
| Clown | 1820.5 |
| Clown | 940.3 |
| Clown's Choice | 1821 |
| Cluster of Lilies | 2058 |
| Cluster of Stars | 1710 |
| Cluster of Stars | 767 |
| Coarse Patchwork | 403 |
| Coarse Woven | 403 |
| Cobblestones | 2429 |
| Cobblestones | 3060 |
| Cobweb | 2729 |
| Cobweb | 2730 |
| Cobweb Quilt, A | 247 |
| Cock's Comb | 2303 |
| Cockcomb | 4053 |
| Cockleburr | 4073 |
| Coffee Cups | 941 |
| Coffin | 172 |
| Coffin Star | 2382 |
| Cog Block, The | 2141 |
| Cog Wheel | 3439 |
| Cog Wheel Quilt, The | 3455 |
| Cog Wheels | 3660 |
| Cogwheels | 3430 |
| College Chain | 3198 |
| Collinsville Rose Star | 269.5 |
| Colonial Basket | 622 |
| Colonial Basket | 672 |
| Colonial Basket | 762.5 |
| Colonial Block | 2573 |
| Colonial Bouquet | 160 |
| Colonial Bow Tie | 2533 |
| Colonial Flower Garden | 153 |
| Colonial Garden | 153 |
| Colonial Garden | 243 |
| Colonial Garden | 2449 |
| Colonial Garden Quilt | 445 |
| Colonial Pavement | 2557 |
| Colonial Pineapple | 2635 |
| Colorado | 3729 |
| Colorado Quilt, The | 1140 |
| Colorado's Arrowhead | 1677 |
| Colt's Corral | 1112 |
| Colt's Corral | 1620 |
| Columbia | 2745 |
| Columbia Puzzle | 1152 |
| Columbia Puzzle | 2197 |
| Columbia Star | 3708 |
| Columbia, The | 3708 |
| Columbian Puzzle | 2196 |
| Columbian Star | 1776 |
| Columbian Star | 3708 |
| Columbus | 1387 |
| Columns | 3735 |
| Combination Feathered Star | 3772 |
| Combination Square | 282.7 |
| Combination Star | 1641 |
| Comet Star | 236 |
| Comfort Quilt, The | 2031 |
| Compass | 301 |
| Compass | 3110 |
| Compass | 3524 |
| Compass | 3548 |
| Compass | 3847 |
| Compass | 3902 |
| Compass | 4075 |
| Compass Point | 1549 |
| Compass Star Quilt | 3657 |
| Compass and Chain | 1072 |
| Completed Square | 2897 |
| Compote Quilt | 762 |
| Concord | 2733 |
| Concorde Star | 225.5 |
| Cone Tree | 851 |
| Confederate Rose | 2651 |
| Connecticut | 1260 |
| Connecticut | 2123 |
| Connecticut Star | 3769 |
| Constellation | 1433 |
| Constellation | 1436 |
| Constellation | 3281 |
| Constellation | 1038.6 |
| Contemporary Butterfly | 924.7 |
| Continental, The | 1949 |
| Continuous Star | 441.8 |
| Contrary Husband | 2597 |
| Contrary Wife Quilt | 1687 |
| Conventional | 1027 |
| Conventional Rose | 2651 |
| Coral Court Friendship Star | 2140 |
| Corn and Beans | 1206 |
| Corn and Beans | 1859 |
| Corn and Beans | 2486 |
| Corn and Beans | 3162 |
| Corn and Beans | 4075 |
| Corner Posts | 3034 |
| Corner Star | 1952 |
| Corner Star, The | 2059 |
| Cornerstone, The | 4179 |
| Cornflower | 3591 |
| Cornucopia | 4051 |
| Coronation | 2169 |
| Coronation | 2691 |
| Coronation | 1043 |
| Coronation Block | 42185 |
| Cosmos | 274 |
| Cottage Tulips | 3848 |
| Cotton Boll Quilt, The | 4103 |
| Cotton Reels | 1326 |
| Counter Charm | 3923 |
| Counterpane | 2021 |
| Country Charm | 1113 |
| Country Checkers | 2426 |
| Country Church | 885 |
| Country Cousin | 1461 |
| Country Cross Roads | 2675 |
| Country Crossroads | 231 |
| Country Fair | 1035 |
| Country Farm | 418 |

# Index

| | | |
|---|---|---|
| Country Farm | 2831 | |
| Country Gardens | 1031 | |
| Country Husband | 1461 | |
| Country Lanes | 1829 | |
| Country Meeting House, The | 226.72 | |
| Country Roads | 1912 | |
| Country Tile | 160 | |
| Country Village | 880 | |
| County Fair | 2077 | |
| County Fair | 2481 | |
| County Farm | 2077 | |
| Court House Lawn | 2818 | |
| Courthouse Square | 2414 | |
| Courthouse Square | 881 | |
| Courtyard | 3432 | |
| Courtyard Square | 2605 | |
| Coverlet Quilt | 2098 | |
| Coverlet, The | 3262 | |
| Cowboy's Star | 2973 | |
| Cowboy's Star | 3912 | |
| Cowboy's Star | 3913 | |
| Cowboy's Star | 3921 | |
| Coxey's Army | 2035 | |
| Coxey's Camp | 2035 | |
| Crab Apple Block | 2552 | |
| Cracker | 2380 | |
| Cradle Quilt | 1066 | |
| Cranberry Patch | 412.5 | |
| Crayon Box, The | 3212 | |
| Crazy Ann | 1856 | |
| Crazy Ann | 2322 | |
| Crazy Ann | 2487 | |
| Crazy Ann | 3238 | |
| Crazy Flower Patch | 4137 | |
| Crazy House | 1931 | |
| Crazy Loon | 4164 | |
| Crazy Patch Star | 1063 | |
| Crazy Pieces | 2354 | |
| Crazy Quilt | 1461 | |
| Crazy Quilt | 2707 | |
| Carzy Quilt Bouquet | 4137 | |
| Crazy Quilt Star | 3873 | |
| Crazy Star | 2716 | |
| Crazy Star Quilt | 3873 | |
| Crazy Tile | 152 | |
| Creole Puzzle | 1679 | |
| Crimson Rambler | 2798 | |
| Criss Cross | 2316 | |
| Criss Cross | 2518 | |
| Criss Cross | 2884 | |
| Criss Cross | 2926 | |
| Criss Cross Patchwork | 1053 | |
| Criss CrossQuilt | 2023 | |
| Crockett Cabin Quilt | 1123 | |
| Crocodile | 940.1 | |
| Crocus | 786 | |
| Crooked Path | 1461 | |
| Cross | 2817 | |
| Cross Bar and Square | 1070.5 | |
| Cross Bars | 1184 | |
| Cross Patch | 1765 | |
| Cross Patch | 2813 | |
| Cross Patch | 2969 | |
| Cross Patch, The | 2414 | |
| Cross Plains | 1952 | |
| Cross Purposes | 3981 | |
| Cross Roads | 1148 | |
| Cross Roads | 1753 | |
| Cross Roads | 2883 | |
| Cross Roads | 2946 | |
| Cross Roads | 2947 | |
| Cross Roads | 3940 | |
| Cross Roads to Bachelor's Hall | 2946 | |
| Cross Roads to Jerico | 2385 | |
| Cross Roads to Texas | 2802 | |
| Cross Stitch | 2880 | |
| Cross, The | 949 | |
| Cross, The | 949.3 | |
| Cross Within A Cross | 1855 | |
| Cross and Chains | 1655 | |
| Cross and Crown | 949.7 | |
| Cross and Crown | 1382 | |
| Cross and Crown | 1863 | |
| Cross and Crown | 1864 | |
| Cross and Crown | 1871 | |
| Cross and Crown | 1891 | |
| Cross and Crown | 2069 | |
| Cross and Crown | 2802 | |
| Cross and Crown | 3234 | |
| Cross and Crown | 3261 | |
| Cross and Crown | 3805 | |
| Cross and Diamond Star | 2333 | |
| Cross and Square | 2160 | |
| Cross and Star | 1919 | |
| Cross in the Square | 1829 | |
| Cross of Geneva | 2953 | |
| Cross of Temperance | 2100 | |
| Cross Upon Cross | 2068 | |
| Cross Within A Cross | 2495 | |
| Crossed Canoes | 1251 | |
| Crossed Chains | 1379 | |
| Crossed Square | 1904 | |
| Crossed Squares | 2893 | |
| Crosses | 1230 | |
| Crosses and Losses | 1142 | |
| Crosses and Losses | 1313 | |
| Crosses and Losses | 1316 | |
| Crosses and Star | 1915 | |
| Crossroads | 1754 | |
| Crossroads | 1889 | |
| Crossroads America | 4025 | |
| Crossword Puzzle | 2281 | |
| Crossword Puzzle | 2285 | |
| Crosswords | 2282 | |
| Crow's Foot | 1262 | |
| Crow's Foot | 1358 | |
| Crow's Foot | 1889 | |
| Crow's Foot | 4184 | |
| Crow's Nest | 1647 | |
| Crow's Nest | 1674 | |
| Crow's Nest, The | 1850 | |
| Crowfoot, The | 1952 | |
| Crown | 2054 | |
| Crown and Thorns | 1806 | |
| Crown of Thorns | 1077 | |
| Crown of Thorns | 1088 | |
| Crown of Thorns | 1806 | |
| Crown of Thorns | 2048 | |
| Crown of Thorns | 2152 | |
| Crown of Thorns | 1077 | |
| Crown of Thorns | 1080 | |
| Crown of Thorns, A | 3654 | |
| Crowned Cross | 3261 | |
| Crystal Star | 2141 | |
| Cube Lattice | 4026 | |
| Cube Lattice | 1013 | |
| Cube Work | 3714 | |
| Cubes and Bars | 1942 | |
| Cubes and Tile | 4026 | |
| Cubes and Tile | 3799 | |
| Cubework | 142 | |
| Cubic Measure | 1543 | |
| Cumberland Gap | 416.9 | |
| Cup and Saucer, The | 941 | |
| Cupid's Arrowpoint | 1062 | |
| Cupid's Dart | 115 | |
| Cupid's Own | 2948 | |
| Cups and Saucers | 1663 | |
| Cut Glass Dish | 1703 | |
| Cypress | 2122 | |
| Cypress, The | 2121 | |
| D This Time, A | 981.7 | |
| D.A.R. Quilt, The | 4002 | |
| Daffodil | 777 | |
| Dahlia | 1542 | |
| Dahlia | 2522 | |
| Dainty Quilt, A | 3497 | |
| Daisy Block | 460 | |
| Daisy Chain | 275 | |
| Daisy Chain | 2652 | |
| Daisy Fan | 3322 | |
| Dakota Star | 2731 | |
| Dancing Bear | 939.2 | |
| Dancing Cubes | 281 | |
| Dancing Pinwheels | 4036 | |
| Dandelion Quilt | 2525 | |
| Dandy, A | 3124 | |
| Dandy Quilt Block, The | 1680 | |
| Danger Signal | 1277 | |
| Daniel Boone Quilt | 3994 | |
| Danish Stars | 3891 | |
| Darting Birds | 1738 | |
| Darting Minnows | 1059 | |
| Darts and Squares | 3069 | |
| David & Goliath | 1950 | |
| Day Lily Block | 765.21 | |
| Day Lily Garden | 4079 | |
| Day and Night | 1425 | |
| Delaware | 2012 | |
| Delaware Crosspatch | 2563 | |
| Delaware's Flagstones | 1001 | |
| Delectable Mountains | 1357 | |
| Delectable Mountains | 2401 | |
| Delectable Mountains | 3986 | |
| Delectable Mountains | 3987 | |
| Delectable Mountains | 3990 | |
| Denver | 2726 | |
| Democrat's Fancy | 1085 | |
| Depression | 132 | |
| Depression | 1204 | |
| Depression | 2608 | |
| Dervish Star | 3895 | |
| Des Moines | 2058 | |
| Desert Flower | 427.7 | |
| Desert Rose | 427.7 | |
| Desert Rose | 2204 | |
| Desert Rose | 729 | |
| Desert Rose | 730 | |
| Design for Light and Dark | 3805 | |
| Design for Patriotism, A | 2176 | |
| Designer's Choice | 176 | |
| Dessert Plate, The | 3452 | |
| Devil's Claws | 1952 | |
| Devil's Claws | 3220 | |
| Devil's Dark Horse | 1130 | |
| Devil's Footprints | 3635 | |
| Devil's Puzzle | 1130 | |
| Devil's Puzzle | 1183 | |
| Dewey Block | 3214 | |
| Dewey Dream Quilt | 1803 | |
| Dewey, The | 2473 | |
| Dewey's Victory | 2147 | |
| Diadem | 2405 | |
| Diadem Star | 3809 | |
| Diadem Star | 4007 | |
| Diagonal Path | 1834 | |
| Diagonal Square | 2278 | |
| Diagonal Stripes | 1459 | |
| Diamond | 3735 | |
| Diamond | 3924 | |
| Diamond Beauty Quilt | 416 | |
| Diamond Chain | 3910 | |
| Diamond Cross | 4212 | |
| Diamond Cube | 240 | |
| Diamond Design | 141 | |
| Diamond Design | 3735 | |
| Diamond Fan | 3317 | |
| Diamond Field, A | 3927 | |
| Diamond Field, The | 160 | |
| Diamond Friendship | 217 | |
| Diamond Head | 1552 | |
| Diamond Hexagon, The | 244.5 | |
| Diamond Knot | 4202 | |
| Diamond Nine Patch | 232.2 | |
| Diamond Nine Patch | 411.6 | |
| Diamond Panes | 1849 | |
| Diamond Plaid Block | 4187 | |
| Diamond Point | 2601 | |
| Diamond Quilt Pattern | 4020 | |
| Diamond Ring | 1939 | |
| Diamond Rows | 271.7 | |
| Diamond Solitaire | 3908 | |
| Diamond Star | 413 | |
| Diamond Star | 2507 | |
| Diamond Star | 2539 | |
| Diamond Star | 2975 | |
| Diamond Star | 3007 | |
| Diamond Star | 3751 | |
| Diamond Star | 3757 | |
| Diamond Star | 3863 | |
| Diamond Star | 4199 | |
| Diamond Star #2 | 3757 | |
| Diamond String | 266 | |
| Diamond Stripe | 1178 | |

# Index

| Name | Page |
|---|---|
| Diamond Stripe | 3227 |
| Diamond, The | 252 |
| Diamond Wedding Block | 3737 |
| Diamond and Star | 413 |
| Diamond and Star | 414 |
| Diamond in the Square | 2375 |
| Diamonds | 141 |
| Diamonds | 231 |
| Diamonds | 232 |
| Diamonds Galore | 1258 |
| Diamonds and Arrow Points | 256 |
| Diamonds and Shadows | 412.8 |
| Diamonds in the Corners | 3739 |
| Diana's Pride | 2252 |
| Dinah's Choice | 2855 |
| Dinah's Pride | 2252 |
| Dinner Plate | 3490 |
| Dirty Windows | 1454 |
| Disappearing Blocks | 142 |
| Dish of Fruit | 3186 |
| Disk, The | 725 |
| Diversion Quilt, The | 2595 |
| Divided Cross | 1166 |
| Divided Star, The | 3745 |
| Doe and Darts | 1950 |
| Does Double Duty | 3211 |
| Dog Quilt, The | 226.7 |
| Dog Tooth Violet | 2455 |
| Dog's Tooth | 112 |
| Dog's Tooth | 114 |
| Dogtooth Violet | 3044 |
| Dogwood | 793 |
| Dogwood | 3611 |
| Dogwood | 2972 |
| Dogwood | 4109 |
| Dogwood Bloom | 3572 |
| Dogwood Blossom | 2223 |
| Dogwood Blossoms | 1016 |
| Dolley Madison's Star | 1640 |
| Dolly Madison's Star | 251 |
| Dolly Madison's Star | 2241 |
| Dolly Madison's Workbox | 1519 |
| Dolly Madison's Workbox | 1520 |
| Dolly Madison's Workbox | 2685 |
| Domino | 3066 |
| Domino and Square | 2821 |
| Domino Chain | 1016 |
| Domino Net | 1370 |
| Domino and Square | 2891 |
| Domino and Squares | 2891 |
| Doors and Windows | 2428 |
| Doris's Delight | 1626 |
| Dottie's Choice | 2403 |
| Double Anchor | 2396 |
| Double Arrow, The | 2120 |
| Double Aster | 4206 |
| Double Ax | 185 |
| Double B, The | 1826 |
| Double Basket | 4135 |
| Double Bit Axe | 185 |
| Double Cross | 1318 |
| Double Cross | 2775 |
| Double Cross Quilt, The | 3068 |
| Double Fans | 3355 |
| Double Four Patch | 1143 |
| Double Four Patch | 1312 |
| Double Hour Glass | 1687 |
| Double Hour Glass | 1695 |
| Double Hour Glass | 1701 |
| Double Irish Chain | 2028 |
| Double Irish Chain | 2284 |
| Double Irish Chain | 1013 |
| Double Irish Chain | 1014 |
| Double Irish Chain | 1018 |
| Double Irish Chain | 1022 |
| Double Irish Chain | 1024 |
| Double Link | 4189 |
| Double Monkey Wrench | 1646 |
| Double Nine Patch | 1601 |
| Double Nine Patch | 1604 |
| Double Nine Patch | 1606 |
| Double Paeony | 770 |
| Double Peony | 765.23 |
| Double Pineapple, The | 2992 |
| Double Pinwheel | 1279 |
| Double Pinwheel | 2624 |
| Double Pinwheel Whirls | 1267 |
| Double Poppy | 3131 |
| Double Poppy | 3460 |
| Double Pyramid | 1702 |
| Double Pyramids | 1700 |
| Double R, The | 1826 |
| Double Rainbow | 3383 |
| Double Square | 2029 |
| Double Square | 4129 |
| Double Square, The | 1193 |
| Double Squares | 2472 |
| Double Star | 415.32 |
| Double Star | 1304.3 |
| Double Star | 2586 |
| Double Star | 3729 |
| Double Star | 3784 |
| Double Star | 3799 |
| Double Star | 3809 |
| Double Star | 3884 |
| Double Star | 4213 |
| Double Star | 1038 |
| Double Star Bed Quilt | 3809 |
| Double Star Flower | 3889 |
| Double T | 1392 |
| Double T | 1662 |
| Double T | 2901 |
| Double T | 3261 |
| Double Triangle | 2338 |
| Double Triangle | 3203 |
| Double Tulip | 1437 |
| Double Tulip | 766.2 |
| Double Tulip Bouquet | 770 |
| Double Tulip, The | 765.2 |
| Double Wedding Bands | 302 |
| Double Wedding Ring | 302 |
| Double Wedding Ring | 2686 |
| Double Windmill | 1293 |
| Double Windmill | 2600 |
| Double Windmill | 4204 |
| Double Wrench | 1850 |
| Double X | 1692 |
| Double X | 2128 |
| Double X | 2179 |
| Double X & 1 | 1689 |
| Double X & 2 | 1316 |
| Double X & 3 | 1315 |
| Double X's | 231 |
| Double Z | 3017 |
| Double Z | 3220 |
| Double Z | 3221 |
| Double Z | 3225 |
| Dove | 1459 |
| Dove, The | 1458 |
| Dove, The | 3767 |
| Dove at the Crossroads | 1889 |
| Dove at the Window | 1629 |
| Dove at the Window | 726.5 |
| Dove at the Windows | 2539 |
| Dove in the Window | 295 |
| Dove in the Window | 415.21 |
| Dove in the Window | 1880 |
| Dove in the Window | 1889 |
| Dove in the Window | 3766 |
| Dove in the Window | 3768 |
| Dove in the Window | 3828 |
| Dove in the Window | 4214 |
| Dove of Peace | 2407 |
| Dover | 2943 |
| Dover Quilt Block | 2943 |
| Doves | 3766 |
| Doves at the Window | 3767 |
| Doves in the Window | 1946 |
| Dragon Fly, The | 1251 |
| Dragon's Head | 1646 |
| Dragonfly | 2087 |
| Dramatic Patch | 3056 |
| Dream Ship | 916 |
| Dresden Basket | 653 |
| Dresden Fan | 3324 |
| Dresden Plate | 3411 |
| Dresden Plate | 3478 |
| Dresden Plate | 3488 |
| Dresden Plate | 3489.5 |
| Dresden Plate | 3628 |
| Dresden Plate | 3629 |
| Drucilla's Delight | 3916 |
| Drunkard Trail | 2228 |
| Drunkard's Patchwork | 2220 |
| Drunkard's Path | 1461 |
| Drunkard's Path | 3366 |
| Drunkard's Path | 1039 |
| Drunkard's Trail | 1461 |
| Drunkard's Trail | 3350 |
| Drunkard's Trail | 3351 |
| Drunkard's Trail | 1039 |
| Dublin Steps | 1698 |
| Duck Creek Puzzle | 2566 |
| Duck Paddle | 1889 |
| Duck and Ducklings | 1859 |
| Duck and Ducklings | 1860 |
| Duck and Ducklings | 2439 |
| Duck's Foot in the Mud | 1879 |
| Ducklings | 1859 |
| Ducks Foot in the Mud | 1945 |
| Ducks and Ducklings | 1206 |
| Ducks and Ducklings | 1859 |
| Duke's Dilemma | 2676 |
| Dumbell Block | 1429 |
| Dumbell Block | 2935 |
| Dusty Miller | 3078 |
| Dutch Boat | 918 |
| Dutch Mill | 887 |
| Dutch Mill | 1001 |
| Dutch Mill | 2966 |
| Dutch Nine Patch | 1604 |
| Dutch Puzzle | 2192 |
| Dutch Rose | 1500 |
| Dutch Rose | 3807 |
| Dutch Rose | 3812 |
| Dutch Tile | 255 |
| Dutch Tile | 268 |
| Dutch Tile | 2375 |
| Dutch Tulips | 3108 |
| Dutch Tulips | 3636 |
| Dutch Windmills | 1269 |
| Dutch Windmills | 1500 |
| Dutchman's Breeches | 3506 |
| Dutchman's Puzzle | 1319 |
| Dutchman's Puzzle | 1339 |
| Dutchman's Puzzle | 3506 |
| Dynametry | 2591 |
| E-Z Quilt, The | 1895 |
| Early Peony | 768.1 |
| East and West | 2978 |
| East to Eden | 1752 |
| Easter Lilly Quilt | 457.9 |
| Eastern Star | 263.5 |
| Eastern Star | 1631 |
| Eastern Star | 3735 |
| Eastern Star | 3772 |
| Eastern Star | 4001 |
| Eastertide Quilt | 1922 |
| Easy Quilt | 1601 |
| Easy Ways | 2201 |
| Eccentric Star | 1683 |
| Eccentric Star | 2597 |
| Eccentric Star | 2603 |
| Eccentric Star | 3807 |
| Ecclesiastical | 152 |
| Economy | 1873 |
| Economy | 2443 |
| Economy Jumble | 189 |
| Economy Nine Patch | 1714 |
| Economy Patch | 2376 |
| Economy Star | 2240 |
| Eddystone Light | 2073 |
| Effective Square, An | 2902 |
| Eight Diamonds and a Star | 2504 |
| Eight Hands Around | 2168 |
| Eight Hands Around | 2934 |
| Eight Hands Around | 3106 |
| Eight Points All Over | 1171 |
| Eight Point Design | 1631 |
| Eight Point Snowflake, The | 445 |
| Eight Point Star | 1631 |
| Eight Point Star | 3735 |
| Eight Pointed Broken Star | 3810 |
| Eight Pointed Star | 1237 |
| Eight Pointed star | 2141 |

534

# Index

| Name | Number |
|---|---|
| Eight Pointed Star | 2901 |
| Eight Pointed Star | 3415 |
| Eight Pointed Star | 3735 |
| Eight Pointed Star, The | 1624 |
| Eight Points in a Square | 3413 |
| Eight-Pointed Star | 1059.5 |
| Eisenhower Quilt | 142 |
| Electric Fan | 2703 |
| Electric Fans | 1513 |
| Elephant | 938.6 |
| Elephant foot | 36664 |
| Elgin Maid | 3575 |
| Eliza's Star | 2833 |
| Ella's Star | 2492 |
| Elsie's Favorite | 2687 |
| Emerald Block | 1243 |
| Emmond's Floor | 421 |
| Empire Star | 3222 |
| Empress | 3341 |
| Empty Spool | 2594 |
| Empty Spools | 3609 |
| End of the Century Patch Work | 2211 |
| End of the Day | 1287 |
| Endless Chain | 160 |
| Endless Chain | 272 |
| Endless Chain | 434 |
| Endless Chain | 1532 |
| Endless Chain | 2716 |
| Endless Chain | 3076 |
| Endless Chain | 3079 |
| Endless Chain, The | 302 |
| Endless Squares | 2888 |
| Endless Stair | 1110 |
| Endless Trail | 1461 |
| English Ivy | 1330 |
| English Wedding Ring | 1806 |
| Enigma | 3882 |
| Enigma Star | 2079 |
| Envelope Motif, An | 1176 |
| Envelope Quilt | 1195 |
| Envelope Quilt, The | 220 |
| Eternal Triangle | 1355 |
| Etoile de Chamblie | 2244 |
| Eureka | 416.8 |
| Eva's Delight | 2790 |
| Evening Flower | 788.5 |
| Evening Star | 296.9 |
| Evening Star | 2138 |
| Evening Star | 2736 |
| Evening Star | 3585 |
| Evening Star | 3997 |
| Evening Star, The | 3951 |
| Evening Starr | 296.7 |
| Everglades | 1521 |
| Evergreen | 2670 |
| Evergreen Tree | 815.5 |
| Evergreen Tree | 815.8 |
| Everybody's Favorite | 2112 |
| Exea's Star | 2492 |
| Expanding Star | 4008 |
| Exploding Star, The | 2332 |
| Exploding Stars | 2612 |
| Explosion, The | 3400 |
| Ezekial's Wheel | 3683 |
| F Block | 3180 |
| F Patchwork | 2395 |
| Fair Play | 3260 |
| Fair and Square | 2034 |
| Fair and Square | 2189 |
| Fairy Star | 3057 |
| Fairy Tale | 2549 |
| Faithful Circle | 431 |
| Fala | 938.2 |
| Falling Star | 3758 |
| Falling Timbers | 1459 |
| Falling Timbers | 1465 |
| Fan | 3320 |
| Fan | 3331 |
| Fan Crazy Quilt | 3354 |
| Fan Mill | 1262 |
| Fan Patchwork | 3307 |
| Fan Quadrille | 3303 |
| Fan Quadrille | 3364 |
| Fan Quilt | 3306 |
| Fan and Ring | 1797 |
| Fan of Friendship | 3304 |
| Fan of Many Colors | 3307 |
| Fancy Fan | 3317 |
| Fancy Fan | 3333 |
| Fancy Fan, The | 3318 |
| Fancy Flowers | 1889 |
| Fanfare | 3006 |
| Fanny's Fan | 454.3 |
| Fanny's Fan | 1892 |
| Fanny's Favorite | 1939 |
| Fanny's Favorite | 1085 |
| Fans and a Ring | 1797 |
| Fantastic Patchwork | 432 |
| Far West | 1650 |
| Far West | 1974 |
| Farm Friendliness | 1682 |
| Farmer's Daughter | 3034 |
| Farmer's Fields | 3073 |
| Farmer's Puzzle | 1905 |
| Farmer's Wife | 4088 |
| Farmer's Wife | 4172 |
| Father's Choice | 1802 |
| Favorite | 256 |
| Favorite of the Peruvians | 1130 |
| Favorite of the Peruvians | 2577 |
| Feather Bone Block | 1292 |
| Feather Edge Star | 2247 |
| Feather Edge Star | 2260 |
| Feather Star | 2244 |
| Feather Star | 2249 |
| Feather Star | 2251 |
| Feather Star | 1065.7 |
| Feather Star-Blazing Sun Centers | 2271 |
| Feathered Star | 2259 |
| Feathered Star | 2260 |
| Feathered Star | 3389 |
| Feathered Star | 3605 |
| Feathered Star, The | 2254 |
| Feathered Star of Bethlehem | 2244 |
| Feathered Stars | 459.13 |
| Feathered Variable Star | 2257 |
| Featheredge Stripe | 135 |
| Federal Chain | 1015 |
| Federal Square | 2793 |
| Fence Posts | 1111 |
| Fence Rail | 135 |
| Fence Row | 1645 |
| Fence Row Quilt | 114 |
| Fence Row Star | 3749 |
| Ferris Wheel | 3435 |
| Ferris Wheel | 3555 |
| Field and Stream | 1073.5 |
| Field of Daisies | 796 |
| Fields and Fences | 1965 |
| Fifty-Four Forty or Fight | 1627 |
| Fifty-Four Forty or Fight | 1645 |
| Fig Leaf | 1440 |
| Fine Woven Patchwork | 135 |
| Fire Lily | 765.4 |
| Fire Lily, The | 765.25 |
| Fireball | 1507 |
| Firecrackers and Rockets | 3122 |
| Fireflies | 1316 |
| Fireside Visitor | 1677 |
| Fish | 226.75 |
| Fish | 3828 |
| Fish Block | 3828 |
| Fish Circle | 3828 |
| Fish Tails | 3784 |
| Fisherman's Reel | 1646 |
| Fishing Boats | 913 |
| Fishscale | 181 |
| Five Cross | 433 |
| Five Cross | 4106 |
| Five Crosses | 2812 |
| Five Crosses | 4106 |
| Five Diamonds | 3236 |
| Five Lilies | 2202 |
| Five Patch | 1223 |
| Five Patch | 1611 |
| Five Patch Beauty | 261 |
| Five Patch | 1802 |
| Five Pointed Star | 3675 |
| Five Spot | 1653 |
| Five Square | 2781 |
| Five Stripes | 1112 |
| Five-Point Star | 3676 |
| Flag In, Flag Out | 1723 |
| Flags | 478 |
| Flags and Ships | 226.8 |
| Flagstones | 1001 |
| Flaming Star | 2133 |
| Flaming Sun | 3540 |
| Flamingo's Flight | 1365 |
| Flashing Star, The | 4112 |
| Flashing Windmills | 1264 |
| Flat Iron | 204 |
| Flat Iron Patchwork | 201.7 |
| Flat Iron Patchwork | 3186 |
| Fleur de Lis | 789 |
| Flight of Swallows | 1322 |
| Flight of Wild Geese | 3845 |
| Flo's Fan | 3315 |
| Flo's Fan | 3319 |
| Flo's Fan | 3321 |
| Floating Clouds | 249 |
| Floating Star | 3250 |
| Flock of Birds | 2340 |
| Flock of Geese | 1321 |
| Flock fo Geese | 1322 |
| Flock of Geeses | 3161 |
| Flora's Favorite | 2353 |
| Floral Bouquet | 777.6 |
| Floral Centerpiece | 751 |
| Floral Elegance | 2761 |
| Floral Patchwork | 799 |
| Florentine Diamond | 3907 |
| Florida | 266 |
| Florida Forest | 855 |
| Florida Star | 269 |
| Flower Basket | 658.2 |
| Flower Basket | 662 |
| Flower Basket | 663 |
| Flower Basket | 664 |
| Flower Basket | 665.4 |
| Flower Basket | 671 |
| Flower Basket | 674.8 |
| Flower Basket | 675 |
| Flower Basket | 678 |
| Flower Basket | 704 |
| Flower Basket | 710 |
| Flower Basket | 725 |
| Flower Basket | 728 |
| Flower Basket | 749.8 |
| Flower Bed | 3058 |
| Flower Bed | 3063 |
| Flower Fields | 4025 |
| Flower Garden | 160 |
| Flower Garden Block | 252 |
| Flower Garden Path | 1158 |
| Flower Petals | 1527 |
| Flower Pot | 151 |
| Flower Pot | 709 |
| Flower Pot | 713 |
| Flower Pot | 725 |
| Flower Pot | 730 |
| Flower Pot | 732 |
| Flower Pot | 733 |
| Flower Pot | 2127 |
| Flower Pot Quilt, The | 752.5 |
| Flower Ring, The | 459.2 |
| Flower Star | 276 |
| Flower Vase | 745 |
| Flower of Autumn | 3359 |
| Flower of Christmas | 4043 |
| Flower of Friendship | 779 |
| Flower of Spring | 3132 |
| Flower of Spring | 799 |
| Flower of the Woods | 779.2 |
| Flower of the Woods | 3337 |
| Flowering Cross | 1165 |
| Flowering Nine Patch | 3021 |
| Flowering Snowball | 3081 |
| Flowering Star | 4061 |
| Flowers in a Basket | 737 |
| Flowing Ribbon, The | 220.6 |
| Fluffy Patches | 457.3 |
| Flutter Wheel | 1708 |
| FlutterBye | 1381 |

# Index

| Entry | Page |
|---|---|
| Fluttering Butterfly | 924.5 |
| Fly | 1262 |
| Fly Away | 4174 |
| Fly Away Feathers | 1894 |
| Fly Foot | 1183 |
| Fly Wheel | 3390 |
| Flyfoot | 1130 |
| Flyfoot | 1027.5 |
| Flying Barn Swallows | 3758 |
| Flying Bat | 3766 |
| Flying Bats | 411.5 |
| Flying Bats | 2601 |
| Flying Birds | 1322 |
| Flying Birds | 1700 |
| Flying Birds | 3034 |
| Flying Birds | 3161 |
| Flying Cloud | 2149 |
| Flying Crow | 1631 |
| Flying Darts | 1950 |
| Flying Dutchman | 1352 |
| Flying Dutchman | 2584 |
| Flying Fish | 1231 |
| Flying Fish | 3828 |
| Flying Geese | 1373 |
| Flying Geese | 1967 |
| Flying geese | 2902 |
| Flying Geese | 3161 |
| Flying Geese & LeMoyne Stars | 1066 |
| Flying Goose | 3160 |
| Flying Kite | 1294 |
| Flying Leaves | 1757 |
| Flying Saucer | 1300 |
| Flying Shuttles | 1699 |
| Flying Squares | 2581 |
| Flying Star | 3758 |
| Flying Star | 3766 |
| Flying Star | 3957 |
| Flying Swallow | 3758 |
| Flying Swallows | 3107 |
| Flying Swallows | 3758 |
| Flying Swallows | 4009 |
| Flying X | 1127 |
| Flying X | 1675 |
| Flying X | 1959 |
| Folded Stars | 3586 |
| Follow the Leader | 1856 |
| Fool's Puzzle | 1466 |
| Fool's Puzzle | 3224 |
| Fool's Square | 2129 |
| Fool's Square | 3231.5 |
| Foot Bridge | 3228 |
| Foot Prints in the Sands-Time | 1695 |
| Foot Stool | 1820 |
| Forbidden Fruit Tree | 846 |
| Ford's Quilt | 141 |
| Forest Path | 1354 |
| Forest Path | 2584 |
| Forest Paths | 2036 |
| Forest for the Trees, The | 835 |
| Forget Me Not | 4145 |
| Forgotten Star | 2977 |
| Forgotten Star | 2985 |
| Forks | 3125 |
| Formal Garden | 2598 |
| Formosa Fan | 3306 |
| Formosa Tea Leaf | 3765 |
| Fort Sumter | 2461 |
| Fortune's Wheel | 3577 |
| Forty-second Street | 223 |
| Foundation Rose | 1541 |
| Foundation Rose | 3421 |
| Four Baskets | 652 |
| Four Birds | 1880 |
| Four Birds | 3768 |
| Four Block Star | 1245 |
| Four Buds | 1151 |
| Four Buds Quilt | 3096 |
| Four Clowns | 1870 |
| Four Corner Puzzle, A | 1212 |
| Four Corners | 1637 |
| Four Corners, The | 4191 |
| Four Cross | 3265 |
| Four Crowns | 2056 |
| Four Darts | 1950 |
| Four Doves | 3767 |
| Four E Block | 1404 |
| Four H | 1402 |
| Four H Club Quilt | 2780 |
| Four Knaves | 1197 |
| Four Leaf Clover | 306 |
| Four Leaf Clover | 2764 |
| Four Leaf Clover | 3897 |
| Four Leaf Clover | 4082 |
| Four Leaf Clover | 4083 |
| Four Leaf Clover | 1006 |
| Four Leaf Clover, The | 2759 |
| Four Leaf Clover, The | 3061 |
| Four Little Baskets | 652 |
| Four Little Birds | 934.4 |
| Four Little Fans | 4068 |
| Four Mills | 2543 |
| Four O'Clock Quilt | 3547 |
| Four Part Strip Block | 1111 |
| Four Patch | 1101 |
| Four Patch | 1103 |
| Four Patch | 1106 |
| Four Patch | 2276 |
| Four Patch Fox and Geese, The | 1176 |
| Four Petals | 2715 |
| Four Point | 2423 |
| Four Point | 2672 |
| Four Pointed Star | 1237 |
| Four Pointed Star | 3899 |
| Four Pointer Quilt, The | 3607 |
| Four Points | 1246 |
| Four Points | 2423 |
| Four Queens | 3119 |
| Four Square | 2589 |
| Four Square | 4104 |
| Four Squares | 2457 |
| Four Squares | 2611 |
| Four Squares | 2857 |
| Four Squares | 1025 |
| Four Star Block | 3876 |
| Four Star Square | 1062.3 |
| Four Stars Patchwork | 3736 |
| Four Stars, The | 3736 |
| Four Swallows | 3768 |
| Four T Square | 1662 |
| Four T's | 2650 |
| Four Triangles | 2498 |
| Four Tulips | 3114 |
| Four Vases | 3127 |
| Four Windmills | 238 |
| Four Winds | 1308 |
| Four Winds | 3903 |
| Four Winds, The | 3092 |
| Four X Star | 1802 |
| Four Z Patch | 1405 |
| Four and Nine Patch | 1001 |
| Four-X Quilt, The | 1632 |
| Four-four Time | 2421 |
| Fox | 940.15 |
| Fox and Geese | 2132 |
| Fox Chase | 1516 |
| Fox and Geese | 1313 |
| Fox and Geese | 1316 |
| Fox and Geese | 1859 |
| Fox and Geese | 3022 |
| Fox and geese | 3574 |
| Fox and geese | 1075.2 |
| Framed Cross | 4111 |
| Framed Squares | 2183 |
| Framed X | 3220 |
| Fredonia Cross | 2003 |
| Free Trade | 1137 |
| Free Trade Block | 2169 |
| Free Trade Patch | 2169 |
| French 4's | 1850 |
| French Bouquet | 160 |
| French Log Cabin | 3241 |
| French Rose Garden | 160 |
| French Star | 3540 |
| French Star | 3659 |
| Friday the Thirteenth | 2383 |
| Friendly Hand | 1142 |
| Friendship | 1187 |
| Friendship | 2674 |
| Friendship Album Quilt | 2375 |
| Friendship Basket | 749 |
| Friendship Block | 3230 |
| Friendship Bouquet | 4136 |
| Friendship Chain | 185 |
| Friendship Chain | 2813 |
| Friendship Chain | 4170 |
| Friendship Circle | 3086.5 |
| Friendship Circle | 3600 |
| Friendship Circle | 3629 |
| Friendship Daisy | 3543 |
| Friendship Fan | 3346 |
| Friendship Fan | 3347 |
| Friendship Garden | 3597 |
| Friendship Hexagon | 251 |
| Friendship Knot | 4045 |
| Friendship Knot | 4046 |
| Friendship Knot | 4047 |
| Friendship Links | 4189 |
| Friendship Medley Quilt | 3092 |
| Friendship Name Chain, The | 3254 |
| Friendship Quilt | 160 |
| Friendship Quilt | 185 |
| Friendship Quilt | 1503 |
| Friendship Quilt | 1648 |
| Friendship Quilt | 1662 |
| Friendship Quilt | 2812 |
| Friendship Quilt | 2895 |
| Friendship Quilt | 3471 |
| Friendship Quilt | 4182 |
| Friendship Quilt | 4189 |
| Friendship Quilt, A | 2673 |
| Friendship Quilt, The | 2410 |
| Friendship Ring | 2550 |
| Friendship Ring | 3471 |
| Friendship Ring | 3488 |
| Friendship Ring | 3640 |
| Friendship Ring | 3652 |
| Friendship Star | 1989 |
| Friendship Star | 2833 |
| Friendship Star | 3588 |
| Friendship Star | 4038 |
| Friendship Wreath | 4047 |
| Friendship's Chain | 2484 |
| Friendship Flowers | 779.1 |
| Fringed Aster | 3335 |
| Fringed Square | 2539 |
| Fruit Basket | 650.3 |
| Fruit Basket | 668 |
| Fruit Basket | 674.9 |
| Fruit Basket | 707 |
| Fruit Basket | 708 |
| Fruit Basket | 712.5 |
| Fruit Basket | 714 |
| Fruit Basket | 722 |
| Fruit Basket, The | 720 |
| Full Blown Rose | 3527 |
| Full Blown Tulip | 2343 |
| Full Blown Tulip | 2973 |
| Full Blown Tulip | 3640 |
| Full Blown Tulip | 3641 |
| Full Blown Tulip | 3653 |
| Full Moon, The | 3511 |
| Fundamental Nine Patch | 1606 |
| Galahad's Shield | 2517 |
| Galaxy | 4025 |
| Game Cocks | 1822 |
| Garden Basket | 727 |
| Garden Basket, The | 686 |
| Garden Beauty | 3128 |
| Garden Bloom | 3113 |
| Garden Maze | 1054 |
| Garden Maze | 3030 |
| Garden Maze | 1054 |
| Garden Patch | 1627 |
| Garden Patch, The | 2815 |
| Garden Path | 484 |
| Garden Path | 2200 |
| Garden Paths | 2890 |
| Garden Spot | 3440 |
| Garden Treasure | 800.1 |
| Garden Tulip | 796.7 |
| Garden Walk | 160 |
| Garden Walk | 1627 |
| Garden of Eden | 1873 |
| Garden of Eden | 1932 |
| Garden of Eden | 3229 |

# Index

| Name | Ref |
|---|---|
| Garden of Friendship | 758 |
| Gardener's Prize, The | 3437 |
| Garfield's Monument | 888 |
| Garret Windows | 1190 |
| Gate, The | 2384 |
| Gay Cosmos Quilt | 274 |
| Gay Pinwheel, The | 1262 |
| Gay Scrap Quilt | 1312 |
| Gay Two Patch Quilt | 2181 |
| Geese in Flight | 480 |
| Geese in Flight | 4127 |
| Gem Block | 2471 |
| Gem Block, The | 3946 |
| General Sherman's Quilt | 132 |
| Gentleman's Fancy | 1815 |
| Gentleman's Fancy | 2838 |
| Geometric | 3166 |
| Geometric Block | 2025 |
| Geometric Garden | 1815 |
| Geometric Patchwork | 1692 |
| Geometric Star | 2978 |
| Geometrical Star | 3875 |
| George Washington Cherry Tree | 850 |
| George Washington Quilt | 3484 |
| Georgetown | 3443 |
| Georgetown Circle | 1806 |
| Georgetown Circle | 2048 |
| Georgetown Circle | 3433 |
| Georgetown Circle | 3443 |
| Georgetown Puzzle | 2048 |
| Georgia | 1957.5 |
| Ghost Walk | 1468 |
| Ghost's Walk | 1039 |
| Giant Amethyst | 3998 |
| Giant Dahlia Quilt, The | 4015 |
| Giddap | 226.77 |
| Gig Prong | 3468 |
| Gingham Dog | 938.2 |
| Giraffe | 938.8 |
| Girl's Joy | 2191 |
| Gleaming Sun | 3540 |
| Glistening Star | 241.2 |
| Glitter Star | 3778 |
| Glittering Star | 3738 |
| Glorified Nine Patch | 1611 |
| Glorified Nine Patch | 2689 |
| Glory Block | 285 |
| Glory Design | 285 |
| Glory Vine | 4193 |
| Glove Design | 3942 |
| Goblet | 943 |
| Going Around The Mountain | 3979 |
| Going to Chicago | 1312 |
| Gold Brick | 3232 |
| Gold Fish | 3828 |
| Gold Nuggets | 2594 |
| Gold and Silver | 3746 |
| Golda, Gem Star | 2741 |
| Golden Chains | 1239 |
| Golden Circle Star | 441 |
| Golden Cubes | 142 |
| Golden Dahlia | 4007 |
| Golden Gate | 1838 |
| Golden Gates | 293 |
| Golden Gates | 1703 |
| Golden Glow | 1840 |
| Golden Glow | 3423 |
| Golden Glow | 3426 |
| Golden Splendor | 2270 |
| Golden Stairs | 1227 |
| Golden Stairs | 1695 |
| Golden Stairs | 3245 |
| Golden Steps | 1606 |
| Golden Wedding Quilt | 1259 |
| Golden Wedding Ring | 313 |
| Golgotha | 2068 |
| Good Cheer | 1983 |
| Good Luck | 2321 |
| Good Luck | 3157 |
| Good Luck Block | 1006 |
| Good Luck Token | 1286 |
| Goose Creek | 1002 |
| Goose Track, The | 3270 |
| Goose Tracks | 1863 |
| Goose Tracks | 1889 |
| Goose in the Pond | 1815 |
| Goose in the Pond | 2911 |
| Gorgeous Chrysthanthemum Quilt | 4012 |
| Goshen Star | 1852 |
| Gothic Pattern | 1167 |
| Grand Right & Left | 1270 |
| Grandma's Brooch | 3756 |
| Grandma's Choice | 1862 |
| Grandma's Dream | 2286 |
| Grandma's Fan | 4096 |
| Grandma's Favorite | 1862 |
| Grandma's Favorite | 3349 |
| Grandma's Favorite Compass | 3661 |
| Grandma's Hop Scotch Quilt | 3183 |
| Grandma's Hop-Scotch | 2607 |
| Grandma's Square | 2286 |
| Grandma's Star | 1627 |
| Grandma's Tulips | 3503 |
| Grandmother Percy's Puzzle | 4122 |
| Grandmother Short's Quilt | 1001 |
| Grandmother's Basket | 654 |
| Grandmother's Basket | 660 |
| Grandmother's Basket | 662 |
| Grandmother's Brooch of Love | 2944 |
| Grandmother's Choice | 1817 |
| Grandmother's Choice | 1855 |
| Grandmother's Cross | 2610 |
| Grandmother's Cross | 2789 |
| Grandmother's Dream | 1733 |
| Grandmother's Dream | 4107 |
| Grandmother's Dream | 766.1 |
| Grandmother's Engagement Ring | 2529 |
| Grandmother's Engagement Ring | 2680 |
| Grandmother's Engagement Ring | 1087 |
| Grandmother's Fan | 3305 |
| Grandmother's Fan | 3306 |
| Grandmother's Fan | 3307 |
| Grandmother's Fan | 3310 |
| Grandmother's Fan | 3323 |
| Grandmother's Fan | 3325 |
| Grandmother's Fan | 3330 |
| Grandmother's Favorite | 2126 |
| Grandmother's Favorite | 797 |
| Grandmother's Flower Basket | 271.5 |
| Grandmother's Flower Garden | 160 |
| Grandmother's Flower Garden | 425.2 |
| Grandmother's Flower Garden | 425.4 |
| Grandmother's Irish Chain | 1014.2 |
| Grandmother's Own | 4104 |
| Grandmother's Pinwheel | 1356 |
| Grandmother's Pride | 2413 |
| Grandmother's Pride | 3341 |
| Grandmother's Prize | 2367 |
| Grandmother's Puzzle | 4122 |
| Grandmother's Quilt | 2157 |
| Grandmother's Quilt | 3638 |
| Grandmother's Rose Garden | 160 |
| Grandmother's Star | 4101 |
| Grandmother's Sunbonnet | 3488 |
| Grandmother's Sunburst | 3488 |
| Grandmother's Tulip | 3504 |
| Granny's Choice | 2309 |
| Granny's Favorite | 3039 |
| Grape Basket | 712 |
| Grape Vines | 2460 |
| Gray Goose | 3220 |
| Great Circle Quilt, The | 2995 |
| Great Circle Quilt, The | 734 |
| Great Divide, The | 1083 |
| Grecian | 1646 |
| Grecian Cross | 3084 |
| Grecian Designs | 1646 |
| Grecian Square | 1646 |
| Grecian Square | 2777 |
| Grecian Star | 3643 |
| Grecian Star | 3652 |
| Greek Cross | 1646 |
| Greek Cross | 1802 |
| Greek Cross | 1851 |
| Greek Cross | 19326 |
| Greek Cross | 2969 |
| Greek Cross | 3231 |
| Greek Square | 1646 |
| Green Cross | 3508 |
| Green Mountain Star | 3833 |
| Greenberg Wedding Quilt | 1032 |
| Gretchen | 1292 |
| Grist Mill | 1525 |
| Grist Mill | 2666 |
| Guam | 4029 |
| Guide Post | 231 |
| Guiding Star | 1781 |
| Guiding Star | 3922 |
| Guthrie | 2844 |
| Gypsy Trail | 3353 |
| H Quilt | 2384 |
| H Square Quilt, The | 1175 |
| Hail Stone | 1196 |
| Hail Storm | 1196 |
| Hairpin Catcher | 131 |
| Hairpin Catcher | 2276 |
| Half Moon Block | 4063 |
| Halley's Comet | 2263 |
| Hand | 1831 |
| Hand Weave | 1746 |
| Hand of Friendship | 1879 |
| Handcraft | 1746 |
| Hands | 235 |
| Hands All Around | 3652 |
| Hands All 'Round | 4044 |
| Handweave | 1745 |
| Handwoven | 1746 |
| Handy Andy | 1206 |
| Handy Andy | 1820 |
| Handy Andy | 1859 |
| Handy Andy | 1878 |
| Handy Andy | 2839 |
| Hanging Basket | 668.5 |
| Hanging Basket | 719 |
| Hanging Diamonds | 3735 |
| Happy Hunting Ground | 3024 |
| Happy Memories | 1843 |
| Hard Times Block | 2805 |
| Hard Times Block | 3052 |
| Harlequin Star | 2988 |
| Harmony Square | 1854 |
| Harrisburg | 3887 |
| Harrison Quilt, The | 1700 |
| Harrison Rose | 1700 |
| Harry's Star | 1128 |
| Hartford | 4168 |
| Harvest Home | 4167 |
| Harvest Star | 3781 |
| Harvest Sun | 3344 |
| Harvest Sun | 3660 |
| Harvest Sun | 3773 |
| Hattie's Choice | 2753 |
| Hattie's Sunflower | 773.7 |
| Hawaii | 2747 |
| Hawks in Flight | 216.22 |
| Hayes Corner | 1377 |
| Hazel Valley Cross Roads | 2945 |
| Hazy Daisy | 1213 |
| Heart Quilt | 1547 |
| Heart of the Home, The | 950 |
| Heart's Seal | 1130 |
| Heart's Seal | 2577 |
| Hearth and Home Quilt | 3230 |
| Hearts & Flowers | 1500 |
| Hearts & Gizzards | 1500 |
| Hearts and Darts | 2215 |
| Hearts and Diamonds | 307 |
| Hearts and Gizzards | 1503 |
| Hearts and Rings | 2632 |
| Heather Square | 2924 |
| Heaven Puzzle | 1916 |
| Heavenly Stars | 3801 |
| Heavenly Steps | 281 |
| Hedgework | 1371 |
| Heirloom Pillow | 192 |
| Heirloom Quilt, An | 2956 |
| Helena | 3753 |
| Hen and Chickens | 1206 |
| Hen and Chickens | 1859 |
| Hen and Chicks | 1206 |
| Hen and Her Chicks, The | 2096 |

537

# Index

| Entry | Number |
|---|---|
| Henry of the West | 1128 |
| Henry of the West | 1631 |
| Hens and Chickens | 1882 |
| Herald Square | 2365 |
| Here's Your O | 987.5 |
| Heritage Quilt | 141 |
| Heritage Quilt | 410 |
| Hero's Crown | 4071 |
| Herringbone | 147 |
| Herringbone | 479 |
| Hex Stars, The | 3450 |
| Hexagon | 160 |
| Hexagon | 246 |
| Hexagon Beauty | 246 |
| Hexagon Beauty Quilt | 292 |
| Hexagon Patchwork | 160 |
| Hexagon Snowflake | 241.6 |
| Hexagon Star, The | 263 |
| Hexagon Stars | 251 |
| Hexagon, The | 160 |
| Hexagonal | 142 |
| Hexagonal | 3701 |
| Hexagonal Star | 142 |
| Hexagonal Star | 251 |
| Hexagons | 153 |
| Hexagons | 160 |
| Hexagons | 425 |
| Hexagons and Flowers | 274.5 |
| Hick's Basket | 733 |
| Hickory Leaf | 3110 |
| Hidden Flower | 2361 |
| Hidden Star | 260 |
| Hide and Seek | 1290 |
| Hill and Crag | 2869 |
| Hill and Hollow | 1276 |
| Hill and Valley | 216.11 |
| Hill and Valley | 216.12 |
| Hippopatamus | 939.6 |
| Historic Oak Leaf, The | 857.093 |
| Hit and Miss | 131 |
| Hit and Miss Variation | 146 |
| Hit or Miss | 160 |
| Hit or Miss | 2276 |
| Hither & Yon | 2131 |
| Hobson's Kiss | 2194 |
| Hole in the Barn Door | 1850 |
| Hole in the Barn Door | 2119 |
| Hole-in-the-Barn-Door | 1646 |
| Holland Mill | 2965 |
| Home Again | 3896 |
| Home Art Rainbow Tile | 160 |
| Home Circle Quilt | 1931 |
| Home Maker | 2665 |
| Home Treasure | 2160 |
| Home Treasure | 2927 |
| Homecoming | 4091 |
| Homespun | 1758 |
| Homespun | 2098 |
| Homespun Block | 4161 |
| Homeward Bound | 1310 |
| Honey Bee | 2217 |
| Honeybees in the Garden | 2625 |
| Honeycomb | 160 |
| Honeycomb | 174 |
| Honeycomb | 1417 |
| Honeycomb Patch, A | 160 |
| Honeycomb Patchwork | 171 |
| Honeymoon Cottage | 874 |
| Honolulu | 2516 |
| Hoosier Circles | 3479 |
| Hope of Hartford | 2586 |
| Hopes and Wishes | 2861 |
| Hopscotch | 1133 |
| Hopscotch | 1410 |
| Hosannah | 1304 |
| Hour Glass | 1195 |
| Hour Glass | 1700 |
| Hour Glass | 1705 |
| Hour Glass | 2124 |
| Hour Glass | 2376 |
| Hour Glass | 3239 |
| Hour Glass | 3258 |
| Hour Glass | 3663 |
| Hour Glass | 4081 |
| Hour Glass | 4215 |
| Hour Glass #2 | 1685 |
| Hour Glass, The | 2242 |
| Hour Glasses | 4141 |
| House | 861 |
| House | 863 |
| House Jack Built | 870.2 |
| House Jack Built, The | 2778 |
| House on the Hill | 862 |
| Houses Repeated | 865.5 |
| Housewife's Dream | 4150 |
| Hovering Hawks | 1323 |
| Hull's Victory | 2044 |
| Hummingbird | 445.9 |
| Hummingbird | 1273 |
| Hummingbird | 3056 |
| Hummingbirds | 3552 |
| Hunt, The | 1983 |
| Hunter's Horns | 3085 |
| Hunter's Star | 1284 |
| I Wish You Well | 1466 |
| IXL | 297.5 |
| Ice Cream Bowl | 3195 |
| Ice Cream Cone | 207 |
| Ice Cream Cone | 947 |
| Ice Cream Cone, The | 2709 |
| Ida Red | 299.2 |
| Idaho | 3090 |
| Idaho | 3946 |
| Idaho Beauty | 1952 |
| Idaho Star | 3233 |
| Idaho Star | 3735 |
| Idle Hours | 2942 |
| Idle Moments | 4026 |
| Illinois | 1664 |
| Illinois Road | 1608 |
| Illinois Road | 1615 |
| Illinois Star | 1538 |
| Illinois Star | 2744 |
| Illinois Turkey Track | 1879 |
| Imperial Fan | 3316 |
| Imperial Fan | 3371 |
| Imperial T | 1665 |
| Improved Four Patch | 2381 |
| Improved Nine Patch | 306 |
| Improved Nine Patch | 2689 |
| Improved Nine Patch | 1001 |
| Improved Nine Patch | 424.5 |
| Independence Square | 1621 |
| Independence Square | 2049 |
| Indian Arrowhead | 1284 |
| Indian Arrowhead | 3158 |
| Indian Canoes | 1251 |
| Indian Design | 3272 |
| Indian Emblem | 1130 |
| Indian Hammer | 1646 |
| Indian Hatchet | 2050 |
| Indian Hatchets | 1186 |
| Indian Head | 3793 |
| Indian Mat | 1378 |
| Indian Mats | 2847 |
| Indian Mats | 3062 |
| Indian Maze | 2849 |
| Indian Meadow | 3166 |
| Indian Meadow | 4135 |
| Indian Paintbrush | 3566 |
| Indian Patch | 1007 |
| Indian Plume | 297 |
| Indian Plumes | 2052 |
| Indian Puzzle | 1142 |
| Indian Puzzle | 1769 |
| Indian Raid | 2766 |
| Indian Raid | 3112 |
| Indian Squares | 2870 |
| Indian Star | 2155 |
| Indian Summer | 2662 |
| Indian Sunburst | 227.3 |
| Indian Trail | 1354 |
| Indian Trail | 2584 |
| Indian Wedding Ring | 305 |
| Indian on Horseback | 938.9 |
| Indiana | 2515 |
| Indiana Farmer | 3650 |
| Indiana Pumpkin Vine | 1039 |
| Indiana Puzzle | 1142 |
| Indiana Puzzle | 1450 |
| Indiana Puzzle | 1684 |
| Indiana Puzzle | 2397 |
| Indiana Puzzle | 1039 |
| Indianapolis | 2456 |
| Indians | 940.45 |
| Inlay Star, The | 3862 |
| Inner City | 152 |
| Inspiration Patch | 1431 |
| Interlaced Blocks | 2579 |
| Interlocked Squares | 1111 |
| Interlocked Squares | 2618 |
| Interwoven | 1746 |
| Interwoven Puzzle | 1954 |
| Iowa | 2467 |
| Iowa Star | 2982 |
| Iris | 777.4 |
| Iris Leaf | 3109 |
| Iris Rainbow | 780.5 |
| Irish Chain | 282.5 |
| Irish Chain | 1606 |
| Irish Chain | 1839 |
| Irish Chain | 2020 |
| Irish Chain | 2114 |
| Irish Chain | 3110 |
| Irish Chain | 1013 |
| Irish Plaid | 2558 |
| Irish Puzzle | 1354 |
| Irish Puzzle | 2584 |
| Iron Cross | 2390 |
| Islam | 2596 |
| Island Creek Hustler | 3865 |
| Italian Beauty | 1889 |
| Jack O' Lantern | 452.7 |
| Jack and Six | 1689 |
| Jack in the Box | 1875 |
| Jack in the Box | 1877 |
| Jack in the Pulpit | 2464 |
| Jack in the Pulpit | 2472 |
| Jack's Blocks | 3034 |
| Jack's Chain | 430 |
| Jack's Delight | 2846 |
| Jack's House | 869 |
| Jacknife | 1638 |
| Jackson | 3609 |
| Jackson Star | 3736 |
| Jacob's Coat | 269.8 |
| Jacob's Ladder | 142 |
| Jacob's Ladder | 1153 |
| Jacob's Ladder | 1312 |
| Jacob's Ladder | 1695 |
| Jacob's Ladder | 1964 |
| Jacques in the Boat | 3192 |
| Jam Session | 2089 |
| Jamestown Square | 3020 |
| Japanese Fan | 3309 |
| Japanese Fan | 3329 |
| Japanese Fan | 3332 |
| Japanese Garden | 953 |
| Japanese Lantern | 956 |
| Japanese Lantern | 957 |
| Japanese Morning Glory | 800 |
| Japanese Poppy | 2135 |
| Japanese Sunburst | 229 |
| Jay Walker | 2488 |
| Jefferson City | 2841 |
| Jeffrey's Nine Patch | 1686 |
| Jerico Walls | 210 |
| Jersey Tulip | 725 |
| Jewel | 415 |
| Jewel | 2436 |
| Jewel Box | 1019 |
| Jewel Boxes | 2454 |
| Jewel Quilt, The | 3948 |
| Jewel Star | 2313 |
| Jewel, The | 3552 |
| Jewels in a Frame | 3796 |
| Jig Jog Puzzle, The | 1224 |
| Jig Saw Puzzle, The | 1469 |
| Jigsaw | 185 |
| Jim Dandy | 3036 |
| Jinx Star | 4064 |
| Joan's Doll Quilt | 1646 |
| Job's Patience | 3110 |
| Job's Tears | 1534 |
| Job's Tears | 3079 |

538

# Index

| Name | Number |
|---|---|
| Job's Trouble | 442 |
| Job's Troubles | 160 |
| Job's Troubles | 415 |
| Job's Troubles | 1246 |
| Job's Troubles | 2330 |
| John F. Kennedy Star | 2313 |
| John's Favorite | 3185 |
| John's Pinwheel | 1268 |
| Johnnie Around the Corner | 2186 |
| Johnnie-Round-the-Corner | 1727 |
| Johnny Jump Up | 216.35 |
| Johnny Jump Up | 788.2 |
| Johnny Round the Corner | 1804 |
| Joining Dots | 298.7 |
| Joining Stars | 2141 |
| Joining Stars | 2266 |
| Jonathan Livingston Seagull | 237.5 |
| Joseph's Coat | 111 |
| Joseph's Coat | 431.5 |
| Joseph's Coat | 451 |
| Joseph's Coat | 475 |
| Joseph's Coat | 1671 |
| Joseph's Coat | 2734 |
| Joseph's Coat | 2758 |
| Joseph's Coat | 2922 |
| Joseph's Coat | 3974 |
| Joseph's Necktie | 1712 |
| Journey to California | 2398 |
| Joy Bells | 2934 |
| Judy in Arabia | 1625 |
| July Fourth | 2783 |
| July's Summer Sky | 1256 |
| Jupiter Star | 3583 |
| Jupiter of Many Points | 3585 |
| Jupiter's Moons | 305.9 |
| Jupiter's Moons | 2679 |
| Kaleidoscope | 278 |
| Kaleidoscope | 413.1 |
| Kaleidoscope | 1421 |
| Kaleidoscope | 2505 |
| Kaleidoscope | 2619 |
| Kaleidoscope | 2704 |
| Kaleidoscope | 4208 |
| Kaleidoscope | 1036 |
| Kaleidoscope Patchwork | 413 |
| Kaleidoscope Quilt | 2736 |
| Kaleidoscope Quilt, The | 2240 |
| Kaleidoscope Quilt, The | 4004 |
| Kaleidoscope Silk Quilt | 445.7 |
| Kaleidoscope Patch | 3874 |
| Kangaroo | 939.4 |
| Kankakee Checkers | 1226 |
| Kansas | 1411 |
| Kansas Beauty | 4028 |
| Kansas Beauty, The | 2657 |
| Kansas Dugout | 433 |
| Kansas Dust Storm, The | 3596 |
| Kansas Star | 407 |
| Kansas Star | 1732 |
| Kansas Sunflower | 275.5 |
| Kansas Sunflower | 773.8 |
| Kansas Sunflower | 3448 |
| Kansas Sunflower | 3451 |
| Kansas Sunflower | 3459 |
| Kansas Sunflower | 3480 |
| Kansas Sunflower, The | 3458 |
| Kansas Troubles | 1270 |
| Kansas Troubles | 2584 |
| Kansas Troubles | 3079 |
| Kansas Troubles | 3168 |
| Kate's Butterfly | 924.6 |
| Katherine Wheels | 1333 |
| Kathy's Ramble | 1262 |
| Katie's Choice | 2816 |
| Katie's Favorite | 2815 |
| Kensington Block | 309 |
| Kensington Club Quilt | 309 |
| Kentucky | 3722 |
| Kentucky Cross Roads | 2802 |
| Kentucky Crossroads | 2914 |
| Kentucky Lily | 765.13 |
| Kentucky Quilt, A | 1067 |
| Kentucky's Twinkling Star | 3770 |
| Key West Beauty | 2731 |
| Key West Star | 2719 |
| Keyhole | 1159 |
| King David's Crown | 3032 |
| King David's Crown | 3465 |
| King David's Crown | 3649 |
| King Solomon's Temple | 2441 |
| King Tut | 302 |
| King Tut Ankh | 966 |
| King Tut's Crown | 1468 |
| King Tut's Crown | 1039 |
| King's Cross | 2390 |
| King's Crown | 1809 |
| King's Crown | 2039 |
| King's Crown | 2054 |
| King's Crown | 2394 |
| King's Crown | 2691 |
| King's Crown | 3184 |
| King's Crown | 3902 |
| King's Crown | 1043 |
| King's Crown, The | 3761 |
| King's Hiway | 1835 |
| King's Star | 3762 |
| King's X | 1290 |
| Kissing Lanes | 1157 |
| Kitchen Woodbox, The | 2627 |
| Kite | 1246 |
| Kite | 2980 |
| Kite Quilt, The | 3892 |
| Kite, The | 3915 |
| Kite's Tail | 482 |
| Kite's Tail | 2290 |
| Kites in the Air | 400.5 |
| Kitty Corner | 1728 |
| Klondike Star | 3038 |
| Knapp Quilt | 3243 |
| Knickerbocker Star, The | 3809 |
| Kuli Pauo | 135 |
| L Patch, The | 176 |
| L Quilt | 2541 |
| Lightning in the Hills | 1156 |
| Lace Edge Quilt | 112 |
| Lace Fan | 3732 |
| Lacy Lattice Work | 2583 |
| Ladder of Success | 477 |
| Ladie's Wreath | 1131 |
| Ladies' Aid Block | 1221 |
| Ladies' Beautiful Star | 308.5 |
| Ladies' Chain | 3071 |
| Ladies' Aid Album | 1719 |
| Ladies' Delight | 1917 |
| Ladies' Delight | 1994 |
| Ladies' Fancy | 2002 |
| Lady Bug | 932 |
| Lady Finger, The | 1085 |
| Lady Fingers and Sunflowers | 2680 |
| Lady in the White House | 1146 |
| Lady of the Lake | 1342 |
| Lady of the Lake | 2493 |
| Lady of the Lake | 2517 |
| Lady of the White House | 1145 |
| Lafayette Orange Peel | 301 |
| Lafayette Orange Peel | 1527 |
| Land of the Pharoahs | 112 |
| Land's End | 2840 |
| Landon Sunflower, The | 3473 |
| Lantern | 954 |
| Lantern | 955 |
| Large Star | 3707 |
| Lattice | 1181 |
| Lattice Block | 433 |
| Lattice Fan | 3313 |
| Lattice Square | 1407 |
| Lattice Weave | 2843 |
| Lattice and Square | 2423 |
| Latticed Star | 3727 |
| Laurel Wreath | 2538 |
| Laurel Wreath | 2539 |
| Lawrence Star | 3839 |
| Lawyer's Puzzle | 1363 |
| Lazy Daisy | 3740 |
| Le Jet | 1441 |
| LeMoyne Star | 3593 |
| LeMoyne Star | 3745 |
| LeMoyne Star | 3806 |
| LeMoyne Star & Windmill | 1282 |
| Leaf Design, The | 1879 |
| Leafy Basket | 752 |
| Leap Frog | 1909 |
| Leap Frog | 1910 |
| Leavenworth Nine Patch | 2280 |
| Leavenworth Star | 3838 |
| Left and Right | 1188 |
| Lehigh Maze | 2172 |
| Lemon Star | 142 |
| Lemon Star | 3593 |
| Lemon Star | 3735 |
| Lena's Choice | 2862 |
| Lend and Borrow | 3166 |
| Leopard | 937.7 |
| Letha's Electric Fan | 3522 |
| Letter F | 2353 |
| Letter H | 2384 |
| Letter L | 2409 |
| Letter X, The | 1675 |
| Lewis and Clark | 2922 |
| Liberty Star | 3748 |
| Light and Dark | 1522 |
| Light and Dark | 2701 |
| Light and Shadows | 2022 |
| Lighthouse | 2851 |
| Lighthouse Block | 2748 |
| Lightning | 112 |
| Lightning | 1028 |
| Lightning Streak | 114 |
| Lightning Strips | 112 |
| Lightning in the Hills | 2868 |
| Lilies | 3204 |
| Lillian's Favorite | 3188 |
| Lily | 756.5 |
| Lily | 765.2 |
| Lily Corners | 745.5 |
| Lily Corners | 766.3 |
| Lily Corners | 1889 |
| Lily Pond | 1889 |
| Lily Quilt, A | 765.25 |
| Lily Quilt Pattern | 2058 |
| Lily, The | 857.04 |
| Lily of the Field | 1397 |
| Lincoln | 2819 |
| Lincoln Quilt, The | 3742 |
| Lincoln's Log Cabin | 863 |
| Lincoln's Hat | 2827 |
| Lincoln's Platform | 1646 |
| Lincoln's Platform | 1935 |
| Lindbergh's Night Flight | 906 |
| Lindy's Plane | 2349 |
| Linked Diamonds | 3910 |
| Linked Squares | 4070 |
| Linoleum | 3031 |
| Linton | 1208 |
| Lion | 937 |
| Little Basket | 650.3 |
| Little Beech Tree | 839 |
| Little Beech Tree | 840 |
| Little Boy's Breeches | 2961 |
| Little Cedar Tree, The | 1311 |
| Little Church on the Ridge | 884.5 |
| Little Foxes | 412.7 |
| Little Girl's Star, A | 239 |
| Little Girl's Star, A | 3701 |
| Little Penguins | 1285 |
| Little Red House | 870 |
| Little Red Schoolhouse | 865 |
| Little Red Schoolhouse | 866 |
| Little Red Schoolhouse | 882 |
| Little Rock Block | 3904 |
| Little Saw Tooth, The | 3166 |
| Little Ship o' Dreams | 912.3 |
| Little Star | 3772 |
| Little White House on a Hill | 862 |
| Live Oak Tree | 849 |
| Lock and Chain | 1792 |
| Locked Squares | 405.5 |
| Locked Star, The | 3934 |
| Log Cabin | 270 |
| Log Cabin | 863 |
| Log Cabin | 865 |
| Log Cabin | 871 |
| Log Cabin | 877 |
| Log Cabin | 1114 |
| Log Cabin | 2573 |

539

Index


Log Cabin ....2574
Log Cabin ....2576
Log Cabin ....3240
Log Cabin, The ....870.3
Log Cabin Star ....3749
Log Cabin Star ....3755
Log Cabin and Album Pattern ....3268
Log Patch, The ....2573
Lola ....2387
London Bridge ....1523
London Roads ....1658
London Roads ....1677
London Square ....1209
London Square ....3164
London Stairs ....1110
Lone Eagle Airplane ....901
Lone Star ....415.3
Lone Star ....1631
Lone Star ....1710
Lone Star ....2141
Lone Star ....2915
Lone Star ....2918
Lone Star ....4003
Lone Star ....4005
Lone Star, The ....3776
Lone Star of Paradise ....3809
Lone Star of Texas ....415.3
Lone X ....1968
Lonely Star ....3398
Lonesome Pine ....216
Long Nine Patch ....2435
Long Pointed Star, The ....3920
Lorna Doone ....1033
Lost Children ....415.27
Lost Children ....2984
Lost Goslin', The ....1717
Lost Paradise ....2999
Lost Ship ....1361
Lost Ship, The ....1362
Lotus ....1086
Lotus Block ....4126
Lotus Blossom ....1086
Lotus Star ....4041
Louisiana ....1335
Louisiana Star ....3745
Lounge Throw ....1026.3
Love Chain ....1023
Love Entangled ....2067
Love Knot ....1646
Love Knot ....2350
Love Knot ....2594
Love Ring ....1469
Love Ring ....1519
Love in a Mist ....3792
Love in a Tangle ....2066
Love's Chain ....4094
Love's Dream ....2622
Lovely Patchwork ....4106
Lover's Chain, The ....453
Lover's Knot ....301
Lover's Knot ....1500
Lover's Knot ....2963
Lover's Knot ....3010
Lover's Knot ....3953
Lover's Lane ....1157
Lover's Links ....453
Lover's Quarrel ....3086
Lozenge ....171
Lozenge Tree ....845
Lucinda's Star ....3834
Lucky Block ....1006
Lucky Clover ....1369
Lucky Knot ....4190
Lucky Pieces ....3752
Lucky Quilt ....1006
Lucky Star ....1301
Lucky Star ....2989
Lucky Star ....3903
Ludlow's Favorite ....1646
M & W Block ....3011
M Quilt Block ....986.2
Ma Perkins Flower Garden ....257
MacKenzie's Square ....2195
Macaroon Patchwork ....2621
Madison ....250
Madison Quilt Block ....250
Magic Box ....2118
Magic Circle ....1429
Magic Circle ....1526
Magic Cross ....2889
Magic Cross Design ....2150
Magic Squares ....411
Magic Squares ....2291
Magic Squares ....3065
Magic Triangles ....1204
Magical Circle ....1429
Magnolia ....4125
Magnolia Block ....2513
Magnolia Blossom ....3530
Magnolia Bud ....1793
Magnolia Bud ....1978
Magnolia Bud ....2208
Magnolia Leaf ....1735
Maiden's Delight ....2191
Maine ....2524
Maine's Spreading Pine Tree ....846
Maltese Cross ....2063
Maltese Cross ....2390
Maltese Cross ....2635
Maltese Cross ....2638
Maltese Cross ....2969
Maltese Cross ....3005
Maltese Cross ....1724
Malvina's Chain ....2305
Man in the Moon ....299.9
Manila Quilt Design ....2616
Many Pointed Star ....2538
Many Roads to the White House ....1182
Maple Leaf ....245.1
Maple Leaf ....857.02
Maple Leaf ....1273
Maple Leaf ....1735
Maple Leaf ....1740
Maple Leaf ....1887
Maple Leaf & Rose ....4042
Maple Leaf Quilt ....1734
Maple Leaf, The ....3277
Maple Leaf, The ....3736
Marble ....1504
Marble Floor, The ....4141
Marcilla's Friendship Quilt ....3254
Margaret's Choice ....1141
Marigold Garden ....4131
Marigold Garden ....4132
Mariner's Compass ....1237
Mariner's Compass ....3400
Mariner's Compass ....3402
Mariner's Compass ....3404
Mariner's Compass ....3404.5
Mariner's Compass ....3444
Mariner's Compass ....3445
Mariner's Compass ....3463
Mariner's Compass ....3601
Mariner's Compass ....3603
Mariner's Compass ....3656
Mariner's Compass ....3658
Mariposa Lily ....765.25
Mariposa Lily ....765.4
Mariposa Lily ....765.6
Market Square ....1289
Martha Washington ....2147
Martha Washington ....791.5
Martha Washington Design ....2147
Martha Washington Rose ....791.5
Martha Washington Star ....2147
Martha Washington's Flower Garden ....160
Martha Washington's Rose Garden ....160
Martha Washington's Star ....2149
Martha's Basket ....744.7
Martha's Choice ....1501
Mary Moore's Double Irish Chain ....1017
Mary Strickler's Quilt ....3404.5
Mary Tenny Gray Travel Club Pattern ....2886
Mary's Block ....2838
Mary's Fan ....3307
Mary's Fan ....3328
Mary's Star ....3328
Maryland ....1957
Maryland Beauty ....3169
Maryland Beauty ....3170
Massachusetts ....2053
Massachusetts Priscilla ....2976
Maud's Album Quilt ....2880
May Basket ....666
May Basket ....710
May Basket ....712
May Basket ....733
May Basket Design ....714
May Basket, The ....651
May Festival ....1025.9
May Time Quilt ....449.5
May Time Quilt ....4031
Mayflower ....2009.5
Mayflower Quilt ....459.15
Mayflower Quilt, The ....2991
Mayflower, The ....3052
Mayflower, The ....912
Mayor's Garden ....2415
Meadow Flower ....4143
Meadow Lily ....765.4
Meadow Lily, The ....765.25
Mechanical Blocks ....442
Medieval Walls ....1872
Meeting House Square ....1955
Melon Patch ....1524
Melon Patch ....1527
Melon Patch Quilt ....2667
Melon Patch, The ....1530
Memory ....1772
Memory Blocks ....2462
Memory Blocks ....2850
Memory Chain ....436
Memory Fruit ....2048
Memory Quilt ....2550
Memory Wreath ....1806
Memory Wreath ....2048
Memory Wreath ....2392
Memory's Chain ....1162
Merrie England ....1228
Merry Go Round ....1355
Merry Go Round ....2726
Merry Go Round ....3467
Merry Go Round ....3475
Merry Kite ....4034
Meteor Quilt ....1347
Mexican Block ....1817
Mexican Rose ....2937
Mexican Siesta ....3526
Mexican Star ....1713
Mexican Star ....2937
Mexican Star ....3703
Michael's Joke ....1432
Michigan ....2547
Michigan Beauty ....2538
Michigan Star ....2752
Michigan's Pontiac Star ....3870
Michigan's Water Wonderland Star ....4092
Midget Necktie ....1900
Midnight Stars ....2705
Midsummer Night ....3070
Milady's Fan ....3340
Milkmaid's Star, The ....1257
Milky Way ....271
Milky Way ....1142
Mill Wheel ....1806
Mill Wheel ....2786
Mill and Stars ....1214
Mill and Stars ....2324
Miller's Daughter ....1975
Miller's Daughter ....1025
Millwheel ....1262
Millwheel ....1452
Milly's Favorite ....1202
Milwaukee's Own ....3635
Mineral Wells ....1951
Minnesota ....1979
Minnesota ....2608
Miss Jackson ....3609
Missionary Baptist ....3885

# Index

| | |
|---|---|
| Mississippi | 1749 |
| Mississippi Daisy | 3506 |
| Mississippi Oak Leaf | 3633 |
| Mississippi Oak Leaves | 3635 |
| Mississippi Pink | 765.1 |
| Mississippi Star | 2478 |
| Missouri | 3743 |
| Missouri Beauty | 1087 |
| Missouri Corn Field | 3213 |
| Missouri Daisy | 3426 |
| Missouri Daisy | 3427 |
| Missouri Daisy | 3587 |
| Missouri Puzzle | 1673 |
| Missouri Puzzle | 1817 |
| Missouri Puzzle | 2090 |
| Missouri Puzzle | 2099 |
| Missouri River Valley | 4119 |
| Missouri Star | 2154 |
| Missouri Star | 3829 |
| Missouri Trouble | 4085 |
| Missouri Windmills | 1205 |
| Missouri Wonder | 444 |
| Missouri's Gateway Star | 2318 |
| Mixed T | 1392 |
| Mixed T | 3274 |
| Mixed T's | 217.7 |
| Mock Orange Quilt | 460.3 |
| Modern Blocks | 1112 |
| Modern Broken Dish | 2415 |
| Modern Daisy | 4086 |
| Modern Design | 1112 |
| Modern Envelope | 1266 |
| Modern Flame | 3177 |
| Modern Peony | 847 |
| Modern Star | 2538 |
| Modern Star | 3866 |
| Modern Tulip | 141 |
| Modern Tulip | 1892 |
| Modernistic Acorn | 959 |
| Modernistic California Poppy | 788 |
| Modernistic Iris | 216.37 |
| Modernistic Pansy | 783 |
| Modernistic Rose | 780 |
| Modernistic Star | 268.5 |
| Modernistic Trumpet Vine | 784 |
| Modernized Poppy | 3131 |
| Mohawk Trail | 3302.5 |
| Mohawk Trail | 3369 |
| Mollie's Choice | 1672 |
| Mona and Monette | 1832 |
| Mona's Choice | 1782 |
| Monastary Windows | 1026.7 |
| Monk's Puzzle | 152 |
| Monkey | 940 |
| Monkey Puzzle | 3188 |
| Monkey Wrench | 1142 |
| Monkey Wrench | 1646 |
| Monkey Wrench | 1868 |
| Monkey Wrench | 2397 |
| Montana | 299 |
| Montana Maze | 2199 |
| Montana Star | 269.6 |
| Montgomery | 1666 |
| Montpelier | 1732 |
| Monument, The | 889 |
| Moon & Star | 2212 |
| Moon Block | 4063 |
| Moon Flower | 3688 |
| Moon Over the Mountain | 948 |
| Moon and Star | 3680 |
| Moon and Stars | 454 |
| Moon and Swastika | 2514 |
| Moorish Mosaic | 3794 |
| Moorish Star Quilt, The | 4011 |
| Morning Glory | 429 |
| Morning Glory | 1500 |
| Morning Glory | 2998 |
| Morning Glory | 797.5 |
| Morning Glory Quilt, The | 784.3 |
| Morning Glory Square | 788.4 |
| Morning Patch | 4105 |
| Morning Star | 248 |
| Morning Star | 254 |
| Morning Star | 269.3 |
| Morning Star | 427 |
| Morning Star | 427.2 |
| Morning Star | 1057 |
| Morning Star | 1058 |
| Morning Star | 1302 |
| Morning Star | 1775 |
| Morning Star | 2008 |
| Morning Star | 2265 |
| Morning Star | 2736 |
| Morning Star | 3049 |
| Morning Star | 3091 |
| Morning Star | 3700 |
| Morning Star | 3772 |
| Morning Star | 3777 |
| Morning Star | 3807 |
| Morning Star | 3931 |
| Morning Sun | 3665 |
| Mosaic | 160 |
| Mosaic | 1634 |
| Mosaic | 2054 |
| Mosaic | 2319 |
| Mosaic | 3581 |
| Mosaic | 3794 |
| Mosaic #1 | 2130 |
| Mosaic #1 | 2319 |
| Mosaic #1 | 2469 |
| Mosaic #2 | 2434 |
| Mosaic #2 | 2464 |
| Mosaic #3 | 2469 |
| Mosaic #3 | 2775 |
| Mosaic #4 | 1219 |
| Mosaic #4 | 2475 |
| Mosaic #5 | 1338 |
| Mosaic #5 | 2445 |
| Mosaic #5 | 2536 |
| Mosaic #6 | 2470 |
| Mosaic #6 | 2475 |
| Mosaic #7 | 2142 |
| Mosaic #7 | 2464 |
| Mosaic #8 | 1658 |
| Mosaic #8 | 2125 |
| Mosaic #9 | 1262 |
| Mosaic #9 | 1338 |
| Mosaic #10 | 1123 |
| Mosaic #10 | 2785 |
| Mosaic #11 | 2788 |
| Mosaic #12 | 1338 |
| Mosaic #12 | 2124 |
| Mosaic #13 | 3752 |
| Mosaic #15 | 2784 |
| Mosaic #16 | 2123 |
| Mosaic #17 | 1132 |
| Mosaic #19 | 2142 |
| Mosaic #20 | 1102 |
| Mosaic #21 | 2470 |
| Mosaic #22 | 3223 |
| Mosaic Block | 2286 |
| Mosaic PW #1 | 1631 |
| Mosaic Patchwork #3 | 438 |
| Mosaic Patchwork #4 | 434 |
| Mosaic Rose | 2280 |
| Mosaic Rose | 2379 |
| Mosaic Squares | 4037 |
| Mother's Choice | 2539 |
| Mother's Choice | 3051 |
| Mother's Choice | 3812 |
| Mother's Choice Quilt | 3416 |
| Mother's Delight | 1237 |
| Mother's Dream | 1733 |
| Mother's Fancy | 2104 |
| Mother's Fancy Star | 2104 |
| Mother's Favorite | 2474 |
| Mother's Favorite | 3422 |
| Mother's Oddity | 185 |
| Mother's Own | 3125 |
| Mound Builders | 1130 |
| Mound Builders | 2577 |
| Mountain Homespun | 1837 |
| Mountain Lily | 765.4 |
| Mountain Lily, The | 765.25 |
| Mountain Maze | 2199 |
| Mountain Peak, The | 2880 |
| Mountain Pink | 3560 |
| Mountain Pink, The | 3561 |
| Mountain Star, The | 258 |
| Mowing Machine Quilt, The | 111 |
| Mr. Roosevelt's Necktie | 1129.5 |
| Mr. Roosevelt's Necktie | 2534 |
| Mrs. Fay's Favorite Friendship Block | 4034 |
| Mrs. Anderson's Quilt | 1932 |
| Mrs. Cleveland's Choice | 2481 |
| Mrs. Dewey's Choice | 1766 |
| Mrs. Ewer's Tulip | 3105 |
| Mrs. Hardy's Hanging Basket | 719 |
| Mrs. Hoover's Colonial Quilt | 1014 |
| Mrs. Keller's Nine Patch | 1860 |
| Mrs. Lloyd's Favorite | 2156 |
| Mrs. Morgan's Choice | 1351 |
| Mrs. Morgan's Choice | 4030 |
| Mrs. Roosevelt's Favorite | 2935 |
| Mrs. Taft's Choice | 3271 |
| Mrs. Thomas | 2922 |
| Mrs. Wolf's Red Beauty | 1815 |
| Mushroom Shell | 181 |
| Mushrooms | 1456 |
| My Country | 1973 |
| My Country | 3803 |
| My Favorite | 1939 |
| My Graduation Class Ring | 3627 |
| My Mother's Apron | 960 |
| My Mother's Star | 3794.7 |
| My Nova | 3553 |
| Mystery Flower Garden | 1635 |
| Mystic Maze | 2726 |
| Mystic Maze | 2728 |
| Name on Each Friendship Block | 3230 |
| Nameless | 2047 |
| Nameless Star | 2138 |
| Narcissus | 3525 |
| Nashville | 1512 |
| Nashville | 2764 |
| National Star | 3780 |
| Nativity Star | 3877 |
| Nautilus | 2400 |
| Nauvoo Lattice | 4110 |
| Navajo | 2847 |
| Nebraska | 1941 |
| Nebraska | 1943 |
| Nebraska Windmill | 2587 |
| Necktie | 1152 |
| Necktie | 1376 |
| Necktie | 2533 |
| Necktie Patchwork | 3397 |
| Neil's Diamond | 237 |
| Nellie's Choice | 1014 |
| Nelly Bly | 3436 |
| Nelson's Victory | 1125 |
| Nest and Fledgling | 1806 |
| Net of Stars | 3860 |
| Nevada | 1898 |
| Nevada | 3501 |
| New Album | 1660 |
| New Album | 2033 |
| New Barrister's Block | 1364 |
| New Cross & Crown | 1667 |
| New Double Irish Chain | 2427 |
| New Double Irish Chain | 2428 |
| New Four Patch | 1312 |
| New 4-Pointer, The | 4153 |
| New Hampshire | 266 |
| New Hampshire's Granite Rock | 1727 |
| New Hour Glass | 2310 |
| New Jersey | 1191 |
| New Jersey | 2952 |
| New Jersey Star, The | 1053.9 |
| New Mexican Star, The | 1817 |
| New Mexico | 1817 |
| New Moon | 1506 |
| New Moon | 2684 |
| New Nine Patch | 1001 |
| New Snowball | 1001 |
| New Star | 1249 |
| New Star | 1916 |
| New Star | 3837 |
| New Star | 3838 |
| New Star Quilt | 3883 |
| New Star of North Carolina | 3040 |
| New State | 1040.5 |
| New Waterwheel | 1649 |
| New Wedding Ring | 3086 |
| New York | 1383 |
| New York Beauty | 1077 |

541

# Index

| | | |
|---|---|---|
| New York Beauty | 1079 | |
| Next Door Neighbor | 1337 | |
| Next Door Neighbor | 2787 | |
| Night & Noon | 2837 | |
| Night Heavens | 3815 | |
| Night and Day | 1210 | |
| Night and Day | 2496 | |
| Nightwatch | 4025 | |
| Nine Patch | 424.5 | |
| Nine Patch | 1601 | |
| Nine Patch | 2020 | |
| Nine Patch | 1071.3 | |
| Nine Patch Chain | 1605 | |
| Nine Patch Checkerboard | 2413 | |
| Nine Patch Diamond | 232.2 | |
| Nine Patch Kaleidoscope | 2732 | |
| Nine Patch Nose Gay | 4121 | |
| Nine Patch Star | 2435 | |
| Nine Patch Star | 3018 | |
| Nine Patch Star | 3935 | |
| Nine Patch Straight Furrow | 1706 | |
| Nine Patch T | 1718 | |
| Nine Patch Variation | 306 | |
| Nine Patch Variation | 1607 | |
| Nine Patch Variation | 1706 | |
| Nine Patch Snowballs | 4149 | |
| Nine and Four Patch | 1001 | |
| 1941 Nine Patch, The | 1720 | |
| Nineteen Oh Four (1904) Star | 2795 | |
| Ninety-Nine Times Around the World | 2293 | |
| No Name | 3495 | |
| No Name Quilt | 4154 | |
| Nocturne | 2006 | |
| Nonesuch | 1469 | |
| Nonsense | 2811 | |
| Nonsuch | 1751 | |
| Noon Day Lily | 765.4 | |
| Noon Day Lily | 3563 | |
| Noon Day Splendor | 3519 | |
| Noonday | 3457 | |
| Noonday | 3480 | |
| Normandy Girls | 940.41 | |
| North Carolina Beauty, The | 2913 | |
| North Carolina Lily | 765.12 | |
| North Carolina Lily | 765.4 | |
| North Carolina Star | 3045 | |
| North Dakota | 3873 | |
| North Star | 1242 | |
| North Star | 2938 | |
| North Star | 3745 | |
| North Star | 3882 | |
| North Star | 3950 | |
| North Star, The | 4197 | |
| North Wind | 1354 | |
| North Wind | 2584 | |
| Northern Lights | 1237 | |
| Northern Lights | 3498 | |
| Northern Lights | 4139 | |
| Northern Lights | 4175 | |
| Northumberland Star | 2901 | |
| Northumberland Star | 3956 | |
| Northwind | 3162 | |
| Norway Pine | 805 | |
| Nose Gay | 1976 | |
| Nose Gay Quilt | 4052 | |
| Nose Gays, The | 4052 | |
| Nose-Gay | 1399 | |
| Nosegay | 766 | |
| Nosegay | 777.7 | |
| Nothing Wasted | 480.7 | |
| Novel Star | 3700 | |
| Noxall | 3557 | |
| Oak Grove Star, The | 3412 | |
| Oak Leaf | 3110 | |
| Oak Leaf, The | 857.093 | |
| Oblong | 3975 | |
| Ocean Wave | 160 | |
| Ocean Wave | 282.7 | |
| Ocean Wave | 283 | |
| Ocean Wave | 2341 | |
| Ocean Wave | 2398 | |
| Ocean Wave | 2628 | |
| Ocean Wave | 3163 | |
| Ocean Wave | 3895 | |
| Ocean Waves | 113 | |
| Ocean Waves | 3150 | |
| Octagon | 283 |
| Octagon | 294 |
| Octagon | 442 |
| Octagon Block | 442.8 |
| Octagon Star | 3855 |
| Octagon Star | 3856 |
| Octagon Tile | 448 |
| Octagonal | 442 |
| Octagonal Star | 2117 |
| OctagonalStar | 2258 |
| Octagonal Star | 3807 |
| Octagons | 442 |
| Octagons | 2704 |
| Octagons | 4141 |
| Octagons | 4146 |
| Odd Fellow's Cross | 2903 |
| Odd Fellow's Quilt | 2414 |
| Odd Fellows | 2902 |
| Odd Fellows Chain | 2170 |
| Odd Fellows Cross | 2902 |
| Odd Fellows March | 2170 |
| Odd Fellows Patch | 2902 |
| Odd Fellows Quilt | 283 |
| Odd Fellow's Cross | 2897 |
| Odd Patchwork, An | 2098 |
| Odd Scraps Patchwork | 1806 |
| Oddfellows | 171 |
| Odds and Ends | 283 |
| Odds and Ends | 1310 |
| Ogden Corners | 433 |
| Ogee | 188 |
| Oh Susannah | 2534 |
| Ohio | 1232 |
| Ohio Beauty | 300 |
| Ohio Star | 1232 |
| Ohio Star | 1631 |
| Ohio Star | 2141 |
| Ohio Star | 3731 |
| Ohio Trail | 1025 |
| Oil Fields of Oklahoma | 2515 |
| Oklahoma | 1548 |
| Oklahoma Boomer | 218.2 |
| Oklahoma Dogwood | 1475 |
| Oklahoma Dogwood | 2223 |
| Oklahoma Dogwood | 1037 |
| Oklahoma Star | 3390 |
| Oklahoma Star, The | 258 |
| Oklahoma Sunburst | 3480 |
| Oklahoma Trails and Fields | 1004 |
| Oklahoma Twister | 1154 |
| Oklahoma's Square Dance | 2702 |
| Ola's Quilt | 3095 |
| Old Colony Star | 3717 |
| Old Country Church | 884 |
| Old Crow | 1262 |
| Old English Wedding Ring | 1806 |
| Old Fashion Fruit Basket | 656.4 |
| Old Fashion Quilt | 1896 |
| Old Fashioned Daisy | 4209 |
| Old Fashioned Flower Garden | 160 |
| Old Fashioned Garden | 777.2 |
| Old Fashioned Garland | 784.5 |
| Old Fashioned Goblet | 944 |
| Old Fashioned Nose Gay | 4052 |
| Old Fashioned Pieced Block | 2790 |
| Old Fashioned Quilt | 433 |
| Old Fashioned Star Quilt | 4044 |
| Old Fashioned Wagon Wheel, The | 3381 |
| Old Fashioned Wedding Ring | 1806 |
| Old Fashioned Wheel Quilt, An | 246 |
| Old Favorite | 1939 |
| Old Garden Wall | 132 |
| Old Glory | 285 |
| Old Gray Goose | 3220 |
| Old Grey Goose | 2144 |
| Old Home | 863 |
| Old Home | 864 |
| Old Homestead, The | 868 |
| Old Indian Trail | 1443 |
| Old Indian Trail | 1444 |
| Old Indian Trail | 973 |
| Old Italian Block | 2881 |
| Old Italian Design | 2880 |
| Old Kentucky Home | 863 |
| Old King Cole's Crown | 3184 |
| Old Maid's Patience | 3736 |
| Old Maid's Puzzle | 1149 |
| Old Maid's Puzzle | 1314 |
| Old Maid's Puzzle | 1317 |
| Old Maid's Puzzle | 1461 |
| Old Maid's Puzzle | 1013 |
| Old Maid's Puzzle | 2225 |
| Old Maid's Puzzle | 3220 |
| Old Maid's Puzzle | 1039 |
| Old Maid's Ramble | 2170 |
| Old Maid's Ramble | 2338 |
| Old Maid's Ramble | 2339 |
| Old Maid's Ramble | 2584 |
| Old Maid's Rambler | 3159 |
| Old Mail | 2413 |
| Old Mexico | 2905 |
| Old Mill Design | 1646 |
| Old Mill Wheel | 3551 |
| Old Mill Wheel | 4090 |
| Old Missouri | 1539 |
| Old Missouri | 3280 |
| Old Poinsettia | 2319 |
| Old Rail Fence | 3286 |
| Old Rugged Cross, The | 2801 |
| Old Snowflake | 1642 |
| Old Spanish Tile Pattern, The | 2075 |
| Old Staffordshire | 4147 |
| Old Star | 1918 |
| Old Time Block | 2791 |
| Old Tippecanoe | 1176 |
| Old Windmill | 1266 |
| Olympia | 2743 |
| On The Square | 2026 |
| One Dozen Napkins | 1119 |
| One Way | 1692 |
| Open Book | 2597 |
| Open Box | 2539 |
| Open Box, The | 2597 |
| Open Window | 1177 |
| Open Window | 2602 |
| Optical Illusion | 1240 |
| Optical Illusion | 2545 |
| Optical Sawtooth | 2138 |
| Orange Bud | 777.5 |
| Orange Peel | 207 |
| Orange Peel | 1519 |
| Orange Peel | 1527 |
| Orange Peel | 2683 |
| Orange Peel | 3110 |
| Orange Peel | 3539 |
| Orange Pekoe | 136 |
| Orange Slices | 3110 |
| Orange Squeezer | 1041 |
| Orchid Hemstitch | 2280 |
| Order #11 | 3110 |
| Oregon | 3242 |
| Oregon Trail | 1461 |
| Oregon Trail | 1462 |
| Oriental Poppy | 788 |
| Oriental Puzzle | 2418 |
| Oriental Puzzle | 4116 |
| Oriental Rose | 780.3 |
| Oriental Splendor | 266 |
| Oriental Star | 2504 |
| Oriental Star | 3640 |
| Oriental Star | 3647 |
| Oriental Star | 3894 |
| Oriental Tulip | 286 |
| Original, The | 2057 |
| Original Design, An | 2057 |
| Original Double T | 2803 |
| Oriole Window, The | 4068 |
| Ornate Star | 1641 |
| Orphan Star | 3807 |
| Ostrich | 936.95 |
| Our Country | 1991 |
| Our Editor | 2175 |
| Our Village Green | 2451 |
| Out of This World | 151 |
| Over and Under | 1746 |
| Over and Under Quilt Design | 1758 |
| Over the Rainbow | 4069 |
| Over the Waves | 182 |
| Overall Star Pattern | 4005 |
| Owl Quilt, The | 4201 |
| Ozark Cobblestones | 442 |

# Index

| | |
|---|---|
| Ozark Diamonds | 257 |
| Ozark Mountains | 1372 |
| Ozark Puzzle | 1469 |
| Ozark Star | 257 |
| Ozark Star, The | 259 |
| Ozark Sunflower | 3579 |
| Ozark Tile Pattern | 433 |
| Ozark Trail, The | 1823 |
| Ozark Trails | 2903 |
| Pinwheels | 1142 |
| Pacific Rail Road | 1695 |
| Paducah Peony | 4087 |
| Paducah Peony | 4207 |
| Paeony Block | 848 |
| Pain in the Neck Quilt | 460 |
| Painted Snowball | 3556 |
| Paisley Shawl | 2825 |
| Palm | 1304 |
| Palm Leaf | 1304 |
| Palm, The | 3174 |
| Panama Block | 2937 |
| Pandora's Box | 281 |
| Paneled Roses | 2661 |
| Pansy | 783 |
| Pansy Quilt | 781 |
| Papa's Delight | 3082 |
| Paper Flowers | 2539 |
| Paper Pinwheels | 1121 |
| Paragon | 4099 |
| Parallelogram | 3805 |
| Parallelogram W, A | 992.5 |
| Parasol Block | 3395 |
| Parquetry Design for Patchwork | 290 |
| Party Plate Quilt | 3846 |
| Patch Blossom | 801 |
| Patch Houses | 876 |
| Patch Quilt Design | 2105 |
| Patch as Patch Can | 1274 |
| Patchwork Bedspread | 4123 |
| Patchwork Butterfly | 931.5 |
| Patchwork Cushion Top, A | 1756 |
| Patchwork Fantasy | 1815 |
| Patchwork Fence, The | 890 |
| Patchwork Posy | 4200 |
| Patchwork Sofa | 3550 |
| Path Through the Woods | 3991 |
| Path Thru the Woods | 1275 |
| Path and Stiles | 1650 |
| Path of Fans | 3302.5 |
| Path of Fans | 3369 |
| Pathfinder | 2317 |
| Pathfinder | 3115 |
| Paths to Happiness | 445.2 |
| Paths to Peace | 3264 |
| Paths to Piece | 1187 |
| Pathway to the Stars | 422.5 |
| Patience Corners | 281 |
| Patience Corners | 4023 |
| Patience Nine Patch | 1601 |
| Patience Quilt, The | 1053.3 |
| Patriot's Pride | 310 |
| Patriot's Quilt | 442.8 |
| Patriotic Quilt | 3983 |
| Patriotic Star | 1297 |
| Patriotic Star | 3772 |
| Pattern of Chinese Origin, A | 3715 |
| Pattern Without a Name | 1855 |
| Pattern Without a Name | 2386 |
| Patty's Star | 3780 |
| Patty's Summer Parasol | 951 |
| Pavement Pattern | 2375 |
| Peach and Plenty | 1201 |
| Peaceful Hours | 2078 |
| Peaceful Valley Quilt, The | 291 |
| Peach Blow | 4178 |
| Peacock Patchwork | 935 |
| Peacock Patchwork | 935.7 |
| Peafowl Quilt, The | 935 |
| Peary's Expedition | 3901 |
| Peekaboo | 1730 |
| Peekhole | 2533 |
| Peeled Orange | 451 |
| Peeled Orange | 3532 |
| Peggy Anne's Special | 3797 |
| Penelope's Favorite | 2519 |
| Penelope's Favorite | 2520 |
| Penguins | 936.9 |
| Penn Mennonite Feather Star | 2271 |
| Penn's Puzzle | 2519 |
| Pennsylvania | 2023 |
| Pennsylvania | 2548 |
| Pennsylvania Hex | 239 |
| Pennsylvania Pineapple | 2908 |
| Pennsylvania Tulip | 765.31 |
| Pennsylvania Wheel Quilt | 3660 |
| Pennsylvanian, The | 1065.3 |
| Peony | 796.5 |
| Peony | 2216 |
| Peony | 2362 |
| Peony, The | 733 |
| Peony Variation | 857.04 |
| Peony and Forget Me Nots | 4207 |
| Pepper and Salt Shakers | 251 |
| Periwinkle | 445 |
| Periwinkle | 446 |
| Perpetual Motion | 1216 |
| Pershing | 2839 |
| Persian | 3027 |
| Persian Star | 3027 |
| Petal Circle in a Square | 3624 |
| Peter and Paul | 1520 |
| Peter and Paul | 2685 |
| Peter's Quilt | 1229 |
| Peter's Quilt | 3155 |
| Petit Park | 2102 |
| Pharlemia's Favorite | 2858 |
| Philadelphia Block | 2032 |
| Philadelphia Patch | 3001 |
| Philadelphia Pavement | 2032 |
| Philadelphia Pavement | 3078 |
| Phillipine Islands | 4166 |
| Phillipines | 2993 |
| Phoenix | 1639 |
| Picket Fence | 175 |
| Picket Fence | 220.4 |
| Picket Fence | 890 |
| Picket Fence | 1325 |
| Picket Fence Border Block | 890 |
| Picket and Posts | 1996 |
| Pickle Dish | 304 |
| Pickle Dish | 2692 |
| Picnic Basket | 712 |
| Picture Frame | 1646 |
| Picture Frame | 2116 |
| Pictures in the Stairwell | 1474 |
| Pieced Baskets | 664 |
| Pieced Bouquet | 1399.2 |
| Pieced Butterfly | 923 |
| Pieced Butterfly | 930 |
| Pieced Flower | 3019 |
| Pieced Flower Basket | 691 |
| Pieced Iris | 216.37 |
| Pieced Pyramids | 203 |
| Pieced Rocking Horse | 939.15 |
| Pieced Star | 1140 |
| Pieced Star | 2146 |
| Pieced Sunflower, The | 3579 |
| Pieced Tulip | 3103 |
| Pierre | 2250 |
| Pierrot's Pom Pom | 1500 |
| Pierrot's Pom Pom | 1503 |
| Pig's Tail | 2379 |
| Pigeon Toes | 1825 |
| Pigeons in the Coop | 3152 |
| Pike's Peak | 3835 |
| Pilot Wheel | 3538 |
| Pilot's Wheel | 3640 |
| Pin Wheel | 1654 |
| Pin Wheel, The | 1717 |
| Pin Wheel Star | 3818 |
| Pin Wheels | 1708 |
| Pincushion | 301 |
| Pincushion | 1519 |
| Pincushion | 2683 |
| Pincushion and Burr | 3103 |
| Pine Burr | 1253 |
| Pine Burr | 2440 |
| Pine Burr | 3002 |
| Pine Cone | 2246 |
| Pine Cones | 3003 |
| Pine Forest, The | 834 |
| Pine Tree | 216.31 |
| Pine Tree | 806 |
| Pine Tree | 807 |
| Pine Tree | 809 |
| Pine Tree | 810 |
| Pine Tree | 810.7 |
| Pine Tree | 816 |
| Pine Tree | 818 |
| Pine Tree | 821 |
| Pine Tree | 822 |
| Pine Tree | 823.5 |
| Pine Tree | 825 |
| Pine Tree | 834 |
| Pine Tree | 840 |
| Pine Tree Quilt | 854 |
| Pine Tree Quilt Design | 808 |
| Pine Tree, The | 819 |
| Pineapple | 784.5 |
| Pineapple | 1844 |
| Pineapple | 2635 |
| Pineapple | 2638 |
| Pineapple Cactus | 2996 |
| Pineapple Quilt | 1060 |
| Pineapple Squares | 1845 |
| Pineapple, The | 2637 |
| Pineys | 768.2 |
| Pink Magnolia | 2208 |
| Pink Magnolias | 1978 |
| Pinwheel | 192 |
| Pinwheel | 272.8 |
| Pinwheel | 1121 |
| Pinwheel | 1195 |
| Pinwheel | 1202 |
| Pinwheel | 1262 |
| Pinwheel | 1266 |
| Pinwheel | 1294 |
| Pinwheel | 1341 |
| Pinwheel | 1857 |
| Pinwheel | 2213 |
| Pinwheel | 2214 |
| Pinwheel | 2314 |
| Pinwheel | 2487 |
| Pinwheel | 3008 |
| Pinwheel | 3476 |
| Pinwheel | 3751 |
| Pinwheel Parade | 1296 |
| Pinwheel Quilt | 1202 |
| Pinwheel Quilt | 1299 |
| Pinwheel Quilt | 3394 |
| Pinwheel Skew | 2038 |
| Pinwheel Star | 3866 |
| Pinwheel, The | 264 |
| Pinwheel, The | 2537 |
| Pinwheel, The | 2718 |
| Pinwheels | 1129 |
| Pinwheels | 1264 |
| Pinwheels and Squares | 1200 |
| Pioneer Block | 2317 |
| Pioneer Block | 2576 |
| Pioneer Patch | 1850 |
| Plaid | 1827 |
| Plaid Star | 3888 |
| Plain Sailing | 1261 |
| Plaited Block | 4195 |
| Plane Thinking | 1790 |
| Play Block | 142 |
| Pleasant Paths | 212.3 |
| Poinsetta | 3009 |
| Poinsettia | 440 |
| Poinsettia | 4043 |
| Poinsettia Quilt | 416 |
| Poinsettia Quilt | 768.3 |
| Poinsettias | 3814 |
| Pointed Oblong | 171 |
| Pointed Ovals | 4094 |
| Pointed Tile | 420 |
| Pointing Star | 262 |
| Pointing Star | 427.5 |
| Points and Petals | 4060 |
| Polar Bear | 939.3 |
| Polaris Star | 3766 |
| Pole Star | 3825 |
| Polka Dots | 1451 |
| Polly and Her Cage | 936.8 |
| Pond Lily | 796.2 |
| Pontiac Star | 3871 |
| Poor Boy | 160 |

543

Index

Poppy....756.7
Pork and Beans....1195
Port and Starboard....1176
Posey Quilt, The....2526
Posies Round the Square....2525
Postage Stamp....2276
Postage Stamp....2286
Postage Stamp....2293
Postage Stamp....2430
Posy Plot....2356
Pot of Flowers....744.5
Pot of Flowers....765.4
Potomac Pride....2691
Potomac Pride....1043
Potted Star Flower....748
Powdor Puff....192
Practical Orchard....1685
Practical Orchard....1707
Prairie Flower....1755
Prairie Flower....798.5
Prairie Lily....765.4
Prairie Lily, The....765.25
Prairie Queen....1656
Prairie Queen....3047
Prairie Star....460.5
Prairie Star....3773
Prairie Sunrise....3939
Premium Star....1881
President Carter....1721
President Roosevelt, The....3094
President's Block....2241
President's Quilt....769
President's Quilt....1043
President's Quilt....2691
Presidential Armchair, The....1914
Pretty Patchwork, A....415.35
Pretty Pussy....937.5
Pretty Triangles....1193
Prickly Path, The....479
Prickly Pear....1948
Prickly Pear....2584
Pride of Holland....2792
Pride of Italy....1889
Pride of Ohio, The....2419
Pride of Texas....4005
Pride of the Bride....3190
Primrose....3523
Primrose Patch Quilt....751.5
Primrose Path....2940
Primrose Path....3273
Print and Plain....3886
Priscilla, The....2975
Priscilla's Choice....800.9
Priscilla's Dream....2082
Priscilla's Prize....3015
Progressive....3623
Proof Through the Night....1761
Propeller....1934
Prosperity Block....1779
Prosperity Quilt....1779
Proud Pine....815
Providence....1819
Providence....2920
Providence Quilt Block....2920
Providence Star, The....2921
Prudence's Star....3048
Puff....192
Puff Ball....192
Puffed Squares....191
Pullman Puzzle....1508
Pullman Puzzle....1001
Pumpkin Vine, The....1461
Pure Symbol of Right Doctrine....1130
Pure Symbol of Right Doctrine....2577
Puritan Maiden....2009
Puritan Star Quilt....3735
Purple Cross, The....3880
Puss in the Corner....1603
Puss in the Corner....1613
Puss in the Corner....1614
Puss in the Corner....1669
Puss in the Corner....1728
Puss in the Corner....2110
Puss in the Corner....2111
Puss-in-the-Corner....1646
Pussy in the Corner....1603
Puzzle....2812
Puzzle Quilt....3284
Puzzle Tile....434
Pyramids, The....4102
Pyramid Patchwork....205
Pyramid, The....201
Pyramids....111
Pyramids....203
Pyramids....2448
Pyramids....2512
Pyrotechnics....3461
Q Quilt....404
Quail's Nest....1646
Quartered Star....2585
Quatrefoils....2523
Quatrefoils....4180
Quebec....2567
Queen Charlotte's Crown....1810
Queen Charlotte's Crown....4134
Queen Victoria's Crown....2071
Queen of the May....3598
Queen of the May....3645
Queen's Crown....1810
Queen's Crown....1818
Queen's Crown....2221
Queen's Crown....3666
Queen's Crown Quilt....4097
Queen's Delight....3442
Queen's Favorite, The....2413
Queen's Petticoat....1697
Queen's Pride....1795
Queen's Pride....2222
Queen's Star....3763
Queen's Treasure....4138
Quilt Made of Scraps, A....954
Quilt Mosaic, A....2539
Quilt Star....3873
Quilt Without a Name, The....1427
Quilt in Light and Dark....3253
Quilt Of Four Birds....438.7
Quilt of Variety, A....1181
Quilt of Variety, A....3250
Quilt of the Century....3772
Quilted Butterfly, A....923.5
Quilter's Delight....1473
Quilter's Delight....1836
Quilter's Delight....1995
Quilter's Pride....4093
Quint Five Quilt, The....1181
Quintettes....432
R There....989.5
Radiant Star....2248
Radiant Star....3000
Radio Windmill, The....2560
Ragged Robin....2941
Rail Fence....112
Rail Fence....145
Rail Fence....432
Rail Fence Quilt....4163
Railroad....1312
Railroad, The....1695
Railroad Around Rock Mountain....3352
Railroad Crossing....299.4
Railroad Crossing....1009
Railroad Crossing....2337
Railroad Crossing....2779
Railroad Crossing....2932
Railroad Crossing....2939
Railroad Crossing....3263
Railroad Quilt, The....1627
Rain or Shine....2930
Rainbow....303
Rainbow....475
Rainbow....3356
Rainbow....3374
Rainbow....3974
Rainbow Block....3112
Rainbow Block....3153
Rainbow Cactus....725
Rainbow Quilt....2289
Rainbow Quilt Design....3315
Rainbow Quilt, The....3350
Rainbow 'Round the World....2293
Rainbow Square....2688
Rainbow Square, The....2502
Rainbow Star....3778
Rainbow Star Quilt....3712
Rainbow, The....302
Rainbow, The....2766
Rainbow Tile....160
Rainbow Weave....209.6
Rainbow Wedding Ring....303
Raised Patchwork....191
Raised Patchwork....193
Raised Patchwork....194
Raleigh....3083
Rambler....2798
Rambling Road....1354
Rambling Road....2584
Rambling Rose....2584
Range's Pride, The....2341
Ratchet Wheel, The....2091
Rattlesnake....3352
Ray....3618
Ray of Light....3463
Razzle Dazzle....4171
Rebecca's Fan....3345
Red Barn....883
Red Basket....653
Red Buds....305.7
Red Cross....437
Red Cross....483
Red Cross....1861
Red Cross....1874
Red Cross....2030
Red Cross....2894
Red Cross Quilt, The....1901
Red Cross, The....1107
Red Robin....936.4
Red Shields....111
Red White and Blue Criss Cross....2776
Red and White Cross....1415
Red and White Quilt....3985
Red, White 'n Blue "V" Quilt....991.9
Red, White and Blue....3156
Red, White and Blue....4055
Red, White and Blue Quilt....3677
Red, White and Blue Quilt, A....2677
Reel, The....3110
Refractions....222
Reindeer....939.7
Reminiscent of the Wedding Ring....3620
Repeat X....3053
Repeating Square....429
Resolutions....1883
Return of the Swallows....1340
Reverse X....1210
Rhode Island....2836
Rhode Island Maple Leaf Star....1926
Rhododendron Star....3441
Ribbon Border....4130
Ribbon Quilt....1160
Ribbon Quilt....1657
Ribbon Square....2207
Ribbon Star....1138
Ribbon Ribbons....4023
Richmond....1654
Richmond Beauty....1086
Right Angle Patchwork....152
Right Angles Patchwork....177
Right Hand of Friendship....2831
Right and Left....2406
Ring Around the Rosy....3589
Ring Around the Rosy....3590
Ring Around the Star....2509
Ring Around the Star....3794
Rising Star....142
Rising Star....2167
Rising Star....3514
Rising Star....3729
Rising Star....3772
Rising Star....4005
Rising Star....4062
Rising Sun....2852
Rising Sun....3165
Rising Sun....3339
Rising Sun....3390
Rising Sun....3445
Rising Sun....3480
Rising Sun....3584

# Index

| Name | Number |
|---|---|
| Rising Sun | 3604 |
| Rising Sun | 3729 |
| Rising Sun | 3791 |
| Rising Sun | 3989 |
| Rising Sun | 3995 |
| Rising Sun | 3996 |
| Rising Sun | 4005 |
| Riviera | 1241 |
| Road Home, The | 1477 |
| Road of Fortune | 1299 |
| Road to California | 1687 |
| Road to California | 1963 |
| Road to California | 2210 |
| Road to California, The | 146 |
| Road to California, The | 2098 |
| Road to Fortune | 1299 |
| Road to Heaven | 1324 |
| Road to Jerusalem | 2537 |
| Road to Oklahoma | 1123 |
| Road to Oklahoma | 2644 |
| Road to Oklahoma City | 2086 |
| Road to Paradise | 1626 |
| Road to Paris | 4194 |
| Road to Paris, The | 2471 |
| Road to the White House | 1639 |
| Roads to Berlin | 2597 |
| Rob Peter and Pay Paul | 1519 |
| Rob Peter and Pay Paul | 2683 |
| Rob Peter to Pay Paul | 1450 |
| Rob Peter to Pay Paul | 1472 |
| Rob Peter to Pay Paul | 4141 |
| Robbing Peter to Pay Paul | 1461 |
| Robbing Peter to Pay Paul | 1512 |
| Robbing Peter to Pay Paul | 1520 |
| Robbing Peter to Pay Paul | 1771 |
| Robbing Peter to Pay Paul | 2685 |
| Robbing Peter to Pay Paul | 2764 |
| Rock Garden | 298 |
| Rock Garden | 3056 |
| Rock Star | 222.5 |
| Rock Wall | 272.5 |
| Rockingham's Beauty | 2987 |
| Rocky Glen | 1362 |
| Rocky Glen | 3166 |
| Rocky Glen | 3269 |
| Rocky Mountain | 1079 |
| Rocky Mountain | 1083 |
| Rocky Mountain | 3152 |
| Rocky Mountain | 1079 |
| Rocky Mountain | 1083 |
| Rocky Mountain High | 224.5 |
| Rocky Mountain Puzzle | 2180 |
| Rocky Mountain Road | 1076 |
| Rocky Mountain Road | 1077 |
| Rocky Road to California | 1639 |
| Rocky Road to Dublin | 1461 |
| Rocky Road to Dublin | 1696 |
| Rocky Road to Jerico | 3372 |
| Rocky Road to Kansas | 415.25 |
| Rocky Road to Kansas | 2979 |
| Rocky Road to Kansas | 3079 |
| Rolling Nine Patch | 2088 |
| Rolling Pinwheel | 3602 |
| Rolling Pinwheel | 1348 |
| Rolling Pinwheel | 1349 |
| Rolling Pinwheel | 1413 |
| Rolling Square | 1932 |
| Rolling Squares | 1731 |
| Rolling Star | 296.5 |
| Rolling Star | 2509 |
| Rolling Star | 3704 |
| Rolling Star | 3795 |
| Rolling Star | 3805 |
| Rolling Star Quilt | 4088 |
| Rolling Stone | 1727 |
| Rolling Stone | 1806 |
| Rolling Stone | 2188 |
| Rolling Stone | 3034 |
| Rolling Stone | 3805 |
| Roman Cross | 2814 |
| Roman Pavement | 2935 |
| Roman Pavements | 1508 |
| Roman Roads | 1918 |
| Roman Square | 477 |
| Roman Square | 1111 |
| Roman Square, The | 1619 |
| Roman Stripe | 477 |
| Roman Stripe Zig Zag | 1111 |
| Roman Stripes | 3153 |
| Roman Wall Quilt | 486 |
| Rope | 435.2 |
| Rope and Anchor | 1677 |
| Rosalia Flower Garden | 430 |
| Rose | 755 |
| Rose | 780 |
| Rose | 2623 |
| Rose Album | 3438 |
| Rose Album | 3651 |
| Rose Arbor | 209 |
| Rose Basket | 753 |
| Rose Dream | 1532 |
| Rose Garden | 4211 |
| Rose Star One Patch | 153 |
| Rose Star One Patch | 243 |
| Rose Tellis | 2555 |
| Rose Windows | 3129 |
| Rose and Trellis | 2360 |
| Rose in Summer | 3949 |
| Rosebud | 1273 |
| Rosebud | 1775 |
| Rosebud | 1884 |
| Rosebud Patchwork | 774 |
| Rosebud Quilt, The | 2710 |
| Rosebud Quilt, The | 2711 |
| Rosebud, The | 2095 |
| Rosebud, The | 2659 |
| Rosebuds of Spring | 3102 |
| Rosemary | 2925 |
| Roses of Picardy | 275.8 |
| Rosette | 192 |
| Rosette | 3502 |
| Roulette Wheel Star for Nevada | 3721 |
| Round Robin | 3509 |
| Round Table | 3376 |
| 'Round the Corner | 1804 |
| 'Round the Twist | 1028.5 |
| 'Round the World | 1467 |
| Royal Aster Quilt, The | 3999 |
| Royal Cross | 3084 |
| Royal Diamonds | 3854 |
| Royal Dutch Tulip and Vase | 743 |
| Royal Gems | 3012 |
| Royal Japanese Vase | 743 |
| Royal Star Quilt | 2453 |
| Royal, The | 3084 |
| Ruby Roads | 1988 |
| Ruby's Star | 2327 |
| Ruins of Jerico | 4188 |
| Russian Sunflower | 3480 |
| Rustic Wheel | 2615 |
| S | 990.2 |
| Sapphire Quilt Block | 2628 |
| Sacramento | 2007 |
| Sacramento | 3872 |
| Sacramento City | 2007 |
| Saddlebag | 3067 |
| Sage Bud | 1713 |
| Sage Bud of Wyoming | 1890 |
| Sail Boat | 3172 |
| Sail Boat Block | 1393 |
| Sailboat | 919 |
| Sailboat Quilt | 915 |
| Sailboat Oklahoma, The | 914 |
| Sailing Darts | 1990 |
| Sailing into Dreamland | 910 |
| Sailor's Joy | 3760 |
| Salal | 2219 |
| Sally's Favorite | 2311 |
| Salt Lake City | 3226 |
| Salute to Loyalty | 211 |
| Salute to the Colors, A | 2159 |
| Sam's Quilt | 3725 |
| Samoa | 3512 |
| Samoan Poppy | 3410 |
| San Diego | 2170 |
| Sandhills Star | 2540 |
| Santa Fe | 2241 |
| Santa Fe Block | 1725 |
| Santa Fe Trail | 1726 |
| Sapphire Net | 3117 |
| Saracen Chain | 2967 |
| Sarah's Choice | 2145 |
| Sarah's Favorite | 2311 |
| Sargeant's Chevron | 4129 |
| Sassafras Leaf | 1831 |
| Saturn's Rings | 2666 |
| Savannah Beautiful Star | 3719 |
| Savannah Beautiful Star | 3720 |
| Save A Piece | 1527 |
| Save All | 1842 |
| Saw, The | 1363 |
| Saw Tooth | 3166 |
| Saw Tooth Patchwork | 1652 |
| Saw Toothed Star | 1136 |
| Saw Teeth | 3844 |
| Sawtooth | 2138 |
| Sawtooth | 2185 |
| Sawtooth | 2249 |
| Sawtooth | 2648 |
| Sawtooth | 3167 |
| Sawtooth | 3168 |
| Sawtooth | 3843 |
| Sawtooth | 3984 |
| Sawtooth | 3985 |
| Sawtooth | 4125 |
| Sawtooth Diamond | 3985 |
| Sawtooth Pattern | 3723 |
| Sawtooth Squares | 1068 |
| Sawtooth Star | 1238 |
| Sawtooth Star | 3730 |
| Scarlet Carnations | 773.2 |
| Schoenrock Cross | 1993 |
| School House | 878 |
| School House | 879 |
| Schoolhouse | 867 |
| Schoolhouse | 870.5 |
| Schoolhouse | 873 |
| Scotch Heather | 1956 |
| Scotch Plaid | 2463 |
| Scotch Quilt | 1390 |
| Scotch Squares | 2463 |
| Scottie Patchwork | 938.2 |
| Scottie Quilt | 938.3 |
| Scottish Cross, The | 1220 |
| Scrap | 2378 |
| Scrap Bag | 1815 |
| Scrap Bag Squares | 2842 |
| Scrap Basket | 728 |
| Scrap Cats | 937.2 |
| Scrap Zig Zag | 1334 |
| Scrapbag | 1671 |
| Scrapbag | 2825 |
| Scroll Work | 2981 |
| Scuppernong Hull | 301.7 |
| Sea Shell Quilt, The | 3357 |
| Sea Shells | 1457 |
| Sea Shells on the Beach | 181 |
| Sea Star | 3904 |
| Seal | 939.8 |
| Seashell | 181 |
| Seasons, The | 1907 |
| Secret Drawer | 2804 |
| Seesaw | 1336 |
| Semi-Octagon | 2704 |
| Seminole Square | 4177 |
| Sentry's Pastime | 2616 |
| Setting Sun | 2662 |
| Setting Sun | 3661 |
| Seven Sisters | 241 |
| Seven Stars | 241 |
| Seven Stars in a Cluster | 241 |
| Shaded Diamonds | 212.5 |
| Shaded Trail | 4032 |
| Shaded Box | 1366 |
| Shaded Box | 2642 |
| Shaded Box | 3152 |
| Shaded Boxes | 2377 |
| Shadow Quilt | 3153 |
| Shadow Star | 3434 |
| Shadow Trail | 232 |
| Shadows | 3153 |
| Shady Lane | 1032 |
| Shasta Daisy | 1283 |
| Shasta Daisy | 3025 |
| Shasta Daisy Quilt, The | 458 |
| Sheepfold Quilt | 2020 |
| Shell | 181 |
| Shell Chain | 181 |

# Index

| Name | Page |
|---|---|
| Shepherd's Crossing | 4104 |
| Shepherd's Light | 3434 |
| Sherman's March | 1646 |
| Shifting Cubes | 142 |
| Shining Hour | 2938 |
| Shining Star | 3829 |
| Shining Star, The | 2986 |
| Ship, The | 911 |
| Ship at Sea | 3181 |
| Ships Wheel | 3773 |
| Ships a Sailing Quilt | 2722 |
| Ships at Sea | 3181 |
| Ships in the Night | 916 |
| Shoemaker's Puzzle | 1250 |
| Shoo Fly | 1171 |
| Shoo Fly | 1202 |
| Shoo Fly | 1206 |
| Shoo Fly | 1645 |
| Shoo Fly | 1646 |
| Shoo-Fly | 1859 |
| Shoofly | 1631 |
| Shoofly | 2375 |
| Shoofly Variation | 1847 |
| Shooting Star | 225.3 |
| Shooting Star | 1152.7 |
| Shooting Star | 1347 |
| Shooting Star | 2556 |
| Shooting Star | 3290 |
| Shooting Star | 3917 |
| Shooting Stars | 1248 |
| Sickle, The | 1327 |
| Signal | 1863 |
| Signal Lights | 2983 |
| Signature Friendship Quilt, The | 2040 |
| Signs of Spring | 2499 |
| Silent Star, The | 1633 |
| Silk Quilt | 4128 |
| Silver & Gold | 4003 |
| Silver Maple | 1442 |
| Silver and Gold | 3746 |
| Simple Cross | 2023 |
| Simple Design | 3063 |
| Simple Design | 3162 |
| Simple Design | 4144 |
| Simple Flower Basket | 705 |
| Simple Star | 3735 |
| Simplicity | 1202 |
| Simplicity | 1645 |
| Simplicity's Delight | 160 |
| Singing Corners | 3107 |
| Single Chain and Knot | 1811 |
| Single Irish Chain | 1019 |
| Single Irish Chain | 2023 |
| Single Lily | 1386 |
| Single Star | 1136 |
| Single Sunflower | 3481 |
| Single Wedding ring | 1727 |
| Sirius Star, The | 4013 |
| Sister Nan's Cross | 949.5 |
| Sister's Choice | 1930 |
| Sitka | 3857 |
| Six Point String Quilt | 3718 |
| Six Pointed Star | 239 |
| Six Pointed Star | 273 |
| Six Pointed Star | 3723 |
| Six-Sided Patchwork | 160 |
| Sky Rocket | 2454 |
| Sky Rocket | 2508 |
| Skyrocket Design | 3044 |
| Skyscrapers | 4169 |
| Slanted Diamond | 1311 |
| Slanted Diamonds | 1692 |
| Slashed Album | 2601 |
| Slashed Star | 3463 |
| Slashed Star | 3401 |
| Slashed Star | 3850 |
| Slave Cabin | 3079 |
| Small Business | 1225 |
| Small Hand | 1879 |
| Small Triangles Quilt | 1193 |
| Smoothing Iron, The | 266 |
| Snail's Trail | 2091 |
| Snail's Trail | 2397 |
| Snail's Trail | 2398 |
| Snail's Trail | 2399 |
| Snake Fence | 112 |
| Snake Fence | 114 |
| Snake Trail | 1459 |
| Snake Trail | 3352 |
| Snake in a Hole | 3353 |
| Snow Block | 2880 |
| Snow Crystals | 244 |
| Snow Crystals | 3802 |
| Snowball | 1246 |
| Snowball | 1450 |
| Snowball | 1452 |
| Snowball | 1453 |
| Snowball | 1500 |
| Snowball | 1507 |
| Snowball | 1508 |
| Snowball | 1517 |
| Snowball | 1518 |
| Snowball | 2672 |
| Snowball | 4057 |
| Snowball | 1001 |
| Snowball Flower | 1540 |
| Snowball Wreath | 1515 |
| Snowball and Nine Patch, The | 1001 |
| Snowballs | 442 |
| Snowballs | 4142 |
| Snowbound | 1030 |
| Snowdrop | 754 |
| Snowflake | 234 |
| Snowflake | 2880 |
| Snowflake Continuity | 3414 |
| Snowflake Quilt | 266.5 |
| Snowy Windows | 1454 |
| Soldier Boy | 218 |
| Soldiers | 940.44 |
| Solomon's Garden | 427.7 |
| Solomon's Puzzle | 1039 |
| Solomon's Puzzle | 1461 |
| Solomon's Puzzle | 1462 |
| Solomon's Star | 2149 |
| Solomon's Temple | 2441 |
| Solomon's Temple | 3986 |
| Sombrero Appliqué | 3526 |
| Some Pretty Patchwork | 727 |
| South Carolina | 2929 |
| South Carolina's Album Block | 1812 |
| Southern Plantation | 3719 |
| Southern Star | 2569 |
| Southern Star | 3408 |
| Southern Star, The | 3735 |
| Space Capsule | 968 |
| Space Ships | 3041 |
| Spanish Fleet | 3361 |
| Spanish Squares | 1384 |
| Sparkling Jewel | 3946 |
| Sparkling Dew | 277 |
| Sparkling Jewels | 415.6 |
| Spice Pink | 1081.5 |
| Spice Pinks | 2527 |
| Spider | 1130 |
| Spider | 1691 |
| Spider Web | 246 |
| Spider Web | 247 |
| Spider Web | 1306 |
| Spider Web | 1307 |
| Spider Web | 2723 |
| Spider Web | 2726 |
| Spider Web | 2727 |
| Spider Web | 2749 |
| Spider Web | 3491 |
| Spider Web | 3546 |
| Spider Web, The | 1075 |
| Spider Web, The | 2544 |
| Spider Web, The | 3498 |
| Spider Web, The | 3842 |
| Spider and the Fly | 3520 |
| Spider's Den | 1940 |
| Spider's Web | 2728 |
| Spiderweb Star | 3754 |
| Spindles and Stripes | 2391 |
| Spinner, The | 1265 |
| Spinning Arrows | 1155 |
| Spinning Ball | 3535 |
| Spinning Ball | 3537 |
| Spinning Color Wheel | 1295 |
| Spinning Hour Glass | 4205 |
| Spinning Jenny | 2347 |
| Spinning Jenny | 2588 |
| Spinning L | 1406 |
| Spinning Star | 3759 |
| Spinning Stars | 2319 |
| Spinning Stars | 2497 |
| Spinning Stars | 3932 |
| Spinning Stars | 3933 |
| Spinning Tops | 1858 |
| Spinning Wheel | 1351 |
| Spinning Wheel | 3625 |
| Spinster's Spindle | 971 |
| Spiral | 3537 |
| Spirit of 1849 | 3092 |
| Spirit of St. Louis | 1111 |
| Spiritus Mundi | 1194 |
| Split Bars | 475.5 |
| Split Nine Patch | 1688 |
| Split Nine Patch | 1690 |
| Split Rail | 1079 |
| Spokane | 2909 |
| Spool | 1407 |
| Spool | 2131 |
| Spool | 2594 |
| Spool, The | 185 |
| Spool, The | 1681 |
| Spool | 1681 |
| Spool And Bobbin | 1179 |
| Spool And Bobbin | 1758 |
| Spool Block | 1970 |
| Spool of 1966 | 3571 |
| Spools | 185 |
| Spools | 2351 |
| Spools | 2804 |
| Spring | 1062.5 |
| Spring Beauty | 1528 |
| Spring Beauty | 2798 |
| Spring Fancy | 790 |
| Spring Flowers | 680 |
| Spring Has Come | 2062 |
| Spring and Fall | 216.27 |
| Springfield | 4035 |
| Springfield Patch | 4035 |
| Springtime | 3130 |
| Springtime Blossoms | 1500 |
| Springtime Blossoms | 1502 |
| Springtime in the Ozarks | 141 |
| Springtime in the Rockies | 1076.5 |
| Sprite, The | 1380 |
| Square Cross | 1057 |
| Square Cross | 1058 |
| Square Dance | 1867 |
| Square Dance | 2085 |
| Square Dance | 2702 |
| Square Deal, The | 1966 |
| Square Diamond, The | 2617 |
| Square Diamonds | 173 |
| Square up | 2787 |
| Square Upon Square | 422 |
| Square and Circles | 3510 |
| Square and Compass | 2366 |
| Square and Half Square | 1763 |
| Square and Points | 2138 |
| Square and Star | 2046 |
| Square and Swallow | 772 |
| Square and a Half | 2137 |
| Square on Square | 2378 |
| Square within Square | 2092 |
| Squared Chain | 1616 |
| Squared Chain | 1651 |
| Squared Circle | 4056 |
| Squared Star | 2620 |
| Squares | 2289 |
| Squares Around the World | 2286 |
| Squares Upon Squares | 1104 |
| Squares and Crosses | 2521 |
| Squares and Lily | 3104 |
| Squares and Oblongs | 2025 |
| Squares and Square | 1902 |
| Squares and Triangles | 2046 |
| Squares within Squares | 1102 |
| Squash Blossom | 1773 |
| Squire Smith's Choice | 1291 |
| Squirrel | 939.9 |
| Squirrel in a Cage | 1727 |
| St. Elmo's Cross | 3126 |
| St. Elmo's Firs | 3793 |

# Index

| Entry | Page |
|---|---|
| St. John Pavement | 2810 |
| St. Louis | 1237 |
| St. Louis Block | 2740 |
| St. Louis Block | 3882 |
| St. Louis Star | 2737 |
| St. Louis Star | 2740 |
| St. Louis Star | 3830 |
| St. Paul | 2493 |
| Stained Glass | 432 |
| Stair Step Quilt | 142 |
| Stairs of Illusion | 142 |
| Stairstep Quilt | 142 |
| Stanley, The | 4181 |
| Star | 415 |
| Star | 1631 |
| Star | 2331 |
| Star | 3735 |
| Star | 3799 |
| Star | 3947 |
| Star and Box Quilt, The | 142 |
| Star & Pinwheels | 2148 |
| Star, A | 1722 |
| Star Bed Quilt | 3735 |
| Star Bouquet | 424 |
| Star Bouquet | 759 |
| Star Bouquet | 3773 |
| Star Bouquet Quilt | 427 |
| Star Center on French Bouquet | 244 |
| Star Chain | 1715 |
| Star Chain, The | 312 |
| Star Crescent | 3902 |
| Star Dahlia | 3428 |
| Star Design | 1631 |
| Star Diamond | 2243 |
| Star Fish | 233 |
| Star Fish, The | 222.2 |
| Star Flower | 791 |
| Star Flower | 857.04 |
| Star Flower | 2134 |
| Star Flower | 2746 |
| Star Flower | 3423 |
| Star Flower | 3424 |
| Star Flower | 3427 |
| Star Flower Wreath | 4196 |
| Star Flowers | 3816 |
| Star Garden | 251 |
| Star Kites | 1246 |
| Star Kites | 3892 |
| Star Lane | 2105 |
| Star Net | 3831 |
| Star Over the Mountain | 4050 |
| Star Pattern | 3023 |
| Star Points | 1309 |
| Star Premo | 2405 |
| Star Puzzle | 2146 |
| Star Quilt Block | 3809 |
| Star Rays | 266 |
| Star Shower | 3823 |
| Star Spangled | 1631 |
| Star Spangled Banner | 2268 |
| Star Spangled Banner | 2270 |
| Star Spangled Banner, The | 1783 |
| Star Studded Beauty | 261 |
| Star, The | 3706 |
| Star, The | 3735 |
| Star Trek | 2158 |
| Star Tulip | 3655 |
| Star Upon Stars | 3773 |
| Star Within Star | 3542 |
| Star Within a Star | 3809 |
| Star X | 1633 |
| Star X | 2835 |
| Star and Arrow | 3829 |
| Star and Block | 1028.7 |
| Star and Block, The | 2792 |
| Star and Chains | 2509 |
| Star and Cone | 3926 |
| Star and Corona | 4039 |
| Star and Crescent | 276 |
| Star and Crescent | 3689 |
| Star and Crescent | 3902 |
| Star and Cross | 438 |
| Star and Cross | 1915 |
| Star and Cross | 1930 |
| Star and Cross | 2005 |
| Star and Cross | 2938 |
| Star and Cross | 2954 |
| Star and Cross | 3230 |
| Star and Crown | 2614 |
| Star and Crown | 3425 |
| Star and Diamond | 2975 |
| Star and Diamond | 3807 |
| Star and Diamond Quilt | 415.23 |
| Star and Diamonds | 216.4 |
| Star and Mill Block | 1435 |
| Star and Planets | 3710 |
| Star and Square | 2605 |
| Star and Stirrups | 3642 |
| Star and Stripe | 1982 |
| Star and Triangles | 3121 |
| Star and Web Quilt | 445.3 |
| Star and Wreath | 3818 |
| Star in a Nine Patch | 1711 |
| Star in a Star | 3993 |
| Star in the Window | 2119 |
| Star in the Window | 3992 |
| Star of Alamo, The | 2609 |
| Star of Bethlehem | 255 |
| Star of Bethlehem | 2245 |
| Star of Bethlehem | 2248 |
| Star of Bethlehem | 2249 |
| Star of Bethlehem | 3655 |
| Star of Bethlehem | 3715 |
| Star of Bethlehem | 3724 |
| Star of Bethlehem | 3648 |
| Star of Bethlehem | 3777 |
| Star of Bethlehem | 3796 |
| Star of Bethlehem | 3809 |
| Star of Bethlehem | 4005 |
| Star of Bethlehem | 4007 |
| Star of Bethlehem, The | 2161 |
| Star of Chamblie | 415 |
| Star of Chamblie | 2244 |
| Star of Destiny | 400.2 |
| Star of Destiny | 2896 |
| Star of Diamonds | 3706 |
| Star of Erin | 1298 |
| Star of Fortune | 2746 |
| Star of '49 | 3841 |
| Star of France | 4000 |
| Star of Home | 3165 |
| Star of Hope | 1061 |
| Star of Hope | 1631 |
| Star of Hope | 3773 |
| Star of Hope | 3861 |
| Star of LeMoyne | 3735 |
| Star of Manhatten | 2482 |
| Star of Many Points | 1255 |
| Star of Many Points | 2538 |
| Star of Mexico | 3406 |
| Star of Montana | 269.6 |
| Star of Mystery | 2866 |
| Star of North Carolina | 2962 |
| Star of North Carolina | 3045 |
| Star of Spring | 1217 |
| Star of St. Louis | 3830 |
| Star of St. Louis | 3883 |
| Star of Stars | 4005 |
| Star of Sweden | 3582 |
| Star of Star of Texas | 3592 |
| Star of Victory Quilt | 3771 |
| Star of Virginia | 2578 |
| Star of West Virginia | 3533 |
| Star of the Bluegrass Quilt | 3772 |
| Star of the Decathalon | 4048 |
| Star of the East | 2705 |
| Star of the East | 3702 |
| Star of the East | 3705 |
| Star of the East | 3716 |
| Star of the East | 3745 |
| Star of the East | 3772 |
| Star of the East | 3808 |
| Star of the East | 3947 |
| Star of the East | 4003 |
| Star of the East | 4005 |
| Star of the Four Winds | 3902 |
| Star of the Magi | 3796 |
| Star of the Milky Way | 1282 |
| Star of the Night | 3937 |
| Star of the Night | 4183 |
| Star of the Orient | 3895 |
| Star of the Sea | 3904 |
| Star of the West | 1128 |
| Star of the West | 1631 |
| Star of the West | 3222 |
| Star of the West | 3679 |
| Star of the West | 3681 |
| Star of the West | 3902 |
| Star's Exhibition House | 862 |
| Starbright Quilt, The | 3813 |
| Starfish | 3828 |
| Starflower | 3678 |
| Starlight | 2454 |
| Starlight | 3858 |
| Starlight | 3867 |
| Starlight Quilt, The | 3858 |
| Starry Crown | 3595 |
| Starry Crown | 3668 |
| Starry Crown | 4045 |
| Starry Heavens | 3779 |
| Starry Lane | 2105 |
| Starry Lane | 2206 |
| Starry Night | 415.21 |
| Starry Night | 2702 |
| Starry Path | 2346 |
| Starry Path | 2352 |
| Starry Pavement | 3074 |
| Stars Upon Star | 3777 |
| Stars Upon Stars | 3773 |
| Stars Within Stars | 3687 |
| Stars and Blocks | 143 |
| Stars and Cubes | 2076 |
| Stars and Cubes | 3799 |
| Stars and Cubes | 3801 |
| Stars and Squares | 2167 |
| Stars and Stripes | 1250 |
| Stars and Stripes | 3244 |
| Stars and Stripes | 3748 |
| Stars of Alabama | 3773 |
| Stars of Twilight | 423.5 |
| Stars over Tennessee | 1923 |
| State Fair | 2631 |
| State House | 1143 |
| State of California #2 | 4040 |
| State of Georgia | 1801 |
| State of Kentucky | 241.4 |
| State of Nebraska Quilt Block | 3938 |
| State of North Carolina | 2962 |
| State of Ohio | 1232 |
| State of Ohio | 857.09 |
| State of Oklahoma | 3554 |
| Steeplechase | 1450 |
| Steeplechase | 1504 |
| Steeplechase | 1520 |
| Steeplechase | 2685 |
| Stepping Stones | 1153 |
| Stepping Stones | 1695 |
| Stepping Stones | 1963 |
| Stepping Stones | 1976 |
| Stepping Stones | 1983 |
| Steps to Glory | 1025 |
| Steps to the Altar | 142 |
| Steps to the Altar | 1694 |
| Steps to the Altar | 2288 |
| Steps to the Altar | 3186 |
| Steps to the Garden | 2284 |
| Steps to the Light House | 2027 |
| Steps to the White House | 2825 |
| Stockade, The | 4084 |
| Stockyard's Star | 2163 |
| Stone Mason's Puzzle | 1903 |
| Stonewall Jackson | 1061.5 |
| Storm Signal | 1196 |
| Storm at Sea | 1071 |
| Storm at Sea | 2187 |
| Storm at Sea | 2188 |
| Storm at Sea | 2584 |
| Strawberry | 3634 |
| Strawberry | 3641 |
| Strawberry Basket | 3187 |
| Streak 'O Lightning | 112 |
| Streak 'O Lightning | 132 |
| Streak of Lightning | 135 |
| Streets of New York | 1072.5 |
| Strength of Union | 1807 |
| Striking Pattern, A | 3457 |
| String Quilt | 1303 |
| String Quilt | 2326 |

547

# Index

| | |
|---|---|
| String Quilt | 2327 |
| Strip Squares | 1830 |
| Striped-Plain Quilt, A | 1192 |
| Stripes and Squares | 1830 |
| Strips and Squares | 1746 |
| Strutting Peacock | 935.5 |
| Stylized Eagle | 3247 |
| Sue's Delight | 3116 |
| Suffolk Puffs | 192 |
| Sugar Bowl | 660 |
| Sugar Bowl | 701 |
| Sugar Bowl | 702 |
| Sugar Bowl | 1519 |
| Sugar Bowl Quilt | 2406 |
| Sugar Bowl, The | 702.5 |
| Sugar Cone | 1252 |
| Sugar Loaf | 201 |
| Sugar Loaf | 204 |
| Sugar Loaf | 2292 |
| Sugar Loaf | 2721 |
| Sugar Loaf | 4021 |
| Sugar Scoop | 181 |
| Sugar Scoop | 184 |
| Sugarbowl | 1262 |
| Sultan's Block | 416.7 |
| Summer Fancy | 3112 |
| Summer Garden | 2284 |
| Summer Sun | 2261 |
| Summer Sun | 4010 |
| Summer Trees | 403.5 |
| Summer Winds | 1668 |
| Summer's Dream | 2042 |
| Sun Burst Quilt, The | 4014 |
| Sun Dial | 1054 |
| Sun Ray's Quilt | 1623 |
| Sun, The | 3487 |
| Sun and Shade | 1208 |
| Sun and shadow | 2286 |
| Sun, Moon and Stars | 3507 |
| Sunbeam | 1791 |
| Sunbeam | 2620 |
| Sunbeam Crossroad | 2931 |
| Sunbonnet Girl | 940.8 |
| Sunbonnet Girls | 940.6 |
| Sunbonnet Girls | 940.7 |
| Sunburst | 1992 |
| Sunburst | 2663 |
| Sunburst | 3373 |
| Sunburst | 3400 |
| Sunburst | 3402 |
| Sunburst | 4303 |
| Sunburst | 3449 |
| Sunburst | 3462 |
| Sunburst | 3466 |
| Sunburst | 3469 |
| Sunburst | 3470 |
| Sunburst | 3480 |
| Sunburst | 3486 |
| Sunburst | 3491 |
| Sunburst | 3543 |
| Sunburst | 3851 |
| Sunburst | 4006 |
| Sunburst Quilt, The | 3456 |
| Sunburst Star | 3777 |
| Sunburst, The | 415.3 |
| Sunburst And Mills | 3782 |
| Sundance | 2864 |
| Sundial | 1754 |
| Sunflower | 795 |
| Sunflower | 2663 |
| Sunflower | 2678 |
| Sunflower | 3425 |
| Sunflower | 3425.5 |
| Sunflower | 3427 |
| Sunflower | 3449 |
| Sunflower | 3453 |
| Sunflower | 3473 |
| Sunflower | 3481 |
| Sunflower | 3482 |
| Sunflower | 3489 |
| Sunflower | 3492 |
| Sunflower | 3559 |
| Sunflower | 3564 |
| Sunflower | 3809 |
| Sunflower Quilt, A | 3594 |
| Sunflower, The | 3541 |
| Sunflower, The | 3645 |
| Sunlight and Shadows | 3735 |
| Sunny Lanes | 1144 |
| Sunrise | 1076 |
| Sunrise | 1081 |
| Sunrise | 3343 |
| Sunrise | 3373 |
| Sunrise | 3402 |
| Sunrise Pattern | 3463 |
| Sunrise, The | 4098 |
| Sunrise in the Pines | 1081 |
| Sunrise, Sunset | 3302 |
| Sunset | 3336 |
| Sunset | 3483 |
| Sunset Glow Quilt | 3336 |
| Sunset Star | 3014 |
| Sunshine | 2055 |
| Sunshine | 3347 |
| Sunshine & Shadows | 2636 |
| Sunshine and Shadow | 1464 |
| Sunshine and Shadow | 1514 |
| Sunshine and Shadow | 2286 |
| Sunshine and Shadow | 3093 |
| Sunshiny Day | 2720 |
| Surprise Package | 1882 |
| Susannah | 1332 |
| Susannah | 2534 |
| Susannah | 2535 |
| Suspension Bridge | 2663 |
| Suspension Bridge | 1010 |
| Swallow | 3914 |
| Swallow, The | 2646 |
| Swallow, The | 2647 |
| Swallow, The | 3099 |
| Swallow at the Window, A | 3785 |
| Swallow in Flight | 934 |
| Swallow's Flight | 933 |
| Swallow's Nest | 3107 |
| Swallows in the Window | 2433 |
| Swamp Angel | 1632 |
| Swastika | 1118 |
| Swastika | 1130 |
| Swastika | 1763 |
| Swastika | 2577 |
| Swastika Patch | 2577 |
| Sweet Clover | 4089 |
| Sweet Gum Leaf | 857.031 |
| Sweet Gum Leaf | 857.032 |
| Sweet Gum Leaf | 3289 |
| Sweet Sultan | 800 |
| Sweetheart Garden | 2528 |
| Sweetwater Quilt | 305 |
| Swing in the Center | 2782 |
| Swing in the Center | 2933 |
| Swing in the Center | 2934 |
| Swing in the Center | 2935 |
| Swing-in-the-Center | 1767 |
| Swinging in the Center | 2935 |
| Swiss Patchwork | 191 |
| Swiss Patchwork | 193 |
| Swiss Patchwork | 194 |
| Sylvia's Beige and Brown | 3217 |
| Sylvia's Bow | 225 |
| Sylvia's Choice | 3719 |
| T Blocks | 2650 |
| T Design | 1850 |
| T Quartette | 3275 |
| T Quilt | 1403 |
| T Quilt Pattern, The | 1385 |
| T Quilt, The | 2650 |
| T Square | 2951 |
| Table for Four | 1937 |
| Tad Lincoln's Sailboat | 912 |
| Tahitian Postage Stamp | 2283 |
| Tail of Benjamin Franklin's Kite, The | 1695 |
| Taking Wind | 1272 |
| Tall Pine Trees | 215 |
| Tall Pine Trees | 216 |
| Tall Ships of '76 | 917 |
| Tallahassee Quilt Block | 2960 |
| Tam's Patch | 1117 |
| Tangled Arrows | 1643 |
| Tangled Cobwebs | 1074 |
| Tangled Garter | 1054 |
| Tangled Garter | 1754 |
| Tangled Lines | 2193 |
| Tangled Squares | 416.6 |
| Tangled Stars | 1244 |
| Tangled Tares | 2584 |
| Tangled Trails | 1554 |
| Tapestry | 2824 |
| Target | 1304 |
| Tassal Plant | 1739 |
| Tea Basket | 761 |
| Tea Box | 240 |
| Tea Leaf | 301 |
| Tea Leaf | 857.06 |
| Tea Leaf | 857.07 |
| Tea Leaf | 857.08 |
| Tea Leaf | 3201 |
| Tea Leaves | 1734 |
| Tea Leaves | 1737 |
| Tea Rose | 1884 |
| Tea Time | 217.7 |
| Tea for Four | 1665 |
| Teapot | 218.4 |
| Teddy's Choice | 3912 |
| Telephone | 962 |
| Television Quilt | 224.7 |
| Telstar | 1235 |
| Temperance Tree | 807 |
| Temperance Tree | 811.5 |
| Temperance Tree | 815.3 |
| Temple Court | 2044 |
| Tennallytown Square | 2813 |
| Tennessee Circles | 3083 |
| Tennessee | 1689 |
| Tennessee | 3748 |
| Tennessee Mine Shaft | 4124 |
| Tennessee Mountain Laural | 3881 |
| Tennessee Pine | 829.5 |
| Snowball | 1500 |
| Tennessee Star | 3822 |
| Tennessee Star | 3954 |
| Tennessee Star | 3955 |
| Tennessee Tulip | 785.7 |
| Tents of Armageddon | 113 |
| Tents of Armageddon | 3150 |
| Terrapin, The | 1479 |
| Tête à Tête | 1933 |
| Tête à Tête | 2281 |
| Tête à Tête | 3275 |
| Texas | 1627 |
| Texas | 1631 |
| Texas | 3682 |
| Texas Bicentennial Star | 3684 |
| Texas Bluebonnet | 775 |
| Texas Cactus Basket | 728 |
| Texas Cactus Basket | 750 |
| Texas Daisy | 3429 |
| Texas Flower | 1395 |
| Texas Pointer | 3111 |
| Texas Puzzle | 1848 |
| Texas Ranger | 2982 |
| Texas Ranger's Badge | 3685 |
| Texas Republic | 3686 |
| Texas Rose | 729 |
| Texas Star | 142 |
| Texas Star | 251 |
| Texas Star | 424.7 |
| Texas Star | 2141 |
| Texas Star | 2830 |
| Texas Star | 3709 |
| Texas Star | 3849 |
| Texas Sunflower | 2565 |
| Texas Sunflower | 3477 |
| Texas Tears | 3079 |
| Texas Tears | 3261 |
| Texas Treasure | 729 |
| Texas Treasure | 1748 |
| Texas Trellis, The | 245 |
| Texas Tulip | 3499 |
| Texas Tulip | 3500 |
| Thirteen Squared | 1409 |
| Thirteen Squares | 1409 |
| Thirteenth Summer | 1555 |
| This is for the Peases | 988.5 |
| This Ol' House | 872 |
| This Way, That Way | 405 |
| This and That | 2376 |
| Thorny Thicket, The | 2205 |

# Index

| | |
|---|---|
| Thousand Islands | 2867 |
| Thousand Pyramids | 111 |
| Thousand Pyramids, A | 112 |
| Thousand Stars | 3055 |
| Thousands of Triangles | 113 |
| Thousands of Triangles | 3150 |
| Three Cheers | 2479 |
| Three Crosses, The | 2068 |
| Three in One Quilt Pattern, A | 1073 |
| Three Irish Chains | 1019 |
| Three Little Kittens | 937.1 |
| Three Patch | 242 |
| Three Patch | 1036.5 |
| Three Steps | 1834 |
| Three and Six | 1689 |
| Three by Three | 1111 |
| Three in One Quilt Pattern, A | 1073 |
| Three-Flowered Sunflower | 773.5 |
| Thrift Block | 2376 |
| Thrifty | 1602 |
| Thrifty Wife, The | 3496 |
| Thunder and Lightning | 1774 |
| Tic Tac Toe | 1003 |
| Tic Tac Toe | 1728 |
| Tic Tac Toe | 2363 |
| Tick Tack Toe | 1833 |
| Tiffany Butterflies | 449 |
| Tiger Lily | 1018.5 |
| Tiger Lily, The | 756.25 |
| Tile Patchwork | 438 |
| Tile Puzzle | 1003 |
| Time and Energey | 1480 |
| Time and Tide | 3899 |
| Tinted Chains | 2815 |
| Tiny Pines | 833 |
| Tiny Star | 143 |
| Tippecanoe | 863 |
| Tippecanoe | 1251 |
| Tippecanoe and Tyler Too | 1631 |
| Tirzah's Treasure | 1054 |
| Tit for Tat | 213 |
| Toad in a Puddle | 2797 |
| Toad in the Puddle | 2464 |
| Tobacco Leaf | 2760 |
| Tombstone Quilt | 2447 |
| Tomorrow's Heirlooms | 411 |
| Tonganoxie Nine Patch | 1828 |
| Top Hat | 2826 |
| Topaz Trail | 226.6 |
| Topeka | 3660 |
| Topiary Garden | 227 |
| Tote a Tote | 1933 |
| Touching Stars | 1061.5 |
| Towers of Camelot | 1704 |
| Toy Balloon Quilt, The | 275 |
| Tracy's Puzzle | 2103 |
| Trail of Friendship | 1039 |
| Trail of the Covered Wagon | 1695 |
| Trail of the Lonesome Pine | 856 |
| Travel Star | 3909 |
| Travel Star | 3912 |
| Treasure Chest | 1638 |
| Tree | 819 |
| Tree Everlasting | 479 |
| Tree Quilt Pattern | 768.2 |
| Tree and Truth | 3278 |
| Tree of Life | 1398 |
| Tree of Life | 814 |
| Tree of Life | 820 |
| Tree of Life | 823 |
| Tree of Life | 824 |
| Tree of Life | 826 |
| Tree of Paradise | 216.31 |
| Tree of Paradise | 811 |
| Tree of Paradise | 811.7 |
| Tree of Paradise | 812 |
| Tree of Paradise | 813 |
| Tree of Paradise | 815.3 |
| Tree of Paradise | 819 |
| Tree of Paradise | 820 |
| Tree of Paradise | 820.5 |
| Tree of Paradise | 821 |
| Tree of Paradise | 822.5 |
| Tree of Paradise | 827 |
| Tree of Paradise | 829.9 |
| Tree of Paradise | 830 |
| Tree of Paradise, The | 831 |
| Tree of Temptation | 836 |
| Tree of Temptation | 837 |
| Tree of Temptation | 852 |
| Trees in the Park | 2639 |
| Trenton | 4065 |
| Trenton Quilt Block | 4065 |
| Trey's Quilt | 4076 |
| Trials and Troubles | 247.5 |
| Triangle | 1206 |
| Triangle Beauty | 1176 |
| Triangle Combination | 1193 |
| Triangle Design | 2375 |
| Triangle Flower | 765.5 |
| Triangle Mosaic | 111 |
| Triangle Puzzle | 1824 |
| Triangle Puzzle, The | 2568 |
| Triangle Quilt | 202 |
| Triangle Squares | 2041 |
| Triangle Star | 2243 |
| Triangle Trails | 2568 |
| Triangle Weave | 1316 |
| Triangle of Squares | 1187 |
| Triangles | 111 |
| Triangles | 1271 |
| Triangles | 2483 |
| Triangles & Stripes | 2118 |
| Triangular Trees | 202 |
| Triangular Triangles | 202 |
| Tricolor Block | 1111 |
| Tricolor Star | 3586 |
| Trip Around the World | 2286 |
| Trip Around the World | 2293 |
| Trip Around the World, A | 2286 |
| Trip to Egypt, A | 111 |
| Trip to the Altar | 1692 |
| Triple Irish Chain | 1019 |
| Triple Irish Chain | 2283 |
| Triple Irish Chain & Eight Point Star | 1021 |
| Triple Link Chain | 2511 |
| Triple Rose | 1741 |
| Triple Star | 3807 |
| Triple Star Quilt, The | 3826 |
| Triple Stripe | 2778 |
| Triple Sunflower | 773.6 |
| Triple X | 1323 |
| Triplet | 1716 |
| Tropical Sun | 3493 |
| Trout and Bass Block | 3828 |
| True Lover's Buggy Wheels | 3386 |
| True Lover's Knot | 1429 |
| True Lover's Knot | 1532 |
| True Lover's Knot | 1831 |
| True Lover's Knot | 1850 |
| True Lover's Knot | 2097 |
| True Lover's Knot | 2579 |
| True Lover's Link | 458.7 |
| Trumpet Vine | 784 |
| Tudor Rose | 2393 |
| Tulip | 756.3 |
| Tulip | 765.01 |
| Tulip | 765.02 |
| Tulip | 766.3 |
| Tulip | 785.5 |
| Tulip Basket | 692 |
| Tulip Basket | 734 |
| Tulip Basket, The | 747.5 |
| Tulip Block | 800.2 |
| Tulip Design, The | 3573 |
| Tulip Garden | 787 |
| Tulip Lady Fingers | 2198 |
| Tulip Pattern in High Colors, A | 799 |
| Tulip Quilt, The | 3097 |
| Tulip Ring | 2551 |
| Tulip Tile | 2101 |
| Tulip Wheel | 3576 |
| Tulip Wheel | 4080 |
| Tulip in Vase | 740 |
| Tulip in Vase | 744 |
| Tulips | 1865 |
| Tumbler | 151 |
| Tumbler | 406 |
| Tumbler | 944 |
| Tumblers | 111 |
| Tumble Weed | 1466 |
| Tumbling Blocks | 142 |
| Tumbling Blocks | 282 |
| Tumbling Blocks | 1951 |
| Tumbling Hexagon | 243 |
| Turkey Giblets | 1305 |
| Turkey Tracks | 1438 |
| Tumbling Blocks | 1883 |
| Tumbling Blocks | 3098 |
| Tumbling Blocks | 3109 |
| Tumbling Blocks | 3631 |
| Turkey in the Straw | 1733 |
| Turkey in the Straw | 2782 |
| Turn About Quilt | 1519 |
| Turn About Quilt | 2683 |
| Turnabout T | 2863 |
| Turnstile | 1266 |
| Turnstile | 3072 |
| Turtle | 3836 |
| Turtle on a Quilt | 1479 |
| Twelve Crowns | 1359 |
| Twelve Triangles | 2377 |
| Twentieth Century Star, The | 3680 |
| Twenty T's | 1784 |
| Twenty Tees | 1784 |
| Twenty-four Triangles | 2838 |
| Twin Darts | 2323 |
| Twin Sisters | 2314 |
| Twin Stars | 2477 |
| Twinkle, Twinkle Little Star | 3735 |
| Twinkling Star | 241.1 |
| Twinkling Star | 276 |
| Twinkling Star | 1251 |
| Twinkling Star | 2249 |
| Twinkling Star | 2252 |
| Twinkling Star | 3747 |
| Twinkling Star | 3930 |
| Twinkling Star, The | 2164 |
| Twinkling Star, The | 2165 |
| Twinkling Stars | 3809 |
| Twinkling Stars | 3861 |
| Twinkling Stars | 3899 |
| Twist | 2660 |
| Twist Patchwork | 443 |
| Twist and Turn | 481 |
| Twist and Turn | 1535 |
| Twist and Turn | 1550 |
| Twist and Turn | 1856 |
| Twisted Ribbon | 3243 |
| Twisted Ribbons | 444.5 |
| Twisted Ribbons | 2344 |
| Twisted Rope | 443 |
| Twister | 2177 |
| Twisting Star | 4165 |
| Two Colors | 3750 |
| Two Crosses | 3034 |
| Two Patch Quilt | 1136 |
| Uncle Sam's Hour Glass | 2045 |
| Under Blue Mountain Skies | 4025 |
| Underground Railroad | 1695 |
| Unfolding Star | 4157 |
| Union | 2056 |
| Union Block | 2056 |
| Union Square | 2056 |
| Union Square | 2417 |
| Union Star | 2074 |
| Union Star | 3675 |
| Union Union Star | 3680 |
| Unique Quilt, A | 865.2 |
| Unknown Star | 3772 |
| Unknown Star | 3807 |
| Up and Down Blocks | 1112 |
| Utah | 4077 |
| Utah Star | 1152.8 |
| Utility Block | 2411 |
| V Block | 2329 |
| V Block | 2717 |
| Valentine Quilt | 4072 |
| Valley Forge Quilt | 3484 |
| Variable Star | 1631 |
| Variable Star | 2141 |
| Variable Star | 3735 |
| Variable Star | 3830 |
| Variable Triangles | 284 |
| Variation of Sail Boats | 2388 |
| Variegated Diamonds | 142 |
| Variegated Hexagons | 160 |

# Index

| Name | Page |
|---|---|
| Vase of Flowers | 760 |
| Vase of Flowers | 763 |
| Vase of Flowers | 763.2 |
| Vegetable Soup | 1511 |
| Venetian Design | 3581 |
| Venetian Quilt, The | 429 |
| Vermont | 2338 |
| Vermont | 2739 |
| Vermont Maple Leaf, The | 1944 |
| Verna Belle's Favorite | 2738 |
| Vestibule | 1057 |
| Vice President's Block | 1806 |
| Vice President's Quilt | 2500 |
| Victoria's Crown | 458.5 |
| Victoria's Crown | 3644 |
| Victoria's Crown | 3648 |
| Victorian Maze | 1430 |
| Victory | 4058 |
| Victory Quilt | 226 |
| Victory Quilt | 991.7 |
| Victory Quilt | 991.9 |
| Victory Quilt | 2717 |
| Victory Quilt, A | 1371 |
| Victory Star | 3800 |
| Village Green, The | 2542 |
| Village School House | 886 |
| Village Square | 2403 |
| Vine Block | 416.5 |
| Vine of Friendship | 1459 |
| Vines at the Window | 1207 |
| Viola's Scrap Quilt | 1020.2 |
| Violet Blossoms | 2668 |
| Violet's Dream | 3031 |
| Virginia | 1775 |
| Virginia Reel | 1339 |
| Virginia Reel | 2193 |
| Virginia Reel | 2379 |
| Virginia Reel | 3054 |
| Virginia Reel | 3805 |
| Virginia Snowball | 2672 |
| Virginia Star | 3773 |
| Virginia Star | 3774 |
| Virginia Stars | 3775 |
| Virginia Worm Fence | 1618 |
| Virginia's Choice | 1501 |
| Virginia's Star | 3773 |
| WCTU | 1666 |
| WCTU Patch | 1666 |
| WCTUnion | 1666 |
| Wagon Tracks | 1695 |
| Wagon Wheel | 241.9 |
| Wagon Wheel | 431.8 |
| Wagon Wheel | 3390 |
| Wagon Wheel Quilt | 3580 |
| Wagon Wheels | 2946 |
| Wagon Wheels Carry Me Home | 3381 |
| Walk Around | 231 |
| Walls of Jericho | 1853 |
| Wampum Block | 1762 |
| Wanderer, The | 3370 |
| Wandering Flower | 3873 |
| Wandering Foot | 3100 |
| Wandering Foot | 3109 |
| Wandering Foot | 3631 |
| Wandering Jew | 3786 |
| Wandering Paths | 429 |
| Washington | 2860 |
| Washington Pavement | 2635 |
| Washington Pavement | 2636 |
| Washington Pavement | 2813 |
| Washington Quilt Pattern | 3278 |
| Washington Sidewalk | 2813 |
| Washington Sidewalk | 2822 |
| Washington Snowball | 305 |
| Washington Stamp Quilt, The | 2286 |
| Washington Star | 1958 |
| Washington Tree | 815.3 |
| Washington's Elm | 815.3 |
| Washington's Own | 2691 |
| Washington's Puzzle | 2562 |
| Waste Not, Want Not | 3152 |
| Water Beauty | 785 |
| Water Glass | 943 |
| Water Lily | 3431 |
| Water Lily | 798 |
| Water Mill | 1760 |
| Water Wheel | 1262 |
| Water Wheel | 1763 |
| Water Wheel | 2314 |
| Watered Ribbon & Border | 4130 |
| Watermill | 1262 |
| Watermill | 1938 |
| Waterwheel | 2928 |
| Waterwheels | 4151 |
| Wave | 145 |
| Waverly Star | 1977 |
| Waves of the Ocean | 283 |
| Waves of the sea | 1353 |
| Waving Plumes | 1544 |
| Wavy Navy | 213 |
| Weather Vane | 2584 |
| Weathervane | 1780 |
| Weathervane | 4033 |
| Weathervane and Steeple | 4027 |
| Web of Diamonds | 231 |
| Wedding Chain | 1032 |
| Wedding March | 1359 |
| Wedding Ring | 301 |
| Wedding Ring | 303 |
| Wedding Ring | 1806 |
| Wedding Ring | 1869 |
| Wedding Ring | 3235 |
| Wedding Ring Bouquet | 2761 |
| Wedding Ring Chain | 301 |
| Wedding Ring, The | 2392 |
| Wedding Ring Tile | 445 |
| Wedge and Circle | 3075 |
| Wedgewood Tiles | 1551 |
| Weeping Willow | 817 |
| Weeping Willow | 846 |
| Weeping Willow Quilt, The | 843 |
| West Virginia | 3798 |
| West Virginia Star | 3798 |
| West Wind | 1393 |
| Western | 871 |
| Western Rose | 3632 |
| Western Spy | 3859 |
| Western Star | 256 |
| Western Star | 1631 |
| Westward Ho | 3840 |
| Whale Block | 1531 |
| Wheel | 1727 |
| Wheel | 3461 |
| Wheel of Chance | 1876 |
| Wheel of Chance | 3386 |
| Wheel of Destiny | 2345 |
| Wheel of Fate | 3911 |
| Wheel of Fortune | 1299 |
| Wheel of Fortune | 1500 |
| Wheel of Fortune | 1960 |
| Wheel of Fortune | 2098 |
| Wheel of Fortune | 2664 |
| Wheel of Fortune | 2852 |
| Wheel of Fortune | 3378 |
| Wheel of Fortune | 3379 |
| Wheel of Fortune | 3382 |
| Wheel of Fortune | 3384 |
| Wheel of Fortune | 3387 |
| Wheel of Fortune | 3454 |
| Wheel of Fortune | 3461 |
| Wheel of Fortune, The | 2854 |
| Wheel of Fortune, The | 3391 |
| Wheel of Life | 3390 |
| Wheel of Life, The | 160 |
| Wheel of Luck | 2852 |
| Wheel of Mystery | 1512 |
| Wheel of Mystery | 2764 |
| Wheel of Time | 1796 |
| Wheel of Time | 2143 |
| Wheel of Time | 3393 |
| Wheels | 1278 |
| When Circles Get Together | 305.3 |
| Whig Rose | 311.5 |
| Whig's Defeat | 1085 |
| Whig's Defeat | 4074 |
| Whippoorwill | 2620 |
| Whirl Around | 296 |
| Whirligig | 1130 |
| Whirligig | 1279 |
| Whirligig | 1877 |
| Whirligig | 3828 |
| Whirligig | 4203 |
| Whirligig Design | 1346 |
| Whirligig Quilt | 2398 |
| Whirling Blade | 1195 |
| Whirling Diamonds | 142 |
| Whirling Fans | 3355 |
| Whirling Five Patch | 1859 |
| Whirling Hexagon | 245 |
| Whirling L | 2889 |
| Whirling Nine Patch | 220.7 |
| Whirling Pinwheel, The | 3418 |
| Whirling Pinwheels | 1350 |
| Whirling Square | 2178 |
| Whirling Square | 2590 |
| Whirling Star | 1279 |
| Whirling Star | 2491 |
| Whirling Star | 3758 |
| Whirling Star | 3925 |
| Whirling Star | 3950 |
| Whirling Star, The | 1297 |
| Whirling Triangles | 245 |
| Whirling Wheel | 3639 |
| Whirling Wheels | 3643 |
| Whirling Whirlpools | 2444 |
| Whirlwind | 222.8 |
| Whirlwind | 1266 |
| Whirlwind | 2314 |
| Whirlwind | 2799 |
| Whirlwind | 3536 |
| Whispering Leaves | 305.5 |
| White Blossom Coverlet | 195 |
| White Cross, The | 212 |
| White Hemstitch | 2151 |
| White House | 1146 |
| White House Rope | 784.6 |
| White House Steps | 2027 |
| White House Steps | 2572 |
| White House Steps | 2606 |
| White Lily | 857.04 |
| White Mountains | 442.8 |
| White Rose | 311.5 |
| White Square Quilt, The | 1866 |
| Widower's Choice | 1908 |
| Wild Cat | 937.6 |
| Wild Duck | 1124 |
| Wild Geese | 1682 |
| Wild Geese Flying | 480 |
| Wild Goose | 2796 |
| Wild Goose Chase | 213 |
| Wild Goose Chase | 214 |
| Wild Goose Chase | 480 |
| Wild Goose Chase | 1075 |
| Wild Goose Chase | 1339 |
| Wild Goose Chase | 1859 |
| Wild Goose Chase | 2051 |
| Wild Goose Chase | 2184 |
| Wild Goose Chase | 2800 |
| Wild Goose Chase | 2905 |
| Wild Goose Chase | 2906 |
| Wild Goose Chase | 2907 |
| Wild Goose Chase | 2912 |
| Wild Goose Chase, The | 113 |
| Wild Iris | 2203 |
| Will of the Wisp | 2704 |
| Wind Blown Square | 2444 |
| Wind Power of the Osages | 1130 |
| Wind Power of the Osages | 2577 |
| Wind Star for New Hampshire | 1925 |
| Windblown Daisy | 3392 |
| Windblown Star | 2476 |
| Windflower | 1476 |
| Winding Blade, The | 1505 |
| Winding Blades | 1130 |
| Winding Blades | 3786 |
| Winding Path Quilt, The | 458.2 |
| Winding Stairway | 1110 |
| Winding Trail | 1424 |
| Winding Trail, A | 3368 |
| Winding Trail, The | 1481 |
| Winding Walk | 1516 |
| Winding Walk | 2584 |
| Winding Ways | 1512 |
| Winding Ways | 2764 |
| Windmill | 887.5 |
| Windmill | 1126 |
| Windmill | 1185 |
| Windmill | 1198 |

# Indexes

| | |
|---|---|
| Windmill | 1199 |
| Windmill | 1203 |
| Windmill | 1210 |
| Windmill | 1262 |
| Windmill | 1266 |
| Windmill | 1420 |
| Windmill | 1500 |
| Windmill | 1709 |
| Windmill | 2314 |
| Windmill | 2560 |
| Windmill Star | 3873 |
| Windmill Star | 3945 |
| Windmill, The | 2704 |
| Windmill, The | 3077 |
| Windmill, The | 3873 |
| Windmill and Outline | 2315 |
| Window Squares | 4066 |
| Windows and Doors | 2428 |
| Windows and Doors | 2655 |
| Wine Glass | 945 |
| Winged 9 Patch, The | 1987 |
| Winged Arrow | 2536 |
| Winged Square | 293 |
| Winged Square | 1426 |
| Winged Square | 1703 |
| Winged Square | 2494 |
| Winged Square | 2546 |
| Winged Star | 3796 |
| Wings of Victory Quilt | 1042 |
| Winner's Circle | 1533 |
| Winter Cactus Quilt | 3175 |
| Winter Cactus Quilt | 3176 |
| Winter Stars | 3746 |
| Wisconsin | 2968 |
| Wisconsin Star | 3609 |
| Wisconsin Star | 3726 |
| Wishing Ring | 1805 |
| Wishing Ring, The | 2626 |
| Wishing Star | 3883 |
| Wishing Well, The | 459 |
| Witches Star | 3766 |
| Wonder of Egypt | 206 |
| Wonder of the World | 305.6 |
| Wonder of the World | 1039 |
| Wonder of the World | 1040.7 |
| Wonder of the World | 1461 |
| Wonder of the World | 1466 |
| Wonder of the World | 1514 |
| Wood Lily | 765.4 |
| Wood Lily | 3793 |
| Wood Lily, The | 765.25 |
| Woodland Path | 1962 |
| Work Box | 4022 |
| Work-basket | 2970 |
| World Fair Quilt, The | 219 |
| World Without End | 2554 |
| World Without End | 2975 |
| World's Fair | 1312 |
| World's Fair | 2014 |
| World's Fair | 2334 |
| World's Fair | 2465 |
| World's Fair Block | 1104.5 |
| World's Fair Quilt | 2013 |
| World's Fair, The | 1516.5 |
| World's Wonder | 1461 |
| Woven Pattern | 425.7 |
| Wreath, The | 3758 |
| Wreath of Lilies | 4044 |
| Wrench | 1850 |
| Wyoming | 3407 |
| Wyoming Patch | 3565 |
| Wyoming Valley Block | 1768 |
| X Quartet | 1127 |
| X Quisite, The | 3250 |
| X, The | 2887 |
| Yankee Charm | 2115 |
| Yankee Pride | 3799 |
| Yankee Puzzle | 1130 |
| Yankee Puzzle | 1195 |
| Year's Favorite | 1129 |
| Yellow Clover | 2459 |
| Yellow Lilies | 2923 |
| Yellow Lily | 222.4 |
| Yellow Lily | 770 |
| Yo Yo | 192 |
| Yokahama Banner | 1172 |
| Yorkshire Daisy | 192 |
| Young Man's Fancy | 1815 |
| Young Man's Fancy | 2037 |
| Young Man's Invention, A | 3667 |
| Yreka Square | 2427 |
| Yuletide | 1509 |
| Z Cross | 1931 |
| Zebra | 939.1 |
| Zig-Zag | 112 |
| Zig Zag | 114 |
| Zig Zag | 132 |
| Zig Zag | 147 |
| Zig Zag | 1111 |
| Zig Zag | 2848 |
| Zig-Zag | 4216 |
| Zig Zag Blocks | 402 |
| Zig Zag Shell | 181 |
| Zig Zag Tile Quilt | 2475 |
| Zodiac Stars | 267 |

INDEX TO PATTERN CATEGORIES

| | |
|---|---|
| All Over | Categories 1- 4 |
| Bar Quilt | (See Sash & Block) |
| Equal Nine-Patch | Category 9 |
| Fans | Category 19 |
| Feathered Star | (See Nine-Patch) |
| Four Patch | Category 8 |
| Four X | Category 13 |
| Maltese Cross | Category 15 |
| Miscellaneous | Category 25 |
| Multi-Patch | Category 3 |
| Nine X | Category 16 |
| Non-Square Blocks | Category 2 |
| One Patch | Category 1 |
| One Patch Square | Category 12 |
| Realistic Patterns | Category 5 |
| Sash and Block Designs | Category 7 |
| Square in a Square | Category 14 |
| Stars, Eight-Pointed/ 45° Diamond | Category 22 |
| Stars, Five- & Six- Pointed Blocks | Category 21 |
| Stars, Other | Category 23 |
| Strip Quilts | Category 14 |
| Three Patch | Category 18 |
| Two-Block Patterns | Category 6 |
| Two Patch | Category 17 |
| Unequal Nine-Patch with Large Center Square | Category 11 |
| Unequal Nine-Patch with Small Center Square | Category 10 |
| Wheel | Category 20 |
| Whole Top Design | Category 24 |

# ~American Quilter's Society~
## dedicated to publishing books for today's quilters

*The following AQS publications are currently available:*

- **Adapting Architectural Details for Quilts,** Carol Wagner, #2282: AQS, 1991, 88 pages, softbound, $12.95
- **American Beauties: Rose & Tulip Quilts,** Gwen Marston & Joe Cunningham, #1907: AQS, 1988, 96 pages, softbound, $14.95
- **America's Pictorial Quilts,** Caron L. Mosey, #1662: AQS, 1985, 112 pages, hardbound, $19.95
- **Applique Designs: My Mother Taught Me to Sew,** Faye Anderson, #2121: AQS, 1990, 80 pages, softbound, $12.95
- **Arkansas Quilts: Arkansas Warmth,** Arkansas Quilter's Guild, Inc., #1908: AQS, 1987, 144 pages, hardbound, $24.95
- **The Art of Hand Applique,** Laura Lee Fritz, #2122: AQS, 1990, 80 pages, softbound, $14.95
- **...Ask Helen More About Quilting Designs,** Helen Squire, #2099: AQS, 1990, 54 pages, 17 x 11, spiral-bound, $14.95
- **Award-Winning Quilts & Their Makers: Vol. I, The Best of AQS Shows – 1985-1987,** #2207: AQS, 1991, 232 pages, softbound, $24.95
- **Award-Winning Quilts & Their Makers: Vol. II, The Best of AQS Shows – 1988-1989,** #2354: AQS, 1992, 176 pages, softbound, $24.95
- **Award-Winning Quilts & Their Makers: Vol. III, The Best of AQS Shows – 1990-1991,** #3425: AQS, 1993, 180 pages, softbound, $24.95
- **Classic Basket Quilts,** Elizabeth Porter & Marianne Fons, #2208: AQS, 1991, 128 pages, softbound, $16.95
- **A Collection of Favorite Quilts,** Judy Florence, #2119: AQS, 1990, 136 pages, softbound, $18.95
- **Creative Machine Art,** Sharee Dawn Roberts, #2355: AQS, 1992, 142 pages, 9 x 9, softbound, $24.95
- **Dear Helen, Can You Tell Me?...all about quilting designs,** Helen Squire, #1820: AQS, 1987, 51 pages, 17 x 11, spiral-bound, $12.95
- **Dye Painting!,** Ann Johnston, #3399: AQS, 1992, 88 pages, softbound, $19.95
- **Dyeing & Overdyeing of Cotton Fabrics,** Judy Mercer Tescher, #2030: AQS, 1990, 54 pages, softbound, $9.95
- **Flavor Quilts for Kids to Make: Complete Instructions for Teaching Children to Dye, Decorate & Sew Quilts,** Jennifer Amor #2356: AQS, 1991, 120 pages, softbound, $12.95
- **From Basics to Binding: A Complete Guide to Making Quilts,** Karen Kay Buckley, #2381: AQS, 1992, 160 pages, softbound, $16.95
- **Fun & Fancy Machine Quiltmaking,** Lois Smith, #1982: AQS, 1989, 144 pages, softbound, $19.95
- **Gallery of American Quilts 1830-1991: Book III,** #3421: AQS, 1992, 128 pages, softbound, $19.95
- **The Grand Finale: A Quilter's Guide to Finishing Projects,** Linda Denner, #1924: AQS, 1988, 96 pages, softbound, $14.95
- **Heirloom Miniatures,** Tina M. Gravatt, #2097: AQS, 1990, 64 pages, softbound, $9.95
- **Infinite Stars,** Gayle Bong, #2283: AQS, 1992, 72 pages, softbound, $12.95
- **The Ins and Outs: Perfecting the Quilting Stitch,** Patricia J. Morris, #2120: AQS, 1990, 96 pages, softbound, $9.95
- **Irish Chain Quilts: A Workbook of Irish Chains & Related Patterns,** Joyce B. Peaden, #1906: AQS, 1988, 96 pages, softbound, $14.95
- **The Log Cabin Returns to Kentucky: Quilts from the Pilgrim/Roy Collection,** Gerald Roy and Paul Pilgrim, #3329: AQS, 1992, 36 pages, 9 x 7, softbound, $12.95
- **Marbling Fabrics for Quilts: A Guide for Learning & Teaching,** Kathy Fawcett & Carol Shoaf, #2206: AQS, 1991, 72 pages, softbound, $12.95
- **More Projects and Patterns: A Second Collection of Favorite Quilts,** Judy Florence, #3330: AQS, 1992, 152 pages, softbound, $18.95
- **Nancy Crow: Quilts and Influences,** Nancy Crow, #1981: AQS, 1990, 256 pages, 9 x 12, hardcover, $29.95
- **Nancy Crow: Work in Transition,** Nancy Crow, #3331: AQS, 1992, 32 pages, 9 x 10, softbound, $12.95
- **New Jersey Quilts – 1777 to 1950: Contributions to an American Tradition,** The Heritage Quilt Project of New Jersey; text by Rachel Cochran, Rita Erickson, Natalie Hart & Barbara Schaffer, #3332: AQS, 1992, 256 pages, softbound, $29.95
- **No Dragons on My Quilt,** Jean Ray Laury with Ritva Laury & Lizabeth Laury, #2153: AQS, 1990, 52 pages, hardcover, $12.95
- **Oklahoma Heritage Quilts,** Oklahoma Quilt Heritage Project #2032: AQS, 1990, 144 pages, softbound, $19.95
- **Old Favorites in Miniature,** Tina Gravatt, #3469: AQS, 1993, 104 pages, softbound, $15.95
- **Quilt Groups Today: Who They Are, Where They Meet, What They Do, and How to Contact Them; A Complete Guide for 1992-1993,** #3308: AQS, 1992, 336 pages, softbound, $14.95
- **Quilting Patterns from Native American Designs,** Dr. Joyce Mori, #3467: AQS, 1993, 80 pages, softbound, $12.95
- **Quilting with Style: Principles for Great Pattern Design,** Gwen Marston & Joe Cunningham, #3470: AQS, 1993, 192 pages, 9 x 12, hardcover, $24.95
- **Quiltmaker's Guide: Basics & Beyond,** Carol Doak, #2284: AQS, 1992, 208 pages, softbound, $19.95
- **Quilts: Old & New, A Similar View,** Paul D. Pilgrim and Gerald E. Roy, #3715: AQS, 1993, 40 pages, softbound, $12.95
- **Quilts: The Permanent Collection – MAQS,** #2257: AQS, 1991, 100 pages, 10 x 6½, softbound, $9.95
- **Sensational Scrap Quilts,** Darra Duffy Williamson, #2357: AQS, 1992, 152 pages, softbound, $24.95
- **Show Me Helen...How to Use Quilting Designs,** Helen Squire, #3375: AQS, 1993, 155 pages, softbound, $15.95
- **Sets & Borders,** Gwen Marston & Joe Cunningham, #1821: AQS, 1987, 104 pages, softbound, $14.95
- **Somewhere in Between: Quilts and Quilters of Illinois,** Rita Barrow Barber, #1790: AQS, 1986, 78 pages, softbound, $14.95
- **Stenciled Quilts for Christmas,** Marie Monteith Sturmer, #2098: AQS, 1990, 104 pages, softbound, $14.95
- **A Treasury of Quilting Designs,** Linda Goodmon Emery, #2029: AQS, 1990, 80 pages, 14 x 11, spiral-bound, $14.95
- **Wonderful Wearables: A Celebration of Creative Clothing,** Virginia Avery, #2286: AQS, 1991, 184 pages, softbound, $24.95

*These books can be found in local bookstores and quilt shops. If you are unable to locate a title in your area, you can order by mail from AQS, P.O. Box 3290, Paducah, KY 42002-3290. Please add $1 for the first book and 40¢ for each additional one to cover postage and handling. (International orders please add $1.50 for the first book and $1 for each additional one.)*